Video Collection Development in Multi-type Libraries

Video Collection Development in Multi-type Libraries

A HANDBOOK

Second Edition

EDITED BY

Gary P. Handman

THE GREENWOOD LIBRARY MANAGEMENT COLLECTION

GREENWOOD PRESS
Westport, Connecticut • London

Library of Congress Cataloging-in-Publication Data

Video collection development in multi-type libraries : a handbook / edited by Gary P. Handman—
   2nd ed.
      p.   cm.—(The Greenwood library management collection, ISSN 0894–2986)
   Includes bibliographical references and index.
   ISBN 0–313–31658–9 (alk. paper)
   1. Libraries—United States—Special collections—Video recordings.   I. Handman, Gary,
   1950–   II. Series.
   Z692.V52V48   2002
   025.2'873—dc21   2001040562

British Library Cataloguing in Publication Data is available.

Library of Congress Catalog Card Number: 2001040562
ISBN: 0–313–31658–9
ISSN: 0894–2986

First published in 2002

Greenwood Press, 88 Post Road West, Westport, CT 06881
An imprint of Greenwood Publishing Group, Inc.
www.greenwood.com

Printed in the United States of America

The paper used in this book complies with the
Permanent Paper Standard issued by the National
Information Standards Organization (Z39.48–1984).

10 9 8 7 6 5 4 3 2 1

Contents

Acknowledgments

Compiling and distilling the experience, wisdom, and counsel of 25 diverse experts, each with an incredibly busy professional and personal life, is no simple task, even given the fact that the Internet has made it wickedly easy and practical for an editor to wheedle, exhort, and plead incessantly and at long distances. Still, whatever my role was in mustering the troops, cracking the whip, and rearranging semicolons, the bottom line is that this book belongs to its individual authors. I owe an enormous debt to the generous, smart, and dedicated colleagues who have contributed their time, energy, and insight to the enterprise (many for the second time around). I'd like to express my particular thanks to Jeff Clark, who answered my frantic prayers, fearlessly jumped into this project in the eleventh hour, and produced a wonderful chapter on preservation.

It is unlikely that I could have pulled this project off without the able support of Ann Moen, UCB Media Resources Operations Supervisor, who kept the Media Resources Center spinning like a celluloid top during my book-related absences.

Longer-Term Debt Department: One of my big regrets in life, particularly as my beard has grown grayer, is that I haven't been more diligent in thanking my teachers over the years. The two mentors who exerted the strongest influence on my life at the movies were Lou Stouman and Bob Epstein, both of the UCLA Television and Film Department, and both, unfortunately, gone now to some Big Screening Room in the Sky. In Epstein's class I had the life-altering experience of watching *Citizen Kane*, *Potemkin*, and *The Bicycle Thief* for the first time. Stouman taught me how to look at non-fiction films and how to think and write intelligently about them. Bob and Lou, wherever you are in the cosmos, I owe you.

Last, my thanks and all my love go to my best pals in the world, Pam and Becky: for putting up with my frequent fits of distraction and craziness at home during the thick of editing; for bearing with my insufferably snobby behavior in video rental stores; and for just being. Here's looking at you, kids.

Introduction

Moving with the Image: Some Millennial Thoughts about Video in Libraries and Video Librarians

Gary P. Handman

This is where we are. The Twentieth Century is on film. . . . You have to ask yourself if there's anything about us more important than the fact that we're constantly on film constantly watching ourselves.

—Don Delillo, *The Names*

By the time these words see the light of print sometime in mid-2002, the invention of home video will be close to three decades old, the inclusion of video in library collections only a few years more recent. In 1994, the year that the last edition of this book was published, videocassette recorders (VCRs) were ensconced in well over 90 percent of all U.S. households. As of this writing, that figure approaches 100 percent, with upstart digital technologies such as Digital Versatile Disc (DVD) gaining an even more astoundingly rapid entry into the living rooms, classrooms, tap rooms, and boardrooms of America and the world.

Writing a general (or at least succinct) introduction to video as a cultural and commercial phenomenon is no easy task at this late date in the Sight and Sound Century, for, in a sense, the medium and its messages have become meta-phenomena (please bear with me, I'm an academic and can't help myself). Like the air we autonomically consume with each breath, video just seems to be there, all the time, everywhere—a kind of low sociocultural hum and an omnipresent glow in the center and corners of our lives. It is the very ubiquity and transparency of these media, their tight weave into the warp and weft of modern life, that make them difficult to pin down and analyze in short order.

The introduction to the last edition of this book spilled a rather extravagant amount of ink outlining the monumental cognitive, cultural, and economic shifts precipitated by video and its broadcast adjunct, TV. Riffing on the ideas of earlier mass communications theorists such as Marshall McLuhan and his slightly daffy mentor, economist Harold Adam Innis, the discussion put forward the notion that new technologies—particularly new communications technologies such as video—have a way of rewiring cultural circuitry, creating new societal valences, new social and political relationships. In taking even a quick leaf through the bountiful post-McLuhanian academic and popular literature dealing with video, TV, and society, one finds that these media have been assigned responsibility for a mind-boggling array of tremors and tectonic shifts in the bedrock of twentieth-century global culture. These effects have variously included the attenuation of childhood; the subversion of family dynamics; the conflation and confusion of public and private space; and the evaporation of boundaries between fact and fiction, information and entertainment, sign and meaning. Read further and you'll find other videffects cited: political and cultural globalization; shifts in the locus of media control (either toward democracy or fascism, depending on whom you read); and radical changes in the perception and use of leisure time. And those are just for openers.

So, what impact have the media-incited revolutions and sea changes discussed above had on libraries and library collections over the course of the past three decades? The answer is maddeningly paradoxical: depending on how you're looking at it, the impact has been at once both profound and trivial. Let me explain.

Viewed in a broad cultural context, film and video have had an inestimably large impact on libraries, very simply because they have inexorably changed the lives and habits, the worldviews, the needs, and the wants of library users. In *theory*, the impact of these media on libraries is enormous because they have become perhaps the most significant and unique forms of storytelling, myth-making, and historical and cultural documentation in the past century (read on in this book and you'll find that Walt Crawford takes issue with this statement; I firmly believe it's true).

On the other hand I offer here for your consideration a notion that was only politely hinted at in the previous edition's introduction (I'm older and more curmudgeonly, after all): the notion that there has never been a video revolution in libraries (regardless of what the ballyhooing articles in the 1980s professional literature told you). While the universe of video materials has exploded like some cinematic supernova in the last 30 years, and while library video collections have blossomed in that same time, as pointed out in the introduction to the first edition (xv):

[The] mere presence of cassettes on the shelf hardly qualifies a library for membership in the revolutionary vanguard. Revolution, after all, generally implies radical discontinuity, changing evolutionary trajectories, or at the very least, intense rethinking and shifting of priorities, directions, and philosophies. The manner in which libraries have dealt with video is frequently less revolutionary than it is an uneasy continuation of notions approaches, and practices applied to earlier media formats and earlier cultural formats.

Like the poor little tramp in *Modern Times* innocently waving the dropped red flag and unwittingly joining the revolutionary parade, libraries have often half-heartedly signed on to the movement without fully understanding its nature, its extent, or the library's effective roles in it.

After 30 years of living with video collections and a thoroughly video-ized public, there is, in fact, still something distinctly Procrustean about the treatment of the medium in libraries. Procrustus was the monstrous mythic Attic high-wayman who wantonly cut off the head and feet of visitors to match the size of his bed. More libraries than I'd care to think about seem, either by design or unwittingly, to have adopted this same gambit when it comes to dealing with video collections. In the sorriest cases, they've cut off the head and feet (the diverse needs and wants) of visitors (patrons) to match a bed clothed exclusively in print. In other cases, they've built video collections on a fiscally short-sheeted bed feathered with conservative public service and collections policies. Lop! Off with anything too controversial, too non-mainstream, too expensive or difficult to acquire.

A decade ago, the marginalization of video in library collections could be—and was often—written off to the relative newness of the medium; lingering print bias; concerns about literacy; and the difficulty and cost of acquiring, processing, and maintaining the materials. Today, given the increasing abundance of superb programming (much of it very affordable), the expanding sources for video acquisition, and the continuing high demand for the stuff, this neglect is just plain perplexing and frustrating. Yet, despite the above gloomy jeremiad, it would be fool-headed and incorrect to view the evolution of library video collections as dead in the water, or even fatally sidetracked. Video collecting and video collections are very much alive and well in all types of libraries, if not necessarily realistically funded or well-staffed. Circulation figures in most large urban public libraries and most academic library video collections will, I think, bear me out on this (although, concrete data, like professional literature about video in general, have become as scarce as Beta video players in the past decade). Overview chapters in this book by Michael Vollmar-Grone, Kristine Brancolini, Anita Ondrusek, and Suzanne Crow provide further evidence that video is well-entrenched and circulating like tape-n'-disc hotcakes in public, academic and special libraries of all sizes.

Interestingly and oddly enough, while library video collections continue to flourish, the same can't really be said of video librarians—those rare professionals whose jobs are centrally involved with selecting, providing access to, and teaching about video content (as opposed to fiddling with the mechanisms via which that content is delivered). Even in the format's palmy honeymoon days in the 1980s and early 1990s, this group of dedicated videoslingers inhabited a tiny professional enclave. Many of us in that group grew into our jobs or insinuated ourselves into a gig as the importance and size of video collections continued to expand; many fewer were hired into positions specifically earmarked "Media." Almost all of us learned the craft on the job (media librarianship has historically ranked right up there with puppetry and papermaking in the curricula of most library schools and erstwhile library schools). Today, however, the specialization seems to be going the way of the spotted owl, the nickel ice cream cone, and the rotary dial phone. I have some not-too-startling theories about why this has come to be.

Beat bard Allen Ginsberg saw the best minds of his *Howl*-ing generation"—"angelheaded hipsters"—destroyed by madness; I saw the best minds of my generation—mediaheaded hipsters—deployed into administrative positions (which may be the same thing as madness). Other colleagues have been tapped for service in new media centers, educational technology programs, digital library initiatives, and the ever-mysterious domain of "special projects." This type of professional attrition may well be the natural, even the logical, evolutionary state of things: video librarians are among the most competent, ambitious, and visionary librarians I know. Unfortunately, it has been my observation that the considerable vaccuum left in the wake of such staff changes and rearrangements is seldom filled, either in full or in part.

Particularly in public libraries, except perhaps for children's and young adult librarians, public service specialization seems to be on the wane generally, a casualty of economic hard times and the attendant impulse to do more with less. Academic libraries, on the other hand, continue to thrive on subject specialization, and that's precisely the round hole into which video's square peg is increasingly being shoved (either there or into the narrow operational slot of course reserves). In all types of libraries, video collections and services—already on unsteady budgetary ground—have become a disturbingly easy mark for staff cuts or "reorganizations." It is somewhat ironic, given the continuing outsider status of video, that the administrative modus operandi in such cases has often been to pronounce the medium officially mainstreamed: it's popular, it's available everywhere, everyone watches it—who needs specialists?"

Then there's the little matter of the Internet and the World Wide Web, both of which have risen like some all-consuming rough beast since the last edition of this book. Widespread naiveté (yes, even among some library administrators) about the current and future nature and capabilities of Web-based media, and the rather insidious confusion between media content and media delivery, have often provided further convenient pretexts for collapsing, evaporating, or generally rejiggering media librarian positions. In casting an eye around the field, it's obvious that there is a general tendency to view the Internet as some kind of universal media Cuisinart, capable of efficiently blending all forms and formats of information and entertainment into some smoothly textured, richly flavored, easily consumable puree. This appliance-centered view would have librarians acting as cyberchefs, pushing the buttons and teaching the master classes in fusion cuisine. (At the risk of bludgeoning this particular metaphor into senselessness, it should be pointed out that there's a corollary game that's frequently played out in libraries: throw everything with a plug into the same room, the hell with content and function: Cuisinarts and vacuum cleaners, VCRs and microform readers.) Lori Widzinski, editor of the excellent *MCJournal: Journal of Academic Media Librarianship*, relates a story about meeting a library director who, when queried about his views on the future of media librarianship, enthusiastically offered the opinion that "All librarians in the 21st Century are media librarians." This sentiment seems to be in the air a lot these days. What it seems to imply is: the magic box contains all; the magic profession knows how to find, use, and teach all (or at least it's economically expedient to believe so). *All Librarians/Media Librarians.* Unfortunately, that's rather like saying all librarians are rare book librarians—after all, you can access sundry manuscript facsimiles on the Web.

The Internet *has*, in fact, revolutionized video librarianship, but not in ways that might be hoped for or expected, if you were to believe everything the microchip makers, the software vendors, or the unidentified library administrator cited above are pitching. The Net has vastly improved and facilitated communication and information sharing between colleagues, and between librarians, educators, filmmakers, and distributors. It has exponentially increased the venues for marketing and buying video, and has brought higher visibility to existing independent distributors. It has provided an enormous and tremendously useful new resource tool kit for video collection development librarians and for film studies scholars: just take a look at the ubiquitous URLs scattered throughout this book.

All of this is very well and cool. Nonetheless, even when the Web is ready for video prime time (read Chapter 24 to see why it isn't currently), there are things that it will never do or replace. Assuming that moving images will continue to occupy a significant role and place in library collections and/or services, there will be an ongoing, perhaps an intensified, need for librarians who understand the unique properties, power, and impact of these media, regardless of how they're served up. Whether it involves licensing online content or buying content in boxes and jewel cases, building effective and responsive video collections will continue to require a familiarity with the genres, history, evolution, and impact of the moving image, and its relationship to other media, including print. Digital media convergence (whatever that means and whenever that happens) will not obviate the need for librarians adept at wading through the muddy and twisting streets and alleys of the video marketplace, with its perplexing mix of mega-enterprises, institutional vendors, and tiny cottage industries. No matter what type of screen video is beamed from or where the images reside, video in libraries will persistently call out for committed advocates—lobbists for informed viewing, for diverse, quality programs and programming; and whatever the future holds for media in libraries, someone has to stand watch and take arms whenever Old Man Procrustus comes lumbering ominously along with his whetted blade.

Onward . . .

The rationale for undertaking a revision of this book at this time lies fairly close to the surface of the preceding discussions and rants: new formats, new resources, new approaches and concerns. Except for a scattering of brief articles in recent professional journals heralding the coming of DVD, there has been a rather ominous silence on the topic of video in libraries since the last edition of this book (the reasons for this dearth should be discernible between the lines of the anxious arguments made above). Not surprisingly, the few substantive exceptions have been penned by contributors to this book, Brancolini, Pitman, and Scholtz among them. One of the aims of this revision is, like its predecessor, to fill this egregiously yawning gap, and to investigate the collection, uses, and users of video in a considerably broader range of contexts than is currently available elsewhere in the literature.

As was the intent of the previous edition, it is hoped that this book will serve as a sort of road map and multifunctional travel guide for working media librarians, media specialists, and others involved one way or another in "doing video" in libraries and schools. In charting the realm of video collection development and management, there has been an attempt to include snapshots of the lay of the land in specific provinces (public, academic, school, and special libraries), as well as more closely focused investigations of significant cultures, landmarks, and points of interest along the way. In addition to these views of the video mainland, there has also been an effort to provide brief forays into the outback—those topical regions seldom visited in print or around the professional conference table (Chapters by Debra Franco (16) and Jon Cecil (17) on the arcane workings of the video marketplace; and the chapter by Helene Whitson (21) on stock footage sources lie in this latter terra incognita).

Like most Baedekers, this volume is liberally interspersed with general wisdom and practical hints for intrepid travellers from all backgrounds (don't drink the water; don't program features without performance rights), as well as more philosophical considerations of the voyage (why travel is broadening; why develop a separate video collection development policy). In most of the writing included, these two approaches—practical and theoretical—coexist peacefully and effectively. Although the organization of this work is geared toward highlighting collection and acquisition issues and resources that are unique or largely specific to a particular library context or clientele, the hope is that much of the information and advice embodied in these chapters will prove to be useful to video selectors across the spectrum of library types. And because the universe of tools and issues relevant to video librarians is a fairly circumscribed one, there is something positively *Roshomon*-like throughout these discussions: the same resources, concepts, controversies, bêtes noires, and experts in the field have an odd way of recurrently popping up in disparate places, albeit with different spins and emphases, and reported from different angles and perspectives, depending on the author's institutional or professional affiliation.

A FAST-FORWARD CONTENTS SCAN

Part I. SEE ALSO: The Nature of Video, the Nature of Video in Libraries

Putting Walt Crawford's chapter first in the batting line-up is somewhat of an intentionally subversive act. It would have been fairly easy—perhaps even expectable—to a put a rosy, evangelical chapter on the power and glory of video in the lead position. It would have also been less provocative and fun to read than Crawford's intelligent, opinionated, and lively non-video librarian's thoughts on video and its place in library collections.

Part II. The Wide Angle: Video Collection in Multiple Contexts

Part II offers a series of wide-angle views of the history and direction of video collection development, video services, and video librarianship in specific types of libraries. Michael Vollmar-Grone, Cassandra Keith, Kristine Brancolini, and Anita Ondrusek and Suzanne Crow consider the issues faced, and the strategies and tools utilized by public, school, academic, and specialized libraries in attempting to build video collections to meet the diverse client and program needs.

In Chapter 2, Michael Vollmar-Grone begins his far-ranging meditation on public library video collections by briefly chronicling the history and use of earlier media formats in these settings. He proceeds by considering the various internal and external obstacles and challenges faced by public library video collection developers, and provides a thoughtful look at central concerns and activities ranging from strategic planning to core collection development, from collection maintenance and management to intellectual freedom issues.

Chapter 3 offers a particularly welcomed (because particularly rare) investigation of the various roles of school media specialists in building video collections that are responsive to teaching and learning needs. Cassandra Keith offers useful views on the importance of partnerships between media specialist/school librarians and teachers, and tips for facilitating these relationships. She also provides a discussion of the practical and philosophical need for developing effective video collection policies in school settings.

Chapter 4 deals with media in academic libraries, a topic that has almost completely evaded scrutiny in the professional literature of the past 30 years. Kristine Brancolini redresses this lack with an in-depth look at the evolution and current status of media on campus. Brancolini's chapter describes the various functional and administrative models that have developed for handling media in colleges and universities, and discusses the changing nature of these media operations in the face of new technologies and shifting teaching and research priorities. Using the 1999 Association of College and Research Universities *Guidelines for Media Resources in Academic Libraries* as a basis, Brancolini presents a thorough analysis of the primary requirements for building effective media collections and services in academic institutions and other library contexts as well.

Among the earliest uses of non-theatrical motion pictures was their utilization as a means of documenting medical practices and providing both professional and lay instruction in medical and health-related fields. In Chapter 5, Anita Ondrusek and Suzanne Crow offer an impressively comprehensive look at the collection and use of film, video, and digital moving image technologies in health-content media collections. Ondrusek's and Crow's broad coverage of the topic includes discussions of the various clientele served in health science settings, the primary collection areas of health sciences video, and the selection and acquisition methodologies and resources for these materials.

Part III. Close Focus: Specialized Collections and Special User Needs

In contrast to the fairly broad overviews presented in Part II, the seven chapters in Part III deal with specific collection emphases, specialized types or genres of video materials, as well as with collecting to meet the specialized needs of particular clientele.

Thomas Harrington's presentation in Chapter 6, dealing with materials for the deaf and hearing-impaired, includes a short history of visual materials for the deaf; a discussion of the deaf community and of the specific needs of deaf library patrons; and a look at the current state of video software and captioning hardware, including current legislation related to the latter. Included in Harrington's chapter are several helpful appendixes of hardware, software, and institutional resources, and a short core listing of videos for the deaf and about deaf culture.

While most of us have become at least passingly familiar with closed-caption video and its benefits for the deaf and hearing-impaired (and for others, such as non-native speakers of English), video for the blind and visually impaired—described video—is a considerably more recent and lesser-known development. In Chapter 7, Mary Watkins and Kim Charlson provide an enlightening discussion of the history, nature, and various uses of described video programming, along with a short overview of current federal legislation concerning described TV programming. Included also are sections on cataloging and processing issues, a useful series of questions and answers related to library video services for the blind and visually impaired, and a listing of resources.

One can easily argue that regardless of the power, stature, and venerable history of print journalism, most of us currently get the majority of our news from the tube. While access to broadcast news has become increasingly important in academic research and teaching, and for various political and commercial purposes, the sources for obtaining current and historical news on videotape are extremely limited. In Chapter 8, Robert Browning describes one of the most significant broadcast news archives and distribution sources in the United States, the Public Affairs Video Archive (PAVA) at Purdue University. Since 1987, the archive has served as the chief repository and distributor of programming on the Cable-Satellite Public Affairs Network (C-SPAN). In addition to describing the services of the Archive, Browning also offers brief descriptions of other important news archives in the United States.

The uses of film and video to foster an understanding of the complex history and intersections of race, ethnicity, gender, and sexuality in society is the theme of Chapter 9, by Diana Vogelsong and Christopher Lewis. The chapter also investigates the role of film and video in building a sense of cultural connection and pride within historically marginalized groups. Vogelsong and Lewis outline some of the considerations in building a video collection of feature films and documentaries on culturally diverse topics, including the role of collecting movies as "social texts"—reflections and promulgators of cultural images and attitudes.

From the days of the earliest public library 16mm film collections and co-operatives in the 1920s to the present days of omnipresent tape and disc collections, feature films—the movies—have dominated the shelves and the circulation statistics. Early enthusiasts of movies in libraries touted the form as a surefire way to entice a celluloid-drunk public into the stacks, a means of leading the masses toward print versions of the visions on the screen. The public, on the other hand, has always loved the flicks on their own unique and entertaining terms—cultural uplift be damned. The advent of home video and video-culture has only served to intensify this frequently manic, century-old love affair.

In their respective chapters, Randy Pitman and Oksana Dykyj offer flip-side views—public and academic—of cinema collection development. In Chapter 10, Pitman addresses a weighty roster of issues facing public libraries involved in building movie collections on tape and DVD, from censorship and ratings, to budget concerns and the need to build balanced, representative collections. The appendixes to his chapter offer concise listings of key selection, evaluation, and acquisition tools for building cinema collections, including a useful sampling of such works devoted to DVD.

For Freud, a cigar was sometimes just a cigar; for academicians (and for Freud, too), a movie is rarely just a movie. Over the course of the past century, film has been studied from an often dizzying array of theoretical and disciplinary vantage points: film as aesthetic form; as a form of modern/postmodern authorship; as pop culture artifact, political force, social indicator; as history, and as psychology. In Chapter 11, Oksana Dykyj provides an edifying historical long view of the changing nature of academic film studies and film scholarship in other disciplines. Among the topics covered in her chapter are the aesthetic and practical differences between various formats (from film to digital); the development of core cinema collections; preservation; and the role of cinema librarians as partners in the processes of film studies teaching and research.

One thing all existing film and video collections have in common, regardless of format, content, or venue: they'll all eventually degrade and crumble into dust if unattended, some horrifyingly sooner than later. In Chapter 12, Jeff Clark addresses the immediate preservation needs of circulating collections. Clark provides valuable information about the physical properties of tape-based media and DVD, and offers wise counsel regarding practical measures for extending the effective life of these resources.

Part IV. Laying the Ground Rules, Picking What Plays: Policies, Criteria, and Methods for Selecting, Evaluating, and Acquiring Video

Librarians have often tended to demonstrate a certain degree of philosophical schizophrenia when it comes to developing policies and criteria for evaluating, selecting, and acquiring video. On the one hand, the argument has frequently been made for eschewing a separate set of video collection policies in favor of incorporating the medium into the general bibliographic policy and procedures fold (this is the idealistic "information regardless of format" approach). On the other hand, the uniqueness of the medium in terms of content and construction, cost, publication universe, and use militates strongly for the development of a separate, format-specific cluster of policies. The relative newness of the medium and its frequently precarious state in libraries are further reasons for closely defining the goals and parameters of video collecting. In Chapter 13, James Scholtz presents a thorough and insightful analysis of the component features of selection and collection development policies in general, and those geared to defining and guiding video collecting in particular. His chapter touches upon techniques for evaluating current collections and for assessing client needs. Scholtz offers an outline of the various types of video selection and collection development policies, and illustrates these models with ample and apposite samples.

A key element of the collection development process for all media is the evaluation of materials. For video and film, this task is often fairly involved and time-consuming. As with books, video evaluation requires an assessment of a work's quality (a complex mix of factors) and its anticipated short- or long-term value (a complex mix of factors) for a particular clientele, program, or purpose. But because film and video engage a multiplicity of senses in getting their messages across, the evaluative process for these media can be substantially more complex than for print resources. In considering video materials, the reviewer must focus at once on what is being said, how the message is technically constructed, and how content and production technique interact. It has been argued by various media theorists that each medium employs a specific grammar: each uses a unique system of symbols and syntax for conveying messages and for codifying experience and reality. Evaluating film and video requires an understanding of the special grammar of those media forms, and an understanding of the types of tales those languages tell best. In Chapter 14, on evaluation, Beth Blenz-Clucas offers helpful guidelines for librarians engaged in this demanding process, and discusses the place of evaluation in the larger collection development context.

In building video collections, there are a number of unique and extremely significant connections between selection and acquisition issues, and those centering on access and use. As Gary Handman comments in Chapter 15, on copyright: "What is very often being acquired when one purchases a video is not only an addition to the library's physical inventory, but also the right to use or perform all or part of that intellectual property in certain contexts or for certain audiences." Handman focuses on video collection and use in libraries and educational contexts in terms of both the rights of the copyright holder and the more nebulously defined fair-use exceptions to these rights granted by the law. He also touches briefly upon the even murkier area of copyright and fair use in the age of digital reproduction, and discusses the 1996 *Educational Fair Use Guidelines for Multimedia*. A core listing of Web and print resources related to current and evolving copyright issues is provided.

Part V. Behind the Box Office: The Nature of the Video Market

For both new and veteran video librarians, as well as those brave souls in the Acquisition Department, the process of negotiating the video marketplace is definitely a "We're not in Kansas anymore, Toto" proposition. The structure, practices, and economics of the video marketplace bear little if any resemblance to print publishing or to other forms of electronic media distribution. In dealing with this highly segmented and anarchistic market, institutional video buyers regularly find themselves facing a bewildering tangle of distribution sources, use rights, and often capricious pricing schemes. In her "Primer on the Home Video Market" (Chapter 16), Debra Franco effectively manages to remove some of the mystery from the market (if not the frustrations inherent in doing business with it). Her piece offers a clear set of answers to frequently asked questions regarding the organization and operation of the home, special interest, and educational video rental and sales markets, as well as a quick look at new developments and changing market trends.

The Public Broadcasting Service (PBS), one of the largest and most powerful sponsors of quality video production and programming, has also evolved into one of the largest distributors of non-theatrical video materials. In Chapter 17, Jon Cecil provides a history of PBS and a discussion of its organization and operation. Cecil offers a valuable discourse on the economics of marketing programs aired on PBS. He details the factors which militate either for or against a program becoming available on the video market, and generally explains pricing structures employed by both home and educational video markets.

Part VI. Resources

Although the advent of the Internet and the Web have, as discussed previously, built a certain number of bridges over the videographic void, sizeable uncharted black holes and gray areas still exist (still no national videography—no Videos in Print—after all these years!). Rebecca Albitz, Gary Handman, and Nancy Goldman and Jason Sanders attempt to fill at least some of this information gap by pointing to a very broad spectrum of finding tools, evaluation sources, current interest literature, organizations, and programs concerned with video production, distribution, and exhibition. It should also be noted that many of the other chapters in this book also contain valuable appendixes listing resources for specific types of material or specific collection emphases (see, for example, Chapters 5, 6, 8, 10, and 21).

In Chapter 18, Rebecca Albitz provides a detailed bibliographic essay covering central current awareness sources, directories and catalogs, review and evaluation materials, videographic databases, core lists, and monographic works in the area of video collection development. Included in her chapter is an interesting discussion of the uses of OCLC WorldCat as a video reference tool.

Print, online, and media resources for the study of diverse American cultures have expanded tremendously over the past decade. In Chapter 19, Gary Handman has compiled a large bibliography and videography of materials that complement the broader discussion of cultural diversity and video collection presented by Diana Vogelsong and Christopher Lewis in Chapter 9. The resources cited in Handman's chapter include those useful for building both documentary collections and feature film collections that reflect the changing representations of race, ethnicity, gender, and sexuality in the movies.

Many of the most exciting and challenging video titles currently available are not found in the pages of the standard videographies described in Albitz's chapter. In Chapter 20, Nancy Goldman and Jason Sanders deal with both printed and organizational resources for locating these "alternative" film and video works. Included in this category are works by independent filmmakers with non-mainstream social and political perspectives, and works that utilize experimental and avant-garde approaches to the medium. Goldman and Sanders concentrate in particular on strategies for identifying both those works which have made it into the video and broadcast mainstream, and those which continue to reside firmly underground.

The primary stock in trade of most video librarians has typically been "store-bought" titles—commercially distributed, prerecorded video. In academic libraries and some special libraries, there is an increasing demand for another type of moving image materials: primary source footage, such as news broadcasts, clips of historical events, and other specialized film/video sequences. Because the acquisition of this type of stock or archival footage is generally beyond the collecting scope of the library, referral to commercial and institutional sources for these materials has become an important part of media reference work. In Chapter 21, Helene Whitson discusses the concept of stock footage, and provides a useful description of the various uses of and sources for these materials.

In many instances, the most effective assistance in building video collections is obtained from organizational connections and collegial networks rather than from the printed or digital page. Gary Handman (Chapter 22) has compiled a basic list of associations and organizations concerned with video and film production, distribution, exhibition, and access. Many of the groups listed also distribute independently produced films and videos and play a strong advocacy role in national and regional arts arenas. Also included in this chapter is a brief listing of online discussion lists devoted to the study and use of film and video in libraries and in educational institutions.

Part VII. Fast Forward: The Future of Moving-Image Distribution and Access

DVD: it ain't the future, it's now (purportedly the fastest selling consumer electronic gizmo ever). In a sense, DVD is every media librarian's worst nightmare—a new format to contend with. On the other hand, there's that glorious picture and that perfect sound! Those supplementary features! That compactness, ease of use, and longevity! In Chapter 23, Kristine Brancolini describes the history of DVD development, and the nature and technical properties of this hot new format. In the course of this discussion, she offers a number of thorough, practical answers to likely questions about DVD collections in libraries, including the inevitable "Why?"

In some sense, undertaking the writing of a book dealing with video collection in an age of digital creation and reproduction is an existential enterprise. There are changes in the fundamental nature of moving image capture, storage, and transmission and display (not to mention marketing) looming just around the next corner. These changes threaten to make much of what has been discussed in this work as quaintly obsolete as a treatise on the collection and use of lantern slides. Rick Provine's conclusion to this book (Chapter 24) provides a glimpse of the new revolution to come—an ultimate move away from artifactually based collections and toward network access and video on demand. Included in his discussion is a basic explanation of streamed media, a look at the current wobbly state of video on the Web, and a discussion of what "preservation" means in a digital environment. Provine also looks at the various potential roles of libraries as producers of Web video content or as developers of gateways to the Web media resources.

In one of the many patently self-serving interviews he was fond of giving, Thomas Edison, who steadfastly claimed to have invented motion pictures (but didn't), offered an oddly dismissive view of the invention as "A silly little device for making pictures that would dance" (as quoted in *The Wizard Who Spat on the Floor*, Time-Life Video 1974). In the ensuing century, that "silly little machine" was to change the world and our perceptions of it thoroughly and irrevocably. The invention of home video in its various guises has only served to bring the dance more intimately and regularly into our daily lives. In increasing numbers, libraries have also come to the Moving Image Ball (or vice versa). It is hoped that the advice and resources in this book will assist in building and managing video collections and services that step wisely, lively, and in good time.

Part I

SEE ALSO: The Nature of Video, the Nature of Video in Libraries

Chapter 1

"Watch This, It's Good for You": Thoughts on Video and Libraries

Walt Crawford

Does video have a place in most library collections? Of course—and most of this book will provide ways to select and use video effectively. Is video now truly the "predominant recorder, conveyer, and manipulator of the cultural message," as Gary Handman put it in his introduction to the first edition of this book—or is it true that, as Handman's e-mail signature file quotes Gregory Ulmer (1989), "Everything wants to be television"? Not in my book.

I don't believe in a video revolution. I do believe that video adds to library services. I don't believe the flickering light of the tube has transformed us—at least, I desperately hope not. I regard "visual literacy" as a silly phrase: video makers do their best to make viewing as painless as possible, and the other meaning of "video literacy" comes down to critical thinking. The importance of *literacy* ("print literacy" is redundant) has not declined; those who cannot or do not read will always be at the mercy of those who can and do.

I'm no more anti-video than I am anti-computer. I watch television—and I do mean TeeVee: not the refined atmosphere of PBS and Bravo but the down-and-dirty of The WB, TNT, CBS, ABC, and occasionally even Fox and UPN. I admit preferring the debased commercial claptrap of *The West Wing, Buffy the Vampire Slayer*, and *Futurama* to the deep intellectual exercises of *Antiques Roadshow*, cooking shows, *NOVA, Mystery, Austin City Limits*, and the world's talkiest TV news hour. My wife and I watch movies on video, usually once a week—on awful old VHS (for the moment) rather than the subversive medium of DVD.

It's worth quoting part of a February 2000 e-mail exchange about this project:

Gary Handman: I *do* think everything in post-post-mod culture *does* have a bias toward televisionness. I think the act of watching, of spectatorship, of projection of real upon reel and vice versa is the defining characteristic of the last century. I know you don't agree with this, but I think it's absolutely futile for librarians (and others) to ignore these facts, and to continue pitting new media against old in a kind of duel to the death contest.

Crawford: Ah, now, there, you see: I *don't* pit one medium against another: my slogan continues to be "And, Not Or." No, I don't think all of life/all of media use fits into the "watching as it goes by" mold or tends toward that mold. I think there's more and more evidence that people appreciate choices, that life tends toward complexity, that good books aren't defective television just as public libraries aren't defective academic libraries. . . . Then again, I'm not your real curmudgeon. Your real curmudgeon sez that video is the ruination of western civilization . . . but I don't watch a lot of UPN, and I don't watch Fox reality shows, so I don't quite fall into that camp.

Video can tell stories that books can't tell as effectively. The best video (and the best television) can enlighten, inform, and even ennoble viewers. But I will assert that the "six o'clock news" is a pathetic substitute for a good metropolitan newspaper; that most people will gain understanding and wisdom faster and more permanently from print than from television; and that video has several strikes against it in moving beyond entertainment, none of which makes video worthless or not worth treating seriously as part of library collections; it's never that simple.

When it comes to thinking about video, culture, and libraries, I find myself in the radical middle: somewhere between tradition and the video believers, with strong sentiments about both extremes.

THE MISSING FOOTNOTES

The scholarly apparatus goes here. I can give you footnoted quotes from more than a dozen books arguing every side of television as a medium. Neil Postman and Mark Crispin Miller cry out against TV. George Gilder expects us all to be producing our own individual TV programs by now, and to prefer those to scripted programs. Tony Schwartz thinks print literacy is irrelevant, and so on: pundits crying out against TV, pundits ennobling TV, both sides assuming that only TV matters.

Then there are Douglas Davis' remarkably sensible *The Five Myths of Television Power* (1993) and David Bianculli's *Teleliteracy: Taking Television Seriously* (1992), both of which present informed perspectives from the middle.

I'm not quoting from any of these for several reasons:

• With the exception of the Davis and Bianculli books, I don't think most of the stuff mentioned here is worth reading. Oversimplification and extremism on either side of the video debates becomes dreary rather quickly.

- Nearly all of the books and articles on these topics are about *television*, specifically commercial broadcast and cablecast television. Video, as collected and circulated by libraries, is not the same medium as broadcast television. Some of the arguments for and against television don't work equally well for video.
- You can look up these authors, and you'll gain more by looking at the full list of books or articles that they've published, and by reading more than the specific page I might footnote.
- I'm not a scholar (at least not most of the time), and this chapter is not intended to be a scholarly article.

Instead of scholarly reflection, here are some semi-random thoughts about video, other media, and libraries. Hang on: it may be a bumpy ride!

TELL ME A STORY

Stories are what video does best—and stories (broadly defined) are what libraries do best. Stories aren't just facts strung together. A good story has a beginning, middle, and end. It has a narrative thrust: an arc, if you will. When you reach the end of a well-told story (whether fact or fiction), you should know, feel, or be aware of something more than when you began.

Good stories hold your attention, both because you want to see how they end and because you find the narrative arc engrossing. Essays and articles can be good stories; they can also be less structured, building a viewpoint or set of conclusions without a formal narrative arc.

Good storytelling—whether fiction or fact—involves much more than plot. One sign of a well-told work of fiction is that you still enjoy it after you know the conclusion. If a "spoiler" spoils your enjoyment, it's a second-rate story.

Strengths of Video for Storytelling

Video brings pictures, motion, sound, and timing to storytelling. That can offer much broader range to narration. Good video stories rely on more than words, and use scenery and action to flesh out a story in ways that words may not do as well.

Instructional video adds richness to lessons by showing what happens rather than talking about it. Ideally, documentary video shows the reality of events together with narrative interpretation—or, in some cases, may claim to show reality directly by omitting narration. Dramatic video adds the visual elements of stage plays, going further to provide broader scenic vistas and the unreal visions and sounds that special effects can provide. Travelogs show destinations more effectively and concretely than words alone.

For those who are visually oriented, video offers a more appropriate route to enlightenment, entertainment, and wisdom. For the rest of us, video offers an alternative approach that suits certain kinds of stories exceptionally well.

These strengths are all common to motion pictures as well as video. It's not clear to me that videocassettes and other video on television offer their own strengths, with two exceptions: you can pause a video in much the same way that you can set aside a book, and videos bring stories to the comfort of your home.

Weaknesses of Video for Storytelling

Most weaknesses of video for storytelling are also those of other "moving media" in general. The most obvious, for non-fiction (especially news) and the richest fiction, is that video conveys text and ideas at relatively slow rates. Even mediocre readers can read and understand printed text much faster than they can take in speech—and the best videos are *never* simply full-speed speech.

A good speaker will deliver 100 to 130 words per minute, typically 6,000 to 7,800 words in a full-hour speech, maybe a little more. An hour-long commercial news broadcast amounts to less than 45 minutes of program time and the need for visual interest substantially reduces the ability to convey text. I'd be surprised if an average commercial news hour contains 4,000 words of text. In one case, a TV station that makes its transcripts available on the Web, I counted 3,000 words for a news hour. But a reader can easily go through a metropolitan newspaper in less than an hour—even though the *front page alone* of that paper may include more text than the evening news.

That may be an extreme case, but consider movies based on novels. In general, such movies convey only a few highlights of the books, unless the books fall into that special modern category of written screenplays (e.g., much of Michael Crichton's fiction). You can make a good two-hour movie from a short story, including all that's in the short story; most novellas include too much material.

A second weakness relates directly to the multimedia strength of video and movies. By providing sound, vision, and motion, all set in a specified running time, movies and videos may use more of our senses than print—but they don't typically *involve* us in the way that the written word can. When you read good fiction and some of the best non-fiction, your mind is part of the creative act, adding your own sights and sounds based on the words you read. Video removes those possibilities; the choices have been made for you.

One other weakness may relate more to television than to packaged videos. To wit, television seems to *disengage* most viewers. Nobody talks about "vegging out" with a good book or interesting conversation, and you don't go to a movie to sink into a semi-comatose state. But that's what frequently happens with television, and may require a little effort for the storyteller or viewer to overcome. Advertisers seemingly want viewers to be so relaxed that we're more suggestible; networks want us to Not Touch That Dial. In either case, we work at a lessened state of consciousness, making it harder to convey a rich, complex story.

The alternative use of television—but presumably *not* video—is death to storytelling and meaning. That's when television becomes background, radio with pictures: a household companion droning on in the background while we read, converse, knit, study, or nap. I won't return to that particular case, because it doesn't make sense for prerecorded video (although there are videos intended to act as pet-sitters).

Video and Other Media

Video for libraries has equated to videocassette, more specifically VHS videocassette, for quite a few years. The package is changing, but the change to DVD does more than simply change the carrier. For now, let's consider how VHS video relates to other media.

The most popular library video collections, and the bulk of the video marketplace, consist of movies (and possibly "films" for the enlightened): multimillion-dollar entertainment projects normally created on film and originally screened in theaters. Add to that a growing number of "direct to video" projects, either because they were intended that way (e.g., most Disney cartoon sequels) or because they never found a home in theaters.

The problem is that videos, while adding convenience and selection, subtract from the original movies. Most home viewers see movies on screens measuring 27" to 36" diagonal, or possibly rear-projection screens as large as 50 to 60 inches. That's not much compared to movie screens. Worse yet, NTSC screen resolution (as used in pre-HDTV U.S. and Canadian television) is so bad that smart viewers sit at least twice as far from the screen as its diagonal size: otherwise, you see the scanning lines; and VHS provides half the visual detail that NTSC sets can display.

Put it all together, and the best home televisions offer a fuzzy little window on the action in a movie, no more than one-quarter or one-fifth the apparent width (that is, visual arc) of a good movie screen and with much less detail in the picture.

Of course, most videocassettes don't show the whole picture in any case. The original picture, typically filmed in proportions between 2.35:1 and 1.8:1 (16: 9) is reduced to 1.3:1 (4:3) by eliminating substantial portions of the picture. Some of us haven't seen movies as they were filmed in years!

But that's carping. Film on video has made it possible for libraries to offer classics, independent films, and all the other films that aren't available at the local multiplex cinema—or on TV, which can offer higher resolution than VHS but otherwise suffers the same drawbacks.

Good video collections offer many projects that did not start out as movies. In my own local library, most non-fiction videos are repackaged TV shows from PBS, A&E, the History Channel, and others, or releases from MacArthur Foundation video projects. There are also videotapes of city council meetings and instructional videos, along with a handful of travelogs.

Instructional videos offer new possibilities for education and specific instruction, but can suffer from popular expectations for video. We've come to expect at least cable-quality video production, and that doesn't come cheap; some of us won't sit still for a talking head or a simple lecture. Good video doesn't come cheap; while the equipment is getting much cheaper (thanks to computers), the talent is getting more expensive. Anybody *can* produce a video these days—but most of us lack the talent to produce one that anyone else would want to watch.

TV News and Newspapers

Do television and video now constitute the "primary chronicle" of our times? I don't believe so. Video (whether packaged or televised) certainly provides the primary *visual* chronicle of contemporary events, but it is in the nature of video to leave out the details behind the visuals. That's partly a matter of density.

As I was writing this—on a slow news day in late summer—I checked today's copy of the *San Francisco Chronicle*, a newspaper long derided (unjustly) for not providing enough text. As I measure it—excluding photos, ads, headlines, stock listings, weather, comics, classifieds, and special sections—today's paper had *at least* 88,000 words of text. Some newspapers would have less; several of the most important newspapers would have considerably more. Even PBS' talking-heads news hour totals around 8,000 words of an evening; commercial news broadcasts probably average half that.

Has TV news affected newspapers? Of course it has, in a variety of ways. Newspapers probably don't circulate as many copies as they would without TV—but that's a hard case to prove. Some newspapers have the pacing and "feel" of video, notably *USA Today*, and what newspaper can avoid dealing with video and television? In the *Chronicle*'s case, there's an odd interaction, one that the paper has stated in some detail. The *Chronicle* has largely abandoned the traditional inverted-pyramid approach to newspaper journalism in favor of more narrative stories. Why? Because the paper's editors assume that readers already know the key points for the big stories, either from TV, radio, or the Internet: in essence, for the biggest stories, the tip of that pyramid has already been communicated. That leaves the newspaper free to do what newspapers do so much better than TV: provide depth, background, and analysis that comes to more than the shouting matches that seem to dominate *Crossfire, Hardball*, and the like.

Print: No Clear Effect

How does video affect print beyond newspapers? That's just not clear. There are, of course, books and magazines *about* television and video—indeed, far too many books that seem to be about media are really books about television. Clearly, television hasn't destroyed the magazine industry; clearly, most books and magazines aren't the print equivalents of video. Some recent magazines do seem to have the jumpy feel of MTV or the Internet, but there's nothing new about magazines for people with short attention spans.

Television can bring people to books; Oprah's book club is a phenomenal example, but C-SPAN's weekend book programming also bridges any gap between print and video cultures. Movies and their video equivalents have spawned hundreds of novels; while most of these may be genre fiction in the worst sense, quite a few offer good-quality writing and can stand on their own as popular literature. Videos, movies, and TV shows also result in many nonfiction books, bridging the gap between media in yet another fashion.

I'm a "print person" in many ways. I don't collect books as objects, but I do read far too many magazines and borrow a fair number of books from my local library. I don't believe that video has undermined literature or non-fiction; I also don't believe that video has the *power* to supplant the best fiction and non-fiction books and magazines.

Tending Away from Massness

Libraries celebrate the unusual—or at least they should. A library video collection may include some of the biggest box office hits, but that's not what makes it worthwhile, any more than a good public library can be defined by having hundreds of copies of every best-seller. Good library collections go beyond the big hits to include more specialized items. Good library collections go beyond the mass to serve specialized interests.

You all know that (or you should). What I see happening over the past couple of decades it a tendency away from "massness" in *all* media—including video and television. It happened years ago for magazines: the big general-interest magazines (*Life, Saturday Evening Post, Collier's*) disappeared while special-interest magazines proliferate. It's always been true for books: a handful of books each year reach mass-market proportions, but publishers continue to publish tens of thousands of new titles.

It turns out to be true for TV as well. One telling statistic came out in the 1999–2000 season. No series—*not one*—had a 30 percent share of the viewing audience taken over the season as a whole. Fifteen years ago, a 30 percent share would be the *minimum* for a show to be renewed. In other words, the most popular show in today's television market would have been cancelled in 1985.

Back then, there were three commercial networks, one public network, and a handful of struggling cable networks and independent stations. People decided among ABC, CBS, and NBC: anything else was on the fringes. Now, there are six *or more* commercial broadcast networks (does PAX count?), but there are also successful new series originating on a growing number of cable channels. The number of cable and satellite options keeps growing, giving television viewers more and more choices.

At home, I need cable to have any TV at all—and the minimum plausible cable combination includes 67 channels (without premium, digital, or pay-per-view options). After removing religious, foreign-language, shopping, and sports channels from the television's click-through menu, I find that Bruce Springsteen is *precisely* on the money: there are 57 channels, and much of the time "nothing" is on.

But "nothing" has taken on an entirely new flavor. With reruns of *Northern Exposure*, *Law and Order*, and *China Beach* available, will I really stare at *Big Brother*? Original movies on TNT may not be Oscar material, but they're as good as most original movies on ABC. *Biography* may be on A&E, ads and all, but it's as well done and worthwhile as many PBS programs. And so it goes.

What's happening with television is also happening with video. Naturally, libraries buy specialized videos that would never be on the big screen—but there's more to it than that. Films from independent studios proliferate in every video rental store; these "indie" features may hold up better for long-term library circulation than their big-studio cousins. Direct-to-video features sit between the indies and the majors; on VHS (or even DVD), you don't know whether $50 million was spent on promotion. Made-for-television features, documentaries, and other videos enrich the mix.

This is a very good thing. It begins to give video some of the breadth of books. It's all part of the flight from massness toward complexity and specialization—a flight that appears to benefit every medium it touches.

DVD: A Subversive Medium?

Libraries are moving from VHS to DVD and will continue to do so. DVD simply works better as a circulating medium: it's less prone to ordinary wear-and-tear and it's completely immune to malign pranks. No borrower can possibly record *Debbie Does Dallas* over your copy of *Bambi*: manufactured DVD can't be rerecorded.

Additionally, most DVDs present the *whole* film, in its original aspect ratio, not just the central half or panned-and-scanned portion. Well-mastered DVDs provide twice the resolution of VHS, offering all the clarity that NTSC television can display; and, at least for now, almost all DVDs sell for rational prices, not the "rental" gouging that has characterized the VHS market for most theatrical releases (and, unfortunately, too many specialized videos). Very few DVDs cost more than $30; a growing number cost less than $20.

But DVD is not the same medium as VHS, and in some ways it's a subversive medium. Most DVDs include extras—alternative endings, scenes cut from the theatrical release, trailers, "Making of" documentaries, even alternate sound tracks where directors or stars talk about the film as it proceeds. Almost all theatrical DVDs offer scene-by-scene access, and all DVDs make it easy to view individual frames for as long as you want: unlike VHS, you won't hurt the disc.

Those extras and that flexibility tends to undermine the passive nature of most video. People become *engaged* with DVDs: paying attention to scenes, tracking problems with continuity, going back to particular spots, and in general ignoring the commandment to Just Sit There and Watch.

Potentially, that makes DVD a far more interesting carrier for instructional and specialized video material. It makes DVD a peculiar carrier for movies: wonderful for film students, magnificent when you watch, but a little bit subversive. When you start thinking about how a picture is put together, you may think more critically about the picture and its message. That's not what Hollywood wants—but it's a great thing for libraries.

CONCLUSION

Videos make awful substitutes for good books. Books make terrible substitutes for good videos. Libraries should include both, along with other media, as they serve the mission of each library. I can't imagine any public library with no good use for video, and it's getting harder to imagine video-free academic libraries. Video provides a different kind of cultural record, one that's just as valid for libraries as print—but video does not *replace* print as the primary tool for enlightenment. Video does many things exceptionally well; analysis, argument, and understanding are not among its strengths. But video can *show*—and that's worth a lot.

REFERENCES

Bianculli, David. 1992. *Teleliteracy: Taking Television Seriously*. New York: Continuum.
Davis, Douglas, 1993. *The Five Myths of Television Power, or, Why the Medium Is Not the Message*. New York: Simon & Schuster.
Ulmer, Gregory L. 1989. *Teletheory: Grammatology in the Age of Video*. New York: Routledge.

RECOMMENDED READING

Gilder, George F. 1994. *Life after Television*. Rev. ed. New York: W. W. Norton.
Miller, Mark Crispin. 1988. *Boxed In: The Culture of TV*. Evanston, IL: Northwestern University Press.
Miller, Mark Crispin, ed. 1990. *Seeing through Movies*. New York: Pantheon Books.
Postman, Neil. 1982. *The Disappearance of Childhood*. New York: Delacorte Press.
Postman, Neil. 1985. *Amusing Ourselves to Death: Public Discourse in the Age of Show Business*. New York: Viking.
Postman, Neil. 1988. *Conscientious Objections: Stirring Up Trouble about Language, Technology, and Education*. New York: Knopf.
Postman, Neil. 1992. *Technopoly: The Surrender of Culture to Technology*. New York: Knopf.
Postman, Neil, and Powers, Steve. 1992. *How to Watch TV News*. New York: Penguin Books.

Part II

The Wide Angle: Video Collection in Multiple Contexts

Chapter 2

Public Library Video Collections

Michael Vollmar-Grone

Stop reading now if unfamiliar faces in the library are undesirable. However, if increased community support, new users, and more return trips by present customers are of interest, read on. While video collections cannot guarantee these results, that has historically been the effect.

PAST, PRESENT, AND FUTURE

Visual formats have a long, albeit peripheral, history in public libraries. Here in the twenty-first century, we may visualize a nineteenth-century progenitor setting up for a lecture utilizing the latest in visual aids—a Magic Lantern projector. A device with roots in the seventeenth century, the slide projector became widely available and affordable by the 1880s, but in 1895 two French brothers, Louis and Auguste Lumiere, made that stagnant technology look instantly quaint and obsolete with their revolutionary invention, moving pictures.[1]

Some progressive librarians embraced the new moving image format early in the twentieth century. Patrick Williams, in his book *The American Public Library and the Problem of Purpose* (1988), excerpts ALA president Hiller C. Wellman's 1915 conference speech.

Photographs and prints of all kinds, music rolls, scores, lantern slides, phonograph records . . . stereoscopes, radiopticons, and lanterns . . . are often supplied. Concert giving by libraries with victrolas is becoming not unusual; and now we are introducing moving picture shows.

Due to the cost of equipment and film reproduction, film was not to find its way immediately into every home; that would have to wait until the video revolution. Film was initially limited to centers that could afford and support such a luxury—libraries, churches, and schools. These venues were often the primary places in communities, other than movie houses, for viewing films. A showing was a major event, and an expensive one at that.

Videos eventually brought the cinema to the living room, but the process required 20 years of technological innovations. Many librarians currently working with media have witnessed the various transitions of the format, from two-inch tapes to the current cutting-edge technology, Digital Versatile Disks (DVD). Massive two-inch reel-to-reel videotapes were introduced in 1956, largely as a broadcast and industrial standard. The first appearance of a more widely accessible video standard was the 3/4-inch (U-MATIC) format, introduced in 1971. Both U-MATIC recorders and players were very large, heavy, and inconvenient to use. It was a technology found in schools and industrial training centers rather than in homes (one impetus for the development of this technology was to show in-flight movies on transcontinental flights). The first convenient home system was the Sony Betamax, introduced in 1975. A year later, a competing standard, 1/2-inch VHS, was introduced. Although Beta was judged technically superior to the VHS format (and is still beloved by many diehard enthusiasts), it is generally agreed that Sony made several major tactical errors in developing its invention: Beta tape could record a maximum of three hours, while VHS tapes could hold two, four, or six hours of programming, depending on the speed— enough for one, two, or even three movies on one tape. Major missteps were also made in marketing Beta technology.[2]

The far-sighted, risk-taking librarians of the 1980s who began adding videotapes to their collections were rewarded almost immediately with high usage rates. New customers were attracted to institutions that formerly had little, if any, relevance for them. It was not uncommon for audiovisual departments to account for 25 to 35 percent of total library circulation. As the audiovisual departments grew, the responsibility of managing the services also expanded. Larger budgets and special knowledge of the format were required to address the needs and demands of patrons who grew up with video in the home.

Until the recent rise of DVD, VHS held the distinction of being the fastest growing consumer electronic technology in history. While video in its various formats opened library services to a whole new category of consumers, it also brought not a little controversy. Some traditionalists felt threatened by this new role for the library, one that involved things electronic and suffused with the stamp of popular culture. Like the Luddites of the previous century, some librarians rejected materials with great popular appeal based on suppositions that such items could not contain thoughts and ideas worth preserving for the ages.

This type of latent and overt print bias often continues to surface with particular vigor in the process of defining the institution's primary purpose, and as battle lines are drawn for budgets.

Even within media librarian circles, not everyone immediately recognized the specific merits of the new video format. Videos were approached either with the paradigm of 16mm film, or by designing the video department as a carnival mirror reflection of a commercial video store. Some boosted library circulation by adding a preponderance of popular titles, using videos as dangling carrots for the movie-hungry, tax-paying masses. Virtually ignored were the unique properties and power of the medium—the power to open new vistas, expand knowledge, and utilize visual learning styles. As Pat Lora (1994: 18) has stated:

Public libraries are funded by taxes paid equally by citizens who relish reading, as well as those for whom reading is a task or perhaps even impossible; we are not in the business of providing books, we are in the business of meeting our patrons' information needs. Video information and entertainment provides cultural appeal and important learning options for the full spectrum of readers and non-readers using the library.

Beyond the fundamental question of media's role in the library, there have been other, persistent controversies and concerns. What will be the hot format in ten years, or even five years? One sure bet is that delivery systems will change over time, be they an offset printed book, an electronic database, or a Digital Versatile Disc. While technology provides signposts we should watch carefully, the issue is ultimately less important than others that face video librarians. For good reasons, librarians are seldom on the cutting edge of technology. Rather than becoming too entangled in our own idiosyncratic technological web, it is best to remember that the mission of librarians remains fundamental, while specific technologies are merely tools. Whatever the nature of the delivery systems we employ, content and evaluation concerns remain constant.

Besides the format wars, video librarians face other challenges. Basic collection development decisions must be made. What types of videos will compose the collection? Will it offer educational titles, documentaries, classic and international movies, or popular features? Is entertainment a significant enough reason to establish and maintain a collection? How do we address our adamant, book-bound colleagues who justify the inclusion of popular authors such as Danielle Steel and John Grisham, while decrying *Erin Brockovich* and such as reprehensible Hollywood confection?

A related question concerns the role of the library video collection vis-à-vis commercial rental operations in the community. In the late 1800s some bookstores rented books. One hundred years later, videos in libraries presented another, more serious challenge to commercial enterprise. Some librarians believe that such competition cheapens the library. Some believe that, in any case, the crass, popular culture offerings of commercial enterprises such as video stores have no place among the library's hallowed shelves. Librarianship is often more about collaboration than competition. Most public librarians are fully aware that competition with the commercial sector is not realistic or even desirable. Instead, they select their niche in the neighborhood. Settling into this niche involves specializing in those titles that video stores are unlikely to carry: foreign-language films, documentaries, and educational titles that could be used in collaboration with local schools or as resources for individuals pursuing continued intellectual growth independently.

The cost of videos has historically been raised as a red flag warning against the medium, and in fact, a simple truth stands out: videos, particularly non-feature videos, often cost more than books (with the possible exception of reference works). Upon scrutiny of video prices in light of usage, however, the argument against video based on its relatively high cost becomes specious at best. A $75 video that circulates 100 times in a year is indeed less expensive than a $15 book that is borrowed 15 times. Some budget-stretching methods that can be used to fulfill patrons' wants, needs, and expectations will be discussed later in this chapter.

If materials costs have been waved in front of library administrators as a warning sign, the cost of processing videos has often closed the door completely. Fortunately, as the profession matures and collections develop, many of the early problems related to cataloging and bibliographic access have virtually disappeared. The scarcity of tools for identifying titles and locating sources for purchasing videos continues to present problems for those involved in acquisitions, although the Internet has improved things considerably in the area of feature films. On the other hand, cataloging records for many entertainment and mainstream educational and documentary videos have become increasingly available through bibliographic utilities such as Online Computer Library Center (OCLC).

Access to video collections has consistently presented its own set of problems and pitfalls. In its "Freedom to View Statement" (http://www.ala.org/alaorg/oif/freedomtoview.html), the American Library Association (ALA) states that all people ought to have free access to all library materials. There are at least four major policy issues for librarians raised in that statement: Will the collection be age restricted? Will videos have rental fees? Will there be fines for late returns? Will the library collect R and X/NC-17 rated films and videos that are sexually graphic or explicit? Unfortunately, there is evidence that many librarians sidestep the labeling issues simply by purchasing few, if any, videos with R or X/NC17 ratings (Kreamer 1992). Others use parental consent contracts to allow minors access to the video collections. Besides content labeling and restrictions, there are other access issues that must be addressed: Are there significant reasons to double charge taxpayers? Are fees a significant roadblock to access for some patrons?

The 1990s were a time of change within the public library community. Many video librarian positions were created during that period, especially in the boom time early in the decade. Despite the changes in the field, many past challenges and fundamental issues remain. While many of these challenges, such as the dependence on constantly evolving formats and continuing anti-media sentiment in libraries, are unique to video and video librarianship, many are universal to the profession: the changing nature of both user needs and collections which meet those needs; intellectual freedom and censorship; preservation of the collections; copyright and intellectual property issues; access and fees issues; competition for materials budgets and for space; the increasing scarcity of library education and the future of professional specialties. We have much to learn from our past successes and failures in dealing with these challenges. To borrow from the great library educator S.R.R. Ranganathan, via Crawford and Gorman (1995), we should examine the past when interpreting the present to envision the future.

STRATEGIC PLANNING

The past decade also witnessed the focus on strategic planning in institutions, from *Fortune* 500 companies to small public libraries. While the terminology and specific planning functions may not be standardized, the core concepts are.

Basically, planning is a reiterative process. The organizational direction is determined through internal and external assessments. From these assessments the vision/mission statement, goals, and objectives are formulated. These elements form the foundation upon which specific plans are detailed, critical success factors established and measured, and resource requirements determined. The plans are then implemented. The third step is to evaluate the implementation and performance of the plans. Finally, the knowledge gained through these processes is used to corroborate or modify the organizational direction. And so the process continues.

This is the "Vision Quest." The term refers to the Native American ritual by which divine guidance is sought through tribulation and intense introspection. In this process, only those who desire and work toward greatness will achieve it. So, too, the hard work of implementing the vision and goals of a library must entail the efforts of individuals at all levels. The fruits of this labor must be planted within individual library operations in order for the institution to be successful. Video collection development and maintenance must be reflective of those core values central to the library system as a whole.

Because the primary mission of public libraries ought to be serving all constituents, and because library constituencies are widely diverse, a step-by-step strategic planning guide cannot be written to cover all libraries everywhere. Instead, a thematic approach to planning utilizing guiding principles can be presented. This methodology allows individual institutions to apply broad planning principles and to develop goals based on the priorities they have set to meet user needs, wants, and expectations.

Ideally, the determination of a library's mission is guided with community input, whether through surveys, focus groups, or simply a suggestion box. Depending on the library, surveys may be internal or external. Surveys may focus on current users only, or they may attempt to gather information from the entire community, users and non-users alike. An important group to remember when surveying are library employees; their insights are invaluable and their participation is crucial to planning and to the overall success of the organization.

Community surveys and profiles are essential to needs assessment and invaluable as a tool for developing and targeting programs and services. The size of the community, its socioeconomic profile; ethnic, racial, or national mix; age makeup; and other factors should directly inform collection development and other essential services and resources within the library. The nature of the community will, for example, determine the mix of fiction and non-fiction videos, videos for a particular age group, videos reflecting particular community characteristics and interests. If, for example, a snapshot of the community reveals an active arts involvement, there may be a need to serve this population with an emphasis on collecting fine arts videos. If a community demographics profile reveals a predominance of individuals over 50, it stands to reason that more videos related to aging than to parenting and schooling (or X-treme sports!) might be appropriate. Higher-income communities may be more inclined to spend money on new consumer technologies and may be looking for a library that supports that inclination with new collection formats. An "environmental scan" of the community should take in the institutional as well as the individual landscape. Who are the other media providers in the community, and how much of the community's attention are they getting? How abundant or lacking are the movie houses, the film societies, and the rental shops? Answers to these questions are bound to have implications for the library video collection development.

As mentioned earlier, in order to meet the needs of users and to function effectively within the overall library, the mission of the video department must reflect the library's overall mission. To that end, the goals of video services and collections must be specifically incorporated in the strategic planning process. For example, a library may adopt the concept of a one-stop shopping center for the family's information and entertainment needs and wants, be they reading, listening, or viewing. The role of media operations in helping to realize this goal should be expressly developed and stated. If the goal of the library is to foster literacy programs or continuing education programs for the community, the directions of the video collections and services should reflect this mission.

What are the present and future roles of public libraries? Are libraries destined to be dusty storage facilities, or active community centers and cultural gathering places? Is our primary mission to serve as an oasis amidst the cultural deserts and chaos of modern life? Can we compete with the commercial book-and-espresso havens popping up in every mall in America? How will the advent of broadband telecommunications affect library usage and our overall mission? Is it our mission to be keepers of the traditional cultural flame? Or will librarians function as teachers and as pathfinders through the often bewilderingly overgrown and overloaded jungles of digital information?

Whatever the future holds for libraries, it is clear that we are at a Darwinian juncture. What is at stake is the very survival of public libraries as institutions. In a culture that is increasingly influenced and shaped by sights and sounds, in which entertainment and information are rapidly converging, video librarians have the opportunity to play a unique role, perhaps a leadership role, in shaping this future. A primary challenge to future generations—to democratic society in general—will be media literacy: the ability to critically navigate and assess the images and the information that assault us daily. Video librarians are uniquely positioned to play critical roles in the acquisition and delivery of formats that enhance visual literacy. Even more significant is the importance of our roles as advocates and as teachers in the evolving and increasingly complex information environment.

The discussion above has touched on what has been, what is, and what may be. Through vision and mission statements, through well-defined goals and objectives, we determine what the library is trying to accomplish. Once we know what we are trying to do, then and only then does it become time to just do it.

BUILDING THE COLLECTION

How is a video collection built? A collection that represents the entertainment and information needs and wants of users, from child to adult, may incorporate feature films and educational and documentary titles, blending mass-market releases with the independent and educational offerings.

In earlier days, the limited nature of the video publication universe defined the nature of library collections. Many early video collections consisted primarily of popular feature films on video, a situation not unlike the building of fledgling DVD collections today. As the market grew, more participants brought more products to market; in fact, the market exploded. This videographic big bang brought with it an enormous body of documentary and educational titles, primary source videos, as well as a broader range of international and independent feature films.

A collection development policy and plan are crucial to navigating and selecting from this expanding universe. Such a document should not merely be modified book policies. Video is unique. It is a medium with its own strengths and weaknesses, its own way of telling stories and imparting information. Those factors ought to be reflected in policy.

A selection plan is essential. Some of the questions that must be answered in this planning process include: Is there a core aspect to the collection? How is that core determined? For damaged or lost materials, which will be replaced, which won't? Are all aspects of the Dewey classification spectrum to be covered (do they need to be)? Are all genres of feature films to be offered? Are the major writers, directors, cinematographers, composers, actors, and actresses represented in the entertainment portion of the collection (and is it necessary to do so)? Are major literary adaptations to be routinely included? Are major award winners to be routinely included?

Well-defined collection development procedures should designate who selects what and how. The procedures should also define specific criteria upon which selection decisions are to be made. Examples of these criteria might include the use of reviews, particular award winners, or wholesale acquisition of broad categories or genres of material. The criteria might entail, for example, automatic selection for all Academy Award Best Pictures, or routine purchase of all ALA notable video winners.

As with any building, the most important element is the foundation. The foundation of a library's bibliographic or videographic structure is often referred to as the "core collection." This core is typically a group of best and brightest titles that reflects the wide breadth and scope of humankind's artistic and intellectual accomplishments. The core should centrally serve the library's mission and, as with other parts of the collection, should address public demand (what good is a collection of the best works, after all, if people do not use it?). The core collection—the foundation—must be preserved. When attrition occurs, the components of a core collection are repaired, replaced, or restored immediately. But how are these titles determined?

Start with the fundamental question, "What is the purpose of this collection?" Will the library's emphasis be on information, on entertainment, or both? Is it for the amusement and/or edification of pre-schoolers as well as elders? Is it to support school curricula or other educational programs? Is it to serve as a community information and outreach resource? A self-help resource? Is it to offer the best foreign-language film collection in the state?

For the answer to these and other collection-related questions, go to the mission statement, if the library's management has struggled to produce one. Chat with the boss, and the boss's boss. The core values of an institution must be known before the basic values of a department can be established and a core collection built. Everything revolves around those values; consistency throughout the library system is imperative.

Foundations are built on budgets. For video librarians in particular, budget time is not the time to be shy—polite, certainly, but never passive. The historically marginal position occupied by video in libraries of all types makes a certain aggressiveness at budget time imperative. There are various methods of determining a video budget ranging from zero-based (i.e., from scratch) models, to models based on specific needs, individually identified titles, percentage of library circulation, or other elements and criteria. The crucial task is to have an understandable plan to present to the financial decision makers. Be prepared to be an advocate for your clearly defined goals and objectives.

Collections have traditionally been divided into Entertainment and Information. Determining the proportion and size of each category will be one of the first decisions to be made. The cost of videos can vary widely, from ten dollars for older feature films to hundreds of dollars for independently produced documentaries. In light of this disparity, the decision must be made on how to allocate the budget: a percentage per category of material, or an allocation based on a determined number of titles per category. Perhaps an even more difficult decision is how to allocate funds for new or evolving formats within these categories. At least in their earliest years, DVDs, like other electronic media, represent collection add-ons; they augment rather than replace earlier formats. Assuming that it is part of the library's larger collection policy and mission, this obligation to support concurrent formats should be prominently and clearly stated when making the case for a realistic piece of the budgetary pie.

The practice of establishing price ceilings for individual titles is commonplace in public libraries. That practice is every bit as limiting, ill-conceived, and as much a disservice to the public as using the Motion Picture Association of America's (MPAA) rating system for collection development (more on this later). Selecting the best and most appropriate materials is a fundamental privilege and responsibility of our profession. Otherwise, why not out-source?

Evaluating and Selecting Videos

In selecting videos for a collection, four central considerations are: critical reviews, major awards, popularity, and local interest. Reviews can be extremely useful in assessing the effectiveness and worth of a video for a particular collection. If reviews are the sole criteria for selection, however, decision making can be severely hamstrung. For instance, the only video on a topic known to be of local interest received a less-than-average two-star review. If the procedure for acquisition requires three stars for a particular review source, should your patrons have to do without? Or will maintaining the review criteria guarantee a quality collection that can be more easily defended should challenges arise?

Popularity of a feature may be determined from box office receipts, video sales and rental charts, and use of existing library materials. Local interest materials include subjects important to residents, or materials that document the community, whether that is defined as city, state, or region. Circulation figures for both print and audiovisual materials are primary indicators in determining user needs and wants. Knowing the community—an often intuitive rather than quantifiable task—is helpful, too.

Generally speaking, most librarians have precious little time for previewing video titles, a regular practice in the days of expensive 16mm films. While time spent in previewing may still be justified when considering expensive videos, in these days of $20 tapes and discs, an hour of staff time may not be a sound fiscal investment. Instead, as mentioned earlier, many librarians rely on reviews. The better evaluations examine two primary areas: content and technical aspects. In selecting videos, it is important to remember the power of the visuals, but the marriage of words (narration) and pictures should be considered, too. When the two are disharmonious, the results may be unintentionally laughable. The central consideration in evaluating any medium should be the power of the format to communicate.

Whether previewing a video or using evaluative reviews, the STARFAC model (Scope, Treatment, Authority, Relationship to similar materials, Format, Attitude, and Cost) may be useful for content evaluation. Content must be organized and accurate. The words and pictures must work together. If the audio and visual work at cross-purposes, the video becomes less than useful. For instance, if the video is talking about a pollution problem and the visuals are stunningly beautiful depictions of polluted streams and rivers, what message is being transmitted? The intended audience for a video must also be considered. Will a children's video be useful in a collection serving mostly adults? Is there suitable subject coverage in each age group that is being served by the library?

Technical aspects to be evaluated include the quality of visuals, sound, editing, and acting and narration. The technical aspects of a video require separate consideration, because without effective production technique, a video is often poor. The best-written and most informative production will be useless if the audio is garbled, the acting stilted, or the video image washed out or blurred.

Feature Films

Libraries are not, and will never be, video stores. Video rental stores specialize in recent theatrical releases. They traffick in multiple copies of these high-demand titles, and their motivation is the fiscal bottom line. Rental stores are, in short, in the business of moving large numbers of big Hollywood movies for maximum profit. Finding a niche that does not compete with these commercial operations has been a common avenue taken by many public libraries. Opportunities lie in directions other than the video store mass-market, multiple copy approach. Taking this direction often entails taking the road less travelled—collecting older classics and foreign features, or seldom seen independent features. There are also reasons for collecting movies other than entertainment. Movies can be viewed as social or cultural "documents"—snapshots of the times that created them. Collecting movies as history and as primary historical or cultural texts is another collecting direction that can separate the library from the video store.

The rise of public interest in independently produced films may afford opportunities for expanding parts of the feature collection in exciting new directions. Although a few rare films, such as *The Blair Witch Project*, achieve widespread distribution and huge cash returns, most independent films never make it to the shelves of mainstream rental stores; they need a home in libraries. Hollywood is very, very good at what it does, but what it does is not the sum total of all creative film expression. Often the independents try untested concepts and take chances to further the art of filmmaking. Because they sell substantially fewer copies than mainstream releases, independent films on video are often, by necessity, more expensive. The high cost is often well worth it: "indies" can offer exciting perspectives and artistic visions that are seldom or never seen in less adventuresome Hollywood offerings.

The collection development policy should serve as a road map to Hollywood offerings as much as to non-fiction films. Depending on the size of the collection and the intensity of collecting, the criteria for collecting movies may either be broad or specific. It may specify the level of collecting for works of individual directors, actors, actresses, screenwriters, or cinematographers. It may also define collecting levels and scope for particular genres of films (e.g., musicals, westerns, gangster films, war films) or films from certain eras.

While the U.S. movie world is widely represented on video and widely reviewed, selecting foreign film titles presents a unique set of challenges and requirements, such as the choice between subtitles and dubbed. Subtitled foreign-language films are virtually always preferable to dubbed versions. Even decent dubbing can be jarring and detrimental to the experience of watching the film (examples are not limited to the Japanese rubber monster epics and Italian *Hercules* sagas). Dubbing almost always runs counter to the artistic intentions of the filmmakers. Fortunately, many DVDs are providing us with the option of multiple versions and multiple language dubbing for foreign feature films.

Editing is another element which can completely change a film. It is increasingly common for films on video to be re-edited from their original theatrical release. An example is the most recent release (the Director's Cut) of *Blade Runner*, in which the voice-over narration of the original is eliminated, and the ending completely changed. Similarly, Francis Ford Coppola re-edited his two films, *The Godfather* and *Godfather 2* into a single *Godfather Saga*, a film, which some critics called better than the sum of the two Best Picture Academy Award–winning films.

Some videos are released in multiple versions over time. *Star Wars* has at least three different releases; the pan-and-scan version, the original theatrical wide screen edition, and the 1997 special edition with updated special effects and additional footage. Additional footage may be a suitable reason to purchase a new version, or it may add nothing but length and tedium. All editions ought to be individual decisions, each based on the same selection criteria. Again, DVDs, with their multiple version options and abundant supplementary inclusions, often provide the best (and most inclusive) of all possible cinematic worlds.

Libraries are consummately print-centered places, and because of this, there is often a tendency to automatically acquire any film based on a critically acclaimed book. While it may be that the library's collection development policy specifies such automatic acquisitions, it is still important to remember that the film is not the book, nor, for that matter, are the book and the audiobook the same thing. All these forms of expression are related to each other, but each is unique and possesses its own strengths and weaknesses as a storytelling medium.

A concern for quality has long been a hallmark of public libraries. Quality can, however, be a slippery, multidimensional concept when it comes to feature films. The awards of film festivals and other such organizations—the Academy Awards, Emmy Awards, Golden Globe Awards, Cannes Film Festival, and Sundance Film Festival, for example—offer one definition of quality that may be useful in building feature film collections.

As mentioned earlier, the popularity of specific films is sometimes used as one criterion for selection. Sales and rental charts are readily available in publications such as *Billboard* magazine. How much money a film has earned can be ascertained on the Internet with a search-engine search using "Box office revenues." Sites such as Movie Box Office (http://movieboxoffice.about.com/movies/movieboxoffice) feature a wealth of statistical data. Many Web DVD and tape sales sites offer similar weekly top box office lists (see the appendix to Chapter 10 for a list of some of these). Selection procedures could incorporate acquisition of videos that have been on the sales/rental charts for selected periods of time or have generated specified revenues at the box office during their theatrical runs. While box office data, like festival award information, can be broadly useful in the selection process, they do not, of course, necessarily ensure the popularity or appropriateness of a film for a particular community of users or a particular library.

Documentary and Educational Videos

Some subjects are simply more conducive to the video format than others. For some topics, there may be no videos (or at least no suitable videos) at all. Topics that have proven to be ubiquitous in the mass-market video world over the years include travel, how-to's, biographical works, popular histories; and performances, such as plays, ballets, operas, and musical concerts. Regardless of the subject or the genre of video, to virtually guarantee dust bunnies on your shelves, all you need to do is add discussion videos that feature "talking heads" rather than visually informing or exciting images (there are exceptions, of course, such as the various productions featuring the redoubtable Bill Moyers). This is another area where judgment based on a thorough understanding of the medium will be required.

Cable television channels are fueling the growth of non-fiction videos, adding quality, reasonably priced titles to a market that once offered little beyond PBS programs and expensive specialty titles. The offerings of the Arts and Entertainment (A&E) and Discovery channels are good examples of this trend.

Some specialty non-fiction titles, particularly independently produced videos, are still very high priced when compared with mass-market releases. Are these worth the extra costs? That is an individual decision which must take into account budgets and collection development goals. It is true, however, that these higher-priced works, like their "indie" fiction counterparts, often offer the kind of individual vision, emotional impact, and unique approaches to the medium not always present in more generic mass-market works. A final note: many independently produced documentaries and educational videos are distributed exclusively by one firm (for example, Women Make Movies, California Newsreel, First Run/Icarus Films, Cinema Guild, Filmmakers Library). In dealing with these firms the high sticker price of independent documentary works is in some instances negotiable, particularly if the library buys a large number of titles from the distributor. It always pays to ask (and to haggle).

Children's Video

As with adult titles the children's video market has exploded, and the quality of titles in this market varies dramatically. Many children's videos are produced and sold solely because they are adaptations of popular children's books or tie-ins with popular children's TV programming. Again, a decision needs to be made as to whether these are sufficient reasons to purchase the video.

The same basic critical components apply to selecting children's video as adult videos, with particular attention paid to age appropriateness. In the case of children's video, particularly works geared to pre-readers or beginning readers, visuals often carry the day. The creative use of images and narration are key points to look for. In all cases an engaging basic story or topic is essential (visuals mean nothing if the storytelling falls flat). In selecting children's titles, video librarians need to be particularly sensitive to ways in which the video portrays the world. Subtle or overt gender, racial, or other social and cultural biases can slip into even the most well-intentioned work. An older but still very useful publication for selecting videos that steer clear of these pitfalls is *Facets Non-violent, Non-sexist Children's Video Guide* (1996).

Copyright

Copyright can be a thorny problem for public library video librarians. The issue of video copyright in public libraries generally rears its head in one or two cases only. Perhaps the most common of these relates to showing—"publicly performing"—a video for a group within the library.

Unless otherwise specified by the copyright owner or owner's agent, public performance rights (PPR) are generally necessary when showing a video to a group within the library (or any public group outside of the library, for that matter). Some non-theatrical video distributors include PPR with their videos; others may offer them for an additional charge. Performance rights are seldom included with entertainment videos. For some feature film producers/studios, umbrella licenses are available for a yearly fee. One supplier of such licenses is the Motion Picture Licensing Corporation (MPLC) (http://www.mplc.com). MPLC bases its rates on factors such as type of organization, anticipated number of viewers, and frequency of showings.

Over the years, there has been a tremendous amount of controversy and confusion about whether individual viewing of videos in a public place such as a library constitutes public performance. While there has been no specific case law regarding this point, the general (although not universal) consensus seems to be that such use would stand up under the fair-use provisions of copyright law (see the discussion of this point in Chapter 15 on copyright).

Other copyright issues related to video include off-air taping of television programming as a means of acquiring materials for the library's collection. The guidelines developed to govern off-air taping (the Kastenmeier Guidelines) are exclusively focused on use of such materials in formal classroom settings. Off-air taping is not, consequently, an option for public libraries. Fortunately, because an increasing amount of television programming, both network and cable, is available for purchase as prerecorded tape, off-air taping is not nearly as much a necessity as it was 10 years ago.

Generally, copying currently copyrighted audio or video material is a practice which the library should actively discourage, and should avoid doing itself. Digital technologies are making the temptation and the ability to transfer, copy, and manipulate visual and audio materials a fact of life. Because of this, and because of the increasingly litigious nature of the world, it is a good practice to develop a clear copyright policy within the library, and to post this prominently for the public to see.

Budget Stretching

In recent years, used videotapes have become widely available. Some companies use professional evaluation equipment to check the quality of the tape. Although buying used tape means that new releases will be added to the collection at least 30 to 60 days after the "street date" of the video, most libraries tend to position themselves for the long term rather than short term. Costs of "pre-viewed" tapes of first run features are about half that of new tapes priced for the rental market, running between $30 and $40. The tapes will typically have been used 15 to 20 times. As industry experts expect the life of a VHS tape to be about 250 plays or 15 years, a tape purchased at half price can be a bargain. Anecdotally, reports indicate that some tapes have survived 1,000 circulations, and who knows how many plays.

There are a number of reputable used and out-of-print tape vendors currently in business. Some of these are listed in UC Berkeley's video distributor database: http://www.lib.berkeley.edu/MRC/Distributors.html. Online auctions such as eBay (http://www.ebay.com) and Amazon.com can be a source for out-of-print titles, too. Unfortunately, many online sources require payment by credit card, an option not always available for public libraries. Whenever dealing with out-of-print or auction sources, caveat emptor! Be sure to check the video as soon as it arrives—strange stuff happens.

Another option, particularly if emphasis is on long-term collecting, is to wait until a title is priced for the "sell-through" market, usually around $20 (see Chapters 10 and 16 for a discussion of sell-through). Be forewarned, however, that customers gain a sense of how quickly new releases are added to video collections. A long delay may send your customers to the video stores as fast as not having enough copies in the collection to satisfy demand.

COLLECTION MAINTENANCE

Once the Collection Is Built, Then What?

Unfortunately, tapes wear out, some are never returned, and accidents do happen. Getting replacements can be easy, difficult, or impossible. Some titles—classic Disney animation, for woeful example—are available for a short while, subsequently disappearing for years, resurfacing briefly, and disappearing again. Some foresightful librarians buy storage copies of such titles. On the other hand, certain titles have lower borrowing demand because so many parents have decided that $20 for a video that will be watched dozens, if not hundreds, of times is a pretty good bargain after all.

How is the decision made whether to replace or remove a video? This is another important application of the collection development policy. Just as those standards come to bear on initial acquisition, they can be used to decide if replacement or weeding is justified.

When acquiring replacement titles, the new videos may or may not need new cataloging. The replacement copy may, for one thing, be distributed by another source. It may be a revised, expanded, or otherwise different version of the film-on-video originally purchased (e.g., directors' cuts, widescreen rather than "pan-and-scan" versions, dubbed or subtitled versions, colorized editions, restored versions, and versions with new or additional footage added). For example, the original *Star Wars* (1977) was chosen for the National Film Register, not the 1997 version with additional footage and new special effects. An added conundrum may be the fact that there is likely to be more consumer interest in the 1997 version than the original. Of course, both versions could productively find homes in the collection.

Fortunately, the Internet makes replacing materials (or determining if a title can be replaced) easier than ever. Large online video sources such as Facets (http://www.facets.org) and Movies Unlimited (http://www.moviesunlimited.com) can be searched for the hard-to-find theatrical titles and some popular documentary and educational videos. Midwest Tape Exchange (http://www.midwesttapes.com) is a particularly library-friendly vendor, and features easy online ordering. For a wonderful set of links to online movie vendors see the Indiana University Media Center's Web page: (http://www.indiana.edu/~libreser/film/buying.html).

Although finding specific information for videos on the Internet is a hit-and-miss proposition (like any general Web search), there can be occasional, surprising success. Metasearch engines, such as Dogpile (http://www.dogpile.com) and Copernic (http://www.copernic.com) are particularly useful ways to concurrently search a large number of sites with various search engines. In searching, try putting quotes around the title being searched and including the word "video" (e.g., *The Ryan White Story* video). In addition to large distributor sites, mega-retailers, such as Amazon.com, and studio sites, many independent producers are using the Internet to their advantage. The recent marketing phenomena of *The Blair Witch Project* resulted in a more than $150 million-dollar box office, largely attributed to initial Internet word of mouth.

SECURITY

Unfortunately (or fortunately), most collections have a large number of titles that are good enough to steal. All the work of building balanced collections can be undone by a frustrating few, nimble-fingered individuals. How to provide easy access while preserving the collection has been an ongoing issue in public libraries.

Closed stacks are one answer. With that answer, however, comes additional costs. These costs are both financial (in terms of staff salaries and/or security hardware), and political (in terms of a decrease in access and the freedom to browse for the patrons). Options, such as browseable binders with copies of video covers, may be used. Alternatives almost always consume that most precious, finite resource—space. Some libraries use the illusion of security in place of actual security. Fake cameras and security detectors, signs, and convex mirrors can create the impression of vigilance.

There are several types of security systems on the market. One type uses radio frequencies to trigger alarms; the other uses electromagnetic detection sensors. Unfortunately, the latter detection method can strip videos of their programming. Both technologies use pass-through gates, an increasingly commonplace sight even in small-town America. Wal-Mart and other major retailers have installed such systems, referring to them with such euphemisms as "inventory control systems."

DVDs are providing their own, unique security headaches. Many of the qualities that make DVDs the attractive medium that they are—compact size, popularity, high-profile movie content—also make them attractive and easy targets for theft. The limited space available on the DVD disc or package for placing detection strips provides even more problems than videotape. As with tape, there are currently a number of cleverly designed cases which may frustrate potential thieves to some extent. For an interesting, ongoing discussion of DVD security, see the VIDEOLIB discussion list archive: http://www.lib.berkeley.edu/VideoLib/archive.html (search on the phrase "DVD security" or "DVD theft").

In the end, if somebody wants something badly enough, a way around most systems can be found. Balancing access and collection preservation and security will continue to be problematic for the foreseeable future.

PRESERVATION

Librarians are beginning to feel the impact of the finite shelf-life of videotapes. Industry experts have predicted that videotapes and other tape-based media have a life span of about 15 years, or 250 plays, depending on environmental and use factors. After that, the tape will deteriorate, losing the coating that holds the electromagnetic information. While anecdotal evidence indicates that some tapes borrowed more than 500 times and played who-knows-how-many times are still going strong after 20 years, those tend to be the exceptions. Regardless of the medium, collections are seldom viewed or treated as totally disposable commodities. The lesson to be learned is that budgeting for preservation and maintenance of video collections needs to be an integral part of the collection development process (a more radical case could also be made for making equipment replacement and upgrade an integral part of this same process). This fact of collection life is not likely to change with the shift to DVD. Although DVDs theoretically promise a longer shelf-life, the medium is still susceptible to damage and wear in heavy use situations over time.

What is the proper way to store videotapes? According to the Eastman Kodak Company (1994–2000), a few simple precautions should be observed. Videotapes should be kept out of direct sunlight and away from any magnetic fields. The mechanism inside a cassette is fairly delicate, and rough handling (such as dropping onto a hard floor) can cause a malfunction. The tape should never be touched with your fingers, and broken tapes should not be spliced and reused. The splice can damage the heads inside a video recorder. If moisture condenses on the surface of a tape from extremely high humidity or a sudden change of temperature, it can stick to the video head drum. When going from a cold, dry environment to warm, moist air (coming in from outdoors on a winter day, for example), it is usually necessary to let the tape and equipment warm up for a couple of hours before use.

According to a study by the Society of Motion Picture and Television Engineers (1995), the optimal storage conditions are 63 degrees Fahrenheit ($+/-4$ degrees) and 30 percent relative humidity. Fortunately for those in public libraries, collections are for use rather than long-term storage. The support of conditions more suited to humans than videotapes is less problematic in these circumstances than in archives. For a fuller discussion of videotape preservation requirements and strategies see National Film Preservation Board (1997).

For optimal storage, videotapes should be re-tensioned every year. This process, sometimes called "wiffling," involves fast-forwarding and then rewinding a tape. The process can help keep tapes supple and correct minor tracking problems. Mechanical rewinders are not recommended because they do not generally have the type of gentle shutoff mechanisms that VCRs do. The quick stop can break or detach a tape from the reel.

A professional cleaning machine, such as the RTI Tape Chek, is a recommended tool for heavily circulating collections. The unit removes oxidation and some other contaminants from the tape while re-tensioning it. Public service personnel can easily load the machine during slow periods or between customers. The length of the cleaning process depends upon the length of the tape, but usually takes less than 10 minutes. More information is available from Research

Technology International (800) 323–7520, (http://www.rtico.com). Repairs can save thousands of dollars. Employees with a modicum of mechanical aptitude can easily do simple repairs such as replacing video shells and leader splicing. With many catalog feature films costing under $20, expending too much effort repairing an already older tape might not be cost-effective.

Preservation of a tape by periodically transferring it to a new tape or a new format is probably a viable strategy for certain materials in the collection, such as locally produced programming. Always check with the copyright holders first! In the case of a tape produced by the local history society, for example, the producers will probably be thrilled to have their efforts preserved in the library. On the other hand, Hollywood has a strong stance against piracy of its products (format transfer or duplication of materials is piracy in Hollywood's book). An example of Hollywood's protectiveness of its wares is the recent rapid legal action against a Web site owner who was distributing a computer program that allowed DVDs to be copied to computer hard discs and other storage media (see Parker 1999; Grossman 2000).

As is discussed in the copyright chapter of this book, copying physically at-risk copyrighted materials that are out of distribution (and that have been legally acquired in the first place) is generally considered to be one of the few instances in which a copy may legally be made without permission. Nonetheless, in such instances, it is wise to fully document attempts to acquire a replacement before copying.

What does one do when a cassette is far past its prime? Money can be saved by recycling these items. Weeded videos and those donations unsuitable for the collection are great sources for spare parts (select those tapes with little apparent wear). Another option for the ecologically minded is sending old tapes to a commercial tape recycler (this doesn't save the library money, but it helps save the earth!). Such firms usually pay the postage costs for sending discards to them. The tapes are either bulk erased and sold as used materials, cannibalized for parts, or recycled completely. Companies that perform this service include CFS Media Services (http://www.cfsmediaservices.com), AmerAgain (Water-bury, CT; 203–755–3123), Global Zero, Inc. (Sanford, ME; 207–324–5200), Intermedia Video Products (http://www.intermediavideo.com), and Greendisk (http://www.greendisk.com).

RATINGS SYSTEMS AND CENSORSHIP ISSUES

Despite best practices and efforts, other forces may negatively affect video collections and services. Impediments come in two flavors: internal and external. The internal obstacles have been alluded to earlier; they include continuing print bias, competition for space and money, and administrative support. External obstacles are often even more insidious, centering on issues of intellectual free-dom and access.

The best-known ratings system is the Motion Picture Association of America's (MPAA) Classification and Rating Administration (CARA), which labels films with the familiar G, PG, PG-13, R, and NC-17 (previously X) ratings. The MPAA/CARA ratings are the subjective opinions of an 11-member board hired by the MPAA and the National Association of Theater Owners for terms ranging from six months to two years. The ratings are not critical judgments of the films; they are copyrighted codes or labels reflecting the committee's tally of a film's treatment of violence, drugs, nudity, sensuality, language, and theme in relation to its suitability for children.

Despite ALA's opposition to labeling and ratings systems, more than half of American public libraries admit that the MPAA's system has an effect on the selection of videos and even more admit to effects on access to their video collections (Kreamer 1992). Recent polls commissioned by the MPAA confirm that most parents use the ratings system to guide their children's viewing options (Valenti 1999).[3]

Recent research into the video purchasing patterns of Ohio public libraries found that less than 20 percent of feature films acquired by Ohio public libraries are MPAA rated for those older than 13 years and less than 3.5 percent for those older than 17. Surprisingly, Not-Rated films were acquired only slightly more than R-rated films. That may be due to either using the ratings system for collection development or a lack of interest in pre-1968 movies (Vollmar-Grone 1999).

Former President Clinton and other politicians have called on Hollywood to enforce the MPAA ratings system. It currently does not have legal standing, and the MPAA insists its value is only advisory. MPAA spokesman Jack Valenti emphasizes that the ratings system is for parents to use in making decisions regarding what their children may view (Valenti 1999).

For those libraries that offer equal access regardless of age, furnishing age-appropriate material may be an issue. Some libraries require a signed parental consent form rather than providing automatic access to video collections by minors. By signing the contract, parents accept responsibility for what their children borrow.

Some Ohio public libraries have posted signs that R-rated films are not available because of obscenity laws. However, the Ohio Revised Code seems to give protections to librarians, teachers, and others involved with education. This may be an area in which consulting with the library's legal counsel is appropriate.

Librarians limiting their video collections to G, PG, or even PG-13 rated videos lose many quality films. MPAA ratings began in 1968. Because most films released before 1968 have not been submitted for ratings, they would be excluded from acquisition. Many television movies and others not submitted for subjective valuation would also be prohibited.

The argument can be made that restrictive collection practices can serve library patrons while providing safer fare for the youngsters. While collecting "family-oriented" programming—videos appealing to multiple age groups—is often an important part of a library's collecting mission and strategy, these titles represent only part of the larger range of available materials, and serve only part of the clientele of most libraries. As Pat Lora (1994: 25) has insightfully commented:

Fortunately for libraries, books are not rated. If they were, surely some would earn the dreaded "R", or perhaps MPAA's latest invention—NC 17. And if they were so labeled, would the public be denied access to certain works . . . ? Would D.H. Lawrence, Henry Miller, Salman Rushdie, and a long list of other once and future controversial authors be allowed space on hallowed library shelves? It is a frightening question. "What if" scenarios aside, selecting or rejecting a title on the basis of an industry marketing tool—a label—rather than on its own intrinsic merits and a careful consideration of its value for the collection is a clear violation of professional ethics. Censorship complaints and protests occur daily in libraries across the country. Building collections based on what the film industry perceives as palatable for children 13 and under is no guarantee that the censor will not knock on the library door. It is however, a certain guarantee that fewer individuals over 13 will want to bother to walk through the AV library door.

Under scrutiny, the MPAA ratings system has been found to have significant shortcomings in terms of its relationship to both child development and current social realities. Wilson, Linz, and Randall (1990) have conducted research that indicates that the current MPAA ratings system needs four specific changes:

1. Change the age groupings of the categories following the patterns of cognitive development to 3 to 7, 8 to 12, 13 to 17, and over 17;
2. Specify the types of horror, violence, sex, and sex and violence so that the perceptions of each age group can be adequately addressed;
3. Integrate allowances for the context of sex and violence in the rating scheme; and
4. Reverse the current evaluation that sex is more problematic than violence. Their research found that violence is more troublesome than sex.

While both hard-line critics and proponents of the MPAA system have found the scheme sorely lacking, many individuals continue to use it regularly for guidance. According to recent polls, more than 75 percent of parents use ratings to guide their children's feature film viewing. Despite ALA's firm and unequivocal opposition to ratings, more than half of American public libraries admit that the MPAA ratings system has an effect on the selection of videos and even more admit to effects on access to their video collections. For those interested in the various ratings schemes, the Web site Parental Media Guide (http://www.parentalguide.org) offers links to descriptions of ratings for electronic games, music, television programming, and movies. Ratings schemes include those developed by the Entertainment Software Rating Board for computer, video and Internet games; Recording Industry Association of America: Parental Advisory for music; Parental Guidelines for television programs; and MPAA/

CARA system for movies. The MPAA site features a searchable database of movies and their ratings.

Be advised, there is no such thing as video that is absolutely exempt from challenge. Objections have been raised over magic in fairy tales on video; over particular biblical interpretations or video discussions of scientific evidence that contradicts scripture; and over the use of non–politically correct terminology or representation. One thing is certain: the censor's knock usually comes under the premise of protecting somebody from something.

What do you do when the knock comes? The question is, "What should you have done?" The answer is to emulate the Boy Scouts and be prepared: the library must have a challenge policy and a collection development policy in place *before* a challenge occurs. The ALA's Office for Intellectual Freedom (http://www.ala.org/alaorg/oif) offers a wealth of resources for responding to challenges.

MARKETING

Building a stellar video collection is a wonderful accomplishment, but it ultimately does little good if no one knows about it. If you are hiding your video lamp under the proverbial basket, it may be time to set that basket on fire and draw some attention to your collection. An effective marketing plan is essential. A three-pronged attack consisting of programming, promotions, and publicity, supported by special services, direct communications, and collateral materials, can be highly effective. Activity suggestions include programming based on videos from the collection, production of thematic videographies, and news releases about aspects of the collection.[4]

To create a marketing plan, start with the basics. Determine who the current customers and potential customers are. An overriding question is, "How is the video collection valuable?" Brainstorming the Who, What, Where, When, Why, and How can provide promotional opportunities by adapting Ranganathan's Laws to videos: "Every viewer his video" and "Every video its viewer."

In determining answers to the above questions, as in any marketing endeavor, a familiarity with user demographics is essential. This information can be ascertained through past library surveys and by conducting new surveys, both internal and external. The local Chamber of Commerce and economic development groups often offer a wealth of such information. Combining these data with the library's vision and mission, and with the video collection philosophy will indicate directions to explore.

If the library's niche in the video world is to collect beyond the mainstream— engaging materials not readily found on the video store shelves or Amazon. com—this enterprise should be specifically publicized and promoted. Use the strengths of the collection creatively. Let those who can use your resources know about them. Recently, a significant donation was made to our library specifically for the acquisition of fine arts videos. Once the videos were added to the collection, letters and videographies were sent to every art and music teacher in the area. Of course, the local newspaper covered the $10,000 donation.

Another local example: our library recently came to the rather startlingly obvious realization that foreign-language films are not foreign to native speakers of those languages. New businesses have brought many Japanese people to this area. Although acquiring foreign-language films has long been an area of collection emphasis, more representatives of the Japanese cinema were purchased. The library collaborated with appropriate local businesses to publicize these materials to their employees.

Video librarians can learn from their retail counterparts. By forming professional relationships with video store managers, concerns about the competition between the two enterprises may be allayed. At the very least, returns of library materials erroneously left at their stores will be expedited (that service should, of course, be reciprocated by the library).

One lesson quickly learned is that video stores have made browsing a number one priority. Video store managers know their customer base. If lack of library space limits browseability in your library, look for methods of segmenting the collection. Create subject or genre videographies, such as lists of award-winning feature films, seasonally influenced videos, hobby or how-to works, or live performance videos. The possibilities are unlimited. Emphasize the strengths of your collection. For instance, if films named to the National Film Registry (http://lcweb.loc.gov/film/filmnfr.html) are automatic acquisitions, displays of those titles with videographies should be prominently and regularly mounted.

Use large, high-impact signage so that the message is quickly and easily understood. A word of caution: signage is wonderful unless there is too much or the staff relies on pointing instead of explaining. Face-out displays with attractive packaging can create interest. Use video cases that show the professionally designed packaging that the videos are shipped in rather than plain brown boxes. Another method of creating interest is a just-returned videos display. The quick turnaround also saves reshelving time.

THE FUTURE

In the first (1994) edition of this book, Pat Lora, in writing about video in public libraries, presciently envisioned the shift toward digital access and away from ownership of artifacts stuffed into little plastic boxes. While that day is undoubtedly coming in all of its streamed media glory, it is still a long way off. In the digital future, the realities of the consumer electronics market, telecommunications infrastructure limitations, and public media biases are, as much as anything, likely to determine what happens in the home first, and only by extension in libraries. Several things are certain in this uncertain future, however. Technological change will continue to happen, most likely at a greatly intensified pace and scope; video, film, and broadcast media will continue to exert a major impact on people's information and entertainment lives; and last, video librarians will be faced with increasing opportunities for exerting leadership and vision in this changing media environment. Whether or not librarians are responsive to these challenges and opportunities may define the success or failure of libraries as public institutions in the future. In a discussion on the American Library Association Video Round Table listserv (VIDEOLIB), University of California Berkeley media librarian Gary Handman (2000) contended:

The bald fact of the matter is that the last 50 years have been largely informed by media other than print. We have, for better or worse, become a post-literate (world) culture. Libraries can approach this fact in three basic ways: a) try to ignore the fact, b) try to stem the rising tide . . . c) hire informed professionals who understand the role of non-print media in shaping the Century and who can go to the mat for informed/critical viewing and intelligently built collections.

Video is closing in on its third decade in libraries. Much has changed in the field of video librarianship and in the perception of the role of video in libraries. In some sense, the specific technological changes in the past 30 years have seemed trivial in comparison to these broader professional changes. Some things have also remained constant in the past 30 years. Video librarians—all librarians—have a number of crucial continuing roles to play: as builders of collections, as access providers, and as teachers. In a world in which information and entertainment are increasingly converging, and in which both are becoming alarmingly commercialized and privatized, video librarians, more than ever, need to be strong advocates both within our libraries and in the larger professional world. We need to be advocates for diverse, quality video collections and programs within our libraries. This advocacy includes finding effective ways of supporting the independent arts community that has given us a good portion of our most engaging stories, voices, and visions on video.

In the face of new media, new messages, and new roles for video librarians, our mission remains unchanged. This mission is determined as much by the direction of our individual libraries as by guiding principles of our profession. The bottom line is service to our constituents—providing relevant, exciting, and accessible content that enriches and informs their lives.

NOTES

1. For an excellent overview of the history of media technology, see the Media History Project (http://www.mediahistory.com).

2. The demise of the Beta format was rooted in economic as well as technological causes. In releasing its product to the consumer electronic market, Sony staunchly refused to license the technology to other manufacturers. The Sony-or-nothing marketing strategy was in marked contrast to the approach of VHS developers, such as Matsushita Corporation, that widely licensed to other hardware manufacturers (see Fasoldt 1988; Wyver 1989). Interestingly, Sony and Matsushita are again battling over DVD standards (see Cheek 1999).

3. For two useful discussions of the nature and impact of video censorship in libraries, see Office of Intellectual Freedom (1989: 160+); Pitman (1992).

4. Programming in public libraries has never been commonplace in the video era, perhaps a result of video's small screen nature. With the advent of large screens and large-scale projection equipment, however, programming seems to be making a resurgence—and happily so. Video screenings in connection with broader programs can be a particularly effective way of highlighting the collection and bringing patrons in the door. For a superb group of timely programming packages assembled by experts in various fields for public libraries and other institutions, see National Video Resources (NVR) Web site (http://www.nvr.org).

REFERENCES

Cheek, Michael. 1999. "VHS vs. Betamax Redux." *Government Computer News* (May 3): 22

Crawford, Walt, and Gorman, Michael. 1995. *Future Libraries: Dreams, Madness & Reality*. Chicago: American Library Association.

Eastman Kodak Company. 1994–2000. "Frequently Asked Questions: Video Tape Storage." http://www.kodak.com/global/en/service/faqs/faq0071.shtml.

Facets Non-violent, Non-sexist Children's Video Guide. 1996. Compiled by Virginia A. Boyle. Chicago: Facets Multimedia; Academy Chicago Publishers.

Fasoldt, Al. 1988. "How Sony Killed Betamax." *The Syracuse Newspapers*. http://www.twcny.rr.com/technofile/texts/howbetadied.htm.

Grossman, Wendy. 2000. "DVDs: Cease and DeCSS?" *Scientific American* (May): 44–46

Handman, Gary. 2000. VIDEOLIB (listserv) discussion, July 5.

Kreamer, J., ed. 1992. *The Video Annual*. Santa Barbara, CA: ABC-CLIO.

Lora, Pat. 1994. "Public Library Video Collections: Evolving Issues in Media Management." In *Video Collection Development in Multi-type Libraries: A Handbook*. Edited by Gary Handman. Westport, CT: Greenwood Press, pp. 17–32.

National Film Preservation Board. 1997. *Television/Video Preservation Study: Volume 1: Report*. http://lcweb.loc.gov/film/tvstudy.html.

Office of Intellectual Freedom (ALA). 1989. "Freedom to View, Instinct to Censor." *Newsletter on Intellectual Freedom* (September): 160.

Parker, Dana J. 1999. "Cease and DeCSS: DVD's Encryption Code Cracked." *EMedia Professional* (December): 23.

Pitman, Randy. 1992. "We Are the Censors." *Video Librarian* (June–July): 1.

Society of Motion Picture and Television Engineers. 1995. *Care, Storage, Handling and Shipping of Magnetic Recording Tape for Television*. White Plains, NY: SMPTE.

Valenti, J. 1999. "New Survey Shows Strong Parental Support of Motion Picture Ratings." http://www.mpaa.org/jack/99/99_9_8b.htm.

Vollmar-Grone, Michael. 1999. *X and the AV Librarian: A Study of the Relationship Between the Acquisition of Feature Films by Ohio Public Libraries and the Influence of the Motion Picture Association of America (MPAA) Rating System*. Master's Research Paper. Kent, Ohio: Kent State University School of Library and Information Science. http://www.bright.net/veegee/ratings.doc.

Williams, Patrick. 1988. *The American Public Library and the Problem of Purpose*. Westport, CT: Greenwood Press.

Wilson, B. J., Linz, D., and Randall, B. 1990. "Applying Social Science Research to Film Ratings: A Shift from Offensiveness to Harmful Effects." *Journal of Broadcasting & Electronic Media* 34(4): 443–468.

Wyver, John. 1989. *The Moving Image: An International History of Film, Television, and Video*. New York: B. Blackwell; London: BFI.

Chapter 3

School Library Video Collections

Cassandra M. Keith

As the use of video in the classroom has become as much a part of instructional method as the more conventional approaches of lecture, example, and discussion, both the size and the expectations placed on school video collections have grown. Video is used for purposes of supplementing and, indeed, complementing texts, whether it is Ken Burns' *The Civil War* to enhance a history class, or a production of a Shakespearean play to bring the written page to life. Video has also become a research tool for students, with documentary films being viewed and cited for information along with books and journals. As multimedia presentations by both teachers and students increasingly become a part of classroom content, a video collection in the library is essential.

Video use in schools began to appear in the 1960s and 1970s, initially as a passive medium (Triche, 1993). English classes, film courses, and fledging student-produced films were among the first uses of video in schools, particularly at the secondary level. Whether it is the nature of teaching or the nature of teachers, new approaches to instruction often take time to be accepted and integrated into the classroom. Like any new medium, video took some time to gain a foothold in schools, but by the 1980s it was being used across the curricula and continues to grow.

In many schools today, the library's video collection is accessed through the online catalog and included in the research materials a student might use for a paper. Teachers of virtually all disciplines use video in their classrooms. The versatility of video as well as the increased availability of subjects covered by video has opened up its instructional applications. As both the technology and its worth develop, it is important that the school library provides a collection that is relevant and timely.

The mission of a school library is, first and foremost, to support the curricular needs of teachers and students. To that end, the school media specialist needs to be an active and involved member of the school community, particularly in her relationships with the faculty and her awareness of curriculum issues. These goals are best accomplished through communication that is ongoing. Knowing the needs of users, and even anticipating changes in course offerings, is key to developing the library's video collection. Attending faculty meetings, working with department chairs and individual teachers, and being part of a curriculum committee are all ways in which the media specialist can determine how best to develop a collection that will be useful and balanced. Additionally, a collection policy for videos should also be in place, in much the same way that a collection policy exists for print media.

In order to avoid a collection that is the result of individual teacher requests or trends, devise a collection policy that supports the curriculum as a whole and includes the potential for growth. By having a written statement that reflects the library's commitment to developing a video collection, the librarian has a document that can be used to review requests in terms of relevance to the current curriculum and with an eye to future use. Too often, requests are made from a narrow perspective, and a collection policy can support the decision to deny a request that is tied to one teacher or one course offering, which may not be offered again. As the curriculum shifts and changes with time, review the policy to determine that it continues to be appropriate to the selection process.

A collection policy for videos also provides a rationale or defense in terms of challenges to the library's materials. Some schools may decide on the basis of their communities that R-rated videos cannot be a part of the collection; others, with greater latitude, may choose to include R-rated materials, leaving their classroom use to the discretion of the teachers. While even the best-constructed and board-approved policies may not decrease the likelihood of a challenge to specific controversial titles in the collection, the presence of such a policy will, however, increase the likelihood that challenged materials will be rarely reviewed and more often retained (Callison, 1990). In writing a video collection policy for the library, get as much input as possible from administrators, teachers, and school board members beforehand, in order to have a policy that best serves your school community.

In addition to a collection policy that helps to shape the selection process, another useful tool is a request form. Having a request form as part of the procedure for video acquisition provides a standardized format for all requests and neutralizes the process. The form should include spaces for the date of the request, the teacher's name, department, phone and/or e-mail address. There should be a slot for as much information as possible regarding the title(s) being requested: producer/distributor; date; cost; whatever information would be helpful in locating and ordering the item. If the teacher has ordering material, indicate that that should be submitted with the request. The request form should also ask for information that supports the acquisition of the video. This can be done by including a checklist that asks if the requestor has seen the video; has read reviews of it; has a colleague's endorsement; whether it has interdepartmental uses. The point is to get the requestor to think about the use of the item and its inclusion in the collection as a whole. Request forms should be made readily available within the school library as well as distributed to departments.

While a collection policy and the use of request forms can contribute to the selection of a video collection, the budget for such a collection determines much of the acquisition process. As technology has developed in leaps and bounds in recent decades, the materials for the school library have become increasingly diverse in nature. Books and periodicals now share the library media center with computers, online resources, and audiovisual items such as videos and CDs. The variety of print and non-print resources on the market, and expected to be available for use in school libraries, continues to grow. Library budgets, which were originally determined for the acquisition of print materials, are now being stretched to the limit in order to provide the necessary media resources that teachers and students require. Dollars are being shifted from one part of the budget to another, as opposed to new dollars being added, and the overall library media collection suffers (Callison, 1990). Having separate lines or categories for different material types within your library's budget helps to target areas of demand more clearly as well as provide support for future increases.

A video budget is recommended, as it keeps video purchases separate and distinct. The video budget may be a lump sum from which all video requests are purchased, or may be divided among departments for the purpose of equalizing requests. Having a budget to refer to when video requests from one teacher or one department begin to dominate the collection can support your decision to turn down or temporarily postpone a purchase. In creating a video budget, the biggest line item will certainly represent adding new titles to the collection; however, other costs should also be considered, such as replacement of older titles, processing materials (including cases and security devices). Unless covered by another area of the budget, viewing equipment and its maintenance should also be included. *School Library Journal* publishes a biennial national survey of school library spending which might provide a basis for comparison in creating or reviewing your video or audiovisual budget. The American Library Association Web-site offers a Library and Research Center Fact Sheet entitled "Library Operating Expenditures: A Selected Annotated Bibliography," which is generally revised annually and includes figures for school libraries (http://www.ala.org/library/fact4.html).

The process of video selection should reflect a partnership between the librarian and teachers. Student input may be a factor as well, but as the video collection is tied most directly to the curriculum, the teaching faculty are essential to the selection process. There will certainly be individual teachers and departments (most often history, English, and science) that take an active role both in requesting titles for the collection and in using video as an instructional material; but in order to develop a collection that complements the curriculum as a whole, the librarian needs to be pro-active.

As school cultures vary greatly, no one method will work for every librarian, but the key to involving teachers is always communication and accessibility. If attending curriculum committee meetings, or better yet, being a member of that committee, is an option, then pursue that course. That forum provides knowledge of both current and future course content, and allows you to highlight library resources that can help support the curriculum. It also makes you a visible presence and gives you a voice. Working with department chairs is another way to learn about the needs of a particular discipline and to determine how the library can best meet those needs. Keeping an eye out for videos that might be of interest to a teacher and then providing a copy of a review for that title opens a dialogue and involves the teacher in the process. Teachers often have limited time for searching and reviewing on their own, but when specific materials are suggested and reviews provided, they have some input without too many demands.

Ideally, the selection process should involve several participants: the librarian, teachers, and students. In reality, that is not the decision-making process for every video that makes its way into the collection. Often the librarian must take the initiative for developing parts of the collection. Consulting reviews in the professional literature can help you make a more informed decision. Periodicals such as *School Library Journal* (http://www.slj.com/index.asp), *Library Journal* (http://www.ljdigital.com/), *Booklist* (http://www.ala.org/booklist), *Media and Methods* (http://www.media-methods.com), and *The Video Librarian* (http://www.videolibrarian.com) all provide video reviews. Reading reviews outside of the library literature is also helpful; a different perspective can be gained from other sources. Many disciplines or broad subject fields have their own journals which review subject-specific videos; for example, the American Association for the Advancement of Science's *Science Books and Films* (http://ehrweb.aaas.org/~sbf/). Time and availability, however, may limit the number of reviews you can realistically read. Taking that into consideration, read what is at hand, keep channels of communication open with your teachers, and consult other school librarians for recommendations.

Access and use of the video collection are also factors that have an impact on its development. As most video collections will exist to support the curriculum, teachers are the primary users. In many schools the video collection is kept separate from the print collection and circulates only to faculty, as it is considered instructional material. Other schools may make the video collection available to students as well, and integrate all print and non-print media on the shelves. The questions of access and use of videos should be addressed by the librarian and the faculty in order to determine an appropriate video circulation policy for the school community. Who may borrow videos? What is the lending period for a video? Are videos cataloged and searched on the online catalog? If not, how do your users know what is in the collection? Where are the videos shelved and what security methods are in place for videos?

As information media become more diverse, it is important to acknowledge that students need access to these diverse materials, especially at the secondary level. In doing research, students may consult books, online resources, and the video collection in order to find the information they need. Teachers are putting an emphasis on primary source materials as part of student research, and videos often include interviews, first-person narratives, and historical footage that provide those accounts. Multimedia presentations are also becoming the end product of student research, in addition to the traditional written paper. If students are expected to include video in these presentations, they need to have access to the collection. A broad base of users benefits the development of the library's video collection by demonstrating its utility and desirability as a source of information, and as support for its budget.

Two issues relevant to the access and use of the video collection are security and preservation. Depending on circulation policy, the level of security for the collection will differ. A non-public area to house the collection or open shelving will determine the vulnerability of the videos. Available money will also be a factor in the type of security you will be able to afford. Preservation is another matter to keep in mind. Videotape has a limited shelf-life, depending on use and storage conditions. Checking the condition of videos periodically is suggested, as well as making allowance in your budget for replacement of titles that are used repeatedly. Keeping viewing equipment clean and in proper working order will also extend the life of videotape.

The development of the video collection offers the librarian the opportunity to expand the library's resources, to provide an alternative medium of information, and to attract additional users with this format. In adding to this collection, include others in the process, both from within the school and without. The greater the diversity of input, the richer the collection content will be. Colleagues at other schools, including local colleges and universities, library organizations at both the local and national levels, and, in this era of electronic communication, e-mail and listservs, put you in touch with others who share your work and concerns in minutes. You do not need to re-invent the wheel as your collection evolves; others have encountered the same problems and are likely to be willing to share their experiences.

In collaboratively building the video collection, it is easy to lose sight of the knowledge and expertise that the librarian brings to the process of selecting and effectively using video. Working closely with teachers and students to develope a wide range of resources in the library and to devise suitable applications of various formats makes the librarian an active participant in a learning environment. Communication, action, and involvement are key to the success of the school librarian's vital role in the teaching and learning process.

REFERENCES

Callison, Daniel. 1990. "A Review of the Research Related to School Library Media Collections: Part 1." *School Library Media Quarterly* 19 (Fall): 57–62.
Triche, Charles. 1993. "Video in the Schools: An Evolutionary View." *Wilson Library Bulletin* 67 (June): 39–40.

RECOMMENDED RESOURCES

Annual Video Reviews

Audio Video Market Place: A Multimedia Guide. New York: R. R. Bowker Co.
Educational Media and Technology Yearbook. Littleton, CO: Libraries Unlimited.
The Video Source Book. Syosset, NY: National Video Clearinghouse.

Associations

American Library Association (ALA). http://www.ala.org.
American Association of School Librarians (AASL). http://www.ala.org/aasl. Publishes *School Library Media Research* [online only]. http://www.ala.org/aasl/SLMR.
Video Round Table (VRT) of ALA (see ALA Web site). *VRT Bulletin* [online only] is available as part of membership in VRT.

Recommended Reading

Berdahl, Ingrid et al. 1990. "Steps in Integrating Video into the Secondary Foreign Language Curriculum." *IALL Journal of Language Learning Technologies* 23 (Winter): 17–23.
Bialo, Ellen R., and Sivin-Kachala, Jay. 1996. "The Effectiveness of Technology in Schools: A Recent Summary of Recent Research." *School Library Media Quarterly* 25 (Fall): 51–57.
Buhler, Stephen M. 1995. "Text, Eyes, and Videotape: Screening Shakespeare Scripts." *Shakespeare Quarterly* 46 (Summer): 236–244.
Callison, Daniel. 1991. "A Review of the Research Related to School Library Media Collections: Part II." *School Library Media Quarterly* 19 (Winter): 117–121.
Evans, G. Edward. 1987. *Developing Library and Information Center Collections*. 2nd ed. Littleton, CO: Libraries Unlimited.
Graham, Ted et al. 1992. "Using Video in the Teaching of Mathematics." *Mathematics in School* 21 (May): 19–21.
Herron, Carol et al. 1995. "A Comparison Study of the Effects of Video-Based Versus Text-Based Instruction in the Foreign Language Classroom." *French Review* 68 (April): 775–795.
Hughes, Margaret J., and Katz, Bill, eds. 1994. *A.V. in Public and School Libraries: Selection and Policy Issues*. New York: Haworth Press.
Kozma, Robert B. 1994. "The Influence of Media on Learning: The Debate Continues." *School Library Media Quarterly* 22 (Summer): 233–239.

Paris, Matthew J. 1997. "Integrating Film and Television into Social Studies Instruction." *ERIC Digest* ED415177 97. http://www.ed.gov/databases/ERIC_Digests.

Scholtz, James C. 1995. *Video Acquisitions and Cataloging: A Handbook*. Westport, CT: Greenwood Press.

School Library Media Quarterly [predecessor to *SLMR*]. Past full-text articles available at: http://www.ala.org/aasl/SLMR/slmr_resources/slmr_select_toc.html.

VRT: Newsletter Archive. http://www.lib.virginia.edu/dmmc/VRT.

Wolcott, Linda L. 1994. "Understanding How Teachers Plan: Strategies for Successful Instructional Partnerships." *School Library Media Quarterly* 22 (Spring): 161–165.

Woolls, Blanche. 1996. *Ideas for School Library Media Centers: Focus on Curriculum*. 2nd ed. Castle Rock, CO: Hi Willow Research and Publishing.

Zimmerman, Lynne W. 1997. "Guidelines for Using Videos in the Classroom." *School Library Media Activities Monthly* 13 (January): 32–33.

Chapter 4

Video Collections in Academic Libraries

Kristine R. Brancolini

INTRODUCTION

More than 20 years after the introduction of the videocassette player and re-corder, video collections and services in academic libraries remain uneven in size and quality. This is not a shocking statement, given the overall differences among academic libraries in terms of size, curricula, and faculty supported, and other academic and administrative factors. One might, however, expect a meas-ure of consistency in the support of media collections and services within aca-demic libraries of similar size: libraries with large budgets and large collections might be expected to invest proportionately in media resources. Surveys and other studies conducted over the past 10 years reveal that the commitment to current and emerging video and multimedia technologies varies widely, even among the largest academic libraries in North America, the members of the Association of Research Libraries (ARL). This is despite the fact that although circulation of traditional print collections is declining, the circulation of video-recordings continues to increase.[1] While some academic libraries are busy cre-ating digital libraries and virtual collections, many of our users still do not have access to tens of thousands of essential publications. Why? Because these publications are motion pictures, distributed on videocassette and optical disc. Academic libraries almost never build collections of motion media with the same intensity devoted to print materials.

Academic institutions (along with industry) were among the earliest to adopt video as a form of instructional technology. While video in its early ¾-inch (U-MATIC) incarnation was not practical for home use or as a consumer format, its application as a teaching and research tool and its advantages over earlier media formats were almost immediately seized upon by many campus media operations and services. These services rarely included the library, however. One of the earliest academic library studies conducted after the advent of videocassettes was *The Integration of Nonprint Media* (ARL SPEC Kit 33), published in May 1977. It described the bleak condition of audiovisual collections and services in academic research libraries. Most of the 27 members of ARL who were surveyed for the SPEC Kit had established specialized audiovisual collections to support instruction in art, music, and the medical sciences. However, less than half reported collecting audiovisual materials to support the general undergraduate and graduate curriculum. Audiovisual collections in most research institutions, particularly film collections, were established in units outside the library. In the 1977 SPEC survey, librarians reported that the impetus for developing audiovisual collections included faculty support and the growing number of appropriate materials, particularly at the graduate level. However, librarians cited three significant obstacles to the establishment and growth of audiovisual collections in their libraries. First, the existence of well-established book collections and the fear that the purchase of expensive audiovisual materials and equipment would lead to the decline of print collections. Second, many libraries lacked the physical space needed to house a new collection that requires special equipment and handling. Third, biases on the part of faculty toward traditional instructional methods and print information sources (ARL 1977).

While the current literature still reflects some of these concerns, technological changes have altered the course of audiovisual collection development in academic libraries. The most recent surveys of audiovisual collections in academic libraries found that approximately 95 percent of the respondents collect audiovisual materials to support the general curriculum (ACRL 1991; ARL 1990, 1993; Brancolini and Provine 1997), with video being the predominant format. Given the age of these studies, it is likely that video collection building approaches 100 percent in academic libraries of all types. The tide has turned, and video has been the major contributing factor.

As younger professors have begun teaching, resistance to the use of audiovisual materials in the classroom has diminished; the greatly simplified nature of the hardware and the rise of home video have also had much to do with this trend. Home video has, furthermore, produced an entire generation of students raised on videoculture, for whom video has become an expected part of the education process. Faculty have begun to accept that video offers unique instructional and research possibilities in a broad range of subject fields beyond art history, drama, and other performance fields—the traditional strongholds of instructional media on campus. Feature films are increasingly used as teaching tools by faculty in a broad range of disciplines, both as an art form in themselves, and as political, social, and cultural texts. The use of documentary materials and primary source footage such as broadcast news is also on the rise. The Public Broadcasting Service (PBS) has been particularly instrumental in exposing faculty to the wide array of excellent educational programs available at the undergraduate and graduate levels. The proliferation of documentary and performing arts programming on cable channels such as the Discovery Channel and the Arts and Entertainment channel (A&E) has further encouraged the use of quality media resources in the postsecondary classroom.

One major obstacle to the establishment and development of significant video collections in academic libraries continues to be the fear that these collections will divert funds from print and other resources. Even in those academic libraries with established and relatively well-funded video collections, expenditures for video lag proportionately far behind those for print materials. In addition to print materials, video collections must now compete with CD-ROM databases, databases mounted on networks, and Web-based resources for funding. The development of digital library programs and the necessity of supporting expensive hardware and software may also divert funds from traditional collection building and services. Ironically, the high cost of these electronic resources has forced libraries to deal with incorporating new technologies into the traditional funding patterns of academic libraries at a time when funding for all formats is decreasing.

BACKGROUND

The course of video collection development in academic libraries cannot be charted without reference to educational motion pictures. Early in the history of motion pictures, colleges and universities in the United States recognized the value of moving-image materials to their teaching mission. However, as mentioned earlier, rather than incorporate motion pictures into the library acquisitions program, most institutions established separate film collections outside of the library. By 1924, at least 12 colleges and universities had established film collections, and by 1936 that number had increased to 25 (Lemler 1948).

In 1947, Ford L. Lemler, then director of the Audio-Visual Education Center at the University of Michigan, conducted a survey of 138 colleges and universities with film centers (Lemler 1948). He received replies from 75 institutions, 65 of which yielded useable results. These film centers included regional or state distribution centers, departments that serve one campus only, and departments that promote and sell films produced by the university. Unlike print libraries, most of these film collections served more than the parent institution. While only 5 percent served the institution only, 19 percent served more than one state, 26 served one state only, 23 percent served part of a state. The other 4 percent produced and distributed educational films.

For a variety of reasons, some of which were noted above, film collection was seen as outside the scope of responsibility of the library. College and university film centers performed a variety of services in addition to supplying educational films. Fifty-five percent loaned slides, 63 percent offered projection services on campus, 72 percent provided film previews, 75 percent offered assistance in selection for classroom use, 60 percent offered formal courses in audiovisual methods, 53 percent provided audiovisual materials for student teachers, to specify only the most commonly offered services. Of the 56 reporting libraries that indicated the department or unit to which they report administratively, over one-half indicated that they were units of extension divisions. Four reported to the college or university library. Seven reported to the School of Education; seven to the president or vice-president; four to a dean of the faculty; one to the registrar; one to the biology department; and one to a special administrative board.

By 1940, librarians had begun to question the placement of audiovisual collections in one location under one administrative unit and the book and journal collections in another location under the library. In an article published in 1940, M. Lanning Shane wrote that "audio-visual aids are themselves books of a kind." Calling audiovisual aids "unconventional books," Shane asserted that "the person best equipped to service audio-visual aids is a member of the library staff. No other faculty member has the training which every librarian has received— training which is indispensable to an efficient long-range audio-visual program" (Shane 1940: 145). In 1948, Marion B. Grady, a librarian at Ball State Teachers College in Muncie, Indiana, reported on the rationale behind the audiovisual collections in the Ball State library. Established in 1939, "the decision to incorporate the non-book materials with the books was based on the logical reasoning of the former librarian and the college administrative authorities that there was no justification for separating related materials designed to serve similar if not identical purposes. They recognized the fact that the packaging did not necessarily change the nature of the contents" (Grady 1948: 314). While the reason for building an audiovisual collection in the library at a teacher's college was to familiarize future teachers with the use of such materials, the collection was used by faculty and students throughout the entire instructional program.

Two surveys provide information about the status of audiovisual collections in college and university libraries during World War II and the late 1940s. The first of these studies, conducted by B. Lamar Johnson and published in 1944, surveyed all colleges that were members of the Association of American Colleges and all junior colleges with enrollments of more than 200. He received responses from 324 four-year colleges and universities and 74 junior colleges. In order to contain the scope of his "quick survey," Johnson limited his questionnaire to motion pictures and sound recordings. Although "practically all" (numbers unspecified) of the responding institutions offered their faculty access to a motion picture collection, only 29 of 398 had centralized the motion picture service in the library. This group included junior colleges and universities, colleges with large enrollments, and those with small enrollments. More importantly, half of the respondents indicated that they believed that the library should be the centralizing agency, particularly for their own institutions. Respondents were not asked for their arguments in support of their judgments regarding the proper role of the library in supplying educational films, but a number presented their reasons. The objections to the library assuming this role included: lack of time on the part of librarians, inadequate space and lack of proper facilities, the other situation works well, lack of training, and the service is handled best by those more knowledgeable about faculty teaching needs. Reasons cited in favor of centralizing the film service in the library included: the librarian's contacts with all departments of instruction, the library's central location, the role of visual aids in supplementing the use of books, ease of handling motion pictures, the availability of the library, the library's role in promoting effective use of books, and the philosophical position that the library should be the center for all instructional materials. Many of the respondents predicted that the library would become the centralizing agency for motion pictures on campus in the foreseeable future (Johnson 1944).

In 1947, Sister Mary Winifred Grass completed a master's thesis at the Columbia University School of Library Service based, in part, upon Johnson's survey. Grass went beyond simply finding out which libraries collect motion pictures and recordings. For the libraries housing such collections, she wanted to "ascertain the current practices in the acquisition, organization, and distribution of educational films and recordings." Grass surveyed all libraries serving a college or university with an enrollment over 170 students. Her survey does not state the total number of libraries sampled, but she received usable responses from 63 libraries, of which 27 centralize the institution's motion picture collection in the library. However, of those 27 only 16 purchase films; the others offer rental service only. Unfortunately, from Johnson's description of his study it is impossible to determine whether his sample included libraries that rent films only. Grass supplies some interesting supplemental information. Most of the film collections in her study were small, ranging in size from one to 2,014 prints, with a median of 121. Grass also found a wide range in expenditures for films, from $100 to $5,000 per year, with a median of $191. For half of the 27 libraries, film service had previously been centralized elsewhere on campus. Only six stated that prior to establishing the collection in the library none had been available on campus. Asked whose suggestion it had been to centralize motion pictures in the library, seven cited the campus administration, seven cited the librarian, five cited a combination (administration, librarian, library staff, faculty, other users), two cited faculty, and six did not specify (Grass 1947).

The widespread practice of separating print and audiovisual collections persisted until the mid-1970s and the advent of video recording and playback technology. The convenience and relatively low cost of videocassettes prompted academic libraries to begin collecting moving-image materials in that format, rather than on 16mm film.

Campus film centers primarily support classroom instruction and continue to offer the range of audiovisual services documented by Lemler's survey. Since the late 1940s, television services have also been established on many college and university campuses. Sometimes these services are part of the audiovisual center, but they may also reside within a separate television support service. At some institutions all of these services—audiovisual collections, audiovisual production, audiovisual equipment, television production, satellite downlinking and uplinking (to specify only some of the most common) may be housed in the library, often with separate staff. All of these services may be housed in a separate audiovisual center. However, it is more typical, particularly at larger institutions, for these services to be divided among the library, the audiovisual center, and the television center. The administrative configurations are as varied as the colleges and universities they serve.

Academic libraries have always focused on individual users rather than group instruction, although this distinction has blurred somewhat as activities in bibliographic instruction have increased. Videotape and DVDs conform to this individual user orientation more easily than 16mm film. Both tapes and discs are easy to handle by individual users, and playback equipment requires little if any training to operate. Cassettes, and particularly DVDs, are easier to stop and start, allowing the viewer to pause to take notes. Pertinent sections can be viewed again and again, conveniently found by scanning backward. By scanning forward or using the counter on the player or the random access features of DVDs, the viewer can skip portions of the work. Videotape/DVD playback in library media centers allows individuals or small groups to watch programs during hours the campus film center is closed. Many of the titles in a film center collection are suitable for large-group showings in class, but what about the student who is absent from class the day the film was shown, or the student who wants to review the film for an exam or use it as source material for a paper? And what about the titles that are more suitable for individual viewing due to their length, such as feature length films and performances of plays? Once faculty began to switch from film to video, the campus library became a more reasonable location to house these materials—either in addition to or in place of the film center. Today most college and university film centers have expanded their holdings to include video formats; most no longer purchase 16mm films at all.

The Consortium of College and University Media Centers (CCUMC), composed of film and video centers responsible for the distribution of educational media to an institutional or extra-institutional audience, provides the best source of information on the status of these services campuswide. Founded in 1971 as the Consortium of University Film Centers (CUFC) by 29 universities, the organization changed its name in 1988 to reflect changing collections. It broadened its membership to all types of two- and four-year postsecondary institutions. In 1993 the constituent membership (representing institutions) stood at 184 members. By 2000, membership had grown to 546 institutional members from 297 institutions and 45 corporate members from 28 corporations, one associate member, one student member, and 37 life members for a total membership of 630. The membership includes "all sizes of institutions in higher education that provide media/instructional technology-related support services, as well as companies providing related products" (http://www.indiana.edu/~ccumc/). Unfortunately, only 12 members still rent films and videorecordings. *The College and University Media Review* (1994–present) is the professional journal of CCUMC and includes articles that focus on media and technology, related research, instructional development, and management and supervision, as related to the operation of instructional support service units in higher education. In contrast to Lemler's findings, approximately one-third of the film and video centers in the Consortium report to the college or university library. Fifty-four percent of the respondents to the 1990 SPEC survey reported that they share responsibility for audiovisual collection building with another unit on campus, usually a media center (ARL 1990).

The administrative distinctions between *media center* film and video collections and *library* film and video collections are changing. Ten years ago, a study of educational media centers in four-year colleges and universities by Mike Albright (1991: 4) found that "the most common reporting senior for [38.6% of] responding centers was the dean or director of the academic library, or subordinate in the library." Even at doctorate-granting universities, which traditionally separated film collections from the academic library, 36 percent (28/77) of the media center directors reported to the library. In early 1997, Albright and Lynn Milet (Milet and Albright 1997) surveyed constituent member institutions again. Of 292 possible respondents, they received 191 usable surveys, for a 66 percent response rate. Of these respondents 82 percent had experienced significant organizational change in the previous seven years or anticipated significant change by the year 2000. The percentage of media centers reporting to the library had increased to 46 percent. The next most common reporting line was the Chief Academic Officer, 28 percent. At doctorate-granting universities, 37 percent of the media center directors report to the library, which is unchanged from 1990, but 35 percent report to the Chief Academic Officer. Overall, the trend seems to be toward reporting to information technology, which saw a net gain of 22 institutions reporting to that administrative unit. As might be expected, changes in organizational reporting lines have led to changes in services. Services no longer provided by these media centers include equipment repair, video/media production, and film/video collections, among others. New services include multimedia production, high-tech classrooms, Web site development, distance education, faculty development and training, management of computer labs, and instructional development. Clearly, these organizations seem to be moving away from the development and support of media resource collections to instructional technology.

Academic libraries have been slow to develop audiovisual collections despite a number of compelling reasons for them to do so. In an effort to support the work of academic librarians who are building audiovisual collections and developing services, the Association of College and Research Libraries (ACRL) Audiovisual Committee (later the Media Resources Committee) drafted guide-

lines. The American Library Association (ALA) published the earliest set of
guidelines as a separate monograph in 1968, with extensive revisions in 1987
and 1999. The authors of the 1967 guidelines wrote, "The philosophy of library
services that has evolved through the years can readily be applied to audiovisual materials. The librarian's ability to select, organize, and service materials
applies to all types of learning resources" (iv). The authors of the 1999 guidelines wrote,

We agree with these statements. Rather than dwelling on the similarities between print
and media collections, we covered those points in the assumptions. In the guidelines
themselves, we focused on the differences. Furthermore, research and experience over
the past 30 years have taught us that some practices are more effective than others in
building useful collections and meeting our users' needs for media-related services. The
guidelines reflect this knowledge. ("Guidelines for Media Resources in Academic Libraries" 1999)

The following is Assumption 1:

All academic libraries will collect media resources. Some academic libraries exclude
some or all media formats from their collections. However, ACRL standards for academic
libraries specify that the library shall select and acquire materials in all formats. If only
one media collection exists on a college or university campus, that collection and its
attendant services should be part of the library. The library staff is uniquely qualified to
provide the best access to that collection, both physical and bibliographic. The library is
also the most qualified to build planned collections, responsive to both immediate and
anticipated programmatic needs. If another administrative unit on campus also collects
media, it is assumed that the library will coordinate its efforts with that unit.

This assumption is based upon four factors: bibliographic control, hours of service, policy-based collection development and selection, and access.

First, libraries can provide superior bibliographic control with thorough descriptive cataloging and subject analysis. While the sophisticated search capabilities of most online catalogs have improved access to all formats, print and
non-print; the impact on access to media materials has been particularly marked.
The online catalog allows retrieval of all versions of a work (the print, video,
and sound recording versions of *Don Quixote*, for example), or provides the
ability to limit a search to one format only. Web-based catalogs permit links to
supplemental materials, such as producer or distributor Web sites (including
video clips for online previewing), or online credit and review information. In
contrast to libraries, few campus media centers offer the same level of cataloging
as the library or universal access to their catalog. On the other hand, collections
in departmental libraries and campus computing centers often receive no cataloging at all.

The second factor to consider is the fact that libraries offer better hours of
service and easier access to materials. Because they primarily support classroom

instruction, campus media centers usually operate during typical office hours, Monday through Friday, 8:00 A.M. to 5:00 P.M. Libraries, on the other hand, typically have extended hours, including nights and weekends. It is not uncommon for media center operations to separate services and collections. The latter are sometimes stored off-site, requiring users to order films and videos for viewing the day before so they can be delivered to an on-campus viewing center. Libraries deliver the videorecording to the user on demand, with no waiting period. Libraries are more likely to circulate videorecordings to faculty for a limited time period. Most media centers and archives require in-house viewing of all users.

Third, library collections are generally developed specifically to support campus curricula and research. Because librarians who select video for library collections need not worry about the appeal of these collections to potential off-campus borrowers or renters, their collections can be more directly responsive to specific teaching and research needs of the college or university community. Libraries are more likely to support graduate and faculty research than a campus media center, or even a departmental library, both of which are more likely to build collections exclusively to support classroom instruction.

Fourth, libraries extend access to all members of the campus community and, in the case of some public universities, to any resident of the state. Departmental libraries and private archives, on the other hand, exclude most users. Multimedia resource centers operated by computing services often limit access to faculty or to students enrolled in specific courses. By centralizing video collections in the library, libraries extend access to a significantly larger user population, which is a more efficient use of scarce campus resources.

The 1999 "Guidelines for Media Resources in Academic Libraries" were developed by the 1995–1997 ACRL Media Resources Committee, with input from a variety of media and library professionals. The 1997–1998 Media Resources Committee revised and refined the document based on further discussions with an exceptionally wide range of interested and knowledgeable individuals and groups within and beyond the ALA. They form the basis of many of the recommendations in this chapter (some of the specific guidelines themselves appear at the beginning of a section in boldface).

BUDGETING

4.1 An Ample and Stable Budget for the Acquisition of Media Resources Should Be Based Either on a Percentage of the Total Library Acquisitions Budget or on a Formula Related to Collection Use as Measured by Circulation Statistics

Despite the expanding interest in video on campuses and the rapid increase of quality video programming, academic libraries continue to be tenaciously print-oriented (even if this print is in digital form), and academic librarians very often continue to discriminate against audiovisual materials in collection building. Given the expansive universe of available and appropriate titles, and increasing user demand, collections budgets for video in most academic libraries remain unrealistically low.

Since 1989, three surveys have been conducted that describe and analyze the status of audiovisual collections and services in academic libraries, including expenditures for materials. The first two (ARL 1990; ACRL 1991) were broader in focus, covering all audiovisual formats. The third (ARL 1993; also reported and expanded in Brancolini and Provine 1997) focused specifically on video recordings. These surveys revealed that although 95 percent of the libraries in the surveys collect audiovisual materials, spending averages less than 1 percent of total acquisitions budgets. *Audiovisual Policies in ARL Libraries* (1990) reports the results of a survey of academic library members of the ARL. With total acquisitions budgets for the sample ranging between $1,330,069 and $6,500,000, expenditures for audiovisual materials ranged between $1,000 and $150,000. *Audiovisual Policies in College Libraries* (1991) reports the results of a survey of college and small university libraries with enrollments ranging between 1,000 and 5,000. With total acquisitions budgets for the sample ranging between $36,680 and $1,220,000, expenditures for audiovisual materials ranged between $100 and $55,584. The 1993 ARL survey found the situation to be similar for the purchase of videorecordings alone. With total materials budget expenditures for the sample ranging between $2,167,349 and $10,215,000, expenditures for videorecordings ranged between $500 and $75,000. Bear in mind that these expenditures are for the largest academic libraries in North America.

An important factor in determining the amount of money spent on audiovisual materials is the existence of a separate fund for the purchase of these materials. Both of the SPEC surveys and the CLIP Note survey described above found that libraries with a separate audiovisual budget spend more than twice as much on audiovisual acquisitions as libraries without a separate budget. Sixty percent of the libraries in the CLIP Note sample have a separate audiovisual budget. The median expenditure for libraries without an audiovisual budget was $2,750; with an audiovisual budget it was $6,000. Fifty-seven percent of the libraries in the 1990 SPEC survey have a separate audiovisual budget. The median expenditure for libraries without an audiovisual budget was $12,591; with an audiovisual budget it was $32,000.

The 1993 SPEC survey asked a similar set of questions. The analysis of these data was reported in a separate publication, *Video Collections and Multimedia in ARL Libraries: Changing Technologies* (Brancolini and Provine 1997). Regardless of the total size of a library's materials budget, libraries with a separate audiovisual or video budget spent statistically higher amounts on video in 1991/ 1992 than libraries without a separate budget (Brancolini and Provine 1997: 12). This confirms the findings of the 1990 SPEC survey, suggesting that this phenomenon is stable over time. Sixty-four percent of the libraries in the 1993

SPEC survey have a separate audiovisual budget. The median expenditure for libraries without either a video or an audiovisual budget was $2,750; with an audiovisual budget it was $23,000, and with a separate video budget it was $29,175. One difficulty encountered in analyzing these data related to the small number of respondents who were able to provide the information in the absence of a separate media acquisition budget (only 8 out of a total of 22 libraries supplied this figure). The authors note, "One possible explanation may be that when libraries do not have a separate budget for audiovisual materials or video, figures on video expenditures are not readily available; we suspect that no one is tracking video purchases" (Brancolini and Provine 1997: 12).

Other factors that may influence audiovisual budgets were also tested, including size of university enrollment, and size of the library as measured by total volumes and amount of the acquisitions budget. To test these hypotheses, the 1990 SPEC survey data were analyzed further. Statistical analysis determined that as the number of students increased, the size of the audiovisual budget or the amount of expenditures for audiovisual materials did not increase. As the number of total volumes increased, the size of the audiovisual budget or the amount of expenditures for audiovisual materials did not increase. As the size of the total acquisitions budget increased, the size of the audiovisual budgets or the amount expended for audiovisual materials did not increase. There is no statistically significant relationship between any of these three factors and budget or expenditures for audiovisual materials. When the purchase of these materials must compete with the purchase of print materials, print materials receive priority.

The results of these studies are reflected in Guideline 4.1 from the ACRL "Guidelines," (1999) quoted at the beginning of this section. Academic libraries should establish a fund for the purchase of video and other media resources. The size should be a percentage of the overall materials budget or based upon an objective measure of use. A minimal level would be 1 percent; for more serious collection building, 3 to 5 percent is recommended. This represents the financial commitment of the largest and best-funded media collections among the ARL. Even these libraries do not have large collections measured against the universe of available and appropriate videorecordings. However, their students and faculty receive significantly better video support than the typical academic library provides.

RESOURCE SHARING

5.1 Media Resources Should Be Accessible through Resource Sharing, in Accordance with the ALA Video Round Table, "Guidelines for the Interlibrary Loan of Audiovisual Formats"

Why is strong support for video collection building so important to the overall quality of an academic library's media resource program? Resource sharing for video and other media materials is in its infancy. The 1993 SPEC survey asked, "Does your library lend videorecordings on interlibrary loan?" Out of 60 respondents, 20 (33%) answered yes and 40 (66%) answered no. Out of the 20 that lend videorecordings, 95 percent place some restriction on their loan, either by type of library (95%), categories of users (65%), or type of use (50%) (ARL 1993: 13). Asked to explain the various restrictions on lending, respondents were most likely to limit lending within a state university system, within a consortium, or within a geographical region—the local area or the state. One university lends only among three universities within the same geographic area. Restrictions by user group focused on faculty; three respondents noted that they lend to faculty only. One lends to faculty and students from their state system only. Restrictions by type of use include support of "face-to-face" instruction (classroom use) and other instructional use (Brancolini and Provine 1997: 13). Lending may be further restricted by individual licenses signed at the time of purchase. Some distributors prohibit the interlibrary loan of their videorecordings in order to protect existing or potential markets (among these are several distributors of expensive business and training materials, and documentary superstar Frederick Wiseman). Consequently, libraries must build strong media collections on-site, if they want to meet the needs of their users for rich and diverse content.

Recognizing the restrictions that most libraries place on the interlibrary loan of media resources, the ALA Video Round Table developed and guided through the ALA approval process, "Guidelines for the Interlibrary Loan of Audiovisual Formats" (http://www.ala.org/vrt/illguide.html), which were approved in January 1998. Library users benefit when media collections are included in resource-sharing programs. No library can meet all of its users' needs for media resources, but libraries are reluctant to lend to our users if we do not lend to their users. The guidelines recognize that some materials may be excluded, but in general, there is no reason to exclude entire formats from interlibrary lending.

COLLECTION DEVELOPMENT

6.1 The Library Should Have a Separate, Written Collection Development Policy Statement to Serve as the Basis for Selection and Acquisition of Media Resources

Whether establishing a new video collection or expanding an existing one, the video librarian must begin with a collection development policy. The policy will delineate the boundaries of the collection and enable the video librarian to communicate effectively with other librarians and with faculty. The video librarian may actually be a media librarian with responsibility for collecting more than one format. If video is part of a media collection, the video collection development policy should be a subpolicy of the overall collection development policy for media. It is insufficient to mention video briefly in the library's print collection development policy. A statement that the library collects material in all appropriate formats is not a collection development policy for video or any other audiovisual format. It does not provide the necessary guidance for the selection process, nor is it specific enough to function as a communication tool. This type of policy may represent a lack of commitment on the part of the library to systematic collection development of audiovisual materials.

As recently as 1985, Mitchell Whichard reported that he could locate no comprehensive audiovisual collection development statements from academic libraries in the library literature (Whichard 1985). In an effort to rectify the situation, the ACRL Audiovisual Committee commissioned a survey, which became the basis for the 1990 SPEC Kit, *Audiovisual Policies in ARL Libraries*. This publication includes samples of collection development and selection policies from 16 ARL libraries, which provide examples of the wide variety among library policies. *Video Collections and Multimedia in ARL Libraries* (1993) compiled 11 collection development policies, some of them updated versions of the policies published in the earlier SPEC Kit and some of them completely new examples. Although these policies come from ARL libraries, they are applicable to any academic library. Some collection development policies are on the Web, including those of Indiana University (http://www.indiana.edu/~libreser/media/media-col-dev-policy.html), the University of California, San Diego (http://orpheus-1.ucsd.edu/fvl/COLLDEVL.HTM), the University of Washington (http://www.lib.washington.edu/media/mccolldev.html), and the University of Montana (http://www.lib.umt.edu/dept/colldev/ims.htm).

The following considerations apply to the development of a general video collection to support the curricula in all disciplines. This discussion of policy coverage omits feature films (see Chapters 11 and 13 in this book). However, feature films have become an integral part of most academic video collections and, if included, should be a part of the library's video collection development policy. Many academic libraries have participated in the ARL North American Collections Inventory Project (NCIP) using the Conspectus methodology developed by the Research Libraries Group (RLG). Media librarians in NCIP libraries found the methodology to be entirely inappropriate for describing audiovisual collections, due to the generally small size and uniform lack of comprehensiveness of these collections. Media librarians in NCIP libraries typically completed only the narrative section, leaving description by call number ranges to the print selectors. The narrative section does provide a useful framework for describing audiovisual collections in academic libraries.

General Objectives and Subject Boundaries

General objectives of the collection and its subject boundaries. The first section of the policy should describe the collection's overall goals. At colleges and universities with subject-specific collections on campus, such as law or music, the policy for an interdisciplinary video collection may state that those subjects are not collected.

Programs and endeavors supported by the collection. The collection may support instruction and faculty research or just instruction. It may support faculty research in some disciplines and not in others

Scope of Coverage

Scope of coverage includes statements regarding languages, chronology, and geography, as well as additional factors specifically relevant to video collection building.

Languages. Does the collection include video recordings with or without subtitles? Most academic audiences prefer subtitled to dubbed video recordings. The policy may, consequently, state that dubbed films are purchased only if no subtitled version can be obtained. Video recordings in some languages may be collected more comprehensively than others. For example, a college or university with a particularly strong Italian-language department may collect more Italian-language video recordings than other languages. Feature films in foreign languages without subtitles may be the responsibility of one selector and those with subtitles the responsibility of another.

Chronology. Videos released within a certain time frame may receive priority. Often, older films are released on video years after their production. The policy should state the priority the librarian gives these productions.

Country of origin. Due to incompatibility problems, the librarian may decide to purchase motion pictures produced in any country only as long as they are distributed on video in the United States or available in the NTSC television standard (see below).

Home video and public performance rights. The policy should state whether or not the collection will include videos licensed for home use only. It should also stipulate when public performance rights will be purchased and whether an umbrella license will be purchased for titles unavailable with public performance rights.

Closed Captioning. Given the provisions of the American with Disabilities Act, many libraries are stipulating that videorecordings available with closed-captioning are preferred over those without them.

Formats and Standards Collected

Video formats. The policy should state the specific video formats to be included in the collection—VHS, laser disc, DVD. While many academic libraries still have U-MATIC tapes and laser discs in their collections, few are buying them. DVD statements should specify regional encoding (see the DVD chapter for an explanation).

Television standards. In addition to video recorded in the American television standard (National Television Standard Committee [NTSC]), foreign titles may be purchased in the other standards employed in other parts of the world; PAL (Phase Alternation Line rate) and SECAM (Sequential Color with Memory). PAL and SECAM videorecordings are incompatible with NTSC playback equipment, despite the fact that they may all be VHS. If the librarian decides to purchase videocassettes in non-NTSC standards, it is advisable to provide multi-standard playback equipment in the library. On many campuses, this equipment will be unavailable otherwise.

Categories of Material

Genres. Although it is assumed that the academic library video collection will include documentary films, it is useful to state explicitly other types of content that will be purchased: dance, drama, feature films, short and experimental films (fiction), video art, opera, other music performances, television programs, political oratory and persuasion, and dramatizations of literary works. Due to curricular strengths and faculty interest in video, certain genres may receive priority. Within these genres, describe any special policies that might apply. Titles within some genres may be purchased only upon the request of faculty.

Treatment. Some videorecordings are instructional rather than educational, meaning they are designed to meet very specific, usually quite narrow, behavioral objectives. For example, in the area of nursing, an instructional videorecording may teach students how to conduct an abdominal examination. The policy should state whether the collection will include or exclude this type of material. It may include instructional video for some disciplines and exclude it for others.

Related Collection Development Policies

The policy should state the relationship between the video collection development policy and those of other library departments and campus units that purchase videorecordings. The video librarian may coordinate purchases with these other departments and units, trying not to duplicate titles. The policy may state areas and degree of overlap with these other collections.

Other Resources

The section on other resources should describe the other video collections available on campus, going beyond the statement of collecting responsibilities. Other video resources might include the film and video center, departmental collections, and specialized archives. Cooperative collection building relationships with these campus collections should be described. Restrictions on the use of these collections should be noted in order to justify the library's purchase of titles held in these collections. For example, a departmental collection may be accessible only to faculty in one department, leaving the library to purchase many of the same titles for use by students and other faculty. Beyond describing the relationship of library video collections to other campus collections, the section on other resources may also include a description of other significant regional or national collections, including specific cooperative arrangements—either formal or informal—between the library and these collections.

SELECTION

6.2 The Selection of Media Resources Materials Should Be the Shared Responsibility of Librarians Specifically Charged with Building the Media Resources Collection and the Subject Selectors

Selection criteria may be covered in a separate collection policy but are often included as part of the collection development policy. Within the scope of the overall collection development policy, the selection policy states who will select videorecordings and how the librarian or other selectors make purchase decisions concerning individual titles. The collection development and selection policies are often tied to a media fund. That fund may be a general fund designated to build a broad, core collection or it may be a subject-specific fund designated to build a specialized collection in one discipline. Video selection may be the responsibility of a subject specialist, a format specialist, a committee comprising both types of selectors, or even faculty. Given the special knowledge needed to select videorecordings, it is desirable to hire specially trained and knowledgeable librarians to the select the format. Faculty tend to have very narrowly defined subject interests; if given too much control over the process, they can skew the collection toward their academic specialty. Subject specialists tend to be extremely print biased. Even when they are convinced of the value of video, most lack the specific knowledge needed to build a strong collection, or the time and willingness to consistently monitor the video production/distribution universe. Some videorecordings may, however, be selected by the subject specialist, and others by the format specialist. The subject specialist may suggest the purchase of titles to the format specialist and vice versa. The format specialist and one or more subject specialists may contribute funds to purchase an especially expensive series. The selection policy should state when each of these conditions applies.

Even in ARL libraries, where selection is generally firmly in the hands of librarians, selection of media resources tends to fall outside of the exclusive purview of the library. Faculty are often actively involved in requesting videorecordings for purchase, and most media librarians encourage this involvement in selection. However, during the pilot test of the 1993 SPEC survey, the investigators received anecdotal information suggesting that in some libraries, virtually all of the videorecordings purchased are faculty requests. The survey included the following question: "What percentage of the videorecordings your library purchased in 1991/92 were requested by faculty?" Forty-six respondents estimated the percentage of videorecordings requested by the faculty compared with those selected independently. The percentage of purchases requested by faculty ranged from 5 percent to 100 percent, with an average of 60 percent and a median of 68 percent. The percentage of purchases selected independently by a librarian ranged from 10 percent to 95 percent, with an average of 44 percent and a median of 40 percent. Is it a coincidence that only 40 percent of the respondents have a media/video librarian? The investigators hypothesized that libraries with a media/video librarian would be less likely to rely on faculty requests than libraries without a format specialist. Although further statistical analysis did not confirm this hypothesis, libraries without a media librarian have a higher percentage of videorecordings requested by faculty than those libraries with a media librarian.

Clearly, in some institutions faculty have far more influence over selection decisions for video and other media resources than they do for the print collections. Generally, the strongest and most responsive video collections are found in libraries where they are selected and managed by a librarian with format expertise, or where selection by committee is coordinated by such a librarian. Video selection requires an interest in feature, documentary, and educational films, and a thorough knowledge of the often eccentric system of film and video production and distribution. Effective video selection also requires thorough familiarity with the curricula supported by the collection, technical knowledge of cinematic expression, and expertise in evaluating educational media for purchase and for use. If the collection includes feature films on video, the selector should also be familiar with the discipline of film studies and knowledgeable about film as art. Beyond selection for purchase, the media librarian must actively promote use of the collection by faculty. This role entails ongoing discussions with faculty about their current uses of video in the classroom and about new resources and new uses of materials. The media librarian must be generally familiar with the entire collection, and certainly with the most significant individual works and with the areas of particular strength. Effective media librarianship includes close work with other librarians to establish contacts with the faculty and to coordinate print and video purchases. Subject specialists are more likely to know about new degree programs or curricular trends. The media librarian should work with these bibliographers to ensure that current and new programs and courses receive video coverage as well as print coverage.

Selection criteria may be more important for a video collection than the overall collection development policy. Video librarians, in their zeal to promote the legitimacy of their special format, often overstate the similarities between print and non-print information sources. Selection represents one aspect of video librarianship that departs dramatically from the selection of print librarianship. Due to the price of some videocassettes and the relatively small size of video budgets, video purchases tend to be much more selective than book purchases, particularly in academic research libraries. Few subject specialists in research libraries consult book reviews; titles are selected for purchase from prepublication sources based upon subject matter, publisher, and author's reputation. Many books are purchased through approval plans. In contrast, most video librarians consult reviews or actually preview potential purchases. Consequently, it is important to articulate clear and concise selection criteria. Just what does the librarian look for in the selection of a videocassette or a videodisc? The selection policy should primarily address content and technical quality variables (creative use of the medium, editing, photography, and sound quality, to name only a few) rather than format variables (VHS versus DVD).

Selection criteria may differ among categories of material. For documentary videos, selection criteria often include accuracy, timeliness of the information, level of treatment (descriptive versus analytical), sound and picture quality, aesthetic appeal, and relative cost. Although these variables have been listed in no particular order, relative cost should be the last consideration. Often librarians who select video allow themselves to focus too intently upon price. This should be only one factor, not the overriding factor in selection.

For fiction films, selection criteria include acceptable levels of print quality, depth of coverage for directors, depth of coverage for genres, the balance among the various genres, and the balance between English-language and foreign-language productions. For drama, selection criteria include the playwright, the director, the theater company responsible for the production, and the completeness of the production (an uncut version versus excerpts). For dance, opera, and music, selection criteria include the composer, the principal performers, the choreographer, title of the ballet or the opera, the themes presented in the work, and the dance company or the opera company.

The selection policy may include a statement about the use of review sources, with or without listing specific titles. The disadvantage of listing specific sources is that the policy rapidly becomes obsolete as new titles are adopted or dropped for various reasons. The selection policy should address such issues as whether the video librarian will preview potential purchases or ask faculty to preview them, in addition to or in lieu of using reviews. The statement should also designate the weight given to faculty requests, as well as how requests from subject specialists are evaluated. In lieu of previewing each title, the librarian may preview only those videorecordings that received mixed reviews. A list of review sources recommended for academic librarians appears at the end of this chapter. The librarian may also rely on attending film festivals and film and video markets to preview videorecordings, rather than ordering them for preview at the library (see Chapters 20 and 22 for listings of some of the more notable festivals and markets).

As with books and other print materials, libraries may purchase multiple copies of particular videorecordings in order to meet demand, or for other reasons. It is often useful to specify these conditions in the selection policy. As libraries adopt new formats and abandon others, librarians find that they are duplicating titles in the new format to ensure that demand does not exceed available equipment. The selection policy might describe how long this practice will persist and provide specific indicators for determining that this practice is no longer necessary.

Depending upon the nature of the collection, the librarian must decide how to handle decisions regarding replacement and weeding. Given the relative fragility of videotape and the vagaries of video distribution patterns, replacement is likely to offer more challenges than weeding. The policy should include a statement about replacement. How does the librarian decide which damaged or worn-out titles to replace? Do the original selection criteria apply or are replacements evaluated differently? How does a library replace a title that is on "moratorium" or out-of-print? Many public libraries and some academic libraries are beginning to purchase used videocassettes to replace out-of-print titles, particularly feature films.

Most academic library video collections require little or no weeding. The collections are small relative to the print collection, and highly selective. Most titles are selected for their anticipated lasting value. However, if the academic program supported by the collection changes, the librarian should have procedures in place for re-evaluating the collection, particularly if storage space is at a premium. Because video titles routinely go out of print (i.e., out of distribution), replacement of worn or damaged materials is often problematic. The policy should state procedures for locating the current distributor in order to reach a reliable conclusion about either weeding or replacing titles.

Section 108 of the Copyright Law was amended in late 1998 by the Digital Millennium Copyright Act, Pub. L. 105–304, 112 Stat. 2860, and the Sonny Bono Term Extension Act, Pub. L. 105–298, 112 Stat. 2827. This amendment does two things relevant to video collections in libraries. First, the original statute permitted the duplication of an out-of-print videorecording under certain circumstances; the amendment adds digitization to the possible methods of duplication. The right of reproduction under this section applies to three copies or phonorecords of a published work duplicated solely for the purpose of replacement of a copy or phonorecord that is damaged, deteriorating, lost, or stolen, or if the existing format in which the work is stored has become obsolete, if

(1) the library or archives has, after a reasonable effort, determined that an unused replacement cannot be obtained at a fair price; and

(2) any such copy or phonorecord that is reproduced in digital format is not made available to the public in that format outside the premises of the library or archives in lawful possession of such copy.

For purposes of this subsection, a format shall be considered obsolete if the machine or device necessary to render perceptible a work stored in that format is no longer manufactured or is no longer reasonably available in the commercial marketplace. (http://loc.gov/copyright/title17/chapter01.pdf; p. 16)

Therefore, libraries should develop procedures that, in the opinion of the college or university legal counsel, constitute a reasonable investigation to determine that an unused replacement cannot be obtained. Note that the definition of an obsolete format is fairly strict. Although ¾-inch U-MATIC playback equipment is scarce, it is still available for purchase, so it is still necessary to seek permission to reformat U-MATIC videocassettes.

RESERVATIONS AND RESERVES

As academic libraries move away from providing video collections exclusively for in-house users, the department housing the video collection may need to develop a reservation system and/or a reserve system. A reservation system allows instructors to ensure that videorecordings will be available on a particular day for classroom use. Given the volume of classroom showings, this system may be automated (perhaps interfaced with the online catalog) or manual. Many academic libraries allow instructors to reserve videorecordings for classroom showings via the Web. For an example of a Web-based reservation form, see the University of Virginia (http://www.lib.virginia.edu/clemons/RMC/coll-reserve.html). The elements of the system will include the instructor's name, department, and telephone number; the names of the videorecordings and the call numbers; and the date needed. If videorecordings are to be sent through campus mail, they will have to be reserved for a long enough period of time to reach the instructor and be returned. On many large campuses this may take as long as one week. In order to shorten turnaround time, many libraries require that videorecordings be picked up from and returned to the library. This procedure also eliminates the possibility that the videorecording will be lost in campus mail and increases the probability that any playback difficulties will be reported to library staff. By using a reservation system, academic libraries can usually avoid placing their own videorecordings "on reserve"—segregating them in the way that reserve books in the collection generally are. However, some academic libraries have begun circulating them to students, which has meant placing videorecordings on reserve, in order to assure their availability for students in particular classes.

A reserve system for personal copies allows instructors to place in the library for limited use their own videorecordings or videorecordings owned by their department. The usual reserve issues must be addressed in a video reserve policy, plus a few specific to video collections:

- *In-house versus circulating.* Will reserve videos be restricted to viewing in the library or will users be permitted to take them home or to another library? For libraries with enough playback equipment, it is probably desirable to restrict use to the library. However, small branch libraries with reserve video collections may find it impossible to house enough equipment to meet users' needs and may decide to allow users to take videos to other locations for a limited period of time.

- *Loan lengths.* How long will the videos circulate? Given the variable lengths of videos, it may be necessary to circulate parts individually and establish a loan length equal to the length of most parts—two hours. To allow time to rewind and review, the library may select a loan length of three hours. Libraries that do not allow users of reserve videos to leave the library may choose to have no loan length; the user is instructed to return the video whenever he or she has finished with it. An automated circulation system may establish a date due for each video on the following morning, so that the library will receive an overdue notice for any video taken from the library.

• *Number of items.* Most reserve policies restrict users to one video at a time, based upon the concept of maximizing the number of users who have access to the materials. There is no need for users to have multiple videos when the items will be due in less time than it would take to view them. Nor does it make sense for users to have a pile of videos in a video carrel when other users may be waiting to use them.

• *Legal versus illegal videocassettes.* Faculty may have recorded a videocassette at home, off-air, off-cable, or off-satellite, or may have duplicated a videocassette or a laser disc. Personal use of programs taped at home and use of them in certain classroom settings are permitted by the copyright guidelines. There is, however, a continuing and often heated debate about the general legality of using programming taped off-air in academic settings outside of the classroom—in a library reserve viewing operation, for example. Regardless of which side of the debate the library chooses to side with, unless off-air videorecordings are in the public domain, they should certainly not be used with students beyond the time period stipulated in the Off-Air Taping Guidelines (see Chapter 15). Reserve viewing operations pose other equally knotty problems and questions, such as whether it is permissible to put rented materials—"home use only" titles in particular—on short-term reserve for use by specific courses. Reserve collections frequently contain a large proportion of personal copies of videos deposited by faculty, and it is often difficult to monitor the legality of submitted tapes. It is, for this reason, important to stress to faculty that duplication of copyrighted videorecordings is illegal under any circumstances. The copyright policy regarding videocassettes should be consistent with the policy for books and photocopies that are placed on reserve.

PROFESSIONAL SUPPORT FOR ACADEMIC MEDIA LIBRARIANS

3.1 The Librarian Responsible for the Media Resources Program Should Be Encouraged to Belong to and Participate in Media-Related Professional Associations and Other Professional Development Activities

Media librarians often find that they have no professional colleagues within their library who share their interests and from whom they can seek guidance on professional issues. They may not even have peers in other academic libraries in their state. One effective remedy for this type of format specialist's isolation is participation in professional activities that encourage interaction with media librarians and media specialists at other institutions. A number of professional organizations, including the ALA and the CCUMC offer this type of professional support. Within the ALA, the ACRL Media Resources Committee is the most relevant place for academic media librarians to connect with colleagues. This committee has, in the past, sponsored surveys of audiovisual collections in academic libraries, presented numerous programs of interest to academic media librarians, and recently published new "Guidelines for Media Resources in Academic Libraries."

The ALA Video Round Table (VRT) (http://www.ala.org/vrt/) brings together video librarians working in all types of libraries, as well as video producers and distributors. The broad nature of VRT's constituency is extremely useful, given the fact that many issues related to video cut across library types. The inclusion of representatives from the video production and distribution industry in this group provides an unparalleled opportunity for video collection development librarians to communicate their needs and concerns, and to learn about the forces shaping the market. VRT usually sponsors a major program at the ALA annual conference. In 1998, VRT established the annual Notable Videos for Adults list, as a means of providing guidance to public and academic librarians involved in building dynamic and balanced video collections for an adult clientele. The first list was announced in January 1999. All selections are listed on the VRT Web site (http://www.ala.org/vrt/criteria.html).

In addition to these formal organizations, listservs provide a more informal means of communicating with other professionals interested in media. One of the best uses of a listserv is to conduct a quick survey or a general inquiry on a particular topic: "How many subscribers circulate camcorders for faculty/student use?" "Would you be willing to send us your collection development policy (copyright policy, circulation and use policy, etc.)?" What are your favorite Web-based review sources?" "Can anyone recommend a DVD security device?" This kind of information is often unavailable in published sources. Another use of a listserv is to ask help with collection development or reference questions: "I am trying to compile a list of women directors working in Spanish-speaking countries; I have consulted reference works and other books, but would be interested in hearing your recommendations of names to be included." "A German professor wants to acquire German-language films on video without subtitles; do you know of any mail order sources in the United States?" "Does anyone know the current distributor of a video on Japanese World War II internment entitled . . . ?"

For a listing of listservs relevant to the work of media librarians in academic and other libraries, see Chapter 22.

VIDEO TRENDS IN ACADEMIC LIBRARIES

Technology used in teaching, learning, and research has created new challenges and opportunities for managers of college and university library media resource collections and services. Faculty and students need traditional media formats—audiocassettes, audio compact discs, videocassettes, laser discs, and so on—but librarians must also consider computer technology and emerging digital formats.

Within the library, the boundary between media collections and services and computer software collections and services has blurred. Academic librarians are also working closely with other agencies on campus to support faculty and student information needs. In some institutions, librarians have become true partners in the delivery of instruction, working with faculty, technologists, and instructional developers to create "new learning communities."

—Foreword, "Guidelines for Media Resources in
Academic Libraries" (1999)

The development of video collections in libraries has been influenced heavily by consumer trends. In addition to collection issues, the media librarian must also stay abreast of technological changes that will affect the nature of the video collection and attendant services. Ten years ago, it appeared that multimedia CD-ROMs were going to be the next major format to impact academic media librarians, but the rapid rise of the Internet and the World Wide Web slowed CD-ROM collection development to a trickle. DVD basically eliminated laser disc collection development overnight. Multimedia production facilities, on the other hand, have broadened the focus of some academic library media centers from collection repositories to instructional technology centers. Many media librarians wonder how digital library development will impact their work: When will we begin digitizing our collections for network delivery? When will we begin incorporating elements of our collections into new digital teaching, learning, and research tools? For some librarians, the answer is, "Now." A 1993 ARL survey (ARL 1993) revealed that as early as 1992, 24 libraries (35%) responding to the survey were offering multimedia services and products to users and/or staff and another 14 (20%) were in the planning stages.

Multimedia are by nature a collaborative endeavor. Therefore, it is not surprising that of 66 respondents to a 1995 ACRL survey (Brancolini and Provine 1997: 17), 61% were working with units outside the library to develop or provide multimedia services and equipment. Asked to specify which other units, 20 respondents listed the following: computing center or information technology (55%); academic schools and departments (35%); instructional technology unit (10%); media resources (10%); human resources (10%); student services (5%); individual faculty and staff (5%). Nine respondents listed only one partner; 11 respondents noted that they were working with more than one unit or with individuals.

The investigators of the 1995 survey hypothesized that libraries with large collections of media resources might be among the first to offer multimedia production services, since these collections could provide source materials for multimedia presentations. However, they discovered that libraries were somewhat wary about allowing their materials to be used in multimedia productions. With regard to videorecordings, only 3 libraries (10%) allowed unrestricted use of the collection; 18 (56%) had some restrictions; and 11 (34%) had none at all. The reasons cited were copyright (25; 81%); circulation/policy restrictions (10; 31%); and preservation (8; 25%). The figures were very similar for sound recordings, which is somewhat surprising given the complex rights issues surrounding musical recordings: 5 libraries (17%) responded yes; 20 (67%) responded with restrictions; and 5 (17%) responded no. The reasons cited were virtually identical to the responses for videorecordings.

The 1995 multimedia survey is fascinating in light of recent multimedia software developments. Although public libraries quickly embraced multimedia CD-ROMs, academic libraries were more skeptical. In an effort to update their data and draw comparisons between formats, the investigators asked: "Does your library collect videorecordings?" Of the 56 respondents, 52 (93%) collect videorecordings, 4 (7%) do not. Asked "Does your library collect multimedia CD-ROMs?"; 40 (71%) responded yes, 16 (29%) do not. Eight additional libraries anticipated beginning a multimedia CD-ROM collection within the next two years. Twenty librarians, 50% of those with multimedia CD-ROM collections, offered comments and observations about their experiences with these materials. Because of the way the request for comments was worded ("Please tell us any concerns you have about collecting or circulating multimedia CD-ROMs"), the investigators suspected that they received more complaints than they would have if the question had been worded more neutrally. Some respondents pointed out that despite the difficulties, "it's interesting work," and in many libraries staff were dealing successfully with the problems. As expected, numerous librarians cited the same issues. Some of the concerns were specific to multimedia CD-ROMs and some pertain to the adoption of any new format. The concerns ranged from the often considerable hardware and technical support demands involved, to budget issues, to concerns about the variable quality of products and varying ease of use. These concerns generally foreshadow the culture shift that media librarians are experiencing as their lives become dominated by computer technology; a multimedia computer is significantly more complex than a VHS VCR.

The 1995 survey focused on one aspect of multimedia in libraries, the collection of multimedia CD-ROMs. However, there is another aspect that deserves exploration—multimedia production. Interestingly, some academic libraries that have chosen not to adopt multimedia CD-ROMs *have* made a major commitment to the support of multimedia production. In May 1995, Rick Provine, Director of Media, Clemons Library, University of Virginia, conducted phone interviews with librarians from five ARL libraries that were currently offering multimedia collections and services. The interviewees were asked to offer suggestions to others who are developing or expanding their own multimedia operations. Based upon these comments and his own experiences developing two multimedia centers in the University of Virginia's Clemons Library (http://www.lib.virginia. edu/clemons/RMC/dml.html), Provine presented "Recommendations for Integrating Multimedia Services" in *Video Collections and Multimedia in ARL Libraries: Changing Technologies* (Brancolini and Provine 1997). Among the issues discussed in this document are the need for careful planning and outreach; the importance of library multimedia services developing well-defined and articulated service agreements when serving or partnering with other campus units;

the central role of the unit in training; and the importance of developing and maintaining software and hardware standards.

What about digitization for purposes other than incorporating video into multimedia classroom presentations and projects? When and why might librarians want to digitize videorecordings? Disregarding for the moment the still considerable technical obstacles (digital capture, storage, and retrieval) and the daunting copyright issues involved, academic libraries might want to digitize videorecordings in the following situations:

- A program in your collection is deteriorating. It is out of print and you cannot find a replacement copy anywhere. It is on VHS, so transferring to another videotape will result in serious degradation of quality. Depending on the length of the work and other factors, digitization might be the answer. The Digital Millennium Copyright Act (DMCA) permits this preservation activity (see Chapter 15 for a short discussion of DMCA provision for preservation copying).
- Your library has acquired a collection of rare 16mm films from a collector. Among the thousands of films are many short films from the silent era. A professor who teaches a two-semester course on Hollywood would like to use some of these films in class, then make them available to his students later for papers and exams. Many of the films are not available on videotape or DVD. You might want to have them transferred to videotape and you might want to digitize the short films.
- Your rare book library owns the archive of a well-known film director, now deceased. Among the filmmaker's papers and other personal effects, there are also many 16mm color home movies that he shot in the 1940s. A scholar from a university in California is interested in seeing these films, but only wants to travel to your campus in the Midwest if the films are germane to his research. You might want to digitize selected films, place them on a secure server, then stream them on Internet2 to the scholar's workstation in California.

Some university libraries are already creating these kinds of digital video resources for faculty; within a few short years, these services may be mainstream in many media centers. At a July 2000 Video Round Table program on digital video (*Byting into Video: DVD and Network Delivery*), Claire Dougherty, Director of Digital Media Services and Director of the New Media Center at Northwestern University Library, reported on her work over the past few years in digitizing media resources from the library's collection and making them available via the campus network (see also Dougherty 2000). Dougherty described efforts to digitize the *Video Encyclopedia of the Twentieth Century* and other library-owned media resources with the involvement of institutional and corporate partners and the publisher of the original work (see http://nmc.nwu.edu/videoencyclopedia for a fuller description of this program).

These digital video initiatives represent the type of support for student learning that will undoubtedly become increasingly common and part of mainstream services as the technology matures. In follow-up conversations, Dougherty offered these insights into the challenges presented by library-based digital projects.

- *Establishing partnerships.* Setting the stage for working on large digital projects involves agreeing on ground rules and responsibilities with the partners. It is difficult to reach agreement on a realistic timetable. Digital video projects are, by definition, complex and resource-intensive. Finding ways to give all partners access to the data they need to produce their respective pieces usually demands an excruciating analysis in order to properly sequence activities.

- *Negotiating intellectual property.* This is a particularly thorny issue for video. Some libraries have materials of questionable origin in their collections, perhaps donated to the institution or taped off-air. There may be many rights holders associated with a particular production. In the case of the *Video Encyclopedia of the Twentieth Century*, the current copyright holders were unclear whether they had the authority to grant permission to digitize the content, which they had purchased from a news archive.

- *End-user support.* An interesting by-product of creating gateways to digital information is an increased demand for technical support. With text resources, such as databases and electronic journals, technical support usually centers around problems of access control and firewalls. With video and audio, however, the number of potential technical problems increases dramatically. Bandwidth, players and plug-ins, and platform compatibility have all been issues for staff providing access to digital video at Northwestern University. They have found it necessary to spend more time than anticipated providing technical support to users via phone and e-mail.

- *Access.* Developing title-level or item-level meta-data in order to provide access to digital video objects involves choosing a meta-data format, describing the objects, and either building a new repository to store the data or adding recordings to an existing repository. In the case of the *Video Encyclopedia*, they converted existing meta-data to an SGML-tagged format, but created a new repository to hold it. This presented communication problems, as most students and researchers at Northwestern were unaware that the library had mounted a significant new digital resource. They had to find ways to publicize the new site, directing traffic to it. The other option would have been to add new records to the online catalog. However, that would have created another user-education challenge.

- *Stability of file formats.* Technical standards for digital video are not well established. Unlike the digitization of text and images, there is a feeling of uncertainty regarding the file formats chosen for digital video. Will they be forward-compatible? No one is certain. As online storage costs drop, librarians will be less concerned about the longevity of our physical media, but file formats and codecs are constantly evolving and changing.

Another *Byting into Video* speaker, Karen Lund, from the Library of Congress's National Digital Library, described the *American Memory Project* (http://lcweb2.loc.gov/ammem/ammemhome.html), which represents another type of digital video activity, the digitization of archival film or video. To date, the Library of Congress has digitized nine collections of short films, including a Coca-Cola advertisement, early Edison films, the Westinghouse Works (circa

1904), vaudeville and popular entertainment (1870–1920), and much more. Most of these films are short and in the public domain, meaning they are no longer covered by copyright. Lund described the need to provide the films in a variety of formats, because different types of users have access to faster or slower machines and a different array of plug-ins. Academic libraries are beginning to explore the possibility of digitizing archival and rare films from their collections, but they face the same issues confronted by the Library of Congress, including technical and copyright concerns. In general, we will want to start with short films that are in the public domain.

A third type of digital video content that may become part of academic library collection building is "born digital." The Web is filled with sites where student and professional independent filmmakers display their work—digital films that were created for network delivery and probably do not exist in any other form. Sites like *inet: Internet Film Community* (http://www.inetfilm.com/), *Spherevision* (http://www.supersphere.com/TV/), and *ifilm: The Internet Place for Film* (http://www.ifilm.com offer) are dilemmas for media librarians. Faculty are beginning to teach with these films, especially film studies faculty. What will we do when faculty want the library to acquire some of these films? What will it mean to "acquire" them? Is anyone archiving these films for future access? Should libraries be archiving these films?

CONCLUSION

Despite the often considerable obstacles, both institutional and individual, library video collections and services have become an integral part of the information and teaching landscape of many colleges and universities. Many of the obstacles still remain, however, and those of us who are committed to bringing visual resources to our faculty and students must devise effective strategies for overcoming them. Despite the theoretical acceptance of video as a valid and vital part of academic library collections, the competition for funds to support these collections in the face of competing and intensified budgetary demands remains fierce. In an era of shrinking materials budgets due to recession, price increases, and an explosion of new publications and new publication formats, media librarians must be prepared to make a convincing case for increased funding for video collections and digital video/multimedia services. Although prices for many videos—particularly independently produced documentary and educational works—continue to exceed the price of a typical monograph, some distributors of educational videos have drastically reduced their prices in recent years, enabling libraries to purchase more than a handful of programs per year. This development has been offset, however, by the dramatically increasing teaching and research demands for lower-price home videos, particularly feature films. The advent of new formats such as DVD has also had an impact on budgets; we are, in a sense, facing the prospect of "re-buying" large portions of existing collections. Until video collections receive a higher percentage of overall acquisitions budgets, they will continue to represent a mere fraction of the important materials available to support teaching and research. And as we venture into new realms such as multimedia production and digital video initiatives there will be new requirements, including a need for new service models and a commitment to building staff with new skills. The good news is that most media librarians have the right stuff—the content expertise and the willingness to embrace new tools and technologies—to make this future work.

NOTE

1. In a recent white paper, "How and Why Are Libraries Changing," Denise Troll (2001) notes, "Use of print resources is decreasing. Use of video and other media appears to be increasing" (p. 7). In e-mail communication, Troll reported that she found this information in annual reports published on the Web.

REFERENCES

Albright, Mike. 1991. "Results of a 1990 Survey of College and University Media Centers." *Leader: Newsletter of the Consortium of College and University Media Centers* 20 (Fall): 3–5.

American Library Association (ALA). Video Round Table. 1998. "Guidelines for the Interlibrary Loan of Audiovisual Formats." http://www.ala.org/vrt/illguide.html.

Association of College and Research Libraries (ACRL). 1991. *Audiovisual Policies in College Libraries.* CLIP Note #14. Compiled by Kristine Brancolini. Chicago: The Association.

Association of Research Libraries (ARL). 1990. *Audiovisual Policies in ARL Libraries.* SPEC Kit 162. Compiled by Kristine Brancolini. Washington, DC: The Association.

Association of College and Research Libraries (ACRL). 1999. "Guidelines for Media Resources in Academic Libraries" http://www.ala.org/acrl/guides/medres.html.

Association of Research Libraries (ARL). 1977. *The Integration of Nonprint Media.* SPEC Kit 33. Washington, DC: The Association.

Association of Research Libraries (ARL). 1993. *Video Collections and Multimedia in ARL Libraries.* SPEC Kit 199. Compiled by Kristine Brancolini and Rick E. Provine. Washington, DC: The Association.

Brancolini, Kristine R., and Provine, Rick E. 1997. *Video Collections and Multimedia in ARL Libraries: Changing Technologies.* Occasional Paper 19. Washington, DC: Association of Research Libraries, Office of Management Services.

Copyright Law of the United States of America. United States Copyright Office. Library of Congress. Text revised to April 2000. http://www.loc.gov/copyright/title17/chapter01.pdf.

Dougherty, M. Claire. 2000. "Video on Demand: Streaming Media at Northwestern University." http://staffweb.library.northwestern.edu/staff/cdougherty/ala2000/dv/index.html.

Grady, Marion B. 1948. "Nonbook Materials in a Teacher's College Library." *College and Research Libraries* 9 (October): 311–315.

Grass, Sister Mary Winifred. 1947. *The Administration, Organization, and Distribution of Educational Films in College Libraries.* Master's thesis, School of Library Science, Columbia University, New York.

"Guidelines for Audio-Visual Services in Academic Libraries." 1968. Prepared by the Audio-visual Committee of the ACRL. Chicago: ACRL, American Library Association.

"Guidelines for Audiovisual Services in Academic Libraries" (ACRL). 1987. Prepared by the ACRL Audiovisual Committee, Margaret Ann Johnson, Chair. *C&RL News* 48 (October): 533–536.

"Guidelines for Media Resources in Academic Libraries." 1999. *C&RL News* 60 (April): 304–312. http://www.ala.org/acrl/guides/medresg.html.

Johnson, B. Lamar. 1944. "Audio-Visual Aids and the College Library." *College and Research Libraries* 5 (September): 341–346.

Lemler, Ford L. 1948. "The College or University Film Library." In *Film and Education.* Edited by Godfrey M. Elliott. New York: Philosophical Society, pp. 501–521.

Milet, Lynn K., and Albright, Michael J. 1997. "Media Center in Transition: Results of a 1997 CCUMC Member Survey." *College and University Media Review* 4 (Fall): 11–42.

Shane, M. Lanning. 1940. "Audio-Visual Aids and the Library." *College and Research Libraries* 1 (March): 143.

Troll, Denise. 2001. "How and Why Are Libraries Changing?" Draft. Washington, DC: Digital Library Federation. http://www.clir.org/diglib/use/whitepaper.htm, January 9.

Whichard, Mitchell. 1985. "Collection Development and Nonprint Materials in Academic Libraries." *Library Trends* 34 (Summer): 37–66.

Chapter 5

The Expanding Domain of Health-Content Video Collections

Anita Ondrusek and Suzanne J. Crow

INTRODUCTION

Since the release of the first edition of this chapter on video collection development in health sciences settings (Ondrusek 1994: 85–124), health-content video development has expanded its horizons. New modalities of video delivery, revisions in health professional education and accreditation, audiences that now include home video consumers, and changes in the medical media markets have all contributed to this expansion of health-related video services. As a result, media librarians in health centers and medical schools are faced with new video-related decisions, such as whether to replace photographic image collections with video-based image data discs; what percentage of the budget should be allocated for VHS cassette acquisition; and how to accommodate requests for acquiring digitized video simulations as learning materials. In addition, a heightened public awareness of personal health has resulted in partnerships between librarians in medical facilities and institutions such as public libraries, the aim being to train library users to retrieve health-related information. Where this information is available in a video format, collection development concerns such as selection, budget, and maintenance become considerations in overall program development. Finally, widespread access to network connections and advances in digital video storage and retrieval methods are together contributing to shifting practices in media delivery. In this shift, the computer, a multi-modal device that serves as a viewing window as well as a portal to locating video information, is better suited to "seek-find-view" user habits than are stand-alone video or traditional broadcast media.

MEDICINE AND THE MOVING IMAGE

Medicine is a profession that has historically woven a rich assortment of moving picture materials into its educational programs. This tradition dates back to as early as the 1890s, when the French physician Etienne Jules Marey filmed a turtle heart kept beating under artificial circulation (Nichtenhauser 1953: 25), and the French surgeon-cinematographer Eugene Louis Doyer invented filming techniques to document his surgeries. By the turn of the nineteenth century, filming of other medical phenomena, such as human gait disorders and epileptic seizures, for the purposes of review and study was becoming an accepted practice in medical circles (Nichtenhauser 1953: 40–65). Other venues for producing films with medical themes followed.

Using film to communicate social implications of medical practice had its start with films such as the 1940 U.S. film production of Paul DeKruif's book *Fight for Life*, "a bitter indictment of slum conditions and a gripping plea for greater medical knowledge in the field of obstetrics" (National Audiovisual Center (NAC) 1978: 80). During World War II, military physicians assigned to units in the South Pacific needed to learn how to identify and treat the tropical diseases to which the troops were exposed. Film was the medium chosen to provide this information, and the body of films that resulted from this mass training project added significantly to medical documentation on infectious disease. In addition, this effort showed that film was an effective instructional medium. By the middle of the twentieth century, film was also employed to record psychological aspects of human behavior. A prominent example is the work of British psychoanalyst James Robertson, who filmed hospitalized children and very young children whose mothers were hospitalized, in order to study the effects of mother-child separation on the child's behavior (Mason 1991).

The need for systematic collecting, indexing, and preservation of materials in biomedicine led to the establishment of the National Library of Medicine (NLM) in 1956, a major event in instituting federal leadership and commitment in this area (*United States Code Annotated* 1957: 136–140). NLM's collection included audiovisual programs, signaling that media were an accepted component of a medical library collection. Other U.S. federal agencies joined this movement by establishing media collection centers, one of which was the National Medical Audiovisual Center. These agencies published holdings catalogs and offered program loans and rentals. Motion pictures covering medical topics composed a major part of these collections. During the 1960s and 1970s, an infusion of federal monies helped medical libraries to fund audiovisual divisions, and administrators realized the need to assign the curatorship of an audiovisual collection to a professional trained in the selection of educational media. By 1980, many of these programs were self-sustaining. The National Medical Audiovisual

Center closed, and its collection was transferred to NLM's Historical Audiovisuals Collection. Some titles remain in a catalog maintained by the NAC, U.S. Department of Commerce, and may be purchased through the National Technical Information Service (NTIS).

Meanwhile, the physician-as-filmmaker tradition continued, attracting scientists and medical educators as well. Programs such as the *Guides to Dissection* series, with Carmine D. Clement as its principal author, and Edward A. Mason's psychiatric interview documentaries, still in circulation, indicate the staying power of these films as teaching materials. In fact, the creation of instructional video spawned a lasting partnership between medical specialists and media producers. With the arrival of videorecording technology, a host of collaborations between media departments and clinicians produced video footage. In fields such as medical imaging, where visual interpretation of data is vital to confirming a diagnosis, a video librarian is likely to find: (1) videotapes housed in hospital departments which are on file for internal use by house staff only; (2) taped conference lectures illustrated with imaging scans procured from a professional organization (e.g., American Institute of Ultrasound Medicine); (3) video showing imaging procedures produced by an institution (e.g., the Mayo Clinic echocardiography series); and (4) instructional videos on topics such as examination of the pregnant abdomen which includes clips of ultrasound scans. In essence, the medical specialist's relatively easy access to videotaping support has created a vast visual record released through a variety of production outlets.

Imagine the reactions of those filmmaker physicians from the late 1800s looking on a century later as medical students view ultrasound sequences as part of a radiology lecture. They might express astonishment at the lack of awe seen in contemporary audiences. In their day, people filled theaters just to see images move across the screen. Today, access to motion pictures is an educational norm, and medical video designers have learned that engaging the viewer requires incorporating meaningful content and including opportunities for viewers to interact with the presentation. Further, demands for medical content video programs are no longer confined to specialists. By the end of the twentieth century, terms such as "consumer health," "public health," and "wellness" became part of the popular vernacular. Conditions such as pregnancy, infection, obesity, and many more which were once discussed only among physicians or with a patient in the privacy of the doctor's office, became the subjects of popular books and television broadcasts. Modern diagnostic methods might even include a "video moment" between a physician and a patient such as viewing mammogram results on a digital monitor as the scans are being taken (Ritter 2000). Combining this new public mind-set with the evolution of videotape from a medium used by professional videographers to a "video home systems" (VHS) format, we find the reach of videotaped health information in the twenty-first century extending from the medical science lecture hall out into the community of health information seekers.

INFLUENCES ON VIDEO COLLECTION DEVELOPMENT

Collections versus Clientele Factors

There are a number of approaches to library collection development that contribute to the practices currently accepted by librarians. Scholtz (1994: 235–236) draws distinctions between a collection-centered development plan, based upon concepts such as depth-of-subject coverage and inclusion of standard titles, versus a client-centered development approach, which uses data-gathering techniques such as user surveys and collection-use analysis. The NLM's materials collection policy, which governs its acquisition of both print and audiovisual items, is an example of a collection-centered scheme. In its collection development manual, NLM identifies the biomedical subjects within its collection scope and includes under each subject heading a statement on coverage depth (NLM 1993). As new topics appear in the biomedical literature, they are assigned medical subject headings (MeSH) which are then incorporated into the subject scope-and-coverage outline. When media programs on those subjects materialize, they are considered for inclusion in NLM's audiovisual collection. Large biomedical media collections, that is, those collections funded to serve conglomerated clinical-teaching-research needs, generally incorporate aspects of NLM's subject coverage approach into their media acquisition policies.

The client-centered approach to library collection development is reflected in schemes such as the model described by Evans (1987), who places community (collection user) analysis at the beginning of the collection development cycle. Eakin (1983: 28) refers to this initial stage in collection development as examining "institutional characteristics." The client-centered approach is most appropriate for health-content media collections with a narrow user focus. For example, a neighborhood library considering video acquisition for its consumer health collection should conduct an analysis of potential user characteristics to guide the video selection process. As video libraries such as these expand, procedures that keep the collection's manager in tune with user needs should be part of the collection plan.

Video collections with a specific focus but with broader-based user groups might consider a modified client-centered collection approach. For example, in a health sciences professional school where the video collection is primarily used for teaching and training, user groups normally include faculty, students, and administrators. In this type of institutional environment, the most important factors to consider are the size, nature, and extent of the instructional programs to be supported by that collection. Subjects to be collected should be directly related to the school's curriculum. Since teaching missions are shaped by accreditation standards and national trends in health care practices, the video programs selected should reflect the current state of affairs in these areas as well. Equally important is an understanding of how video utilization fits into a teaching institution's administrative structure; that is, what funding and reporting relationships are in effect.

Organizational Structures

Health-content video collections generally function under the auspices of a larger administrative organization, most commonly managed by a hospital, a health professions school, or a health sciences library. There is, at present, so much cross-fertilization among video loan programs that it is difficult to describe the attributes that make the video users from each of these institutions unique. To illustrate, patient education videos that were once accessible exclusively through hospital collections may now be found in public libraries. Nonetheless, librarians interested in health/medical media services will find that hospitals, health professions schools, and health sciences libraries differ in their approaches to collection management for reasons related to their missions and administrative structure. These differences are highlighted in the sections which follow.

Hospitals

At the heart of a hospital's mission is exemplary patient care, or as the Hippocratic Oath states, to "first do no harm" to those under the physician's care. To assure that this mission is upheld, hospitals are periodically subjected to a stringent accreditation process overseen by the Joint Commission on Accreditation of Healthcare Organizations (JCAHO), and a document entitled *The Comprehensive Accreditation Manual for Hospitals* (CAMH) outlines the current JCAHO accreditation standards. "Professional Library Services" was once a discreet category in the *Manual* (JCAHO 1990: 209–212), but this designation did not survive changes in the accreditation process enacted during the 1990s. JCAHO's evaluation process now centers upon a hospital's ability to carry out "functions"—a term defined by JCAHO as "[a] goal-directed, interrelated series of processes such as continuum of care or management of information" (JCAHO 1999: PF-1). Under these new standards, a hospital librarian's role is defined in terms of "knowledge-based information" directives, an "Organization Function" according to the JCAHO accreditation services organization chart.

In a number of ways, the new JCAHO standards can be used to help a hospital librarian focus on collection development issues, including video collection development. For example, the new guidelines accentuate optimizing patient care through patient education and hospital staff performance improvement—two areas where video utilization has traditionally found a place in hospital services. In fact, an examination of the JCAHO's organization chart reveals at least three mandated services in which video collections can be used to help meet accreditation needs. These three areas include: "Patient and Family Education and Responsibilities"; "Orienting, Training, and Educating Staff"; and "Credentialing" (of medical staff). Brief background information in each of these services is outlined next.

Patient education was officially recognized in the American Hospital Association's declaration, a *Policy Statement on the Hospital's Responsibility for Patient Education Services* (AHA 1982). This document states: "The hospital has a responsibility to provide patient education services as an integral part of . . . care." To meet this responsibility, many hospitals have established patient education units where video programs addressing the medical needs of a hospital's patient population are made available for patient viewing or for use between clinicians or counselors and their patients. Some institutions maintain their own closed-circuit patient education channel and distribute their programs on videotape. Other hospitals depend upon the librarian to collect patient education videos and provide viewing areas. With an increased emphasis on patient education and consumer health information, hospitals may look toward expanding audiovisual collections. In this situation, a librarian with expertise in video utilization is a valuable resource as a video collector and consultant.

Orienting, training, and educating hospital staff can be driven by government mandates to educate hospital personnel in areas such as chemical hazards and infection control, or by an individual hospital's staff training priorities, which may range from recognizing and reporting sexual harassment to training on the newly installed telephone system. If the hospital library is designated as the central depository for training videos, the video manager will need to assure that budget and storage needs for training videos are articulated in the library's collection policy. In institutions where individual units, such as the office of infection control, maintain their own video collections, the library's video manager may act as a consultant for review and selection of these programs. In either instance, it is advisable for the video manager to maintain close contacts with hospital administrators from offices such as right-to-know, risk management, and quality assurance programs. Since materials on these topics date quickly, direct contact with government agencies that set standards such as the Centers for Disease Control and Prevention (CDC) and the Occupational Safety and Health Administration (OSHA) is the most effective means of determining accuracy of video programs under consideration.

Credentialing of physicians, nurses, and certain allied health positions begins with passing national board examinations in order to obtain a license. Throughout their careers, these health professionals are, then, required to renew their licenses through a continuing education process administered by certified providers, sometimes referred to as sponsors. These providers operate from health sciences centers, medical societies, professional organizations, or as private companies. In medicine, the process is referred to as CME (continuing medical education), and the Accreditation Council for Continuing Medical Association (ACCME) "set[s] standards to certify providers, monitor compliance, and connect CME to medical care" (Biddle 2000: 63). Nurses, pharmacists, and other hospital professionals who must be re-certified have their own accrediting coun-

cils. Self-learning via video programs is one approved method for earning continuing education credits, so many CME providers either distribute their own
video programs or enter into partnerships with commercial distributors to market
their CME videos. Hospital-based organizations such as the Hospital Satellite
Network and the AHA broadcast continuing education courses and, then, make
these programs available on videotape. A caveat on CME video library purchasing is that these programs are relatively expensive, specialized in content,
and tend to date quickly. CME credits are accumulated based on viewing hours,
and earning one credit may mean viewing several two-hour video programs.
The acquisition and maintenance of a comprehensive CME video collection is
better handled by a CME unit or individual clinical departments. For all these
reasons, the Internet is an attractive alternative for CME delivery, and video
"webcasts" are now available through certain CME providers.

Health Professions Schools

Video technologies have played a part in modifying the learning environment
in health professions schools at several junctures in medical education development. For instance, the lower cost and portability of videotaped programs,
when compared to films, expanded motion picture uses from what previously
consisted of a small number of films viewed in a large-group lecture hall to a
wide array of videotapes acquired for small-group and individualized viewing.
The beginning of mass marketing of video programs in the early 1980s actually
coincided with changes occurring in medical education itself. In 1984, the Association of American Medical Colleges (AAMC) released its report, "Physicians for the Twenty-first Century." The report was a review and comment on
the General Professional Education of Physicians (also called the GPEP Report)
as studied by a panel of medical school and university educators (AAMC 1984).
Its findings precipitated a shift in the philosophy of medical education away
from rote memorization and lecture methods toward self-directed learning methodologies such as case-based and problem-based learning. Recommendations
from the GPEP Report on the importance of computer technologies added mo-
mentum to the movement among media developers in the health sciences to
design computer-based programs with problem-solving and interactive elements
(O'Neill 1990: 624–627; Woods et al. 1988: 853). This advance, along with
rapid refinements in the personal computer's video capabilities, paved the way
for the incorporation of the digitized moving image into computer programs.
This format, as it proliferates, continues to influence video viewing and video
collecting in health sciences school settings.

Like medical schools, schools of nursing and allied health incorporate video
programs into their curricula. According to a 1999 National League for Nursing
statement, entitled "The Future of Nursing Education: Ten Trends to Watch," it
is imperative that educators emphasize information technologies, particularly
those that encourage distance-independent communication and those that enable

clinical simulations (Heller et al. 1999: 2). Educators are beginning to incorporate such technologies. For instance, a major trend in nursing and allied health education is the offering of distance education courses, in which video programs often play a significant role (Rosenlund et al. 1999: 194). In addition, pedagogical emphasis in these fields is increasingly placed on problem-based learning, which encourages the practical application of knowledge, requires the development of critical thinking skills, and uses real or simulated professional situations to stimulate student learning (Brandon and Majumdar 1997: 1). Video, particularly interactive video, is a powerful tool for problem-based learning because it enables students to practice their professional actions and hone their decision-making skills in simulated professional situations (M. Dornbaum, personal communication, July 11, 2000).

The content of video programs selected for use in health professions schools generally corresponds to curricular content. Courses referred to as the basic sciences are covered in the first two years of medical school and are either courses or prerequisites for nursing and allied health students. These courses include anatomy, physiology, biochemistry, microbiology, pathology, and human development/behavior. Although considered important, less course time is usually devoted to topics such as embryology, genetics, epidemiology, and bioethics. Under older curricular regulations, students learned these "basics" in the classroom and through laboratory exercises, and then entered a period of clinical training. However, many health professions schools have opted to integrate the basic sciences more closely with the acquisition of clinical skills by assigning students to clinical practicums while they are still receiving their basic science education.

In basic sciences studies, which are rich with visual information, video programs enhance learning by using close-ups and labels to highlight information such as vessels and musculature. In the area of clinical performance, video remains an effective presentation vehicle for demonstrating procedures, especially in areas such as interviewing and history-taking; physical examination and assessment; medication, infusion, and injection administration; blood pressure, temperature and pulse/respiratory rate measurements; intubations; complete blood counts; fluid-electrolyte and blood gas interpretation; medical asepsis; bedmaking and bathing; lifting and transfers; and catheter and ostomy care. More advanced clinical procedures, which students are expected to master in their final years of training, have also been recorded as video programs, covering areas such as airway maintenance; interpreting diagnostic information (ultrasound, X-rays, electrocardiograms, heart/lung sounds, etc.); sterile techniques and surgical procedures for the operating room; managing pregnancy, labor, and delivery; and specialized pediatric and psychiatric assessment protocols.

In health professions schools where a variety of nursing and allied health programs are supported, advanced courses focus upon recovery, therapies, physical and psycho-social aspects of illness and disease, family relations, and professional theories and processes. Also, some curricula now include survey courses on topics such as health care systems or the sociology of particular populations (e.g., AIDS patients, battered women, the aged). Topics such as these tend to be the subjects of documentaries, produced and marketed through different venues than the biomedical sciences demonstration programs previously described.

Specialized health sciences professions such as dentistry, pharmacy, optometry, and osteopathy each have unique areas of video collecting. Video collections supporting these programs generally include a core collection of tapes from the basic medical sciences, with variations depending on specialized areas. For example, osteopathic training currently follows a curriculum similar to allopathic medical education but with manipulation techniques taught. Anatomy tapes are standard items in all medical school libraries with an emphasis on the head and neck tapes in dental collections, and a similar emphasis on neuroanatomy in optometry collections. Video collectors in these schools seek out commercial distributors that market video series specific to their curricula such as neuroanatomy, dental procedures, and miopacial pain, and supplement these selections with productions made by professional organizations, other professional schools within their specialty, and manufacturers of products related to each specialty.

Health Sciences Center Libraries

Health science(s) centers, or medical centers, encompass a wide range of activities that may include scientific research, testing new drugs or procedures, hospital services, and health professions education. The libraries that serve these centers must contend with a much broader user population than the users of hospital or professional school libraries, and health sciences centers libraries are subject to review by more than one professional board. Thus, a health sciences center library serving a teaching hospital, or a network of affiliate hospitals, will be evaluated by JCAHO; if a medical school is part of the health sciences center, the library will be visited by the AAMC accreditation team. Traditionally, video collections served to strengthen a medical center's teaching programs, positioning faculty and students as major video collection users. Video users may come from colleges of medicine, nursing, and allied health as well as graduate and other certificate-granting programs. In this situation, the librarian responsible for the video collection will receive requests for videotapes, and, if the library oversees computer facilities, everything from interactive video "courseware" to an electronic file containing links to Internet video sites may be routed to the video librarian for dispensation. That same librarian may be obliged to review and acquire video materials for other endeavors to which the Center has pledged support, such as community health programs, continuing education for physicians and nurses, resource-sharing through health consortia, health careers recruitment, or mandated training on workforce safety.

Since the health sciences center library serves so many constituencies, it is essential that the video collection developer establish parameters for video acquisition. If the health sciences center library houses a centralized, multi-health topic collection, the video manager needs to identify what (if any) other video collections exist outside the library and how responsibilities for video collection are delineated among those varying collections. This investigation provides the central library's video manager with an overview of special-service collections which can sometimes lead to productive partnerships. For example, if the hospital maintains its own patient education video center, it may be willing to loan certain titles to help fill viewing requests received by the centralized library's video center. On the other hand, this process identifies video units that cannot strike reciprocity agreements with the library's video center (sometimes funding restrictions or use patterns make this impossible). Information such as this helps the video manager to make collection decisions regarding video program location and purchase requests. These will be discussed in more detail in this chapter under "The Collection Development Policy."

Consumer Health Videos

Consumer health information, intended for the lay audience, has proliferated in today's era of managed care. Both because less time is spent in consultation with physicians and because high-quality health information has become widely available, consumers are actively educating themselves about health issues, and audiovisual information is a vital part of this trend (Rees 1994; Stolberg 2000). The subject matter for consumer health video programs varies widely. Perhaps the strongest emphasis is on health promotion, an area that includes disease prevention, nutrition and physical fitness, and the effects of behavior on health (e.g., substance abuse and sexual behavior). Many self-care programs address the realities of living with certain conditions, such as diabetes or asthma, and introduce strategies for coping with these disorders. Others address diseases and conditions that affect both body and mind, dealing with aspects such as treatment, diagnosis, and emotional reactions. Videos also allow viewing of recorded medical procedures, including surgeries and alternative medical treatments.

Videos are frequently a significant component of health education programs which are offered though organizations including community-based health education centers, schools, and businesses. Consumer health videos are also used in the context of patient education services provided by hospitals and other health care facilities. Studies indicate that videos are an effective means of communicating health information, particularly when they are produced with the intention of reaching specific audiences (Biglan et al. 1988; Freimuth et al. 1997; Noell et al. 1997; Resnicow et al. 1997; Schinke et al. 1992). Target audiences frequently include different ethnic groups, genders, and age groups (Freimuth et al. 1997; Noell et al. 1997; Ramirez et al. 1997; Resnicow et al. 1997; Schinke et al. 1992). Examples of this sort of video program include a substance abuse prevention program developed specifically for seventh graders (Freimuth et al. 1997) and a smoking cessation program designed for urban African Americans

(Resnicow et al. 1997). Target audiences may also consist of those with common concerns, such as pregnant women, parents, caregivers for the aged, or those affected by a particular disease or condition (Lewis and Nath 1997; Maslin 1998). Examples of such programs include an interactive multimedia kiosk used to educate diabetes patients about their condition (Lewis and Nath 1997), an interactive videodisc used to inform breast cancer patients about treatment options (Maslin 1998), and a video designed to inform patients about advance directives (Cugliari et al. 1999).

Videos are effective in educating consumers about health issues for additional reasons. They provide a consistency for health information content (Cugliari et al. 1999: 106; Freimuth et al. 1997: 556), and, unlike print materials, they are capable of reaching all reading levels (Schinke et al. 1992: 324). Videos also provide behavioral models for viewers (Freimuth et al. 1997: 555–556). Another advantage of videos is that they can be viewed independently or in a group, and they provide the opportunity for repeated viewing. Many videos are designed with interactive components, and these programs are particularly effective for the dissemination of health information because they require users to participate actively, they allow immediate feedback to users, and they can be tailored for specific individuals (Noell et al. 1997: 87–89). Interactivity is emphasized by formats such as interactive videodiscs, which enable user customization and branching story lines, and video games designed to teach children about health information (Dorman 1997: 135). Several studies have shown that, while video programs are effective in communicating health information, their effectiveness increases when they are viewed in conjunction with either supplementary print materials and/or an educator that can facilitate discussion (Cugliari et al. 1999: 112–113; Ramirez et al. 1997: 610–611; Resnicow et al. 1997: 215–216).

Consumer health videos are also collected by public libraries. One interesting example of a public library's involvement with consumer health information is the "CHOICES" (Community Health Onsite Information) project, sponsored by the New York Public Library. (http://www.nypl.org/branch/health). CHOICES "provides the public with open access to reliable and up-to-date health information on a variety of topics" (CHOICES Brochure). A multifaceted project, CHOICES offers health information skills training for librarians; sponsors community outreach programs that address health topics and information resources; and provides branch libraries with recommendations for health-related acquisitions (J. Fisher, personal communication, June 28, 2000). The acquisition recommendations include printed materials and videos. The video recommendations are based on published reviews and on relevancy. The subject matter of videos that are recommended by CHOICES varies, but all programs are tailored for the lay audience. Videos that are acquired by the New York Public Library branches may be checked out and viewed by patrons in private.

The Kris Kelly Health Information Center, located in California, is another example of a public library that provides consumer health information. The Kris Kelly Health Information Center is a joint effort of the Humboldt County Library System and the St. Joseph Health System. Open to the public at no charge, the Center is "designed to help people get the information they need to make informed decisions about their lifestyles and health care choices" (Kris Kelly 2000). In addition to other information services and programs, the Center provides a collection of books, audiotapes, and videos. This circulating collection can be accessed by library card holders through the Humboldt County Library System.

Increasingly, there are opportunities to view health video programs outside of an institutional setting. Individuals can purchase videos from physical and virtual bookstores, or they can view televised health-related programs on channels such as the Health Network, PBS, or Discovery. Today, a growing number of programs can also be accessed via the Web, with several consumer health Web sites providing streaming videos. The following annotated list is a small selection of resources that are currently available via the Web.

- *WebMD* (http://www.webmd.com) serves as an Internet portal for cable television's Health Network. The site broadcasts both live and on-demand programs such as "Cybersurgery Suite," which allows a direct view into a wide range of surgical procedures, and "The Beat Goes On," which addresses medical, nutritional, and behavioral issues surrounding the heart. The site even broadcasted a natural birth online. WebMD provides a weekly program schedule and a weekly list of recommended programs, and certain programs can be purchased on videocassette.

- *LearnFree.com* (http://www.learnfree.com) provides another example of free health-related streaming video. This site offers "vidbooks," described as "multimedia learning environments [that] offer an innovative teaching approach and mix text and pictures with streaming video clips . . . [resulting in] a serve-yourself learning experience that is easy to use and available any time" [http://www.learnfree.com/vidbook.html]. Within their small but useful "Health & Medicine Channel," the site provides video presentations on CPR techniques, how to conduct a breast self-exam, what can be expected in a mammogram, and multimedia information on how alcohol affects the brain.

- *HealthSCOUT* (http://www.healthscout.com), part of a "Healthology" series, offers audio or video "discussions" that are moderated by health professionals. Users can send e-mail messages before or during the discussion, and the health professionals will respond. All programs are broadcast live initially. After the live presentation, the site provides the shows on-demand, along with thorough descriptions of each. HealthSCOUT.com also offers e-mail reminders of upcoming discussions.

- *CancerEducation.com* (http://www.cancereducation.com) provides streaming presentations by medical experts on a wide variety of cancer-related topics.

All these developments in increased open access to consumer health information have led to expanding expectations from a library's video clientele in terms of health-content programs. To satisfy the demands of this audience, a video librarian must have a clear vision of what materials can be made available directly to patrons through the library's resources, and health information in video format to which clients may have to be referred. A collection development policy provides a vehicle for articulating a video collection's purpose, for documenting resource selection priorities, and for identifying referral practices that suit the collection's user needs.

THE COLLECTION DEVELOPMENT POLICY

When a 1989 survey was conducted among health sciences media collection managers, 35 respondents (68 percent) reported written selection policies; however, non-print selection was often combined with print policies (Reit and Semkow 1989: 8). Responses to the "E-mail Survey" (Ondrusek and Crow 2000) showed that 9 of the 20 health media collectors had a written policy pertaining to video selection. There are a number of reasons for submitting media or video collection guidelines to be incorporated into a library's collection development policy at some level. As Eakin points out: "The scope of an audiovisual collection is likely to be considerably narrower than that of a print collection. It is therefore necessary to define explicitly its special purposes and limitations" (Eakin 1983: 57). A separate policy on audiovisuals may also be used to point out the strengths and values of such a collection, thereby justifying its worth and funding.

Nature of the Collection

Formal collection development statements open with a brief overview of the collection, which may give the library's mission statement (if one exists) and a brief history of the library itself. If the library's media facility has been separately supported or has historical ties to other institutions, acknowledgment of these events is appropriate. However, this opening statement should focus upon identifying the user groups to be served by the collection. If the media/video collection serves clientele different from the print collection's users, it should be noted within this section. Richards and Eakin (1997: 62) point out that in selecting library materials, "[p]redictions of use are best made based on a solid knowledge of the user group"; and on audiovisual selection, the same authors remark that "[it] is usually more user-driven than that of other formats." In certain video collection situations (especially where managers adopt a client-centered collection approach), articulation of the collection's user groups is essentially all that is needed to guide collection development decisions. The question next raised is how to identify potential users and their needs.

Strategies for analyzing a user community requesting access to health-related video programs will vary according to the video manager's assignment. The video consultant hired to establish a core collection may want to conduct a formal needs assessment within the institution using questionnaires or focus groups. Video or media librarians assuming responsibility for an established collection may inherit a system for communicating with its constituents, such as a library newsletter. Further tactics for identifying user patterns include: (1)

being introduced to policy makers in the organization; (2) meeting with curriculum and credentialing committees within the institution; (3) requesting copies of, or electronic access to, institutional bulletins, newsletters, college catalogs, and annual reports; (4) visiting other video collections with similar clientele; (5) searching the professional literature; and (6) joining professional organizations (see http://www.lib.berkeley.edu/MRC/health.html for a listing of key organizations).

Collection Location(s)

In certain instances, departments of a medical facility identify a need for their own video collections. Within a university setting, for instance, colleges may opt for decentralized audiovisual collections. Such proposals should be discussed in terms of the philosophy and objectives of the institution, consistency of funding, hardware and software care, and fulfillment of accreditation requirements (McGinn 1975: 38–39). If videos are to circulate beyond a departmental viewing area, a staffing plan and borrowing guidelines must be formulated. If better access to videos is the primary argument for a separate facility, alternative viewing plans might be considered. For example, at the Bowman Gray School of Medicine, underutilized audiovisual programs on emergency medicine were relocated to a room adjacent to the emergency room at North Carolina Baptist Hospital. The reception to this was so positive that a similar collection was set up near the obstetrics clinic (Parker et al. 1981: 393–395). Ultimately, the location chosen for a video collection should offer the best options for ease of video retrieval and viewing, sufficient video storage and security, and continued administrative support. Although important, accessibility, in itself, does not justify subdividing a video collection.

Scope and Coverage

Clarification of a collection's scope (breadth) and coverage (depth) is essential to the video librarian who has adopted the collection-centered approach to program selection. The NLM defines *scope* as "the range of subjects [collected]" and *coverage* as "the extent of . . . collecting effort within the biomedical subjects" (NLM 1993: 2). The most current *Collection Development Manual* for the NLM is found on the Internet at http://www.nlm.nih.gov/pubs/libprog.html. This document contains a policy statement (NLM 1993: 40) which defines NLM's collection of audiovisuals as "less broad" than its collection of print items, and defines its user focus as "health professionals" and "historians." Consistent with this tone, the NLM statement explains its definitions of "audiovisuals of historical interest" and "[c]ontemporary examples of authoritative audiovisuals."

Most health-content video librarians will need more than the NLM model to fashion their own collection development guidelines. For academic subject collectors, the Research Libraries Group (RLG) recommends six collecting levels based on the level of academic scholarship the collection supports: 0–Out of Scope; 1–Minimal; 2–Basic Information; 3–Instructional Support; 4–Research; and 5–Comprehensive. Health sciences and hospital libraries with media collections will find the RLG levels combined with the NLM *Manual*'s "Selection Guidelines by Subject" outline to be useful documents for articulating their own scope and coverage guides. In health sciences teaching institutions, for example, Instructional Support should be considered as a collecting level for all subjects identified as required courses of study. Basic Information and Minimal levels are generally not collected in health sciences settings where researchers and health professionals are the primary users; however, a medical facility committed to community health outreach programs may want to include these lower levels in its video collection development policy.

Formats Collected

As mentioned in earlier sections of this chapter, health-related video presentations are not confined to a single production format. The video format question from the "E-mail Survey" (Ondrusek and Crow 2000) showed that all 20 respondents acquire VHS programs, but one medical center respondent had instituted Web-based video streaming and one hospital librarian indicated that closed circuit television is an alternative video delivery method. On the other end of the format spectrum, old formats such as ¾-inch and Beta videotapes still arrive as donations. Guidelines that spell out what formats are supported by a video/ media collection accompanied by rationales for the selection of these formats help the video collection manager to respond to requests for videos produced in formats not supported in the video center.

NLM's "Special Consideration in Selection" guidelines state that audiovisual programs acquired for its general (non-historical) collection must be produced in the United States in all U.S. format, and in English (NLM 1993: 40). This language makes it clear that requests for European videotapes which use formats (PAL and SECAM) not compatible with U.S. video players can not be honored. NLM places similar limitations on electronic format items by specifying a U.S. format as one using "widely available equipment and protocols," and those same criteria exclude "health instruction materials [that] are intentionally designed to be altered by the user" or "[which are] useful only . . . with additional equipment, programs, and documentation" (NLM 1993: 42).

However, the lines between viewing video images and reading electronic files begin to blur when video-based CD-ROM programs are included in a health media collection. Events such as the transfer of medical image slide collections to the CD-ROM medium have transformed photographic image projection into a digital video display. In CD-ROM format, that video display can include hyperlinks connecting its video images to additional material residing on the compact disc itself, the computer's hard drive, or a remote server. In video libraries where electronic video files are managed, collection guidelines should include a statement that spells out software and hardware requirements.

Selection Criteria

In their article "Attributes of Quality in Audiovisual Materials for Health Professions Education," Suter and Waddell (1981: 6) identified *content* as the "essence of educational material." Content, they found, must also be "valid, relevant and current." The findings of the NLM study found overall agreement between health educators and consultants who ranked accuracy and relevancy as first and second in importance, respectively, when selecting materials. In this same study, technical quality and availability ranked in the middle, whereas credibility of authors and cost ranked of least importance (Bratton and Brooks 1985: 51). In the much more limited "E-mail Survey," the factors marked by 18 or more of the 20 respondents as ones which they consider when selecting a video program were accuracy, content, recency, audience, and cost. In terms of cost, two respondents qualified the influence that cost might have by saying, "we don't have a ceiling price—it all depends on the program" and, "if a program is very good and is going to meet our needs, but is expensive, we won't not get it simply because it's pricey." A third respondent indicated that cost-sharing for video or CD-ROM products between the library and the requester is a practice. These comments speak to the flexibility that a media selector may be able to negotiate, where a program that is important to furthering the goals of the institution can be demonstrated.

Suter and Waddell (1981) also discuss *program design* as an important factor in audiovisual program selection. Program design includes attributes such as creative treatment of the subject matter, logical content organization, fulfillment of objectives, provision of guides and manuals, and appropriate length. Translating these design elements into an effective video presentation requires technical and artistic talent in areas such as scripting, editing, directing, acting, camera action, sound mixing, lighting, and the incorporation of animation, graphics, special effects, and music selections. These technical merits of a media program are referred to as *production values*. A lack of attention to program design and production techniques results in ineffective programs such as teaching videos that run longer than a typical class or patient education programs that use complex medical terminology. It is, therefore, important to include these elements in video evaluation criteria.

If a computer system is to be the viewing unit for a video program, *system requirements* for the program must be compared to the hardware capabilities of the video purchaser's facility. Promotional brochures for CD-ROM videos, for example, usually list required computer features such as the operating system, memory size, and hard drive space. If video monitor resolution and color-bit requirements are not given, the developer should be queried for these details. Video playback accessory files (called "plug-ins") are often needed to display video on a computer. If the program is packaged as a CD-ROM, these files may be on the CD-ROM disc, but they usually need to be copied to a drive on the computer system. Sometimes these plug-in files must be copied and/or purchased from the producer's Web site. Plug-in standards such as RealPlayer and QuickTime are used for video playback on discs as well as for live video streaming from the Web. Other plug-ins such as Macromedia's Shockwave and Flash are more commonly used for animations or interactive user options. Caveat emptor to the video librarian who purchases computer-driven video programs that use accessory software still undergoing testing.

Selection Authority

The question on the "E-mail Survey" (Ondrusek and Crow 2000) on who was charged with video selection for the institution revealed a wide range of answers among the 20 respondents. Seven people indicated that a unit head acts as the video selector, and five of these unit titles were related to media services or the learning resource center. Six respondents gave an individual with a librarian title as the designated video selector. Another six answers to this question cited some form of joint decision-making arrangement channeled either through librarian(s) accepting selections from other selectors (e.g., faculty, educators, subject specialists) or through two library managers (e.g., the Associate Library Director for Collection Development and the Microcomputer Services Coordinator). Only one respondent indicated selection of video via a committee. Nevertheless, in many health science centers, the library director meets regularly with a library committee, an advisory group consisting of representatives from various programs in the center. These committees can help keep acquisition librarians apprised of new programs. If a library committee exists, the video manager might consider making periodic appearances at committee meetings, at which time questions about the video collection can be answered and suggestions from the committee can be discussed.

Selection Request and Preview Procedures

Most libraries have a "request for purchase" form for print materials. A form for media requests will need to include more than the standard author (which usually does not apply to video), title (which the requester may not recall verbatim), and production company/date (which the requester usually cannot supply). In fact, where a video selection request is a subject rather than a title request, the request form should be filled out by the librarian and the requester together. In a teaching setting, the request form should be used to record the intended use (large-group versus individual, required versus suggested viewing, long-term versus one-time activity, etc.) and proposed audience (students, professionals, hospital personnel, patients, etc). Other questions on the form may focus upon educational objectives to be met, whether there is a need for interactivity in the program's design, and how fast changes occur in the field that is the subject of the request.

The librarian must then decide whether the requested program merits purchase consideration, that is, where does it fall within the matrix of scope and coverage levels established in the selection policy? If the decision is weighted toward acquisition, a preview of the program should be arranged whenever possible. Although it can be problematic for health sciences professionals to find time to preview programs, the 1985 NLM *Manual* indicated that 89 percent (634) of the health educator respondents and 66 percent (147) of the library/media consultants surveyed previewed audiovisuals before making a decision about them (Bratton and Brooks 1985). The "E-mail Survey" results showed that 18 of the 20 respondents preview programs on some level, and would do so where there is no firsthand account of the program available. Keeping a record of programs previewed, their dispensation, and accompanying reviewer remarks is important for future reference. In fact, a place on the request form could be designated for this purpose.

Collection Evaluation and Preservation Guidelines

When describing collection policy formulation, Eakin (1983: 35) points out that "[h]ealth care and teaching institutions . . . are affected by improvements in medical treatment, changes in teaching methods, new developments in research, [and] shifts in professional concerns." As changes in these areas occur, the video collection developer will need to re-examine the content, design, and format attributes of the collection's programs.

Health sciences media/library managers can create opportunities for collection evaluation and avoid turning this responsibility into an impossible chore. One evaluation method is to ask health professionals who regularly request video purchases to review segments of the collection covering their areas of expertise. Preview sessions for new programs can be combined with the review of older selections from the collection. Health specialists can often determine content accuracy by a program's title and release date, so submitting lists with that information to a subject specialist is yet another evaluation method. A final source of information is the distributor of the program. A sales representative can often find out whether programs are still actively marketed, have been superseded by new editions, have changed distributors, or are no longer produced.

Replacement and weeding decisions are handled by health sciences media librarians in a variety of ways. Responses from the "E-mail Survey" of health sciences librarians and media professionals (Ondrusek and Crow 2000) reinforced findings from an older survey on weeding media collections in health sciences libraries (Reit and Semkow 1989: 8), in which health-content media librarians ranked reasons for withdrawing a program. On both surveys, top reasons for program de-selection were that a faculty or subject specialist recommends withdrawal, the content is outdated or the information has been superceded, or the poor physical condition of a program. The surveys, taken together, show other factors such as circulation history and obsolete format receiving lower rankings as reasons to deaccession a program. Lack of shelf space was not a factor that respondents on either survey felt would influence weeding decisions.

SELECTION PRACTICES

Earlier in this chapter, the selection criteria considered most important to health-content video collectors were identified as content, cost, program design, production values, and system requirements. With a video program in hand, applying the criteria from the preceding list appears to be a straightforward exercise. However, the science of collection development (and some librarians would argue that this is an art) relates to the developer's ability either to locate a video that matches a request submitted by a user or to recognize a program as a "good fit" to the video user community being served. This expertise develops, in part, by becoming more knowledgeable about the institution served and potential video users (as discussed in previous sections). However, an expert selector also judges video programs according to style elements inherent in the program's presentation. In addition to this critiquing skill, the expert health-content video selector knows how to locate programs in the video marketplace. This next section covers these two aspects of selection practice in health-content video librarianship.

Presentation Style as a Factor in Video Selection

For the purposes of this discussion, *presentation style* may be thought of as an attribute that gives each video program its own "look" or "tone" or "feel." Style, in this sense, is similar to what film critics identify as genre. It is a combination of "how the medium works" and "the way it affects the people watching it" (Armour 1980). In a review of interactive patient simulation video programs, Harless et al. (1990: 329) pointed out that "the practice of medicine is inherently dramatic . . . [and that] [g]ood dramatic portrayal of [medical] situations will capture the students' imaginations and compel them to become involved in the situations." In this same review, students were asked to rate the "sense of reality" they experienced while engaged in the video simulation.

The degree to which drama and reality are used to communicate the message of a health-content video depends upon its purpose. For example, a video on preparing medications must be authentic in its depiction, but its audience might be distracted by the use of overly dramatic effects (showing a patient suffering the ill effects of an overdose). A second illustration is a nursing administrator seeking a video outlining the indicators of physical child abuse for elementary teachers. She needs a program delivered in an instructional, expository style. A documentary on children who survived child abuse, no matter how well-designed it is, will not be an appropriate match to this need. Videomakers employ a number of techniques for achieving authenticity and drama in health-content presentations, and it is useful for the health-content video selector to be able to match a user need with a program produced in a style appropriate to that need.

Selection Aids

When the 1985 NLM study asked health media consultants to rank the sources they used most to keep informed about audiovisual materials, 79 percent (606) of the consultants ranked vendor catalogs first, followed closely by colleagues and promotional mailings. Databases were used least frequently (Bratton and Brooks 1985: 23). In the "E-mail Survey" (Ondrusek and Crow 2000), librarians were given a list of selection sources/tools and were asked to check off any of the items they use to select videos. In this slightly different context, the "Vendor catalogs/brochures" item was checked by all 20 respondents. However, the "Internet" got the next most responses (17 of 20), followed by "User requests" (16 of 20) and "Colleagues" (15 of 20). Two respondents cited "User requests" as the most consulted selection source, and comments from several other respondents indicated user-request-centered (client-centered) selection practices. After these categories, the "E-mail Survey" contributors indicated medium use (7 to 12 responses each) of health and medical journals, online catalogs (OCLC and NLM LOCATORPlus) and online/print directories. In the next section, these popular sources will be described along with lesser-used selection aids such as review serials, festivals, and a core list.

Vendor and Distributor Sources

The vendor information included in this section should be considered representative, not exhaustive. Contact information and Internet addresses for the vendors cited here and in other parts of this chapter are listed in the Appendix.

The video librarian who manages a multi-health subject collection will find a wealth of biomedical sciences, nursing and allied health, clinical skills, and patient education video programs in the inventories of a relatively select group of distributors of health sciences media. These distributors have ties with the health sciences community at large and have established reputations as service-oriented enterprises. Customer services that are vital to a media librarian include publishing catalogs (in print and/or on the Internet), accepting institutional purchase orders, announcing sales promotions, handling preview requests, making follow-up calls to clients, and negotiating dubbing and archival-copy rights. Vendors that fit this profile and carry large inventories of health care/medicine/ nursing video are marked with (#) in the Appendix listing. Vendors of more specialized health-content video programs are indicated with (*); those which might be consulted for general-audience health care, health education, and psycho-social videos are indicated with (**).

In addition to commercial vendors, many professional associations and organizations distribute video programs. For a short listing of these organizations, see http://www.lib.berkeley.edu/MRC/health.html. Medical societies' CME and conference video distributors are additional important sources of programing. These sources include:

- *Cine-Med* (distributor for the American College of Surgeons, Society of American Gastrointestinal Endoscopic Surgeons, subsidiaries of the Davis and Geck services such as the American Congress of Obstetricians and Gynecologists, and the Association of periOperative Registered Nurses).

- *CME Unlimited*, a nonprofit division of Audio-Digest Foundation (distributor for American College of Physicians-American Society of Internal Medicine, American College of Chest Physicians, Society of Critical Care Medicine, American College of Rheumatology, and the American Academy of Allergy, Asthma, and Immunology).

A comparison of the health-content video marketplace in the year 2000 to that same market 10 years ago reveals major changes. There were consolidations, such as The Altschul Group and United Learning venture; expansions, such as print publishers like Mosby Yearbook making a push into the media marketplace; and losses, including the demise of the *American Journal of Nursing*'s multimedia division. The influence of digital video is evident in that suppliers of interactive video (e.g., FITNE and the University of Washington) report that their programs once available on laser videodiscs have been transferred to the CD-ROM format, and titles on DVD now appear in some vendor catalogs. On the Internet, AGC/United Learning has launched a subscription-based service giving subscribers access to more than 800 videostreamed programs for K–12 school audiences (about 25% cover health content), and Medcom Inc. is developing videostreamed continuing education courses. These developments currently complement the still-flourishing health-content video-cassette market, but also are indicative of the growing digital video delivery movement.

Online Databases: NLM LOCATORPlus and OCLC

In 1975, the NLM established AVLINE, its online catalog containing mediographic information for audiovisuals. NLM has re-organized its online catalogs so that records for all print and non-print materials owned by NLM can now be searched through a single system called LOCATORPlus (http://www.nlm.nih.gov/locatorplus/locatorplus.html). NLM also administers a Cataloging-in-Production (CIP) service that assigns a provisional mediographic citation to programs about to be released, and provides timely acquisitions information of new audiovisual titles to media librarians (Tashjian and Simon 1983: 10–15).

Procurement information for material received in CIP form is corrected when the actual item is received and the final record is prepared for the database. OCLC, the trade name for the Online Computer Library Center Inc., is another national online catalog consisting of millions of records contributed by its members. The OCLC database (known as WorldCat) can be searched by its subscribers using either its menu-driven FirstSearch interface or its command-based Prism system (http://firstsearch.oclc.org).

For media items, the records of both NLM LOCATORPlus and OCLC can assist a librarian in verifying video program procurement information. Both search systems have advanced search forms which contain options for limiting a search to media items and for keyword searching. Since many video requests are presented as a title fragment or by a series name, the keyword searching option is a blessing to media collectors. As one "E-mail Survey" participant observed, "using OCLC and NLM LOCATORPlus are crucial for finding candidate programs efficiently . . . then with publisher info[rmation] in hand, [librarians] go to catalogs and vendor [Web] sites to get more information on specific titles" (Ondrusek and Crow 2000). One caveat is that health sciences video programs often change hands following entry into these databases. NLM, by policy, does not update source information after its final record entry. The OCLC database enters as many records as are submitted by its contributors. This results in multiple entries for the same title due to variants in format, producer, release date, and title fields. Therefore, a procurement source identified through either database should always be confirmed with the producer or distributor before a purchase order is submitted.

Print Directories: The *Video Source Book* and the *Complete Video Directory*

The two print directories that stand out as comprehensive guides to video programs are Gale's two-volume *The Video Source Book* and *Bowker's Complete Video Directory*, a four-volume set. Bowker's Volumes 3 and 4, covering Education/Health, may be purchased separately. *The Video Source Book* integrates all its contents, including educational programs and feature films, into a single alphabetical title list. Both sources contain a Subject Index, with the *The Video Source Book*, 24th Edition, listing more health/medical topics and classifying topics with more specificity than Bowker's *Directory 2000*. Other differences in indexing style of interest to the health-content video selector include: (1) Cross-referencing occurs in the *The Video Source Book*'s Subject Index, but not in the Bowker *Directory*; (2) A Credits Index in the *The Video Source Book* makes it possible to check for a program under practitioners and theorists such as Drs. Elisabeth Kubler-Ross, Terry Brazelton, and Carl Rogers; (3) A Series Index in the Bowker *Directory* can locate, for example, the *Video Seminar Series* by the American College of Cardiology, the *Discussions on Bioethics* series, and some titles from the *Doctor Is In* series; and (4) The Bowker *Directory* includes a Laser Videodisc Index (with very few health-content programs), an 8mm Index, and a Closed-Caption Index. To check for redundancy in listings between the two directories, three health-content subject headings were compared: (1) "Child Care/Parenting"; (2) "Dentistry/Dental Care"; and (3) "Physically Challenged/Handicapped." There was a low percentage of overlap (6 to 8% on average) between the listings from these two directories, indicating that video librarians with the funds to purchase both sources should do so.

Review Serials

Association journals such as the *Journal of Biocommunications* (HeSCA), and *Science Books and Films* (AAAS) periodically review health-related videos. For reviews of consumer health videos, standard library trade journals such as *Booklist*, *Choice*, and *Library Journal* are helpful in selection. Unfortunately, many of the printed guides to health-related audiovisuals and review journals devoted exclusively to health media review that were once published regularly have proven to be too expensive and time-consuming to continue.

Festivals

Competitions that recognize and publicize quality productions are part of the filmmaking tradition, and health-content film and video producers compete in their own forums. The International Health and Medical Film Competition (formerly the biennial John Muir Medical Film Festival) is comparable to the Academy Awards for health-related film and video productions. In 1998, Time Inc. Health, a division of Time Warner, purchased this festival from the American Medical Association (AMA), and corporate sponsors help to fund this competition. On a smaller scale, other festivals are sponsored by various special-interest groups. Events sponsored by health organizations include the Health Sciences Communications Association's Media Festival; the National Health Information Awards (sponsored by CareWise Inc. and the American Custom Publishing Corporation); the Association of American Medical Colleges' (AAMC) festival; chapters of the American Medical Writers Association; and the American College of Obstetricians and Gynecologists. Broader-ranging organizations such as the National Educational Media Network and the National Media Owl Awards (aging topics) include health categories in their festivals. Some regional film/video festivals, such as the New York Festivals and the Columbus (Ohio) International Film and Video Festival, also accept entries on health and medicine topics.

Core List

Creating a core list suitable as a selection aid for health sciences audiovisual collections is a venture that has been undertaken by the Education and Media

Technology Specialists (EMTS) of the Medical Library Association. EMTS surveyed members of several professional groups, including their own members and the Biomedical Librarians Interest Group (BLIG) of the Health Sciences Communications Association, to gather titles of media programs considered essential or extremely useful as resources. The resulting program recommendations have been posted on the Web as "Highly Recommended AV and Computer-based Tutorial Programs." Titles are posted in two lists, one for audiovisuals and one for computer-based programs. The list, along with an online form for submitting additional program titles and a publisher's list, are available on the EMTS Web site http://research.med.umkc.edu/media_center2/emts/emts.html.

ACQUISITION OF MATERIALS

Budget

Richards and Eakin (1997: 159–165) divide methods for health sciences collection development allocations into these categories: (1) by discipline (pediatrics, surgery, etc. where cost variances in materials are taken into account); (2) by department (similar to discipline, but the size of each department is also a factor in allocation); (3) by material type (monographs, journals, and media have separate allocations); and (4) by location (usually used to set aside funds for special purposes such as building up a reference or reserve collection). Allocation by material type is probably the most common method used to define audiovisual budgets in a health science library, but this practice does not preclude a video manager from seeking funding using the other methods.

For example, the library's budget might consist of funds from various sources such as institutional monies, private or governmental grants, endowments, departmental contributions, research funds, or charge-backs from fees. Each one of these funding categories might carry with it unique spending guidelines. As a part of the library's budget, the video collector may be entitled to portions of funding from a mixture of sources available to the library. If these resources are tied to disciplines or departments that depend upon video program acquisition, this may serve as a justification for expanding the video budget. Where the video collection is a separately administered unit in a health science institution, the video manager may have to compete for funding from these same institutional sources.

In a time of shrinking budgets in health sciences institutions, the pressure is on librarians to show that library collections are an essential service. As Richards and Eakin (1997: 164) point out, the preparation of a highly structured budget may not serve the purpose it once did in health sciences libraries. Automated acquisition systems can track and sort expenditure data for collection managers. However, the need for accountability on spending has increased. In a video collection where the average cost of a videotape is $100 or more and expensive equipment must be maintained to view that program, accountability demands may be even more rigorous than for print materials.

Acquisition Alternatives

There are several avenues for obtaining a health video program that cannot be purchased by the health media selector, and these should be discussed with video users who place an acquisitions request that cannot be met. If the program is needed for a one-time use, or if the program is no longer distributed, interlibrary loan (ILL) could be suggested. The health video liaison can help ILL staff by locating all the information required to submit an ILL request (i.e., title, producer, distributor, and production release date). Online catalogs, OCLC and NLM's LOCATORPlus, are good starting points for finding this information. If these sources fall short, a record of the program might be located through online catalogs of other health sciences libraries or by searching the print health video directories. ILL requests for video works are generally submitted through the OCLC interlibrary loan network, and patrons should expect to pay the standard ILL fee.

Rental of health sciences programs are another solution to many selection dilemmas. First, it allows for reviewing a program from a distributor that does not provide free or low-cost preview privileges. Second, a rental fee allows for program viewings with students and clients, so the reaction of the intended audience can be observed and assessed. Next, for programs no longer in production or for programmers who prefer 16mm film prints for large-group screenings, rental may be the only route to obtaining them. The rental option, also, is an answer to the video user who needs programs that are out of scope and are not likely to be purchased. Last, rental fees that generally vary from $40 to $100 per rental can be deducted from the purchase price if a purchase agreement follows. (Some of the small or independent distributors may not be aware that this is a standard practice but will negotiate it, if asked.)

Yet another alternative route that libraries can take to gain access to video programs is through participation in consortia. A consortium usually involves multiple institutions joining together for the purpose of sharing resources, pooling expertise, or negotiating for reductions in price for resources. Sponsored by New York's Mid-Hudson Library System, the Health Information Project (formerly known as the Video Health Information Project) is an excellent example of a resource-sharing consortium. An important part of the Health Information Project's mission is to provide free access to consumer health information in a large collection of videotapes (Video Health 2000). The collection, composed of more than 180 titles, is primarily designed to meet the diverse health needs of adolescents (B. Clapp, personal communication, July 25, 2000). The videos are used by adolescents as well as health educators, teachers, and the general public. In order to take the users' perspectives into account, the library system hires teenage interns to review current titles in the collection as well as prospective video acquisitions (B. Lindsley, personal communication, October 9, 2000). Reserve, borrowing, and return transactions for videos may be done from any library in the Mid-Hudson system using intralibrary loan channels. Certain libraries in the system have health information centers, and these libraries may elect to purchase selected Health Information Project titles in order to have on-site copies. For those users who live outside the Mid-Hudson Library System and have active public library cards within New York State, videos can be borrowed for free through interlibrary loan channels. On their Web site, the Health Information Project provides an annotated catalog, arranged alphabetically and by subject (http://www.sebridge.org/~vhip).

The Illinois-based Winnetka Alliance for Early Childhood is an example of a local, resource-sharing consortium. The Winnetka Alliance is a not-for-profit community organization that encourages healthy child development. Its 28 institutional members include schools, daycare centers and other providers of services for children in Winnetka and Northfield, Illinois. With funding from donations and newsletter subscriptions, the Winnetka Alliance maintains a video collection that includes more than 80 titles. These tapes are available for seven-day loan periods, free of charge, to "parents, grandparents, teachers, and other early childhood professionals" (Winnetka Alliance 2000). While a limited number of tapes are stored in the organization's office, the majority are housed in a local bookstore. The annotated collection catalog is available on the Alliance's Web site: http://www.winnetkaalliance.org.

The Library Media Project, known during its grant-funded period as the MacArthur Foundation Library Video Project, is an example of a different sort of consortium. According to its Web site, this not-for-profit program seeks to "assist in the development of video collections in public libraries, and to increase the public access to the Independent film and video community" (Library Media 2000). The Project sponsors the development of subject-specific "collections," consisting of titles that have been "curated" by panels of experts. Collections include the "Health Video Collection" and the "Issues in Aging Video Collection," and both are organized alphabetically and by subject. For limited time periods, the Project joins with video distributors to make these titles available to public libraries at a substantially discounted price. The Library Media Project effectively treats public libraries as a consortium, affording them discounts for titles in the video collections. Title lists for each collection, contact information for video distributors, and supplementary information remain posted on the Project Web site even after the special pricing arrangements have ended (http://www.librarymedia.org).

Some consortia require libraries to pay a membership fee in order to gain access to resources. One example of such a consortium is the Consortium for Health Information and Library Services (CHI), based in Upland, Pennsylvania. In addition to other services, CHI offers membership to libraries and information centers in hospitals, academic institutions, health care businesses, and non-profit organizations in 32 states. CHI's video collection includes more than 1,600 titles in the fields of nursing, medicine, health care administration, library management, business, and information technology training. In order to borrow video programs, member libraries submit orders to CHI by fax. CHI then confirms the order and sends the video via UPS. The catalog is accessible to members and to the general public on CHI's Web site, where lists of recommended video programs can also be found: http://www.chi-info.org. According to the Web site, there are currently more than thirty institutions that subscribe to this consortium.

Finally, there is the Health Sciences Consortium (HSC), which is a "nonprofit publishing cooperative founded in 1971 and dedicated to sharing instructional materials in the health sciences. The Consortium has grown from twelve founding members to nearly 400 institutions representing more than 1,000 schools, hospitals, and other institutions around the world. Anyone can purchase from the Consortium's library of nearly 1,000 videotape and computer-based instructional programs, however, institutions that become members receive discounts on every purchase" (Health Sciences Consortium 2000).

Notes

In the early 1990s, video development for the health sciences seemed to be moving in the direction of sophisticated, interactive simulation programs, some of them computer-based and others self-contained laser videodisc productions. Over the past decade, there has not been a sweeping movement to bring these programs into the mainstream in health sciences schools or training programs. Instead, health-content media providers remain focused on the development and marketing of portable, easy playback video resources such as the VHS videocassette and the CD-ROM. These continue to provide affordable programs for many health-content video collections, while the new wave of health-content information delivery is occurring over digital channels such as local institutional networks and the Internet. Media librarians who serve health-related programs must prepare to act as consultants and advocates for their clientele who wish to take advantage of the programs that are becoming available through these means. Meanwhile, librarians can expect to observe many positive effects of this digital transformation. Two advantages are that video stored digitally, either on DVD or on a computer, uses a standard, internationally accepted format; and that the capability of sending and receiving video across networks encourages endeavors important in health settings such as scientific collaboration and distance education. All in all, the new video technologies are exciting, but the implications of adopting, or not implementing, these technologies have not been well researched. As Chessell (1990: 18) observed, "What still seems to be missing is an analysis of the factors needed to make audiovisual technology intrinsically valuable in medical education." The profession could benefit from an in-depth study that examines the use of media in higher education, as did Britain's 1965 Brynmor Jones Report (see Chessell 1990: 17–19) and Harvard University's eight-year (1964–1972) Program on Technology and Society study (see International Business Machines Corp. 1972), both of which were long-term studies that included medicine in the fields examined. The results of an updated study would supply health-content media librarians, among other professionals, with much-needed information about who is using video, in what formats and applications, and with what results. This type of information may also reveal trends that would help video collectors participate knowledgeably in planning for video collections in this changing theater.

APPENDIX: DISTRIBUTORS AND DEVELOPERS

#*AGC/United Learning* (merger of The Altschul Group Corporation and United Learning), 1560 Sherman Avenue, Suite 100, Evanston, IL 60201; (800) 323–9084; http://www.agcmedia.com/agc_99/index.htm.

**AIMS Media*, 6901 Woodley Avenue, Van Nuys, CA 91406–4878; (800) 367–2467; http://www.aims-multimedia.com.

American College of Cardiology (ACCEL), P.O. Box 79231, Baltimore, MD 20814; (301) 897–5400; http://www.acc.org/login/index.taf.

American Journal of Nursing (AJN) (Print publications now managed by Neodata, (800) 627–0484; some video programs still available from Lippincott/Williams & Wilkins).

Appleton & Lange. *See* McGraw-Hill Medical.

Baxley Media Group (Leo Media, Inc.), 110 W. Main Street, Urbana, IL 61801–2715; (800) 421–6999; http://www.leomedia.net/.

Bradshaw Cassettes, P.O. Box 720947, Houston, TX 77272; (800) 6-BRADSHAW; http://www.bradshawcassettes.com.

Carle Medical Communications. *See* Baxley Media Group.

Cine-Med, 127 Main Street North, P.O. Box 745, Woodbury, CT 06798; (800) 253–7657; Fax: (203) 263–4839; http://www.cine-med.com.

CME Unlimited, 74–923 Hovley Lane East, Suite 250, Palm Desert, CA 92260; (800) 776–5454; http://www.CMEunlimited.org.

Dartnell Corporation, 360 Hiatt Drive, Palm Beach Gardens, FL 33418; (800) 621–5463; http://www.dartnellcorp.com/.

**Direct Cinema Ltd.*, P.O. Box 10003, Santa Monica, CA 90410; (800) 525–0000; http://www.directcinemalimited.com.

Educational Research, New York State Psychiatric Institute, 722 West 168th Street, New York, NY 10032; (212) 960–2575; http://www.nyspi.cpmc.columbia.edu.

**Facets Multimedia*, 1517 W. Fullerton Avenue (2400N, 1500W), Chicago, IL 60614; (773) 281–4114; http://www.facets.org.

Fanlight Productions (health care and mental health), 4196 Washington Street, Suite 2, Boston, MA 02131; (800) 937–4113; http://www.fanlight.com.

**Filmakers Library*, 124 East 40th Street, New York, NY 10016; (212) 355–6545; http://www.filmakers.com.

**Films for the Humanities and Sciences*, P.O. Box 2053, Princeton, NJ 08543–2053; (800) 257–5126; http://www.films.com.

Focus International. See Sinclair Intimacy Institute.

**Foto-Comm Corporation* (Radiology and nuclear medicine), 2000 York Road, Oak Brook, IL 60521; (800) 272–2920 (no Internet address available).

#*Fuld Institute for Technology in Nursing Education* (FITNE), 5 Depot Street, Athens, OH 45701; (800) 691–8480; http://www.fitne.net/index.html.

Gale Research Inc., World Headquarters, 27500 Drake Road, Farmington Hills, MI 48331; (248) 699–4253; http://www.galegroup.com.

#*Harcourt Health Sciences Division*
Includes: *Mosby*, 11830 Westline Industrial Drive, St. Louis, MO 63146; (800) 325–4177; http://www.mosby.com; *W. B. Saunders*, West Washington Square, Philadelphia, PA 19105; (215) 238–7800; http://www.wbsaunders.com.

#*Health Sciences Consortium* (HSC), 201 Silver Cedar Court, Chapel Hill, NC 27514; (919) 942–8731; http://www.hscweb.org/.

Hospital Satellite Network (HSN), 2020 Avenue of the Stars, Suite 550, Los Angeles, CA 90067; (800) 537–5329; (800) 537–9628.

Kaiser Permanente, Audio Visual Services, 825 Colorado Boulevard, Los Angeles, CA 90041; (213) 259–4546.

#*Lippincott/Williams & Wilkins*, East Washington Square, Philadelphia, PA 19105; (800) 527–5597; http://www.lww.com.

McGraw-Hill Medical, 2 Penn Plaza, New York, NY 10121; (212) 904–2000; http://www.books.mcgraw-hill.com/medical/.

#*Medcom Inc.*, P.O. Box 3225, Garden Grove, CA 92642; (800) 541–0253; http://www.medcominc.com.

**Menninger* (psychotherapy), P.O. Box 829, Topeka, KS 66601–0829; (800) 351–9058; http://www.menninger.edu/.

**Milner-Fenwick, Inc.* (patient education), 2125 Greenspring Drive, Timonium, MD 21093; (800) 432–8433; http://www.milner-fenwick.com.

Mosby. See Harcourt Health Sciences Division.

National Audiovisual Center, 5285 Port Royal Road, Springfield, VA 22161; (800) 788–6282; http://www.ntis.gov/nac/.

National Technical Information Service (NTIS), Technology Administration, U.S. Department of Commerce, Springfield, VA 22161; (703) 605–6000; http://www.ntis.gov.

Network for Continuing Medical Education (NCME), One Harmon Plaza, Secaucus, NJ 07094; (201) 867–3550; http://www.ncme.com/index4.html.

NIMCO, Inc., P.O. Box 9, 102 Highway, 81 North, Calhoun, KY 42327–0009; (800) 962–6662; http://www.nimcoinc.com.

NOVA. See PBS Video. *NOVA* DVD programs: http://www.pbs.org/wgbh/shop/novavideodvd.html.

Novartis, Summit, NJ, (888) NOW-NOVA; http://www.novartis.com/.

Parthenon Publishing Group, One Blue Hill Plaza, P.O. Box 1564, Pearl River, NY 10965; (914) 735–9363; or Casterton Hall, Carnforth, Lancashire LA6 2LA, United Kingdom; Tel.: +44 (0)15242 72084; http://www.parthpub.com/.

**PBS Video*, 1320 Braddock Place, Alexandria, VA 22314–1698; (800) 344-3337; http://www.pbs.org/.

Penn State Media Sales (ethics and psychology), 118 Wagner Building, University Park, PA 16802–3899; (800) 770–2111; http://www.mediasales.psu.edu/.

Polymorph Films (obstetrics and neonatal topics), 95 Chapel Street, Newton, MA 32158; (617) 370–3456.

Psychological Cinema Register. See Penn State Media Sales.

The Psychological Corporation (a Harcourt Assessment Company), P.O. Box 9954, San Antonio, TX 78204–0954; (800) 233–5682; http://www.hbtpc.com/.

Pyramid Media, P.O. Box 1048, Santa Monica, CA 90406–1048; (800) 421-2304; http://www.pyramidmedia.com/.

Radiological Society of North America (RSNA), http://www.rsna.org. *See also* Foto-Comm Corporation.

RAmEx Ars Medica, Inc., 1714 South Westgate Avenue, #2, Los Angeles, CA 90025–3852; (800) 633–9281; International: 1–310–826–4964; http://www.ramex.com/.

Routledge, 7624 Empire Drive, Florence, KY 41042; (800) 634–7064; http://www.routledge-ny.com/.

Sinclair Intimacy Institute (human sexuality), P.O. Box 8865, Chapel Hill, NC 27515; (800) 955–0888, ext. 8NET2; http://www.bettersex.com.

Springhouse Corporation (nursing skills), 1111 Bethlehem Pike, Springhouse, PA 19477; (215) 646–4670; http://www.springnet.com.

SVE/Churchill Media, 6677 North Northwest Highway, Chicago, IL 60631–1304; (800) 829–1900; http://www.SVEmedia.com/.

Taylor & Francis Group (UK Head Office), 11 New Fetter Lane, London EC4P 4EE, United Kingdom; http://www.carfax.co.uk/.

Teacher's Video Company (a division of Global Video, Inc.), P.O. Box ENL–4455, Scottsdale, AZ 85261; (800) 262–8837; http://www.indiana.edu/~libmps/order/teac.html.

Terra Nova Films, Inc. (gerontology), 9848 South Winchester Avenue, Chicago, IL 60643; (800) 779–8491; http://www.terranova.org/.

Trace Research and Development Center, University of Wisconsin at Madison, S-151 Waisman Center, 1500 Highland Avenue, Madison, WI 53705; (608) 262–6966; http://www.trace.wisc.edu/.

Vida Health Communications (family and parenting), 6 Bigelow Street, Cambridge, MA 02139; (617) 864–4334; http://www.vida-health.com.

Vital Source Technologies, 133 Fayetteville Street, Suite 600, Raleigh, NC 27601; (919) 755–8105; http://www.vitalviewer.com.

University of California, Extension Center for Media and Independent Learning, 2000 Center Street, 4th Floor, Berkeley, CA 94704–1223; (510) 642–1340; http://www-cmil.unex.berkeley.edu/media/.

University of Utah, Spencer S. Eccles Health Sciences Library, Building 589, Salt Lake City, UT 84112–1185; (801) 581–8694; http://www-medlib.med.utah.edu/sol/.

University of Washington, Health Sciences Center for Educational Resources, T-252 Health Sciences, Box 357161, Seattle, WA 98195; (206) 685–1156; http://www.hscer. washington.edu/hscer.

W. B. Saunders. See Harcourt Health Sciences Division.

Williams & Wilkins. See Lippincott/Williams & Wilkins.

ACKNOWLEDGMENTS

Several colleagues provided helpful information for this chapter. For their very thoughtful comments in interviews and conversations, many thanks go to Jane Fisher of the New York Public Library, Barbara Clapp and Barbara Lindsley of the Health Information Project, Karin Wiseman of the Veterans Administration Medical Center (New York) Medical Library, and Martin Dornbaum of Hunter College. Also, the authors greatly appreciate those librarians and media specialists who completed our e-mail survey.

REFERENCES

AIMS Multimedia. 2000. *AIMS Multimedia Unveils Internet Video-on-Demand Library for Schools* [Press release, February 29]. Retrieved July 24, 2000 from the World Wide Web: 209.130.57.27/aims/news/releases/digitalcurriculum.htm.

American Hospital Association (AHA). 1982. *AHA Policy Statement on the Hospital's Responsibility for Patient Education Services*. Chicago: AHA.

Armour, R. A. 1980. *Film, A Reference Guide*. Westport, CT: Greenwood Press.

Association of American Medical Colleges (AAMC). 1984. "Physicians for the Twenty-first Century." *Journal of Medical Education* 59 supp. (November): 9.

Biddle, S. 2000. "CME at a Glance: A New System of Accreditation." *Feedback* 26 (May–June): 1, 3.

Biglan, A., James, L. E., LaChance, P., Zoref, L., and Joffe, J. 1988. "Videotaped Materials in a School-Based Smoking Prevention Program." *Preventive Medicine* 19 (September): 559–584.

Bowker's Complete Video Directory. New York: R. R. Bowker. Annual.

Brandon, J. E., and Majumdar, B. 1997. "An Introduction and Evaluation of Problem-Based Learning in Health Professions Education." *Family and Community Health* 20 (April): 1–16.

Bratton, B., and Brooks, C. M. 1985. *A Study of the Audiovisual Selection and Acquisition Processes in Health Professions Education*. Springfield, VA: National Technical Information Service.

Chessell, G. 1990. "Audiovisual Resources for Learning—A Brave New World Realized." *Journal of Audiovisual Media in Medicine* 13 (January): 17–19.

Cugliari, A. M., Sobal, J., and Miller, T. 1999. "Use of a Videotape for Educating Patients About Advance Directives." *American Journal of Health Behavior* 23 (March–April): 105–14.

Dorman, S. M. 1997. "Video and Computer Games: Effect on Children and Implications for Health Education." *Journal of School Health* 67 (April): 133–137.

Eakin, D. 1983. "Health Science Library Materials: Collection Development." In *Handbook of Medical Library Practice, Vol. 2*, 4th ed. Edited by L. Darling, D. Bishop, and L. A. Colaianni. Chicago: Medical Library Association, pp. 27–91.

Evans, G. E. 1987. *Developing Library Collections.* 2nd ed. Littleton, CO: Libraries Unlimited.

Freimuth, V. S., Plotnick, C. A., Ryan, C. E., and Schiller, S. 1997. "Right Turns Only: An Evaluation of a Video-based, Multicultural Drug Education Series for Seventh Graders." *Health Education & Behavior* 24 (September–October): 555–567.

Harless, W. G., Duncan, R. C., Zier, M. A., Ayers, W. R., Berman, J. R., and Pohl, H. S. 1990. "A Field Test of the TIME Patient Simulation Model." *Academic Medicine* 65 (May): 327–333.

Health Sciences Consortium Web site. 2000. *About HSC.* Retrieved August 14, 2000 from the World Wide Web: http://www.hscweb.org/stan/info/info.htm.

Heller, B. R., Oros, M. T., and Durney-Crowley, J. 2000. *The Future of Nursing Education: Ten Trends to Watch.* National League for Nursing Web site. Retrieved June 25, 2000 from the World Wide Web: http://www.nln.org/infotrends.htm.

International Business Machines Corp. 1972. *Harvard University Program on Technology and Society 1964–1972. A Final Review.* Cambridge, MA: Boston Programming Center (ERIC microfiche ED 064 932).

Joint Commission on Accreditation of Healthcare Organizations (JCAHO). 1999. *The Comprehensive Accreditation Manual for Hospitals: The Official Handbook.* Oakbrook Terrace, IL: Joint Commission on Accreditation of Healthcare Organizations.

Kris Kelly Health Information Center Web site. Retrieved July 15, 2000 from the World Wide Web: http://www.humboldt1.com/~kkhic/home.html.

Lewis, D., and Nath, C. 1997. "Feasibility of a Kiosk-based Patient Education System in a Busy Outpatient Clinic Setting." *The Diabetes Educator* 23 (September–October): 577–585.

Library Media Project Web site. Retrieved October 15, 2000 from the World Wide Web: http://www.librarymedia.org.

Maslin, A. 1998. "Using an Interactive Video Disk in Breast Cancer Patient Support." *Nursing Times* 94 (November): 52–55.

Mason, E. 1991. "Where's Mummy? The Robertson Studies on Mother-Child Separation." University Park: Pennsylvania State University Audio-visual Services.

McGinn, H. F. 1975. "A/V Materials: Where Should They Be Kept?" *Nursing Outlook* 23 (January): 38–39.

National Audiovisual Center (NAC). 1978. *A Reference List of Audiovisual Materials Produced by the United States Government.* Washington, DC: National Archives and Records Service.

National Library of Medicine (NLM). 1993. *Collection Development Manual of the National Library of Medicine.* 3rd ed. Edited by Duane Arenales et al. Bethesda, MD: U.S. Dept. of Health and Human Services, National Institutes of Health, National Library of Medicine.

National Library of Medicine (NLM). Technical Services Division. 1985. *Collection Development Manual of the National Library of Medicine.* Bethesda, MD: U.S.

Department of Health and Human Services, Public Health Service, National Institutes of Health.

Nichtenhauser, A. 1953. "A History of Motion Pictures in Medicine." Unpublished manuscript prepared for Audio Visual Training Section, Professional Training Division, Bureau of Medicine and Surgery, U.S. Department of the Navy.

Noell, J., Ary, D., and Duncan, T. 1997. "Decision-making and Social Skills Program: 'The Choice is Yours—Preventing HIV/STDs.' " *Health Education & Behavior* 24 (January–February): 87–101.

Ondrusek, A. L. 1994. "Video Collection Development in a Health Sciences Setting." In *Video Collection Development in Multi-type Libraries.* Edited by G. P. Handman. Westport, CT: Greenwood Press, pp. 85–124.

Ondrusek, A. L., and Crow, S. 2000. "Health Content Video Collection E-mail Survey." Unpublished document.

O'Neil, P. N. 1990. "Developing Videodisc Instructions for the Health Sciences: A Consortium Approach." *Academic Medicine* 65 (October): 624–627.

Parker, C., Lee, S. K., and Sprinkle, M. D. 1981. "Emergency Medicine Audiovisual Satellite Library at Bowman Gray School of Medicine." *Bulletin of the Medical Library Association* 69 (October): 393–395.

Ramirez, A. G., Gallion, K. J, Espinoza, R., McAlister, R., and Chalela, R. 1997. "Developing a Media- and School-based Program for Substance Abuse Prevention Among Hispanic Youth: A Case Study of *Mirame!/*Look at Me!" *Health Education & Behavior* 24 (September–October): 603–612.

Rees, Alan M. 1994. *The Consumer Health Information Sourcebook.* 4th ed. Phoenix, AZ: Oryx Press.

Reit, J., and Semkow, J. 1989. "A Weeding Survey Summary." *@MLA News* (June/July): 8.

Resnicow, K., Vaughan, R., Futterman, R, Weston, R. E., Royce, J., Parms, C., Hearn, M. D., Smith, M., Freeman, H. P., and Orlandi, M. A. 1997. "A Self-help Smoking Cessation Program for Inner-city African Americans: Results from the Harlem Health Connection Project." *Health Education & Behavior* 24 (March–April): 201–217.

Richards, D. T., and Eakin, D. 1997. *Collection Development and Assessment in Health Sciences Libraries.* Lanham, MD: Medical Library Association and The Scarecrow Press.

Ritter, J. 2000. "Computers Replacing Film for Mammograms." *Chicago Sun-Times,* [February 22, online]. Retrieved from Lexis-Nexis [June 25, 2000].

Rosenlund, C., Damask-Bembenek, B., Hugie, P., and Matsumura, G. 1999. "The Development of Online Courses for Undergraduate Nursing Education." *Nursing and Health Care Perspectives* 20 (July–August): 194–198.

Schinke, S. P., Orlandi, M. A., Schilling, F, and Parms, C. 1992. "Feasibility of Interactive Videodisc Technology to Teach Minority Youth about Preventing HIV Infection." *Public Health Reports* 107 (May–June): 323–329.

Scholtz, J. C. 1994. "Formulating a Video Collection Development Rationale and Policy." In *Video Collection Development in Multi-type Libraries.* Edited by Gary P. Handman. Westport, CT: Greenwood Press, pp. 227–275.

Stolberg, S. G. 2000. "Patient Power: The Big Decisions? They're All Yours." *New York Times* (June 25): 1.

Suter, E., and Waddell, W. H. 1981. "Attributes of Quality Audiovisual Materials for Health Professionals." *Journal of Biocommunication* 8 (July): 5–11.

The Video Source Book. Farmington Hills, MI: Gale Group. Annual.

Tashjian, S. A., and Simon, K. 1983. "Library-Media Production Interface." *Journal of Biocommunication* 10 (September): 10–15.

United States Code Annotated. 1957. Title 42, Section 275–80: 136–140.

Video Health Information Project. 2000. Retrieved July 20, 2000 from the World Wide Web: http://www.sebridge.org/~vhip/about/frame.htm/.

Winnetka Alliance for Early Childhood. 2000. Retrieved July 7, 2000 from the World Wide Web: http://www.winnetkaalliance.org.

Woods, J. W., Jones, R. R., Schoultz, T. W., Kuenz, M., and Moore, R. L. 1988. "Teaching Pathology in the 21st Century: An Experimental Automated Curriculum Delivery System for Basic Pathology." *Archives of Pathology and Laboratory Medicine* 112 (August): 852–885.

RECOMMENDED READING

Chandler, G. E., and Hanrahan, P. 2000. "Teaching Using Interactive Video: Creating Connections." *Journal of Nursing Education* 39 (February): 73–79.

Joint Commission on Accreditation of Hospitals (JCAH). 1990. *Accreditation Manual for Hospitals.* Oakbrook Terrace, IL: Joint Commission on Accreditation of Healthcare Organizations.

Souter, G. A. 1988. *The DISConnection: How to Interface Computers and Video.* White Plains, NY: Knowledge Industries Publications.

Part III

Close Focus: Specialized Collections and Special User Needs

Chapter 6

Video Services for the Deaf

Thomas R. Harrington

WHAT IS THE DEAF AND HEARING-IMPAIRED COMMUNITY?

Deafness is more than just an inability to hear. It is a very complex phenomenon, involving not only communication but also psychology, demography, education, economics, minorities, social attitudes, and culture. Deaf people do not make up a single, homogeneous population, but are characterized by diversity equal to that of the hearing population among which they live. No comprehensive treatment of the subject can be given in the limited space available here (for a short but fairly comprehensive overview of deafness and deaf people, see *Gallaudet Encyclopedia* 1987). This introduction will attempt instead to discuss the major facets of deafness that affect the selection of video materials for this population.

Definition

No universally accepted definition for deafness exists. For the purpose of this chapter, *deaf* and *deafness* refer to "the inability to hear and understand speech through the ear alone" (Schein 1987: 251). For simplicity's sake here, other terms for this condition—*hearing-impaired, deafened, aurally handicapped, hard-of-hearing*—will also be covered by the generic term *deaf*. The common thread is an inability to understand spoken language through hearing alone, though many deaf people can understand speech with the assistance of lipreading, aural amplification, or other aids.

Demography

Reliable figures for the number of deaf people in the United States are hard to come by, as the definition and the methods of counting are extremely variable. Estimates range from a low of 500,000 to a high of 21 million. The U.S. Census has not counted deaf people since 1930. The last reliable census of deaf people in the United States was privately funded by the National Association of the Deaf. It took place in 1971 and identified over 13 million Americans with some form of hearing impairment. Almost two million of those had a profound hearing impairment (Schein and Delk 1974). The general U.S. population has grown substantially since then, and the numbers of deaf people are proportionally larger today; however, the precise number of deaf individuals in the United States is unknown. The National Organization on Disability gives 21 million as its current estimate of persons having some type of deafness from any and all causes.

On the other hand, the U.S. Census Bureau, in a 1994/1995 "model-based" estimate using statistical manipulation of data from the 1990 Census (no actual counting), says 10.9 million Americans *16 years of age or older* "have difficulty hearing normal conversation" (i.e., hard-of-hearing) and another 918,000 are "unable to hear normal conversation" (i.e., deaf), for a total of 11,798,000. It is impossible to figure out how many children under age 16 to add to those numbers, since the Census Bureau does not estimate them the same way. It has separate estimated figures for children aged 6 to 14 and for children aged 15 to 21, the latter group obviously overlapping substantially with the 16-and-over group. Children aged 5 and under are not estimated at all, "due to the difficulties of statistically identifying disabilities in young children" (U.S. Census Bureau 2000).

Categories of Deaf People

Again, there is no universally accepted method of sorting deaf people into uniform groups; however, the following list is generally representative:

- Sign language users
- Oralists (those who rely totally upon lipreading and speech)
- Later-deafened adults (deafness occurred after about age 18)
- Hard-of-hearing (able to hear and understand speech with or without amplification)

Each of these groups can be further subdivided. For example, sign language users may include native users of American Sign Language (ASL) with limited written English skill; bilingual users fluent in both ASL and written English;

and users of English-based sign systems instead of ASL. Sign language users can also be divided on the basis of education: high school level or less, college degree, and postgraduate degrees. Other divisions are possible, such as by ethnic origin, religion, hearing status of family (e.g., hearing parents or deaf parents), and age (children or adult; a lifelong deaf person now aged versus a lifelong hearing person now deafened by age). These divisions can be made for each of the other groups also.

The point of all this is simply that there is no "typical" deaf person, anymore than there is really a typical hearing person. This fact needs to be kept in mind when developing video collections for use by deaf people: what serves one deaf person may not necessarily be of value to another deaf person. Just as the hearing population requires a diversity of video programming, so the deaf population also requires a diversity of video programming.

Language

Not all deaf people use sign language. Not all deaf people can lipread well. Not all deaf people can read and write English well. There is a centuries-long controversy in deaf education circles about the best way to teach deaf children. This controversy basically centers on what communication mode and language deaf people should use. The "oralists" insist on spoken English and lipreading exclusively; the sign advocates promote sign language as the natural and clearest means of communication. Both groups are passionate about their beliefs, and sometimes the debate approaches the atmosphere of a religious war. The library seeking balance in its video collection generally will want some signed videos but rely primarily upon captioned videos. The captioned videos are not only much more numerous and more available but are accessible to both the oral deaf and to most signing deaf people, in addition to regular hearing audiences. However, signed videos still are needed for those deaf people having low English-language skills, just as a library will have high-interest/low-vocabulary books for adults with low English-reading skills, and signing deaf people with good English-language skills may still prefer programs in the language they are most comfortable with—signs. Some signed videos also have captions, to better serve both signing and oral deaf people.

Education

Just as with hearing people, deaf people have a wide variety of educational levels. These may range from bare survival skills all the way to an earned doctorate degree. Some are educated in state residential schools, some in special day schools; others are "mainstreamed" with hearing children, to varying degrees and varying success, in regular schools. For over a century, Gallaudet University in Washington, DC, the world's only liberal arts university for the deaf, was virtually the only option for college education of deaf people. However, in the mid-1960s, the National Technical Institute for the Deaf in Rochester, New York, became a technical-college alternative; and since the mid-1970s, federal legislation mandating increasing access to educational opportunities has given deaf people a larger choice of postsecondary educational programs in regular colleges and universities around the country. As a group, however, deaf people have a lower level of education than their hearing peers, owing to the communication difficulties and the frequently inadequate basic schooling they get.

Interests and Vocations

Deaf people are found in virtually every field of work. They may be day laborers or college professors, printers or publishers, physicists or physicians. As a group, however, deaf people have a higher rate of unemployment and underemployment than the general hearing population, due to long-standing social discrimination and misunderstanding.

Deaf people generally have the same interests that hearing people do. Every field of recreation and hobbies has its deaf participants—even music has its deaf performers and listeners. Do not make the mistake of excluding any subject because you think a deaf person wouldn't be interested or can't use it. As a quotation attributed to deaf Gallaudet University President I. King Jordan goes, "Deaf people can do anything but hear."

Deaf People as Library Users

Historically, deaf people have not been users of libraries. Despite what logic may say, their visual orientation does not automatically convert them into readers. English, a phonetically based language, is difficult to learn if one cannot hear it, and many deaf people never do learn it fluently. For many, their first language is American Sign Language, an unwritten language very different from English. These deaf people have much in common with other "English as a Second Language" library patrons. If a potential library patron is not comfortable with reading English, that person tends not to visit a library; it matters little whether that person's first language is Spanish, Cambodian, or American Sign Language.

In addition, other factors may discourage a deaf person from visiting the library: staff who cannot sign or are insensitive to the special needs of deaf people; poor directory and explanatory signage; inaccessibility of the library's telephone reference service; inaccessibility of special programs hosted by the library; ignorance of the library's many services; lack of good exposure to good school libraries during childhood; and, of course, the inaccessibility of the library's audiovisual resources. (For information on providing and promoting general library service to deaf patrons, see Dalton 1985; Goddard 1995; Wright 1989.)

Those few deaf people who are avid readers are generally later-deafened people who already had a good command of English prior to becoming deaf, or those who have only a relatively mild hearing impairment.

A BRIEF HISTORY OF VISUAL MATERIALS FOR THE DEAF

Film

When the motion picture was invented, it was silent. For the first time ever, deaf people found themselves able to share the same entertainment that hearing people did, on equal grounds. Educators of the deaf quickly found this newfangled resource to be of great value with their deaf students, who could be exposed to the wide world around them through newsreels. However, with the advent of the "talkies" (beginning with Al Jolson's *The Jazz Singer* in 1926), deaf people found themselves increasingly shut out again from public entertainment and educational films.[1] By the end of 1930, Hollywood had stopped making silent theatrical films altogether (Walker 1979). Not until the 1980s and the spread of "closed captioning" on television and videos did deaf people again have wide access to popular films, though there had been limited access to a few open-captioned films since the middle 1960s.

Early on, deaf people recognized that this new medium was ideal for capturing stories, speeches, and other expressions in sign language. Out of concern for preservation of sign language, which then was under attack by educators attempting to stamp it out in favor of strictly oral methods, the National Association of the Deaf (NAD) initiated and funded a project to film notable deaf leaders of the day signing a collection of poems, lectures, memoirs, and stories. This project began in 1910 and ran for 11 years. The resulting films were widely exhibited throughout the American deaf community, and today this preserved collection of 14 films forms a valuable resource for researching the history, culture, and sign language of American deaf people in the early twentieth century (Schuchman 1988). The core NAD collection, augmented by additional films of NAD activities from 1937 to 1955, is currently housed in the Gallaudet University Archives, Washington, DC.

After the "talkies" took over the film industry, deaf people perpetuated the old silent films through showing them at deaf club meetings, deaf schools, and other social events of the deaf community. Some deaf individuals also attempted to make up for the lack of new material by making original, low-budget silent films with deaf casts signing their lines (Schuchman 1988: 18).

Television and Video

From its commercial beginnings around 1940, television was a sound medium, and deaf people were left out from participation for its first four decades.

As with film, television proved well suited for presentations in sign language, but very few signed programs were made. This was a consequence of the (hearing) broadcasters' monopoly on the airwaves and on the stations and transmitters, and of the fact that the television audience was overwhelmingly hearing and uninterested in signed or captioned programs. Indeed, the few times that captions were broadcast, the television stations regularly got complaints about the "distracting" captions from hearing viewers. The rare broadcasts of signed programs would draw complaining letters from people believing only in the oral method of communication for deaf people, and from hearing people objecting to the displacement of their normal programming.

Not until the development of closed-captioning technology in the mid-1970s did deaf people finally get access to television programs that didn't also bother intolerant hearing viewers. The spread of home video in the 1980s brought a variety of closed-captioned programming to deaf viewers, who were no longer dependent upon the whims of television broadcasters for captioned programming. Home video also created a new niche product: the relatively low cost of producing and distributing videos for the consumer market led to the appearance of several companies specializing in videos for the deaf and for hearing people desiring to learn sign language and about deaf people.

A BRIEF HISTORY OF CAPTIONED FILMS FOR THE DEAF

In 1950, Edmund B. Boatner and Clarence O'Connor, two educators of the deaf, conceived the idea of captioned films for the deaf, paralleling the "talking books for the blind" that already existed. With support from colleagues and a small private grant, Boatner founded Captioned Films for the Deaf (CFD), a non-profit corporation, to develop the best method for captioning films for the deaf and to begin a collection of loanable films for use in schools for the deaf. At first, these films were entertainment films only. Their popularity soon outstripped the non-profit group's ability to support the demand, and Boatner felt that the only practical answer was government support. Through the help of Senator William Purtell of Connecticut, Public Law 85–905 was enacted in 1958, establishing CFD as a government-funded agency. Low funding levels hampered the program in its first few years, but eventually, with support from Elliott Newcomb of Encyclopedia Britannica Films and Senators Edmund Muskie and Claiborne Pell and Representative John Fogarty, both funding and scope were expanded to include educational as well as entertainment films. President John F. Kennedy signed the amended bill into law in 1962. Four regional media centers and 60 educational film depositories followed; CFD also held workshops and institutes to train teachers in the use of these films and other media for deaf education. (For a fuller account of the history of captioned films, see Gannon 1981.)

CMP Today and Its Limitations

Today, after many years of being contracted out to private industry, and now renamed the Captioned Media Program (CMP) (http://www.cfv.org/), the CMP functions are administered by the National Association of the Deaf through a special office in Spartanburg, South Carolina. Government oversight is through the Captioning and Adaptation Branch, Office of Special Education and Rehabilitative Services, in the U.S. Department of Education.

Several schools for the deaf around the country continue to be "depository" collections of educational films, serving not only their own schools but also other deaf education programs in their respective regions. Entertainment captioned films are borrowed directly from CMP's central collection in Spartanburg. The collection originally consisted entirely of 16mm films, but in the 1980s and 1990s, CMD shifted to open-captioned VHS videotapes, with emphasis on titles that are not already available commercially with closed captions.

Valuable as the CMP service is, it does have its limitations and disadvantages. Only films selected by a panel of evaluators are captioned and made available. The necessity to negotiate permissions and fees with each individual film distributor for each title also limits the number of titles that can be made available. No more than 12 copies of each theatrical film are available to serve deaf audiences over the entire country. The mail order system requires planning for a film's use months in advance; there is little flexibility for changing situations or spontaneity. The requirement for a minimum group size of six deaf people likewise limits access to the theatrical films; and the educational films are selected to support elementary and secondary schools only, leaving collegiate, adult, and family audiences mostly unserved in the educational and "special interest" areas. Fortunately, closed-captioned videos have emerged during the past quarter century to overcome some of these problems (discussed below).

To borrow a captioned film from CMP, registration for an account is required. The captioned educational films are, in general, available to all types of handicapped children (not just deaf) who can benefit from them. However, because of commercial restrictions on them, the captioned entertainment (feature) films are restricted to deaf persons only.

The captioned feature films require a group of six or more deaf persons (a school, a deaf club, etc.) to qualify for loans. There is no group size limit for the educational films, however. For more information on the CMP program, registration, and catalogs, contact Captioned Films for the Deaf (see Appendix A, this chapter).

Signed Productions

A few companies have taken advantage of the home video revolution to produce original programs, with a narrator or cast using sign language, expressly for deaf audiences. Many of these aim to teach deaf people various life and social skills; others are religious instruction or general interest videos. A few are strictly for entertainment, descendants of those homemade signed film productions made by deaf individuals or deaf clubs to fill the entertainment void after Hollywood converted to "talking" movies.

Related to the above are videos produced for the purpose of helping hearing people learn sign language. These may consist of formal lessons, supplementary material for practice in reading signs, or auxiliary material for learning more about deaf culture and the deaf world.

SPECIAL NEEDS AND CONSIDERATIONS FOR THE DEAF AND HEARING IMPAIRED

Captioning

Captioning is the process of adding textual information to a film, television, or video image to provide additional information not present in the normal image or on the soundtrack. There are three different types of captions.

Open Captions

Open captions are part of the image, and always appear when the program is run. They are called "open" in contrast with "closed" captions (see below). Reference works older than about 1980, that refer to "captioned" programs, always refer to what are now called open captions. In films for the deaf, open captions provide a visual rendering of the spoken soundtrack, sometimes edited for space and timing considerations or to adjust the language to the target audience's level. Captions for the deaf will also indicate sounds that are not visible but nevertheless important to the understanding of what is happening; for example, a character on screen may react in startlement to the slamming of an off-screen door. Deaf viewers will not know about the door-slamming unless the caption informs them of that sound; only then does the on-screen character's frightened response make sense. Some films are distributed in two versions, a non-captioned version and an open-captioned version.

Subtitles

Subtitles are a specialized form of captions. They provide a printed translation of a spoken foreign-language soundtrack, nearly always for the benefit of hearing viewers rather than deaf viewers. Subtitles do not include visual cues of other sounds not visible on screen, since hearing audiences are expected to hear them anyway. Although deaf people can follow a subtitled foreign film far better than one not captioned at all, it is important to keep in mind that the subtitling is done for the benefit of hearing audiences not knowing the language of the film's soundtrack, and is not done with the needs of deaf people in mind. This did not prevent deaf people from being avid patrons of theaters showing subtitled foreign films; they still go today, though the ready availability of closed-captioned videos in the home has substantially reduced this attendance in recent decades.

Closed Captions

Closed captions are called that because they are invisibly encoded into a television or video image and can be retrieved and displayed only through the use of a special decoding device. In the standard 525-line (NTSC) video image as used in the United States and Canada, Line 21 in the vertical blanking interval (the black bar visible when the TV picture "rolls") is reserved for carrying digital data, which can be translated by a decoder into captions and superimposed on the video image. The great advantage of closed captions over open captions is that both deaf and hearing audiences can enjoy the same programming, without the distractions of captions for people who don't want them; only one version of the program is required to satisfy both deaf and hearing viewers.

Because of their electronic nature, true closed captions are available only from television programs and video programs. Due to their physical nature, optically projected films cannot be directly closed-captioned. However, experimentation in the late 1980s and early 1990s with various methods of captioning films in theaters led to the development of the "Rear Window" captioning system, which provides a similar experience in appropriately equipped theaters. The Rear Window system consists of a transparent acrylic panel mounted on a long gooseneck that is clipped to the theater seat or plugged into its cup holder. The acrylic panel is adjusted by the viewer so as to reflect captions displayed on a reversed light-emitting diode (LED) text display at the back of the theater, and may be positioned anywhere relative to the film screen that the viewer desires. The theater's existing DTS audio system reads the captions from a CD-ROM along with the other CD-ROMs that provide the film's digital audio track, and commands and synchronizes the display of the captions on the LED display. In this way, deaf filmgoers can watch the film with captions while their hearing seat-neighbors get the film without captions. This system began to appear in a few specialty and high-end theaters in 1998 and is gradually spreading. For more information on the Rear Window theatrical captioning system, see http://www.wgbh.org/wgbh/pages/ncam/mopix/faq.html.

DVD Subtitles

The appearance of the DVD has also introduced a new wrinkle in the provision of text for video: what might be called "closed-captioned subtitles." These are encoded onto the DVD disc and are normally invisible unless and until specifically requested, just as with closed captions. However, they have the appearance of traditional "open" subtitles, and share the same flaw as traditional subtitles: they are designed for hearing audiences only, and lack indications of environmental and other off-screen sounds that may be important to a deaf person's understanding of the video. Many video programs on DVD now come with closed-captioned subtitles in English and often in other languages as well. Unfortunately, these are usually not identified in bibliographic data, and can consequently be difficult to find if you are seeking a deaf-accessible DVD. Just to confuse the matter further, some DVDs actually come with both closed *captions* and closed *subtitles*, both in English! It is even possible to display both at the same time, though usually the closed captions will overlay the subtitles. Unlike closed captions, which require special decoding circuitry either built into the TV receiver or in a stand-alone decoder, DVD subtitles are extracted and displayed by the DVD player itself as part of the video signal it sends to the TV. If a DVD has subtitles, they will be accessible through the DVD's setup menu.

A special problem arises with deaf people from foreign cultures who do not know English. They cannot take advantage of regular captioned films, as they not only cannot understand the soundtrack but also cannot read the English, though usually they can read captions in their native country's language. A very few films are available in the United States with subtitles in languages other than English, but these are difficult to locate. Fortunately, as noted above, many programs on DVD now come with closed-captioned subtitles in languages additional to English, and these can help meet the need of this special group of deaf people, with the usual caveat that these subtitles do not include information on environmental and off-screen sounds. The main problem here is identifying which DVDs have foreign-language subtitles and which languages are available. This information is usually missing from advertising and bibliographic sources, and often can be found only by examining the text on the DVD box itself.

Closed-Captioned Television

Closed captions were developed during the mid-1970s to give deaf people access to television programming without the objections that hearing people usually have to captions on their programs. Under the instigation of the late Malcolm J. Norwood, deaf chief of the Media Services and Captioned Films Division of the Bureau of Education of the Handicapped, Department of Health, Education and Welfare, the WGBH Educational Foundation in Boston, Massachusetts, worked with the National Bureau of Standards to develop a system that could transmit caption information piggybacked on standard television signals. The Public Broadcasting System (PBS) took a major guiding role in this work, supported by the American Broadcasting Company (ABC) (Gannon 1981: 385–386). In 1976 the Federal Communications Commission officially set aside Line 21 of the television screen for transmission of caption information. The non-profit National Captioning Institute (NCI) (http://www.ncicap.org/) was set up in the same year with the charge to caption regular and special television programming and to promote the use and spread of closed captions. Sears, Roebuck & Company accepted the responsibility for manufacturing and marketing a caption decoder to the public; a few years later, this responsibility was assumed by NCI, which is still the primary manufacturer of stand-alone closed-caption decoders. In 1979, regular closed captioning of popular TV shows began on the ABC, NBC, and PBS networks. CBS held out for a few years, favoring a different and incompatible teletext-based system that ultimately failed in the marketplace. CBS now participates in "Line 21" captioning too. The new Fox Broadcasting System also initiated captioning of its programs within its first year of existence. The Canadian Broadcasting Corporation (CBC) also broadcasts programs closed-captioned in this system. Today, all prime-time network programming on all American networks is closed-captioned, as well as a few (but not all) non-prime-time programs. However, most syndicated and locally produced television programs still lack closed captions.

Closed captions can also be found on a couple of cable TV networks. For example, most HBO programming is closed-captioned; a few movies on Showtime are captioned, and the majority of the Disney Channel programs likewise are captioned. Lack of captions is still the rule on most cable TV programs, however.

Closed-Captioned Videos

Closed-captioned videotapes first appeared publicly in 1980, when RCA/Columbia released *Chapter Two* and *The China Syndrome* with closed captions. Since then, many more have appeared from many different sources, roughly 10,000 titles, past and present. Although this may seem like a large number, it is in fact less than 6 percent of all the home video and educational video titles released onto the market.

In addition to their small numbers, awareness and use of closed-captioned videos is severely hampered by a lack of publicity for the presence of closed captions on those programs that do happen to have them. Most advertising catalogs and other publicity material for captioned videos neglect to show this fact; it is also not uncommon for the video box, sleeve, or label to omit it. While some video vendors do make efforts to indicate the presence of closed captions, those efforts tend to be uneven or intermittent. Even where the original distributor indicates closed captions, secondary advertisers, such as video stores and retail dealers, usually do not bother to show this information in their own advertising and catalogs. This is particularly true for "non-fiction" videos, which are mostly distributed by smaller companies having smaller publicity budgets.

Without knowledge of which few of the many available videos have closed captions, it is difficult for deaf persons, as well as educators, librarians, parents, and other interested people, to identify videos they can use. Most closed-captioned videos bear some kind of identification of this fact; it may be the words "closed captioned," the initials "CC," or the NCI closed-captioning symbol (a small stylized TV set with a cartoon-caption balloon point on the bottom).

There is no doubt that captioned films and videos, in both open-captioned and closed-captioned forms, are of enormous benefit to the hearing-impaired.

From this author's own personal experience as a deaf person, captions are essential to bringing understanding and comprehension of film, television, and video to a deaf person. This is of particular importance in our society, where so much information, education, and cultural and social attributes are presented and shaped by television, film, and video. Without full access to these media, hearing-impaired persons are left in ignorance and in the backwaters of our society, unable to make full use of their potential.

Several studies have consistently shown great improvements in reading skills and English-language ability in deaf persons exposed to captioned films and videos, as well as improvements in their general knowledge and functioning skills (see, e.g., Koskinen et al. 1986: 15–19). Benefits have been demonstrated for special populations other than the hearing-impaired, too: captions are of great help to learning-disabled students, in remedial English teaching, in teaching English as a second language to immigrants, and for literacy teaching (see, e.g., National Captioning Institute 1990). The benefits of captioning extend considerably beyond deaf audiences. They also indirectly benefit our society at large, in helping to improve and broaden the education of the hearing-impaired and other groups, making them more productive members of our society, more able to participate in a labor pool increasingly in need of educated persons, and returning the investment to society through greater independence, increased productivity, and less reliance on social services.

One problem with closed-captioned videos is that, with only a few known exceptions, all are captioned in English only. They will be of only limited benefit to deaf persons from non-English-speaking backgrounds who do not themselves know English (Hispanics, immigrants, etc.). Although the caption decoders include the ability to display characters peculiar to Spanish and a couple of other languages, only a few dozen video titles are known to be closed-captioned entirely in a language other than English, and nearly all of these are in Spanish only. Some are identified in the closed-captioned video list available from the National Captioning Institute. Fortunately, many DVDs are now appearing with subtitles in languages other than English (see "DVD Subtitles"), which will alleviate this problem to some extent, at least for major western European languages.

Closed-Caption Decoders

The decoder for closed captions is available in two different forms. *Stand-alone* decoders can be connected to a TV receiver and used with any standard videocassette recorder, videodisc player, DVD player, cable TV system, or satellite TV receiver. Current manufacturers of stand-alone consumer decoders are Mycap (see http://www.cpcweb.com/mycap.html) and Universal (see http://www.hacofamerica.com/ad09.htm). The National Captioning Institute was once the largest manufacturer of stand-alone closed-caption decoders, but has now left the market.

At this writing, there are two models of consumer decoders available: the Universal Model V7310 and the Mycap Jr. The V7310 is a classic small, plain "black box" that installs between the video signal sources (antenna, VCR, DVD player, cable TV outlet, etc.) and the inputs on the TV receiver. The stylish Mycap Jr. is little larger than a pack of cards and installs similarly but requires separate audio/video jacks on the TV receiver. Older models of stand-alone decoders that had their own channel tuner, for use with plain antenna or cable TV input, are no longer available; the current models rely on the video player, cable converter, or satellite receiver for channel tuning.

The second type of decoder is *built into a TV receiver*, with special decoder circuitry integrated right into a regular TV receiver. For a brief time in the late 1970s and early 1980s, Sears Roebuck offered a 19-inch tabletop TV receiver with a built-in decoder. This model was not a great success, probably because, apart from the decoder circuitry, the TV itself was an undistinguished model with little to recommend it above others. TVs with built-in decoders did not appear again until 1992.

The National Captioning Institute, together with friends in the Congress (notably Congressman Major Owens [Democrat, New York] and Senator Tom Harkin [Democrat, Iowa]), saw the need to break the logjam of closed-caption accessibility through mandating more universal access to the closed captions. The resulting Television Decoder Circuitry Act of 1990 mandated that all new television receivers manufactured for sale in the United States after July 1, 1993, and having screens of 13 inches or larger, must have built-in decoder circuitry for closed captions (see http://www.ncicap.org/docs/dcb.htm for text of the Act). This was made practical by NCI's development of a decoder-on-a-chip that could be added to TV sets at a cost of only $5 to $10 each in mass production. Zenith was the first manufacturer to introduce the new generation of consumer TVs having built-in decoders, in early 1992. Most other manufacturers waited until near the deadline to introduce their upgraded models.

If you are uncertain whether an older TV is equipped with decoder circuitry, first examine its remote control for a button labeled "CC." If it does not have such a button, use the remote to call up the menu of functions on the TV and scan it for the "Closed Captions" function. (Do not confuse this with the "Channel Caption" functions on some TVs, which merely shows on-screen which channel it is tuned to and the identity of the broadcasting station.)

A third type of decoder, *built into a VCR*, was never very popular and is no longer available. It consisted of special circuitry built directly into a VCR, which automatically decoded any closed captions on videotapes being played in the VCR. It also decoded captions on regular TV, cable TV, or satellite TV signals being passed through the VCR to the television receiver.

Signed Videos

Some videos produced for deaf audiences have sign language presented in them. This signing may take one of two different forms. Using *sign interpretation*, an interpreter renders into signs what is being spoken. This interpreter may be seen standing near the speaker or may be in an inserted "window" placed in the corner or on one side of the screen. Such a program is obviously one produced for regular hearing audiences, with deaf accessibility "tacked on." Alternatively, *sign language productions* are presented directly in sign language. The speakers use signs, camera angles and scene cuts are made with deaf viewers in mind, and no reliance is made on music or other sound effects for conveying a meaning. Most such productions have voice-overs added by interpreters, so non-signing hearing audiences can understand the dialogue. A few programs are presented in signs, have voice-overs, and also have captions; those aim to reach the widest possible audience by offering a communication mode for everyone.

Non-Narrated and Non-Verbal Programs

Prior to the general availability of open- and closed-captioned films and videos, educational programs for the deaf made use of non-verbal and non-narrated films, as these do not depend on a spoken soundtrack for conveying information. They are still useful with deaf audiences, though caution must be taken when evaluating a film for suitability for deaf audiences. Some of them, though non-narrated, still depend on sound effects for conveying a message. Those, obviously, are inappropriate for deaf audiences.

Unfortunately, access to information about available non-narrated videos is difficult. Only one directory is known. It covers only 16mm films, and it is nearly three decades old (Parlato 1973).

LEGAL ASPECTS

Several federal laws affect libraries with respect to providing access to video and film collections for deaf persons. Following are some brief descriptions of major laws and what they mean to libraries in terms of video collections.

The author of this chapter is not a lawyer, and the interpretations that follow are not to be considered legal advice. As far as possible, conclusions drawn here are from the texts of the acts, published government guidelines, and court decisions. In case of any question or doubt, check with your legal counsel first.

Rehabilitation Act of 1973 (P.L. 93–112); Amended and Extended 1978 and 1983

Section 504 of this Act prohibits discrimination against persons with handicaps by any group or agency, public or private, which receives federal funds.

Handicapped people, including deaf people, have a right to "learn, work, and compete on a fair and equal basis." (The Americans with Disabilities Act of 1990 [below] extends this concept to include almost all groups or agencies, public or private, not just those receiving federal funds.) In terms of videos in libraries, the Rehabilitation Act means that libraries using federal funds for video collection development have an obligation to provide videos accessible to the deaf, otherwise deaf people will not have fair access to the library's collection.

Copyright Act of 1976 (P.L. 94–553) (Off-Air Recording and Fair Use)

Prior to the development of closed captioning, deaf people had virtually no access to television or videos. Beginning in the early 1970s, a few schools for the deaf attempted to meet this need for their deaf students by copying broadcast television programs off the air and adding open captions for use by their students. The legality of this use was uncertain, as it fell into an ambiguity in the original Copyright Act of 1909, which never forecast the possibility of television, let alone of copying television programs. It was generally felt that "fair use" permitted this copying and captioning, but in the absence of specifically written law or test court cases, its legality remained uncertain.

The extensively revised Copyright Act of 1976 (Title 17 of the U.S. Code) addressed the new technologies that had emerged since 1909, and also legitimized this specialized interpretation of "fair use." The 1976 Act itself makes no direct references to the access needs of deaf people. However, at the time the bill was reported to the floor of Congress for its final vote, the House Committee on the Judiciary set forth several guidelines under which "nonprofit educational institutions for the deaf and hearing impaired" could take advantage of the law's "fair-use" provision to copy broadcast television programs "off the air," add captions, and make these captioned programs available to the institution's deaf students. These guidelines were published in the U.S. *Congressional Record* (1976: H 10875). The following is an encapsulation of the major points:

1. This special use is covered under Section 107 of the act, the "fair-use" provision.
2. Television programs may be recorded off-the-air by a non-profit educational institution serving the deaf or hearing-impaired for the purpose of producing one master and one work (use) copy of a captioned version of the program.
3. This captioned version must be "performed" (used) solely within the confines of the institution.
4. The use of the captioned recording must be "noncommercial in every respect, and educational in the sense that it serves as part of a deaf or hearing-impaired student's learning environment within the institution."
5. The institution is responsible for ensuring that the master and work copies are kept "in the hands of a limited number of authorized personnel within the institution," for

preventing unauthorized reproduction or distribution, and for preventing use for other than educational purposes within the institution.

6. Copies may be made, by the originating institution, of the captioned version of the program for sharing with other non-profit educational institutions serving the deaf or hearing-impaired that agree to abide by the above constraints.

Since 1976, the nearly simultaneous home video revolution and the development and spread of closed captioning on TV programs and videos have largely negated the need for schools to meet their deaf students' needs through copying and captioning off-the-air TV programs. However, as suitable closed- (or open-) captioned programs are not available for every possible subject or every possible grade level, an educational institution may still have occasion to take advantage of "fair use" in this manner.

Education for All Handicapped Children Act of 1976 (P.L. 94–142); Amended and Renamed in 1992 as the Individuals with Disabilities Education Act (P.L. 101–476)

This act affects libraries in schools that educate deaf children, whether a regular school with "mainstreamed" deaf children or a special school for deaf children. These schools are mandated to provide a "substantially equal" educational environment for deaf children. This would include access to videos that are used in school programs, whether in or out of the classroom. Such videos must be made accessible to the deaf students in some way, such as a sign language interpreter or through captioning at an appropriate language level.

Americans with Disabilities Act of 1990 (ADA) (P.L. 101–336)

The ADA mandates, among other things, that places of public accommodation must make their facilities and services accessible to persons with disabilities. Title II of the Act applies to publicly funded libraries; and Title III applies to libraries that are privately funded, but offer services, programs, and activities to the public. Accessibility requirements are similar in both cases.

A library is not required to replace its existing non-captioned films and videos with open- or closed-captioned or signed titles, as this would mean a "substantial alteration" of the collection (as well as being an "unreasonable financial burden," in most cases). However, this author believes that libraries are obligated to take the needs of deaf people into consideration when purchasing *new* titles, as the library is required to ensure accessibility to the "goods" offered. If a library orders certain video titles upon request from its patrons, it can be obligated to order accessible videos upon request from a deaf patron. Libraries showing films or videos in public meeting rooms may be required to make the verbal information accessible to deaf persons, through provision of an interpreter, through captions, or through an assistive listening system, depending on the aggregate needs of the various individuals attending. If a library customarily provides video players in its facility for patrons to view videos, it must provide closed-caption decoding equipment to allow access to closed-captioned videos (U.S., *Federal Register* 1991: 35567, 35571, 35573, 35690).

Television Decoder Circuitry Act of 1990 (P.L. 101–431)

As already described elsewhere in this chapter, this law requires all television receivers of 13-inch or larger screens, manufactured on or after July 1, 1993 for sale in the United States, to have built-in decoder circuitry for closed captions. Libraries buying such television receivers will automatically provide access to closed captions on TV shows and videos, as mandated by other laws. Older televisions still in use may be "retrofitted" by adding stand-alone decoders. See "Closed-caption Decoders" for more details.

Telecommunications Act of 1996 (P.L. 104–104)

Section 305 of this Act concerns "video programming accessibility" of broadcast television, cable television, and prerecorded videotapes and discs. It provides that the Federal Communications Commission (FCC) complete an inquiry on the extent to which existing or previously published programming is closed-captioned, the size of the video programming provider or owner, and the size of the market served; report its findings to Congress; and prescribe regulations to maximize the amount of closed-captioned video programming, including setting deadlines. The FCC in fact performed this inquiry, made its report, and issued final rules on August 22, 1997, mandating that by January 1, 2006, 95 percent of all new programming must be closed-captioned. By January 1, 2008, 75 percent of "prior" programming (that originally released before the FCC's rules effectiveness date of January 1, 1998 and re-published or re-exhibited after that date) must also be closed-captioned.

Unfortunately, Section 305 of the Act also provides for several exemptions to the requirement of captioning, crafted in such a way that many video programming providers will be able to weasel out of providing captions, causing de facto results of significantly less than 95 percent and 75 percent respectively. Still, libraries may expect eventually to see an increase in the availability of closed-captioned videos as a result of this legislation.

CONCLUSION

Deaf people are a large but severely underserved population in libraries generally, and in libraries' video services especially. The chief barrier—that of communication—may be overcome in a library's video collection by selecting videos that are captioned or in sign language, by provision of appropriate assistive devices such as caption decoders and listening systems, and, not least, by staff awareness and consideration of their needs. It is important to keep in mind that deaf people are not all alike; they have a variety of communication methods and different needs and interests, just as hearing people do, and the video services provided to them must recognize and meet this diversity.

APPENDIX A: SOURCES OF VIDEOS

Open-Captioned

Captioned Media Program, National Association of the Deaf, 1447 East Main Street, Spartanburg, SC 29307; Tel.: (800) 237–6213; TTY: (800) 237–6819; Fax: (800) 538–5636; E-mail: info@cfv.org; URL: http://www.cfv.org/.

Closed-Captioned

National Captioning Institute (Attn.: Home Video), 1900 Gallows Road, Suite 3000, Vienna, VA 22182; Tel.: (800) 756–7619 or (703) 998–2400; TTY: (800) 374–3986 or (703) 998–2400; E-mail: mail@ncicap.org; URL: http://www.ncicap.org.

Not a source, but a free simple title list of thousands of home videos that NCI has captioned since 1980. Does not contain the thousands of videos captioned by other captioning services, but still the largest list currently available. A shorter list of more current videos is also available online at NCI's Web site.

Review Sources Identifying Closed-Captioned Videos

It is very difficult to determine from review sources whether or not a given video has closed captions. Most review sources do not seem to be aware of, let alone try to list, the presence of closed captions. Even the library profession's flagship periodical, *Library Journal*, does not bother to identify reviewed videos as closed-captioned. The number of review sources showing closed-caption information has actually declined during the past decade. Although the first edition of this book (1994) was able to list four reviewing periodicals showing captioning information, at this writing, only one surviving periodical, *Booklist*, still attempted to show closed-caption information. Although *Booklist* frequently identifies whether or not a reviewed title is closed-captioned, it is not infallible, and very often fails to identify titles that are in fact closed-captioned. Most reviewers do not run their review videos through a closed-caption decoder to check for the presence of captions.

Signed Videos (Selected List)

The following are some major sources of videos produced in sign language. In addition to these resources, see Chris Wixton's useful annotated Web listing, "Where to Buy ASL Videos" via the ASL Access Web site (http://www. aslaccess.org/sources.htm).

ASL Access, 4217 Adrienne Drive, Alexandria, VA 22309; E-mail: mailto:aslaccess @aol.com; URL: http://www.aslaccess.org.

ASL Access is a non-profit organization dedicated to promoting the placement of videos in American Sign Language in libraries, to allow community members better access to materials for learning and practicing ASL. They have a collection of over 200 screened and selected videos in ASL from various producers that are purchased through private fund-raising and placed in cooperating libraries for public access. This is a good way for libraries to obtain a good number of quality sign language videos at little or no cost. Beginning on June 15, 1999, by October 2000 ASL Access had already placed collections in four public libraries around the country. For more information, contact ASL Access or visit its Web site, which has a FAQ section especially for librarians.

DawnSign Press, 6130 Nancy Ridge Drive, San Diego, CA 92121–3223; Tel./TTY: (858) 625–0600; Fax: (858) 625–2336; E-mail: comments@dawnsign.com; URL: http:// www.dawnsign.com.

DeBee Communications, 3900 Monet Court South, Pittsburgh, PA 15101–3221; Tel./ TTY: (412) 492–8214; Fax: (412) 492–8215; E-mail (customer service): customer@ debee.com; URL: http://www.debee.com.

Gallaudet University, Department of Television, Photography and Digital Media, 800 Florida Avenue NE, Washington, DC 20002–3695; Tel./TTY: (202) 651–5115; URL: http://tv.gallaudet.edu.

Harris Communications, Inc., 15155 Technology Drive, Eden Prairie, MN 55344– 2277; Tel./TTY: (800) 825–9187; Fax: (952) 906–1099; URL: http://www.harriscomm. com.

Sign Media Inc., 4020 Blackburn Lane, Burtonsville, MD 20866; Tel.: (800) 475– 4756; (301) 421–0268; TTY: (301) 421–4460; FAX: (301) 421–0270; E-mail: mailto: signmedia@aol.com; URL: http://www.signmedia.com.

T. J. Publishers, Inc., 817 Silver Spring Avenue, Suite 206, Silver Spring, MD 20910– 4617; Tel./TTY: (301) 585–4440 or (800) 999–1168; FAX: (301) 585–5930; E-mail: TJPubinc@aol.com; URL: http://www.bowker.com/lrg/home/entries/t.j._publishers_inc, children_s_sign_language.html.

The Oral View

Alexander Graham Bell Association for the Deaf, 3417 Volta Place, NW, Washington, DC 20007–2778; Tel./TTY: (202) 337–5221; Fax: (202) 337–8314; URL: http://www. agbell.org.

Offers videos for learning speechreading, and other videos espousing the oral-only philosophy for the deaf.

APPENDIX B: SOURCES OF OTHER MATERIAL

Stand-Alone Closed-Caption Decoders

These can be special-ordered through Radio Shack stores; purchased through the catalog at Sears Roebuck; from dealers of assistive devices for the deaf such as Harris Communications; or directly from the National Captioning Institute

(NCI). If you have trouble locating a dealer, NCI can assist you with locating one near you.

Harris Communications, Inc., 15159 Technology Drive, Eden Prairie, MN 55344–2277; Tel.: (800) 825–6758; TTY: (800) 825–9187; Fax: (952) 906–1099; E-mail (customer service): mail@harriscomm.com; URL: http://www.harriscomm.com.

National Captioning Institute, 1900 Gallows Road, Suite 3000, Vienna, VA 22182; Tel.: (800) 756–7619 or (703) 998–2400; TTY: (800) 374–3986 or (703) 998–2400; E-mail: mail@ncicap.org; URL: http://www.ncicap.org.

TV Receivers with Built-in Decoders

Since July 1, 1993, all television sets of 13-inch or larger size manufactured on or after that date have been required to contain closed-caption decoding circuitry. Check the manufacturer's data sticker on the back of the TV for its manufacturing date. If it is dated before January 1992, it will not have decoding capability. If it has a date between January 1992 and June 1993 inclusive, it may or may not have decoding capability. See "Closed Caption Decoders" in the main chapter text for how to check for decoding capability.

APPENDIX C: CAPTIONING SERVICES

The following companies will caption videos with either open or closed captions. Most will also do subtitling for DVD videos. This is not a complete list; over 100 more captioning services exist, but these are believed to be the major ones.

The Caption Center, WGBH Boston, 125 Western Avenue, Boston, MA 02134; Tel./ TTY: (617) 300–5400; Fax: (617) 300–1026; URL: http://www.wgbh.org/wgbh/pages/captioncenter/.

Computer Prompting & Captioning Co., 1010 Rockville Pike, Suite 306, Rockville, MD 20852; Tel.: (800) 977–6678) or (301) 738–8487; TTY: (301) 738–8489; Fax: (301) 738–8488; E-mail: mailto:info@cpcweb.com; URL: http://www.cpcweb.com.

National Captioning Institute, 1900 Gallows Road, Suite 3000, Vienna, VA 22182; Tel.: (800) 756–7619 or (703) 998–2400; TTY: (800) 374–3986 or (703) 998–2400; E-mail: mailto:koconnor@ncicap.org; URL: http://www.ncicap.org.

Real-time Captions, Inc., 901 West Alameda Avenue, Burbank, CA 91506 (see Web site for other national locations); Tel.: (818) 729–9501; Fax: (818) 729–9519; URL: http://www.captionsinc.com.

VITAC/CaptionAmerica, 101 Hillpointe Drive, Canonsburg, PA 15317–9503 (Corporate Headquarters) (see Web site for other national locations); Tel.: (800) 278–4822 or (724) 514–4000; TTY: (724) 514–4100; Fax: (724) 514–4111; URL: http://www.vitac.com.

"Do-it-yourself" captioning software is available from:

Computer Prompting & Captioning Co., 1010 Rockville Pike, Suite 306, Rockville, MD 20852; Tel.: (301) 738–8487; TTY: (301) 738–8489; Fax: (301) 738–8488; E-mail: info@cpcweb.com; URL: http://www.cpcweb.com.

External Captioning Projects, The Caption Center, WGBH Boston, 125 Western Avenue, Boston, MA 02134, Tel./TTY: (617) 300–5400; URL: http://www.wgbh.org/wgbh/pages/captioncenter/.

These software programs run on personal computers. Adding a pair of VCRs, a closed-caption decoder, and a TV monitor with audio/video inputs provides a low-cost way to create captioned videos in-house. The results are not of professional captioning quality, but are suitable for the consumer and local institution level.

APPENDIX D: RECOMMENDED CORE VIDEOGRAPHY

The following videos are suggested as the core of a collection aimed specifically at the needs of the deaf community and at persons interested in the deaf. This core collection is to be augmented by regular video programming having closed captions, and by additional deaf-specific videos selected to suit the needs of your local deaf patrons. Unless otherwise noted, addresses for the distributors for these titles are cited in Appendix A.

Deaf Culture

American Culture: The Deaf Perspective, 4 videocassettes, each 28 to 30 min., 1984.
Four parts: *Deaf Heritage* traces the development of American Sign Language and focuses on some of the individuals who have contributed to American deaf heritage. *Deaf Folklore* illustrates how the traditions and values of deaf people are passed on through the humor, tales, games, and personal stories of deaf individuals. *Deaf Literature* samples poetry, drama, and visual literature of the deaf as witnessed on stage and screen. *Deaf Minorities* shares the experiences of deaf persons who are also members of other minority groups. Closed-captioned and with English voice-overs. Friends of SFPL: Video Account, c/o Special Media Services, San Francisco Public Library, Civic Center, San Francisco, CA 94102.

ASL Poetry: Selected Works of Clayton Valli, 105 min., signed, voice-over, 1998. ISBN 0–915035–23–5 (VHS).
Deaf linguist and acclaimed sign language poet Clayton Valli presents several of his works, while host Lon Kuntze guides viewers through the hidden meanings in these ASL poems, revealing differences and similarities with English-language poetry. DawnSignPress.

In the Land of the Deaf, 99 min., 1994.
Directed by Nicolas Philibert. A unique and privileged look inside the world of (French) deaf people. A teacher, a woman treated for mental illness because of her

deafness, and a newly wed deaf couple offer compelling portraits of the deaf community in a film which is revealing, moving, and often funny. French and French Sign Language with English subtitles. FACETS (http://www.facets.org) and other video distributors.

Introduction to American Deaf Culture, 5 videocassettes, each 60 min., 1986.

Five parts: *Rules of Social Interaction* introduces selected aspects of social interaction among deaf people; *Values* addresses the importance of clubs for deaf people, their perspectives on deaf children's socialization and education, and the importance of eyes and hands; *Language and Traditions* examines the way that unique aspects of deaf culture are expressed through American Sign Language; *Group Norms* reviews some of the "rules" and norms for behavior of deaf people; *Identity* discusses self-identity and membership within the American deaf culture. Sign Media, Inc.

An Introduction to the Deaf Community, 30 min., 1993.

A much briefer introduction to deaf culture and how and why deaf people behave the way they do, for more casual students of deaf culture. Sign Media, Inc.

Laurent Clerc (1785–1869), 30 min., 1995.

A historical documentary about the remarkable deaf Frenchman who brought sign language from France to America in 1817, established the first permanent school for the deaf in America, and directly or indirectly taught the founders of most other schools for the deaf in America, leaving an indelible mark on American deaf people and deaf people throughout the world. DeBee Communications.

The Preservation of American Sign Language, 1997.

Presents eight old films dating back to the period 1910–1920, showing master signers of the past in a variety of sign language stories and narrations. Brian Malzkuhn introduces each film with a brief biographical sketch of the signer; the film is shown; and Malzkuhn comments on each, including showing the differences between old and present-day signs. Sign Media, Inc.

Sound and Fury, 60 and 90 min. versions available, 2000.

Sound and Fury deals with the painful struggle of one family over a controversial medical technology called the cochlear implant. Some family members celebrate the implant as a long overdue cure for deafness while others fear it will destroy their language and way of life. *Sound and Fury* explores this seemingly irreconcilable conflict as it illuminates the ongoing struggle for identity among deaf people today. Filmakers Library, 124 East 40th Street, New York, NY 10016 (http://www:filmakers.com).

When the Mind Hears, 13 videocassettes, 1993.

Based on Harlan Lane's book of the same title, the series presents a study of the history of deaf people in Europe and America. Traces the beginning of formal education for deaf students in France and the United States, and the prejudices and hardships faced by the deaf. Each tape provides a detailed American Sign Language synopsis of a single chapter in Lane's book, in addition to voice-over narration. Sign Media, Inc.

Feature Films with Deaf Characters

Unfortunately, few good films with deaf characters have been released on video. Most films portraying deaf characters use old stereotypes or outright misunderstandings about the deaf. Many of the good ones that are on video are not captioned and thus not accessible to deaf people themselves. This list is restricted to available films that give a reasonably unbiased image of deaf people *and* are captioned. Titles listed are available from most home video distributors.

Beyond Silence, 107 min., 1997. Directed by Caroline Link, 1996. ISBN 0–7888–1394–3 (VHS).

An Academy Award–nominated German film about the love and tensions that develop between deaf parents and their hearing daughter who wishes to pursue her dream of a career in music. In an unusual case of internationalism, American deaf actor Howie Seago and French deaf actress Emmanuelle Laborit were cast as the deaf German parents, both learning German Sign Language for their roles. In German with English subtitles and closed-captioned. Miramax Home Entertainment.

Children of a Lesser God, 110 min., 1986. ISBN 0–7921–0034–4 (VHS).

The movie version of the Tony Award–winning play about the complex relationship between a hearing male teacher of the deaf and a deaf woman with a chip on her shoulder. Deaf actress Marlee Matlin won an Academy Award for this, her first movie role. Closed-captioned. Paramount Home Video.

Hear No Evil, 98 min., 1993. ISBN 0–7939–1988–3 (VHS).

Deaf actress Marlee Matlin is the target in this suspense-thriller. She is stalked by a killer who wants a stolen gold coin that, unknown to her, is hidden inside her pager, while a hearing police agent tries to simultaneously protect her and find out who the villain is. Closed-captioned. Fox Video.

His Bodyguard, 88 min., 1998. ISBN 0–7921–5260–3 (VHS).

This film makes an interesting comparison with the previous one, *Hear No Evil*. In this one, deaf actor Anthony Naturale is the only eyewitness to a major theft, and a beautiful security agent is assigned as his bodyguard against the thieves who are trying to eliminate the sole witness. Their initial animosity turns to mutual respect and eventually deep affection. Closed-captioned. Paramount Home Video.

For Children

Beauty and the Beast, 59 min., 1994.

The Spectrum Deaf Theatre, directed by award-winning deaf actress Elizabeth Quinn, performs a sign language version of the classic tale. In sign language and with closed captions. Gibbe Productions, 3101 North Fitzhugh, Suite 550, Dallas, TX 75204 (http://www.gibbe.com).

Four for You: Fables and Fairy Tales, 5 videocassettes, each 60 min., 1988.

Each video presents internationally renowned American Sign Language performers and storytellers retelling four fables of Aesop, each told two different ways, and two traditional fairy tales. Voice-over narration makes these enjoyable to hearing audiences too. Sign Media, Inc.

Sign and ABCs: A New Way to Play, 50 min., 1998. ISBN 0–932314–97–X (VHS).

A deaf actor and a deaf actress show both deaf and hearing children how to sign "The Alphabet Song" and "Before the ABCs." Aylmer Press, Box 2302, Madison, WI 53701 (http://www.signit2.com.)

Sign-Me-a-Story, 30 min., 1987. ISBN 0–394–89232–1 (VHS).
"Goldilocks and the Three Bears" and "Little Red Riding Hood" are presented by talented deaf actors, with closed captions and voice-overs for all audiences. Random House Video.

Twice Told Stories, 5 videocassettes, various lengths.
Noted deaf actor and mime Bernard Bragg presents five children's stories in both American Sign Language and Signed English. Gallaudet University, Department of Television, Photography and Digital Media, 800 Florida Avenue NE, Washington, DC 20002.

Learning American Sign Language

ASL Video Series, 12 videocassettes, each 60 to 90 min., 1994.
Suggested for the serious and committed student of sign language. Follows the Robinson family throughout life at work, home, and school, presenting many deaf people in natural settings. In addition to the ASL lessons, "Deaf History Segments" introduces many famous deaf people of the past and present and "Basic Rules of Grammar" helps with the understanding of the underlying structure of ASL. DeBee Communications.

Fingerspelling: Expressive and Receptive Fluency, 120 min., 1991.
Focuses entirely on fingerspelling, which uses various hand shapes to represent the letters of the English alphabet and is used to represent proper names and English words having no corresponding sign. Appropriate for both beginning and intermediate audiences. Does not teach fingerspelling from scratch, but rather supplements the initial learning of fingerspelling from a teacher or from other videos. DawnSignPress.

Say It by Signing, 60 min., 1985.
Suggested for the casual student of sign language. Teaches very basic ASL through dramatized settings from everyday life. From the Crown Living Language series. Random House Video. Available from FACETS (http://www.facets.org) and other video distributors.

You Can Sign! American Sign Language for Beginners, 3 videocassettes, total ca. 5 hr. 17 min., 1998.
Lessons present the daily routines of a family with a deaf father, a hearing mother, and two deaf children, introducing new vocabulary, grammatical information, practice sentences, a practice story for reinforcement, and immediate ASL skills. Harris Communications, Inc., 15159 Technology Drive, Eden Prairie, MN 55344–2277 (http:// harriscomm.com).

Non-Narrated

Although not made with deaf audiences in mind, the following two non-narrated films are excellent choices, not least because they are considered cinema classics.

An Occurrence at Owl Creek Bridge, 27 min., b&w, 1962.
An adaptation of Ambrose Bierce's short story of a hanged Civil War soldier's last minutes. Telecast on TV's Twilight Zone series and winner of several awards. Video

Yesteryear, Box C, Sandy Hook, CT 06482 (http://www.yesteryear.com) and other distributors.

The Red Balloon, 34 min., 1956.

An award-winning fantasy about Pascal, a lonely French boy who befriends a wondrous red balloon that follows him everywhere. Video Yesteryear, Box C, Sandy Hook, CT 06482 (http://www.yesteryear.com) and other distributors.

Special Interest

Assistive Devices for Hearing-Impaired Persons, 17 min., 1988.

Provides an overview of the types of assistive devices available for deaf people, including timers with lights, doorbell devices, telephone accessories (including signal lights, amplifiers, and inductive listening coils), direct audio input devices, TTYs/TDDs, infrared and FM listening systems, closed-caption decoders, and central communication units. New York League for the Hard of Hearing, 71 West 23rd Street, New York, NY 10010–4162 (http://www.lhh.org).

Deaf Mosaic, 30 min. each, 1985–1995.

A monthly television-magazine program featuring a variety of American and worldwide subjects related to the deaf community, in sign language, spoken English, and open captions. A total of 122 programs were produced. Individual programs of particular worth include #312, *Deaf President Now*; #411, *Performing Arts Special*; #505–506, *The Deaf Way*; #707, *The Age of AIDS*; #909, *The 1993 World Games for the Deaf*; and #912, *The National Theatre of the Deaf*. Gallaudet University, Department of Television, Film and Photography, 800 Florida Avenue NE, Washington, DC 20002–3695.

Using Your TTY/TDD, 20 min., 1989.

A training video for both deaf and hearing people in how to use a Telecommunications Device for the Deaf (TTY or TDD). Open captions and spoken narration explain how to make calls, TTY etiquette and rules of use, and directories of TTY numbers. Telecommunications for the Deaf, Inc., 8630 Fenton Street, Suite 604, Silver Spring, MD 20910–3803 (http://www.tdi-online.org).

NOTE

1. Not until Gallaudet University produced an open-captioned videotape of *The Jazz Singer* for viewing by its deaf students—over half a century after the original release of the film—did deaf people have access to this first "talky."

REFERENCES

Dalton, Phyllis I. 1985. *Library Service to the Deaf and Hearing Impaired*. Phoenix, AZ: Oryx Press.
Gallaudet Encyclopedia of Deaf People and Deafness. 1987. New York: McGraw-Hill.
Gannon, Jack R. 1981. *Deaf Heritage: A Narrative History of Deaf America*. Silver Spring, MD: National Association of the Deaf.
Goddard, Martha L., ed. 1995. *Guidelines for Library and Information Services for the*

American Deaf Community. Chicago: Association of Specialized and Cooperative Library Agencies, American Library Association,

Koskinen, Patricia. 1986. "Using Captioned Television in Classroom Reading Instruction." *Teaching English to Deaf and Second-Language Students* 6 (Spring): 15–19.

National Captioning Institute. 1990. "Using Captioned Television to Improve the Reading Proficiency of Language Minority Students." Falls Church, VA: The Institute. Available through the ERIC Document Reproduction Service, ED332542.

Parlato, Salvatore. 1973. *Films—Too Good for Words: A Directory of Non-narrated 16mm Films.* New York: Bowker.

Schein, Jerome D. 1987. "Deaf Population—Demography." In *Gallaudet Encyclopedia of Deaf People and Deafness.* New York: McGraw-Hill.

Schein, Jerome D., and Delk, Marcus T. 1974. *The Deaf Population of the United States.* Silver Spring, MD: National Association of the Deaf.

Schuchman, John S. 1988. *Hollywood Speaks: Deafness in the Film Entertainment Industry.* Urbana: University of Illinois Press.

U.S. Census Bureau. *Disability 1990 Census Table 3* (2000, June 6). Washington, DC: U.S. Census Bureau. Retrieved October 15, 2000 from the World Wide Web: http://www.census.gov/hhes/www/disable/census/tables/tab3us.html.

U.S. *Congressional Record.* 1976. 122, no. 144 (September 22): H10875.

U.S. *Federal Register.* 1991. 56: 144 (July 26): 35567, 35571, 35573, 35690.

Walker, Alexander. 1979. *The Shattered Silents: How the Talkies Came to Stay.* New York: Morrow.

Wright, Kieth C. 1989. *Library and Information Services for Handicapped Individuals.* Littleton, CO: Libraries Unlimited.

RECOMMENDED READING AND WEB SITES

Brentano, Michael R., and McConnaughey, Jefferson. 2000. "TV Access for the Deaf, Blind Reaches New Heights." *National Law Journal* (October 30): B12.

"Closed Caption Issues." http://www.deafmillennium.net/closedcaption/. Includes useful information of issues, legislation, court cases, and resources related to captioning.

Closed Captioning Web. http://www.captions.org/. Includes a wealth of information and links to resources related to captioning, including legislative updates, information about captioned movies and movie distributors, job information, information related to assistive technology hardware.

Kovalik, Gail, and Kruppenbacher, Frank. 1994. "Complying with the ADA: Strategies for Libraries to Serve Individuals with Hearing Impairments." *MC Journal: The Journal of Academic Media Librarianship* (Winter): 1–19. http://wings.buffalo.edu/publications/mcjrnl/v2n1/kovalik.html.

Mack, Tara. 1996. "Getting the Word Out: Closed-captioners Let Their Fingers Do the Talking (National Captioning Institute)." *Washington Post* (August 23): D1.

Reed, C. A., and Davenport, S. E. 1999. "American Sign Language on the Web: A Guide to the Best Sites for Your Library." *Internet Reference Services Quarterly* 4: 97.

Chapter 7

Accessible Video Services for People Who Are Blind or Visually Impaired

Mary Watkins and Kim Charlson

Full enjoyment of television, videos and other forms of popular culture has been denied to people with visual impairment; now the technology is available to turn that situation around.
—*Who's Watching? A Profile of the Blind and Visually Impaired Audience for Television and Video* (Packer and Kirchner 1997)

For 12 million blind and visually impaired Americans, 1990 marked the debut of a new era promising fuller access to television programming through an innovative service called Descriptive Video Service, developed by Boston public broadcaster WGBH. In this service, specially added voice-over descriptions convey key visual elements in a program that a visually impaired viewer would ordinarily miss. These descriptions are carefully inserted into the natural pauses in dialogue, and do not interfere with the soundtrack. Actions, costumes, gestures, and scene changes are just a few of the crucial elements described—vital information that helps to engage the viewer who is blind with the story.

Described programs and films inform and entertain people who previously were unable to gain access to a medium that continues to define our culture as we enter the twenty-first century. Description is also available in other forms of media including theatrical releases, live theater performances, multimedia content on Web sites, and training videos. The terms "video description," "audio description," and "narrative description" are sometimes used interchangeably.

For the purposes of clarity, the term "audio description" is used throughout this chapter. Descriptive Video Service® refers to the department at WGBH in Boston responsible for producing described programs and videos.

BACKGROUND OF AUDIO DESCRIPTION

Audio description for television is the brainchild of Dr. Barry Cronin of WGBH. When stereo television was developed in 1984, Cronin began seeking ways to provide broadcast services to all audiences via the second audio program channel (SAP) available on stereo TVs and VCRs. Cronin recalled an announcer named Whispering Smith on a New York television station bowling show, who would describe what was happening for the viewer. Cronin realized a similar concept could be used to benefit blind and visually impaired people by employing the new audio channel to broadcast narrated descriptions.

In the late 1980s, Cronin and WGBH, already pioneers in developing television captioning for deaf and hard-of-hearing viewers in the 1970s, worked with The Metropolitan Washington Ear, Inc., which had been providing "live" audio description of stage performances since 1981. Other organizations also began applying this audio description concept for video formats, including the Narrative Television Network (NTN) of Tulsa, Oklahoma in 1989 and the late Gregory Frazier's AudioVision.

In 1990, WGBH launched Descriptive Video Service® (DVS®) as a free national service. (Note: Descriptive Video Service and DVS are registered trademarks of WGBH/Boston.) Blind and visually impaired audiences were overwhelmingly enthusiastic about the service and immediately began lobbying for more described programs. During these years, the availability of closed captioning was mushrooming (the major broadcast networks first announced 100 percent of prime time and then virtually their entire schedules as accessible to deaf and hard-of-hearing viewers). Advocates in the blindness community began to question why the concept of accessible TV programming did not include them and their families.

Since 1990, DVS has described more than 2,200 PBS programs, including *The American Experience, Arthur, ExxonMobil Masterpiece Theatre, Mystery!, Nature, and more than 80 films for the Turner Classic Movies cable channel, including Casablanca, Citizen Kane, National Velvet,* and *King Kong.*

Audio description is available to home viewers who turn on (or select) the SAP channel; the regular program audio is unaffected for those who don't activate SAP. Second Audio Program reception and audio playback is a standard feature on most television sets and VCRs built since 1990.

Since 1991, DVS has made available home videos for purchase by individuals and institutions to facilitate development of private or organizational accessible video collections. DVS provides more than 200 openly described home videos through funding from the U.S. Department of Education and through arrangements with most of the major Hollywood studios. These videos are available via direct mail purchase and for loan at over 1,200 libraries nationwide.

An additional description service provider, the Narrative Television Network (NTN), describes selected episodes of television series including *Bonanza, Matlock, The Andy Griffith Show*, and *The Streets of San Francisco*, which appear on the GoodLife TV cable network (formerly the Nostalgia Channel). NTN programs are normally provided with open description, meaning there is no need for use of the SAP feature. Open description means all viewers listen to the narration and do not have the option to turn off the added narration. NTN also provides a selection of public domain television shows and movies as openly described VHS videos for use by libraries and other institutions. These videos may be copied by these organizations at no charge, through an NTN agreement with the producers, for loan to blind and visually impaired borrowers. NTN also makes these films available through streaming technology on its Web site, www.narrativetv.com. Major support for DVS and NTN comes from the U.S. Department of Education.

AUDIENCE FOR VIDEO DESCRIPTIONS

It is estimated that more than 12 million visually impaired people can benefit from descriptive video, according to the American Foundation for the Blind (AFB) and other professionals in the field of blindness and visual impairment. AFB has analyzed a variety of data on blindness and visual impairment and has written a widely used resource manual on the subject (Kirchner 1988; Packer and Kirchner 1997, 1998).

The figure of 12 million visually impaired persons is based primarily on an annual measure collected by the Health Interview Survey (HIS) of the National Center for Health Statistics (NCHS). It includes people with any problem in seeing that is not correctable with ordinary glasses or contact lenses.

Some basic demographic characteristics about the non-institutionalized visually impaired population have been reported. For example, most are 65 years of age and older and female. Also, the non-white population's rate of vision loss is higher than for whites of all ages.

Among the estimated 12 million in the target population for video description, there is, of course, a wide range of visual loss or impairment. Nearly 400,000 people report they are totally blind in both eyes. In addition, 45,000 persons in nursing homes are reported to be totally blind (LaPlante 1988).

The NCHS indicates that eye problems now rank third, after heart disease and arthritis, among chronic conditions that restrict the normal daily activities of people 65 years of age and older. The National Eye Health Education Program's (NEHEP) Glaucoma Awareness Project, a program of the National Eye Institute, National Institutes of Health, states, "Over 50 million Americans are at high risk of losing their eyesight to glaucoma or diabetes-related eye disease. For glaucoma, this includes African Americans over age 40 and everyone over age 60, and for all people with diabetes." (National Eye Health Education Program: http://www.nei.nih.gov/gam2001/index.htm).

OTHER POPULATIONS USING AUDIO DESCRIPTION

Throughout the history of research and development in media access technologies, many valuable alternate uses of audio description have been encountered. Like captioning, audiences outside of the core group have turned to the service for their own needs.

Elders

A significant additional audience for audio description can be found in the elder population. Many in this group experience losses in vision as a natural result of the aging process, but are unlikely to identify themselves with—or be identified as—visually impaired. While many older people are reluctant to use assistive devices, the discreet nature of descriptions and the fact that no special equipment is needed to use it increase the likelihood of use among this population.

People with Learning Disabilities

Films and videos that contain video description appear to be especially well suited to the needs of children with learning disabilities. Because the medium has high visual appeal along with rich audio description, it has a great potential for both capturing a child's attention and enhancing information processing. By providing similar information in two modes, audio description capitalizes on the different perceptual strengths of children with learning disabilities (LD), utilizing their stronger learning capability and pairing it with their less-developed modality to reinforce their comprehension of information. From a teacher's perspective, the learning acquired through viewing educational videos in the classroom could be particularly meaningful for students with learning disabilities.

Since so little work has been done in the field of audio description for students with learning disabilities, WGBH sought to test the concept by interviewing 22 professionals in the fields of learning disability, attention disorders, and head injury; 17 watched a described videotape sampler before the interview (Morse 1996). Experts noted that audio description supplies multiple extra cues about what's important during the program, and about how people interact, including visual and behavioral cues. It was felt that this additional information might help students with learning disabilities grasp or figure out causal links for themselves.

The consensus among the study's professionals who were familiar with nonverbal learning disabilities was that this population is likely to benefit greatly from described videos, especially descriptions that provide focus on body language, gesture, and facial expression. These subtle behavioral nuances, while challenging for students to interpret, are essential for understanding the dynamics of social interaction. Nonetheless, further research is needed to determine specific effects and benefits of audio description for individuals with learning or cognitive disabilities.

Non-Disabled Viewers

One viewer wrote to WGBH's DVS department with the following comment:

> Even though my wife and I are fully sighted, as are our two children, we have found that the concise but colorful descriptions of the action on the screen helped us to enjoy our programs with a whole new dimension of perception. Often the narrator describes little details that we would certainly have missed, details which enhance our viewing pleasure. Our children have also increased their working vocabulary and have learned to be more observant participants in the shows they watch with DVS.
> —Ira Marc Goldberg, Los Angeles, CA

Descriptions can also be useful when a viewer is doing several things at once, needs to attend to something, or leaves the room during a program. Some viewers with limited English proficiency have found description helpful in clarifying vocabulary and increasing their understanding of the language. While these uses are not the original intent of the service, they need to be taken into account when considering the potential audience for and potential benefits of audio description.

This has certainly been the case for closed captioning: the majority of beneficiaries of this now pervasive service are people who watch captions in health clubs, sports bars, airport lounges, and other places where ambient audio makes captioned TV an ideal solution.

COLLECTION DEVELOPMENT ISSUES

The addition of described videos to your library's video collection is an excellent method for providing people who are blind or visually impaired with access to the library's overall video collection services. At the present time, distributors who sell described videos are limited to the pioneering DVS Home Video out of Boston, Massachusetts, (800) 333–1203, access@wgbh.org. Hundreds of described videos are presently sold to thousands of libraries, individuals, and organizations across the country.

In determining how much of your budget can be designated for described videos, you will have to evaluate your potential user group and title availability. Also keep in mind the added advantage of DVS Home Videos—that they include closed captioning on their titles, so your accessibility can be further expanded to deaf and hard-of-hearing patrons.

CATALOGING ISSUES

After your described videos have been ordered and received, they will need to be cataloged and made available for circulation. If your library does original cataloging of its described videos, you should be clear and consistent in identifying the video title as "described." It is helpful to staff and library borrowers alike, if cataloging entries indicate clearly that the video is described. Whichever term your library chooses to use—"described video," "audio described video," or "DVS video"—be consistent. It should be evident when the title appears on the screen that the specific holding is a described video. Staff may opt to enter the designation under "edition," or under the information relating to the producer. Whichever option your library selects, consistency will help when staff or patrons choose to search for described videos. It will also assist staff in identifying a complete and up-to-date listing of all described videos in your library's collection or available to patrons through your library's regional or cooperative library network that can be ordered through interlibrary loan.

The issues outlined above are also relevant if your library uses MARC records entered by another library to prepare your library's catalog records for described videos. If the MARC record doesn't indicate that the video is described, you should modify the record to clearly reflect that information. It is certainly possible that the MARC record your library utilized to prepare its catalog record for a specific title was not a described video. It therefore would not have indicated such information, and it will be necessary for staff to add the designation of described video.

PREPARING THE VIDEO FOR SHELVING

All titles purchased from DVS Home Video should arrive with two strips of clear adhesive braille that is the title label. These labels should be affixed to both the videotape itself and the container. These braille labels are very important to blind and visually impaired borrowers and assist them in keeping the library's video safe and out of their own personal collections. Your library may also choose to design a printed label that is in large, clear print—in 16- to 18-point type, with the type style being a simple, straightforward, readable font. Such large print labels will assist low-vision borrowers to more easily identify the described videos.

SHELVING ISSUES

When the videos are ready to be placed on the library shelves, many library staff have then needed to make some policy decisions as to where and how they would be shelved. Some libraries have opted to place all described videos for children as a distinct group within the children's collection where all videos for children are shelved. Likewise, the described videos for young adults would be shelved with other young adult videos. Adult described videos would also then be shelved as a group among the adult video collection.

Other libraries have opted to intermix described videos within the regular video collection, thus not indicating that there is any difference between regular and described videos. Still other libraries have opted to completely separate described videos within the children's, young adult, or adult collections in a distinct area.

Justification for the decision to place described videos among all of the other videos in the library's collection is based on a philosophical concept that this integrates the described videos into the library's full collection. It then keeps the described videos in the "mainstream" circulation and does not make them separate or special collections.

If patrons then want to borrow described videos they would go to the shelves where all videos are kept to find the described videos—not to a separate and distinct shelf area for the described videos. However, the drawback to this policy is that if the described videos are on the shelf with all other videos, anyone can borrow them at any time. This means that for the patron with a visual impairment who wants to borrow a described video, there may not be any available because they are checked out to other library patrons. Conversely, general patrons may not realize that they are checking out a described video, and will get home and put the video in for viewing and be quite surprised that there is a voice telling them what's happening on the screen. Library staff must decide if they feel the so-called advantage of an integrated collection outweighs the disadvantages of not having described videos available when the patron with a disability wishes to borrow them.

Still other libraries have opted to keep described videos separate and distinct and have placed them in a designated area specifically for described videos, regardless of age level. This method can be a plus for the target population, because they can become familiar with where the described videos are shelved and can search through them by using the braille and large-print labels to independently make a selection. Feedback from the disability community has been quite strong that they do not mind sharing described videos with other library borrowers, but when they come into the library to check out one for themselves, they really want something to be available.

If your library's described video collection is housed separately, and is distinct from other videos, you should design signage that is clear, with large print for easy identification. The signs should say "Audio Described Media" or "DVS Home Videos," and you might opt to place the DVS logo or the audio description icon on the signs as well. It would also be helpful to the general public if there were a sign that explains what described videos are and how they work— whichever shelving method you employ. Educating the public will be very important, particularly if your described videos are intermixed with the overall video collection.

LENDING POLICIES

Libraries must make a number of lending policy decisions regarding the circulation of described videos. We have already discussed some areas where possible policy decisions must be made by library staff.

The library's loan period may also need to be reviewed. If your general lending period for videos is seven days, you may wish to extend the loan period for described videos to fourteen days to accommodate borrowers who find it more difficult to get to the library. Many people with disabilities do not drive and must plan their travel or must arrange transportation to the library to return materials. Friends or family members may also return borrowed materials for them. Is your library willing to consider loaning described videos through the mail to people who have disabilities or who have difficulty traveling to the library?

Many libraries do not allow patrons to place videos on reserve. It is recommended that your library consider adoption of a policy that makes it possible for borrowers with disabilities to place described videos on reserve. In turn, if borrowers reserving videos have visual impairments, the library should notify them by phone rather than through the mail when the video is available. It could even be arranged for library staff to send videos directly to patrons when they become available.

FEDERAL MANDATES FOR DESCRIBED TELEVISION AND CABLE PROGRAMMING

In conjunction with a national celebration of the tenth anniversary of the Americans with Disabilities Act (enacted July 26,1990. See http://www.usdoj. gov/crt/ada/adahom1.htm), the Federal Communications Commission (FCC) took steps to increase the accessibility of television for persons who are blind or visually impaired.

On July 21, 2000, the FCC voted to mandate the provision of described programming on TV stations (ABC, CBS, Fox, NBC affiliates) in the top 25 television major markets, effective between April and June 2002.[1] This rule requires participating broadcasters to provide a minimum of 50 hours of described prime-time and/or children's programming per calendar quarter, which amounts to approximately four hours per week.

Multichannel video programming distributors (MVPDs)—such as satellite and cable systems—with at least 50,000 subscribers will follow the same guidelines for each of the top five national non-broadcast networks they carry. PBS stations already air approximately 10 hours of described programming per week and are exempt from the rule.

Incorporated into the rule is the mandatory broadcast of accessible emergency announcements (e.g., storm warnings) by all TV stations and MVPDs that typically provide local emergency information. This requires that by early 2001 the crucial details of emergency announcements be made accessible to those who are blind or visually impaired living within the affected local area.

Similar mandates to increase the amount of closed-captioned programming to nearly 100 percent by 2006 are now in place. For further information on efforts to increase the amount of accessible television and cable programming, visit http://access.wgbh.org, or the FCC's Web site, http://www.fcc.gov.

In 1993, in partnership with the Corporation for Public Broadcasting (CPB), WGBH established the CPB/WGBH National Center for Accessible Media (NCAM). NCAM is a research and development facility designed to extend the Boston public television station's previous media access efforts into new media, and to further the uses of captioning and audio description in the home, classroom, workplace, and community. Current projects involving video description include Web access efforts, developing access specifications for distance learning, development of design guidelines for making educational software and rich media accessible and "eDescription"—creating extended, enhanced, descriptive passages that will give blind and visually impaired children more context and richer language and cultural learning opportunities.

LIBRARIES AND THE BLIND/LOW-VISION COMMUNITY

The following are some fundamental questions that might help in thinking about library services and collections for blind and low-vision members of the community:

How Does a Viewer Watch DVS on Television?

A viewer must live within range of a PBS station that carries DVS and must have a stereo TV or a stereo VCR that includes the Second Audio Program (SAP) feature, standard on most new stereo televisions and videocassette recorders. Inexpensive receivers that convert TV sets to stereo with SAP also can be purchased. Viewers who subscribe to cable should ask the cable company to "pass through" stereo with SAP.

How Do Viewers Find Out if They Have SAP Capability?

To find out whether or not a TV or VCR has SAP capability, consult the owner's manual. Most TVs or VCRs purchased since 1995 are SAP equipped. To hear the narrated visual descriptions via a stereo TV or VCR, simply activate its SAP feature.

An SAP receiver is a device that is able to tune in, similar to a radio, an SAP channel. It can be used with or without a TV, depending on whether or not you want to receive the video picture. These are available either pre-tuned or adjustable.

The following companies produce SAP receivers:

Compol, Inc. (pre-tuned), (800) 972–0881; http://www.compolinc.com/.

Avocet Instruments, Inc. (pre-tuned), (800) 443–0728; http://www.avocetinst.com.

FM Atlas* (adjustable), (800) 605–2219; http://members.aol.com/fmatlas/home.html.

*This device can also receive the signal from Radio Reading Services (see International Association of Audio Information Services Web site [http://www.ukans.edu/~arnet/arrslinx.htm] for listing of radio reading services).

Where Are Described Television Broadcasts Available?

DVS is broadcast free to viewers by 168 participating public television stations reaching 80 percent of U.S. television households. To carry DVS, a station must be equipped to broadcast in stereo with SAP.

How Does a Viewer or Institution Get Described Movies on Home Video?

Over 200 described popular Hollywood movies and PBS programs are available for purchase by direct mail. *A viewer needs a regular VHS videocassette recorder (VCR) and a television to watch these videos and hear the descriptions. The SAP feature is not required.* Described home videos are also available for loan at over 1,200 libraries nationwide.

Which Television Programs, Feature Films, and Video Releases Are Described?

Television: Currently, you can find descriptions on select PBS programming including *Arthur, ExxonMobil Masterpiece Theatre, The American Experience, Nature, NOVA,* and *Zoom.*

Cable: WGBH's Descriptive Video Service has described over 80 feature films which run on the Turner Classic Movies cable network, including the DVS Showcase offered every Saturday evening at 8:00 P.M. (ET). The DVS Showcase has offered classics such as *Casablanca* and *North by Northwest.*

NTN has described selected episodes of popular series such as *The Andy Griffith Show, Matlock,* and *The Streets of San Francisco,* which appear on the GoodLife TV cable network.

Feature Films: Through WGBH's Motion Picture Access efforts (or MoPix), DVS has provided descriptions for 20 first-run film releases, including *Star Wars Episode 1: The Phantom Menace* and *The Patriot,* in time for their debut in theaters equipped with the DVS Theatrical® system. More movie theaters are installing the necessary equipment to accommodate described movies. The blind or visually impaired viewer checks out a special FM receiver headset at the theater and is able to listen to the description along with sighted moviegoers. In addition, more than 20 described films are now in distribution at IMAX®, OMNIMAX®, and other large-format theaters in cities such as Denver, Boston, Washington, DC, St. Louis, New Orleans, and Seattle. A complete list of theaters with access system installations is available at http://www.mopix.org.

Home Video: DVS sells described videos through a direct mail catalogue that offers more than 200 titles, including new and classic feature films and public television titles.

DVS Home Videos are also available for loan at over 1,200 libraries nationwide. WGBH is working to ensure description tracks are included in future DVD releases as well.

The World Wide Web: Narrative Television Network offers descriptions of a sizable number of films now in the public domain on its Web site, www.NarrativeTV.com. WGBH is working on several projects that will increase the amount of described multimedia available on Web sites.

How Is a Program or Video Described?

Describers watch a program and write a script describing key visual elements. They carefully time the placement and length of the description to fit within natural pauses in the dialogue. After a script is completed it is edited for continuity, clarity, and style conventions.

Narration is recorded and mixed with the original program audio in a unique "mix to pix" process to create a full description track. The description track is then laid back to the master either on a spare audio channel (for broadcast) or to a separate master (for home video distribution). For descriptions intended for large format or theatrical films, a full program mix is not created. The descriptions are kept as a separate track and delivered to theaters as part of the motion picture sound track.

What Special Skills Do Describers Have?

Describers are a diverse group of individuals, among them former educators, writers, trained musicians, and avid travelers. They possess degrees in a variety of fields, but share key skills for describers. They must be tireless researchers, demonstrate strong writing skills, and be very detail-oriented. When hired, each describer undergoes an extensive training program.

In What Other Venues Are Descriptions Provided?

Descriptions are available for selected live theater productions around the country, for museum exhibits, and for live events such as parades.

RESOURCES: MAJOR AUDIO DESCRIPTION PROVIDERS AND INFORMATION RESOURCES

CPB/WGBH National Center for Accessible Media (NCAM), Media Access Group at WGBH, 125 Western Avenue, Boston, MA 02134; (617) 300–3400; (617) 300–2459 (TTY); E-mail: access@wgbh.org; http://ncam.wgbh.org.

Descriptive Video Service (DVS), Media Access Group at WGBH, 125 Western Avenue, Boston, MA 02134; (617) 300–3600; E-mail: access@wgbh.org; http://access. wgbh.org.

To request a Home Video Catalogue in braille, call toll free: (888) 818–1181, or in large print, call toll free: (888) 818–1999. To hear an audio version of the catalogue, or to obtain taped information about DVS, call (800) 333–1203.

Metropolitan Washington Ear, Inc., 35 University Boulevard East, Silver Spring, MD 20910; (301) 681–6636, (301) 681–5227; E-mail: washear@his.com; http://www.his. com/~washear/.

Narrative Television Network (NTN), 5840 South Memorial Drive, Suite 312, Tulsa, OK 74145–9082; (800) 801–8184; (918) 627–1000; Fax: (918) 627–4101; E-mail: webmaster@narrativetv.com; http://www.narrativetv.com.

MAJOR ADVOCACY AND CONSUMER ORGANIZATIONS

American Council of the Blind, 1155 15th Street NW, Suite 1004, Washington, DC 20005; (202) 467–5081, (800) 424–8666; Fax: (202) 467–5085; E-mail: info@acb.org; http://www.acb.org.

American Foundation for the Blind, 11 Penn Plaza, Suite 300, New York, NY 10001; (212) 502–7600, (800) 232–5463; Fax: (212) 502–7777; E-mail: afbinfo@afb.org; http://www.afb.org.

National Association of Parents of Children with Visual Impairments, P.O. Box 317, Watertown, MA 02272–0317; (800) 562–6265; Fax: (617) 972–7444; E-mail: Napvi@ perkins.pvt.k12.ma.us; http://www.spedex.com/NAPVI.

National Federation of the Blind, 1800 Johnson Street, Baltimore, MD 21230; (410) 659–9314; Fax: (410) 685–5653; http://www.nfb.org.

ACCESS-RELATED WEB-BASED LISTSERVS

Audio Description List (AUDIODESCL), the list for audio description, allows describers, consumers, presenters, and others to create a network in the international community now using description services. To subscribe, send an e-mail message to listproc@lists.acs.ohiostate.edu. The body of the message must contain only the following line: subscribe audiodescl Yourfirstname Yourlastname.

NOTES

Mention of a product or service in this chapter does not constitute an endorsement. The intent is to increase awareness of items that may be helpful to viewers.

1. For the text of this Report and Order and other documents pertaining to it, see http: //www.fcc.gov/cib/dro/video-description.html. For discussions of this mandate and its implications for users, see "FCC Adopts Rules" (2000).

REFERENCES

"FCC Adopts Rules for Video Description." 2000. *Journal of Disability Policy Studies* (Fall): 127.

"Letter from the Director, Glaucoma Awareness Month." 2001. Rosemary Janiszewski, M.S., CHES, Director, National Eye Health Education Program (NEHEP), National Eye Institute, National Institutes of Health, January. http://www.nei.nih. gov/gam2001/index.htm.

Kirchner, Corinne. 1988. *Data on Blindness and Visual Impairment in the U.S.: A Resource Manual on Social Demographic Characteristics, Education, Employment and Income, and Service Delivery.* New York: American Foundation for the Blind.

LaPlante, Mitchell P. 1988. *Data on Disability from the National Health Interview Survey, 1983–85.* Washington, DC: National Institute on Disability and Rehabilitation Research.

Morse, Ann B. 1996. *Described Video Programming: Potential Application for Learning Disabled Students.* Boston: CPB/WGBH National Center for Accessible Media.

Packer, Jaclyn, and Kirchner, Corinne. 1998. "Executive Summary: Project to Conduct Research on Described Video's Audience and Methods of Distribution" (U.S. Department of Education Grant). http://www.igc.org/afb/dv_exec.html.

Packer, Jaclyn, and Kirchner, Corinne. 1997. *Who's Watching? A Profile of the Blind and Visually Impaired Audience for Television and Video.* New York: American Foundation for the Blind.

Chapter 8

Accessing Primary Source Public Affairs Programming

Robert X. Browning

Modern history is televised history. Virtually every significant public event of the last 50 years has been televised. The advent of videotape in the 1960s, ironically never contemplated as an archival medium, made possible the preservation of the political events that allow us to re-experience and re-analyze events first experienced on television.

Before the advent of satellite and cable television technology in the late 1970s, very few events were seen in their entirety. Occasionally, the broadcast networks would interrupt their daily programming to cover news events. It was the creation of C-SPAN in 1979 that took the medium of television and used it to transmit daily public affairs events in their entirety. C-SPAN was followed a year later by CNN which added news reports, interpretation, and advertising to the mix. Twenty years later we would find multiple cable news networks including MSNBC, Fox News Channel, and CNBC.

It is the uninterrupted, unedited, balanced coverage of C-SPAN that creates an unrivalled historical video record. These events range from the ordinary to the extraordinary activities of government. They include the White House briefings, congressional news conferences, congressional hearings, presidential speeches, appearances, and news conferences. Political campaigns, conventions, victory and concession speeches are covered in their entirety. The complete coverage of all House and Senate sessions is the daily staple of the network.

The extensive televised coverage of public affairs events, such as the Persian Gulf War or the impeachment of a president, raised to a new level the interest in video archives as a research resource for primary source documents. Interest is high in documents that move—or moving-image documents, as they have been termed. Just as we assume that yesterday's newspapers are preserved in libraries for today's research scholar, many assume that today's videotapes are being preserved for tomorrow's research. With the dramatic growth in the use and reliance on videotaped coverage, it is useful to assess the availability and access of public affairs videotape collections.

The good news is that extensive collections do already exist and that use will become easier and more commonplace as computer and video technology continue to develop rapidly. Thus, today's scholars of impeachment, presidential campaigns, judicial nominations, or the Congress can expect to spend many hours viewing videotapes, much as scholars have spent time perusing boxes of manuscripts and reviewing reels of microfilmed documents. Tomorrow's scholars will have an even easier time reviewing these collections on computers from their own libraries, offices, and homes.

In this chapter, the organization and mission of the C-SPAN Archives will be discussed. In addition, the scope of other public affairs collections will be outlined. Finally, research issues and questions that are now possible because of the existence of these primary source collections will be covered.

THE ORIGIN AND EVOLUTION OF THE C-SPAN ARCHIVES

The Public Affairs Video Archives was created in 1987 at Purdue University to record, catalog, and distribute all programming of the Cable Satellite Public Affairs Network (C-SPAN) for educational and research use. The Archives thus built on the tradition established over 30 years ago by the Vanderbilt Television News Archive of recording all the television programming off-site, indexing it, and making it available to scholars for academic purposes. However, the Public Affairs Video Archives differed from other collections such as Vanderbilt or deposit collections such as the Library of Congress and the National Archives in significant ways. The Archives operated at Purdue University from 1987 until 1998. In 1998, the Archives separated from Purdue University and became an operating unit of C-SPAN. The change altered the financing of the Archives, but the mission and operating philosophy remained much the same.

The idea for the Archives originated in a discussion on the Purdue University campus with the chairman and founder of C-SPAN, Brian Lamb. Lamb, a 1964 Purdue University graduate, started C-SPAN in 1978 as a non-profit, cable industry–sponsored cooperative. Its mission was to allow citizens to watch public affairs events, in their homes, via cable television or home satellite dish, without editing and without commentary, as if they were at the event themselves. C-SPAN first telecast via satellite on March 1979, when the U.S. House of Representatives first provided news organizations video access to its proceedings through a signal originating from House-controlled and -operated cameras.

Table 8.1
State-of-the-State Speeches Aired during the Clinton Impeachment Coverage (2000)

Program Type	First Run	Live	Reairs	Archival
Call-ins	1,101	1,101	968	179
House	1,074	1,074	28	0
Senate	1,016	1,016	51	0
Committees	498	120	1,180	0
White House	58	165	304	44
News Conferences	371	99	371	0
Public Affairs Events	2,575	766	5,351	385
International	73	5	134	1
Interviews	66	10	133	48
Vignettes	20	0	61	25
Promotions			83	0
Other	284	58	699	249
Total	7,136	4,414	9,363	931

Notes: All numbers are in hours.
Live airings are also counted within first run.
Archival hours include programs first airing prior to this year.

C-SPAN transmitted this signal in its entirety whenever the House was in session.

In 1980, C-SPAN began telecasting viewer call-ins with members of Congress, administration, and interest group officials. Coverage of National Press Club speeches and political campaigns began in 1980 and was followed by committee hearings in 1981. The network began 24-hour coverage in 1982. A second network was created in 1986 when the U.S. Senate followed the House lead and began creating a video record of its proceedings similar to the House. Today the two 24-hour networks transmit over 7,000 hours of first-run programming from Washington, around the country, and around the world.

The C-SPAN programming is much more diverse than most people first think. In 2000, for example, it included over 1,200 hours of campaign coverage, including all major debates, gavel-to-gavel convention coverage, and informal candidate appearances. International programming includes newscasts from other countries; British House of Commons Prime Minister's Question Time; and interviews and sessions of the Parliament from Germany, Argentina, Russia, Ireland, Japan, Hungary, France, Israel, Mexico, and Canada. In 2000, 40 state-of-the-state speeches were aired, all during the extensive Clinton impeachment coverage. Table 8.1 details the number and types of this programming.

Because the Archives was initially created not by C-SPAN but by Purdue University, it established an educational institution with direct responsibility for creating the policies for cataloging and use. The Archives was established by educators working with other educators nationwide. Through direct contact with users, we were able to understand how this video record was being used and could be made more accessible for research and teaching.

As the Archives grew, it outgrew its university base. The university did build a new facility for the Archives located in the Liberal Arts and Education Building adjacent to the faculty in political science and communication, who were the most active users of the collection. However, over time the demand for the materials grew rapidly in two non-education sectors. These were requests from consumer and corporate users. Initially, these users were outside the scope of the Archives' academic charter. Since the Archives had built an efficient and automated system for indexing, archiving, retrieving, processing, and duplicating requests, it began to process and fulfill tape requests received by C-SPAN. This contract-service provided revenue to supplement the educational tape sales and support the basic operations of the Archives.

From 1995 to 1998, C-SPAN and Purdue University created a contract to reflect the evolution of the Archives, the importance of the Archives to C-SPAN, and the necessary financial arrangements required to sustain the operation. The contract formalized a new relationship in which the Archives provided tape indexing and duplication services to C-SPAN in return for a portion of the proceeds and a guaranteed annual subsidy. This arrangement allowed the Archives to hire additional staff and invest in new equipment. With this budget, the Archives was able to handle the increased volume of tape requests and achieve financial stability through a guaranteed and adequate budget to sustain the operations. The C-SPAN Education Foundation provided annual research grants to the Archives to further the academic researchers using the collection.

A Licensed Collection

Because C-SPAN is both non profit and committed to encouraging educational use of its material, it agreed to the initial arrangement in which Purdue University would be licensed to distribute its programming for educational use. This arrangement had two major benefits. First, it permitted the Public Affairs Video Archives to retain all fees from the distribution of the programming—and thus to use those fees to finance the operation. Second, it permitted the Archives to provide duplicate copies directly to educators with a very clear license to use the material.

The unique arrangement that was developed between C-SPAN and Purdue University was the first of its kind. There was no other current, ongoing video collection in which the new material was immediately available to educators through a university that was granted rights by the copyright holder to distribute duplicate copies that could be permanently kept by end users at other institutions. Vanderbilt University, which provides an invaluable service through the recording and cataloging of nightly broadcast newscasts and news-related specials, was initially sued by CBS. The Vanderbilt Television News Archive operates under a provision of the copyright law that permits libraries to archive news broadcasts. This provision permits loans but not the permanent transfer of the recorded programs to the library collection of another institution or individual.

An Accessible Collection

The model for the Archives is one that might be followed by other networks that want to provide greater access to their material. Although other significant public affairs programming collections exist, such as the National Archives and the Library of Congress, access to these collections is generally quite limited. Often materials are not available for loan or duplication. Use is often restricted to viewing in-house by recognized scholars. (Refer to the Appendix for more information.)

Balancing the requirements of a university-based archive and the financing it needs is difficult. Ongoing archives such as the Purdue or Vanderbilt archives have continuing acquisition costs. In addition, there are the costs and logistics of maintaining phone, duplication, and shipping services to provide the materials that generate the income. After 11 years, Purdue concluded that the provision of the services that sustained the Archives was not compatible with the school's educational mission. The university valued the access to the collection, but not the operational elements required to sustain it.

The C-SPAN Archives is still located in West Lafayette, Indiana, near the Purdue University campus in the Purdue Research Park. Indexing, acquisition, and access policies remain the same as they were at Purdue University. C-SPAN recognized the value of providing copies of its materials to individuals who wanted to view them after they had aired. The Archives held 11 years of material and a system to maintain, index, and distribute it. C-SPAN acquired all of the inventory, physical, and intellectual property from the university to continue the operation. Purdue University continued to maintain a research collection of videotapes and a center to encourage video-based research in political science and communications.

Other significant collections are detailed in the Appendix. These include the Museum of Television and Radio, UCLA Film and Television Archive, and the George Foster Peabody Collection of the University of Georgia Library. Other museums, universities, and libraries are often depositories for local news collections. Many of these are acquired when the stations change from film to videotape or run out of space. Some institutions tape local news off-air. An effort to encourage and coordinate the preservation of local television news is headed by the Association of Moving Image Archivists. Local news needs to be preserved for its future historical significance, much like local newspapers have been considered for years. Libraries, museums, and historical societies have a significant role to play in their preservation and access.

The difference between most of these collections and the C-SPAN Archives is that the others, with one exception, require users to travel to the institution to use the videotapes. The exception is Vanderbilt, which loans tapes. Thus, each of these collections is important from a reference perspective in allowing libraries to direct patrons to other locations. None of these other collections, however, permit librarians to acquire materials to build their own reference collection.

The C-SPAN Archives is unique in this regard. It has archival and reference components certainly, but it also actively encourages the acquisition of duplicate videotapes by other institutions. Since its creation, over 100,000 duplicate tapes have been distributed. This distribution is of four distinct types.

The Individual Acquisition. A teacher sees something on C-SPAN and has either heard of the C-SPAN Archives or heard of C-SPAN's own education program, C-SPAN in the Classroom, or simply calls the network to ask if it sells tapes. All of the calls by educators to C-SPAN for videotapes are directed to the Archives. More and more of these calls are coming directly to the Archives' 800 telephone number. Since most programming is accessible in our computer system within 24 hours of airing, we can almost immediately identify programs over the phone and quote prices and cataloging numbers. Longer programs often require additional time to break them into smaller units. For example, users might only want one interview of a multihour *Look at Time Magazine.*

The General Inquiry. Since the Archives has such a diverse collection of programming, many inquiries come from teachers and libraries. They generally ask that we "send them a catalog." Since we catalog over 5,000 programs per year, and 75,000 to date, it is not possible to send complete free listings of all programming. We direct users to Web site http://*www.c-span.org/shop*, where 7,000 programs are listed with descriptions. Every program airing in the last 30 days can be found there as well as all book-related programs and other popular titles.

The Specific Inquiry. Many of these inquiries come from media specialists, librarians, and teachers. Someone might call to ask what programs we have on "multicultural diversity," or "ancient forests," or "ethics in journalism," or the "savings and loan failures." Some of these individuals are familiar with C-SPAN, while others will only know that the Archives distributes public affairs videotapes. We respond to these inquiries by using keyword, sponsor, individual name, or affiliation searches. The result is a very specialized "minicatalog," created for this user or in response to an earlier similar request.

The Library Acquisition. Increasingly, college and university libraries are purchasing entire videotape series to add to their own collections. A number of law schools, for example, have purchased the entire Robert Bork, David Souter, and Clarence Thomas nominations to add to the law library collection, much like books. The Bork nomination remains an excellent seminar in constitutional law and judicial interpretation. The Thomas nomination, however, vividly demonstrated the importance of the visual and audio record, and has increased law library awareness and acquisition of the videotape record.

Similarly, the Clinton impeachment was an event where the video record became so important. Librarians who use the *Congressional Record* debate are increasingly aware that the video record is also now available. As librarians become more aware of this resource, they become increasingly important intermediaries between the patron and Archives, helping the user hone the inquiry using our listings that we fax or mail, and our extensive Web site.

A Comprehensive Collection

The C-SPAN Archives is also unique in that it is the first complete archive of an entire network. Parts of the broadcast and new cable networks are available at other institutions. In addition, the networks all maintain their own archives. These archives, however, are primarily to provide footage to their own news programs. They often defray costs by selling footage to independent producers. They are not, however, readily accessible or affordable for scholars, nor would they contain a complete video record of everything ever produced or broadcast. The cost of time, space, and tape prevent this.

An Electronically Indexed Collection

While the Archives is a very large collection, it has the advantage of the use of technology and computers from the first day. The result is that we have no backlog of cataloging records to be input. We are currently exploring options for digitizing the collection and expect that process to begin within a year. That will enable even more opportunities to further expand the indexing, retrieval, and access to the collection.

The programs are indexed by type of program, policy area, keywords, names of individuals, titles, affiliation, organizations and events, committees, and location. These indexes are essentially chronologies in that they list all programs serially. In a particular policy area, one can follow the developments in areas such as judicial nominations, political campaigns, and foreign affairs. Figure 8.1 is an example of an Archives catalog listing.

An Educational Mission

C-SPAN and the C-SPAN Archives have a strong educational mission. The Archives was created because C-SPAN wanted to make its unique video record available for research and education. This is realized through our recording, archiving, and cataloging, without which there would be no easy way to know what has been telecast, find it, and obtain duplicate copies. The vast amount of material is still difficult to use because of the amount and the real time needed to review videotape.

To encourage educational use, C-SPAN develops lesson plans and holds educational seminars for teachers. C-SPAN also has created entire series of pro-

Figure 8.1
Example of Archives Catalog Listing

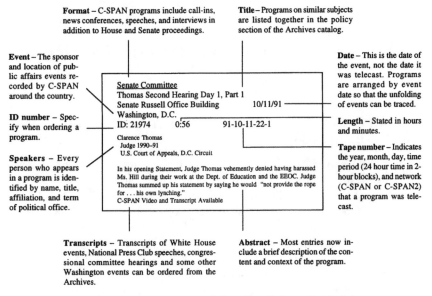

Format – C-SPAN programs include call-ins, news conferences, speeches, and interviews in addition to House and Senate proceedings.

Title – Programs on similar subjects are listed together in the policy section of the Archives catalog.

Event – The sponsor and location of public affairs events recorded by C-SPAN around the country.

ID number – Specify when ordering a program.

Speakers – Every person who appears in a program is identified by name, title, affiliation, and term of political office.

Senate Committee
Thomas Second Hearing Day 1, Part 1
Senate Russell Office Building   10/11/91
Washington, D.C.
ID: 21974   0:56   91-10-11-22-1
Clarence Thomas
    Judge 1990–91
    U.S. Court of Appeals, D.C. Circuit

In his opening Statement, Judge Thomas vehemently denied having harassed Ms. Hill during their work at the Dept. of Education and the EEOC. Judge Thomas summed up his statement by saying he would "not provide the rope for . . . his own lynching."
C-SPAN Video and Transcript Available

Date – This is the date of the event, not the date it was telecast. Programs are arranged by event date so that the unfolding of events can be traced.

Length – Stated in hours and minutes.

Tape number – Indicates the year, month, day, time period (24 hour time in 2-hour blocks), and network (C-SPAN or C-SPAN2) that a program was telecast.

Transcripts – Transcripts of White House events, National Press Club speeches, congressional committee hearings and some other Washington events can be ordered from the Archives.

Abstract – Most entries now include a brief description of the content and context of the program.

Videoguides – Some programs are accompanied by a videoguide that provides a detailed description of the program along with background information, suggested discussion questions and readings.

Searching – The Archives database can be searched on all fields. Programs can also be searched by keywords. The Archives staff performs searches to locate a specific program or to find programs in a particular area.

gramming for educational purposes. In 1994, the network covered the re-enactments of the seven Lincoln-Douglas debates in their original cities. In 1997, it followed the original path of Alexis de Tocqueville as he traveled America in the 1830s. In 1999, C-SPAN profiled the 42 men who have served as president. In 2001, the network will launch a new series on American writers. Each of these series has included related educational materials, educational activities, and related educational videotapes.

C-SPAN is thus a unique institution. As a non-profit organization, it has developed television as a vehicle to document public affairs events in their entirety. Through its archive, the network is preserving and providing access to these moving documents for education and research use. In the future, when we want to access our past, we will increasingly depend upon this invaluable collection.

C-SPAN brings public affairs programming to all parts of the country and now the world, without editing, and without commentary. It is left to the public to interpret and use the information. C-SPAN and its affiliated cable systems have simply lowered the cost of being informed citizens.

The C-SPAN Archives is extending the C-SPAN mission and commitment. We are bringing its public affairs programming to libraries and classrooms where it did not exist before. It is still without editing and without commentary. We have simply lowered even further the cost of educating the informed citizens of today and tomorrow.

Today and tomorrow, librarians nationwide also have an important role to play in helping patrons understand how they can use the primary source video record of the nation's public affairs.

APPENDIX: ADDITIONAL SOURCES OF PRIMARY SOURCE VIDEO COLLECTIONS

The C-SPAN Archives is unique in that it specializes in current primary source public affairs programs. There are other collections that might also be of interest to scholars. A brief summary of the other collections is included here. For further information about access to these collections, contact them directly.

Library of Congress, Motion Picture, Broadcasting and Recorded Sound Division, Room 336, Madison Building, Washington, DC 20540; (202) 707–1000, Motion Picture and Television: http://lcweb.loc.gov/rr/mopic/; Recorded Sound: http://lcweb.loc.gov/rr/record/rechome.html.

The Library of Congress National Archives and Record Service is the official repository for U.S. government-produced films and other federal records. The Library contains many copyrighted television news programs from ABC, CBS, and NBC. The Library's holdings of *CBS News* is the most extensive and includes weeknight and Sunday evening broadcasts, as well as early morning, morning, and midday news programs from 1975 to present. *CBS News* specials and documentaries from the 1950s to the present are also available. The ABC holdings include weeknight news broadcasts from 1977 and news specials from the 1960s to the present. Nightline programs from 1986 and 1987 are also held. Weeknight broadcasts of *NBC News* from September 1986 to the present and limited selections of *NBC Morning News* are also in the possession of the Library of Congress. The Library also holds certain *Today* and *Meet the Press* programs from NBC. Additionally, the Library contains CNN programming from 1989, and up to 200 hours of special programming each year.

Under an agreement with Vanderbilt University, the Library of Congress holds the master copies of all television news material available at Vanderbilt. Therefore, the news programs, held only on master copies, are not readily available to researchers at the Library of Congress. Researchers should contact Vanderbilt University to arrange for viewing the material. The copyrighted news programs may not be purchased or duplicated.

The Library of Congress has a growing collection of international news programs, including Russian newscasts. These holdings are indexed by date of broadcast and include a brief abstract of each program. The Library also houses the Embassy of South Vietnam Collection and the Public Archives of Canada.

Researchers may find newsreels dating from 1910, with hundreds of hours of additional "actuality" films dating from 1894 of interest. There are also MGM and Paramount issues from the 1930s and 1940s and a virtually complete collection of German, Japanese, and Italian newsreels from the same era.

The Library contains the Theodore Roosevelt Association collection acquired in 1967 through the National Park Service. The collection is significant as President Roosevelt was the first U.S. president whose life was extensively recorded in motion picture format. The collection of 381 films from the 1920s and 1930s contains films of many major political events, activities from Roosevelt's "Rough Rider" days, and Roosevelt's funeral.

Persons interested in researching programming at the Library of Congress should plan ahead and begin with inquiries by phone or mail. It often takes as long as three days to retrieve films from Library collections, and viewing time must be scheduled in advance. The researcher should also be aware that much of the Library's collections are copyrighted, and duplication of these materials is often not possible. Duplication of materials may be done only with written permission of the copyright owners and/or donors. Reference librarians and staff in the Public Services Office are available to assist you with questions.

National Archives, Motion Picture, Sound, and Video Branch, 7th and Pennsylvania Avenue, NW, Room 2W, Washington, DC 20408; (202) 786–0041; Information about holdings: http://www.nara.gov/research/bymedia/mo_int.html.

The National Archives collection is dedicated to the preservation of U.S. history. The collection is arranged by Record Group. The Stock Film Collection, which is located in a Washington suburb in Virginia, contains over 10,500 reels of stock film and videotape, which are available for viewing and duplication. The National Archives catalogs its holdings on card catalog and a database system.

As a great deal of the National Archives' holdings are in the public domain, many may be duplicated. Others may contain copyrighted materials, and items in the gift collection will require permission by the donor for duplication. Duplication services are provided through a private lab and take from three to eight weeks. Handouts with information on the National Archives' holdings, cataloging, sources, and price lists are available.

Public affairs researchers will find holdings from the Office of Inter-American Affairs, 1941–45; the U.S. House of Representatives, 1953–86; National Archives Collection of Foreign Records Seized, 1916–51; National Aeronautics and Space Administration (NASA), 1959–74; the President's Commission on the Assassination of President John F. Kennedy; and the United States Information Agency, 1942–86; among others.

Vanderbilt University Television News Archive, Baker Building, Suite 704, 110 21st Avenue South, Nashville, TN 37203; (615) 322–2927; http://tvnews.vanderbilt.edu/.

Vanderbilt Television Archive is composed mostly of network evening newscasts from 1968 to the present. Special newscasts of presidential speeches, debates, press conferences, and so forth, are also included in the collection.

Because of the nature of network news copyrights, material is not available for purchase or duplication. Tapes are loaned for the purpose of research, reference, and classroom instruction, for up to 90 days. There is a fee to borrow the tapes. Videotapes may also be viewed at the Archive during business hours.

Materials are abstracted by network, date, and time in the Archive's publication Television News Index and Abstracts. The publication is available by subscription or through many research libraries. In 1993, the Vanderbilt Archive received a major Ford Foundation grant to convert this index to machine-readable form and to make it available through the Internet. The abstracts and indexes are now online at www.tvnews.vanderbilt.edu.

UCLA Film and Television Archive, 1438 Melnitz Hall, University of California, Los Angeles, Los Angeles, CA 90024; (213) 206–8013; http://www.cinema.ucla.edu/archive.html.

The UCLA Television Archive, founded in 1965, operates as a preservation and research center. Its broad collection of films, studio prints, and newsreel footage makes it the largest university-based repository in the world.

The UCLA Archive has a large collection of documentaries, speeches, and campaign highlights from the career of John F. Kennedy. Material from the 1952 and 1956 presidential campaigns of Adlai Stevenson is also available. The UCLA Archive also holds a substantial collection of newsreels from the Hearst collection. Material from Hearst Metronome News material is available for licensing and reuse. A license fee is charged, depending on the intended use of the material.

Access to the collection is limited to researchers and scholars, in-house only. Research and screening fees may apply. The UCLA Archive Study Center is equipped with viewing machines. As clients must screen film with the assistance of UCLA Archive staff, appointments should be made as far in advance as possible.

Card and microfiche catalogs are available, and there is no fee to use these materials. Reference librarians are available to assist in special requests.

The Museum of Television and Radio, New York: 1 East 53rd Street, New York, NY 10022; (212) 752–4690; http://www.mtr.org/welcome.htm. Los Angeles: 465 North Beverly Drive, Beverly Hills, CA; (310) 786–1025.

The Museum of Television and Radio is operated as a non-profit institution. The collection is available for in-house viewing by the public, but no programs will be loaned or duplicated. Both radio and television programs are preserved. The collection contains news programs, foreign programming, inaugurations, Watergate hearings, and more than 25 years of political commercials.

The Museum utilizes a computer-generated card catalog that is cross-referenced by title, subject, date, network, and other significant categories.

Peabody Awards Collection, University of Georgia Library, Athens, GA 30602; (404) 542–3785; http://www.libs.uga.edu/peabody/pbacoll.html; Computerized catalog: http://gil.uga.edu/.

The Peabody film and videotape collection holds most Peabody Award–winning television and radio programs dating back to 1941. The collection is available for in-house research use only. Original materials may not be viewed, so the researcher's use is limited to those programs that have been transferred to videotape. This is generally limited to programs dating from 1974. No research fees are charged, and research requests may be made by mail or telephone.

Since the rights to all material are held by the original owner, duplication of any programming requires the permission of the original owner. Generally, the materials are not available for licensing or re-use.

Partial cataloging has been completed. Many of the earlier programs have not yet been cataloged.

Political Commercial Archive, Political Communication Center, University of Oklahoma, Department of Communication, 610 Elm Avenue, Norman, OK 73019–0335; (405) 325–3111; http://www.ou.edu/pccenter/index.html.

The Political Commercial Archive began as a private collection in 1956. It holds over 309,000 television commercials from 1950 to the present. The collection contains commercials for candidates running for office in a variety of elections, both local and national; commercials by special interest groups; and even commercials for elections in foreign countries. The length of the various commercials runs from a few seconds to 60 minutes. The material is available for research and re-use, subject to certain restrictions. Material is available for duplication, with the user responsible for securing permission and any clearances for use. The user must state the intended use of the footage and agree that use will be limited to that specific purpose. Usage fees are charged for material that is to be rebroadcast. Although the primary use of the collection is for researchers on-site, in certain, unusual cases, off-site rental may be possible for a fee to cover costs.

A looseleaf catalog lists programming. There is also computerized programming available for use by Political Commercial Archive staff and researchers.

National Jewish Archive of Broadcasting, The Jewish Museum, 1109 Fifth Avenue, New York, NY 10128; (202) 860–1886; http://www.jewishmuseum.org/Pages/ Programs_Media/progmedia_broadcast.html (public affairs pertaining to the Jewish experience).

Founded in 1981, the Jewish Archive of Broadcasting collects and preserves programming on the Jewish culture. The collection includes network television programs, documentaries, religious programs, and public television programs. Also included in the collection are 170 hours of videotape coverage of the trial of Adolf Eichmann.

Access to the Jewish Archive is limited to researchers and scholars, by appointment only. A partial catalog is available to researchers. Museum staffs have computerized cataloging. The Museum holds no rights to any of the material.

Wisconsin Center for Film and Theater Research, Film and Photo Archive, State Historical Society of Wisconsin, 816 State Street, Madison, WI 53706; (608) 264–6466; http://www.shsw.wisc.edu/wcftr/ (no public affairs, you must reserve a viewing machine and the titles you wish to view at least 24 hours in advance. Computerized catalog: http: //arcat.library.wisc.edu/).

Founded in 1960, the Wisconsin Center houses an extensive collection of programming from the United Artists Collection and the collection of the Ziv Television Library. The Center is open to researchers and scholars for in-house viewing. The material is not available for duplication or re-use. All materials must be reserved for viewing in advance.

The collection includes movies and cartoons acquired from Warner Brothers, RKO, and Monogram, and a collection of feature films from independent filmmakers. The Center also holds a collection of Third World newsreels from 1968 pertaining to social and political issues. The Ziv Television Library collection contains more than 2,000 programs of 38 different series. Also available for viewing by researchers are films and 35mm photographs of Soviet features and documentaries dating from 1950 to 1970. The collection is organized on card catalog, primarily by program title.

A valuable reference guide to available sources of film and video footage is Footage 89 and Footage 91, published by Prelinger Associates, Inc., 430 West 14th Street, Room 403, New York, NY 10014.

NOTE

Jennifer Redden provided invaluable research and editing assistance in the preparation of this chapter.

RECOMMENDED READING

"Bringing Government to the People." Interview with C-SPAN founder Brian Lamb. 1989. *Broadcasting* 116 (April 3): 66.

Browning, Robert X. 1989. "Archiving the Video Record of Legislatures." *Canadian Parliamentary Review* 12 (Summer): 9–11.

Corry, John. 1988. "C-SPAN: Electronic Sunshine." *New York Times* (February 21): 2: H31.

Frantzich, Stephen E. 1996. *The C-SPAN Revolution*. Norman: University of Oklahoma Press.

Godfrey, Donald G. 1992. *Reruns on File: A Guide to Electronic Media Archives*. Hillsdale, NJ: Lawrence Erlbaum.

Green, Alan. 1991. *Gavel to Gavel: A Guide to the Televised Proceedings of Congress*. 3rd ed. Washington, DC: Benton Foundation.

Krolik, Richard. 1992. "Everything You Wanted to Know about C-SPAN and Were Afraid to Ask." *Television Quarterly* 25 (Winter): 91.

Lamb, Brian. 1988. *C-SPAN: America's Town Hall*. Washington, DC: Acropolis Books.

Lamb, Brian. 1997. "C-SPAN: From Novelty to Institution." *Congressional Quarterly Weekly Report* (November 29): 2948–2949.

Mansfield, Harvey. 1997. "The Virtues of C-SPAN." *The American Enterprise* 8 (September/October): 46.

National Film Preservation Board. *Television/Video Preservation Study: Volume 1: Report*. http://lcweb.loc.gov/film/tvstudy.html.

Prato, Lou. 1992. "Politics in the Raw." *WJR: Washington Journalism Review* 14 (September): 35–38.

Swerdlow, Joel L., ed. 1988. *Media Technology and the Vote: A Source Book*. Boulder, CO: Westview Press.

Weaver, Warren. 1989. "C-SPAN on the Hill: 10 Years of Gavel to Gavel." *New York Times* (March 28): A10.

West, Don and Brown, Sara. 1997. "America's Town Crier." *Broadcasting & Cable* 127 (July 21): 70–74

Chapter 9

Cultural Diversity and Video Collecting

Diana Vogelsong and Christopher Lewis

INTRODUCTION

As American educational institutions begin to embrace the cultural diversity of the communities they serve, and as new scholarship expands to reflect a greater variety of cultural perspectives, the library can offer a distinct form of support. Through identification and selection of visual media that reflect the plurality of cultures and cultural viewpoints, librarians and media specialists can provide powerful tools for investigating history, for dispelling long-standing stereotypes, for fostering pride and identity within cultures, and for promoting tolerance between cultures. By collecting resources that represent or analyze diverse perspectives, libraries offer viewers an opportunity to expand and enrich their cultural awareness and, ultimately, overcome communication barriers.[1]

This chapter addresses some of the issues and objectives involved in developing multicultural media collections: the importance of developing these collections, the particular strengths of visual media for this purpose, the types of materials to be collected, and the strategies for locating those materials.

Multiculturalism has assumed a popular meaning and is frequently associated with a limited number of minority groups in the United States. By limiting oneself to the popular interpretation of the term one undermines the value of incorporating diversity as a criterion of collection development. In its broadest sense, cultural diversity can be viewed as extending well beyond national boundaries, for technology and other forces have made us all social and political participants on a global scale. For that reason, this chapter will use the term "multiculturalism" to include not only the predominant American minorities but also the wider scope of American cultures, immigrant communities, gender groups, sexual preference groups, and international cultures.

THE ROLE AND VALUE OF MULTICULTURAL VIDEO COLLECTIONS

National organizations representing media professionals have long recognized the importance of a broadly inclusive and balanced approach to collection development as a means of preserving basic democratic freedoms. These concerns have often been incorporated into basic policy statements. The American Library Association's (ALA) "Library Bill of Rights" mandates a library's responsibility to "provide materials and information presenting all points of view on current and historical issues. Materials should not be proscribed or removed because of partisan or doctrinal disapproval." This document also states, "Materials should not be excluded because of the origin, background, or views of those contributing to their creation" (ALA 1948; rev. 1961, 1967, 1980, "age" issues reaffirmed 1996). The Association for Educational Communications and Technology (AECT) similarly supports an inclusive collecting policy in its "Statement on Intellectual Freedom" (1979): "Attempts to restrict or deprive a learner's access to information representing a variety of viewpoints must be resisted as a threat to learning in a free and democratic society. Recognizing that within a pluralistic society efforts to censor may exist, such challenges should be met calmly with proper respect for the beliefs of the challengers." Video collections, which represent a significant information resource, can play a central role in protecting these fundamental rights.

Building a collection to meet the goals and prescriptions outlined in the statements above can be difficult. The history of mainstream mass media—from feature films to the nightly news—has been marked by the underrepresentation and misrepresentation of ethnic, racial, and cultural minority groups. Video librarians involved in building balanced multicultural collections are working to undo (or at least to document and learn from) much of the stereotyping and skewed representation put forth by the mass media.

Any attempt to build a broadly representative collection of video titles must take into account the enormous roles the mass media have played in shaping the social and political histories of various American cultures. Writing about the power that motion pictures wield in influencing beliefs and values, bell hooks (1996) states:

Whether we like it or not, cinema assumes a pedagogical role in the lives of many people. It may not be the intent of a filmmaker to teach audiences anything, but that does not mean that lessons are not learned. It has only been in the last ten years or so that I began to realize that my students learned more about race, sex, and class from movies than from all the theoretical literature I was urging them to read. Movies not only provide a narrative for specific discourses of race, sex, and class, they provide a shared experience, a common starting point from which diverse audiences can dialogue about these charged issues.

Because many media producers do not acknowledge the enormous influence their work has in educating or shaping the perceptions of viewers, the need to entertain has taken precedence over a need to act responsibly. Throughout the history of the electronic media, audience appeal, translated into box office receipts, has consistently been the primary driving force behind production. Thus, the American media have been dominated by programming that, with few exceptions, reflects the values of the predominant culture. Because conformity has proven to be more profitable than the flaunting of conventions or questioning the past, most producers have not been compelled to deconstruct time-honored stereotypes. As Chon Noriega (1999) has commented: "The mass media do not cause racism, of course, but neither do they offer a value-free medium for the exchange of ideas and information. They are marketplaces and we are both their consumers and a product sold to advertisers."

Both the 1971 and 1979 reports of the U.S. Commission on Civil Rights document the dearth of positive images of women and ethnic minorities in American television, despite formal complaints by organizations representing those groups. The disparity in the depiction of cultural minorities on television (or the lack of representation altogether) continues to the present, albeit in modified form (see Hamamoto 1994; Lichter and Amundson 1996; Steenland 1989; Torres 1998). Minorities have been traditionally portrayed in film and video in a limited variety of roles: as primitive and anonymous savages, as exotic outsiders, or as objects of ridicule. Films and videos that romanticize these cultures can be just as damaging as those that depict a more overtly racist viewpoint. Both approaches mythologize rather than convey the truth about those whom they pretend to represent. As Hall and Fifer (1990: 19) have commented:

Television tends to compress the world into simplified equations in which everything is designated as either similar (dominant) or different (other). In this order, universality is ascribed to the dominants' characteristics whereas qualities that belong to the other are marginalized and objectified. The other does not represent, but is rather represented. Thus hierarchy is encoded into the iconography and ideologies of every soap, sitcom, and advertisement. This simulation of hierarchical social relationships fixes identities, mythologies, or stereotypes that serve the interests of the sex, class, sexual preference, or race of the dominant.

This narrow range of viewpoints in the media, representative of the biases and sociopolitical power structure in society, perpetuates the myths of that society. Because of the commercial nature of production, when minority members have been invited to participate in the media, they have often been slotted into stereotypic roles and functions deemed acceptable (and easily recognizable) to mainstream culture. In the video *Color Adjustment* (1991, dist. California Newsreel), filmmaker Marlon Riggs records this tendency, documenting the repeated failure of American television to come to terms with a realistic portrayal of the African-American culture. The video *Slaying the Dragon*, directed by Deborah Gee (1988, dist. National Asian American Telecommunications Association), relates a similar history of Hollywood's negative stereotyping of Asian and Asian American women.

Clearly, the task of building a multicultural video collection embodies a number of interesting challenges and complex requirements for video librarians. Author E. L. Doctorow (1988) warns that when ideas go unexamined and unchallenged for a long enough time, they become mythological and they create conformity. A well-selected multicultural collection can and should challenge viewers to re-examine stereotypes and preconceived notions about other cultures. Video can provide an ideal format for re-examining past cultural perspectives and for achieving a greater cultural understanding of others. Film and video can demystify the "exotic" or "foreign" by revealing individuals in the context of their everyday lives and by wearing down the culturally imposed barriers between "insider" and "outsider." As Professor Carlos Cortes (1992: 7) has commented: "[A]s we rethink, rewrite, re-teach, re-commemorate through history, literature, and the other humanities and arts, we reshape and sometimes recast the very metaphors that form the perceptual guideposts to our multicultural future."

In order to meet these challenges, multicultural video collections must ultimately be diverse not only in subject matter, but also in the cultural and political viewpoints and perspectives represented, in the aesthetic approaches offered, and in the historical contexts provided. Such a collection should make accessible the voices and visions of both cultural "insiders" and those historically assigned to the position of cultural "outsiders." The range of materials included should provide a sense of the historical roles film, video, and broadcast media have played in creating and perpetuating negative images of cultures and ethnicities. The collection should present works that facilitate the shattering of these myths and stereotypes. These goals can only be accomplished by including a wide range of cinematic representations, styles, and genres, from the "real-world" visions of documentary filmmakers and historical chroniclers to the storytelling and myth and image making of the movies.

THE NATURE OF THE COLLECTION

Determining which videos should be collected depends on the needs, policies, and mission of the library or media center. Nevertheless, the development of multicultural collections requires specialized strategies for identifying and locating appropriate materials. The scope of core reference sources and standard subject access has proven too narrow to encompass many of the cultural documents and artifacts that exist beyond the realm of traditional study. In an article on academic library responses to cultural diversity, authors Robert Trujillo and David Weber (1991: 160) stressed the importance of expanding selection to include primary source materials pertaining to ethnic and racial groups; of having a core teaching collection for broad coverage of race and ethnic relations; and of acquiring ethnic materials from marginal, independent publishers. These guidelines are particularly applicable to media collections, since videos play a significant role as both fundamental teaching resources and as essential primary source documents for the study of the twentieth century.

Movies and Television as Mirror, Myth, and History

In her book *The Woman Warrior; Memoirs of a Girlhood among Ghosts* (1976), Chinese American writer Maxine Hong Kingston asks an intriguing question. The protagonist, a young Chinese American girl struggling to span the chasm between her mother's culture and the American world in which she lives, speaks for many when she poses the question, "What is Chinese tradition and what is the movies?"

Much of what we know and believe about others has been forged at the movies and on TV. Film and video by their very nature—their magical ability to emulate or synthesize reality—embody a certain aura of authenticity and authority. What looks real on the screen, in other words, is often accepted and internalized as real, even when we know that the work is fiction. When the movies attempt to openly masquerade as history, the distinction between fact and fiction is even more blurred (see Bernstein 1988; Burgoyne 1997; Carnes et al. 1995; Martin 1997). It is evident that the media affect our perception and comprehension of the world; the risk posed is that the images we see often repeat stereotypes and cultural mythologies rather than cultural or historical reality.

When they are at their most effective and authentic, commercial television and feature films can create stories, contexts, and lessons about particular cultures or peoples that are as enlightening as those created by similar documentary works (in some cases, there is no documentary counterpart). However, these productions can serve as powerful social indicators as well. The formulas they employ and the audiences they address often convey more than any story line about the social, political, or cultural conditions in which they were created. It is clear that a study of materials from the history of film and television production, with its associated historical mythologies, is essential for any broad understanding of cultural and ethnic history. This is particularly the case in academic settings where the mythology is in itself the subject of study. Early films such as D. W. Griffith's *The Birth of a Nation* (1915) and Cecil B. DeMille's *The Cheat* (1915), the 1940s and 1950s westerns of John Ford, and other "innocent" post–World War II entertainments such as *Teahouse of the August Moon* (1956, dir. Daniel Mann) and *My Geisha* (1962, dir. Jack Cardiff) stand as important historic artifacts, however contemptible the prejudices they embody. They can be instructive in demonstrating how cultures create myths and reinterpret history, how they reflect fears and antipathies through visual means.

This mythmaking is by no means limited to the distant Hollywood past. While recent theatrical films demonstrate heightened sensitivity in their portrayal of minority cultures, they must still be viewed with a sharply critical eye. In *Mississippi Burning* (1988), for example, director Alan Parker conveys the powerful emotions and recounts the key events of a pivotal civil rights case. However, the murder of the three civil rights activists is told not from the African-American perspective, but through the fictional story of two white law enforcement agents, thus shifting the emphasis away from the primary story and denying the audience access to the full meaning of the historical event (see Davis 1988; King 1988). Similarly, *Dances with Wolves* (1990, dir. Kevin Costner) broke new ground by introducing Native American actors and language and by portraying a specific Lakota tribe with some sensitivity. Despite these laudable elements, the film retained the traditional focus of the white hero and, in many ways, delivered an updated version of the "noble savage" myth (see Hinckley 1992; Hoffman 1997). Nevertheless, films such as these have a valuable place in media collections, both for the historical events they seek to relive and for the underlying sociological statement created by the choices presented. The historical evaluation of such films, including an examination of how the films were received at the time of their releases, is as important as the literal content in achieving an understanding of the past (see Jackson 1990).

It would be unfair to characterize Hollywood as a singularly rapacious moneymaking machine, responding only to the forces of the market, indifferent to racism and bigotry. Despite the enormous amount of stereotyping and prejudice Hollywood has fostered, there have been more than a few Hollywood films that have challenged the status quo. The history of movies is marked by periodic attempts to deal realistically or sympathetically with major social issues of the day. For example, the enormous changes in American life and society following World War II, combined with the democratic impulses engendered by American involvement in the war, led to the rise of a distinct genre of "social problem" or "social message" in the decades after 1945.[2] Contemporary "message" films, though not as unconventional as they once were, still have the power to deconstruct stereotypes and restore cultural identities. Noteworthy recent examples include *Schindler's List* (1993, dir. Steven Spielberg), *Amistad* (1997, dir. Steven Spielberg), *Philadelphia* (1993, dir. Jonathan Demme), *Rosewood* (1997, dir. John Singleton), *Beloved* (1998, dir. Jonathan Demme), and *The Hurricane* (1999, dir. Norman Jewison).

By including a wide chronological sampling of films dealing with or portraying various ethnic and racial groups and films by directors with varying cultural backgrounds, it is possible to chart Hollywood's response to the historical or social climate and, in turn, to chronicle our changing culture.

For example, a collection supporting Asian American studies would be incomplete without early classics such as D. W. Griffith's *Broken Blossoms* (1919); the infamous Charlie Chan and Mr. Wong series (both egregious examples of white actors playing in "yellowface"); the sundry xenophobic war films of the 1940s, and postwar films such as *The World of Suzie Wong* (1960, dir. Richard Quine), and *Flower Drum Song* (1961, dir. Henry Koster). The same collection should, as a marked contrast, also include a sampling of newer films by Asian American filmmakers, such as Wayne Wang's *Dim Sum* (1984) and *Eat a Bowl of Tea* (1989), Steve Okazaki's *Living on Tokyo Time* (1987), Mira Nair's *Mississippi Masala* (1992), Tony Chan's *Combination Platter* (1993), and Mina Shum's *Double Happiness* (1995).

Similarly, a collection offering a survey of Native American culture would be incomplete without a broad sampling of films reflecting the image of "celluloid Indians" over the past century. Such a collection would include older westerns from sound and silent eras (the films of John Ford alone—from *Drums Along the Mohawk* [1939] to *The Searchers* [1956])—provide a complex textbook example of cinematic myth, stereotype, and prejudice).[3] The evolving image of Native Americans in the often highly polemical films of the Vietnam War era should also be represented. Films such as *Tell Them Willie Boy Is Here* (1969, dir. Abraham Polonsky), *Little Big Man* (1970, dir. Arthur Penn), and *Soldier Blue* (1970, dir. Ralph Nelson) tended to associate the historical plight of indigenous people with U.S. imperialism in Southeast Asia, and marked the beginning of more sympathetic treatment of Native Americans on the screen. This trend continued with the revisionist westerns and other looks at Native American history and culture of the 1980s and 1990s, including *Dances with Wolves* and Michael Mann's take on *Last of the Mohicans* (1993). Finally, no representative collection would be complete without recent works by Native American filmmakers, particularly *Powwow Highway* (1989, dir. Jonathan Wacks) and *Smoke Signals* (1998, dir. Chris Eyre).

The same westerns useful for studying the movie image of Native Americans often contain equally skewed and racist depictions of Mexicans and Mexican Americans. Stereotype and cultural misrepresentation of Hispanics abound in other film genres as well, throughout the history of the movies—from the silent Hispanic cardboard cutouts in *Mark of Zorro* (1920, dir. Fred Niblo), to Jennifer Jones' "brown face" portrayal of a sultry Latina in *Duel in the Sun* (1946, dir. King Vidor) and Marlon Brando's amazingly off-kilter turn in the title role of *Viva Zapata!* (1952, dir. Elia Kazan). As with other racial and ethnic groups, the last decade has seen a move toward more realistic and/or sympathetic representations, particularly in films by Chicano/Latino filmmakers. A representative collection of these newer works would include such videos as *Zoot Suit* (1981, dir. Luis Valdez), *El Norte* (1983, dir. Gregory Nava), *Stand and Deliver* (1987, dir. Ramon Menendez), *Mi Vida Loca* (1994, dir. Allison Anders), and *Mi Familia* (1995, dir. Gregory Nava).

Collections geared to the study of African-American culture and race relations in the twentieth century would be greatly hampered without the long roster of

Hollywood films needed to demonstrate the changing portrayal of African Americans over time and the changing involvement of African Americans in both mainstream and independent film production. This list ranges from Griffith's *Birth of a Nation* (1915) to the 1930s and 1940s mythologies of *Gone with the Wind* (1939, dir. Victor Fleming) and *Cabin in the Sky* (1943, dir. Vincente Minelli). Larger collections concerned with providing a comprehensive look at the image and role of African Americans in motion picture history may also want to include a selection of early African-American independent filmmakers, such as Oscar Micheaux. Many of these early "race films" were produced specifically for African-American audiences. Even though many are low-budget potboilers, they afford a fascinating inside view of black culture during the 1920s and 1930s.[4] A representative historical survey of African Americans in motion pictures would include "socially conscious," post–World War II works such as *Intruder in the Dust* (1949, dir. Clarence Brown), *Pinky* (1949, dir. Elia Kazan), *The Defiant Ones* (1958, dir. David L. Rich), and *Guess Who's Coming to Dinner* (1967, dir. Stanley Kramer). An African-American core video collection should also include a sampling of films representing the growing empowerment of black filmmakers and the rise of powerful black images on the screen, from "blaxploitation" films of the 1970s such as Melvyn Van Peebles' *Sweet Sweetback's Baad Asssss Song* (1971), and contining with works of young African-American filmmakers, such as Robert Townsend's *Hollywood Shuffle* (1987), Spike Lee's *Do the Right Thing* (1989) and *Malcolm X* (1992), John Singleton's *Boyz in the Hood* (1991), and Mario Van Peebles' *New Jack City* (1991).

Over the course of the last 50 years, television as much as motion pictures has been responsible for promulgating and maintaining racial, ethnic, and other cultural stereotypes. Not surprisingly, these stereotypical images have been particularly prominent in comedy programming. *Amos 'n' Andy* is perhaps the most notorious and blatant of the first wave of television programming. Sadly, programs of more recent vintage, such as *The Jeffersons, Sanford and Son*, and *Good Times*, are equally fraught with misrepresentative caricatures of black urban lifestyles. Newer TV offerings—from *Moesha* to *The Hugleys*, from *Martin* to *The Wayans Brothers Show*—have often simply replaced crude older stereotypes with more complex and less immediately obvious ones. A number of early TV series prominently featuring black characters, including *Amos 'n' Andy* and the *Beulah Show*, are currently available on videotape. It is unfortunate for collection builders that later examples of race representation on TV are largely unavailable on videotape, although they can be easily found in syndication on cable channels such as Nick at Nite and TV Land.

Other ethnic and racial groups have faired equally poorly on the small screen. Stereotype-ridden examples of these treatments include *Life with Luigi* (Italian Americans), *The Life of Reilly* (Irish Americans), *Mama* (Norwegian Americans), and *The Goldbergs* (later called Molly) (Jewish Americans). Samples of each of these programs are commercially available on videotape.

The value of older films and television programs to the study of past attitudes toward race and culture is evident. Outside of academic libraries, however, building a collection of titles that reflect negative ethnic and racial images is tricky business. Public libraries, which lack the type of critical and contextual support provided by academic curricula, and which have a considerably different mission, may choose to emphasize more positive, multidimensional, and accurate portrayals that reinforce the cultural heritage of the communities they serve. Fortunately, there are an increasing number of current popular theatrical films, particularly those made by filmmakers of color, that fill this need. Recent examples include *Stand and Deliver* (1987, dir. Ramon Menendez), *La Bamba* (1987, dir. Luiz Valdez), *Selena* (1997, dir. Gregory Nava), *Glory* (1990, dir. Edward Zwick), *The Long Walk Home* (1991, dir. Richard Pearce), *Get on the Bus* (1996, dir. Spike Lee), *A Great Wall* (1986, dir. Peter Wang), and *Smoke Signals* (1998, dir. Chris Eyre).

Whether or not the collection supports the acquisition of earlier Hollywood films for the purpose of tracing negative cultural images in the movies, the video librarian can provide users with important links between movie "reality" and historical and cultural reality. There is currently an excellent and expanding body of printed works dealing with racial, cultural, and gender images in the movies (see Chapter 19 in this book). These works can provide valuable historical and social context and analysis for the materials collected as part of a multicultural collection; video librarians should work closely with print materials selectors to ensure that the library provides this type of context.

Documentary Film: The Camera Eye on the "Real World"

While movies can provide valuable insights into the social, political, and psychological tenor of the times in which they were made, they are ultimately indirect and incomplete means of studying the history and relationship of cultures. The best movies can provide is a highly refracted and stylized view of these histories and relationships. Any collection purporting to provide an effective, balanced approach to the study of American and international cultures must also provide a strong documentary counterpoint to the movies. Well-produced documentary films can provide the scope, the substantive approach, and the insider's vision demanded in such a collection.

Documentary filmmakers (particularly independent filmmakers) typically operate outside of the constraints of box office economics and Hollywood politics and prejudices. Documentaries are a film genre that, by their very nature, seem to encourage democratic participation and the expression of strong and/or nontraditional viewpoints. The best documentaries provide the type of immediate and unique vision that is rarely achievable in other media, such as print. Documentary film can, of course, run the gamut from coolly objective to wildly subjective; from mainstream works aired widely on PBS and network channels to the incendiary or experimental output of independent producers/distributors.

It is the selector's job to achieve a balance in these approaches and styles and to assist users in critically assessing the legitimacy and value of the materials in the collection.

It should be mentioned that achieving this type of balance and breadth of scope in a multicultural video collection (or any type of video collection, in fact) is likely to require some hard economic choices for the video collection development librarian. For many of the reasons outlined in Chapter 17 in this book, independently produced videos often tend to be expensive—more expensive than titles distributed by large organizations such as PBS, and certainly more expensive than home video titles. The fact remains, however, that independently produced works often provide the most interesting and provocative visions and insights available on a topic. There are numerous instances in which the subject matter or focus of an independent video is unique. Notable examples include *Bontoc Eulogy* (1995, dist. Cinema Guild), Marlon Fuentes' amazing quasi-documentary essay on race, spectatorship, and cultural memory; *Halving the Bones*, Ruth Ozeki's moving and humorous meditation on family history and ethnic roots (1995, dist. Women Make Movies); *Coming Out Under Fire* (1994, dist. Zeitgeist Films), Arthur Dong's documentary on gays and lesbians in the World War II military; Beth Harrington's look at the religious and cultural life of Boston's Italian-American community, *The Blinking Madonna & Other Miracles* (1994, dist. University of California Center for Media and Independent Learning); and Stanley Nelson's video history of black journalism, *The Black Press: Soldiers Without Swords* (1998, dist. California Newsreel).

Although there are, to be sure, a large number of multicultural documentaries in the less-expensive home video market, many of these works take fewer risks and offer fewer rewards than the type of independent films cited above. It would be difficult to represent diverse cultures and dissident viewpoints effectively with material from this market alone.

While most independent documentaries offer a strong, often partisan point of view, some works are clearly intended to expose injustice, and to incite action. A number of influential examples of older documentary activism are available on video; for example, *The Quiet One* (1948), Sidney Meyers' film about the bleak life of a 10-year-old African-American boy in Harlem; and *Harvest of Shame*, Edward R. Murrow's groundbreaking 1960 CBS documentary that dealt with the impoverished lives of migrant agricultural workers.

The past decade has seen an intensification in documentary film activism. The topic of *In Whose Honor? American Indian Mascots in Sports* (1997, dir. Jay Rosenstein; dist. New Day Films) is self-evident. *Who Killed Vincent Chin?* (1988, dir. Christine Choy; dist. Filmakers Library) addresses a case of xenophobic violence against a Chinese American. *Dear Jesse* (1999, dir. Tim Kirkman; dist. Facets et al.) is a humorous though impassioned plea for tolerance from a gay North Carolinian to his senator. *Out of the Past: The Struggle for Gay and Lesbian Rights in America* (1998, dir. Jeff Dupre; dist. Facets et al.) uses the case of the Utah high school that chose to ban all student clubs rather than accept one gay and lesbian club as a central metaphor on the history of homosexuality in America. *Natives: Immigrant Bashing on the Border* (1991, prod. Jesse Lerner and Scott Sterling; dist. Filmakers Library) documents violence against undocumented Mexican immigrants. *Not in Our Town* (1994, dir. Patrice O'Neill and Rhian Miller; dist. The Working Group) documents a town's reaction to hate crimes perpetrated against the Native American, African-American, and Jewish citizens of the community.

Historical Documentaries and Primary Source Materials

The documentary camera is never a mute recording mechanism; it is a lens that is manipulated to reflect the viewpoint and the vision of the filmmaker. Like theatrical works, documentary recordings of a particular generation's "reality" can provide fascinating insights into changing attitudes, political stances, and worldviews. Developing a collection of documentaries and feature films that spans a period of history provides a provocative way of looking at how such productions responded to their broader historical context. Frank Capra's *The Negro Soldier* (1944), for example, provides extremely valuable insights into the changing attitudes toward African Americans during World War II. Although the film bears many of the culture-based conventions of earlier works, the more favorable representation of African Americans in this and other war-era films has been linked to the government's desire to symbolize the democratic values for which the war was being fought, and to encourage African-American participation in the armed services and on the home front (Cripps and Culbert 1979; Woll and Miller 1987: 53–55).

Primary source material, such as unedited newsreel, produced news footage, and amateur field recordings, while often difficult to obtain in video formats, is another form of documentary evidence that can be extremely valuable in tracing the social and political history of cultures and groups (see Chapter 21 in this book). MPI Home Video's *The 20th Century: A Moving Visual History* (see http://www.twentiethcentury.net) and *The Video Encyclopedia of the 20th Century* (Sunrise Media, 45 W. 45th St., Suite 808, New York, NY 10036–4602) are two examples of commercially available stock footage collections covering a broad array of significant historical events. The MPI work is an edited and narrated collection of clips, available on both tape and DVD; the *Video Encyclopedia* is a large collection, on both tape and laser disc, of raw, largely unnarrated clips. Both collections include coverage of the Civil Rights Movement, as well as vital speeches of minority political and social leaders. Collections such as those discussed above offer decontextualized images—usually short clips—that, in order to be effective as teaching and research tools, require other forms of supporting documentation. In many cases, this type of raw primary source material is used by documentary filmmakers to provide the visual and historical context against which the documentary story is told.

Educational and Training Video

A significant addition to the field of diversity awareness education was the establishment of the Media Education Foundation (MEF) in 1991 (http://www. mediaed.org). MEF is a non-profit organization that produces videotapes for educators and individuals concerned with media literacy. Many of its releases offer concrete analysis of the stereotyping that is still common in American mass media. Examples of titles include *Off the Straight & Narrow: Lesbians, Gays, Bisexuals & Television* (1998, Katherine Sender); *Killing Us Softly III: Advertising's Image of Women* (2000, Jean Kilbourne); *Dreamworlds II: Desire/ Sex/Power in Music Video* (1999, Sut Jhally). MEF is also notable for releasing programs that give voice to dissident media critics who challenge the status quo and expose the racism and sexism that subtly pervades many current television programs and films. These titles include works featuring bell hooks, Edward Said, and Stuart Hall.

Issues and problems related to living and working in a multicultural society have become the focus of another substantial body of videotapes by educational and training video producers. These works tend to be highly focused on specific issues. Many are intended for building sensitivity to the issues in the corporate or institutional workplace; the best, such as the widely cited *Going International* (1983) and *Valuing Diversity* (1987) series (Copeland-Griggs), offer lessons and skills that can be used in many contexts (Copeland-Griggs, 302 23rd Avenue, San Francisco, CA 94121; (415) 668–4200). A distributor specializing in this field is Big World (http://bigworld.com), whose works focus exclusively on encountering diversity in the global marketplace. Their titles are as general as *Bridging Cultural Barriers: Managing Ethnic Diversity in the Workplace* (1991) and as specific as *How to Welcome Business Guests from Japan* (1990).

BUILDING AND PROVIDING ACCESS TO THE COLLECTION

A first step in developing a multicultural collection may involve an analysis of the existing collection to identify those materials useful to this area of study. Many libraries and media centers already contain a wealth of titles that could be labeled *cross-cultural* or *multicultural*, but these resources are hidden within the traditional categories used to define and describe visual materials. Standard subject headings assigned to documentary films and videos often refer to the literal content of the program but fail to define the issues that make that work particularly valuable for some aspect of cultural study. A feature film such as *Milagro Beanfield War* (1998, dir. Robert Redford), for example, to which many libraries assign only the most general subject headings (e.g., "Comedy Films" on [OCLC]), carries a powerful message about the complexities of land development and control. Despite its setting in the American Southwest, this film could apply equally well to other groups seeking to affirm their rights in the

United States or elsewhere. Documentaries tend to be categorized by the culture represented rather than the issue portrayed. The subject headings for a film such as *Ethnic Notions* (1986, dir. Marlon Riggs; dist. California Newsreel) may refer to the African-American culture, but its topic of visual stereotyping may serve studies of other American ethnic groups.

The creation of a filmography on multicultural issues may help determine useful categories of materials and alert both selectors and catalogers to the necessity of providing alternative access points. Availability of computer resources such as online catalogs, CD-ROMS (e.g, *Variety's Video Directory Plus* and *A-V Online*), subject searching on OCLC, and others provide expanded access through keyword searching, but the searcher must have in mind the range of appropriate terms. Ideally, a thesaurus could be constructed that would strengthen the cataloging of materials and serve as a checklist in the evaluation of materials during the selection process.

To assure maximum use of multicultural materials, the media selector should collect supporting documentation or provide bibliographic links to the print collection for difficult topics and areas that are unfamiliar to many American audiences. The unsophisticated viewer may have difficulty appreciating the norms of another culture or may require historical, social, or cultural background and context. Although filmmakers face pressure to conform to the tastes of the dominant commercial audiences, the language of film can change from culture to culture, as do other forms of communication. African cinema, for example, may feel foreign to the Western viewer not only because of its content but because of its distinctive use of space and time. Audiences may require additional background information to fully appreciate the subtleties of the message.

Information about the filmmaker, the political or social context in which the video was made, the relations of the video to others of a similar genre, and the traditions, folklore, and customs upon which the story is built may be required to fully appreciate the impact of the message. Both the media selector and the viewer must be attentive to potential barriers to effective viewing.

The selector can perform the important task of gathering and disseminating this background information along with video materials. Maintaining an ongoing file of reviews and related articles; an index of titles, useful subject headings, or keywords; and a print collection with supporting documentation may be especially valuable in assisting users of multicultural media. Media selectors should work in cooperation with print selectors to ensure a coordinated collection development effort. The Web provides a valuable tool and an unprecedented opportunity for developing and maintaining links and connections between collections and resources.

Several notable distributors are meeting such needs by providing background documentation about their videos, either in print or via their Web sites. PBS, for example, offers teachers' guides, lesson plans, and a printed index identifying key events and topics on many of its videotapes by minute and second. On its Web site (http://www.pbs.org) PBS offers expanded background and sidebar information about topics covered in many of its programs, from *Frontline* and to *Jewish Cooking in America*. California Newsreel offers facilitators' guides, both in print and on its Web site (http://www.newsreel.com), for nearly all of its titles. Its Web site also includes articles written by its staff and "Notes on Understanding African Cinema." The National Asian Telecommunications Association (NAATA) site (http://www.naatanet.org/) offers a "Filmmaker's Corner" featuring interviews with the producers of selected NAATA titles.

POSSIBILITIES AND CHALLENGES

The growth of culturally diverse populations and the strengthening of the political, social, and economic power wielded by these groups in the United States have had direct impact on the media. Media watch, performing arts, ethnic and social activist organizations, and other interest groups are increasingly monitoring the content and quality of broadcast and theatrical media. This attention, coupled with the increased coverage of culturally sensitive issues by the news media, is placing pressure on producers and directors to be more attentive to accurate representation (see Pristin 1991). These efforts to improve the quality and accuracy of programming are bound to have direct benefits for libraries building multicultural video collections.

The intensified emphasis on multiculturalism has spurred interest in developing programs that focus specifically on cross-cultural concerns.[5] For example, part of the impetus for developing the series *The Buried Mirror* (1991, dist. Facets, et al.), written and narrated by Carlos Fuentes, was to provide an accurate educational resource on Hispanic American cultures and to stimulate cross-cultural discussion. The recent mainstream successes of minority theatrical filmmakers in the commercial market and the wide, mainstream audience for the works of minority documentary filmmakers aired on the public broadcasting network also bode well for the growth of multicultural collections (see *Christian Science Monitor* 1991). Attention and demand by librarians and media specialists for the more elusive films of independent filmmakers may also strengthen this market in the future.

Although video technology has provided an unprecedented opportunity for minority filmmakers to tell their own stories and histories, there are still formidable barriers to telling these stories in the mainstream media. Fortunately, a number of promising alternative outlets for video and television have generated possibilities outside the mainstream media. As Weatherford and Seubert (1988: 7–8) have noted, new forms of telecommunication such as low power and cable broadcast systems offer wider public access to Native American tribal media productions. The growth of multicultural media arts centers such as Visual Communications (Los Angeles), Asian CineVision (New York), Cine Acción (San Francisco), and the Black Film Makers Hall of Fame (San Francisco) have helped support and gain attention for independent works of minority filmmakers. Satellite delivery also opens opportunities for reception of regional or ethnic programming as well as international television through services such as Satellite Communication for Learning (SCOLA) (http://scola.org/). Access to media distribution over the Web and other digital networks holds both great promise and great challenges for maintaining media diversity in the future.

Librarians and media specialists can respond to the plenitude of ideas, people, and viewpoints represented on video by seeking to develop richer collections that reflect the breadth of that diversity. They also have an important role to play in preparing multicultural media guides and improving bibliographic access to videos with alternative viewpoints. It is only through improved access that use of these materials will be assured. By strengthening collections to address culturally diverse needs, media selectors can challenge viewers to appreciate the world in all its complexity and to prepare for the community and global challenges that lie ahead.

NOTES

1. In developing its multicultural collection of video for sale to schools and libraries, the now-defunct Modern Talking Picture Corp. enlisted a panel of 10 educators as advisers. The panel developed a list of six objectives for the collection that are generally useful for video collection builders: (1) Allow (users) to gain an appreciation and understanding for other cultures while developing self-esteem and pride in their own; (2) facilitate understanding that all cultures are significant and that no specific culture or ethnic group is inferior or superior to another; (3) impart an understanding of how differences in cultural values, beliefs, and norms can cause conflicts that affect economic, political, social, and educational development; (4) provide information about the origins of cultures found in the United States and the impact of migration, immigration, and slavery; (5) illustrate how individuals in a complex society can identify and participate in many cultures; (6) encourage critical and creative thinking that leads to meaningful dialogue on multicultural issues (from program prospectus).

2. For useful discussions of Hollywood's liberal social and political impulses as reflected in "social problem" or "social message" films, see Brownlow (1990) and Sloan (1988) (both dealing with silent films and social issues); Roffman and Purdy (1981) (which discusses a broad array of social and cultural issues in the movies); and Cripps (1993) (a study of African-American and race issue films from 1945 to the Civil Rights Movement)

3. For in-depth discussions of John Ford's treatment of Native Americans, see Aleiss (1994); Ellis (1980); Gallagher (1993); Nolly (1998).

4. A collection of these early films is available in video format from Facets (http://www.facets.org) and other feature film video distributors. Film enthusiast Michael Mills has developed an exceptionally well-designed and authored Web site devoted to race movies: *Midnight Ramble: The Negro in Early Hollywood*, http://www.moderntimes.com/palace/black/index.html.

5. Current examples include the National Film Board of Canada's catalog entitled *Multicultural Studies*; the University of California Extension Media Center's *World Cultures on Film and Video*; Facets' *Multicultural Video Catalog*; Films for the Humanities' *Multicultural Studies on Video*.

REFERENCES

Aleiss, Angela. 1994. "A Race Divided: The Indian Westerns of John Ford." *American Indian Culture and Research Journal* (Summer): 167–187.

American Library Association (ALA). "Library Bill of Rights." Adopted June 18, 1948; amended February 2, 1961; June 17, 1967; and January 23, 1980; inclusion of "age" reaffirmed January 23, 1996, by the American Library Association Council.

Association for Educational Communications and Technology (AECT). 1979. "Statement on Intellectual Freedom." In *Media, the Learner and Intellectual Freedom; A Handbook.* Washington, DC: AECT Intellectual Freedom Committee.

Bernstein, Richard. 1988. "Can Movies Teach History?" *New York Times* (November 17): 2: 1.

Brownlow, Kevin. 1990. *Behind the Mask of Innocence.* New York : Knopf.

Burgoyne, Robert. 1997. *Film Nation: Hollywood Looks at U.S. History.* Minneapolis: University of Minnesota Press.

Carnes, Mark C., ed. 1995. *Past Imperfect: History According to the Movies.* New York: H. Holt.

Christian Science Monitor. 1991. "New Era Shaping Up for Black, Hispanic Film makers in U.S." (June 24): 11.

Cortes, Carlos. 1992. "Backing into the Future: Columbus, Cleopatra, Custer, & the Diversity Revolution." *Humanities Network* (Summer): 7.

Cripps, Thomas. 1993. *Making Movies Black: The Hollywood Message Movie from World War II to the Civil Rights Era.* New York: Oxford University Press.

Cripps, Thomas, and Culbert, David. 1979. "The Negro Soldier (1944): Film Propaganda in Black and White." *American Quarterly* 31(5): 616–640.

Davis, Thulani. 1988. "Civil Rights and Wrongs." *American Film* 14(3) (December): 32–42.

Doctorow, E. L. 1988. *World of Ideas Series with Bill Moyers.* Washington, DC: Public Affairs Television, Inc.

Ellis, Kirk. 1980. "On the Warpath: John Ford and the Indians." *Journal of Popular Film and Television* 8(2): 34–41.

Gallagher, Tag. 1993. "John Ford's Indians." *Film Comment* (September–October): 68–72

Hall, Doug, and Fifer, Sally Jo, eds. 1990. *Illuminating Video: An Essential Guide to Video Art.* New York: Aperture Foundation, Bay Area Video Coalition.

Hamamoto, Darrell Y. 1994. *Monitored Peril: Asian Americans and the Politics of TV Representation.* Minneapolis: University of Minnesota Press.

Hinckley, Ted C. 1992. "Vanishing Truth and Western History." *Journal of the West* 31(1) (Janurary): 3–5.

Hoffman, Donald. 1997. "Whose Home on the Range? Finding Room for Native Americans, African Americans, and Latino Americans in the Revisionist Western." *MELUS* 22(2) (Summer): 45–50.

hooks, bell. 1996. *Reel to Real: Race, Sex, and Class at the Movies.* New York: Routledge.

Jackson, Harvey. 1990. "Can Movies Teach History?" *Organization of American Historians (OAS) Newsletter* (November): 4–5.

King, Coretta Scott. 1988. "Hollywood's Latest Perversion: The Civil-Rights Era as a White Experience." *Los Angeles Times* (December 13): II-7.

Kingston, Maxine Hong. 1976. *The Woman Warrior; Memoirs of a Girlhood among Ghosts.* New York: Vintage Books.

Lichter, S. Robert, and Amundson, Daniel R. 1996. *Don't Blink: Hispanics in Television Entertainment.* Washington, DC: National Council of La Raza.

Martin, Phillip W. D. 1997. "Shaking Up the World, or Shaped By It?" (How History and Motion Pictures Influence One Another). *New York Times* (February 2): 2: 1.

Nolly, Ken. 1998. " 'The Representation of Conquest': John Ford and the Hollywood Indian." In *Hollywood's Indian: The Portrayal of the Native American in Film.* Edited by Peter C. Rollins and John E. O'Connor. Lexington: University Press of Kentucky, pp. 73–90.

Noriega, Chon. 1999. "Media Matters." Viewing Race Project (National Video Resources), http://www.viewingrace.org/.

Pristin, Terry. 1991. "Hollywood's Sensitivity Training; Minority Groups Are Changing the Script for Filmmakers." *Washington Post* (December 28): C1.

Roffman, Peter, and Purdy, Jim. 1981. *The Hollywood Social Problem Film: Madness, Despair, and Politics from the Depression to the Fifties.* Bloomington: Indiana University Press.

Sloan, Kay. 1988. *The Loud Silents: Origins of the Social Problem Film.* Urbana: University of Illinois Press.

Steenland, Sally. 1989. *Unequal Picture: Black, Hispanic, Asian and Native American Characters on Television.* Washington, DC: National Commission on Working Women of Wider Opportunities for Women.

Torres, Sasha, ed. 1998. *Living Color: Race and Television in the United States.* Durham, NC: Duke University Press.

Trujillo, Robert G., and Weber, David C. 1991. "Academic Library Responses to Cultural Diversity: A Position Paper for the 1990's." *Journal of Academic Librarianship* (July): 160.

Weatherford, Elizabeth, and Seubert, Emelia, eds. 1981–1988. *Native Americans on Film and Video.* Vol. 2. New York: Museum of the American Indian and the Heye Foundation.

Woll, Allen L., and Miller, Randall. 1987. *Ethnic and Racial Images in American Film and Television: Historical Essays and Bibliography.* New York: Garland.

RECOMMENDED READING

Abash, Barbara and Egan, Catherine, eds. 1992. *Mediating History: The MAP Guide to Independent Video by and about African American, Asian American, Latino, and Native American People.* New York: New York University Press.

Bowser, Kathryn. 1988. *AIVF Guide to International Film and Video Festivals.* New York: Foundation for Independent Video and Film.

Goldman, Nancy. 1991. "Bibliography of Multi-Cultural Film & Video." *SightLines* (Summer/Fall): 29–33.

U.S. Commission on Civil Rights. 1971. *Window Dressing on the Set: Women and*

Minorities in Television; A Report of the United States Commission on Civil Rights. Washington, DC: The Commission.

Worldwide Directory of Film and Video Festivals and Events, 1992–1993. Edited by Richard Calkins. 3rd ed. Washington, DC: The Council on International Nontheatrical Events.

Chapter 10

Cinema Collections: Public Libraries

Randy Pitman

I'm reminded of the title of one of Robin Williams' comedy albums: *Reality! What a Concept!* A quarter century ago, the response to the suggestion that someday people might be able to watch motion pictures on video in their homes whenever they chose might have provoked a similar response: "Video movies! What a concept!" Today, we not only take videocassettes and DVDs for granted, we've even incorporated some of the terminology surrounding the "video revolution" into our daily language. Toddlers with 25-word vocabularies are likely to be able to say some form of the word *video*, while adults, after a particularly grueling weekend in front of the movie machine, might be inclined to say that they were "feeling video'd out."

In short, with VCRs in 93 percent of American homes, and DVD player penetration projected to hit 20 percent by the end of 2001 (with player prices well below the $200 mark), video movies have become as common a feature on the national landscape as Mom, the flag, and apple pie.[1] Grocery stores, gas stations, gift shops, and other independent operations might never consider carrying other media for the public to buy or rent, but many offer videocassettes; and since the mid-1980s, a large number of public libraries have added circulating videocassette collections.

Public libraries are different, in many respects, from the other outlets offering video. Although depth in the range of movies on video found in video stores varies greatly, the smaller to medium-sized outlets concentrate their purchases on that small percentage of video releases that bring in the most amount of revenue: the "A" titles, or recent Hollywood feature films, which generally make their way to video within four to six months after their theatrical run (independent titles and foreign films often take much longer to reach video). With the recent widespread closing of independent video stores (3,624 between January 1998 and December 1999 alone), the homogenized offerings found in the major chains, such as Blockbuster and Hollywood, have even further narrowed the range of choices available to the public.

Fortunately, libraries are not in the "retail" business, nor are they comfortable, at least in the area of print materials, with providing to the public only the newest and most popular items. Serving a broad cross-section of the populace, as libraries do, they are far more conscious of the mandate to build a balanced, diverse collection.

With nearly 20,000 movies released on videocassette, and some 10,000 titles currently on DVD (as of mid-2001), the first step is to establish a set of criteria for making selections. Generally speaking, the optimum video collection should be able to encompass a broad range of classification schemes, including (1) an overall history of the cinema, (2) a sampling of the best of the major genres in film (action/adventure, children's, comedy, cult, drama, foreign, horror, musical, mystery/suspense, science fiction/fantasy, and western), (3) a representation of the work of the best directors making movies, and (4) a popular collection.

Obviously, the key to building a cinema collection that is both good and useful lies in striking a balance. On the one hand, you don't want your collection to merely be a replica of what's available at the local Blockbuster; on the other, you're not really serving the community's needs if all you're offering is Third World cinema or avant-garde video.

Unless you already have a background in film history, you'll probably want to use some of the guides listed in Appendix A to either begin or augment your existing collection. What I'd like to do is concentrate on some of the problem areas you need to be aware of when putting together a cinema collection.

AVAILABILITY

Video movies have a tendency to go "out of print" very quickly, unless they are extremely popular films; and sometimes, even the popular films—many of the Disney animated classics, for example—are put on "moratorium," or taken off the market, after an initial six-month or year-long release. Fortunately, with the wide array of current hits and classic titles continuously being re-released at a low price for the huge legion of video "collectors," sell-through video (and DVD) now accounts for the lion's share of the video business and selectors are faced with a proverbial embarrassment of riches from which to choose. In addition, there are a number of wholesale outlets that have kept their stock of out-of-print video titles on the shelf, as well as a handful of used-tape brokers that carry older, previously viewed titles. (A list of vendors can be found in Appendix B.)

BUDGETS

How much money should you spend on video movies as compared with non-theatrical titles in your collection? Although there are still many libraries out there that are top-heavy in feature films (which may comprise 75 percent or more of the entire collection), the trend has been toward a more responsible, balanced collection mirroring print holdings. For many libraries, the split between non-fiction and fiction runs about 60 percent to 40 percent, respectively, in their print collections—and that should be the model for your video collection.

A more difficult question is how should you split your purchases between video and DVD (which some pundits believe will be the last "hard" format, before broadband streaming video replaces the need for physical copies of movies—a future both uncertain and quite some way off). Presently, feature films on video are variably priced, with most regular movie releases ranging between $89.95 and $109.95 retail (with wholesale prices averaging out to $68 to $84). Occasionally, some foreign and independent films are initially priced in the $59.95 to $79.95 range, making these choices slightly more economical. However, the vast bulk of video movie purchases by public libraries consist of sell-through titles (mostly classics and blockbusters) that are generally offered at $19.95 to $29.95. DVD, by contrast, is priced much lower, with list prices ranging from $14.95 on some older Warner catalog titles to $49.95 on a few of the deluxe edition DVDs from the Criterion Collection and Disney. Most titles, however, price out at under $25 wholesale—a substantial difference from the $100-plus price tag on new video releases.

In addition, many DVD titles offer "extras," ranging from simple text videographies of actors and directors to extensive additional material. Universal Home Video's first quarter 2000 DVD release of Alfred Hitchcock's classic thriller *The Birds*, for example, includes production notes and photos, trailers and newsreels, as well as a stand-alone 80-minute bonus documentary featuring insightful and entertaining interviews with Hitchcock's daughter, Tippi Hedren, Rod Taylor, Veronica Cartwright, scriptwriter Evan Hunter, and others.

Given the rocketing rise of DVD (literally the fastest growing new consumer electronics format in history), my recommendations for stretching the video movies budget would be to seriously consider a few DVD players for checkout and to replace damaged and older VHS titles with DVD whenever possible. The hardware cost will, I think, be outweighed in the long run by not having to make duplicate purchases (in VHS and DVD) of non-current titles. Not only that, but the opportunity to buy new hit DVD titles for under $25 means that you can offer your patrons greater access to a wider range of popular titles than you can with prohibitively priced VHS. Whether this "golden" price scale for DVD will last or not, however, is very much up in the air as of mid-2001, with lots of speculation over whether studios will gradually start raising DVD prices to match VHS rental-priced products once player penetration reaches a comfortable level.

Ultimately, an even bigger "budget" issue lies in how your library divides its overall materials budget. Most likely, your video budget represents less than 10 percent of the overall materials budget, although your video collection may be accounting for 30 percent or more of your library's total circulation. It's pretty hard to build a quality cinema collection (or a quality non-fiction collection, for that matter) on pennies. Angling for a larger slice of the budget pie should be a top priority for anyone planning to build a balanced video collection.

CENSORSHIP, THE MPAA RATINGS, AND ACCESS

Although numerous arguments for or against the Motion Picture Association of America (MPAA) ratings exist, the facts are that (1) many patrons use the ratings as an aid in determining their viewing selections, and (2) many video titles carry the rating on the videocassette box; to ignore—or worse, remove—the rating is, at the very least, a dismissal of what the public has come to accept as usable information about a particular movie, and at the worst, a form of censorship.[2] The argument that ratings constitute labels, and should therefore be removed, is at least partially absurd. (If we really believed this, then we should, by extension, either mask over or remove any publicity tag lines on books—that is, "A sexy, adult thriller" or "A wonderful children's story"—on the grounds that they suggest a particular audience for the material.)

The important thing to keep in mind with the MPAA ratings is that they are only suggestions. They do not now carry, and never have carried, the force of law. To have the ratings as information for patrons is one thing; to enforce the ratings as far as limiting access to video movies is another entirely—and directly in conflict with the principles of intellectual freedom.

However, simply purchasing well-reviewed movies without any regard whatsoever for content is an almost surefire way to end up being crucified by your community. Without necessarily allowing traditional morals and ethics to dictate your movie selections, you still need to be sensitive to your community's standards, as well as the laws in your state.

Take the Japanese film *In the Realm of the Senses*, for example. Lauded by critics (myself included), the film includes graphic sexual scenes of intercourse and fellatio. I do not consider the film to be pornographic, but many would, and in some states, the film would be *legally* considered so. Following the controversy surrounding the releases of *Henry and June*; *The Cook, the Thief, His Wife, and Her Lover*; *Tie Me Up, Tie Me Down*; and *Henry: Portrait of a Serial Killer* in 1990, the MPAA adopted an additional rating of NC-17 (no children under 17) to distinguish films that they felt went beyond a standard "R" rating. None of the films listed above contain graphic sex, but *In the Realm of the Senses* was given, in 1991, an NC-17 rating, and it does contain graphic material.

Further complicating matters is the plethora of "unrated" video releases, most of which are "unrated" for either artistic (i.e., the perception on the part of the filmmaker, producer, and/or distributor that the ratings are either restrictive or irrelevant) or financial (ratings cost money) reasons. Many children's movies are, in fact, "unrated." On the other hand, the 1999 French film *Romance* (released in 2000 by Trimark Home Video), Catherine Breillat's disturbing portrait of a woman's desperate sexual odyssey, was released in both an R-rated 84-minute version and a sexually explicit, "unrated" 98-minute version.

Obviously, purchasing *In the Realm of the Senses* or *Romance* for a small-town library in the Bible Belt would not be a prudent choice. Refusal to purchase *The Cook, the Thief, His Wife, and Her Lover*, on the other hand, because of fear of reprisals from the community would, in most cases, I think, be a clear case of internal censorship. It's an admittedly fine line we're talking about here, and it will require a good dose of common sense and sound judgment to build a cinema collection in the public library that provides a challenging and diversified set of viewpoints—some of which may be unpopular—without outraging the community (or in some cases, breaking the law).

One step you can take in forestalling censorship challenges is to set up a children's video collection in the children's area. Putting your Disney and other quality children's videos near the children's books will not only better serve younger patrons; it's also likely to deter some of them from browsing through the "adult" videos. Without breaking any principles of intellectual freedom, you are still letting parents know that the library understands and respects the differences between children and adults (just as we do with our print collections).

POPULAR VERSUS QUALITY

We sometimes tend to think of *popular* and *quality* as mutually exclusive terms, although they often aren't. Many recent Oscar-winning films are both, obviously, but some blockbusters also straddle the popular/quality fence. It would take a considerable amount of film snobbishness, for example, to maintain that the 1999 Keanu Reeves thriller *The Matrix* is trash. On the contrary, it does precisely what it sets out to do—provide a couple of hours of excellent, thrilling entertainment; no more or less than what any number of popular fiction writers serve up in our print collections.

With a limited budget, however, you really need to be careful about your selections. There's nothing wrong with choosing some movies that are pure entertainment—especially when they have solid critical backing. What you want to avoid are movies that died at the box office but are being promoted on video as if they're the greatest thing since sliced bread, as well as those turkeys that were deemed unfit for theatrical release and went straight into video distribution.

Vendor catalogs published by Baker & Taylor, Follett AudioVisual, Ingram, Midwest Tape, and so on, are excellent places to find out about new movies (although I would also highly recommend you get on the list for the Facets Video catalog, which lists many alternative movies not necessarily carried by the major wholesalers); but they are just the first, not the final, step in making selections. You can't judge a book by its cover, and you can't judge a movie by its ad. Full-page, glossy sell-sheets (as the ads are called) are designed to do just that—sell the movie. Read the fine print. Are the critic's recommendations listed on the ad? Are the credits given (often you might recognize a major director's name in the credits, but it's not prominently displayed in the ad)? Does it star a bunch of name actors, but you've never heard of it (made-for-TV movies are often re-titled for video release, and the fact that it's a made-for-TV movie goes unmentioned)?

Not only can you be sucked into buying a poor movie by an excellent ad; you can also miss a wonderful movie because of the way it's advertised. Just because scantily clad women or giant machine guns are the most prominent aspects of a given ad, it doesn't necessarily mean that the film is some grade-Z sleaze or shooter flick. It's almost human nature to flip past these ads when we're looking for "serious" video movies to add to our collections. Again, read the fine print. Advertising is designed to sell a video, not give an accurate description of its content. Sex and violence sell; therefore, sex and violence will be emphasized. Nine times out of ten, the sleazy ad will indeed be for a sleazy film, but it's that tenth film that will separate the video selector who's on the job from someone that simply picks by the box office numbers.

Once you've made a list of potential purchases (including titles you're unsure about), then it's time to start looking in your reference and review sources. Cross-checking these items will tell you what the ads won't tell you about the movie: the truth.

PUBLIC PERFORMANCE

For most public libraries, public performance of video movies is not really an issue at this point. With video projection equipment priced in the several-thousand-dollars range, few public libraries can afford to hold showings. Too, since the video is presumably also available for checkout, there's far less incentive for people to leave their homes and come to the library to watch a movie.

The sticky part of the public performance issue concerns not group showings but showings for individuals. If a patron wants to sit down in a carrel or use a viewing room to watch a movie, is he breaking the copyright law by engaging in an unlawful public performance? There is no simple answer to that question. To date, there hasn't been a court case involving a library that would decide the question once and for all. The positions are pretty clear: the MPAA holds that any showing in the library is an unlawful public performance (unless a proper license for showing the film has been obtained); the American Library Association (ALA), on the other hand, maintains that single-person or single-family viewings on the library premises do not constitute unlawful public performances.

Legally, I think that the MPAA has the stronger argument, although ethically

I tend to side with the ALA. Yes, the public library is a public place, but does it really matter whether a patron watches a movie in the library or takes it home? Economically, it doesn't, since the studio will not see an additional red cent regardless of where the patron watches the film. Policy-wise, I think it does make a difference, however. We don't require patrons to take books out of the library before they can read them or, God forbid, microfiche. Any materials in the library should be available for use on the library premises, as far as I'm concerned.

Librarians who are interested in holding public performances of feature films on video can purchase "blanket" and/or individual licenses from three sources: the Motion Picture Licensing Corporation (800–338–3870), Swank Motion Pictures (http://www.swank.com; 800–976–5577) or Kit Parker Films (http://kitparker.com; 800–538–5838). Each company holds the "public performance" rights to videos from different major producers (Disney, Warner, Paramount, etc.—though even together, all of the companies do not cover all titles available on video). License fees are computed on a case-by-case basis, taking into account a number of different factors (including number of branches, meeting room capacity, video budget, etc.). It's wise to call each company, compare prices, and even be prepared to bargain a bit if you're not happy with the prices quoted. For smaller, independent labels, such as Kino-on-Video (http://www.kino.com), New Yorker Video (http://www.newyorkerfilms.com), Milestone Film & Video (http://www.milestonefilms.com), Zeitgeist (http://www.zeitgeistfilm.com), and so on, you'll need to contact the distributor directly. For a fuller discussion of performance rights, see Chapter 15.

SLOW-SPEED RECORDING TAPE

Another item is the controversy over video movies recorded in the "extended-play," as opposed to the "standard-play," mode. What this essentially means is that the average feature film can fit on a 60-minute tape rather than a 120-minute tape. It's cost-effective for the distributors, but the process results in a quite noticeable drop in the overall audio and video qualities of the program. Although popular during the late 1980s and early 1990s, movies recorded in the EP or SLP modes are much rarer today (although it's still a common practice on some popular children's titles, such as Paramount's *Blues Clues*). Although the slow speed recording process has improved considerably, I still do not recommend these slow-speed recorded tapes, since some require extensive fiddling around with the tracking adjustment, and many offer a washed-out video image and tunnel-like audio signal. Another option here would be to check for DVD availability, which will also have the advantages of better quality audio and video, on a medium that is less subject to damage than videocassette.

Another problem that, unfortunately, there is no real cure for is the practice of putting long films on a single video. When the home video revolution hit, tape technology was not advanced enough to fit long movies on a 120-minute tape. Today, using much thinner videotape, manufacturers are able to fit a three-hour-plus film on one tape. Two notable "long" films, *The Unbearable Lightness of Being* (171 min.) and *Dances with Wolves* (181 min.), were both cited by video retailers as major "problem" films. The thinner tape was more likely to stretch and cause tears and wrinkles, with the result that many retailers complained that copies of these two films rarely lasted a full month before being trashed. Fortunately, the outcry over *Dances with Wolves*, and the unusually large defective return rate that Orion Home Video suffered, led to more cautious handling of the "long" film problem, though it's still common to see longer titles—such as the 1999 Michael Mann film *The Insider* (158 min.)—on single cassettes.

SUBTITLES

Most of the foreign films on video that have been released on major labels for the past several years offer clear, readable subtitles. However, the quality of earlier and/or non-major label releases can vary widely. Although some titles are available at much lower prices—especially works that are not copyrighted or in the public domain—I recommend that you choose a more expensive but carefully restored and re-subtitled version, where it exists. An example is the many subpar public domain versions of Jean Renoir's 1937 classic *Grand Illusion* that are struck from scratchy prints and feature faded subtitles. Home Vision Arts' VHS and DVD versions, however, are pristine, both in terms of the print and the new subtitles. The VHS version costs twice as much as the public domain versions ($29.95 as opposed to $14.95), but the difference is dramatic: One you can't watch; the other you can relish.

The video revolution has brought an amazing opportunity to our libraries—the ability to offer to their patrons feature films on video that were previously unavailable to them on broadcast television or in local movie theaters (especially many foreign and independent films). As video collections mature, a number of questions that currently plague video librarians will hopefully disappear. Today, libraries worry about ratings, they worry about whether to buy popular or quality movies, they worry about competition with local video stores. In the future, I believe that libraries will make their video movie selections on the same basis that they already make their fiction print selections: they will try to provide the widest variety of materials as their budget will allow, without regard to the subject matter (or ratings) or any outside commercial influence, whether it be a bookstore or a video store.

APPENDIX A: REFERENCE AND REVIEW SOURCES FOR VIDEO MOVIES

Since there are well over 100 books and periodicals that are either exclusively or partially devoted to the subject of video—including such exotic entries as

Cinematherapy: A Girl's Guide to Every Mood, The Guy's Guide to Guy Videos: The Only Guide with Attitude, and *Baked Potatoes: A Pot Smoker's Guide to Film and Video*—a selected bibliography seemed both more appropriate and more useful. To further aid librarians, I have added two symbols—(*) Highly Recommended and (#) Recommended—to denote titles that I feel are either essential or especially helpful. With the exception of David Shipman's *The Story of Cinema*, titles published before 1986 have not been included.

Selection Aids: Books

Connors, Martin and Craddock, Jim, eds. 2002. *VideoHound's Golden Movie Retriever*. Detroit: Gale/Visible Ink. $21.95.

Assigning 1 to 4 bones (as well as a "woof"—zero bones rating), this Saint Bernard of video review guides features nearly 24,000 reviews and comes loaded with extras, including: indexes by category, series, awards, director, cast, writer, cinematographer, composer, and more. Doggone good source. (*)

Doug Pratt's DVD-Video Guide. Harbor Electronic Publishing (available from http://store.unet.net/) $15.97.

Pratt, the publisher/editor of the *DVD-Laser Disc Newsletter*, provides witty capsule reviews of his favorite DVD picks. His print publication purports to be "the world's first in-depth guide to the exciting new medium of DVD-Video."

Ebert, Roger. *Roger Ebert's Movie Yearbook 2001*. New York: Andrews McMeel. $16.95.

Featuring all the reviews published by the most famous critic in America from 1997 though mid-1999, the new format also contains interviews and essays, entertaining questions for the Movie Answer Man, and film festival coverage, as well as a list of all movies previously appearing in earlier editions of *Roger Ebert's Video Companion*. (*) Many of Ebert's *Chicago Sun-Times* reviews (1985–present) are also available online at: http://www.suntimes.com/ebert/index.html.

Facets Non-Violent, Non-Sexist Children's Video Guide. 1996. Compiled by Virginia Boyle. $12.95.

Descriptions of over 800 video releases, including feature films, shorts, and educational videos. Indexed several ways, including thematically (themes of friendship, cooperation, positive self-esteem and peaceful conflict resolution, etc.). Selections geared for kids to age 12. A bit dusty by now, but still useful.

Film Review Annual. 1982—Englewood, NJ: J. Ozer/Film Review Publications. $158.00, annual.

Film reviews released in the United States, and international, from 1981 to the present. The reviews have previously appeared in major newspapers and cinema journals in the United States. Listings are alphabetical by title, and include production, cast, crew, running time, and audience ratings.

Halliwell, Leslie and Walker, John, eds. 2000. *Halliwell's Film and Video Guide 2001*. 15th ed. (in paperback). New York: Harper Resource. $22.50.

Landmark favorite initiated by the late Halliwell now features brief (and often caustic) annotations for over 23,000 feature films, with occasional dialogue excerpts, as well as other critics' comments.

Kael, Pauline. 1991. *5001 Nights at the Movies*. New York: Henry Holt. $27.50.

Capsule reviews of over 5,000 films that originally appeared in *The New Yorker*'s "Goings On About Town" section. Hardcore fans of Kael's feisty and influencial reviewing may also want to check out William J. Slattery et al. (1993), *The Kael Index: A Guide to a Movie Critic's Work, 1954–1991*. Englewood, CO: Libraries Unlimited. $45.00.

Maltin, Leonard. 2000. *Leonard Maltin's TV Movies and Video Guide*. New York: New American Library. $7.99.

For $8 this compendium of capsule reviews for over 20,000 feature films is still one of the best buys on the market. (*)

Martin, Mick, and Porter, Marsha. 2000. *Video Movie Guide 2000*. New York: Ballantine Books. $7.99.

Brief annotations for over 18,000 feature films on video, arranged by genre. In addition to key credit information, this excellent guide includes indexes by cast and director. (*)

The New York Times Guide to the Best Childrens' Videos. 1999. New York: Pocket Books. $16.00.

An annotated and rated guide to more than 1,000 children's videos, including over 500 family films. The book is compiled by KIDS FIRST! an initiative of the Coalition for Quality Children's Media (http://www.cqcm.org). This organization is the only national non-profit organization that uses adult *and* children to evaluate media. Listings are organized by age, from infancy to adolescence.

Shaw, Andrea. 1996. *Seen That, Now What? The Ultimate Guide to Finding the Video You Really Want to Watch*. New York: Simon & Schuster. $25.

Although a bit dated, Andrea Shaw's amusingly arranged video thesaurus of 5,400 titles arranged under headings such as White Flannel Films (*A Room with a View, Out of Africa*, etc.) and *LA Sick Soul of Modern Life* (*American Gigolo, Less Than Zero*, etc.) is still a useful guide. (#)

Selection Aids: Online Periodical Indexes

Most of the standard periodical indexes known and loved by librarians do a fairly good job of covering reviews of current and older (mainstream) feature films in popular journals and newspapers. *The Readers Guide* and the *New York Times* are good places to start delving for such reviews (look under MOTION PICTURES—REVIEWS). The advent of Web-based periodical and journal indexes has expanded the options for finding such reviews, making it possible to search an ever-broadening base of publications for both review citations and—increasingly—the full text of the reviews themselves. The indexes listed below are examples of some of the larger and most generally useful online databases for finding film and video reviews and criticism.

Expanded Academic Index (Information Access Company/Gale) http://www.Gale.com.

Includes citations for articles from over 1,500 core academic journals and popular magazines in the social sciences, humanities, sciences, business, and law. Contains some abstracts, and some full text. Coverage includes 1988 to the present. Journals indexed include *American Film*; *Cineaste*; *Film Comment*; *Film Quarterly*; *Films in Review*; *Historical Journal of Film, Radio, and Television*; *Journal of Film and Video; Journal of Popular Film and Television*; *Literature-Film Quarterly*; *Quarterly Review of Film and Video*; *Sight & Sound*; and *Variety*.

Lexis/Nexis (Academic Universe) (Reed/Elsevier, Inc.) http://www.lexis-nexis.com/.

Indexing and full-text articles from thousands of national and regional publications, including general interest periodicals, newspapers, and newsletters, trade journals, and other industry publications. A separate Arts & Sports category allows searching for book, movie, play, and music reviews. Covers the past 10–20 years to present.

National Newspaper Index (Information Access Company/Gale) http://www.Gale.com/.

Indexes *Christian Science Monitor* (National edition); *New York Times Magazine*, *Los Angeles Times* (Home edition); *Wall Street Journal* (Eastern and Western editions); *New York Times* (Late and National editions); *New York Times Book Review*; *Washington Post* (Final edition), January 1, 1982 to the present. IAC also offers an expanded database of newspapers (InfoTrac) that provides full text for some of the titles indexed.

ProQuest (Bell & Howell Information and Learning Company).

Includes abstracts and indexing to more than 1,100 periodical titles, plus current coverage of *New York Times* articles. It includes some full text. Journals indexed include *American Film, Cineaste, Film Comment, Film Quarterly, Films in Review*, and *Historical Journal of Film, Radio, and Television*.

Selection Aids: Periodicals

Boxoffice, monthly, $40 yr.

Excellent, reasonably priced review source for feature films which, in addition to offering original reviews, collates numerical gradings from several other review sources. (*)

DVD Insider, daily. Free to all interested subscribers. http://www.dvdinsider.com/.

Geared to DVD professionals, *DVD Insider* is a mailing list (*DVD Spotlight*) and Web site that provide useful information about new DVD releases and DVD software and hardware industry developments. Includes reviews of current DVD releases.

DVD-Daily, bi-weekly. Free to all interested subscribers. http://www.dvd-daily.com.

Steven Craig Sickles' useful free e-journal provides detailed information on upcoming DVD releases, in addition to well-written reviews of current releases.

DVD Journal. http://www.dvdjournal.com/.

A useful, free e-journal that provides "DVD news, reviews, commentary, and stuff like that." Includes information on DVD (and other media) hardware, software, and commerce, as well as amusing reviews of current releases.

DVD-Laser Disc Newsletter, monthly, $35 yr.

Doug Pratt's chatty, amusing, and informative reviews of new DVD and laser disc releases. Pratt has put an index to the newsletter and many past reviews on his Web site: http://www.DVDLaser.com/ (Pratt, a man definitely given to hyperbole, claims that his site is the largest DVD review database on the Web). (*)

DVD Review http://www.dvdreview.com/.

Contains news, reviews, release dates, miscellaneous information about DVD technology, downloadable clips, links to related sites.

Entertainment Weekly, weekly, $52 yr. http://www.ew.com/.

EW has slowly grown into one of the indispensable review sources covering what's new each week in various media. Although not comprehensive, *EW* offers a good mix between capsule reviews of pop, independent, and foreign film and video titles. (*)

Library Journal, bi-weekly, $109 yr. http://www.ljdigital.com/.

Jeff Dick's "Fast Scans" column reviews approximately ten lesser-known American independent and foreign feature films per issue. (*)

Sound & Vision, monthly, $24 yr. http://www.soundandvisionmag.com/. Offering nearly two dozen movie reviews per issue, this hybrid magazine built from combining *Video Review* and *Stereo Review* also features excellent layperson-friendly articles explaining new technology. (#)

Variety, weekly, $146.50 yr. http://www.variety.com/.

Extensive reviews of new feature films. (#) A useful reference resource for finding reviews of older titles in *Variety* is Max Joseph Alvarez. 1982. *Index to Motion Pictures Reviewed by Variety, 1907–1980*. Metuchen, NJ: Scarecrow Press. $47.50.

Video Librarian, bi-monthly $47 yr. http://www.videolibrarian.com/.

Randy Pitman's video review magazine for libraries features some 175 reviews per issue, including roughly 40 reviews of upcoming popular, independent, and foreign videos and DVDs. (*)

Video Business, weekly. Free (to qualified subscribers). http://www.videobusiness. com/.

Aimed primarily at video retailers, this informative weekly lists street dates on upcoming feature video releases and addresses issues primarily of relevance to the video industry, some with implications for public libraries as well. (*)

Video Store, weekly. Free (to qualified subscribers).

This is an excellent freebie that lists street dates and pre-order information on upcoming feature video releases, as well as running articles on video industry matters. (*)

For articles about movies and the movie business, you might also want to check out *Cineaste* (http://www.cineaste.com/), *Film Comment* (http://www.filmlinc.com/fcm/fcm. htm), and *Premiere* (http://www.premiere.com). And don't forget major newspapers; many have regular video review columns.

Reference Sources: Print/CD-ROM

Bowker's Complete Home Video Directory. 2000. New York: R. R. Bowker Co. $275.

Boasting entries covering some 200,000 videos, the four-volume Bowker directory includes indexes for genre, cast/director, and awards, among others. Foreign films are also indexed by country of origin. Also available on CD-ROM, updated quarterly ($520). (#)

Media Review Digest. 1970. Ann Arbor, MI: Pierian Press. http://www.pierianpress. com. $395–$595 yearly, 1–8 concurrent users.

An index to reviews and evaluations of documentary, educational, and feature films from over 150 reviewing sources, including journals, festivals, and organizations. The print version of the MRD began in 1970. The Web version of the MRD provides coverage from 1989 to the present, including more than 90,000 media resources with more than 375,000 reviews, evaluations, awards, and prizes.

Shipman, David. 1982. *The Story of Cinema*. New York: St. Martin's Press. $19.95. (*)
Superb one-volume history of cinema for familiarizing oneself with the history of movies. As of mid-2000, available only as special order item, possibly with higher price.

The Video Source Book. 2000. 24th ed. Detroit: Gale Group. $335.
Known within the industry as "The Bible," this hefty reference work lists some 120,000 titles encompassing over 160,000 videos. Each entry includes some 20 different facts about the video (rating, running time, year of release, etc.). Indexes include: alternate title, subject, credits, awards, special formats, and program distributors. (#)

Reference Sources: Web

All Media Guide (http://www.allmovie.com).
All Media Guide's 160,000 title database (which includes special interest titles, though these rarely include reviews) offers search capabilities for title, cast, keyword, and plotline, and listings include these as well as general production information. Although both useful and fun, the plotline searches are not always comprehensive. "Cannibalism," for instance, includes two categories, "lifestyle of" (which inexplicably only includes *Night of the Living Dead*), and "for profit" (which includes 12 entries, but omits the black comedy classic *Motel Hell*). Still, a good resource to use for viewer advisory. (#)

Internet Movie Database (http://www.imdb.com).
Featuring detailed videographic information and sophisticated search functions for over 230,000 movies, the first-to-the-Web giant movie database, IMDB literally transformed video movie reference work with its numerous cross-links (cast, director, reviews, etc.), keyword searches, and now—thanks to being bought by Amazon.com—instantaneous confirmation of whether a movie is available on video. (*)

Movie Review Query Engine (http://www.mrqe.com).
Although not nearly as elaborate as other movie databases, the MRQE offers links to over 140,000 reviews for over 19,000 movies.

TV Guide Online Movie Database (http://www.tvguide/movies.com).
Although the search functions are limited (title, cast), *TV Guide*'s database of over 40,000 movies features starred reviews, general production information, and cross-linked cast listings.

In addition to general movie databases and sites, the Web has spawned a wide variety of review sites, both original (see http://www.ofcs.org for listings of members of the Online Film Critics Society) and spin-offs from existing print publications (Roger Ebert, *Chicago Sun-Times* [http://www.suntimes.com/ebert], the *New York Times* [http://www. nytimes.com], *Variety* [http://www.variety.com/], etc.).

The number of individual fan review sites, review sites attached to commercial and industry enterprises, and hybrids of the two (e.g., Epinions.com and MovieFan [http:// www.moviefanonline.com/dvd_reviews/]) is truly mind-boggling. This online stew includes an increasing number of sites exclusively devoted to reviewing new DVD releases (see, for example, *E!online* [http://aol.eonline.com/Reviews/Dvd/], *DVD-Daily* [http:// www.dvd-daily.com], *DVD Insider* [http://www.dvdinsider.com/insight/movies/reviews/], Doug Pratt's *DVD-Laser Disc Newsletter* [http://www.DVDLaser.com], and *DVD Town* [http://www.dvdtown.com]).

APPENDIX B: VENDORS FOR VIDEO MOVIES

The following vendors have been divided into three groups: wholesale, retail, and used-video dealers. Most wholesale vendors offer a substantial discount on the video movies they carry (often between 25 and 30 percent) but do not always carry as wide a variety of titles. Retail vendors generally charge full list price for video movies (though some will discount a large order) but often have a greater selection of video movies on hand.

Major Wholesale Vendors

Baker & Taylor Video, Five Lake Pointe Plaza, 2709 Water Ridge Parkway, Suite 500, Charlotte, NC 28217; (800) 775–1800; http://www.btol.com.

Follett Audiovisual Resources, 220 Exchange Doctor, Suite A, Crystal Lake, IL 60014; http://www.far.follett.com.

Ingram Video, One Ingram Boulevard, P.O. Box 3006, La Vergne, TN 37086–1986; (800) 937–5300; http://www.ingramlibrary.com.

Midwest Tape, P.O. Box 820, Holland, OH 43528; (800) 875–2785; http://www. midwesttapes.com.

Professional Media Services, 1160 Trademark Drive, Suite 109, Reno, NV 89511; (800) 223–7672; http://www.promedia.com/.

Major Retail Outlets

Amazon.com (online only) (http://www.amazon.com).

Bigstar.com (online only) (http://www.bigstar.com/).

DVD Express.com (online only) (http://www.dvdexpress.com).

Facets Video, 1517 West Fullerton Avenue, Chicago, IL 60614; (800) 331–6197; IL: (312) 281–9075; http://www.facets.org.

Ken Crane Laserdiscs, 15251 Beach Boulevard, Westminster, CA 92683; (800) 624–3078; CA: (800) 626–1768; (714) 892–2283; Fax: (714) 892–8369; discs@kencranes. com; http://www.kencranes.com/.

Movies Unlimited, 3015 Darnell Road, Philadelphia, PA 19154; (800) 668–4344; http: //www.moviesunlimited.com.

Major Used-Tape Dealers

DV&A, 1610 North Myrtle Avenue, Clearwater, FL 33755; (800) 382–8433; http:// www.dva.com.

Tapeworm Video Distributors, 27833 Hopkins Avenue, Unit 6, Valencia, CA 91355; (805) 257–4904; Fax: (805) 257–4820; http://www.tapeworm.com/.

Video Oyster, 145 West 12th Street—basement #1, New York, NY 10011; (212) 976–6800; video@VideoOyster.com; http://www.VideoOyster.com.

NOTES

Portions of this chapter originally appeared in a much different form in *Video Movies: A Core Collection for Libraries*, by Randy Pitman and Elliot Swanson (Santa Barbara, CA: ABC-CLIO, 1990).

1. For those interested in tracking the commercial fortunes of the DVD and VHS industries—such statistics as hardware and software sales—there are a growing number of fairly reliable Web resources which may be consulted: for example, Showbiz Data (http://www4.showbizdata.com); Media Central (http://www.mediacentral.com/); DVD File (http://www.dvdfile.com/); DVD Insider (http://www.dvdinsider.com/).

2. For the official ALA stand on MPAA ratings, see "Access for Children and Young People to Videotapes and Other Nonprint Formats: An Interpretation of the Library Bill of Rights. http://www.ala.org/alaorg/oif/acc_chil.html.

RECOMMENDED READING

Manafy, Michelle. 2000. "Facts, Figures, & Findings: DVD Players, Projection TV Sales Continue to Climb." *EMedia Professional* 13(4) (April): 12.

Mitchell, Rick. "MPAA Ratings Code is Broke." *Variety* 376(6) (September 27, 1999): 6.

Roth, Chris. 2000. "Three Decades of Film Censorship . . . Right Before Your Eyes." *Humanist* 60(1) (January): 9.

Van Horn, Charles. 2001. "DVD Delivers Over 10,000 Reasons to Buy." Speech delivered by the President of the International Recording Media Association at DVD Europe 2001, April 20, 2001, London, England. http://www.recordingmedia.org/speechdvdeur2001.html.

Vroman, D. L. 1995. "To See or Not to See: A Study of Video Collection Censorship in American Public Libraries." *RQ* 35 (Fall): 37–42.

Waldrep, Mark. "DVD: The First Three Years." *EMedia Professional* 13(4) (April 2000): 52. http://www.emedialive.com/EM2000/between4.html.

Chapter 11

Cinema Collections: Academic Libraries

Oksana Dykyj

The intent of this chapter is to address a number of specific issues pertinent to cinema collections in academic libraries and other academic environments. It will also attempt to highlight areas in which cinema collections differ from other academic moving-image collections, particularly in the exceptionally broad range of academic disciplines and endeavors these collections support. In order to understand the current status of film studies on campuses today and how this field is likely to affect collection development, a chronology of its development is provided along with a discussion of current and anticipated future topics for research and teaching.

What is Cinema? is the title of the collected works of one of the preeminent film theorists, André Bazin. What, indeed, is "cinema"?—a term used to designate art, entertainment, commerce, and slice-of-life reality. And what is the significance and role of this technology, art form, societal mirror, and industry as a focus for academic study? Because moving images are the starting point of much of contemporary self-expression and communication, they are studied and used as teaching tools in a multitude of academic disciplines; but, the term "cinema" has undergone many identity permutations since the period when it originally only meant motion picture film. Film as high art or popular culture artifact now includes video art, multimedia performance pieces, and other aesthetics hybrids. The terms used to denote the realm of "cinema"—film, video, digital—have expanded and now appear to be used interchangeably. Furthermore, the boundaries between these forms and genres has continued to blur and mutate: the original work may have been made on film, but is now being delivered digitally as a streamed video via the Web; or the work may have been conceived as an experimental video and subsequently distributed or commercially available on DVD.

In the face of the rapid convergence and flux of moving-image technologies and forms, there is little academic consensus regarding either nomenclature for cinema and its components, or the rightful place of film studies on campus. As Daryl Chin (1996) has commented: "The fact that the movies can encompass so many arts, visual, theatrical, literary, has made the definition of 'cinematic' forever unstable." This situation in some sense mirrors the fact that academic departments themselves are in the process of re-inventing the very nature of who they are and what they teach and study in an intellectually and aesthetically convergent world. Increasingly, the traditional boundaries between disciplines have begun to dissolve, and the scope of inquiry within individual disciplines continues to expand. Film Studies falls squarely and significantly into this context.

Film/movie/cinema continuously re-invents popular culture, and in doing so continues to re-invent its importance and role in academia. Moving images in any incarnation are powerful didactic tools, and increasing numbers of academic courses are incorporating cinema into their curricula. The impact of "the movies" on all aspects of modern life—their recording and reflection of cultural fantasies, fears, and outlooks—has made them an intense focus of study across the disciplinary board. Film Studies departments are no longer unique in looking at and studying fiction, non-fiction, animation, and experimental moving-image works: there are now notable studies of architecture and cinema; political sciences, history, and cinema (Adams 1968); ethnic and women's studies and cinema. Art history, dramatic arts, and dance courses regularly include film, as do historical and theoretical courses in comparative arts. Language courses make extensive use of feature films, to expose students both to spoken vernacular and to the cultures in which the language is spoken (Cockerman 1972). Journals such as *Film and Philosophy* flourish, while listservs dealing with history and film are among the most active on the cinema front. What is cinema? It is clearly the depiction of modern culture, and within a contemporary academic context it has become one of the strongest elements of Cultural Studies.

DEVELOPMENT OF CINEMA AS AN ACADEMIC DISCIPLINE

The study of film began soon after films began being watched. Boleslaw Matuszewski, an early film theorist and philosopher, published two treatises in Paris in 1898 in which he discussed the advantages of film as an educational tool, as well as the necessity of proper collection building to fully utilize its didactic power (Matuszewski 1999 [1898]). Initially, film education was not formal, and consisted of how-to books: how to run a theater, how to get into the film business, or how to write and sell a script. Writer Anita Loos and her husband, film director John Emerson, published a number of these. *How to Write Photoplays* (Emerson and Loos 1920), for example, goes beyond the cursory text to include analysis and criticism. Publications like *Moving Picture World* began printing articles on scriptwriting at the start of the 1910s, and books closely followed. Institutions such as the New York Institute of Photography began giving courses in scriptwriting, and textbooks began to appear to support this teaching (Wright 1922). There were also correspondence courses on this increasingly lucrative subject during the 1910s and 1920s. By the very early 1920s, educational film services were already being provided in two dozen state universities (Nolan 1961) as these types of films proliferated.[1] Publications devoted to the teaching of international film culture in primary and high school, such as *Educational Screen*, began to appear around this same time (Edgar 1935).

In the early 1930s the film archive movement had its beginnings. With the establishment of the Film Library at the Museum of Modern Art (MoMA) in 1935, the emphasis was on the study of films themselves, not simply their preservation. A theater was constructed in the museum in 1939, and MoMA's lending library began shipping films out to film societies and educational institutions (Houston 1994). Shortly prior to this period, the 16mm amateur film gauge also became popular. In 1925, the Kodascope Library was fully operative in the United States and Britain. Sixteen-millimeter films could be rented and watched in the privacy of one's own home or with friends. The categories of films in this library ranged from drama and comedy to popular science, useful arts, and natural history (McKee 1978). The British Film Institute, established in 1935, began to issue a catalog of 35mm and 16mm films available to institutions and individuals. During this period, enthusiasts and filmmakers engaged in discussions in cineclubs and contributed to journals or distributed mimeographed film notes to the regulars gathered to watch films presented by avid collectors or borrowed from a library.

Along with the rise of continuing education courses in various aspects of filmmaking, the late 1920s also saw the slow beginnings of formal, organized academic film study in a small number of universities. In 1929 the Academy of Motion Picture Arts and Sciences (AMPAS), in cooperation with the University of Southern California, offered a course in motion picture appreciation—specifically on the appreciation of the photoplay. The guest lecturers included actors (Douglas Fairbanks, Conrad Nagel), producers (Irving Thalberg), writers (Paul Bern), and directors (J. Stuart Blackton). A similar course was subsequently given at Stanford University, and a textbook published (AMPAS 1929). These programs were among the factors leading to the establishment of academic courses—and in some instances departments—of film, at the University of Southern California (in 1932), at the University of California at Los Angeles, City College of New York, New York University, and Boston University by the end of the 1940s. The increase in academic publications related to film, including scholarly guides and bibliographies, reflect the rise of Film Studies during this period, as well (Christeson 1938; Giroux 1936). By the end of the 1950s, Art and English departments were also offering courses in film appreciation, criticism, or history (Curry 1986), and it was natural for academic libraries to establish film collections to support these curricula. It was pedagogical innovation rather than film research that led the way for the classroom presentation of films in literature, theater, philosophy, and art history courses. Film was introduced as an innovative way of teaching, and as a means of encouraging the study of adaptations of novels and plays. The use of film allowed the inclusion of popular culture in treating traditional topics like genres and myths (Andrew 2000; Jackson-Wrigley and Leyland 1939).

As the demand for film courses grew, the need for fundamental scholarship became increasingly apparent. In Britain, the number of lectures handled by the British Film Institute in association with numerous colleges increased from 343 in 1956–1957 to almost 1,000 in 1963–1964 (Hall et al. 1964). Academic cinema studies is usually given a birth date of around 1968, coinciding with the turbulent period before the Society for Cinema Studies grew out of the Society of Cinematologists. The results of a 1969 American Film Institute survey indicate that in the United States there were 219 institutions of higher learning offering some sort of film course and 51 offering degrees (Spehr 1970). Much of the theoretical work concerning film had up to this point been European, and related to an auteurist approach to film, spearheaded by André Bazin.[2] This canon was more or less supplanted by a North American embrace of Post-Structuralist literary theory, Structuralist semiotics, variants of Althusserian Marxism, and Lacanian psychoanalysis as approaches to analyzing or "reading" films. Christian Metz' *Language and Cinema* (1974), Laura Mulvey's "Visual Pleasure in the Narrative Cinema" (1975), Jean-Louis Baudry's "The Apparatus" (1986), Stephen Heath's "Narrative Space" (1976), and Peter Wollen's *Signs and Meaning in the Cinema* (1969) were some of the more important texts that became the basis of theoretical teaching in Film Studies. The films analyzed in these texts, such as the work of John Ford and Howard Hawks, were intensely watched and discussed. Film Studies allied itself with structural linguistics and comparative literature. Thus, Roman Jacobson, Claude Levi-Strauss, and Roland Barthes bridged textual semiotics with a psychoanalysis of reading by repeatedly addressing cinema in the process (Andrew 2000).

Feminist film theory followed these theoretical trends by initially drawing heavily on European psychoanalytic theory and then diversifying; but, by the 1980s a focus on television had crept into syllabi, challenging the priorities of academics and unleashing an era of pluralism in the late 1980s. If the 1970s addressed theoretical "subject-positioning," then the 1980s argued for "culturalism" along with Postmodernism as its second strand (Bordwell and Carroll 1996). In the past 20 years, plural inquiry has encompassed many areas such as history, with very early cinema or colonial and postcolonial images a particular focus.

In the past 10 years, reception study has been a similarly popular area of research. This academic focus, which examines a variety of topics, ranging from cult films to audience function, is a type of literary sociology that analyzes the variety of ways audiences receive or apprehend a film, rather than the films themselves. Reception study, together with the growing focus on the interrelationships between motion picture and other arts and technologies, has resulted in moving Film Studies toward more of a Cultural Studies approach to research.

In their 1996 anthology *Post-Theory: Reconstructing Film Studies*, David Bordwell and Noel Carroll sought to challenge the prevailing practices of film scholarship by proposing that theories be thought of in terms of a field of activity, tailored to specific goals rather than searching for a unified theory that will explain many films, their production, and reception. Bordwell and Carroll maintain that middle-level research programs have shown that you can do a lot with films besides interpret them.

The study of media platforms and the impact and influence of digital technologies on film is as much a theoretical issue as it is a technical and cultural one. This focus will undoubtedly be a central one for scholars for some time to come. Inquiries into film and the construction of social identity have also been prominent in recent years. Topics related to cinema and gender, nationality, ethnicity, and sexuality continue to be on the front burner as courses, as conference papers, as dissertations, and areas of research. Current trends include studies of the body and of masculinity, an approach that has expanded the concept of gender and film beyond the previous focus of feminist film studies. A related area—queer studies—has also been prominent and diverse. There is a sense of a "theoretical quieting down" in the humanities that is affecting Film Studies. This trend is leading the way to research related to technological advances and, more quietly and slowly, to a small area of cognitive psychology/ analytical philosophy-influenced studies.

Film Studies is presently at a crossroads as a discipline; it is somewhat fragmented, questioning its identity as it prepares to re-invent itself again. New faculty appointments at universities include a generation of professors raised on film and television at home and in the classroom. These faculty are not hesitant to introduce films in their courses whenever appropriate and convenient (Andrew 2000). However, the difference between them and earlier, non-film-studies academics may only lie in their cinema education.

CINEMA OUTSIDE FILM STUDIES

Just as Film Studies was coming into its own as a discipline in the 1960s, other disciplines were beginning to take a much greater interest in films, studying them not only as a communication system, but also for the insight they supplied into the society they depicted (Lovell 1970). As discussed earlier, the study of film—as history, as art form, as societal reflection—spread to an increasing number of disciplines. With this broadening of interest on campuses came an increased demand for resources. Data indicate that even in the mid-1970s, bookings for videocassettes was much higher than records, audiocassettes, or slides relative to holdings (Roberts 1975).

Political Science, Anthropology, and Management are other areas that have reported successfully using films in teaching, either as entire films or excerpted scenes illustrating abstract theories and concepts: films can function effectively as case studies or be used as experiential exercises to be solved in groups (Champoux 1999). Educators often publish material on how to effectively use films in teaching (Fails 1988; Jurkiewicz 1990; Proctor 1990), and report findings about positive course evaluations in courses using films (Champoux 1999). Using film as a didactic tool is now standard practice. Instructors use *Twelve Angry Men* as well as *Mary Poppins* to illustrate decision-making processes and management styles. Fiction films are easily found in which the characters or situations represent theoretical models.

In the last 40 years we have seen a cross-pollination of teaching methods and materials and a cross-disciplinary use of cinema collections in teaching and research. These trends could be defined as an academic embracing of Cultural Studies; they could reflect the general assumption that students entering colleges or universities bring with them a degree of media and cinema literacy (or at least certain expectations regarding the use and availability of media related to their studies). A professor in the History Department giving a course on documentary film can fairly safely assume that most of her students possess a level of understanding of the medium that was not present a generation ago. The area of history is a useful one to examine in terms of teaching and research trends. One of the hottest areas for study is non-Western history, including such popular topics as genocide, Native history, and colonialism. Topics in cultural history, which have traditionally been marginalized, appear to be doing well. There is more published research in this area than previously and courses on film, music, popular culture, and public history are proliferating in history departments. There is also a broader interest in more contemporary periods of history. This latter-day focus lends itself particularly well to the use of moving images, and virtually all the major history journals have begun to review films routinely. However, there still appears to exist a tendency for historians to deal with films as either purely illustrative material, or as easy targets for pointing out and mocking historical inaccuracies and biases.

It is clear that using media has long been popular in certain areas of academia, but in the last five years it has also become an accepted and legitimate practice. Where a generation ago a course about Shakespeare on film might have been scoffed at by the English Department, it most likely would not be today, simply because the scholarly focus on the subject has intensified and the approach to teaching the topic has evolved and matured.

THE CINEMA LIBRARIAN, FACULTY, AND THE FIELD OF CINEMA

For academic librarians working with cinema collections, the last 40 years have necessitated adaptability at every turn. The rapidly successive introduction and obsolescence of moving-image formats have resulted in numerous preservation issues in terms of both material and equipment. The growing interest in film and video in teaching and research has required the development of much closer working relationships with academic departments, and a symbiotic participation in curricular development. In many academic institutions it is the cinema librarian who has been instrumental in first acquiring films on video and other evolving formats, and then bringing the possibilities of these media to the attention of faculty. The media librarian then and now functions as research support, and if the relationship with academic departments is positive, a synergetic outcome is inevitable.

There are many ways of keeping up with developments in academic areas related to cinema. The most obvious is to be aware of the titles that circulate for teaching purposes. Those faculty members who are heavy media users usually have a screening list of titles to be booked for their course. Using screening lists as a starting point, as well as the course description in the institution's catalog, a cursory overview of the topic begins to emerge. This information gathering can be done on a course-by-course basis, depending on department. If the institution has a Film Studies Department, it might be simpler to request a copy of handouts for all the courses being offered. Another source for sample syllabi are the "Course Files," regularly published in the *Journal of Film and Video*, which present examples of a wide variety of Film Studies courses with reading lists, filmographies, modules, and sample assignments (Erens 1986). The third in a series of biannual issues on teaching film and video courses appeared in the Summer 1999 issue of *Cinema Journal*: it contains several articles dealing with teaching national cinema courses and includes screening lists which could be useful as a way of enhancing existing collections (Welsch 1999). Automated booking systems and databases, which provide summary data about titles booked for courses, can also be a source of valuable information regarding the shifts in teaching topics. This type of information can also alert the cinema librarian to subject or discipline areas that need to be further enhanced, or areas in desperate need of core titles.

Communication with faculty is essential and should be considered a crucial part of the collection development process—possibly even formally mandated in the collection policy. Use-analyses tend to confirm that video titles specifically requested by faculty are twice as likely to circulate as non-requested titles (Lloyd 1994). Conversely, studies of low collection use recommend greater liaison with relevant academic departments, including department heads (or chairs) and staff who use media resources (Evans and Del-Pizzo 1999). As helpful as post facto use studies can be, a pro-active approach to collection building tends to be the most beneficial in most cases. Anticipating curricular requirements and possible evolving research areas by staying informed allows the development of a collection that not only meets needs but also provides options.

Joining a select group of academic film associations is a very reliable way of both keeping up with the trends and research in the field and obtaining a better sense of the position or role the various academic institutions play in the development of the field. Association newsletters provide publication information, and annual association conferences are where the most current thought in the disciplines is exchanged. The Society for Cinema Studies (http://www. cinemastudies.org), the University Film and Video Association (http://www. ufva.org), and the Film Studies Association of Canada (http://www.film. queensu.ca/FSAC) are three of the most important Film Studies associations in North America. Even a cursory look at the call for papers of these groups provides an unambiguous snapshot of research trends. Because most Film Studies faculty are members of at least one of these associations, their own concerns and research will be reflected in future courses they will teach.

The awareness of specialized film festivals is another way to increase subject knowledge and to broaden familiarity with specific distribution and reference information for current films. Faculty often learn about new film offerings by attending independent, documentary, and historical film festivals (or at least by reading festival publications and lists). Keeping abreast of the activities of notable local and national festivals will allow a media librarian to anticipate titles likely to be requested. Chapters 19, 20, and 22 in this book provide good listings of some of these festivals.

Specialized or more general academic subject online discussion lists (listservs) provide a more personal and immediate overview of current concerns in the field, and build a sense of professional collaboration. Screen-L and H-Net are the two main and active lists related to Film Studies areas. Other lists are worth looking in on occasionally, but tend to either be too marginal or non-academic. To supplement the perspective from a librarian's point of view, the American Library Association Video Round Table's listserv, (VIDEOLIB) is an invaluable source of information. As both a participator and consumer in this discussion forum, I can honestly say that it may well be the most important reference source for media librarians. One can often learn more in a week of listserv threads than from an organized search of the literature. The immediacy of such online forums cannot be stressed too highly—they effectively bring the research and teaching concerns out in public as they occur, as well as the answers, solutions, or recommendations. The academic process is long and tedious: by the time information is published, particularly as it relates to media librarianship and cinema, a certain percentage of it is no longer pertinent, valid, or accurate. Film distributors may come and go but VIDEOLIB is a constant (see Chapter 22 in this book for information on subscribing to the above-mentioned and other film-related lists).

CINEMA COLLECTIONS AND THEIR USE IN ACADEMIC INSTITUTIONS

There are basically three types of media collections containing cinema materials in academic institutions: video formats only (including laser discs and DVDs) situated in libraries and/or media centers, sometimes under an Instructional Technology (IT) umbrella; 16mm (and occasionally 35mm) films, as well as various video formats located in libraries or IT media centers; and situations where there is a separation of formats: films are housed in an institutional archive or academic department, while video formats are under the library or IT media center umbrella. There is no right way or wrong way of managing cinema collections as long as proper care is exercised, and information about and access to these collections is effectively provided. Historical staffing and budget considerations tend to determine ownership in academic institutions, occasionally resulting in limited access, particularly if a collection is housed within an academic department rather than in the library or separate IT center.

Academic cinema collections tend to be composed of commercially acquired or locally produced materials rather than rare and unique archival material. Rather than being stashed away in a vault, these collections are regularly—often intensively—used in teaching and in research. The teaching process varies from department to department, from course to course, from instructor to instructor, from freshman level to graduate courses, and from institution to institution. If a sociology instructor wants to show part of *Blackboard Jungle* in class to make a point, the quality of the format is generally less important than the quality of the content. When the film is available for rent from a distributor or on video in the institution's collection, even if the rental cost were not an issue, the ease of use of video makes it more desirable as a teaching tool than film. Similarly, if a Film Studies instructor requests the best possible format to project Sergei Eisenstein's *Strike*, it may also not be a 16mm film. The rapid growth of the video market during the past 20 years has greatly impacted the non-theatrical distribution of 16mm film, and it is increasingly rare to find 16mm prints being struck for this market. The media librarian working with cinema collections should be able to advise an instructor of the benefits of showing a new DVD or even a VHS that has been made from the best source material available, rather than using a dark, duped, and possibly incomplete and silent 16mm print of the film. Some academics are under the misconception that film—any film— is always better than video. These misguided purists rarely stop to realize that the film they would normally consider projecting in class might actually be several generations removed from the original, while the newly acquired DVD may have been made from a video master of a restored positive print, and projects beautifully on a video projector. Sometimes a "shoot-out"—a side-by-side comparison—of formats can persuade faculty members to select the best currently available material to show their students. Such comparisons can also act as the catalyst for developing a positive relationship between the librarian and faculty. The best medium for the individual situation ought to be the rule. If a psychology professor wants to show a film to make a point about the effects of horror film visuals and sound on an audience, the best advice might be to forgo showing a class of 50 students a 15-year-old video on a small monitor in favor of securing a budget to rent a 16mm print and having it properly projected to the class (or better still, to move the class to an auditorium equipped with a 35mm or professional 16mm projection booth). The media librarian, in understanding the goal of using film in the classroom, participates in the process.

It must be mentioned that the use of video in the past 20 years has enormously changed the Film Studies teaching and learning process. Despite detractors who maintain that the only true way to teach film is by showing 16mm or 35mm film, there are more positive benefits to the use of video than negative repercussions, as will be discussed below. By using video, more material can generally be covered in class, close analysis can be done more easily, and students can acquire a broader sense of film history. Video has, therefore, enabled the development of a new film culture, much beyond that which was previously offered by cineclubs and art houses. For Film Studies, at least, video has had some of the same impact as the printing press has had on the literary world: it has allowed the close examination of unique texts by the masses and has encouraged textual literacy, in contrast to earlier, limited access to a small body of incunabula by the elite.

In institutions with Film Studies departments, the collection may be used in a variety of ways. Depending on the time allotment per class, an instructor in a course that meets once a week for four hours may want to show an entire work, followed by close analysis of short clips of the film viewed and perhaps several others. In a course that meets twice a week for two hours per class, an instructor may want to show an entire film on one day, and during the following class, analyze the clips, and hold a discussion. Depending on the institution and its budgets and mission (and the background and inclinations of its instructors), an array of classroom projection formats and technologies may be brought into play, including 35mm and 16mm projection (with licensed projectionists); video projection, including multi-standard VHS[3] (PAL [Phase Alternating Line], NTSC [National Television Standards Committee], or SECAM [Sequential Color and Memory]) and ¾-inch U-MATIC videoplayers; laser disc, and DVD players. If the institution has film/video production programs, playback equipment for professional production formats such as Betacam SP or digital video may also be required. It is increasingly common to find a mix of requirements in film courses: if a particular class revolves around the aesthetics of camera movement, for instance, an instructor may show his students the entire film projected in 16mm or 35mm film, and bring to their attention some key sequences or specific camera movements on DVD. After a discussion, the same instructor may show the class other camera movements from other films cued up on a number of videos, or called up by frame or sequence on DVDs. A four-hour class may involve using one main film and clips from 10 or 15 works as additional examples. Film Studies courses may have been the first to intensively use classroom technology, but the world has changed rapidly. The increasing demand for Internet and other computer-based resources and for digital projection equipment in classes has forced an upgrading of classroom infrastructure on most campuses. Even in institutions in which Film Studies has been a relatively low and underfunded programmatic priority, these courses have managed to thrive by piggybacking on the "smart classroom" boom.

On the research side of things, cinema collections are used by undergraduate and graduate students in a variety of ways. The most common research and study uses of collections takes place in media centers. These facilities typically contain multiformat video viewing carrels with small to medium monitors, possibly a few smaller rooms with large screen televisions and/or 16mm projection, and, less frequently, film and video editing suites. Students in carrels typically watch films using headphones, and their work may involve a very close analysis of a few sequences. Students doing close analysis using laser disc have been reported to work with greater interest and success, alone or in small groups, because they have felt that they were able to exercise control over the medium to yield multilayered "texts" (Costanzo 1995). Some students may want to count or track frames if they are dealing with highly edited films. This task is, however, best accomplished with film, and nearly impossible using video. Since the original film frame count of 24 frames per second for sound film is lost when the film is transferred to video's standardized 30 frames, when a VCR is paused or freeze-framed, there is only one chance in four that the image on screen actually corresponds to an actual film frame (Bordwell and Thompson 2000).

FORMATS AND AESTHETIC DIFFERENCES

The facts about film gauges (the width of the actual strip of film measured in millimeters, like still photography) are relatively clear. A piece of 35mm film, the standard commercial gauge, provides significantly better picture quality than a piece of 16mm film, because motion picture image quality increases with the width of the film; the greater the picture surface area, the better the image definition and detail. Seventy-millimeter film is therefore superior to 35mm or 16mm. When a film originally shot in 35mm is transferred to 16mm, degradation occurs not only in the sharpness and clarity of the image, but also in the surface of the image in the frame. In attempting to avoid print frame lines, the top and sides of the image often end up being cropped in the reduction of 35mm to 16mm.

Unlike film, which is a photographic medium, analog video translates light waves into electrical pulses which are recorded on magnetic tape. In North America the National Television Systems Committee (NTSC) has established that the video picture possesses 525 scan lines, each with about 600 pixels (separate dots or picture elements). A standard consumer television monitor has in the vicinity of 425 lines. A 16mm color negative image offers the equivalent of 1,100 video scan lines, while a 35mm color negative equates to anywhere between 2,300 and 3,000 horizontal lines of lightness and color resolution. Furthermore, while NTSC video has a total of about 350,000 pixels per frame, 35mm negative film has the equivalent of about seven million. While a video camera can reproduce a maximum contrast ratio of 30:1, color negative film can reproduce a contrast ratio of over 120:1. When a film is transferred to video, its colors consequently look brighter and "hotter" with fewer true blacks and pastels, while subtle gradations of shadow tend to disappear (Bordwell and Thompson 2001). This explains why videos tend to have a more uniform flat look to them than film does. It also explains why they appear to look lighter and more "lit" than the original film.

High Definition Television (HDTV), DVD, and other evolving technologies may in the near future overcome some of the limitations of video discussed above. The widespread availability and adoption of these technologies may, however, take some time. There is also a very common lag between the release of new hardware and the availability of content to play on it. For these reasons, media librarians will continue to face the need to maintain collections of older formats and the obsolete hardware on which to play them. In introducing DVD to the collection mix and attempting to replace some older VHS titles with new DVD versions of films, care should be taken not to discard an old VHS before establishing that it is not a unique version of the work, even if the image and sound quality are inferior to the DVD. For example, the VHS may have been transferred with the original monophonic soundtrack and the newly restored version on DVD may contain a synthetically assembled stereophonic soundtrack to please the ear of contemporary listeners. Unlike other moving-image subject areas, cinema collections on videotape are likely to be replaced by new technology before they wear out. The fact that the expected life of videotape is on average 15 years becomes irrelevant when one considers the increasingly common practice of major studios to issue re-released versions of films in new formats that are clearer, restored in many instances, more complete, and less expensive. The issue, at least for mainstream cinema, is in many cases more one of weeding than preservation. Dealing with the long-term fate of experimental and independent works, and other titles less likely to make the leap into new formats, will, on the other hand, continue to be a challenge.

One of the reasons media librarians began collecting laser discs in the mid-1980s was that they were a welcome departure from VHS. Although an analog technology like VHS, laser dics provided random non-linear access to their contents by time code or segment (chapter). Laser discs also offered considerably higher resolution (425 lines in comparison to VHS's 240 lines of resolution), as well as the possibility of an aspect ratio (the relationship between a frame's width to its height) that resembled that of the film as it was originally released, rather than the television monitor ratio. A number of laser discs also contained supplementary material, such as stills, storyboards, alternative sound tracks, voice-over commentaries and trailers, and additional moving-image material. They were *the* serious film study format until DVD came onto the consumer market. Unfortunately, unlike DVDs, laser discs did not capture the consumer market. Price is the most likely culprit. The least expensive laser discs were priced at what the most expensive DVDs are today. Laser disc players were also far more expensive than current DVD players, which are in the same price range as middle to top-of-the-line VHS players.

FAMILIARITY WITH THE IMAGE

Almost every American film shot for theatrical release in the last 20 years has used a wide-screen format with an aspect ratio of either 1.85:1, 35mm anamorphic or CinemaScope,[3] frequently with aspect ratios of 2.35:1, as well as 70mm and others. In order to make the film image fit the parameters of a television monitor, a great percentage of the image is lost. Cropping the wide image to the 1.33:1 ratio is only the first step. In broadcasting an image on TV, 6 percent of the image is lost. The television monitor itself crops the image further. Even a 1930s film whose aspect ratio was 1.33:1 will lose 20–30 percent of its picture area by the time it is viewed on the screen. If a film was shot 1.85:1, the television monitor is showing between 41 and 53 percent of what was projected in a theater. In an Ultra 70mm film, the percentage lost to the TV safe title area is 70 percent of the original projected image! (Wilson 1983). Many Film Studies instructors are acutely aware that films broadcast on a television monitor only remotely resemble the original. Apart from the 50 percent loss of the original image and the common practice of censoring nudity and redubbing lines or words in the dialogue, some broadcasters use "time compression," a device that speeds up the film slightly in order to squeeze in more advertising. The announcement at the beginning of the broadcast and on numerous VHS tapes, "This film has been modified from its original version and has been formatted to fit your screen," should be a red flag dissuading instructors from using off-air tapes of films for research. Also to be avoided are prerecorded VHS tapes that do not attempt at least to preserve the original aspect ratio as well as those recorded to preserve as much tape as possible, that is to say on SLP speed.

It would be foolish to assume that simply because a film is letterboxed—formatted on video so that its original wide-screen ratio is retained—the video image displays the entire width of the original image. If the original film had an aspect ratio of 2.55:1, the letterboxed image would be very narrow, and therefore difficult to watch on anything smaller than a 27-inch monitor. It is not unusual, then, to see some cropping at the ends in order to produce a larger image with less masking. The more extreme the wide-screen process on the original film, the more chance that letterboxing will not to be faithful to the original aspect ratio.

With films increasingly being distributed on DVD either letterboxed or with multiple format options, many of the old "pan-and-scan" problems are gradually fading. Because there are still numerous video versions available that employ "pan and scan," the technique and its inherent problems are worth mentioning, nonetheless. The "pan-and-scan" format entails making decisions about which portions of the film image to show. If a decision is made that the action at both ends of the frame is important, then a computer-controlled scanner moves across the image and generates an artificial camera movement, one not intended by the filmmaker. Alternately, a single shot may be cut to show the two people at either end of the frame separately, thus creating editing not originally intended by the filmmaker. It is interesting to watch a film "modified to fit your screen" on video side-by-side with a letterboxed film on video. The composition and the proportion of the elements within the frame are generally different. Actors or objects in the modified version can inadvertently gain more prominence than they have in the letterboxed version, or they can lose the impact of the powerful totality they have in the letterboxed version. In any event, from a cinema studies point of view, the "modified" version is vastly different from what faculty intend their students to see and study.

The concept of "streamed" video—digitally encoded video delivered in real-time over wide-area or local-area networks—is currently receiving a tremendous amount of press in popular, technical, and professional literature. It is a concept which has caused many academic administrators to prick up their ears and start asking questions. The boom in online and distance learning has caused numerous university administrators to wonder why all their media collections cannot be digitized and made available to students. From a cinema collections perspective there are two overriding obstacles in the way of using streamed media in distance learning Film Studies courses: copyright and quality of image. Although there may be certain fair-use provisions for digitizing and streaming short video clips as part of classroom teaching, digitizing full-length works and making these works broadly available over the Web runs the definite risk of copyright infringement. Even if copyright were not an issue, the visual quality of the streamed image is not at present adequate in teaching Film Studies. Streamed video may be of some peripheral use to show a brief clip of a film, but for the next several years it would not be valuable or economical to undertake any projects of this nature, particularly in relation to Film Studies. Television-quality video requires much greater bandwidth than most consumers (or educational institutions, for that matter) have at their disposal. Additionally, the Internet's network structure is not currently robust enough to support reliable access to media. Media streams degrade and bog down as they pass through servers and routers that have not been scaled for this kind of demand. Hopefully, the spread of broadband connections and other initiatives to upgrade the Internet along with hardware improvements and the increasing drop in the cost of digital storage will begin to resolve some of these shortcomings (Forman and Saint John 2000). Some institutions are testing video-on-demand services using material copyrighted by the institutions themselves. La Trobe University in Australia, for example, has embarked on such a program, although the university has found it difficult to provide access to six 20-minute programs for 120 students over a two-week period (Chrisfield 1999). On the other hand, a number of institutions in Canada now have access to 800 streaming videos from the National Film Board of Canada's (NFB) collection. Access to the NFB site is presently limited; if 200 people were trying to access films at the same time, the streaming process would be considerably slowed down. While a psychology instructor interested in showing a group therapy session may not care about the quality of the image or the limitations of streaming the image, a Film Studies instructor interested in the intricacies of the texture of the animation artwork is likely to be frustrated by the great disparity between the online image and the original work.

Remote digital delivery and projection is becoming more prevalent, but is not likely to reach commercial theaters for some time; it will take even longer to penetrate the academic market, as non-theatrical distribution is quite low on the digital totem pole (for a report on the first all-digital distribution of a full-length feature film, see Lyman 2000). The main issues with digital delivery are price and piracy. In 2000, digital projectors cost $250,000 each, while professional film projectors cost $50,000. Digital projectors currently available reportedly produced resolutions approaching 2,000 horizontal lines with contrast ratios (white to black) of 1000:1, matching contemporary 35mm prints and exceeding the U.S. performance parameters of high-definition TV. However, digital cinema still has a long way to go in order to match 70mm prints, which typically run at 3,000 lines and ratios of 1,200:1 (Lubell 2000). Although digital distribution via satellite or fiber-optic lines potentially offers cost-saving simultaneous delivery to theaters (saving the average cost of $2,000 for each 35mm print), there are still concerns about piracy in the process of downloading the film data file (about 1,000 gigabytes for the average feature film, or 42 gigabytes in compressed form). Despite these limitations, the thought of ordering a film for a class and having delivery of a pristine spectacle is tantalizing, and film studies instructors are already salivating at the idea.

The first forays into digital delivery will undoubtedly be blockbuster movies holding the promise of big box office returns. The fate of smaller, non-theatrical films is less certain. When (or if) digital projection reaches the realm of non-theatrical distribution, it will enhance, if not revolutionize, the teaching of cinema. New distribution mechanisms will be created, and access to material from independent distributors will also have to be rethought for the consumer and academic markets. As for doing away with physical copies of films on some video platform, convergence will be determined by the consumer. The consumer chose the substandard VHS over the smaller and better quality Betamax in the 1970s; it's anyone's guess whether history will repeat itself.

STORAGE, PRESERVATION, AND "ARCHIVING" DECISIONS

Until the past decade or so, librarians have tended to be seriously lacking in their familiarity with motion media in general and its preservation in particular. Graduate library school curricula have tended for the most part to follow tra-

Specialized Collections and Special User Needs

ditional (i.e., print-biased) avenues. As a result of the increasingly urgent need for information about preservation of collections, courses of study in this area are now available in many institutions. Some institutions have broadened their programs to include motion media as particular areas of study, while others include it with their computer courses (Adler 1997). The consideration of motion media in preservation courses is due at least in part to the fact that more information on the subject has become available—a result of a visible change in the perception of the value of motion media by academic institutions as well as its producers. Recent graduates of library schools are now better prepared to face the challenges of moving-image management and preservation than their predecessors, most of whom ended up learning through experience.

Many academic cinema collections, particularly the older and more established ones, supported film programs with materials that included 16mm, and occasionally 35mm film. Increasingly, academic administrators have come to view media collections as assets rather than as disparate "teaching aids." In terms of storage and preservation, film and video are, consequently, no longer the administrative pariahs they once were. Administrators are, nonetheless, feeling budgetary pressures, admission pressures, and marketing pressures. Requests for preservation money are not likely to receive higher priority than those for Web course development. New technology excites administrators, and before they support such "low-tech" endeavors as film and video preservation, they need to be assured that such activities are being done in the service of good management. Good management in this view includes anticipating, preventing, stopping, or retarding the deterioration of capital investments and academic assets. The most important strategy in gaining support for preservation funding is to establish a preservation program. Such an undertaking should, like library disaster planning programs, look into the future as well as maximize value from the past.

Some elements of a preservation plan can be implemented without any cost to the institution, such as sensitizing people to the great losses of a deteriorating collection. It is important to get as many campus individuals and units on board as possible, including the library, archives, computing services, and academic departments. It is essential to focus on creating a positive approach that identifies present and future needs and constructively responds to them, at the same time raising awareness of the ways in which preservation contributes to the research at the institution. If it can be demonstrated that library collection activities are one of the reasons that enrollment is up in certain departments, the preservation program will gain more clout. Fostering good relationships with department chairs and faculty deans by showing them statistics on how much use the collections are receiving in supporting teaching and research will also raise opportunities for the services.

Storage is directly linked to the makeup and use of the collections. The various SMPTE (Society of Motion Picture and Television Engineers) and ANSI (American National Standards Institute) standards describe different storage conditions for long-term, medium-term, and active-use storage. There are different qualifications for color and black-and-white film, and a completely different set of standards for videotape. Before making decisions it is important to understand the uses of the collections and to identify which material might be rare (rarity being defined in terms of ease of replacement). If the material is in demand, there is no point in placing it in a long-term or off-site facility. Most librarians have determined that medium-term storage for many items and active-use storage for the bulk of the collection is the best course (Swartzburg and Boyle 1983). Most have determined that the bulk of the collections can be taken care of fairly easily and replaced when necessary. Occasionally, reformatting becomes a necessity, and then the applicable copyright regulations come into play (Forgas 1997).

Since the basics of video preservation are provided in Chapter 12 in this book, they will not be discussed here, except to encourage librarians with moving-image collections to establish storage practices that minimally include a clean, ventilated, and consistently cool and relatively dry environment. Films should be separated from videos and HEPA (High-Efficiency Particulate Air) filters used when possible to eliminate harmful air particles and pollutants. Proper handling techniques should also be posted, and staff and library users should be encouraged to follow them.

The Association of Moving Image Archivists (AMIA), a professional group that includes experts in moving-image archiving, preservation and restoration, research and development, has a listserv on which questions may be posted. AMIA is a very active group and the questions raised and ensuing discussions are often extremely useful (see http://www.amianet.org/ for subscription information).

COLLECTION DEVELOPMENT, SELECTION, AND CORE CINEMA COLLECTIONS

Although the literature dealing generally with video collection development is scant, there are a few basic resources that can serve as a good starting point. The recently revised ACRL Guidelines for Media Resources in Academic Libraries provides useful criteria for standard academic media collections (http://www.ala.org/acrl/guides/medresg.html). The wisdom imparted by video veterans James Scholtz, Randy Pitman, and Sally Mason-Robinson in their writings about selection and acquisition of moving images, although primarily geared toward public libraries, is also quite helpful for academic collections. Beyond the guidance provided in the above-mentioned sources, there are additional points to consider when dealing with cinema collections. Sample policies may be found in Chapter 13 in this book, in Kristine Brancolini's *Audiovisual Policies in ARL Libraries* (ARL 1990), and in William Schmidt and Donald Rieck's *Managing Media Services: Theory and Practice* (2000). Beyond those basic policy models, collection activities must be directed by the particular needs and anticipated research needs of the patrons.

Academic cinema collections are not composed of classics exclusively, nor should a core collection be. The far-ranging and often highly particular nature of academic inquiry leads to the necessity of collecting materials and genres that are highly unlikely to be found in the collections of most public libraries and video rental outlets. As scholars and students examine the cinematic output of the past century, they are looking at an amazing mix: films that reflect outdated and often abhorrent social, cultural, or political attitudes; films that are uplifting and visionary; critically acclaimed films, as well as those that received terrible reviews or did dismally at the box office. With the integration of Cultural Studies into Film Studies there is an increased emphasis on the social, institutional, and other extra-cinematic aspects of film. These aspects can often be best studied by acquiring materials outside the classic canon. Many of the films promoted by the American Film Institute (AFI) as the most important of the century (see http://www.afionline.org/100movies) are seldom used for teaching, although they should be part of a basic and general cinema collection. Many of the film titles appearing in syllabi, in fact do not appear on the AFI best films lists (academics furiously criticized these lists for sins of omission when they appeared recently).

A core academic cinema collection cannot simply mirror "best lists" or Oscar winners and nominees, or even the list of titles government agencies seek to preserve. A core collection needs to be more global, more inclusive, and more varied than a general cinema collection. Culture is made up of the good, the bad, the ugly, and the obscure. To properly study culture, a cinema collection must reflect it. The scholarly study of film has, in fact, taken research and teaching far beyond the mainstream into more fringe areas, such as pornography, cult films, and ultraviolent films. In this environment, films such as *Behind the Green Door* and *Texas Chainsaw Massacre* have become part of a new canon for feminist film studies and other areas of inquiry. Cultural ephemera—films never intended for the arts or the ages—have similarly been re-examined as cultural artifacts. Old 16mm educational and industrial films and 16mm and 8mm amateur movies from the 1950s may be studied, not for their specific content or their technique, but instead for the clear snapshot they present of contemporary 1950s culture. The survival of these "fugitive" and often orphan films in academic libraries ensures the possibility of archival records of the period for future study, just as the current onslaught of horror genre parodies will serve as social text on the end of the twentieth century.

How does one go about establishing a basic core list of titles supporting cinema studies? An effective although not altogether practical method might be to compile a list of titles indexed at the end of an introductory textbook in Film Studies. The films listed often include not only the ones thoroughly analyzed in the text, but also related titles included to expand on the ideas put forth in the book. A cursory examination of Bordwell and Thompson's *Film Art: An Introduction* (2001) provides numerous titles listed by director when applicable, as well as extensive bibliographies related to historical periods and to genres and specialized discussion topics. This textbook is the most well-written, current, and frequently updated work on the market, as well as one of the most widely used. If a media librarian is to read just one textbook on Film Studies, this is the one to read.

Duplication of titles is occasionally necessary, particularly if a better video print, a director's cut, or a restoration becomes available. In cases where multiple versions of a film have been bought for a collection, it is essential that information regarding the various versions appears in the library's catalog. If a "pan-and-scan" version of a film was initially purchased on VHS and a letterboxed director's cut subsequently purchased on DVD, the differences should be clear in the cataloging records. Because multiple versions of a film are often used for comparison in the classroom, or for research, this careful cataloging of videographic successions is perhaps even more important in academic libraries than public libraries.

As academic video librarians are seldom faced with the unfortunate task of dealing with MPAA ratings or other types of rankings, film review sources, although extremely valuable in keeping apprised of titles likely to appear on video, play only a relatively minor part in the selection process in academic libraries. A number of the more useful movie review sources and databases are discussed in Chapters 10 and 18 in this book. Although the *New York Times* film reviews are important to read, particularly because they include independent and foreign releases, the *Times* Home Video Section is a far more useful resource for keeping up with new video releases of value to cinema collections. Similarly, journals and magazines such as *Cineaste, Film Comment,* and *Sight and Sound* all contain video reviews. A publication such as *Classic Images* is more of an enthusiasts' monthly than a scholarly publication, but it contains reviews of new video releases of films from the silent period to the 1950s. The importance of video reviews as opposed to film reviews is that the quality of the video transfer and other technical aspects are often addressed in the former.

Awareness of upcoming video releases is essential to the planning process. Subscription to the electronic mailing lists of online publications such as *Laser Scans* (http://www.laserscans.com) and *DVD Insider* (http://www.dvdinsider. com) is useful for keeping up with new and forthcoming DVD titles, as well as learning about special editions or additional features of the DVDs. This is exactly the type of advance information that instructors are grateful for, because it assists their own planning for upcoming courses. A number of vendors such as Ken Crane (http://www.kencranes.com) will also send weekly announcements of new releases.

Developing a relationship with vendors is key to building personal reference sources in cinema. Specialized distributors have Web sites and catalogs available online. Additionally, many of these concerns contribute to VIDEOLIB and VIDEONEWS listservs with insights about the distribution business and copyright information. There are numerous distributors that sell titles for cinema collections, and if one were to limit oneself to 15 only, that list might include, in no specific order: Milestone, Kino, New Yorker, First Run/Icarus, California Newsreel, Direct Cinema, Canyon, Filmmakers' Library, Women Make Movies, Electronic Arts Intermix, Video Data Bank, Cinema Guild, Museum of Modern Art Circulating Film and Video Library, New Day Films, and Cinema Guild.[4] In Canada, I would also add the National Film Board of Canada, Mongrel Media, and the Canadian Filmmakers' Distribution Center. Naturally, general vendors such as Facets, Movies Unlimited, and Ken Crane should also be mentioned as sources of information and catalogs.

Forging relationships with other agencies and institutions can similarly assist in the collection development process. Developing connections to local film repertory theaters, film archives, or film arts foundations is an example. Collaborations between academic institutions have always existed in terms of interlibrary loans, or even collaborative purchasing, but, for those institutions geographically close to a film archive, there are numerous advantages in combining forces when it comes to programming. As mentioned earlier, it is absolutely clear that commercial 16mm film distribution is a dying enterprise. Fewer and fewer prints exist, making it difficult to rent them for class screenings. Film archives can program screenings on their premises, and may have prints of films no longer available through commercial channels. Collaboration with local archives can benefit Film Studies curricula in other ways also. For example, if a course on documentary film is given during the fall semester, it may be possible to program a series on documentary film at the archive to supplement the class screenings and enrich the students' film culture. If it is not practical or possible to collaborate with a film archive, working with local repertory theaters may be (particularly since these venues tend to be populated largely by students anyway). This kind of outreach into the community should be considered part of the cinema librarian's bag of tricks, an alternative facet of collection development.

SOME SPECIFIC COPYRIGHT ISSUES

Although Chapter 15 in this book deals with general copyright concerns, a few issues specific to cinema collections are worth discussing here. Teaching Film Studies is always constrained by the material resources, particularly the availability of non-theatrical rental prints and commercially released videos of films. Many films of the past century no longer exist, or only exist in fragmented form. Relatively few of these early films are commercially available on video, and fewer still, non-theatrically on film. Some titles are only distributed in Europe. Others have been broadcast on television but have not been released on video. The vagaries of non-theatrical distribution and those of home-use-only markets are uniformly daunting. On the one hand, the extension of copyright and the copyrighting of (mostly) European public domain works under GATT (General Agreement on Tariffs and Trade) sends a clear and highly restrictive picture of owners' rights. On the other hand, academia is clamoring for freedom of access to the complete body of international cinema. Some instructors disregard copyright outright and acquire personal collections of pirated videos, exposing themselves to potential prosecution (Welsch 1999). Some request that the campus library acquire pirated videos, while others resign themselves to focusing only on academic areas well represented by video. The contemporary rediscovery of "hidden" film treasures often occurs simply as a result of the work being released on video. Much of the fairly recent interest in silent films seems to stem from the fact that there are an increasingly large number of titles available with musical accompaniment and struck from good or even restored prints. Twenty-five years ago, *Birth of a Nation, Greed, Metropolis, Sunrise, The General, Battleship Potemkin*, and possibly a handful of others were, by necessity, presented to students as representative of the entire silent period—one-third of the output of the past century. Today, there are new DVD releases from the silent period almost every week.

Dealing with cinema collections always involves compromise on a number of levels. For example, it may be impossible to purchase an experimental 16mm film from a distributor, because the filmmaker has decided that he or she will not allow any more prints of the film to be struck, but, perhaps renting an existing print would be a possibility. Developing relationships with distributors is essential. Knowing whom they represent, and what rights are attached to the works distributed begins to give some shape to the puzzle. A bit of knowledge goes a long way. The fact that a vendor has a Web site and is selling titles not available on Amazon.com certainly does not mean that all the videos are pirated, but, some caution needs to be exercised just the same. Video vendors, particularly vendors dealing with more obscure cinematic fare, are often none-too-particular about the original sources of the materials they sell (they generally deal with products from a wide variety of distributors). It is not at all uncommon to find among their offerings videotapes of suspect lineage, works often poorly transferred from battered 16mm prints, and frequently with parts of the credit information missing. A film like Visconti's *The Leopard* is not legally distributed in the United States currently, yet a pirated tape has been available from various respectable sources. In such cases librarians are often placed in a difficult situation as they attempt to balance requirements of copyright law and the integrity of the collection against often heated faculty demand. Fortunately, in some instances, compromise in dealing with copyright issues is possible; for example, the use of a multi-standard player rather than the unauthorized copying of PAL to NTSC format tape (an infringement of current copyright).

One crucial thing to remember is that copyright laws are different in every country, and that the law of the land applies. The fact that a title is in the public domain in one country does not mean it is necessarily public domain in all countries. It is also important to remember that in some countries, such as Canada, there are no educational exemptions for using home-use-only video in face-to-face teaching situations. The fairly new teaching exemptions in Canada allow public performance in a non-profit educational institution (but only of live performances of a work by students to an audience in the class consisting of mainly students) of a sound recording, or of a live telecommunication (television broadcast) (Canadian Copyright Act, C-42 [29.5]).[5] Students could, for example, perform the theatrical version of *The Rocky Horror Picture Show* in class, or listen to the original cast performance on CD, or even watch the film if it happens to be broadcast on television during class time, but they cannot watch a home-use-only DVD of the film in class without the institution negotiating a public performance license with the appropriate distributor.

CONCLUSION

The convergence of academic disciplines coincides with technological convergence. As both technology and academia struggle to emerge as stronger and more viable entities, the cross-pollination of theoretical models requires increased access to supporting material for teaching and research. In the next few years, the challenge for librarians with cinema collections will be to maintain existing multi-format collections while planning and delivering anticipated services, with a watchful eye to copyright legislation and keeping up with digital realities.

NOTES

1. There are a number of histories of media services and audiovisual libraries. Three worth noting are found in: Brancolini 1994; the overview chapter in Schmidt and Rieck 2000; and the helpful chronology presented in Loucks-DiMatteo 1985.

2. A term coined by film critic Andrew Sarris, the *auteur* theory grew out of the post–World War II theoretical writings of Bazin and Alexandre Astruc, primarily in Bazin's influential journal *Cahiers du Cinema*. The construct, later taken up by Francois Truffaut and other young *Cahiers* critics, focused on the director of a film as its primary shaping force or author (*auteur*).

3. The anamorphic process is a wide-screen process in which filmed images have been optically compressed or "squeezed" by using an anamorphic lens on the camera. During projection the images are restored to their normal wide proportions by an "unsqueezing" anamorphic lens on the projector. Some trade names of anamorphic processes include CinemaScope, Grandscope, Megascope, Naturama, Panavision, and Techniscope.

4. Information on how to contact these distributors has been compiled by Gary Handman and is available as "Film & Video Distributors & Producers," http://www.lib. berkeley.edu/MRC/Distributors.html. Also useful as a general starting point is Brancolini 1999.

5. A useful book about the Canadian copyright scene is Lesley A. Harris, 2000. *Canadian Copyright Law*, 3rd edition. Toronto: McGraw-Hill. The full text of the Canadian Copyright Act is available at http://canada.justice.gc.ca/cgi-bin/folioisa.dll/estats.NFO/ query=*/doc/{@32449}?.

REFERENCES

For a selected bibliography of film studies resources compiled by the author, see http://www.lib.berkeley.edu/MRC/filmstudies.html.

Academy of Motion Picture Arts and Sciences (AMPAS). 1929. *Annual Report 1929.* Hollywood, CA: AMPAS.

Adams, D. 1968. "The Use of Film in American Studies." *University Vision* 1: 15–18.

Adler, Rebecca. 1997. "Media Librarianship: Curricular Responses to the Digital Revolution." *MC Journal: The Journal of Academic Media Librarianship* 5(2). http://wings.buffalo.edu/publications/mcjrnl/v5n2/adler.html.

Andrew, Dudley. 2000. "The 'Three Ages' of Cinema Studies and the Age to Come." *PMLA Publications of the Modern Language Association of America* 115(3): 341–351.

Association of College and Research Libraries (ACRL). 1999. "Guidelines for Media Resources in Academic Libraries." *College & Research Libraries News* 60 (April): 294–302.

Association of Research Libraries (ARL). 1990. *Audiovisual Policies in ARL Libraries.* SPEC Kit 162. Compiled by Kristine Brancolini. Washington, DC: The Association.

Baudry, Jean-Louis. 1986. "The Apparatus." In *Narrative, Apparatus, Ideology: A Film Theory Reader.* Edited by Philip Rosen. New York: Columbia University Press, pp. 299–319.

Bazin, André. 1967. *What Is Cinema?* Berkeley: University of California Press.

Bazin, André. 1971. *What Is Cinema?* Vol. II. Berkeley: University of California Press.

Bordwell, David, and Carroll, Noel, eds. 1996. *Post-Theory: Reconstructing Film Studies.* Madison: University of Wisconsin Press.

Bordwell, David, and Thompson, Kristin. 2001. *Film Art: An Introduction.* 6th ed. New York: McGraw-Hill.

Brancolini, Kristine. 1994. "Video Collections in Academic Libraries." In *Video Collection Development in Multi-type Libraries.* Edited by Gary Handman. Westport, CT: Greenwood Press, pp. 41–69.

Brancolini, Kristine. 1999. "Media Reference Sources for an Academic Library." *The Reference Librarian* 65: 89–101.

Champoux, Joseph E. 1999. "Film as a Teaching Resource." *Journal of Management Inquiry* 8(2): 206–217.

Chin, Daryl. 1996. "As Time Goes By: The Century of Cinema." *Performing Arts Journal* 54 (18:3): 26–40.

Chrisfield, Ted. 1999. "La Trobe University Library Video on Demand Services Trial." *Multimedia Information & Technology* 25(2): 143–147.

Christeson, Frances Mary. 1938. *Guide to the Literature of the Motion Picture.* Cinematography Series no. 1. Los Angeles: University of Southern California.

Cockerman, H. 1972. "A Film Study Course in a French Department." *University Vision* 8: 19–25.

Costanzo, William. 1995. "Teaching Film with Laserdiscs." *Cinema Journal* 34(4): 78–83.

Curry, Ramona. 1986. "25 years of SCS: A Socio-Political History." *Journal of Film and Video* 38 (Spring): 43–57.

Edgar, Dale. 1935. *How to Appreciate Motion Pictures: A Manual of Motion Picture Criticism Prepared for High School Students*. New York: Macmillan.

Emerson, John, and Loos, Anita. 1920. *How to Write Photoplays*. Philadelphia: George W. Jacobs & Company.

Erens, Patricia, ed. 1986. *College Course Files*. Monograph #5, University Film and Video Association.

Evans, Geraint, and Del-Pizzo, Jane. 1999. "Look, Hear, Upon This Picture: A Survey of Academic Users of the Sound and Moving Image Collection of the National Library of Wales." *Journal of Librarianship and Information Science* 31 (September): 152–167.

Fails, E. V. 1988. "Teaching Sociological Theory through Video: The Development of an Experimental Strategy." *Teaching Sociology* 16: 256–262.

Forgas, Letitia. 1997. "The Preservation of Videotape: Review and Implication for Libraries and Archives." *Libri* 47: 43–56.

Forman, Peter, and Saint John, Robert W. 2000. "Creating Convergence." *Scientific American* 283(5): 50–56.

Giroux, Robert. 1936. "Film Theory; Notes for a Bibliography." *Columbia Review* (Columbia University) 17 (May): 10–17.

Grove, Pearce S. 1975. *Nonprint Media in Academic Libraries*. Chicago: American Library Association.

Hall, Stuart, Knight, Roy, Hunt, Albert, and Lovell, Alan. 1964. *Film Teaching*. London: British Film Institute Education Department.

Heath, Stephen. 1976. "Narrative Space." *Screen* 17(3): 68–112.

Houston, Penelope. 1994. *Keepers of the Frame*. London: British Film Institute.

Jackson-Wrigley, M., and Leyland, Eric. 1939. *The Cinema Historical, Technical and Bibliographical: A Survey for Librarians and Students*. London: Grafton & Co.

Jurkiewicz, K. 1990. "Using Film in the Humanities Classroom: The Case of Metropolis." *English Journal* 79: 47–50.

Lloyd, Kim. 1994. "Select or Satisfy? The Video Collection Development Dilemma." *MC Journal: The Journal of Academic Media Librarianship* 2 (Fall): 110–118.

Loucks-DiMatteo, Amy R. 1985. "The History of Media Librarianship: A Chronology." In *Media Librarianship*. Edited by John W. Ellison. New York: Neal-Schuman Publishers, pp. 72–89 (http://www.sils.buffalo.edu/faculty/ellison/Syllabi/519 Complete/readings/historymediab.html).

Lovell, A. 1970. "Film and the Social Sciences." *Social Science Research Council Newsletter* 10: 21–22.

Lubell, Peter D. 2000. "Digital Cinema Is for Reel." *Scientific American* 283(5): 70–71.

Lyman, Rich. 2000. "Digital Distribution of Movie Is Planned by Fox and Cisco." *New York Times* (June 5): C6.

McKee, Gerald. 1978. *Film Collecting*. New York: A. S. Barnes & Co.

Matuszewski, Boleslaw. 1898. "Une nouvelle source de l'Histoire." Reprinted in *A New Source of History—Animated Photography: What It Is, What It Should Be*. 1999. Translated by Ryszard Drzewiecki. Warsaw: Filmoteka Narodowa, pp. 25–30.

Matuszewski, Boleslaw. 1898. "La Photographie animée, ce qu'elle est, ce qu'elle doit être." Reprinted in *A New Source of History—Animated Photography: What It Is, What It Should Be*. 1999. Translated by Ryszard Drzewiecki. Warsaw: Filmoteka Narodowa, pp. 31–65.

Metz, Christian. 1973. "Current Problems of Film Theory." Translated by Diana Matias. *Screen* 14(1–2): 40–88.

Metz, Christian. 1974. *Language and Cinema*. The Hague: Mouton.

Mulvey, Laura. 1975. "Visual Pleasure in the Narrative Cinema." *Screen* 16(3): 6–18.

Nolan, John L. 1961. "Audio-Visual Materials." *Library Trends* 10 (October): 261–267.

Proctor, R. F. II. 1990. "Interpersonal Communication and Feature Films: A Marriage Worth a Course." *Michigan Association of Speech Communication Journal* 25: 1–12.

Roberts, Michael. 1975. "The Use of Audio-Visual Materials by Individual Subject Departments within a University and the Development of Library Services." *University of Sheffield Postgraduate School of Librarianship and Information Service Occasional Publications Series Number Six* (September).

Schmidt, William D., and Rieck, Donald A. 2000. *Managing Media Services: Theory and Practice*. 2nd ed. Englewood, CO: Libraries Unlimited.

Spehr, Paul. 1970. "Feature Films in Your Library." Reprinted in *Audiovisual Media and Libraries Selected Readings*. 1972. Edited by Emanuel T. Prostano. Littleton, CO: Libraries Unlimited.

Swartzburg, S. G., and Boyle, D. 1983. "Videotape." In *Conservation in the Library: A Handbook of the Use and Care of Traditional and Nontraditional Materials*. Edited by S. G. Swartzburg. Westport, CT: Greenwood Press, pp. 155–161.

Welsch, Tricia. 1999. "Techniques and Approaches for Teaching Film and Video Courses." *Cinema Journal* 38(4): 86–108.

Wilson, Anton. 1983. *Anton Wilson's Cinema Workshop: Ten Years of Technical Insight from American Cinematographer*. Hollywood, CA: American Society of Cinematographers.

Wollen, Peter. 1969. *Signs and Meaning in the Cinema*. London: Secker & Warburg; the British Film Institute.

Wright, William Lord. 1922. *Photoplay Writing: Used as a Supplementary Text in New York Institute of Photography*. New York: Falk Publishing Co.

Chapter 12

Preserving the Image: Video Preservation

Jeff Clark

INTRODUCTION

As Oksana Dykyj observes in Chapter 11 in this volume, the preservation of motion media has a higher profile than it once did in professional education and in academic collections, as well as archives and other types of collections. There is a constantly evolving group of research-derived preservation recommendations suitable for the most unique and valuable collections managed in the most controlled environments; many of these standards can be located through the selected resources in the appendix to this chapter.

While occasional reference to preservation measures for long-term archival collections will be found in this discussion, the primary focus of this chapter is on practical preservation measures for "active use" collections of motion media in the VHS videocassette and DVD formats.[1] Typically, several broad aims and conditions characterize such collections:

- They strive to maximize the useful life of their steadily circulating media;
- They are primarily composed of commercially available programming expected to remain in publication, rather than original or unique media;
- Materials are circulated to public or institutional borrowers, often for use outside the collection facility and under conditions that are unpredictable and generally uncontrolled; and

- Such collections are often stored in facilities that are also inhabited by staff and users most of the time. In such environments the atmospheric (heating, air conditioning, humidification) system for the building cannot be rigorously controlled on demand.

The best preservation standard that such collections—whether located in academic or public libraries, public or private archives—can normally expect to meet is that defined as "active use" storage by American National Standards Institute (ANSI) standard IT 9.13–1996.

Recommendations below are organized into two main sections for videotape and DVD, then subdivided for various preservation topics and measures. They are the collective products of various recommendations and readings in the Appendix, discussions with colleagues, and experience with an active-use academic collection over a number of years. Closing this chapter is a short consideration of issues involved in preservation transfer, when original program material no longer has a useful life.

VIDEOTAPE

As a relatively recent major study reiterated, videotape in general has had no professional recognition as a permanent medium of record (Library of Congress 1997). This is especially true in the case of VHS videotape. Surprisingly, there are few if any firm figures regarding the effective life of videotape offered in the available popular and scholarly literature dealing with tape-based media. Anecdotal evidence seems to indicate a maximum expectancy of 150–250 tape plays (see Chapter 15 in this volume; Scholtz 1989). A shelf-life of about 10 years before the onset of severe tape degradation appears plausible under the most favorable combined storage and use conditions. Unfortunately, any expectations regarding the effective life of tapes used under ideal conditions is often compromised by the condition of VCR playback equipment used outside the collection facility. The eventual degradation of VHS audio and video quality due to playback wear may make retention of a particular tape for its entire life less attractive than replacement while this option is practical and inexpensive.

Temperature and Relative Humidity (RH)

Standards for temperature and RH evolve with practical experience and research, differ according to authority, and vary depending on whether long-term, medium-term, or active-use collections are involved. Nonetheless, for most circulating videotape collections, the environmental range which would satisfy most current standards recommendations is 50–70 degrees Fahrenheit, and 20–50 percent RH. Authorities generally agree that a lower RH is more important than a lower temperature.

The most important requirement for storage of circulating collections overall is to keep temperature and RH as constant as possible. This measure can enhance collection longevity more than adherence to specific temperature and RH ranges, particularly in the case of low-circulation tapes that may spend more time on the collection shelves than in uncontrolled environments.

Dust

The absence of dust and other atmospheric debris in areas where videocassettes are stored and used is desirable. If the layout of a circulating facility lends itself to the measure, HEPA (High-Efficiency Particulate Air) filtering (as suggested in Chapter 11) can be employed to enhance the building's air conditioning system. In the case of valuable archives, special filtering should be mandatory.

Storage—Handling and Shelving

In handling cassettes, the tape inside the shell should never be touched with bare hands (oils on the skin can prevent the tape from being "read" effectively, and can lead to quicker physical degradation). The hinged door flap that opens when the cassette is playing inside the VCR should not be opened, except during damage inspection and repair (see the section on cassette repair below).

Shelving of tapes should allow for upright, on-end storage of videotapes. The tape should be fully wound onto the lower, rather than upper spool as the cassette is positioned on the shelf (this helps prevent gravity from stretching the tape over time). Cassettes should never be stored flat on their top or bottom, since, again, gravity may pull the tape pack against the cassette shell and cause one of the tape's edges to become curled or crinkled over time, especially if it was unevenly spooled to begin with. The lower edge of VHS videotape contains recording information called a "control track," which synchronizes the proper playback of the audio and video. It is important to prevent damage to this track, since that will disable playback of an otherwise normal-seeming videocassette.

Under normal conditions, properly grounded metal shelving poses no threat from residual magnetism for videocassette storage. The electromagnetic signal recorded onto videotape and the physical composition of the tape are more robust than those of audiocassettes. These properties will even allow special adaptations of some library security systems (meant for media) to accommodate videotape safely.[2] Wood shelving is less desirable than metal, but still acceptable for active-use circulating collections. Wood shelving should, however, be avoided in archival situations, since, over time, acid vapors from wood finishes or the wood itself can be harmful to videotape.

Tape Tension and "Exercising"

Ideally, videotape should be evenly wound so that tension on all parts of the reel is equal when stored. Proper tension helps tape resist the adverse effects of stretching and of expansion and contraction caused by variable temperature and humidity. The easiest way to achieve even tension is to store tapes in a "tails out" position (not rewound), and to allow the borrower to rewind the tape and play it back to the end, returning it to the original storage state. This technique is, unfortunately, often not practical in most library video operations. As a next best solution, tapes can be wound and/or rewound to one end, with relatively even tension, by using a VCR on fast forward, a high-quality (not inexpensive) cassette rewinder, or an "inspection/cleaning" machine such as manufactured by RTI (see Cassette Maintenance and Repair below). This wind/rewind strategy will help produce a relatively even-tensioned tape pack on the reel, if not quite as good as a tape played through at normal speed from end to end.

"Exercising" or "refreshing" videotape periodically can be an important additional practice for increasing the life of tape. Exercising seldom-circulated tapes helps readjust uneven tension in the tape pack, reduce layer adhesion (from sticky elements in the tape binder), and "print-through" of the magnetic signal between tape layers on the spool. It can be difficult to find time and staff to perform this task, and there is no absolute recommendation on how often it should be done for those tapes that may spend much of their lives unplayed. A rule of thumb is to try and exercise unplayed tapes by winding them through at relatively even tension once a year.

Packaging and Labeling

Whatever style of circulation case is chosen, it should be hard-sided for impact protection, provide a tight seal from dust, and minimize cassette exposure to light. Never store videotapes in the cardboard boxes or sleeves in which they may have been packaged originally. Cardboard packaging tends to expose the tape to atmospheric dust, and, over time, produces debris itself.

A variety of cases both with and without fixed interior hubs are available. Those with hubs are beneficial to the videocassette in that they fix the cassette's tape reels so that the tape does not loosen and tighten during handling. Hubs have a minor drawback, too: they usually require the cassette to be seated in the case in one orientation, thereby increasing the chance that either borrowers or staff will casually force the cassette in the wrong position. A mis-seated tape runs the risk of forcing the case partially open, and subjecting the tape to dust or the danger of accidentally falling out of the case if dropped. Local experience may dictate trying different kinds of cases over time to find a style that achieves the best trade-off between use and storage protection.

Appropriate cases can be found from the usual library vendors (such as Brodart, Demco, Gaylord, and Highmith) and from special vendors such as Specialty Store Services (800–999–0771; http://www.specstoreserv.com) and Tek Media Supply Company (800–323–7520; http://www.rtico.com/tekmda1.html).[3]

Typical labeling products from library, educational media, and specialty vendors should be acceptable for circulating collections, as long as their adhesive is firm. Labels should be applied carefully to minimize curling and catching exposed on playback equipment over time. Labels and security strips should never be applied to the hinged cassette door, either the outside or the inside surface. A label on the door flap may catch inside the VCR as it is opened and closed repeatedly. If applied on the door's inner surface, the label may also catch and damage the tape itself.

Magnetic Damage

Magnetism is the enemy of every videotape, and its presence in areas where tapes are stored and used should be minimized. Tapes should not be left on or near common playback equipment such as television monitors and loudspeakers, particularly when they are in use. These devices can produce magnetism that may cause tape erasure. Electrical appliances, such as vacuum cleaners, are not normally a serious concern, but such devices without properly shielded motors can also harm tapes. Frequently, the effects of magnetic field erasure can be heard in the audio as a cyclical dropout or lowering of the sound volume, and in the video as a cyclical breakup of the picture with a band of white video "noise" running through it.

VCR playback equipment in the facility should be demagnetized (sometimes called "degaussed") from time to time, since the player's video and audio heads (which "read" the program signal) build up residual magnetism that can accelerate tape signal degradation over time. In facilities where technical staff is not available to measure magnetic buildup and determine when to demagnetize equipment, a periodic maintenance schedule can be adopted. For regularly used equipment, a collection facility might adopt the same schedule as for exercising videotapes—once a year for equipment demagnetization as well. When performed properly, this procedure should not harm equipment and tapes, even if it is performed more frequently than necessary. Of course, videotapes should be kept away from a demagnetizer while in operation. Tape head demagnetizers are available from educational and professional audio/video equipment suppliers such as Markertek (800–522–2025; http://www.markertek.com) and Full Compass (800–356–5844; http://www.fullcompass.com).

Cassette Maintenance and Repair

The cassette shell itself can be repaired—or more often replaced—if it suffers damage, which most often occurs to the hinged door. Part replacement is sometimes difficult because of variations in the design of cassette shell parts among different manufacturers. "Retired" cassettes—those removed from the collection due to tape damage or wear-out—are a good source of replacement shells if they are saved for reuse. Very often, the only tool required for cassette repair is a small Phillips screwdriver; however, some cassette manufacturers use tamper-proof screws of several designs for which specialty vendors provide the tools. A set of six screwdrivers sells for around $70 from stores such as Video Store Shopper (800) 325–6867 http://www.shopperinc.com). Additional anti-tamper screws may also be purchased from these sources.

When "transplanting" a commercial videotape on its spools to a new shell, the labeling from the old shell should be carefully removed and reapplied to the new one. Usually this can be done easily by focusing the low heat of a hair dryer on the label until it peels off—but *only* after the tape is no longer in the old shell.

Repair of the videotape itself, using splicing tape or tabs and one of a variety of common repair kits, should be limited to the beginning or end of the tape, where it attaches to the spool. A break in the clear "leader" (attached to the take-up reel, before or after the dark videotape), or in the tape immediately next to the leader usually can be safely repaired to allow indefinite continued use of the program. A carefully applied splice to the tape itself—in the middle of the program content—can be successful for very short-term use, but should not be depended upon long term. Over time the tape stretches, and the splice with it, exposing the splice adhesive to the VCR video and audio heads where it may cause damage to heads or the tape itself. If tape repaired in this way is an original (such as locally produced materials), it can be played back and recorded onto a new cassette for further use, copyright requirements permitting. If it is a commercially available tape, it is wiser to consider the damaged cassette permanently out of circulation and to repurchase it. When using a repair kit, clean hands, or preferably thin cotton gloves, are necessary to prevent dirt and skin oils from being transferred to the tape.

Cassette replacement shells, repair kits and/or special screwdrivers are available from specialty and even standard library supply companies (for kits).

Videotape inspection and cleaning machines, such as those from RTI (800–323–7520; http://www.rtico.com/tekmda1.html), may also be useful for prolonging tape life, although there is no clear consensus on their necessity. The cleaning feature of these machines employs a razor-like blade to gently scrape off loose oxide from the surface of the tape, which might otherwise shed inside a VCR and clog its video heads. However, these machines must be carefully maintained themselves, with their blade surfaces regularly cleaned with lint-free cloth and examined for defects. A rough cleaning blade could permanently damage the videotape passing over it, especially if the tape contains stray creases or other defects already.

Playback Equipment Maintenance

VCRs themselves should undergo a few standard maintenance measures. They should undergo immediate repair by qualified technical staff if they begin to catch and damage tape inside them. A malfunctioning VCR should be taken out of use at once, until it is inspected, and repaired or cleaned.

The video heads and the tape path mechanism inside a VCR require occasional, if not regular, cleaning and maintenance. This should be performed, at the very least, whenever the machine shows signs of mishandling the tape or the picture shows signs of degrading.

Common forms of picture degradation include "drop-out" (snow-like spots randomly appearing on the screen and caused by the oxide layer on the tape wearing through), and picture flutter and roll (generally caused by tape stretching or curling). If tape mishandling is not due to tension misadjustment in the VCR's mechanism (requiring inside technical repair), the parts in the tape path mechanism may need cleaning with a commonly available VCR cleaning cassette. The same cleaning cassettes take care of oxide and other debris that clog the video heads and cause irregular white "noise" in the picture, or completely obliterate the picture when severe. "Dry" and "wet" video head cleaning cassettes each have advantages and drawbacks in their use, but when applied only as needed and according to instructions they are relatively safe for VCRs. Many of the standard library suppliers and specialty vendors supply head cleaners as well.

Demagnetization of VCR heads and tape path—a final routine maintenance procedure mentioned above under Magnetic Damage—should be performed periodically.

DVDs

By all accounts in the trade press, DVD for video programming has become the largest and most rapid success among all formats in consumer electronics history.[4] It seems likely now that as its public acceptance grows, as its life is extended in a few years by a "high definition" version of the DVD, and especially by a recordable version on the near horizon, this new digital optical disc format will have a long run as a carrier of video programming.

"DVD" officially stands for nothing. Political maneuvering among its developers resulted in two primary candidates for these letters—"digital video disc" and "digital versatile disc"—but neither has triumphed. The latter designation, suggesting multiple uses, would have been more apt, however. Besides the popular video format, the DVD audio format is making its official debut in 2001, and several recording techniques for the computer data format, DVD-ROM, are vying for ascendancy, so that a standard for this application of the general format can be set. Nevertheless, the trade organization DVD Entertainment Group (http://www.dvdinformation.com/index.cfm) promotes the two main consumer-oriented formats with the names DVD-Video and DVD-Audio. "DVD" is used here to reference the video software and playback hardware.

In a sense, DVD technology bears more of a relationship to computer technology than to the analog video technology we've known until now. Video DVDs contain digitally encoded media; their consumer players read this data with laser beams and process it with microprocessors. Some DVDs contain material such as screenplays and other textual/numeric data that are encoded for retrieval by a computer DVD-ROM drive. In general, however, the DVD video format and the stand-alone players in particular are in effect sophisticated computer-centered media products. This fact complicates the decision to apply preservation measures, as we shall see below.

Much of what we know about optical disc care and longevity is usually focused on audio compact discs (CDs). Some of this knowledge may be applicable to the DVD, but rigorous study of the format's durability is still in progress at this time, as is our long-term practical experience.[5] As with CDs, the projected life of a DVD (arrived at through accelerated aging research) may prove to be 100 to 200 years; but its usable life, due to comparable obsolescence of format and playback equipment, may be 25 years or fewer.

Both formats have similarities—physical dimensions and compositional materials—but key physical differences make it hard to accept their durability as identical.

DVDs have the same diameter and thickness as CDs. Both formats use polycarbonate plastic as the substrate or protective layer under which a thin metallic reflective layer of aluminum, gold, or silicon carries the digital information. Unlike a CD—but comparable to the nearly obsolete 12-inch laser videodisc— the DVD is composed of two half-thickness sides glued together. This fact, combined with the advanced and complex ways in which DVDs can be configured and recorded, introduces speculative concerns regarding their durability. The thinner protective polycarbonate layer may mean the DVD is more vulnerable to scratches on its surface. Balancing this potential problem is the fact that the format's error correction capability is much greater than the CD's. The two-sided structure of the DVD may eventually introduce a phenomenon like "laser rot" for videodiscs, where oxidation of the metallic layer takes place, probably because of impurities in the binding glue or moist air entering through an imperfectly applied seal. This phenomenon has not been credibly reported as an identifiable problem yet. On the other hand, the commercial DVD, when encoded on only one side and having a label on the other, is probably less vulnerable to label-side scratches than is the CD: the CD's label surface has only a thin coating of lacquer (besides the label printing) to protect the metallic recording layer beneath, whereas the DVD has polycarbonate nearly half the thickness of the whole disc. Finally, DVDs are more susceptible to heat than are CDs. Because of this problem, label application through the silk-screening process, which uses ultraviolet heat, is not recommended.[6]

The above characteristics and other considerations make projections and recommendations regarding the care, durability, and life expectancy of DVD, difficult at this time, but we can extrapolate from research concerning CD optical discs, and from practical experience with CD and DVD collections so far, to form conservative measures that should help preserve an active-use collection.

Temperature and Relative Humidity (RH)

The various recommended temperature and RH ranges for optical discs vary more widely than those for videotape. The most common general recommendations are the same as those listed above for videotapes: 50 to 70 degrees Fahrenheit, 20 to 50 percent RH. As is the case with tape-based media, constant temperature and RH are more important than the exact range for each parameter. DVD collections should thus do well in the same kind of collection environment that serves videotapes.

Dust

While DVDs and their players are not likely to be as susceptible to permanent damage from dust and debris as videotapes and VCRs, keeping the storage and use areas free of contaminants is still important. DVDs that may have finger oils from handling, or other sticky substances on their surfaces, are likely to collect debris in the atmosphere. Again, the same general environment and maintenance measures that apply to videotapes are appropriate here.

Storage—Handling and Shelving

In handling DVDs, the disc surfaces should never be touched. Instead, the disc should be held with the fingertips by its outer rim and/or by the inner rim of the disc's center hole. The disc should not be indiscriminately removed from its case and rested on working surfaces that may be dusty or dirty. These measures will prevent the disc surfaces from accumulating smudges and debris that must eventually be removed by careful cleaning, or scratches that may require repair.

Shelving should allow for upright storage of DVDs in their cases. As with CDs, DVDs are not likely to suffer warping from short-term storage flat on their side, but routine shelving measures should be conservative and avoid this position. Since DVDs are not a magnetic medium like videotape, the composition of the usual library and office shelving alternatives should not present a problem for circulating collections.

Packaging

Although the DVD may be physically comparable to the CD in its general imperviousness to mishandling, it is also a "naked" media carrier without a protective mechanism, such as the cassette shell. The DVD is subject to some cumulative wear, not only from the casual handling habits of multiple users, but also from the packaging from which it is removed and to which it is returned.

As with videocassettes, packaging of choice should be hard-sided, sealed dependably and tightly against dust and exposure to light. In addition, the container should keep the disc sides from touching the surface of the case and thereby contributing to casual abrasion. DVDs that originally came in cardboard-cover casing (the style popularly known as the "snapper" case) should be re-cased in an alternative with more long-term circulation durability.

In choosing a casing style, it is wise to observe one general principle whenever possible: adopt a style that provides the least occasion for accidental scratches and wear in the process of removing or replacing the disc (by either borrowers or staff). Casing that does not seem immediately intuitive to use or that requires special care in disc removal is less desirable. Casing that may exert undue stress on the disc's center hole when it is removed and replaced is also less desirable. There may be no definitive evidence yet, but it is probably wise to avoid unnecessary friction on the disc's center hole, since this might produce tiny fractures in the inner rim over time. As of this writing, professional colleagues are starting to provide anecdotal reports of such damage associated with the standard commercial DVD cases mentioned below. Ironically, the style of casing that likely leads to the least wear on the center disc hole is the CD "jewel box." Unfortunately, an adaptation of its hub is used only in the cardboard case of many DVDs—the commonly termed "snapper" case, which should be discarded for heavy circulation. The jewel case itself has been largely abandoned for commercial DVD use due to marketing considerations (to maintain product distinctiveness from audio and other CD formats).

Presently, there are several styles of hard-sided case popularly known as the "keepcase." These are generally of the same height and width dimensions as videocassette cases, and they permit the inclusion of some printed literature. The two most common styles at this time are the "Alpha" and the "Accura" cases. In this author's experience and opinion, both models present preservation concerns for longer-term repeated circulation. Both models utilize two small flanges to hold the DVD in place, unlike the jewel box hub that exerts more or less even spindle pressure around the disc's center hole rim. The flanges require the DVD to be snapped off and back onto the hubs of these cases, risking sharp, focused stress on several points of the disc's center hole rim. Compounding this problem in the Alpha-style case is its tendency to flex the DVD as it is lifted off the hub—a possible long-term problem for discs made of two bonded sides. While cases with this and even more unfriendly styles of hub may be serviceable for personal collections where discs are handled carefully by their owners, these are not dependable enough for preserving a high-use public collection.

Alternative casing options at this time are few. Special envelopes, like those developed for archival storage of CD-ROMS and offered by archival supply companies such as University Products (http://www.universityproducts.com), are impractical for circulating collections without supplementary packaging. Even then, such alternatives may expose DVDs to casual abrasion when they are removed from and replaced in the envelopes under uncontrolled conditions by users. The CD jewel box is of course available, but likewise requires supplementary packaging to hold at least the program's accompanying literature.

Sturdier cases adapting the jewel box hub, and accommodating the usual DVD print literature, should appear for sale as the DVD market expands.[7]

In the final analysis, the costs of various packaging styles and of the program itself, along with the likelihood of the program's continued availability for replacement, must be weighed together with ideal handling conditions when making a decision about the best packaging option to adopt. Available DVD cases can be acquired from the same library and specialty vendors cited under videotape packaging.

Labeling

Because DVDs are, like CDs, naked media and require balanced spinning inside their playback equipment, caution should be exercised in label application. There have been concerns in the past with CDs regarding interaction between the composition of the disc and label adhesives and inks. These same concerns also apply to the DVD. For archival collections, only the most cautious labeling approach—with archivally formulated materials where appropriate (see University Products, http://www.universityproducts.com)—should be used. But for an actively circulating collection, many of the products from reputable library and specialty media vendors, such as those previously cited, should be safe when applied with sensible measures in mind.

For DVDs with a label side rather than recording on both surfaces, no library labeling of any type should cover the disc's label if possible. Regardless of whether interaction with the adhesive might occur in the longer run, standard library labels used for call numbers or property identification may unbalance the disc's spinning motion in its player, or catch inside the machine if it comes loose. Some vendors provide a circular labeling system that covers only the inner ring around the hole—where the surface is usually clear—and does not reach out into the DVD's own label surface or recorded surface (if a double-sided recording without label). Such labels should be acceptable for use. A slightly more conservative measure is to label only with ink, in the same inner ring around the hole. Dependable permanent ink pens for labeling are the Staedtler Pigment Liner drawing and writing pens, and (especially when a white ink option to mark a dark inner ring is required) the Pentel Milky Gel Roller pens. Both series offer fine-point versions, and can be had from art supply stores and catalogs as well as the companies' own Web sites (http://www.staedtler.com and http://www.pentel.com).

Additional package labeling that provides handling tips for borrowers and staff is useful, too. Wording of directions should be kept concise; better still, simple graphics can be used to remind the borrower how to correctly handle and care for the disc. Pictures such as those found in the instruction manuals for DVD and CD players, or on Kodak's Web pages devoted to CD technical advice (http://www.kodak.com/global/en/professional/products/storage/ped/tech

Info/permanence7.shtml), can serve as a model for drawings or digital snapshots turned into prints.

Disc Cleaning and Repair

When DVDs become dirty or scratched, the measures taken to clean or repair them should match the severity of the damage. In general, the special products mentioned below can often be obtained from the same vendors that supply videotape cleaning and repair accessories.

For moderate dust and fingerprint damage, first try a clean, lint-free cloth or lens-type tissue, using only moisture from the breath. Discs should always be cleaned in a radial direction—from the center hole to the outer rim—and never rubbed in a circle around the disc surface. Tiny scratches in the surface, including those added by cleaning, do not generally cause harm when they are radial in orientation.

If debris on the disc requires stronger cleaning to remove it, a camera lens cleaner or a plastics cleaner, such as Meguiar's Mirror Glaze #17, is acceptable. Mirror Glaze #10 is a mild plastic polish that can be applied afterward to improve a very faintly scratched disc surface.

When disc repair is required for prominent scratches after cleaning, there are several products currently on the market—none of which may be preeminent, but most of which seem reasonably safe without long-term testing experience to provide a definitive answer.[8] These products should be used sparingly, however.

Repair kits mend scratches on the disc playing surface in one or a combination of two ways: by filling in the scratch so that the laser can read the information "pits" beneath the damaged surface more easily, or by literally buffing out the scratches as the general surface is smoothed. Proprietary surface coatings, claimed to be protective, are commonly part of the repair process. Often these kits were first formulated for use on CDs but are perfectly appropriate for DVDs. Two current examples are Wipe Out! (http://www.cdrepair.com/) and CD/DVD Playright (http://www.cdplayright.com/).

Beyond such manually applied repair kits, equipment is available to minimize the skill and time required to perform repairs. These types of repair apparatus range from inexpensive devices such as Skip Doctor (http://www.skipdoctor. com), to elaborate, expensive units such as RTI's DiscCheck Inspector Station (http://www.rti-us.com/discchek/index.html).

In repairing discs, there is a general rule of thumb that should be uniformly observed: whatever the product used, apply it only if a simple disc cleaning alone does not solve the playback problem.

Equipment Maintenance

DVD players, like VCRs, may require professional technical repair if they malfunction, and should be removed from service if such repair is needed. Fortunately, in a format where interaction between the disc and the machine normally cause nothing but very gradual mechanical wear on the latter, routine preventive maintenance procedures are almost non-existent. If a disc does not start up in a player, or if it freezes, skips or otherwise malfunctions during playback, you may try a CD or DVD lens cleaning disc on the chance that dust or other debris particles are blocking the laser lens and causing it to mistrack. (Normally, the operational design of a DVD player does not permit ambient dust particles to settle on the lens due to the circulation of air caused by the spinning disc.) Lens cleaning discs are available from the audio and video specialty vendors.

Beyond this simple measure, if the player is operating smoothly and the disc is clean and undamaged but still will not play, the problem may actually be with hardware/software compatibility. In this event, the problem could reside either in the disc programming or the "firmware" of the player itself.[9]

In order to test if there is a player/disc, hardware/software compatibility problem, try playing the disc in one or more different models of player. If the disc will function properly, the problem is more likely to be a compatibility problem of the player itself (this problem may extend to other players of the same model, which is why different models should always be tried). If the disc will not function in other models of player either, then it may contain a serious defect in its programming or a problem in its physical pressing.

Often such problems are major enough that the player's manufacturer may have a firmware upgrade solution, or (if primarily a disc problem) the DVD's publisher may offer a corrected pressing of the title. At this point in DVD's history, determining the problem and pursuing a solution can be haphazard and tedious, but major Web sites devoted to DVD, such as DVDFile (http://www.dvdfile.com) and DVDTown (http://www.dvdtown.com), offer a database and/or user forum for learning about widely known disc/player compatibility problems to help pursue a solution. Also available is the counsel of consumer listservs such as alt.video.dvd. The manufacturer of either the player or the DVD can be contacted, too. They may have received enough calls regarding their product to have identified a real problem and devised a solution that hasn't been made widely public yet.

In short, DVD disc playing problems do not always involve disc defects and straightforward preservation issues. Carefully try the most obvious maintenance measures for both disc and player, but be prepared to pursue a more complicated compatibility problem and solution if nothing else works.

MIGRATION STRATEGY: WHEN TO TRANSFER, AND IS IT PERMISSIBLE?

The focus of this chapter has largely been on commercially available video programming, rather than unique or out-of-publication works. As mentioned previously, the maintenance strategy for collections that consist primarily of commercially acquired materials is most often "replace" rather than "preserve." However, even in a collection which is actively used and which has no archival pretenses, there may be select materials that warrant transfer for preservation purposes. These program materials fall into three broad categories.

* *Unique video records generated by the institution or acquired by donation.* In public-use collections such as those under consideration in this chapter, copies of such works rather than the original should be circulated (or used within facility). Even with this practice in place, the original recordings will need preservation transfer sooner or later.

* *"Public domain" materials that may be kept and preserved indefinitely because of assignment to this status or the expiration of copyright.* The number of films lapsing into the public domain over time is relatively small. The age of a work alone does not necessarily determine its release from copyright coverage, and second-guessing which titles may or may not be in the public domain is ill-advised. Old feature films that logically seem as if they should be in the public domain may, in fact, contain elements (music, for example) that are still under copyright. Similarly, a restored version of a film seemingly in the public domain may have been newly copyrighted as a unique work. Some older films produced by the federal government, presidential addresses and congressional hearings, television news reporting, C-SPAN television coverage in general, and selected educational programming from cable/satellite channels may be open to public use and preservation under different conditions. Although this subject cannot be covered in detail here, this latter variety of programming may be a candidate for preservation transfer.

* *"Out of distribution" copyrighted video programming.* Under certain conditions, U.S. copyright law permits libraries and archives to preserve such materials by copying them. The recent Digital Millennium Copyright Act (see http://www.loc.gov/ copyright/legislation/hr2281.pdf) extends this prerogative to digital preservation copies of any format original, under severe restrictions. These current DMCA restrictions on library prerogatives in the digital world will need to be addressed and modified if preservation is to remain viable in the future.[10] (See Chapter 15 in this book for further information about copyright matters.)

These general categories can all produce collection materials that may benefit from preservation transfer to the same or other existing video formats, or from digital encoding that helps ensure their availability to new formats and standards. As one study report puts it, the purpose of video preservation should be "a continuing process aimed at protecting information that can migrate from one technology to another as the need arises" (Library of Congress 1997).

The aesthetic and philosophical issue of program "integrity" will not be considered here. Concerns regarding how the transfer format may change crucial "information" in the original have been with us since video replaced film stock as the most widespread medium of public viewing for film.[11] The look and feel—the technology itself—of a recorded format may not only enhance the resolution of detail in the program's content, but also offer insights into its manufacture and sociocultural context. Our migration of video content into dig-

Specialized Collections and Special User Needs

ital form, and from there through a series of digital encoding formats, will doubtlessly introduce other concerns about information "integrity" in the future.

The issue of program integrity aside, the challenge to preservation transfer as we fully enter the digital age is to determine when transfer is necessary and what form it should usefully take. Some general, common-sense principles should apply.

- For unique video materials, physical condition of works should be monitored carefully. This may take the form of periodic inspection and playback of the original material, or disciplined staff observation and reporting of irregular conditions noted whenever the original is handled (e.g., in making use copies).

- For commercial materials, stay abreast of the current video marketplace, including title availability, sources for purchase, and format developments (both software and hardware). This measure also serves unique archival recordings. A large number of resources for staying current in these areas are offered elsewhere in this book (see, for example, Chapter 18).

- When "interim" preservation transfer of analog program materials is warranted, select the transfer format on the basis of: (1) its durability; (2) its general, rather than proprietary, availability; (3) its ability to replicate the original content with maximum fidelity; and (4) its ability to produce good circulating copies with a minimum of program signal degradation. In addition, circulating copies should be made on high-quality videotape or other materials; the longer these remain in circulation, the less frequently the original will need to be worn through replay in order to make more copies.

- Finally, keep current on developing digital (and audio) video standards, both international and proprietary. In the process of digitizing video and other media, there are two primary challenges: (1) faithfully reproducing the original in the process of video encoding, which includes balancing the common need to compress video data with the need to maintain suitable picture quality. (2) Dealing with rapidly evolving media access technologies, which may render today's encoding standards and access hardware obsolete tomorrow. Research into standards and strategies for preservation migration in the digital realm are ongoing. Several of the Internet URLs listed in the Appendix will track the literature in this area and should be consulted frequently.

In summary, video preservation in the digital as well as the analog world has been and remains as challenging as the preservation of any form of information, and perhaps more challenging than most.

NOTES

1. The ANSI (American National Standards Institute) standards for storage definitions (IT 9.13–1996), and storage conditions for magnetic tape (IT 9.23–1998) and optical disc media (IT 9.25–1998) can be purchased via their Web site at http://webstore.ansi. org/. Relevant details of their standards, as well as others, can be found also through the various Web documents and organizational sites included in the Appendix to this

chapter—e.g., the Association of Moving Image Archivists (AMIA) Web site (http://www.amianet.org).

2. For example, the 3M Company's Model 3803DM library detection system uses a weaker form of magnetic security strip and sensitizer/desensitizer mechanism for application to audio and video program materials.

3. Supply companies like these apply repeatedly for both videocassette and DVD preservation accessories. Other companies will be cited in the text only for special products not always handled by the types named here. For a more thorough catalog of suppliers, most still active, see Scholtz 1989, as well as other resources in the Appendix.

4. For example, see the press release, "Industry Celebrates DVD-Video—the Fastest Growing and Most Rapidly Adopted Consumer Electronics Product" (http://www. dvdinformation.com/news/press/010601.html). It points out that by its fourth year of availability (2000), the DVD player had three times as many units in the marketplace as the CD format, and seven times as many as the VCR, during the same period of their own introductions.

5. For example, the National Institute of Standards and Technology (http://www. nist.gov) is studying data preservation and life expectancy of writable DVDs and CDs.

6. For more information on DVD characteristics, see especially Nimbus' "Optical Disc 101" (http://www.nimbus.ltd.uk/nte/101); Sanyo-Verbatim CD Company (http://www.sanyo-verbatim.com/dvd/faq.htm); and "DVD Frequently Asked Questions (and Answers)" (http://dvddemystified.com/dvdfaq.html).

7. One "keepcase" style exception has appeared as of this writing: a full-sleeve DVD vinyl case with a molded interior well that allows the disc to be held on a jewel-box-like hub (no flanges), or stored inside a jewel box itself. Literature can be stored inside the case as well as inserted in the clear outside sleeve covering. This case model can be found from the usual library supply vendors but is generally expensive at this time. Check The Library Store (800–548–7204; http://thelibrarystore.com), stock #89–0094, for the most cost-effective version that the author has found.

8. The author has used one of these products, Bundee International's Disc Repair & Protection System, successfully for many years. CDs and laser discs treated more than five years ago are still playable as of this writing. Though this specific product no longer appears on the market, some of those that have replaced it work in a similar fashion.

9. For a relatively clear explanation of this complicated situation, consult an article at the *DVD Review* Web site, "Working through player/disc compatibility issues" (http://www.dvdreview.com/html/working_through_player_disc_compatibility_issues.html).

10. This concern, in fact, has been addressed in the recent report and general recommendations of the National Research Council, *The Digital Dilemma:Intellectual Property in the Information Age* (2000). The report can be found on the Internet at http://books.nap.edu/html/digital_dilemma/, and is also available in print from the National Academy Press (ISBN 0–309–06499–6). Another study with specific recommendations on changes in copyright law that would facilitate digital preservation in archives is H. M. Gladney's *Digital Preservation Archiving and Copyright: Problem Description and Legislative Proposal (Version 2)*, available at http://www.almaden.ibm.com/u/gladney/ArchCopy.htm/.

11. See, for example, the "CCUMC Policy Statement on the Value of Preserving Film as an Important Document of Our Cultural Heritage," at http://www.indiana.edu/~ccumc/. See also Chapter 11 in this book for a detailed discussion of this issue.

SELECTED VIDEO PRESERVATION RESOURCES

Much of the information in this chapter has been drawn from the print and Internet resources listed below. However, these resources often extend far beyond the preservation basics for the curator of an active-use collection, and can present in-depth research and consideration of a full range of preservation issues: practices and developing standards, evolving recommendations on migration strategies in digital formats, and more. The major comprehensive preservation Web sites below should be monitored for the latest developments on all preservation issues.

Print Sources

Jimenez, Mona and Platt, Liss, eds. 1998. *Magnetic Media Preservation Sourcebook.* New York: Media Alliance. This comprehensive reference work "not only lists vendors, consultants, and organizations who provide services, but also the groups and consortia tackling the issues of preservation through collaborative work." The Media Alliance also maintains its own Web site at http://www.mediaalliance. org/.

Saffady, William. 1991. "Stability, Care and Handling of Microforms, Magnetic Media and Optical Disks." *Library Technology Reports* (January–February): 27. One of the first major library-related preservation studies with recommendations for magnetic media and optical disks.

Scholtz, James C. 1989. *Developing and Maintaining Video Collections in Libraries.* Santa Barbara, CA: ABC-CLIO. Currently out of print, this title continues to provide useful in-depth information on maintaining videocassettes and VCRs, and on supply vendors.

Internet Sources

American Film Institute Online. 2001. *Moving Image Preservation: A Basic Bibliography.* http://www.afionline.org/preservation/about/bib.html. Contains a section on basic print resources related to videotape.

American National Standards Institute. 2000. *Standards Information.* http://web.ansi. org/public/std_info.html. The site for locating and purchasing ANSI standards related to the preservation of tape and optical media.

Association of Moving Image Archivists. 2000. http://www.amianet.org. A major professional organization, AMIA's site includes storage standards for videotape, as well as film and video preservation resources on the Internet.

Digital Library Federation. 2000. http://www.clir.org/diglib/dlfhomepage.htm. Operating under the Council on Library and Information Resources, the DLF focuses on digital preservation by providing access to its own and its sister organizatons' "preservation initiatives, research reports, and related information resources."

Library of Congress. 1998. *Cylinder, Disc and Tape Care in a Nutshell.* http://lcweb. loc.gov/preserv/care/record.html. Includes basic standards for tape and optical disc preservation, with bibliography.

Library of Congress. 1997. *Television and Video Preservation 1997: A Report on the Current State of American Television and Video Preservation. Volume 1: Report.* http://lcweb.loc.gov/film/tvstudy.html. A report of the Librarian of Congress, this crucial volume (ISBN: 0–8444–0946–4; made available online by the National Film Preservation Board) contains substantial information on videotape composition, its longevity and preservation—in chapters 2 ("The Materials and Their Preservation Needs") and 8 ("A National Plan: Recommendations for Safeguarding and Preserving the American Television and Video Heritage").

National Library of Australia. 1999. *PADI: Preserving Access to Digital Information.* http://www.nla.gov.au/padi. An international site for digital preservation topics and resources.

Northeast Document Conservation Center. 2001. http://www.nedcc.org. A general preservation and disaster recovery site that includes some useful resource links, as well as technical leaflets on climate control and suppliers and services for film and video reformatting.

"Permanence and Handling of CDs." Kodak Professional. 1994–2001. http://www.kodak.com/global/en/professional/products/storage/pcd/techInfo/permanence.shtml.

RLG Preservation Program (PRESERV). 2000. http://www.rlg.org/preserv. Maintained by the Research Libraries Group, this Web site offers useful information on media preservation (see the "RLG Magnetic and Optical Media Preservation Manual," published in 2001) and digital preservation issues (the bi-monthly Web newsletter "RLG DigiNews").

SMPTE (Society of Motion Picture and Television Engineers). 2001. *Standards.* http://www.smpte.org/smpte_store/standards/. SMPTE standards related to all aspects of film and video recordings, including storage conditions, are available for sale here.

SOLINET. 2000. *Related Internet Resources.* http://www.solinet.net/presvtn/links/org.htm. The Web site of the Southeastern Library Network, this section includes Web resources on electronic formats, digital imaging, and "Preservation Resources on the Internet: Photographic, Film, and Video Formats" (published in 2001).

Stanford University Libraries, Preservation Dept. 2001. *CoOL: Conservation Online.* http://palimpsest.stanford.edu. Perhaps the foremost U.S. Web site for information on a full range of preservation topics. Includes searchable archives of numerous preservation listservs.

Van Bogart, John W. C. 1995. *Magnetic Tape Storage and Handling: A Guide for Libraries and Archives.* http://www.clir.org/pubs/reports/pub54/index.html. This major report is "a joint project of the Commission on Preservation and Access and the National Media Laboratory, developed within the Commission's Preservation Science Research initiative. The initiative encourages new techniques and technologies to manage chemical deterioration in library and archival collections and to extend their useful life." It also offers substantial technical information on the characteristics of magnetic tape, its care and life expectancy.

Video History Project. 2001. *Video Preservation—The Basics.* http://www.experimentaltvcenter.org/history/preservation/pres_contents.html. A comprehensive, well-organized, but not-too-technical guide to the subject for tape formats.

Part IV

Laying the Ground Rules, Picking What Plays: Policies, Criteria, and Methods for Selecting, Evaluating, and Acquiring Video

Chapter 13

Developing Video Collection Development Policies to Accommodate Existing and New Technologies

James C. Scholtz

INTRODUCTION AND PURPOSE

Since the writing of this chapter in the first edition (1994), there have been three significant changes impacting video collection development/selection practices in libraries. The first change is the evolution and increase in the number of special interest "niche" cable channels, including the History, Discovery, Home & Garden, Golf, and SciFi Channels, the Cartoon Network, and others. These channels have opened up new markets for programming, and have increased the demand for direct sales of videos. Within the next five years, it is likely that the appearance of "smart" programming or programming on demand will have a further monumental impact on the sales and rental of prerecorded videos. The second change is the appearance of the digital videodisc (sometimes known as Digital Versatile Disc [DVD]) in 1995 and its emergence as a viable, albeit fledgling circulating format in libraries in 1999. The third change is the increasing number of collection development and related policies appearing on the Web sites of libraries, from public to academic.

An expanding number of libraries now have Web sites that include various service and collection/selection policies for the public to view. Unfortunately, many of these policies are not up-to-date or well written. The best of these policies can be used as models, but an understanding of the component parts of a collection development policy is still valuable. The intent of this chapter is to give the reader a broad understanding of video collection development policies and procedures. The version of the chapter that appeared in the first edition of this book concentrated on building an understanding of video collection development within a historical framework of the video revolution, and provided a discussion of consumer/patron/producer dynamics. This revision will summarize those historical insights, and will discuss the implications of the new DVD format. It will also discuss some key collection development concepts, define the core collection, and discuss various client- and collection-centered techniques that will work regardless of format. An example of a very comprehensive policy statement that incorporates many of these concepts is provided. For additional examples of policy statements, see: http://www.lib.berkeley.edu/MRC/policies.html. The previous edition of this book should also be consulted for additional samples of collection development policies.

THE PAST PREDICTS THE FUTURE

In a 1992 *Library Journal* column entitled "The Futurecast," Raymond Kurzwell identified seven hierarchical and evolutionary stages in the life cycle of any technology: precursor, invention, development, maturity, false pretender, obsolescence, and antiquity (Kurzwell 1992) All technologies exist within a complex societal and economic context. Because the acceptance of a technology is based on its use or obsolescence (factors which are often radically affected by marketing), the life cycle of a technology can be staggered: old and new technologies can coexist and overlap, at least for a short time. Today, VHS video enjoys unparalleled consumer market penetration, while DVD is in its infant stage, but rapidly assuming a more prominent consumer role. Both formats are, however, coexisting quite nicely at present.

Jacqueline Mancall, a professor at Drexel University in Philadelphia, feels that radical changes are in the works for library collections and their users. She feels that library users are currently very format oriented, choosing to use certain formats for particular reasons. In the future, Mancall predicts that users will become "information oriented" (where format is of secondary concern), as well as "multiple-concept adept" (a skill set involving the use of multiple, linked media to accommodate different learning styles, grade levels, and multicurricular needs) (Mancall 1991: 88).

Ray Serebrin of the Seattle Public Library feels that "the elements are in place for a shift in focus, away from movies . . . toward responsive collection building that focuses on the information needs of the community" (Serebrin 1988: 88). Responsible collection development seeks to find links between the user, the information source, and its uses. At the same time, effective collection building recognizes different levels of use, as well as format appropriateness in terms of the subject and the capabilities of the medium. Within the next 15 years, library services are likely to be transformed into a technological package in which bibliographic and content access are integrated, immediate, and seamless. Neither the technology or delivery systems nor the copyright laws are presently in place to permit this seamless access. It is also currently the case that the public demand leans toward specific formats—specifically VHS video and DVD—and that new technologies are being driven by the industry, and not necessarily by consumer demand.

Back in 1988, Ray Serebrin stated that "Video [was] just the tip of the technological iceberg; how librarians [handled it would] largely determine the degree of success for future technologies and formats in tomorrow's library" (Serebrin 1988: 35). This prophecy will be fulfilled within the next five years as DVD collections evolve and mature within the library environment. DVD will no doubt be the wave of the future; but before (and if) DVD supersedes VHS video, librarians will be forced to support and maintain collections in both formats. As a new library collection and service, DVDs will impact the library on all levels, forcing a reassessment of storage requirements, materials budgets, staffing of both technical and public services, supplies and equipment budgets, and collection development policies and procedures.

THE COLLECTION DEVELOPMENT CONCEPT

In his book *Developing Library Collections* (1979), G. Edward Evans asserts that collection development is a universal process in which librarians acquire diverse materials to meet patron demands. This continuous process consists of six distinguishable, albeit sequential, elements: (1) Community analysis (users), (2) Policies, (3) Selection, (4) Acquisition, (5) Weeding, and (6) Evaluation.

To be successful, a library collection must be a product of community and clientele information and recreation needs and demands. These needs are translated into specific goals and objectives, which should, in turn, be reflected in the nature and shape of the collection. Because both selection and collection development are (or should be) tailored to a specific community of users or a particular set of user contexts, neither is generally transportable; the collection of one library cannot necessarily be overlaid or duplicated with any degree of success in another library. Each collection is unique.

Serving a broad-based clientele, particularly in public libraries, almost always entails balancing the generally high demand for current, "blockbuster" feature titles with other parts of the video collection. It is a given that libraries cannot normally compete with video stores in terms of either quantity or timeliness when it comes to current, popular video releases. Video stores are, after all, profit motivated and focused almost exclusively on high-volume, mass-market commodities. While libraries are not in this same ballgame, they can serve the important role of complementing video store services by providing various cinema "classics," lesser-known and difficult-to-find titles, and foreign features, as well as non-fiction titles.

In the past librarians gave little thought to developing a systematic, goal-oriented collection development approach based on institutional goals and objectives, collection analysis by subject, and patrons' wants and needs. Every service and collection must have a defined purpose or goals, even if that goal is to satisfy the recreational needs of patrons through the purchase of blockbuster movies.

Librarians should ensure that the broad spectrum of patron information needs is being satisfied. To those ends, a policy of integrated collection development should be adopted—purchasing materials in forms and formats that are most suitable to the patron, the subject, and use patterns. It is essential that the public library develop a video policy and goals consistent with its service mission, one that focuses on "video as information." This strategy will assist the librarian in establishing a framework for future collection and service planning. On a larger scale, the collection development policy also helps maintain a dynamic tension and budget equity between formats, and provides a defense against censorship challenges.

GATHERING PRELIMINARY INFORMATION

The first set of questions any librarian should ask before developing any collection is:

1. What do I want this collection to do, and is there a specific patron base I want to serve?
2. Do I want the collection to be fairly ephemeral (a popular/blockbuster collection with high circulation over the short term), or do I want a mixture of popular features and non-fiction programs that fosters a stable, long-term circulation, and a collection with longer-term value?
3. What mix of popular, genre-specific, and non-fiction/special interest titles will work in my library?
5. How do I decide which titles to purchase for a new collection? This is a central question for librarians establishing a new DVD collection coexisting with an established VHS collection.

The above questions should be asked at the outset of building a core collection. While a core collection is a list of basic titles—those determined to be essentials—this defined core is not necessarily the same from library to library. Core collections for libraries with the same types of clientele and goals are, nonetheless, likely to have many similarities in terms of individual titles and the mix of titles. A core collection in any library is based on four basic factors: (1) the initial materials budget; (2) the basic genres, subjects, historical periods, and directors chosen for initial start-up; (3) the depth and breadth of coverage; and (4) the current availability of those titles in the marketplace.

For libraries beginning to establish DVD collections, it is important that the identified start-up collection not only stays within current budget allocations and satisfies current patron demands, but that it also provides a building block upon which expanded collections can be built in the future. The core DVD collection should not simply be a mirror image of an existing VHS collection. This building-block approach should be thought of as acquiring a coherent set of titles or establishing a longer-term wish list, rather than simply acquiring a collection in a title-by-title fashion. Using the former approach allows the collection to be built like a jigsaw puzzle, with each new title serving as an integral part of a planned overall picture.

In starting to build a core collection, it is necessary to first determine which titles, subjects, and genres are currently available on DVD (or any new format under consideration). While it obviously isn't possible to buy titles that are not yet released in a desired format, one *can* create "wish-lists" for future purchases based on the current publication universe and expectations for future production. Second, reviews for those items and formats must be found in order to assess their quality and appropriateness for a particular collection. Patron demand for each subject and genre should then be assessed via survey information. Desiderata lists compiled at AV desks are particularly important in this stage, as they will indicate specific titles, topics, subjects, and genres being requested by users. After all of these preliminaries are completed, the collection development policy can be modified to include the new media with specific collection goals.

This concept of collection development has several advantages. First, it allows librarians to establish measurable and definable goals and objectives in terms of both budget expenditure and number and types of titles purchased within a specific time period. Second, it sets up a process for reasonable goal attainment and success measurement. It is important that specific objectives be attainable within a short period of time, so goal assessment can be regular. It is equally important that only a maximum of three to four objectives be listed at one time so that the budget is not overtaxed or goals diluted.

THE CORE COLLECTION AND SELECTION TOOLS

Building a core collection is one of the most difficult undertakings involved in setting up a new service. The librarian must accomplish several tasks, including surveying the broad range of available products, identifying the scope and depth of client need, identifying all core collection areas, and locating eclectic titles in those core areas.

Once a video core collection is established, how do librarians make choices in building and extending that collection in a systematic and organized fashion? In order to answer that question, we must first define the term *core collection*. As it is defined in this chapter, a core video collection is a small collection (from 250 to 1,000 titles) composed of "essential" titles—an eclectic collection embodying a broad range of subjects and genres that serves the most basic needs of a specific clientele. Essentially, a core collection consists of standard works that represent the best of a genre or subject, or are more authoritative and inclusive in coverage than other titles. The establishment of a video core collection should be considered as a "block" purchase—a library of titles acquired at one time, and serving as the foundation for future collection expansion. Core collections are largely homogeneous; the group of titles as a whole provides a broad representation of many subjects within a few volumes, much like an encyclopedia set. At this writing, there is no one reference book that effectively describes a complete non-fiction video core collection, nor are there any that describe methods for collecting one. Feature films, on the other hand, are in some ways similar to literature: there is substantial agreement on which works, performers, and directors have survived, and will survive, the test of time based on the quality of their work. From the basic core collection, collection analysis can begin and a systematic collection development program can be adopted, reflective of community needs, budget requirements, and library goals.

While there are several books outlining core collection theory and suggesting specific titles for monograph collections, there are, as mentioned above, few works of this type for video. The scattered publications that do deal with video core collections, while somewhat dated, still offer useful conceptual guidance. Of these works, only one, *Video for Libraries* (Mason and Scholtz 1988), provides a list of both features and non-fiction, "special interest" videos. The editors of this annotated list emphasize that the titles listed should not necessarily be considered a "core collection," but rather "representative . . . of videos that are actually being used successfully in [public] libraries across the country." In the above-mentioned book, James L. Limbacher provides an excellent, brief discussion of "what makes up a good feature video core collection" and provides a list of approximately 500 "first-purchase" titles. Randy Pitman, editor of the *Video Librarian*, has compiled a recommended list of 500 feature films in a book entitled *Video Movies: A Core Collection for Libraries* (Pitman and Swanson 1990). Gordon B. Arnold's article in *Library Journal* (1989: 29–35), entitled "From Big Screen to Small Screen," provides a fairly comprehensive list of about 100 features representing the gamut of film history currently available on videocassette. Tom Wiener's *The Book of Video Lists* (1990) provides an excellent list of feature videos that effectively establish and extend the core collection by answering the patron's question, "I took X title out; what do you have that's like it?" A particularly unique book, useful in targeting and obtaining features and non-fiction videos for children and young adults, is *Best Videos for Children and Young Adults* by Jennifer Jung Gallant (1990). Various awards, such as the Oscar (Academy Awards) and Golden Globe awards for feature films, and the ALA Video Round Table's (VRT) Notable Video for Adults (http://http://www.ala.org/VRT), and the Young Adult Library Services Association (YALSA) Notables for YA's (http://www.ala.org/YALSA) for documentary and educational titles, also provide an excellent base of titles for inclusion into a core list.

The tasks of identifying and acquiring video core collections are somewhat more problematic for schools and academic libraries than for public libraries because of the almost complete lack of standardized or authoritative lists for these institutions. An increasing number of states are, however, adopting curricular and teaching competency standards, as well as adhering to national standards already in place. Producers such as PBS are striving to link programs to those competency standards by developing resources such as the 366+ title *PBS Video Database of American History*. In addition to the lack of standards for video acquisition in school settings, varying levels of presentation and use within specific curricula and for specific subjects and grade levels also complicate selection. In these cases, other sources of identifying and evaluating video titles must be used. Among the possible resources for accomplishing these goals are festival and award winners, professional and association videographies, notables lists, and curricular subject lists. In general, any list or festival award arrived at by group consensus rather than by individual review carries more weight as a core recommendation.

In addition to the works cited above, there are a number of serial publications that provide valuable assistance in building core video collections. Since the first edition of this chapter, the pool of printed review sources has shrunk, but the Web has made reviews more accessible. While all of the following sources offer some Web-based access, *Video Librarian* (http://www.videolibrarian.com) offers the most comprehensive, archived, searchable review site for both features and non-fiction titles. It is also the premiere magazine for video reviews. *Booklist* magazine, published by ALA, contains a non-print section that is a semi-monthly review source for multimedia. Two annual issues of *Booklist* stand out as being particularly valuable for core collection development: the audiovisual showcase issue (November 1 issue), and the Editors' Choice issue (January 1). *Booklist* generally only includes favorable reviews. In contrast, *Library Journal*, which continues to be a standard, lists both recommended and panned reviews.

The Web can increasingly be used to gain information about regional and national film and video festivals and awards (see Chapter 22 in this book for an example of some of these sites). Academic library Web sites devoted to film and video can also be useful resources; the best of these often include extensive film and video information, reference, and review sources, and collection development links. Examples of large academic Web sites include:

- Indiana University Film Library (http://www.indiana.edu/~libreser/media/Feature-Film-List.html)
- University of California, Berkeley (http://www.lib.berkeley.edu/MRC)
- University of Michigan Film Library (http://www.lib.umich.edu/libhome/FVL.lib/)
- American University Media Services (http://www.library.american.edu/collects/media/medmenu.html)

The popularity and wide availability of movies on video have fostered a dramatic increase in the number of print publications and online resources devoted to identifying and reviewing feature films. In the appendixes to Chapter 10 in this book, Randy Pitman offers a good short list of some of the more useful among these. It is interesting to note that in a recent discussion on the American Library Association Video Round Table listserv (VIDEOLIB), three movie sources were identified as being the most valuable for collection development and reference: *Halliwell's Film and Video Guide*; Leonard Maltin's *Movie & Video Guide*; and *Video Hound's Golden Movie Retriever*.

VIDEO COLLECTION DEVELOPMENT

Like a profit margin in business, high circulation is often considered to be the hallmark of success in libraries. While high circulation is an important indicator of any collection's overall success, it is only one measurement. It is also important to measure the popularity of any one title or group of titles compared to the relative popularity of its genre or subject group; for example, how popular is X title on home repair compared with others in that category? The number of titles checked out at any given time in proportion to the total number of titles in that category is also very telling. The following section will describe various techniques for determining collection success and for gathering statistics that will help in acquiring titles that will perform well and fill gaps in the collection.

"Collection development is probably the single most important and difficult library theory to effectively put into practice because it requires so much pre-planning and a broad scope of vision" (Scholtz 1989: 35). Collection development seeks to form the entire collection or its component parts based on specific goals and objectives. In a nutshell, the collection development process involves taking a snapshot of the collection at a particular point in time and analyzing its past and present. This process will eventually employ the gathered data to formulate goals and determine the future shape of the collection.

Current assessment of the collection is a necessity, and can be accomplished by using one of four approaches: client-centered; circulation sampling; collection-centered; or a combination of all three. A variety of instruments such as telephone surveys, mailed surveys, in-house surveys, services and collections measurement, circulation data, copyright dates, collection comparison with select bibliographies and citation analysis, and reference success tracking can be used by themselves or in combination to yield valuable data. Each one of these data collection instruments has various advantages and disadvantages and must be chosen wisely to fit the circumstances.

Client-Centered Techniques

Client-centered data can be gathered from current library users, identified non-users, or a combination of both. There are two types of sampling techniques: random and purposive. A purposive sample differs from a random sample in that the former is not necessarily representative of the activity or population being measured, although it is said to be "typical." A library undertaking a community/client/patron survey must relate this enterprise to a set of defined goals and objectives. With these goals and objectives in mind, the survey questions can be tailored to providing information useful in realizing these goals and objectives (for example, increasing the use of the video collection by non-users.), rather than simply providing a gathering of irrelevant and extraneous information. In order for the data gathered to be useful, the data synthesizing mechanism, such as a spreadsheet developed from a relational database, must be similarly well planned and constructed.

Gathering data from non-library users usually takes the form of telephone questionnaires or mailed surveys. In order to be valid, the population sample should represent the broader community/clientele. Questions must be carefully constructed and should avoid using leading questions that result in the "halo effect" (responses that anticipate a desired answer rather than reflecting the respondent's true opinions or experience). In non-user surveys, there are often numerous, uncontrollable variables; therefore, each question must be simply worded, direct, and focused.

The client-centered approach analyzes patron/client use patterns and the degree of patron satisfaction with the collection. This approach measures which materials patrons use, which they don't use, and what they need and demand. It should be noted here that most texts view the "Give 'em What They Want" and the "Give 'em What They Ought to Have" approaches as opposing and irreconcilable. The question often faced by collection developers is "[S]hould they provide what is wanted simply because it is wanted?" (Williams 1990: 55). Patrick Williams feels that "want" and "need" are not opposing positions as long as librarians take the position that patron wants and patron needs can coincide, with the collection reflecting both specific community or institutional needs and demands.

Circulation Sampling and Collection-Centered Techniques

Circulation sampling enables librarians to determine the correlation between collection use and volume count. Particularly valuable in school and academic libraries, these connections can provide the basis for measuring the impact of the media center on the curriculum. Such information can become an important justification for materials budget continuation, increases, and allocation. It answers the following questions:

1. What sections of the collection receive the most use?
2. Do the sections of the collection that receive the highest use correlate with the curricular areas emphasized in the school?
3. Are the sections of the collection with the greatest use those sections with the largest numbers of materials? (Garland 1992: 73)

As in client-centered techniques, either purposive or random sampling methods can be used. If the library has an automated circulation system capable of generating various cumulative or statistical reports, surveying the entire collection is preferable.

The collection-centered approach provides a picture of a collection's overall strengths and weaknesses, matching subject groups against standard videographies and lists. Another collection-centered device, called the "conspectus approach," measures a collection's depth-of-subject coverage against a hierarchy of "study levels," ranging from no coverage to exhaustive. Using a combination of these two approaches will yield the most useful data. Analyzing circulation statistics for books and videos in particular classification ranges—either Dewey Decimal Classification (DDC) or Library of Congress (LC) classification—is likely to reveal important information for purchases in both types of collection. Collections can be further analyzed by looking at circulation by copyright, production, and/or release date of materials. Composite (or average) profiles based on the above factors can be derived, providing the librarian with useful information concerning patron demand, likelihood, and extent of use, and subject coverage. Other measurements that may provide useful information include analysis of owned/not-owned lists; turnover rates (circulation within a specific-subject category divided by the number of titles or volumes/prints in that category); analysis of reference questions; and interlibrary loans.

A unique statistical derivative used to compare the various parts of a collection with their respective circulation is the relative-use factor. This factor is obtained by dividing the percent of circulation in any subject or format category by the size (percentage) of the category relative to the overall collection. A high relative-use factor (greater than 1) would indicate both a demand for materials by users and an area of the collection that may need expansion, while a low relative-use factor (less than 1) would indicate minimal demand (Bertland 1991: 90–92). The relative-use factor is not directly dependent on the number of volumes/titles (as is, for instance, turnover rate) and thus serves as a transition statistic between client- and collection-centered methods.

"Collection mapping," detailed in *Information Power* (American Association of School Librarians [AASL] and Association for Educational Communications and Technology [AECT] 1988: 26–39), and in *Measures of Excellence for School Library Media Centers* (Loertscher 1988: 14–16), is a process whereby the collection is analyzed in terms of subject strengths and weaknesses and depth of coverage. The unique collection map developed for a library can be overlaid onto a collection-use (circulation) map for that same library, thus yielding valuable comparative and interpretive data in terms of use versus subject strengths, weaknesses, and curriculum relevancy. Kathleen Garland (1992: 74) writes of the collection mapping process: "A 'perfect score' is attained when the collection-use map matches the 'ideal' collection map."

In determining specific subject areas in which there is a need for video, as well as in determining the appropriate depth of coverage for those areas, circulation of both the current video collection and other parts of the collection should be examined historically. Collection-centered techniques might also use lists of the type discussed in the Selection Tools section above for collection coverage analysis. Some library vendors, such as OCLC/WLN Pacific Northwest Service Center (http://www.wln.com) and Follett Audiovisual (http://www.far. follett.com), have developed selection lists that can be compared against library catalog holdings and used for compiling acquisition or "wish lists." Again, libraries with computerized circulation systems have a distinct advantage because the entire collection, rather than samples, can be analyzed, and because data are so readily available and easily manipulated in machine-readable form.

Using an automated circulation system, the entire collection and its component parts can be analyzed for a wide variety of factors related to current and historical circulation trends. Some libraries have started using circulation bar codes that include both bibliographic and use statistics; such tools make inventory and statistics gathering particularly easy. Libraries that do not own automated circulation systems must rely on time-consuming volume counting and shelf counting practices. Sampling techniques are very useful for many libraries because of the smaller collection size required and limited data collection periods. In order to be valid, a sample must contain at least 20 percent of the larger collection. The sample must also be truly random and representative of the entire collection. If, for instance, the number of copies of videos within each feature film genre is known, the number of features in each genre checked out at any one time can be easily counted. A certain number of titles in each non-fiction category could be identified (with a green dot on the video case, for example), and tracked for circulation over a certain time period. In many cases, both large automated circulation systems and manual circulation systems allow exportation of data to PC-based databases and spreadsheets, allowing manipulation and analysis of raw data. Most statistical methods rely on the mean or average; however, when the range (minimum and maximum) of a set of numbers is great, it is sometimes beneficial and accurate to substitute the median (midpoint of the set) or mode (the number[s] occurring most frequently). An exceptionally clear, well-written guide to evaluating collections is the *Guide to the Evaluation of Library Collections*, edited by Barbara Lockett (1989).

The best plan for surveying the current status of the collection is to use a combination of collection- and use-centered techniques. This involves looking not only at the video collection and its use, but also the book and serial collections as well. If craft books, such as woodworking and flower arranging, circulate well, it's a good bet that videos on the same subject will circulate equally as well. The community should be assessed for unserved or inadequately served needs. Similarly, specific subject areas or topics that could be appropriately fulfilled using video should be evaluated. Various ethnic and racial groups, disabled patrons, senior citizens, latchkey children, and other identifiable patron groups have specific needs that might be addressed in the video format. Businesses, as well public sector organizations such as police and fire departments, may have a great need for training, continuing education, and motivational videos. Local travel agencies might discover a variety of uses for the travel collection. Populations that are traditionally marginal users or non-users of libraries (such as individuals served in literacy outreach programs), and users seeking continuing basic education (such as patrons involved in general equivalency diploma [GED] training), often find that video is also an attractive and effective learning tool. Children's video, classic features, and foreign films are often largely ignored by mainstream video rental stores in the community. Collection-based goals and measurable objectives can be formulated using this information, thus making selection a measurable, quantifiable process. This collection analysis, evaluation, goal formulating, and selection process is cyclical and builds on itself.

Two terms, *systematic* and *organized*, are key words in collection development. Many librarians see their role in collection building as simply selecting material on a "per title" basis, without thinking about the overall long-range purpose, form, or outcome of the collection, the collection as continuum. This approach is often supported by the fact that most reviews evaluate specific titles as unique, stand-alone entities, rather than comparing, contrasting, and linking those titles to others.

Community and institutional needs and demands must be assessed by examining the existing video collection as well as other collections and community resources. Once the needs of the community have been determined, it is fairly easy to determine the library's role (mission statement) in providing information to fulfill those needs. Specific goals and measurable objectives are then developed with respect to services and collections. Planning documents, such as selection policies, serve to translate goals and objectives into specific operational terms, providing a method through which goals can be concretely met and continuity can be assured.

In most libraries, broader selection activities occur even when no policies exist. A librarian may see a need for materials on standardized test skills and purchase videos and books to meet that need, not realizing that filling this need was actually an objective. Collection development seeks to formalize and prioritize, but not necessarily restrict, the formation of measurable and attainable objectives relating to materials selection. Thus, the purchase of the standardized test videos might be linked to the broader goal of purchasing a certain number of self-help study skills materials.

DEFINING SELECTION AND COLLECTION DEVELOPMENT

What is the difference between a collection development and a selection policy? Historically, the three terms—*collection development, selection,* and *acquisitions*—have been used interchangeably; however, they are radically different. Rose Mary Magrill and John Corbin (1989: 1) state that "[c]ollection development has come to encompass a broad range of activities related to the policies and procedures of selection, acquisition, and evaluation of library collections." Hendrik Edelman suggested that these terms represent a hierarchy, with the highest level, collection development, being the planning function (Magrill and Corbin 1989: 1). In the work cited above, Magrill and Corbin suggest that

from the established collection development plans of the library flow the decisions about inclusion or exclusion of specific items in the collection . . . in other words, selection, the second level of the hierarchy. Acquisitions—the next level—is the process that implements selection decisions. [It is] the process of verifying, ordering, and paying for . . . materials.

Selection and acquisitions can be viewed as single activities, while collection development is neither a single activity nor a group of activities; it is a planning and decision-making process. Charles B. Osburn states that collection development "implies that collection response to changing conditions is to be part of a predetermined definable system of relating the collection to the community man aged by the librarian" (Magrill and Corbin 1989: 2). Essentially, the collection development policy serves to establish an interdependent relationship between information formats (e.g., print and non-print) and disciplines/subject areas. It also links many policies together, such as selection, acquisition, and weeding. Goals, measurable objectives, community analysis, and evaluation are the four key elements that distinguish a collection development document from a selection policy.

A collection development policy serves the following basic functions:

1. It establishes a planning guideline and working tool for selectors;
2. It operates as a communications medium between the library, external administrative bodies, and patrons, as well as between collection development and acquisitions librarians within a single institution;
3. It codifies the rationale for decisions regarding the materials budget;
4. It helps achieve a unified view of the areas of the collection that should be developed;
5. It helps define and coordinate individual responsibilities for developing and maintaining the collection;
6. It helps achieve consistency in materials selection by clarifying specific objectives and reducing the number of ad hoc decisions related to the selection process; and
7. It provides methods for performance evaluation in regard to the collection-building cycle.

A well-written collection development policy may also outline and facilitate both regional and national cooperative collection development and management. Furthermore, such a policy may provide the foundations for responding to censorship challenges. In academic institutions, a collection development policy can help librarians respond to departmental or individual faculty self-interest pressures by focusing on the needs of the broader campus community.

Every library collection should be established for a definite purpose. Most collections strive to serve a wide range of patrons and patron needs by including a broad variety of subjects, genres, and formats. Goals will determine the specific formats to be acquired and the depth of subject or genre coverage within those formats. Depth of collection within subjects should relate to the library mission and goals, who uses the collection, and why they use it. The ALA *Guide to the Evaluation of Library Collections* comments on coverage depth by stating: "The collection may be developed for research, recreation, community service and development, instruction, support of a corporate activity, or a combination of these or other purposes [represented by multilevels of in-depth coverage]" (Lockett 1989: 1)

Librarians involved in building collections should first identify the current levels of service and the collection strengths and weaknesses. This process involves, among other things, attempting to determine the history and evolution of the collection (When and why was it begun? How did it develop?). The makeup of the library's clientele should be analyzed along with the budget picture. Finally, the library's goals and objectives should be overlaid on the gathered information, and goal priorities established.

After specific collection goals have been gathered and prioritized, narrative statements concerning the scope, depth, and limitations of the collection should be developed. These statements should include expectations or goals for collecting specific formats, subjects, or genres of material. An alternative method, known as the *conspectus approach*, has become a standard tool for coordinating collection development based on the library's classification scheme. This approach is used in many academic libraries, and is generally based on Library of Congress Classification scheme (Lockett 1989: 4).

The elements of a collection development policy include the following:

1. *Introduction.* Defines and identifies the purpose and materials policy scope, the audience for the policy, and the governing body adopting the policy. The date of adoption should also be in this section.

2. *Library mission or general philosophy statement and institutional goals for collection management and service.* This statement creates a theoretical foundation on which the more practical sections of the policy will be built. This section may also include statements regarding library policies concerning patrons' rights, including freedom to read or view statements, access policies, and library policies regarding censorship. These statements may be derived internally, or they may be based in part or wholly on statements developed by external organizations. Examples of these latter statements include the ALA/ American Film and Video Association (AFVA) Freedom to View statement (http://www.ala.org/alaorg/oif/freedomtoview.html), ALA's Freedom to Read statement (http://www.ala.org/alaorg/oif/freeread.html), ALA's *Library Bill of Rights* statement on labeling (http://www.ala.org/alaorg/oif/labeling.html), and

other intellectual freedom documents (see ALA's Intellectual Freedom Committee site (http://www.ala.org/alaorg/oif/ifc_inf.html).

3. *Analysis of the library's objectives.* This section describes the external environment and boundaries and limits of the collection as a whole. The section should include:

a. Description of clientele and community to be served.

b. Description of library programs currently available and planned within the next two to three years.

c. Brief overview of the collection, including history, limitations, boundaries, special collections, subjects, formats, genres emphasized/de-emphasized, exclusions, and collection locations. (Narrative statements or a conspectus approach should be used here, delineating levels of collection and levels of users.)

4. *Organization of collection management and development program.* This section should define such elements as staffing, liaison with user groups, and cooperative collection development agreements and programs.

5. *Selection policies.* This section may either be a group of related policies or one all-encompassing general policy. Sources and percentages of materials funds might be mentioned, as well as policy and practice regarding materials duplication and acquisition of multiple copies. Selection methods and departmental or individual selection responsibility should be designated here. Specific criteria for selection based on subject, genre, or format should be included in this section. Challenged materials documents, forms, and policy hierarchy should be delineated.

6. *Relationships to policies and programs for the management of collections.* This section should address such issues and requirements as preservation, weeding, and storage.

7. *Collection evaluation techniques and methods.* In addition to the above elements, the policy should address various measurable objectives, including specific numbers of titles to purchase in specific areas, clientele to be reached, and new formats to be purchased. As mentioned earlier, it is important that objectives be measurable and attainable within time and budgetary constraints. Clearly stated, realistic objectives can prove invaluable in formulating budgets and staying accountable to the bottom line, in measuring success and motivating staff, and in demonstrating achievements to patrons and boards.

THE SELECTION POLICY

Within the collection development policy resides the selection policy. The term *collection* generally refers to the collection as a whole, regardless of formats or subjects and genres. Often, however, the collection development policy is simply a group of selection policies, delineated by format or department, and brought together by a common mission and goals. A selection policy can be transformed into a collection development document by adding a mission statement, a description of the community served, measurable collection goals and objectives, and a set of evaluation methods (making the document cyclical and measuring goal attainment).

A 1980s Rockefeller Foundation survey of video collection and use in libraries revealed that only about one-third of the 17 respondents possessed separate video selection policies, "feeling that the overall materials selection policy was broad enough to cover video collection development" (Pitman 1990). Durbin (1987: 40) writes of the dangers of this practice:

Many policies have been written with the idea that one need only insert the word *nonbook* in order to give equal status . . . but each format has individual characteristics and demands different criteria or basis of selection than the others. Each medium makes its own contribution as a carrier of information, and should be judged accordingly.

In developing collection policies for a library that includes video, the issue *is not* whether to make a general policy broad enough to include the format; it is to develop sections of the policy that are sufficiently narrow or specific enough to accurately represent the special characteristics and uses of video. A separate video selection policy is essential because it reinforces the library's commitment to the medium.

A question many librarians ask is: Do I need both a collection development policy and a selection policy? The answer is: No. A collection development policy should contain all the elements of a selection policy, although such a policy statement may not specifically deal with discrete formats or departments. In many cases, it may be better to develop a general collection development policy than to formulate many specific format or departmental selection policies. A single policy tends to strengthen the concept of collection unity and integration.

TYPES OF COLLECTION DEVELOPMENT POLICIES

The type of collection development policy and the specificity of elements within it depend to a great degree on the administrative and departmental structure of the library for which it is written. Each style has distinct advantages and disadvantages. A library may choose one of the following selection policy styles, or a mix of the three:

1. *A generic policy for the entire collection.* Best suited to small libraries, this type of policy completely eliminates differences in formats, concentrating instead on the shape and coverage of the entire collection. By its nature, the generic policy will be extremely basic and cursory, ignoring the significant differences in format selection criteria.

2. *One policy with specific sections by media format (i.e., film, video, art prints, books, etc.) or specific subjects and genres or locations.* This type of

policy works well in small to medium-sized libraries with several distinct departments. Interdepartmental communication in such environments is generally good, and selection and acquisition policies and procedures for each department are not widely disparate. A department head, sometimes in a committee, frequently does selection in these contexts. This type of policy is the perfect mechanism for outlining different selection criteria for various formats and subjects. It is also effective in reinforcing the similarities and interdependencies between those different groups.

3. *Several distinct selection policies, with separate selection criteria for specific media formats, subjects and genres, or media location.* This type of arrangement works best in highly departmentalized or division/branch libraries where clientele and depth of subject or genre coverage differ widely. In such settings, selection decisions for various parts of the collection are often made by disparate individuals (such as department heads), and specific subject or format collections are housed in separate departments or facilities. Selection and acquisition methods may differ widely from department to department. In focused collections of this type, separate policies are generally easier to use and revise than a broader document that attempts to cover all media and all subjects.

To a great degree, the size of library staff, the departmental structure of the library, departmental budget allocations, inter- and intradepartmental lines of communication, and selection authority determine the overall shape, content, and depth of the selection policy. Large libraries usually have a collection development department to coordinate overall collection development activities within the library. Subject or format specialized libraries and branches, on the other hand, in responding to different purposes and priorities, may be viewed as isolated pieces rather than as parts of a composite "large library." In large library settings, department or division heads may hold authority that extends to specific branch collections. Selection committees may operate with rotating personnel. In small and medium-sized public libraries, librarians are usually involved in the collection development process. However, in these libraries, selection authority is frequently departmentalized into "adult" and "children's" areas.

Regardless of the type of library or the type of selection policy adopted, the policy should contain the following basic elements:

1. A statement of goals and measurable objectives; purpose and use of the collection (both in-house as well as circulating collections).

2. A succinct statement describing the parameters of the community served, unserved parts of the community, and groups destined to be served through the meeting of goals and objectives.

3. A clear statement establishing selection authority and responsibility.

4. A clear statement delineating how selection is performed, including review and evaluation procedures and resources to be used (specific print and online review sources, in-house previewing, etc.), or other methods of selection such as approval plans.

5. Specific selection criteria regarding the following aspects: technical, production, aesthetic, artistic, and use-appropriateness.

5. Collection maintenance concerns, such as branch activities, acquisition and distribution of multiple copies, weeding, copy re-assignment, gifts, and replacement.

6. A statement regarding access to collections, including statements concerning intellectual freedom/censorship, and the principle of building objective and balanced collections.

7. Intellectual freedom and censorship "challenged materials forms," such as a "Patron Materials Reconsideration form."

8. A statement mandating regular evaluation of the collection. It is a good idea to document the data-gathering and statistical analysis techniques so that accurate comparisons can be made from year to year.

SAMPLE COLLECTION DEVELOPMENT POLICIES

The Web has made accessing collection development and selection policies much easier and immediate than in the past—that's the good news. The bad news is that the Web sites for many libraries include seriously outdated, incomplete, and ill-worded policy statements. While a number of excellent best practices examples can also be found (such as the Indiana University policy cited in the Academic Library section below), the fact is that some of the most carefully thought-out and developed policy statements have not yet been mounted on the Web. The Danville Public Library policy below, for example, is a superb model of a statement that incorporates many of the concepts and features discussed earlier in this chapter.

AUDIOVISUAL DEPARTMENT
COLLECTION DEVELOPMENT POLICY [selections]
Danville Public Library
Danville, IL
March 2001

This document will be used to guide the Head of the Audiovisual Department in various aspects of collection development, including selection, acquisitions, and de-selection of materials.

Purpose

In accordance with the mission of the Danville Public Library, the Audiovisual (AV) Department shall provide informational, educational, cultural and recreational nonprint materials in various formats for all ages. Materials are selected in anticipation of and in response to identified community needs. The library presents as many points of view as possible, irrespective of their general social acceptability, to provide a place where anyone may encounter the original, sometimes unorthodox and critical ideas so necessary for a democracy to flourish.

AV materials will seek not only to complement print materials in the library, but also to stand independently as valuable sources of information and entertainment.

Community Served

AV materials are selected to serve the broad, general interest ranges of Danville residents. Danville has a population of 34,000 with a work force approximately 55% blue-collar and 45% white-collar. The median age is 35.4 years, with 26% of the population under 18 and 16% over 65 years old. Whites make up 77% of the population, blacks 18%, Hispanics 3%, and all other groups the remaining 2%.

Responsibility for Selection

AV materials are made available in the AV Department and the Children's Department. Selection of adult AV materials is the responsibility of the AV Department Head. In conjunction with the Children's Department Head, the AV Department Head also selects Children's feature films on videocassette and DVD. Final approval of selections is made by the Director of the library.

General Selection Policy

Selection is a judgmental and interpretative process, involving recognition of the community's needs; general knowledge of the subject and its importance; familiarity with materials in the collection; and awareness of materials available on the subject. Items are selected for various reasons, including permanence of value, currency of interest, diversity of viewpoint, and creative merit, but all items selected should have a reasonable probability of being needed and used by the local community.

Formats Collected

The AV Department shall collect all formats and technologies used by a significant segment of the local community. National and global trends will also play a role in determining new AV technologies housed within the library. Currently, the AV Department actively collects materials on VHS videocassette, compact disc, analog audiocassettes, and CD-ROM. The Department introduced DVDs (digital video discs) during the summer of 2000.

Collection sizes are determined not just by available space and budget but also by use. AV circulation by format is as follows:

Videocassettes: 52% of AV circulation.

CD: 23%

Cassette: 22% (within this, cassette audiobooks comprise 83% and cassette music 17%)

DVD: 2% (but growing rapidly)

CD-ROM: less than 1%

Retention and Weeding

At present, weeding is accomplished primarily through damage assessment and is an ongoing process throughout the year. The AV Department does not automatically replace missing, worn, or damaged materials. The need for replacement is judged by age of the material; availability of more recent and/or comprehensive materials; public demand for the title and circulation figures; and cost of replacement. Weeding will be done to rid the collection of out-of-date, damaged, and unused materials using the criteria outlined above. Specific weeding information per format is discussed in the appropriate format sections below.

Gifts

In accordance with the Library's overall Gifts Policy, the AV Department will accept gifts of AV materials but will apply the same criteria as used in the initial selection of AV materials. Attention will also be given to cleanliness, physical condition and need. Any item that does not fit the needs of the library will be disposed of in whatever manner the library decides. Such gifts will be acknowledged by letter.

Patron Suggestions

A notebook is kept at the AV service desk for patrons and staff to write down suggestions for purchase. Requests for specific AV items are given full attention and will be considered if the request meets the conditions of this policy.

Intellectual Freedom Statements

The Danville Public Library asserts the fundamentals of intellectual freedom and purchases materials representing all sides of a subject/topic when possible. Along with the Library Bill of Rights, the Danville Public Library endorses the following statements as approved by the American Library Association:

Freedom to View Statement

Expurgation of Library Materials: An Interpretation of the *Library Bill of Rights*

Access for Children and Young People to Videotapes and Other Nonprint Formats: An Interpretation of the *Library Bill of Rights*

The choice of AV materials by patrons is an individual matter. A person may reject certain items for himself/herself or for his/her family, but that person does not have the right to restrict access to these materials by others. Responsibility for materials used by children or adolescents rests with their parents, care-givers, or legal guardians.

AV materials are not marked or identified to show library approval or disapproval of their contents. A common example of this issue concerns feature films. Since 1968, The Motion Picture Association of America (MPAA) has maintained a voluntary ratings system (G, PG, PG-13, R, NC-17), which has no legal bearing on the borrowing of videos. If MPAA ratings are included on a video's original packaging they are retained; however, the library will not add MPAA ratings labels, or any other ratings label, to packaging which does not already contain it (Appendix C).

The library takes no responsibility for copyright infringements . . . and other illegal use of library materials by patrons. To aid patrons, a list of videocassettes with public performance rights is maintained by the AV Department and is available at the AV service desk.

Reconsideration of AV Materials in the Collection

If a patron has a complaint about an item and wishes to discuss a matter verbally, it shall be handled first by the Head of the AV Department and then the Head of Adult Services. If the patron wishes to carry the matter further, the complaint shall be submitted in writing on a "Patron Request for Reconsideration" form. The Director shall respond in writing to the patron within ten working days. If the response is unsatisfactory, the patron shall submit a complaint in writing to the President of the Library Board, stating the nature of the complaint and any suggestions for resolving the problem. The Board President shall make the determination how the complaint shall be addressed. Once an item has been selected as qualifying under the selection criteria/policies of the AV Department, it will not be removed unless it can be shown to be in violation of these policies.

VIDEOCASSETTE COLLECTION DEVELOPMENT

The Collection

The Danville Public Library has built a self-supporting collection of approximately 3,400 VHS videocassettes since June 1987 composed of rental and free videocassettes. The rental video collection strives to complement, rather than compete with, local video rental stores by offering a different collection focus. It consists of a mix of feature films, including new releases, classics, family entertainment, and some foreign films that represent all genres as well as major performers and directors; nonfiction videos, including educational, instructional, and travel; and children's video, including live action and animated features and shorts, literature-based video, and an increasing number of nonfiction titles on a variety of subjects.

Because the video budget will only support a medium-sized collection, marginal, expensive, or narrowly focused videos are not cost effective. We will make efforts to acquire works by Danville natives . . . and about other topics of regional and community interest. The video collection does not include materials purchased specifically for school or college curriculum use, with the exception of videotaped lectures provided free of charge by Danville Area Community College; these number a few dozen and change each semester.

A long-term goal of the AV Department is to reduce or, ideally, eliminate fees on videos. Though the current funding structure prevents this, we are continuing to work on the situation.

Videocassette Circulation

Adult and Children's Feature Videos are checked out for 2 days to Danville Public Library cardholders, system reciprocal borrowers, and non-resident borrowers holding a valid library card. Nonfiction videos (both adult and children's) are checked out for 7 days to valid library cardholders. There is a 4-title limit per card with the following fees: $1.00 rental charge per Danville-owned title for new adult features, and .50 per title for all else. A $1.00 per day overdue fine is charged with the highest fine being either the number of working days overdue or the replacement price of the video, whichever is less. Videos may be returned in either the outside or inside drop boxes. Videos may be renewed once *in person only*. Phone renewals are not available. Holds through the online catalog are permitted only for nonfiction titles. End-of-business-day holds are available for nonfiction titles and older features.

Videocassette circulation revenue and overdue fees are recycled directly back to the AV Department budget to purchase more videos for the collection.

Videocassette Selection Policy

In selecting features, children's, and nonfiction videos, favorable reviews from recognized review sources (print, televised, and Internet) are utilized. Standard selection tools and reviewing sources such as *Video Librarian, Booklist, Library Journal, Entertainment Weekly, New York Times*, and/or other periodicals are consulted regularly. Publishers' catalogs (*Baker & Taylor, Ingram, Facets, Midwest Tape Exchange*, etc.) and advertisements are also used to identify current high-interest releases, nonfiction videos, and replacements. Published videographies (*Video Movie Guide, Videohound's Golden Movie Retriever, Leonard Maltin's Movie and Video Guide*), and "Best of" lists are referred to for retrospective selection. Previewing by the AV Department Head is also being used.

Multiple copies of videocassettes are ordered only in rare instances such as with Disney films which are only available for a limited time and then withdrawn from the market, making future replacement difficult. Individual videos priced at more than $100 will rarely be purchased; however, series or multivolume videos for which the price is more than $100 will be occasionally purchased.

Video Selection Criteria—Technical

Imaginative photography, sense of movement and change

Good, clear, understandable sound

Imaginative narration and dialogue

Good picture quality (color and black and white)

Video Selection Criteria—Content

Present and potential relevance to community needs

Accurately presents factual and information

Is useful for intended audience

Provides high quality performances

Currency and timeliness of material presented

Weakness of the collection in a particular area

Video Selection Criteria by Subject of Material

In selection of materials by subject, consideration should be given to such matters as popular (and timely) demand for the item; relationship of the material to the existing collection and to other materials available on the subject; the likely attention of critics, opinion makers, and the public to the item; its importance as a document of our times; and the cost of the item as compared with comparable material on the same subject.

Types of Video Collected

Documentary: Documentary films have been defined as "a creative interpretation of reality." Documentaries of historical importance and those that serve an informational function will be collected.

Plays and Dramatizations of Classic Literature: These will be collected if they meet high standards of play writing, performance, and cinematography, and have classic appeal and long-term interest.

Film Study: Only films that have proved to be of long-term or lasting value and have been produced at least 20 years ago are considered film classics and will be collected as examples of film study. These videos should illustrate the history and development of film as a source of information and as an art form, and should be listed in most books on film study. Videocassettes that have been colorized (changed from their original black-and-white format) will not be purchased unless this is the only format available. Classic silent films will be collected as examples of the earliest stages of filmmaking. The collection will also include the most important works of acclaimed producers, directors, actors and actresses, or other significant personalities in the film world. We will also seek to include the films of Danville natives.

Local and Regional Topics: These will be selected when available. Due to the limited number of these films produced, our standards of quality may be lowered to allow acquisition of these specialized videos.

Holiday: Films that are solely concerned with a specific holiday and for which there is an acute demand only at the time of those celebrations are termed holiday films. A small collection of holiday films is provided, but since the content of these films limits their use, they will not be considered a high priority for the collection.

How-To: A good how-to video must present accurate and appropriate material in an informative and entertaining manner. How-to videos will be selected when the topic can be explained as well or better on video than in another medium.

Concerts, Operas, Ballets, and Other Musical Productions: These videos must meet high standards of sound reproduction and performance. Videos which enhance the enjoyment, appreciation and understanding of the musical event will be collected.

Children's Video: We will collect feature films, both live-action and animated videos based on children's literature, and an increasing number of informational titles on a variety of subjects for preschoolers through eighth grade. Special emphasis will be placed on a child's developmental needs. Video adaptations of children's books, folktales and fairy tales, animated videos, and concept videos (programs teaching basic concept skills) will also be emphasized. Titles that promote a product or are based upon a toy and used primarily as promotional/advertising vehicles will not be purchased. Young adult material will emphasize current, popular, lively themes that contribute to the development and pleasure of this group. Also, programs concerning specific timely health, social and personal issues of interest to teens will be collected.

Contemporary American Classics: Motion pictures produced in America within the past 5 to 20 years which have, over the course of time, gained in importance so that they regularly appear in film texts shall be considered contemporary classics and added to the collection. All films selected should have a 4- to 5-star rating in the sources described above.

American Feature Films: Features will be purchased to satisfy the public's need for recreational materials, and to serve differing tastes and interests. Owing to the relatively high cost of new features and a limited budget, it is impossible for the library to adequately satisfy public demand for high-interest feature films. Because of this, only the best-reviewed films can be collected. Features should receive 3- or 4-star ratings by either three of the country's leading film critics or three of the selection tools described above. Features that have won a major award (e.g., Academy Award, Golden Globe, New York Film Critics Circle, etc.) will also be considered.

Foreign Films: Videocassettes of foreign-made films can be an important source of information on a country and its culture. Because relatively few of these films are shown in Danville movie theaters and because of their limited availability in Danville video stores, we shall work to gradually obtain a representative collection. Foreign films that have won a major award in the U.S. or internationally may be purchased. Foreign films that have received a 4- or 5-star rating in commonly used reference sources will also be collected. In order to retain the integrity of the original film, the subtitled rather than the dubbed version should always be purchased.

Cult Films: These are offbeat films from any genre which, while seldom commercially successful, have developed a strong following among a sizable minority of viewers or critics (probably the most famous example is the musical *Rocky Horror Picture Show*). Because they can be difficult to find elsewhere in Danville, and are often an important part of film history, a small representative number of cult films will be collected.

Closed-Captioned Video

When available, videos with closed-captioning will be purchased to meet the library's commitment to serve the hearing-impaired. Videos with closed-captioning are indicated on the cover art and cassette by a special symbol.

Public Performance Video

A public performance video is any title for which licensing fees (or contractual arrangements by a distributor) have been paid so that it may be shown in public. The majority of the videos purchased for our collection *do not* have public performance rights and will be for *home-use only*. Videos which include public performance rights will only be purchased when the price is not considerably more than the home-use-only version of the title. A limit of 10–20% over the home-use-only price is reasonable. Public performance rights will only be purchased when the title will be useful for adult and children's programming within the library.

Rental-Free Videos

A small collection of rental-free videos has been developed. These are titles the library has received free of charge from government agencies, organizations, or local videographers. A green, Free Rental sticker on the video case indicates its status. A list of rental-free videocassettes is available at the AV service desk.

Video Collection Development Plan

Current space in the AV Department will allow for a collection of approximately 3,900 videocassettes (this includes shelving in the Children's Department for Children's videos). Circulation of videos roughly follows these patterns:

Adult feature films: 47% of video circulation

Juvenile videos: 20%

Adult nonfiction videos: 16%

The goal for the AV and Children's Departments is a 33–33–33% split in acquiring features, children's, and nonfiction titles. Within the AV Department, the desired split is 50% features and 50% nonfiction. Within the Children's Department, the desired split between features and nonfiction has yet to be determined.

Our emphasis is the development of a well-rounded, diverse collection. Areas to be considered for retrospective development are older classics, films that represent outstanding technical and artistic achievement in cinema, foreign films, and quality, literature-based and informational children's video. Also, the nonfiction video collection shall be added to where patron interest is strongest.

DVD COLLECTION DEVELOPMENT

The Collection

During the summer of 2000, Danville Public Library began collecting DVDs (digital video discs). A core selection of nearly 100 DVDs was chosen to begin the collection. These titles are a mix of adult and children's feature films (ranging from classics to foreign to recent releases), plus a handful of musical concerts and documentaries. At the time of this writing, approximately 8,000 DVD titles are available on the market, but the vast majority are feature films. Thus our collection is presently heavy in favor of children's and adult features. As nonfiction titles become more readily available, they will be collected as well.

Like the videocassette collection, the DVD collection is self-supporting through the use of fees (see DVD Circulation below). As described above, we hope to eventually reduce or eliminate these fees in conjunction with videocassette fees.

DVD Circulation

All adult and children's DVDs, whether fiction or nonfiction, are checked out for 2 days to Danville Public Library cardholders, system reciprocal borrowers, and non-resident borrowers holding a valid library card. There is a 2-title limit per card with rental fees of $1.00 per title. A $1.00 per day overdue fine is charged with the highest fine being either the number of working days overdue or the replacement price of the DVD, whichever is less. DVDs may be returned in either the outside or inside drop boxes. DVDs may be renewed once *in person only*. Phone renewals are not available. Holds through the online catalog are not permitted for DVDs. DVD circulation revenue and overdue fees are recycled directly back to the AV Department budget to purchase more DVDs for the collection.

DVD Selection Policy

Most of the selection criteria listed above for videocassette apply to DVD. Special considerations for DVD include:

Multiple copies—in many instances DVD copies will be collected for titles already owned on videocassette if the DVD contains enough bonus material to make it more than a mere duplicate. Also, for the near future both DVD and videocassette copies of popular feature films may be ordered to meet patron demand.

DVD Selection Criteria—Technical

In addition to criteria already listed for videocassettes, special DVD criteria include:

Good, clear, understandable sound, *choosing especially digitally remastered sound.*

Good picture quality (color and black and white), *choosing especially digitally remastered prints, and discs offering both letterboxed and pan-and-scan versions.*

Inclusion of bonus material, especially alternate language and/or dubbing, director commentary, behind-the-scenes info, filmographies, etc.

DVD Selection Criteria: Content; Selection Criteria by Subject of Material; Types of DVD Collected/Closed-Captioned DVDs/Public Performance DVDs

Identical to criteria for videocassette.

DVD Collection Development Plan

DVD circulation is presently small but growing rapidly, with circulation increasing every month. Emphasis is on the development of a well-rounded, diverse collection. Areas to be considered for retrospective development are older classics, films that represent outstanding technical and artistic achievement in cinema, foreign films, and quality, literature-based and informational children's video. The nonfiction DVD collection shall be added to where patron interest is strongest once more titles are on the market. In the future, space availability and changing technology in the video marketplace will also influence the long-range development of the DVD collection.

The Danville (IL) Public Library collection development policy is exceptional in its comprehensive treatment of AV formats, integrating them into the whole library materials policy but effectively segmenting them by format (VHS video and DVD) so that important selection, retention, and weeding issues specifically related to those formats may be highlighted. Collection development concepts, community analysis, collection makeup (as a result of the community analysis), and collection goals and objectives, along with format selection within genres and subjects, circulation issues and intellectual freedom statements/reconsideration policies are all fully integrated into a tightly woven, well-defined package.

SCHOOL LIBRARY MEDIA CENTERS

Surveying the Field

Frequently, the only significant difference between school library media center and public library collection development and selection policies lies in the goal statements. Most of the principles and cognitive elements included in public library collection policies are also relevant in school settings. School-district library media centers are much more like academic libraries or large, departmentalized public libraries than their small, public-library counterparts, in that they receive selection suggestions from a diverse set of people including faculty, staff, and students, and that they serve a defined curricular support mission.

Toward a Service Philosophy

Collections built to support the instructional programs of K–12 schools are usually expected to meet current needs with a diversity of high-quality materials. Many times the expectation is that materials will be selected according to a collection development plan that not only adheres to district-wide policy, but also addresses the needs of the individual school. National curriculum standards have been adopted, but most states have their own state standards for all curriculum subjects and grade levels. Distributors of videos aimed at the K–12 market often tie their products specifically to these standards: for example, distributors exhibiting at the annual National Media Market (http://www.nmm.org). The PBS Video Database for American History (pbsvideodb.pbs.org) includes comprehensive national and state-by-state curriculum- and competency standards information for all of its programming. To emphasize the level of quality expected in the collection, the national guidelines include the following selection criteria:

1. Intellectual content of the material: scope, arrangement and organization, relevance and recency of information, special features, and overall value to the collection.

2. Philosophy and goals of the school district: the resources support and are consistent with the educational goals of the district and with goals and objectives of individual schools and specific courses.

3. Characteristics of the user: the resources are appropriate for the age, emotional development, ability levels, learning styles, and social development of the students for whom the resources are selected.[1]

The following principles place selection of library materials within a broader service philosophy for schools:

Secondary school libraries exist for the support, enrichment, implementation, and supplementation of the curriculum and educational programs of the school system. To that end, books, periodicals, and other library resources exist:

- to provide materials that will stimulate growth in factual knowledge, appreciation of literature, aesthetic values, and ethical standards;

- to provide a varied and diverse background of information which will enable students to make intelligent judgments in their daily lives;

- to provide materials presenting a variety of points of view concerning literary and historical issues in order to develop, under guidance, critical examination, thinking, and informed judgment;

- to provide materials which realistically represent our pluralistic society and reflect the contributions made by groups and individuals to our American heritage;

- to generate an understanding of American freedoms and a desire to preserve those freedoms through the development of informed and responsible citizenship;

- to promote a critical appreciation for, as well as skills in, reading, viewing, listening, and learning which will continue as a lifetime source of education and enjoyment; and,

- to provide a planned program which will arouse in students an interest in books and other types of media, and to broaden this interest through service and guidance in a pleasant atmosphere.[2]

Like public library selection policies, school library media center selection policies reflect both local and district-level organizational structure. In multi-campus school districts, collection development activities are usually distributed between individual schools and the district office, possibly with a district coordinator supervising the entire operation. In smaller districts, each individual building librarian may be responsible for all selection. Collection development activities in these settings may range from involvement in curricular activities, to faculty and student outreach; from securing and routing selection aids, to selection committees to previewing, or setting up previews. While maintaining separate print libraries, some districts centralize AV services and materials purchases. In such cases, a central coordinator is often assigned to take care of selection and circulation of materials. In other states, school districts cooperate to form regional systems, and AV cooperatives to utilize staff and budget more efficiently.

An example of a well-articulated series of selection objectives appears in the Manchester (Iowa) Community School District:

In order to ensure that the school media program is an integral part of the educational program of the school, the following selection objectives are adopted:

1. To provide materials that will enrich and support the curriculum and personal needs of the users taking into consideration their varied interests, abilities, and learning styles.

2. To provide materials that will stimulate growth in factual knowledge, literary appreciation, aesthetic values, and ethical standards.

3. To provide a background of information which will enable students to make intelligent judgments in their daily lives.

4. To provide materials on opposing sides of controversial issues so that users may develop, under guidance, the practice of critical analysis.

5. To place principle above personal opinion and reason above prejudice in the selection of materials in order to ensure a comprehensive media collection appropriate for the users.

These are philosophical goal statements rather than measurable objectives, but they serve to set the stage of service for selecting curriculum and enrichment-based videocassettes.[3]

THE ACADEMIC FILM AND VIDEO LIBRARY

In their 1956 text *The University Library*, Louis Wilson and Maurice Tauber set forth the principles upon which collection development should rest; those principles are still viable today. Academic librarians are increasingly concerned with growth in the size and complexity of collections, as well as the concomitantly complex problems of supplying materials to support individual university courses. Wilson and Tauber felt that academic acquisition programs must ensure the development of collections that are adequate to meet the demands that the universities make upon them. These demands are dictated by specific university functions, including conservation of knowledge, instruction, research, publication, and extension services. In the academic library, the quality, diversity, and quantity of the combined collections are the core around which sound teaching and related educational activities take place. In most academic and research libraries and media centers, circulation and use statistics are less important than the two convergent primary goals of curriculum support and building collections with suitable subject depth and breadth.

Many academic library media centers do not possess a discrete collection development or selection policy (there are notable exceptions: see, for example, the excellent policy developed by Indiana University Library: http://www.indiana.edu/~libreser/media/media-col-dev-policy.html [rev. September 2000]). The reasons are myriad and complex, but some of these will be highlighted in this section. Many academic media departments are part of a larger library unit, rather than existing as a separate budgetary unit of the library or university. As such, internal and external political considerations, the role and status of the department in the larger library context, and budgetary and collection-building priorities play important roles in decision making. In most cases, the academic media librarian has a fair amount of control over materials selection. There may, however, exist more than one media department or departmental library collecting media on campus, resulting in unnecessary duplication of materials and little inter-departmental cooperative effort.

In most academic libraries, video materials selection involves a complicated process including faculty recommendations and peer preview. The responsibility for selecting and acquiring materials in this environment can vary widely, from selection of videos by subject bibliographers (who are also responsible for print selection), to selection by format specialists responsible for selection across the disciplinary spectrum. Involvement of faculty in the selection process also varies. In some instances academic video collections serve primarily as course reserve collections, built exclusively upon the requests of individual faculty to support their specific (and often temporal) curricular needs. In most cases, academic collections reflect a combination of the above-mentioned models.

Methodologies for selecting video in academic settings have been largely shaped by the complex and often highly specialized needs of academic libraries and faculty, the frequent focus in such collections on non-mainstream materials, and the scarcity of vendors who can meet these needs. Selection and acquisition of videos in such settings is most often a title-by-title process: while blanket and approval plans for books are common in such settings, similar plans have not generally been developed for videos.

Because the standing of media in most academic libraries is still tenuous (or misunderstood by administrators), funding tends to be less firmly fixed or certain than for other parts of the collection. Funding may not be consistent from year to year and frequently originates from a variety of sources. The budget may be a "use-it-or-lose-it" proposition. Funding for both print and media in academic libraries is often accompanied by highly defined curricular or programmatic requirements and limitations. These requirements may preclude or limit retrospective or replacement purchases, specialized purchasing, and approval plans.

Media departments frequently must compete with other library or university departments for funding or for the purchase of specific programs and materials. One major obstacle to adopting a collection development/selection policy for video in academic libraries is the complexity and long-term nature of such processes in organizations that are often decentralized and highly bureaucratic. Collection policy revision in such settings is often a protracted and convoluted process, and obtaining consensus among vested administrative bodies is generally difficult.

The essential elements in the collection development policy for academic libraries are basically the same as for school libraries; only the emphases are changed. ALA's Association of College and Research Libraries (ACRL), in its 1999 "Guidelines for Media Resources in Academic Libraries" (http://www. ala.org/acrl/guides/medresg.html), endorses the use of broader general guidelines rather than specific standards. This endorsement recognizes the inability of standards to satisfy the divergent interests, needs, and resources represented by the spectrum of academic libraries and the wide variety of organizational models of audiovisual (AV) services existing in those libraries (Association of Research Libraries [ARL] 1990).

SUMMARY

The potential of audiovisual media is considerable and far-reaching. The realization of this potential depends on the knowledge, enthusiasm, ingenuity, creativity, and tenacity of librarians who make the materials available to patrons in any type of library. Tomorrow's library innovators are today's risk-takers. As previously stated, video is just the tip of the technological iceberg; the warm consumer reception of DVD is a reflection of that trend. Librarians and libraries need not be on the cutting edge of technology, but they *do* need to keep abreast of technological trends and technological impact. They need to follow closely behind in adopting and practically applying emerging technologies once accepted by the mainstream. To these ends, the efforts made in proper planning are vitally important. Such planning entails developing new collections based on a strategic plan and a collection development/selection policy that are dynamic, ever-changing documents. The philosophy of developing "format-appropriate" collections—collections for which the librarian acts as a mediator for the patron, supplying the correct information, in just the right format, at just the right time—should become universal for today's librarians. The degree to which we adhere to this philosophy will determine our success as future information providers for society at large. As we compete with for-profit companies who will no doubt eventually supply audio and video on demand, various multimedia databases, and e-books to consumers, we need to keep an eye on technology and be selective in the services and collections that we offer. The key to the library's success in the future will be the ability to learn from past format and service transitions and changes and to efficiently transfer that knowledge to a new, emerging format, rather than wastefully attempting to create an entire new world. Finally, the formulation of an integrated collection development program for video is just one link in a greater chain. The increased possibilities of service and enhanced collection breadth and depth made possible through new and innovative technological developments, supported by a well-planned collection development process, should excite every librarian.

NOTES

1. These points are part of a policy prepared by the plaintiff's attorney, Ronald R. Coles, for submission in the case of *Sheck v. Baileyville School Committee* (1982) (see Kemp 1986: 36).
2. Ibid.
3. Ibid.

REFERENCES

American Association of School Librarians (AASL) and Association for Educational Communications and Technology (AECT). 1988. *Information Power: Guidelines for School Library Media Programs.* Chicago: ALA.

Arnold, Gordon B. 1989. "From Big Screen to Small Screen: A History of the Cinema on Videocassette." *Library Journal* 114 (May 15): 29–35.

Association of Research Libraries (ARL). 1990. *Audiovisual Policies in ARL Libraries.* SPEC Kit 162. Compiled by Kristine Brancolini. Washington, DC: The Association.

Bertland, Linda H. 1991. "Circulation Analysis as a Tool for Collection Development." *School Library Media Quarterly* 19 (Winter): 90–92.

Durbin, Hugh A. 1987. "Using Policy Statements to Define and Manage the Non-book Collection." In *Policy and Practice in Bibliographic Control of Non-book Media.* Edited by Sheila Intner and Richard Smiraglia. Chicago: ALA, pp. 38–42.

Evans, G. Edward. 1979. *Developing Library Collections.* Littleton, CO: Libraries Unlimited.

Evans, G. Edward. 1987. *Developing Library Collections.* 2nd ed. Littleton, CO: Libraries Unlimited.

Gallant, Jennifer Jung. 1990. *Best Videos for Children and Young Adults: A Core Collection for Libraries.* Santa Barbara, CA: ABC-CLIO.

Garland, Kathleen. 1992. "Circulation Sampling as a Technique for Library Media Program Management." *School Library Media Quarterly* 20 (Winter): 73–78.

"Guidelines for Media Resources in Academic Libraries." 1999. http://www.ala.org/acrl/guides/medresg.html.

Halliwell's Film & Video Guide. 1999. Edited by John Walker. New York: Harper-Perennial.

Indiana University Library. *Film Library Collection Development Policy.* 1998. (rev. September 2000) (Web site) (http://www.indiana.edu/~libreser/media-col-dev-policy.html)

Kemp, Betty, ed. 1986. *School Library and Media Center Acquisitions Policies and Procedures.* 2nd ed. Phoenix, AZ: Oryx Press.

Kurzweil, Raymond. 1992. "The Future of Libraries—Part 1: The Technology of the Book." *Library Journal* 124 (January): 80.

Leonard Maltin's Movie & Video Guide. 2001. New York: New American Library.

Lockett, Barbara, ed. 1989. *Guide to the Evaluation of Library Collections.* Chicago: ALA.

Loertscher, David V. 1988. "Collection Mapping: An Evaluation Strategy for Collection Development." In *Measures of Excellence for School Library Media Centers.* Edited by David Loertscher. Littleton, CO: Libraries Unlimited, pp. 14–16.

Magrill, Rose Mary, and Corbin, John. 1989. *Acquisitions Management and Collection Development in Libraries.* 2nd ed. Chicago: ALA.

Mancall, Jacqueline C. 1991. "(Un)changing Factors in the Searching Environment." *School Library Media Quarterly* 19 (Winter): 88.

Mason, Sally, and Scholtz, James C., eds. 1988. *Video for Libraries: Special Interest Videos for Small and Medium-Sized Public Libraries.* Chicago: American Library Association.

Pitman, Randy. 1990. "Rockefeller Foundation Videocassette Distribution Task Force: Final Report—Library Market." Bremerton, WA (typewritten).

Pitman, Randy, and Swanson, Elliott. 1990. *Video Movies: A Core Collection for Libraries*. Santa Barbara, CA: ABC-CLIO.

Scholtz, James C. 1989. *Developing and Maintaining Video Collections in Libraries*. Santa Barbara, CA: ABC-CLIO.

Serebrin, John. 1988. "Video: Planning Backwards into the Future." *Library Journal* 120 (November 15): 34–35.

VideoHound's Golden Movie Retriever. 2001. Edited by Jim Craddock. Detroit: Visible Ink.

Wiener, Tom. 1990. *The Book of Video Lists*. Lanham, MD: Madison Books.

Williams, Patrick. 1990. "How Should the Public Library Respond to Public Demand?" *Library Journal* 122 (October 15): 55.

Wilson, Louis, and Tauber, Maurice. 1956. *The University Library*. New York: Columbia University Press.

RECOMMENDED READING

Alexander, Bob, and Innerfield, Amy. 1990. "In the Eye of the Beholder." *Video Software Dealer* (May): 36.

American Library Association (ALA). Office for Research. 1988. *Non-Tax Sources of Revenue for Public Libraries: ALA Survey Report*. Chicago: ALA.

Kreamer, Jean Thibodeaux, ed. 1992. *The Video Annual 1991*. Santa Barbara, CA: ABC-CLIO.

Levy, Randy. 2000. DVD Info. VIDEOLIB listserv post (August 25).

Paige, Earl. 1988. "AVA Poll Reveals Viewer Sophistication." *Billboard* (September 17): 48.

Pitman, Randy. 2000. DVD Player Price Drop (Not an Ad). Video listserv post (September 31).

Rochester (MN) Public Library. *Selection Policy for the Audio/Visual Section*, July 1997 (http://www.ci.rochester.mn.us/library/homepage/collect.htm#video).

Scholtz, James C. 1991. *Video Policies and Procedures for Libraries*. Santa Barbara, CA: ABC-CLIO.

Scott, Allen. 2000. DVD Info. VIDEOLIB listserv post (August 22).

Slote, Stanley J. 1982. *Weeding Library Collections—II*. 2d rev. ed. Littleton, CO: Libraries Unlimited.

Chapter 14

Some Guidelines for Evaluating Non-theatrical Videos

Beth Blenz-Clucas

A brief catalog entry, a blurb on Amazon.com, or a colleague's quick recommendation: most of the time, these are all that a video librarian has to rely on when selecting titles for a collection. In an ideal world, a video librarian spends countless hours before the small screen, consulting with a committee of subject experts and carefully previewing titles in question. In the real world of most libraries, evaluating non-theatrical video is a fast-paced afterthought.

When time is precious and there is no plan for evaluation, the result can be a less-than-optimum collection, purchased mainly at the suggestion of promotional materials. Video producers and distributors spend millions of dollars to determine what will sell to the library market, and some of the less scrupulous companies try to pass off poorly made programs as appropriate for library and school needs simply because the subject matter fits the perceived needs in the marketplace. Vendor catalogs can be a helpful resource for determining what's available in certain genres and subject areas; but unless there are specific benchmarks for evaluating non-theatrical videos, patrons may be left with inadequate programming and uneven collections.

A POLICY IS ESSENTIAL

There are a few preliminary steps that a video librarian can take in the evaluation process. A strong collection development policy for audiovisual materials is essential. The policy reflects the library's stated public mission and should clearly define subject and genre areas of interest. Other articles in this book offer guidelines for and examples of video collection development policies for particular types of libraries. Chapters within professional reference books offer ideas: for example, James C. Scholtz' *Video Acquisitions and Cataloging* (1995) or G. E. Evans' *Developing Library and Information Center Collections* (1995). It soon becomes clear that, as is the case with book collections, video evaluation goes hand in hand with collection development and is done most effectively in the context of the goals stated in a policy that is geared for a particular library or school. Patron needs and budget constraints are the first concerns for such a policy.

DETERMINING COMMUNITY NEED

As is true with the process of evaluating any materials for library purchase, it is helpful to think of community and patron needs first. An especially fine documentary about political conflict in Guatemala may be too detailed for high school student patrons with a limited background on the region; they may find a general introduction of Central America more useful. Be aware of patrons' particular interests and then make a comprehensive list of the subject areas and formats that will have top priority in video selection.

In different libraries, this needs assessment will entail looking at different issues. Public librarians should learn all they can about the communities and populations they serve. A video library user-request form might be an easy way to get some of this information, or perhaps a formal user survey would result in a wider awareness of patron needs. Compiling information about people who do not use the library is also important: Why doesn't the library currently meet the non-user's information and entertainment needs?

Some questions to consider might be the socioeconomics of a particular community, urban or rural interests, local student needs, languages spoken in the community, and special needs among patrons. Is attractive video packaging going to drive circulation, and will supplemental materials be a help or hassle for users?

While listening to the community's interests is vitally important in the pre-evaluation process, be wary of patrons who complain about controversial materials. The library's mission to the public includes the responsibility to represent a diversity of viewpoints and cultural backgrounds. For more information on how to develop an anti-censorship policy for a video collection, contact the American Library Association (ALA) regarding its 1992 Freedom to View statement (www.ala.org/alaorg/oif/freedomtoview.html).

School librarians will consider some of the same factors when determining patron needs. For example, the community's demographics and other available resources must be considered when selecting videos, but the main focus for school video librarians will be on the curriculum and developmental levels of the children and young adults they serve. Most media specialists work closely with teachers to determine the curricular areas that will benefit from audiovisuals. Age appropriateness is an important factor in evaluation decisions, and the trends in state educational policy will also determine which subject areas can be enhanced by video.

Many video producers would like to break into the lucrative school market, and media specialists will quickly learn which vendors are reliable and which are simply trying to capitalize on an educational trend with shoddy, poorly conceived programs.

How do you choose only the best? Luckily, there are a host of recent publications that can assist librarians in selecting educational and popular children's videos,[1] and the Young Adult Library Services Association (http://www.ala.org/yalsa) and the Association for Library Services to Children (http://ala.org/alsc) provide annual lists of notable videos that can almost be regarded as checklists for purchase because they are so carefully evaluated by children's specialists. As children's video expert Martha Dewing notes, reviewers of children's videos must be especially aware of child development issues when determining the age appropriateness of a given title. Here again, consultation with teachers is vital (Dewing 1992; see especially her guidelines for selection in chapter 3). You may consider buying a video with important information on dental health, but if it lacks color and humor, it will quickly lose its young audience. Briefer running times, or clearly segmented programs, are also helpful to teachers who are trying to mix lecture and discussion with audiovisual materials during one class period. The availability of expertly produced teachers' guides, workbooks, and other printed instructional materials to supplement the video may also be important considerations.

Like school media specialists, librarians in colleges and universities work closely with instructors in determining audiovisual needs. Again, the educational needs of the students are the primary consideration in evaluating video titles, and some of the same issues involved in public and school library settings apply in the academic setting. At the university level, the faculty's research needs must also be factored in. Dance historians may need videos featuring the Paris Ballet or Baryshnikov to complete their studies on interpretation. Historians find a wealth of primary documents in the newsreel files now available on "video encyclopedias," and political scientists use the treasure trove of U.S. congressional and executive sessions now available on tape.[2] Certainly, the academic librarian will learn the curricular and research emphasis of the college he or she serves, and issues such as running times and instructional level are important in evaluation decision making. The academic library's collection strengths and emphases, programmatic emphases, and the nature of other audiovisual resources on campus are also considerations when you evaluate any new video. Previewing videos is a luxury that not many libraries can afford these days. According to Gary Handman, director of the Media Resources Center at Moffitt Library, University of California, Berkeley, "I don't really preview, and I don't think many academic librarians do, either."

Handman offers this advice from his 20 years of experience in evaluating videos for a major academic library: "I use a fairly limited number of professional review sources. I also scan subject journals that periodically carry reviews of video (e.g., *Journal of American History, American Historical Review, Journalism & Mass Communication Quarterly, Postmodern Culture, Journal of Popular Culture*). I tend to buy in subject areas that I know are hot or otherwise important from distributors whose works I respect. I also pay attention to film festival winners and the annual ALA VRT Notable Videos for Adults list [http: //www.ala.org/vrt]."[3]

PRICE/BUDGET CONSIDERATIONS

Libraries of all types usually work within tight budgets for audiovisual collections. Each purchasing decision is weighed against the projected patron use and benefit of the material, the need for its subject matter, and the amount of money budgeted for purchases of this kind. Many libraries have in fact set price limits for the videos they buy. For a public library, the per-title limit might be $50, while in an academic library, the limit (official or unspoken) may be $100 or $200 per title.

With so many new programs on the market, often well within these price limits, it is usually easy to locate a number of titles to fit community needs. Still, it is wise for library management to allow for special purchase of higher-priced programs. Overly defined dollar limits per title can result in a collection skewed to popular or mass-market works by mainstream producers. Many of the most exciting, controversial, and effective filmmaking is done by independent producers whose work is often self-distributed or sold through an exclusive agent. Typically, the cost of these materials is much higher than mass-market titles. What's more, many of the lower-cost home videos are not available with public performance rights, which is important, especially to public libraries planning programming (schools and colleges using videos as part of face-to-face instruction do not need these rights in most instances). One way to give patrons access to some of the fine but high-priced documentaries and instructional programs might be to form or take advantage of a cooperative buying group with other libraries in a region or school district. Regional media centers and public library audiovisual consortia buy films and videos in bulk orders, and video vendors frequently respond favorably by offering substantial discounts on these multiple purchases.

Still, it pays to seek out the bargains. Randy Pitman, editor of *Video Librarian*, looks at thousands of non-theatrical videos each year. He finds that "there is often no relationship between price and quality. Anyone who shops intelligently—whether a consumer or an institution—should consider price when making purchase decisions. Librarians have a mandate to spend public monies wisely in the acquisition of popular and/or quality materials for their collections. As in any other arena, the more bang you can get for your purchasing buck (whether through negotiating with vendors or consortium buying), the richer your collection will be."

DETERMINING QUALITY

Once patron needs and pricing guidelines are determined, the video librarian still will want to figure out how to judge the content and technical aspects of the videos available on the market. Once again, in an ideal world, a committee of subject experts would preview each video under consideration. More likely, it is the video librarian who makes the evaluation decisions, weighing the subject experts' casual recommendations. Occasionally, you'll have time to preview a video before purchase. When you do, it helps to have established a few guidelines to make it easier to determine quality. Most of the time, your option will be to try to gather enough information about a prospective purchase that you can determine some aspects of quality without previewing.

To do an evaluation effectively, it helps to devise an easy-to-follow worksheet or rating form so that you are not reinventing the wheel each time you look at a new video. Take into consideration various elements regarding program quality—and how each video fits in with community needs and budget constraints as outlined above. It may help to ask yourself these questions, partially borrowed from those that reviewers for *Booklist* follow.[4]

Authoritativeness and Authenticity

- Is it authentic, accurate, and current? Check the video's copyright date on the closing credits, because many educational programs touted as "new" are actually re-releases of old 16mm films or patched-up versions of outdated programs.
- Who are the experts involved in the production? What content specialists are used?
- Is it free from bias, prejudice, or misleading emphasis?
- How believable is the production? These issues are particularly important in viewing historical re-enactments, which can be carefully executed or woefully artificial.
- Are translations and retellings faithful to the original?
- How does it compare with other videos on the subject? A knowledge of the market will be essential here. There is usually a wealth of programs available on more popular subjects.

Utilization

- Will it stimulate and maintain the viewer's interest?
- Will the viewer want to pursue further study or discussion?
- Is it useful with individuals as well as groups?
- Are the format, vocabulary, concepts, and pacing appropriate for the intended audience?
- Will it develop concepts that are difficult to communicate through other media?

- Will it affect attitudes, build appreciation, develop critical thinking, or entertain?
- Look for a stated purpose. Does the production achieve it?

Content

- Is it well organized and well balanced? How are the scenes juxtaposed and layered? Too much jumping around can be confusing, especially for younger viewers.
- Is the script well written and imaginative? Does it present a unique vision of a well-covered topic? Sometimes even an amateurishly produced program is worth considering if it offers a fresh perspective.
- Is the script succinct and to the point? Many otherwise important programs need a good editor to cut through digressions and emphasize the essential points. In general, educational films and videos suffer when the narrative rambles.
- Is it timely or pertinent to library, community, or curricular needs?
- Is the treatment appropriate to the subject matter?
- Could the subject be better treated through another medium? Sometimes the viewer will wonder why a program was ever put on tape. A talking-heads exposition of highly technical material will usually lull a roomful of viewers to sleep unless the speaker is unusually dynamic and the director has found an unusual way to present the lecture. Despite all the hoopla over visual media, some information is best conveyed through a book or interactive CD-ROM.

Technical Qualities

The production values of a video are extremely important, especially to the generations of patrons used to the technical quality of network television. Poor production quality tends to distract viewers, defeating the purpose of an instructional or informational program. Viewers may be forced to look away from a screen plagued by rough-cuts and unstable camera-holding. Poor zooming on a man sorrowfully telling of his son's tragic death will cause viewers to concentrate on the poor man's out-of-focus nose rather than on his words. Sometimes, unusual camera techniques are intentional; the video evaluator must decide for him- or herself whether they work for or against the video's message.

The best programs achieve excellence in videography, including the composition of scenes, focus and exposure, color accuracy, audibility and fidelity of sound, legibility of titling, effective use of graphics, and the quality of special effects (such as multiple camera, black-and-white/color combinations, selective color use in an otherwise black-and-white production, combinations of formats such as animation and live-action or archival footage with new video segments, fade-to-black, split-screen, and special motion effects).

Music should be appropriate to the subject matter and appealing. Although there is a great deal to consider regarding the technical aspects of video, the librarian or media specialist doesn't have to be an expert on production. It does help to learn some of the basics and to become well acquainted with the look and sound of high-quality productions.

The production techniques of an effective video may be extremely simple: one example is the expert mingling of historical stills, period music, and talking-head interviews with articulate experts in Ken Burns' popular documentary series.

If a video is animated, look for fluidity of motion, skillful drawing, and a creative use of the medium. Beware of animation that becomes the main event of a supposedly informational piece; the technique should be used to enhance the message rather than as a surrogate for live action. In some children's videos, limited animation of popular books is done very effectively, though there are others that are stiffly executed.

Of course, many of the technical problems of a video may be rooted in poor tape or disc duplication or poor-quality viewing equipment. For VHS, look for tapes duplicated at the SP (or standard-play) mode. Videos duplicated at the SLP (super-long-play) speed tend to have faded or bleeding color, "snow," sound distortion, and tracking problems. Generally, these lower-cost SLP videos are not acceptable for library purchase because of their poor audiovisual quality. If a tape under consideration is from a reliable vendor but still seems to suffer from visual or audio defects, the video librarian should request another copy in case the problems are due to a duplication error. DVDs, of course, should have superior visual clarity and color. Any problems probably indicate a faulty disc.

Again, some questions to ask include:

- Is the photography satisfactory and effective?

- Are the visuals other than photographs (e.g., paintings, illustrations, maps, charts, etc.) well reproduced?

- Are titles, captions, and other on-screen words readable? Sue-Ellen Beauregard, Media Reviews editor for ALA's *Booklist*, notes that one red flag is when she sees misspellings in captions, demonstrating that the filmmaker didn't pay attention to details.

- Is the sound acceptable? Look for good fidelity, realistic sound effects, lip-synchronization, and the absence of conflict between music/sound effects and the narration or dialogue.

- Is the editing smooth and unnoticeable?

- Are the narrators and actors appealing? Do they speak clearly? Are they believable? Condescending? Are the "real" people featured in the program articulate enough to convey the message, or is their story somehow moving? Videos that interview people whose speech is muffled or otherwise difficult to understand should run captions for clarity.

Packaging and Accompanying Materials

- Is the packaging appealing enough for shelf display? (The type of library you serve will determine whether this is important.)

- Is the packaging durable and easy to open?
- Are the teachers' guides or other printed matter useful? Instructors will often be the best judge of these supplementary materials and may offer guidelines on what they look for.

"In My Opinion"

Be aware of your own personal biases if you decide to pan a title. It is usually easy for others to see when strong opinions impair a person's judgment of a video dealing with controversial issues. It helps if the librarian realizes his or her own conflicts of interest and is willing to get a second opinion. Because of the diverse backgrounds and interests of patrons, librarians should attempt to represent various points of view in their collections and should not decide against buying a video just because it is controversial or expresses an unusual point of view. Again, the video buyer is responsible for upholding the library's mission to serve the broad information needs of its users.

OTHER RESOURCES

Film festival winners can be a helpful resource for locating new and high-quality titles in particular subject areas (several chapters in this book offer listings of festivals devoted to particular genres or topics). Beware, however, of putting your faith in awards alone. Beauregard, of *Booklist*, says, "Since the demise of the American Film & Video Festival, I find it difficult to rely on festival winners as always being top notch." *Video Librarian*'s Pitman agrees. "People joke about the 'numbing cold' at Sundance, wondering whether or not the critical faculties become frozen while watching whining, self-absorbed indie films," he says. "We don't put a huge amount of stock in film and video festival picks. In fact, I find *Booklist*'s annual "Editor's Choice" list more in synch with our own highly recommended titles than any particular festival awards. Beauregard adds, "Certainly, the ALA Notable Lists are reliable, especially because the titles are chosen by librarians who view and discuss the titles. I also take note of the Sundance winners, Academy Award nominees and Montreal Film Festival winners in the documentary category, even though some worthy titles are overlooked."

New online resources can be especially helpful in the evaluation process. With the plethora of libraries on the Web, it is not difficult to locate situations similar to your own.[5] A few state educational agencies also have devised guidelines for evaluation of instructional videos, such as the one used by the California Instructional Video Clearinghouse.[6] The National Association of Regional Media Centers (http://www.aect.org/Affiliates/narmc.html), the Consortium of College and University Media Centers (http://www.indiana.edu/~ccumc), and several groups within the ALA have developed model video selection criteria as well.

When a video librarian is new to the job, or is assigned to develop a collection from scratch, it is always useful to call on more experienced video evaluators for help. A great deal of shared experience is vital to the development of effective selection criteria. In large, urban public libraries, video selection has become a highly developed art, as many of these institutions collect and house thousands of titles. The larger school districts, regional media centers, and individual schools also have long years of experience in collecting educational video. A few academic film librarians have become near legends in the video collection world for their pioneering efforts to standardize the collection development process in an institutional atmosphere that frowns upon non-print educational materials. (Some of their contributions grace this volume.) Many of these experts have contributed to this volume, and the novice may find professional associations such as the Video Round Table of the American Library Association an invaluable resource for sharing video evaluations.

Whenever possible, librarians and media specialists should seek out peer reviews in professional publications. Some library policies require at least two favorable reviews before a purchase can be made. Reliable reviews of non-theatrical programs appear in *Booklist, Video Librarian, Library Journal, School Library Journal, Media & Methods*, and some scholarly journals. Beauregard also notes the treasure trove of reviews posted at the *Booklist* Web site (http://www.ala.org/booklist) and at the *Video Librarian* Web site (http://www.videolibrarian.com). A digest of older *Video Librarian* reviews is located at http://www.elibrary.com. The only index currently devoted exclusively to identifying a comprehensive digest of professional reviews of videos is *Media Review Digest*. The electronic version of the database provides coverage from 1989 to the present, including more than 90,000 media resources with more than 375,000 reviews, evaluations, awards and prizes. It also has a print subscription version (Ann Arbor, MI: Pierian Press, or see http://www.pierianpress.com/mediarev. htm). See also Chapter 18 in this volume.

Video is a firmly established part of most libraries today, but its status is still marginal as compared to other media. If selection and evaluation of videos are done too casually, no one in library management will regard these materials as an integral part of the collection. By setting and following professional guidelines for evaluation, video librarians will assert the status of visual media as a means to inform, educate, and delight. Even better, more stringent buying guidelines set by library customers might induce the special interest and educational video industry to improve its own standards for production.

NOTES

1. Recommended children's videos are not difficult to find these days, thanks to several new guidebooks. The Coalition for Quality Children's Media recently teamed with the *New York Times* to produce *The New York Times Guide to the Best Children's Videos* (1999) (see also www.cqcm.org). High-quality videos for very young children are spotlighted in the annual *Oppenheim Toy Portfolio Best Toys, Books, Videos, Music & Soft-*

ware for Kids (http://www.toyportfolio.com). The guide to *Culturally Diverse Videos, Audios, and CD-ROMs for Children and Young Adults* (Wood 1999) is a valuable resource for those committed to building a balanced collection.

2. For example, C-SPAN's online store offers a wide variety of videos that would be useful for classroom discussion on various governmental issues. Topics include U.S. congressional sessions and hearings, international governmental proceedings, and campaign speeches. Often there are specially priced videos, organized by subject area. See http://www.c-spanstore.com.

3. Handman's comments and those of Randy Pitman and Sue-Ellen Beauregard that follow were gathered in informal telephone conversations and e-mail correspondence, February through June 2000.

4. Special thanks go to Sue-Ellen Beauregard, Media Reviews editor at *Booklist*, who graciously supplied the magazine's guidelines for reviewers and lent her advice and support for this chapter.

5. Some Web sites of note include one developed by the Arizona State Department of Libraries, in which they have outlined a brief and clear set of policies for "Selection of Library Resources: AV." See http://www.lib.az.us/cdt/slrav.htm. Note also the Baltimore County Public Schools' "Selection Criteria for School Library Media Collections Center" at http://www.bcps.org/offices/lis/office/admin/selection.html. The North Carolina Department of Public Instruction's evaluation guidelines for audiovisual materials is succinct and easy to follow. See http://www.sret.sreb.org/criteria/av.asp.

6. The Clearinghouse publishes the *California Index of Instructional Technology* each year, offering their teacher evaluators' ratings of thousands of educational videos. The Clearinghouse has also formed a new California Learning Resource Network to develop new review criteria for various media, including video. In the past, evaluators used such general evaluation criteria as instructional design, content, curricular match, interest level, and technical quality. For more information, visit www.clrn.org/criteria or write to Sandra Burdick, CLRN, 1100 H Street, Modesto, CA 95354.

REFERENCES

Dewing, Martha. 1992. *Beyond TV: Activities for Using Videos with Children.* Santa Barbara, CA: ABC-CLIO. This book is out of print, but copies are available from the Center for Media Literacy (800 226–9494) and many libraries.

Evans, G. E. 1995. *Developing Library and Information Center Collections.* 3rd ed. Englewood, CO: Libraries Unlimited.

The New York Times Guide to the Best Children's Videos. 1999. New York: Pocket Books.

Scholtz, James C. 1995. *Video Acquisitions and Cataloging.* Westport, CT: Greenwood Press.

Wood, Irene. 1999. *Culturally Diverse Videos, Audios, and CD-ROMs for Children and Young Adults.* New York: Neal-Schuman Publishers.

Chapter 15

The Rights Stuff: Video Copyright and Collection Development

Gary P. Handman

In the process of book and serial collection development and acquisition, few librarians are ever forced to traverse the labyrinth of copyright. With the possible exception of the reproduction of out-of-print, ephemeral, or replacement materials, copyright puts few obstacles in the way of acquiring printed works and incorporating them into the collection. On the other hand, when faced with the task of building media collections, video collections in particular, copyright can be a serious deterrent to some aspects of the process. Although the same laws that establish these roadblocks also afford a number of provisions for the use of copyrighted materials in teaching and in scholarly endeavors, there are substantially narrower legal windows of opportunity available in the process of building standing collections of library materials. Understanding the often perplexing dichotomy between copyright strictures and fair-use safeguards and the legal relationship between video acquisition and video use is essential for any librarian involved in acquiring and managing the medium.

The concept of copyright has a long and complex history. Broadly speaking, copyright was "conceived as a set of laws and practices restricting the rights to reproduce or perform individual creations" (Lawrence 1989: 4). These restrictions were established in large part to encourage the development and dissemination of intellectual properties; the laws stand as a form of property protection for the copyright holder. A crucial point for video librarians to understand is that the main focus of the law is the intellectual property embodied in the physical pieces acquired by the library. As will be discussed at length below, the intellectual property owner is afforded a number of exclusive rights under this law. What is very often being acquired when one purchases a video is not only an addition to the library's physical inventory but also the right to use or "perform" all or part of that intellectual property in certain contexts or for certain audiences.[1] Because videos are acquired to be "performed"—in individual homes, in library carrels or meeting rooms, or in classrooms and auditoriums— the process of video collection building is almost always intimately associated with issues related to access and use.

Compared with book acquisition, the channels for acquiring and using video are remarkably varied. The very ubiquity of video, television, and cable broadcasting; and Web-based media, the widespread ownership of video and computer equipment, and the ease with which video from various sources can be captured, manipulated, copied, repackaged, and shown, can easily obscure the fact that a large cluster of rights related to the acquisition and use of the video is exclusively reserved to the copyright holder. According to the Federal Revised Statutes of the United States Copyright Act of 1976, section 106 (90 *U.S. Statutes at Large* [1976]: 2546), a copyright owner has five exclusive rights:

1. To reproduce copies of the work,
2. To prepare derivative works,
3. To distribute copies of the work to the public by sale or other transfer of ownership, or by rental, lease, or lending,
4. To perform the copyrighted work publicly, and
5. To display the copyrighted work publicly.

These rights protect the intellectual property itself and reserve for the creator or owner of the work one or all of these exclusive rights. Copyright owners may choose to exercise only some of these exclusive rights, or they may negotiate some or all of the rights through contractual agreements.

This roster of rights granted the intellectual property owner holds a number of frustrations and sticky logistical problems for collection builders. These problems manifest themselves both directly and indirectly in the selection and acquisition process.

PERFORMANCE RIGHTS

Strictly interpreted, the copyright law specifies that most uses of video outside of the home (including use by a single individual in a library carrel) constitute public performance.[2] Public performance is one of the rights exclusively held by the copyright owner. For libraries that acquire videos exclusively to be circulated for home use, the need to secure rights from the copyright holder is generally not an issue.[3] There are also very explicit (and limited) provisions provided by the law allowing the use of copyrighted works in the classroom and other educational contexts—for example, the "face-to-face" teaching provision of section 110(1) of the 1976 revised copyright law (90 *U.S. Statutes at Large* (1976): 2549). For a good capsule summary of the face-to-face teaching exemption, see http://www.libraryvideo.com/articles/feature_article_sl.asp (via Library Video Company/Schlessinger Media Web site)

Librarians who are building collections to be used for in-house programming or for use in on-site facilities *must*, on the other hand, carefully consider the need to secure performance rights. On-site use of video for programs and instruction held in public libraries—either those sponsored by the library or by an outside group—seldom meets the stringent conditions outlined in the face-to-face teaching provisions mentioned above; rights must consequently be acquired from the copyright holder (or an agent of the holder) to use the work in this context. The fact that the library or the group using the library's facilities is a non-profit organization, that the use of the videos is educational in nature, or that fees are not charged for the program, is inconsequential in these situations. In the case of academic and school libraries, there are also many possible programmatic uses of library video collections that may not meet the conditions specified by the face-to-face teaching provisions of the law; for example, use in extracurricular programs, classroom uses that are not specifically curricular in nature, or programs open to the general student body.

Much murkier is the case of on-site use of videos by a single individual in carrel and related single-user facilities, especially in public libraries. Whether or not such use constitutes public performance is among the most hotly contested issues in video librarianship. As might be expected, there are staunch advocates on both the library side and the industry side of the issue willing to offer opinions in the absence of specific, defining case law. Jerome Miller (1988: 30–36) cites several major cases that support the notion of performances to individuals and small groups in private viewing rooms constituting public performance. In the other camp, Mary Hutchings Reed, former legal adviser to the American Library Association (ALA), has implied that private performance of videos for single individuals or families may be exempt (Reed and Stanek 1986). Similarly, in an informal opinion offered in his address to a 1993 National Video Resources symposium on new media, the late Ivan Bender, legal adviser to the Consortium of College and University Media Centers, suggested that such use would very likely be upheld under fair use.[4]

The issue of individual, in-library use of video gets particularly difficult when academic and school libraries are being considered. Section 107 of the copyright law defines teaching and scholarship as two areas of use falling under the fair-use provisions of the law. Much of the individual viewing of video in school and academic library facilities is directly related to one or both of these endeavors. The question can also be validly raised as to whether use of copyrighted materials for individual study or research in connection with specific curricula can be considered a logical extension of the face-to-face teaching exemption. Confusing this issue is the fact that school and academic video collections are generally open to the student body at large, and often tend to be used on-site for non-curricular and entertainment purposes, as well as for uses that directly support the curriculum. Whatever the long-term legal resolution of this point (if, in fact, such a resolution ever occurs), single-viewer use of video in libraries, particularly academic libraries, has become an almost universal practice in academic libraries with video collections, and in many public libraries as well.

One of the most maddening tasks faced by video librarians is ascertaining which performance rights are currently bundled with specific works. Although the nature of the rights granted the video buyer is usually clearly outlined by large non-theatrical producers and distributors (in the distributor's catalog or Web site, in a separately issued purchase agreement, on the label of the work), the going gets very rough in cases where videos are sold through large second- or third-party jobbers such as Baker & Taylor, Ingram, Facets, or Amazon.com, which are usually not the copyright holders. Identifying available performance rights for independently produced and distributed videos often presents similar challenges. Confusing the matter considerably is the fact that some non-theatrical video titles are sold both with and without performance rights, that is, in both home video and educational market versions. This explains why one may find a home video version of a popular title listing for $24.95 in a jobber's catalog, and the same title for $150 or more in an educational video vendor's catalog; at least in part, the cost difference reflects the rights attached to each. The sale of licenses to publicly perform videos is in large measure an attempt on the part of the copyright owner to compensate for the potential loss of revenue inherent in showing a single copy of a work to a large group of viewers.[5]

The complex nature of video distribution adds other woes to the process of rights tracking and rights acquisition. Unlike book distribution, which tends to be a one-book/one-publisher proposition for the life of the book, distribution rights for video are frequently bought, sold, and shifted with alarming regularity and seeming capriciousness. This is perhaps not surprising, given the time-valued nature of the medium and the size and volatility of the market. What this often means from the video selector's standpoint, however, is the necessity of navigating through a publication and rights universe that is in constant flux and obscurity. This is especially true in the case of non-theatrical video titles, which are often distributed by a single producer or distributor exclusively.

Feature films and the majority of non-theatrical home-use video titles virtually never have performance rights included in the purchase price. For the releases of certain studios, licenses may in some cases be separately available for purchase. The Motion Picture Licensing Corporation (5455 Centinela Avenue, Los Angeles, CA 90066–6970; 800–462–8855; info@mplc.com; http://www.mplc.com) is a firm that offers this type of arrangement for movies. It is frequently the case with independently produced/distributed feature films on videos that the primary distributor is the best contact source regarding licensing information (although it confuses the matter considerably that distributors such as Kino International and New Yorker Films and Videos also sell their catalog of titles through vendors such as Facets).

In the process of ordering video materials, it may be useful to specify the rights desired and the intended use of the video on the purchase document. Such a statement may serve to clarify the nature of the order and facilitate communication between buyer and seller of the video title. It has been suggested, most notably by Reed and Stanek (1986), that an order filled in response to a purchase request that contains such a statement constitutes a kind of implied consent on the part of the vendor. This notion has largely been discredited by Jerome Miller and others. Miller contends that Hutchings' notion is based on "the common mistake of assuming that vendors of videocassettes are the copyright proprietors" (Miller 1988: 29). In all cases, it is sound acquisition practice for the library to maintain a file of past purchase agreements and licenses along with the usual paper trail of purchase requests. A recent interesting discussion on the American Library Association Video Round Table listserv, VIDEOLIB, discussed the practice of tracking videos which have been acquired with performance rights by including this information in the cataloging record for the item (see library. berkeley.edu/VideoLib/archive/0001/0415.html and ensuing discussion).

FAIR USE

Leval (1990: 1105) has commented, "Fair use is not a grudgingly tolerated exception to the copyright owner's rights of private property, but a fundamental policy of copyright law." Basically, the doctrine allows reasonable use of copyrighted materials without the consent of the copyright holder; it essentially permits overriding one or more of the five exclusive rights of the copyright holder in certain cases. The law itself describes fair use as use of "a copyrighted work, including such use by reproduction . . . for purposes such as criticism, comment, news reporting, teaching (including multiple copies for classroom use), scholarship, or research" (90 *U.S. Statutes at Large* [1976]: 2546) (see http://www4 .law.cornell.edu/uscode/17/107.html).

In practice, however, the doctrine of fair use is often a shadowy, moving-target-of-a-concept that has become even more chimerical in the face of rapidly evolving digital technologies. Large sections of the copyright law and its explicatory apparatus are devoted to defining and establishing criteria for "reasonable use." There is frequently a great temptation on the part of librarians and educators to assume that because a particular use of video is in connection with culturally significant, educational, or non-profit efforts, the safety net of fair use universally applies. While the doctrine of fair use *is* often a tremendous boon for educators, scholars, and sundry library *users*, the legitimate applications of the doctrine in library work, including materials acquisition, is extremely limited. Invoking fair use in the name of library collection development is *extremely* risky business.

292 Policies, Criteria, and Methods

The criteria for determining whether a particular use of a work is fair use are outlined in section 107 of the copyright law:

1. The purpose and character of the use, including whether such use is of a commercial nature or is for nonprofit educational purposes;
2. The nature of the copyrighted work;
3. The amount and substantiality of the portion used in relation to the copyrighted work as a whole; and
4. The effect of the use upon the potential market or value of the copyrighted work (90 *U.S. Statutes at Large* [1976]: 2546).

Timberg (1989: 309–310) has restated these criteria in more directly economic terms:

A researcher, educator, or librarian, in order to understand the specific "fair use" situation confronting him, must first identify the economic interests and the specific legal rights of the copyright owner that his contemplated use of the copyrighted material may affect or infringe. Next, he must consider the nature and relative amount of his proposed use, and how much such proposed use would adversely affect the potential market or value of the copyrighted materials, the copyright owner's economic interest, and the copyright owner's general licensing and distribution program. Finally, he must reckon on the normal tendency of the owners of intellectual property rights to secure the maximum financial return from them.

For libraries that are primarily concerned with collecting whole works or substantial parts of works and retaining them permanently, the case for fair use based on the above considerations would seem to be extremely weak.

In its report on the revised copyright law, the Senate elaborated further on the fair-use criteria. In discussing "purpose or character of use" (criteria 1), the report specified spontaneity of use as a prime test of fair use—that is, the duplication or use of copyrighted works by teachers in cases where it would be "unreasonable to expect a timely reply to a request for permission" (U.S. House *Report* No. 94–1476 [1976]: 69). While fair use in libraries could conceivably come into play in the case of bibliographic instruction and related library teaching and research activities, collection development and acquisition endeavors in libraries are, by their very nature, usually far from spontaneous; these latter activities rarely fall within the fair-use guidelines.

OFF-AIR TAPING

The cluster of copyright issues that is generally of most direct interest to video collection developers concerns the taping of materials off the air. The rise of public broadcasting and cable TV, the tremendous sociopolitical importance and influence of broadcast news, and the almost universal availability of inexpensive video recording equipment in the home and in institutions make pushing the record button a convenient and tempting means of capturing the cultural record. There is an understandable impulse on the part of librarians to view the airwaves as a free supermarket of information. This impulse is reinforced by shrinking materials budgets, the ephemeral nature of broadcasting, and the frequent non-availability of television programming through legal purchase channels (see Chapter 17 in this book for a discussion of this latter problem).

The landmark Supreme Court 1983/84 case *Universal City Studios Inc. v. Sony Corporation of America* established the right of individuals to make off-air recordings for home use. For a fascinating, lengthy history of the *Sony* case, see Lardner (1987: 45–71); for a full text of the case see cyber.law.harvard. edu/metaschool/fisher/integrity/Links/Cases/sony.html. Interestingly, however, specific fair-use provisions in the copyright law governing off-air taping for educational and related purposes were never actually developed. Esther Sinofsky (1984: 98–99) provides a thorough discussion of the early impasse reached by educational and industry interest groups in attempting to define such guidelines around the time of the 1976 copyright revisions. To break this stalemate, a congressional subcommittee was constituted, chaired by Representative Robert Kastenmeier. The Kastenmeier Committee, which included educators and industry representatives, eventually developed general guidelines governing off-air taping for educational purposes. These guidelines were inserted into the *Congressional Record* in 1981. For the complete text and a thorough discussion of the guidelines see Sinofsky (1984); the text of the guidelines is also at http: //www.lib.berkeley.edu/MRC/Kastenmeier.html.

It is extremely important to understand that the Kastenmeier guidelines, although useful as reasonable, good-faith parameters for educators, "do not have the force of law, nor are the courts bound by [them]" (Sinofsky 1984: 100). It is also important to note that because the guidelines are predicated on short-term use and retention of materials in connection with classroom teaching, there is little in them that directly applies to the normal processes of library video collection development and maintenance. With the exceptions discussed below concerning the taping of news, the right to tape and retain off-air material for a permanent library collection must in almost all cases be negotiated with the copyright holder.

Fortunately, prerecorded videos of many programs aired on public broadcasting stations are available for purchase for home and/or institutional use through various distribution channels (http://www.pbs.org, http://www.wgbh. org, or through video jobbers such as Baker & Taylor). Other works aired on public broadcasting channels, such as programs shown on the P.O.V. and PBS Independent Showcase programs, may be available for purchase from independent distribution sources. Sources for these programs are often listed as 800 numbers at the end of the program; PBS VideoFinders service (800–343–4727) can also be of service in locating distributors for programs aired on PBS channels.

Obtaining licenses for copying network and cable programming is considerably more problematic. The situation in which a broadcast program is not available through commercial distribution channels or through an off-air license arrangement is, indeed, a frustrating (and increasingly common) one. Unfortunately, in such situations there is usually no legal acquisition alternative for collection development librarians.[6]

OFF-AIR TAPING OF NEWS

There is one very major exception to the narrow fair-use exemptions available to video collection builders—the copying of broadcast news. In 1973, CBS sued Vanderbilt University for taping and archiving television news programs. Vanderbilt countersued for abridgement of academic freedom (see Kies 1989: 165–175). Both of these cases were ultimately dropped with the establishment of provisions for off-air taping of news in section 108(f)(3) of the 1976 revised copyright law: "Nothing in this section . . . shall be construed to limit the reproduction and distribution by lending of a limited number of copies and excerpts by a library or archive of an audiovisual news program" (see http://www4.law.cornell.edu/uscode/17/108.html).

The U.S. House of Representatives report on the revised law established a number of definitions and parameters for off-air taping of news:

This exemption is intended to apply to the daily newscasts of the national television networks. . . . It does not apply to documentary (except documentary programs involving news reporting as that term is used in Section 107), magazine-format, or other public affairs broadcasts dealing with subjects of general interest to the viewing public. (U.S. House *Report* 94–1476 [1976]: 77)

Very specific conditions for this exemption are outlined in section 108: The reproduction and distribution must not be for a profit; the library collection or archive must be open to the public, or open not only to researchers affiliated with the institution but also to other individuals doing research in specialized fields; the reproduction must include a notice of copyright.

In addition to news broadcasting, the copyright law also permits off-air copying of presidential addresses and congressional hearings. This type of material is considered a government publication and, as such, is in the public domain (section 105 of the copyright law). Jerome Miller has pointed out that this issue gets tricky when the broadcast of the address includes introductory or concluding news commentary, although there is some opinion that this augmentation may also be covered under section 108 (Miller 1979: 43–45).

REPRODUCTION

In the days of 16mm film, replacement of materials was a straightforward process. More often than not, the high cost of replacing an entire work made editing the preferred means of dealing with damaged or worn film. For a fixed cost per running foot, a library could purchase replacement footage, which could be easily spliced into place. Because of the cumbersome nature of film processing, few if any institutions outside of large film archives had the equipment, expertise, or inclination to reproduce whole 16mm films in-house.

Video technology has given us another world by making tape imminently reproducible (digital technology, which will be discussed below, has simply upped the ante). It is, in fact, considerably easier and cheaper to reproduce an entire videotape than it is to edit replacement segments onto the tape. The average life expectancy of a videotape played on a machine in good repair is usually well under 200 playings and/or 10 years of shelf-life before there is significant degradation in picture quality. Viewed in light of intensifying library conservation needs, in-house reproduction of video materials seems like a natural collection management solution, particularly given the generally high cost of purchasing replacement copies of non-theatrical materials. With few exceptions, this strategy can only be legally applied in cases where written permission has been secured from the current copyright owner.

There is also a tendency to confuse video with other electronic formats in the matter of reproduction. It is, for example, both a common and, in many cases, a legal practice to make working or circulating copies of computer software from a legally acquired archival copy. Video, however, is a considerably different story. The right to make copies of copyrighted works is one of the five exclusive rights granted to the copyright holder. In most cases, permission must be acquired to make backup or replacement copies of video materials. An alternative way to view this issue is from the standpoint of the fair-use guidelines discussed earlier. Because the practice represents a substantial threat to the potential market for the copyrighted work, reproduction of an entire in-print work would clearly seem to run counter to the guidelines for measuring fair use.

Fortunately, video producers and distributors are generally aware of the need for periodic replacement of materials in library collections. It is fairly common for distributors to offer attractive discounts for replacement copies or multiple-copy purchases. It is also the case that it is practically as cheap to acquire new copies of many home-use video titles as it would be to reproduce these materials in-house.

The above discussion is primarily focused on materials that are still available on the open market. As the video publication and distribution universe has matured and expanded, it is natural that an increasing number of titles in this universe have fallen out of distribution. Anyone attempting to acquire a new or replacement copy of an older *NOVA* program or a title formerly in the catalog of the late, lamented Films Inc. can attest to the frustration of not being able to legally get the "good stuff."

While "out of distribution" categorically does not mean "out of copyright," there may be certain dispensations for replacing existing titles in the collection no longer available in the video marketplace. The provisions in the copyright

law for making reproductions of endangered or out-of-print phonograph recordings may also apply to videotape recordings. Section 108(c) allows for reproduction for purposes of replacing a piece that is "damaged, deteriorating, lost,
or stolen, if the library or archive has, after reasonable effort, determined that
used replacement cannot be obtained at a fair price." Similarly, section 108(e)
allows for reproduction of out-of-print materials that have been determined to
be unavailable at a fair market price. It is crucial to note that in order to take
advantage of these exemptions, a library must meet the section 108 conditions
discussed above in connection with off-air copying of news (see http://www4.
law.cornell.edu/uscode/17/108.html).

Before proceeding with reproduction of out-of-distribution or damaged items,
libraries should in all cases carefully assess the current value of these materials
to the collection. The roster of commercially available video titles is expanding
exponentially, and the availability of related (and perhaps more timely and effective) materials on the market should be investigated as part of this process.
In instances where reproduction of materials is deemed to be appropriate, the
library should maintain thorough written documentation of its preliminary efforts
to obtain the item from standard trade sources or from the copyright holder.

FORMAT TRANSFER

In the last half century, media librarians have witnessed a long parade of
formats running rapidly past their doors—from 16mm to ¾-inch videotape, to
Beta and ½-inch to DVD and the dawn of streamed video on the Web. Unfortunately, while they quite often bring improvements and benefits for users, new
formats create major problems for collection builders and managers, not the
least of which is having to deal with large bodies of materials, and large resource
investments rendered quickly obsolete. Older formats that do survive the onslaught of new technologies face a different kind of peril: analog media do not
physically last forever, nor, often, do the enterprises that produce or distribute
them. With the maturing of VHS collections, video librarians are often faced
with the prospect of managing a medium crumbling to oxide dust before their
eyes.

With the advent of VHS hardware and software and the almost universal
swing of libraries to this format, tape transfer is often viewed as a cost-effective
means of maintaining the utility of collections acquired in earlier formats or
preserving older VHS materials no longer available on the open market. Format
transfer is often relied upon to solve other problems as well. For example, while
there is a growing interest in and availability of international video, much of
the material produced outside of the United States is in formats incompatible
with U.S. standard (NTSC) hardware, such as PAL and SECAM. Despite the
onset of the video revolution, there is still a very large body of material, particularly theatrical titles, that is still currently available only in 16mm format.

It is fairly clear that the general strictures governing the copying of works discussed in the previous section also apply in the case of transferring whole works from one format to another, whether these transfers be analog to analog, analog to digital, digital to analog. Unless permitted by section 108 provisions for copying out-of-distribution or endangered materials, conversion of one format to another would consequently require securing permission from the copyright holder (Bender 1990:10). Again, for material still in distribution, it may ultimately be most cost- and time-effective to acquire a new copy of the title in the format desired, when possible.

Emerging digital technologies have put a new and increasingly complex spin on the issue of format transfer, whether in the service of video preservation or expanded content delivery. Although effective networked digital video delivery and storage technologies and read/write DVD technology are far down the road, the legality of transferring copyrighted analog videos to digital media is beginning to loom large for some libraries (particularly those, such as large academic libraries, fortunate enough to have suitable computing muscle for the job). Particularly interesting and pressing is the issue of digital transfers of at-risk analog video materials to digital formats. The limited provisions of section 108 of the copyright law for copying at-risk media materials (from one format to another or duplication in the same format) were briefly mentioned above. The Digital Millennium Copyright Act (1998) has substantially revised the older law.

Kenneth Crews (1998) has commented:

The amendments to Section 108 of the Copyright Act offer good and bad news for libraries. First, they clarify and assure that preservation copies of unique or deteriorating works may be made in digital formats; however, the digital version may be used only on the library premises. Second, they allow the library to copy works if the works are currently in formats that have become technologically obsolete. Finally, the amendments address a long-standing controversy in Section 108 by specifying that all copies made by the library under Section 108 must include the formal copyright notice, if available, or a specified statement about the applicability of copyright to the work.[7]

As analog video collections continue to age and deteriorate, as older parts of the video publication universe become unavailable on the open market, and as digital video delivery technologies mature, format transfer—a relatively minor blip on the collection development radar in the past—is bound to become a central issue for libraries of all types.

NEW HORIZONS, NEW CHALLENGES: VIDEO, THE CLASSROOM, AND THE DIGITAL WORLD

The enormous buzz concerning the potential for creating and delivering multimedia content via the Web is seemingly everywhere these days. And although the delivery of full-motion, high-resolution video over networks is still on the horizon (despite what the slick TV and magazine ads say), it's a horizon that seems to be getting closer at an exponentially rapid rate (see Chapter 24 of this book for a weather report on this digital front). When we finally get there, video "collection development" is likely to mean something substantially different than it has in the past three decades. Like the current move toward electronic text access in libraries, video collection, at least for some classes of material, is likely to become a matter of selecting content and acquiring (i.e., licensing) remote access to it, rather than selecting and acquiring tape in boxes or discs in jewel cases.

Even in advance of these quantum technological leaps, digital technologies are changing the ways in which media of various sorts are being used in class-rooms and in homes. The advent of digital technologies has put tremendous power in the hands of educators, students, and the public at large—the power to create or appropriate, manipulate, combine, and communicate various media in ways inconceivable as few as five years ago. As significant collectors and repositories of diverse content in varied formats, libraries are increasingly find-ing themselves called upon to provide grist for this multimedia and telecom-munications mill. Not surprisingly, this demand and the operational challenges associated with it are becoming particularly intense in academic and school libraries. In such settings, traditional video and audio collections are routinely being mined for images and sounds that can be digitally incorporated into course and student Web sites, PowerPoint presentations, digital term papers, CD-ROM projects, faculty research projects, and other digital tools used in teaching and learning.

The basic intellectual property issues faced by video collection developers working in this environment are much the same as those outlined above for analog media: what are the allowable uses of the materials selected and acquired or licensed for a library collection? What are the exclusive rights of the copy-right holder and, more importantly, what are the fair-use rights of the end users of this material? Unfortunately, in the digital domain the answers to these fun-damental questions are, at present, still far from clear or universally agreed upon.

Over the last decade, it has become apparent that the Copyright Act of 1976 is seriously inadequate for addressing the complexities of the new digital order and the changing nature of teaching and learning. In September 1994, the Na-tional Information Infrastructure Working Group on Intellectual Property Rights convened the Conference on Fair Use (CONFU) in an attempt to update the 1976 Act to reflect how technologies are used in the classroom and how course material is transmitted over distance learning networks.[8]

Several years before CONFU, the Consortium of College and University Me-dia Centers (CCUMC) had begun work on developing its own set of fair-use guidelines for new media. These discussions, involving representatives from educational organizations, library associations, and copyright proprietary groups, were subsequently incorporated into CONFU negotiations. CONFU ultimately ended rather disastrously in 1997 without any consensus reached on guidelines. The one exception was the CCUMC guidelines, which were finally endorsed by a majority of the industry and educational organizations involved in their development. It is important to note that a number of organizations that actively participated in the guideline negotiations (including the American Library Association) refused to endorse them on grounds that the final product was overly restrictive and did not "maintain the balance between users and owners of copyrighted materials" (Jackson 1997).[9]

The guidelines were adopted as a non-legislative report by the U.S. House of Representatives. Like the Kastenmeier guidelines, the CCUMC document is simply a set of guidelines; it is not law. The guidelines do, however, represent a broadly agreed-upon interpretation of the fair-use provisions of the Copyright Act, and it is felt that they might hold a fair amount of weight in court cases.

As they stand, the CCUMC guidelines only apply to educators and students who incorporate parts of lawfully acquired copyrighted works in not-for-profit multimedia projects for use in educational settings. The guidelines carefully delineate the allowable uses of these materials, and define the nature, duration, and extent of materials which may be incorporated in multimedia projects, as well as the duration these derivative works may be retained and used. Because they were largely developed before the rise of the World Wide Web, issues related to mounting and distributing student/faculty multimedia works via the Web or other online channels are not adequately addressed.

It is clear that evolving uses of media collections are increasingly demanding new ways of thinking about how media content is acquired and managed. New uses of collections will undoubtedly require the forging of new economic relationships with the copyright owners or their agents. At the same time, institutions will need to develop new collection access policies and guidelines that take into account new types of collection use made possible by digital technologies. Regardless of whether or not a school or library chooses to accept the CCUMC guidelines, it is important for library collection managers to become closely involved in these processes.

CONCLUSION

Under the existing copyright laws, educators and scholars (including librarians) are afforded a number of significant opportunities for using copyrighted materials in the course of teaching and research. For educational users of video, the exemptions provided under the umbrella of fair use open the door to a wide range of possibilities for utilizing this powerful medium. Within the limits and guidelines defined by the law, the television airwaves are opened for short-term use in classroom teaching, and educators are provided increased access to the expanding universe of prerecorded video programming in connection with formal instruction. In addition to these more traditional classroom uses of video, newer fair-use guidelines provide some allowance for the incorporation of portions of copyrighted media in new and exciting educational contexts—the creation of multimedia teaching and learning tools and products.

Librarians and libraries operate under considerably greater constraints. The processes through which videos are acquired, the contexts in which they are made available to library users, the uses to which they may be put, and the mechanisms for preserving them are generally closely tied to one or more of the rights exclusively held by the copyright owners of the material. While libraries are often centrally involved in the education process, they are typically sheltered by a much narrower set of exemptions to copyright than is provided to classroom instructors. In many libraries, the right to perform, duplicate, excerpt, transmit, or retain video materials—all centrally important to video collections and services—must be negotiated on a case-by-case basis with the intellectual property owner. These complex requirements force video librarians to view their collections in a unique light. For media librarians, assessing content, and acquiring the artifact or access are only part of the collection-building process. Equally important is a careful consideration of the intended end uses of the material in light of the laws protecting both the rights of the intellectual property owner and the institution's potential rights to fair use of this property.

APPENDIX: WEB SITES RELATED TO VIDEO AND NEW MEDIA COPYRIGHT

Primary Documents

U.S. Copyright Law (Full Text) (http://www.law.cornell.edu/usc/17/).

U.S. Copyright Office Web Site (http://lcweb.loc.gov/copyright).
Includes sections on copyright basics, frequently asked questions. Official description of Fair Use (in PDF format) is at http://lcweb.loc.gov/copyright/fls/fl102.pdf.

Kastenmeier Guidelines for Off-Air Taping (http://www.lib.berkeley.edu/MRC/Kastenmeier.html [via the University of California, Berkeley]).

Tutorials

Copyright Bay/Fair Use Harbor (http://www.stfrancis.edu/cid/copyrightbay/).
A wonderfully goofy and informative site that provides interactive tutorials related to copyright and fair-use issues for various media. The "AudioVisual Lagoon" section provides an excellent introduction to video, fair use, and public performance issues. Includes a good, selective bibliography of print and online sources.

Crash Course in Copyright (University of Texas) (http://www.utsystem.edu/ogc/intellectualproperty/cprtindx.htm).
A thoughtfully developed overview and introduction to copyright law aimed at higher education, but exceptionally useful for teachers and librarians in all settings. Separate tutorial modules are provided for various media, including videos, images, graphics, and music. Higher bandwidth users can listen to a spoken narrative of the tutorial.

Bibliographies

Copyright, Intellectual Property, Video & Multimedia: A Selected Bibliography (UC Berkeley Media Center) (http://www.lib.berkeley.edu/MRC/copyrightbib.html).
An annotated list including includes books, articles, videos, and Web sites related to video and copyright.

Information Policy: Copyright and Intellectual Property (International Federation of Library Associations and Institutions [IFLA]) (http://www.ifla.org/II/copyright.htm).
An extensive bibliography of online texts from IFLA and other sources dealing with copyright and intellectual property issues and policies. Includes a number of resources dealing with digital media.

General Information about Copyright and Fair Use

Association for Information Media and Equipment (AIME) (http://www.aime.org/).
AIME is a media industry organization that acts in the interest of video and software producers and distributors. The organization has produced a number of books and videos dealing with video and digital copyright (available for purchase from this Web site).

Association of Research Libraries (ARL) Copyright and Intellectual Property Site (http://www.arl.org/info/frn/copy/copytoc.html).
Links to information about current copyright legislation and litigation, including the Digital Millennium Act.

Copyright: An Overview (Cornell University) (http://www.secure.law.cornell.edu/topics/copyright.html).
Includes links to full-text documents, organizations, and other resources related to copyright and intellectual property. Useful links to information regarding international copyright agreements (Berne Convention et al.).

Copyright & Fair Use (Stanford University Libraries) (fairuse.stanford.edu/).
Sponsored by the Stanford Libraries and the Council on Library Resources, this is perhaps the most comprehensive and well-organized single Web site related to current copyright law and legislation, including resources regarding evolving copyright issues related to digital information and telecommunications. Includes extensive links to other sites.

Copyright, Fair Use, and Other Legal Matters: Film/Television/Video Topics (http://www.tcf.ua.edu/ScreenSite/res/bib/copyright.htm).
Part of the excellent ScreenSite film studies Web (University of Alabama), this metapage offers links to a wide variety of sites related to copyright, film and video, and the arts in general.

Copyright Resources Online (http://www.library.yale.edu/~okerson/copyproj.html).
An extensive, thoughtfully assembled metasite developed by Ann Okerson, Yale University. Links are provided to both university-related and non-university Web sites.

Copyright Resources on the Internet (Groton Public Schools) (http://www.groton.k12.ct.us/mts/pt2a.htm).
A metasite devoted to copyright resources, particularly focused on K–12 education, but including links of interest to higher education as well.

The Copyright Web Site (http://www.benedict.com/).

Launched in 1995 by attorney Benedict O'Mahoney, this site endeavors to "provide real world, practical and relevant copyright information of interest to infonauts, netsurfers, webspinners, content providers, musicians, appropriationists, activists, infringers, outlaws, and law abiding citizens." Includes an interesting section that discusses "notorious pillagers of copyright on the big screen."

ALA LARC (Library and Research Center) Fact Sheet Number 7: Video & Copyright (http://www.ala.org/library/fact7.html).

Somewhat overly conservative (particularly in its discussions of on-site viewing of video in libraries), but generally useful overview of primary issues related to video copyright in libraries.

Licensing Perspectives: The Library View (http://www.library.yale.edu/~okerson/cni-license.html).

A presentation given by Ann Okerson, Associate University Librarian, Yale University at the ARL/CNI Licensing Symposium (San Francisco, December 8, 1996).

Public Domain (University of North Carolina, Chapel Hill) (http://www.unc.edu/~unclng/public-d.htm).

A useful table developed by Laura Gasaway that outlines the current terms and definitions of public domain. Includes material from new Term Extension Act, P.L. 105–298.

Ten Big Myths About Copyright Explained (http://www.templetons.com/brad//copymyths.html).

An opinionated but useful attempt to answer common myths about copyright seen on the Internet and to cover issues related to copyright and Internet publication, by Brad Templeton.

Digital Media

An Intellectual Property Law Primer for Multimedia and Web Developers (http://www.eff.org/pub/Intellectual_property/multimedia_ip_primer.paper).

A straightforward discussion (with good examples) authored by J. Dianne Brinson and Mark F. Radcliffe and geared primarily to Web and multimedia developers in the commercial sector.

Fair Use and Multimedia (Stanford University) (http://fairuse.stanford.edu/multimed/).

Part of Stanford's superlative copyright and fair-use Web site (http://fairuse.stanford.edu/), this page provides extensive links to various sites and resources related to copyright, multimedia, and digital technologies.

Fair Use in the Electronic Age: Serving the Public Interest (http://arl.cni.org/scomm/copyright/uses.html).

An outgrowth of discussions among a number of library associations regarding intellectual property, and in particular, the concern that the interests and rights of copyright owners and users remain balanced in the digital environment.

Multimedia Fair Use Guidelines

Full text of Guidelines and supporting documentation (Indiana University) (http://www.indiana.edu/~ccumc/mmfairuse.html; http://www.utsystem.edu/mis/ogc/intellectual property/ccmcguid.htm).

CCUMC Copyright Initiatives (http://www.indiana.edu/~ccumc/copyright.html).
Provides historical background on the development of the Multimedia Fair Use Guidelines.

Educational Fair Use Guidelines for Multimedia: A Summary of Concerns (http://www.arl.org/info/frn/copy/mmedia.html).
The Association of Research Libraries' fact sheet in response to the CCUMC guidelines.

Fair Use in Multimedia: Digital Age Copyright (ARL online newsletter) (http://www.arl.org/newsltr/185/fairuse.html).)
An article by Stacey Carpenter, Multimedia Communications, Information Technology Division, Emory University, generally discussing the concept of fair use in an age of digital reproduction, the evolving classroom needs in a digital environment, and the pitfalls of the CCUMC Guidelines.

Library Issues: Multimedia and Fair Use: The Practical Side of a Philosophical Debate (http://www.libraryissues.com/pub/LI9803.asp).
A lengthy discussion of the development and current status of the CCUMC guidelines. Includes discussions of the objections raised by ALA and other groups regarding the limitations and shortcomings of these guidelines. Article includes good selective webliography of sites related to multimedia, copyright, and fair use.

Multimedia Fair Use Guidelines: Background and Summary (http://www.libraries.psu.edu/mtss/fairuse/dalziel.html).
A document authored by Chris Dalziel, Executive Director, Instructional Telecommunications Council, Pennsylvania State University, that provides background information about the development of the Multimedia Guidelines and opinions regarding the interpretation and utility of these guidelines in a university setting.

George Mason University, Department of Instructional Improvement and Instructional Technology (http://www.doiiit.gmu.edu/copyright.htm).
Includes good, brief summaries and reasonable interpretations of copyright and various fair-use guidelines as they pertain to instructional technologies. Site incorporates links to other Web resources for specific points being made.

NOTES

This chapter reflects the informed opinions of the author and does not constitute legal advice.

1. The copyright law (90 *U.S. Statutes at Large* [1976]: 2543) defines *performance* of a motion picture or other audiovisual work as "to show its image in any sequence or to make the sounds accompanying it audible."

2. To *perform publicly* is defined as "to perform or display it at a place open to the public or any place where a substantial number of persons outside of a normal circle of family or friends and its social acquaintances are gathered" (90 *U.S. Statutes at Large* [1976]: 2543).

3. Section 109(a) of the copyright law embodies a concept commonly referred to as the "first sale" doctrine (90 *U.S. Statutes at Large* [1976]: 2548) (see http://www4.law.cornell.edu/uscode/unframed/17/109.html and http://palimpsest.stanford.edu/bytopic/int prop/ipwg/law.html#id3a5b). This provision allows that individuals to whom copies of copyrighted materials are transferred (e.g., sold) may in turn "sell or otherwise dis-

pose of the possession of that copy" without the authority of the copyright holder. Section 109(a) specifically refers to phonograph recordings, but analog videos have also been included under this blanket. Once a video is loaned to a patron, it is largely the patron's responsibility to adhere to the provisions of the copyright law. The issue of first sale coverage for DVDs is still being debated; recent copyright legislation has severely limited first sale exclusions for computer software. For a discussion of the DVD/First Sale debate, see The Openlaw DVD/DeCSS Forum (2000) and Kamarck (1997). For an opinionated discussion of fair use and First Sale erosion under recent copyright legislation, see Besser (1998).

4. It is interesting to note that this opinion reverses earlier pronouncements made by Bender during his tenure as legal adviser to the Association for Information Media and Equipment (AIME), a video industry group: "[a public library] qualifies as a location where a use on the premises constitutes a public performance" (Bender 1987: 8).

5. The practice of "two-tiered pricing"—charging higher prices for institutional use or for use by selected types of institutions—is an often rancorously discussed issue among video librarians and video distributors. One common pretext for such differential pricing schemes is the supposed universal requirement for public performance rights for video use in institutional settings. While charging higher prices for different types of institutions is annoying but within the market rights of video distributors, claiming that this practice stems from the public performance rights requirements is more than a little disingenuous and misleading. Libraries that circulate videos exclusively for home use or for exclusive use in face-to-face teaching generally do not require these rights at all.

6. Although the majority of network and cable programming are not available for purchase or off-air licensing, it's worth checking out Corinne H. Smith's somewhat out-of-date but still useful "I Saw It On TV: A Guide to Broadcast and Cable Programming Sources" (via http://www.library.nwu.edu/media/resources/tvguide.html).

7. The amended section 108 defines *obsolete* as follows: "a format shall be considered obsolete if the machine or device necessary to render perceptible a work stored in that format is no longer manufactured or is no longer reasonably available in the commercial marketplace."

8. For historical background on CONFU and a summary of the conference outcome, see the University of Texas copyright crash course Web site: http://utsystem.edu/ogc/intellectualproperty/confu.htm.

9. For a discussion of the objections of ALA and other groups to the CCUMC guidelines, see *Library Issues: Multimedia and Fair Use: The Practical Side of a Philosophical Debate* (http://www.libraryissues.com/pub/LI9803.html); and *Educational Fair Use Guidelines: A Summary of Concerns* (ARL) (http://www.arl.org/info/frn/copy/mmedia.html).

REFERENCES

Bender, Ivan. 1987. "Public Libraries and Copyright." *Television Licensing Guide* 7 (March): 8.
Bender, Ivan. 1990. "Copying: Setting the Record Straight." *Sightlines* (Winter): 10.
Besser, Howard. 1998. "The Erosion of Public Protection: Attacks on the Concept of Fair Use." Paper delivered at the Town Hall Meeting on Copyright & Fair Use, College Art Association, Toronto, February 1998. http://www.pipeline.com/~

rabaron/ttm/BESSER.htm; also: http://www.gseis.ucla.edu/~howard/Papers/copy right99.html.

Crews, Kenneth D. 1998. "Copyright and Higher Education: Announcement of Recent Development: New Copyright Legislation Directly Affects Teaching and Research. Congress Enacts the Digital Millennium Copyright Act." http://www. iupui.edu/~copyinfo/dmcamemo.html.

Jackson, Mary E. 1997. "Educational Fair Use Guidelines for Multimedia: A Summary of Concerns." http://www.arl.org/info/frn/copy/mmedia.html.

Kamarck, Mitchell D. 1997. "Exceptions Consume the Rule: DVD and the First Sale Doctrine." *The Business of Film* (March). http://www.rmslaw.com/articles/art65. htm.

Kies, Cosette. 1989. "The CBS-Vanderbilt Litigation: Taping the Evening News." In *Fair Use and Free Inquiry: Copyright Law and the New Media.* 2nd ed. Edited by John S. Lawrence and Bernard Timberg. Norwood, NJ: Ablex, pp. 165–175.

Lardner, James. 1987. "Annals of Law: The Betamax Case." *The New Yorker* (April 6; April 13): 45–81.

Lawrence, John S. 1989. "Copyright Law, Fair Use, and the Academy: An Introduction." In *Fair Use and Free Inquiry: Copyright Law and the New Media.* 2nd ed. Edited by John S. Lawrence and Bernard Timberg. Norwood, NJ: Ablex, pp. 3–19.

Leval, Pierre. 1990. "Toward a Fair Use Standard." *Harvard Law Review* (March): 1105–1136.

Miller, Jerome. 1979. *Applying the New Copyright Law: A Guide for Educators and Librarians.* Chicago: American Library Association.

Miller, Jerome. 1988. *Using Copyrighted Videocassettes.* Friday Harbor, WA: Copyright Information Services.

The Openlaw DVD/DeCSS Forum. Frequently Asked Questions (FAQ) List. 2000. http: //www.cssfaq.org/dvd-discuss-faq.html#ss2.6.

Reed, Mary Hutchings, and Stanek, Debra. 1986. "Library and Classroom Use of Copyrighted Videotapes and Computer Software." *American Libraries* (February), special supplement.

Sinofsky, Esther R. 1984. *Off-Air Videotaping in Education.* New York: Bowker.

Timberg, Sigmund. 1989. "A Modernized Fair Use Code for Visual, Auditory, and Audiovisual Copyrights: Economic Context, Legal Issues, and Laocoon Shortfall." In *Fair Use and Free Inquiry: Copyright Law and the New Media.* 2nd ed. Edited by John S. Lawrence and Bernard Timberg. Norwood, NJ: Ablex, pp. 309–310.

U.S. House. *Report.* 1976. 94th Congress. Report No. 94–1476.

U.S. Statutes at Large. (1976). 90: 2541–1760.

Part V

Behind the Box Office: The Nature of the Video Market

Chapter 16

A Primer on the Home Video Market

Debra Franco

This chapter will attempt to describe and demystify *the business of home video*. An in-depth analysis of video marketing would require more room than can be allotted here. Instead, this discussion will present a general overview of how home video is marketed, as well as answer some of the most commonly asked questions institutional purchasers often have about home video, pricing, and non-fiction video.

HOW DOES THE HOME VIDEO MARKET WORK?

Essentially, the home video business is a *mass-market* business. This means that the market is dominated by large companies (movie studios, especially, called "licensors"), who bring out titles that will have mass appeal. As in any mass market, the object is to move the largest possible number of units as efficiently as possible out to the largest possible number of consumers.

The channels through which videos and DVDs get from the studios to consumers include: retail, or sales and rentals through stores; direct marketing, which includes sales through catalogs, ads, direct mail, television broadcast, and, most recently, the Internet.

For mass-market titles (hit feature films, children's programs, and high-profile titles), retail has traditionally been the main channel of distribution. Because the large studios are not in the business of opening their own stores to sell videos and DVDs directly, a network of middlemen exists that buys titles from the studios and sells them to the retailers. These include *wholesalers* (companies such as Baker & Taylor or Ingram), who supply video retail stores as well as other institutions, and *jobbers* (companies such as Handleman), who supply the huge chain stores like Wal-Mart, Target, or Sam Goody.

Customers normally use videos and DVDs in two ways: by renting them, usually from video outlet stores (and a handful of other stores that handle rentals); and by purchasing them, ostensibly for multiple viewing or use. The ways customers purchase have changed greatly over the years, both as channels for selling video and DVD have grown and as customer use has changed. These had an impact on the entire home video marketplace, as we shall see.

HOW DOES THE VIDEO RENTAL BUSINESS WORK?

For the first 10 years of home video's history, most video business was *rental* business, and most of it was carried out through video outlet stores. These are stores whose major business is the rental and sale of videotapes, whether they are small one- or two-store establishments (known in the industry as "Mom & Pops"), local chains of stores, or large national chains (Blockbuster Video, Hollywood Video, etc.).

Here's how the rental business works and how it affects pricing. The video store purchases videos and DVDs from the wholesaler at a discount off the list price. The store puts the tapes and DVDs out for rental to customers for a night or even up to a week, charging anywhere from $0.99 to $4.50 per title. Since the licensors receive nothing from these rentals, but only a percentage of the list price they get from the wholesaler, many studios keep the initial price of their rental videos high (currently, around $100; although at present DVD is more often priced in the $19.95 to $39.95 range). The studios expect to sell large numbers of popular titles to the video rental stores at the higher price over the first few months, then drop the price later in order to reach those consumers willing to purchase titles outright. For their part, the video stores attempt to maximize their revenues by stocking large numbers of big hits for rental during the first three to six months after they are released. Then, as the demand fades, the store will cut the price and try to sell off some of the extra inventory.

The world of home video rental is highly competitive. Network television, cable, pay-per-view, and new technologies such as webcasting all compete for consumer attention with video and DVD rentals. The expanding video sell-through and direct-sales markets (see discussions below) have also presented an increasing threat to the rental industry. Within rental stores, titles compete with each other for "shelf space." In order to survive, then, many video stores need to squeeze as much money out of every title as they can. As a result, the video rental business is often described as "hit-driven"—meaning that it focuses on feature films with well-known stars and a lot of publicity. Titles like *Titanic, The Matrix, Star Wars: The Phantom Menace*, or any film starring a well-known actor are "presold" in home video—customers come into the store already knowing about them, through the massive publicity accompanying their theatrical runs.

Other kinds of videos and DVDs (e.g., documentaries, cultural or instructional titles), as well as lesser-known feature films and foreign films, have traditionally received short shrift in most video rental stores. Even though many of these titles have a longer potential rental life than time-sensitive feature films, these "evergreen" titles do not deliver a big enough return fast enough for many video rental stores to consider them profitable. So, non-mainstream videos and DVDs have had to find other ways to reach an audience than through video stores.

WHAT IS SELL-THROUGH?

Aside from the video retail outlets, whose main products are videos and DVDs, there are numerous other retail stores that stock video and DVD. Most of these other retail outlets do not deal in the rental business but, rather, in what is called "sell-through"—i.e., selling titles priced low enough (generally between $9.95 and $29.99) so that consumers will buy instead of rent. One of the biggest changes in the market since the late 1980s has been the shift from rental to sell-through as a major share of home video revenues. For some segments of the video market, such as children's video, sell-through has become *the* single largest revenue stream (USADATA.com 2000).

The biggest players in the sell-through market have traditionally been the mass merchants, huge retail chains like Wal-Mart, K Mart, and Toys R Us, and shopping clubs, such as Costco, that sell videos and DVDs among many other products and move thousands of units per store. A study by the Video Software Dealers Association (VSDA) estimates that 50 percent of all video sales are logged by large discount chains (Dretzka 1999).

The mass merchants operate in a unique way in their marketing of video, by using *rack jobbers*. Rack jobbers bring preselected videos and DVDs into stores. The jobber selects, prices, stocks, maintains, moves, and removes the inventory as needed. This allows the stores to sell video and DVD without having to train in-house staff to select, purchase, and deal with inventory. Videos and DVDs that are "racked" and sold through the mass merchants are selected on the basis of their mass appeal and price—often at the rock-bottom levels of $4.99 to $9.99. Videos in this category tend to be feature films that have outlived their high-priced lives, brand-name children's tapes, and generic special interest tapes (cooking, exercise, beauty, sports).

Selling through the mass merchants is one key to huge sales for titles with mass appeal, such as well-known feature films, and generic non-feature entries. Other retail outlets are an important venue for sales of *non-mainstream video* (and DVD), even though they do not move such large numbers of units. Video and music stores feature video and DVD sell-through sections, as do some bookstores and many specialty stores, such as museum stores, gift stores, and children's stores.

As consumers have begun to purchase videos and DVDs as much as rent them, other avenues than retail have opened up to get videos and DVDs to buyers. The main growth has been through the many channels of direct marketing. In recent years, there has been an explosion in the sale of video to consumers through catalogs, on-air television spots, video clubs, and Web retailing/marketing. While the bulk of all videos and DVDs sold and rented remains feature films (over 70 percent), the explosion in sell-through video and DVD through direct marketing and the Internet has greatly increased the sale of *special interest video* to consumers.

WHAT IS SPECIAL INTEREST VIDEO?

In home video terminology, a special interest video is any tape or DVD that is not a feature film. This includes a broad range of genres—children's, animation, educational, exercise, beauty, cooking, sports, documentary, cultural—in essence, almost any non-fiction title. Although special interest video has been around since the beginning of home video (Jane Fonda's *Workout* being an early example), there is today a wider range of non-feature titles being used by consumers than ever before. In the mid-1990s, the Special Interest Video Association (SIVA) reported average total consumer sales of over $900 million a year for special interest videos (Liebenson 1995). This continuing growth can be attributed to the maturation of the video market. As the novelty of renting feature films gradually wore off, and as consumers began learning new ways to use video, interest in videos beyond hit feature films began to climb. The rise of Internet video distribution has also had a major role in this growth. As Ed Kirchedoerffer (1999: 60) has commented:

As it has done for books and music, the Internet has flung the doors wide open for the sale of special interest and documentary home video. The endless shelf space offered on the Web gives consumers the change to find videos on niche topics ranging from biography to wildlife, religion to yoga.

Although there is a long way to go before people truly "use videos like books" (the prediction of the 1970s), special interest video is still an expanding segment of the home video marketplace.

In most cases, special interest video gets to the consumer in different ways than feature films and is treated differently. As we saw above, special interest videos are not big renters through video stores. They are not "hit-driven" and cannot compete with the huge initial demand for hit features in video stores. Consumers do not rush to the video store in droves as soon as the latest travel video by Rick Steves is released, the way they will with *Star Wars: The Phantom Menace*, for example. Rather, they will go looking for travel videos or DVDs on an as-needed basis. Still, many special interest titles tend to be evergreens. In other words, they will continue to rent over a longer period of time, even if they never break the bank as blockbuster rentals at any one time.

This points up another difference between the way special interest and feature films are used. Aside from children's films, which are watched over and over, and feature films that inspire multiple viewing (such as the *Star Wars* series), most features are watched once, often on weekends, and so lend themselves to rental activity.

Special interest videos and DVDs, on the other hand, are as likely to be bought as rented. They are often informational and may require more than one viewing to retain or use the information in them. How-to's may be watched in segments during the process of building, making, or cooking something and thus may need to be kept overtime. Other special interest videos, such as cultural titles, are often seen as documents of valuable performances and thus something to collect (concerts on DVD, for example, such as *Dave Matthews Band: Listener Supported*, or *Placido Domingo: Evening*, feature CD quality sound that lends itself to multiple viewing or listening); and many special interest videos are purchased as gift items for an individual's "special interests" (as in "Let's get Dad that video on fly fishing for Father's Day; it's the only thing he's really passionate about.").

HOW IS SPECIAL INTEREST VIDEO SOLD?

Because each title must reach a specific market, the way that special interest video makes its way to consumers must be much more targeted than that of mass appeal videos and DVDs. As opposed to mass marketing, special interest videos and DVDs are generally sold through *niche marketing*. Niche marketing means pinpointing and reaching a specific, specialized segment of the population that will have a special interest in, or need for, the product.

Reaching specific segments of the population can often require more creativity and knowledge about the potential audience than is needed to sell a mass-market title. Say you are selling a hit feature film. By the time it reaches home video, millions of Americans have already heard about it, based on the millions of dollars worth of television, news, and radio publicity that accompanied its theatrical release. If it is a major blockbuster, it will also have commercial tie-ins with other American institutions—McDonald's, Burger King, Coca-Cola. You can therefore sell this title in video stores, of course, but also wherever masses of people shop—supermarkets, drugstores, Wal-Mart, toy stores, and so on.

But when you are selling a title with a very specialized market, say, a program about American painter Jackson Pollock, trying to sell the video or DVD at supermarkets will not get you very far. To sell special interest video, the distributor has to *discover* the program's market, and tapping the places where potential customers go to buy products of similar content does that. This concept is called discovering the *logical point of distribution* (l.p.d.). One retail l.p.d. for the program on Jackson Pollock, for example, might be gift shops at museums of contemporary art, where people go to buy gift items relating to art. The assumption is that people who are interested in art go to museums; therefore, by extension, those interested in buying books, videos, and DVDs on art go to the gift stores at those institutions.

Specialty stores—record stores, museum stores, specialty gift shops—have been growing as the logical points of retail distribution for related special interest videos over the past 15 years. Today, you can find videos on the wonders of the Grand Canyon selling at the gift store at the park itself, as well as at retail outlets such as Discovery Channel Stores and The Nature Company, which sell gift items relating to nature and the environment. Tapes on golfing tips sell at pro shops where people interested in golf go to purchase or rent their sports equipment. Videos and DVDs of performances by Placido Domingo sell at gift shops at opera houses, as well as at record and music stores where people buy classical music. Currently, specialty retail outlets account for anywhere from 5 to 30 of sales of special interest videos.

How do special interest titles fare in video stores? Although sell-through has grown significantly through video stores, most of those sales are still of feature films. Aside from certain blockbusters relating to exercise, sports, and beauty, special interest video has not fared well in these outlets. This is especially true for quality special interest programs—those with cultural relevance. (The one exception is PBS Home Video, which has had some success selling documentaries that have aired on PBS via large displays in video retail stores.)

Although growing in importance, retail has not been the biggest channel for special interest programs. Other, often more important channels have opened up and grown dramatically over the past decade. One is direct mail. For some special interest video producers/distributors, such as National Geographic, direct mail accounts for as much as 75 percent of total sales (Kirchedoerffer 1998). This is in notable contrast to feature films, for which direct marketing sales are relatively insignificant. Much of the direct-mail activity for video and DVD is through *catalogs*. There are thousands of product catalogs mailed to consumers every year, many of which carry special interest videos. A handful of the catalogs contain video or DVD only; most of the ones that carry video and DVD do so in addition to other products. Direct-mail sales—although they are no guarantee of success—have the benefit of allowing distributors to match videos and DVDs with the special interests of consumers via pinpointed customer mailing lists. Companies such as Reader's Digest, for example, have built extremely successful operations creating and selling videos on non-fiction subjects that reflect the tastes and interests of their magazine readership. Another way special interest titles are sold via direct marketing is through video and music clubs, such as Columbia House, which operate similarly to book clubs.

One of the most important sales channels, especially for quality special interest videos, is *television broadcast*. Public television, especially, is an increasingly important venue for 800-number video DVD sales following a broadcast. Although, according to Jon Cecil of PBS Video, the number of sales resulting from a broadcast can range from as few as 150 units to as many as 15,000, selling videos and DVDs this way has a tremendous advantage: it lets consumers view the show in its entirety before purchasing. Especially for culturally relevant and social issue documentaries, selling via PBS broadcast is rapidly becoming one of the most direct and important ways of reaching the home market.

The newest and fastest-growing avenue for delivering special interest programming is over the Internet. It is estimated that Web-based sales currently account for over 10 percent of all video sales (Dretzka 1999). Consumers may purchase videos and DVDs through online retailers such as online-only Amazon.com (which, in 1999, accounted for 40 percent of all fourth-quarter online video and DVD sales), or online arms of traditional brick and mortar retail outlets such as Wal-Mart, and specialized educational distributing aggregates such as Edudex.com. Besides these online warehouses, many individual producers and distributors are taking advantage of the low overhead of selling directly to a worldwide audience online via their own sites, and/or through marketing partners. Video sales on the Internet are said to currently account for approximately $400 million of the $1.4 billion overall online retail sales (Sporich 2000). It is estimated that by 2004, approximately $1.7 billion, about 15 percent of the overall sell-through market, will be sold via e-commerce (Scally 1999). While the individualized sites will surely remain, industry watchers predict that most video and DVD dedicated online operations without a brick-and-mortar presence will fail due to low margins (Sporich 2000a). An ominous portent occurred at the end of June 2000, when Reel.com, arguably the highest profile online retailer of video and DVD, suspended retail operations after parent company Hollywood Video decided to cut its losses (and many dot.coms are in the same financial boat, hemorrhaging cash with no strong profitability in sight) (Mangalindan 2000).

A potentially even bigger role for the Internet, however, will not be in the realm of moving physical units of videos and DVDs, but rather in offering streaming VOD (video on demand). In 2000, several new companies, including VastVideo.com and ShowMeTV.com, were in the process of mounting video clips demonstrating a variety of "how-to" activities, from changing a bike tire to cooking a spinach soufflé. Although the huge bandwidth requirements and low-speed connections (56k modems or less) of most consumers limit the size of the video clips online, the rapid deployment of DSL, ISDN, and high-speed cable modems will make the streaming of entire programs a reality in the not-too-distant future.

The final outlet for certain special interest videos and DVDs is *educational institutions*. While schools, colleges, and public libraries all purchase feature films, institutional sales account for a tiny percentage of the gross of these features. For certain special interest titles, however, the institutional market can account for as much as 25 to 50 percent of sales. In the case of certain educational and documentary titles, it can be the entire market, as we will see below.

WHY AREN'T MORE SPECIAL INTEREST VIDEOS SOLD IN BOOKSTORES?

Bookstores would appear to be one of the most obvious retail outlets for special interest titles. Like libraries, bookstores are venues that attract people who read and are interested in informational and cultural pursuits. These would seem to be prime candidates for purchasing videos and DVDs of similar subjects to which they purchase books. In fact, market predictors in the early days of home video anticipated that bookstores would become the main channel through which non-fiction videos would be sold.

But bookstores have not become a central force for sell-through as many in the field had hoped. The reasons for this have more to do with marketing than with logic. One is the different way the video and book markets do business. Video distributors often cannot afford to offer the same retail discount for video and DVD as booksellers are used to getting from books (50 percent off list). In addition, video distributors usually cannot afford to offer a 100 percent return rate, which booksellers traditionally get from publishers.

Among the other reasons that special interest video has not made big inroads into bookstores is the problem of *cross-merchandising*. This means placing videos and DVDs of a particular subject in the same section as books on that subject. (This is similar to the public library issue of *interfiling*). So a military history buff browsing in the History section of the bookstore would come across both videos and DVDs *and* books on the Civil War or Charlemagne, or air battles of World War II. In this way, each subject section in the bookstore— Cooking, Mystery, Art, and so on—becomes the 1.p.d. for videos on that subject and attracts the most motivated buyers.

Very few bookstores have adopted this practice, however. Most keep videos and DVDs in a segregated area, completely separate from the books. Part of the reason for this is security—video has a higher theft rate than books, but, in addition, many bookstores have simply not yet seen, or been interested in, the potential correlation of selling video and DVD with books.

While certain videos/DVDs with book tie-ins (A&E's *Pride & Prejudice* and Ken Burns' *The Civil War*, for example) have sold extremely well along with their books in bookstores, most special interest videos and DVDs have not yet been given a chance in this venue. Many in the video field expect this to change as sales of special interest videos and DVDs continue to grow and bookstores become aware of their potential. (These experts point out that it took bookstores almost 10 years to embrace audiotapes, which now account for annual revenues of over $2 billion) (Rosenblum 1999).

HOW IS VIDEO PRICING DETERMINED?

A number of factors go into determining pricing for home video. The most important one is, simply, how many units a tape or DVD will sell.

When a Hollywood feature is a *hit film*, it can expect to sell upwards of a half million units in home video through many sources—video stores, the mass merchants, video clubs, specialty stores, catalogs, and online. Major blockbusters, like *Batman*, *E.T.*, or *The Little Mermaid*, have sold in the 10-million-unit range, but even hit "adult" films such as *The Sixth Sense* sell well (one million copies of the DVD of *The Sixth Sense* were sold during the first weekend of release alone).

If a studio decides that a hit feature will do well in sell-through, it will usually price the film low—between $14.95 and $29.95—to encourage consumers to buy it. It will simultaneously go out to video stores for rental and sale, as well as to other outlets for sale. It can price such a film so low because with a title selling a million or so units, it can make serious profits at $19.95, even with the costs of manufacturing and marketing.

For *features that are not big hits*, or for hits that studios believe will not do exceptionally well at sell-through, the studios can expect to sell anywhere from 50,000 to 500,000 units. Since most of the sales activity will come from video stores purchasing the title for rental, the studios will price these titles higher. As we saw earlier, this price may be as high as $100 per tape, or it may be in the $49 to $89 range. While video stores may complain about the price and may order fewer of the higher-priced tapes, they will still purchase them because they need to continually stock new rental titles to satisfy their customers. The one new variable in this mix is DVD. Consumers have taken to the new format very quickly, not only because of the superior video and audio capabilities DVD offers, but also because most new priced-for-rental VHS titles are released on the same day in the DVD format at a sell-through price. The end result is that video stores are beginning to cut back on the number of copies of VHS titles they order, substituting a few lower-priced DVD copies for the growing legion of DVD renters. As of mid-2000, the studios were beginning to see some cannibalization of video sales to DVD, and the industry was rife with speculation concerning the possible raising of DVD prices.

For *special interest titles*, the potential markets vary. Exercise, beauty, and sports tapes have greater markets because they are generic—that is, they appeal across the board to all kinds of people. These titles can expect to sell between 25,000 and 75,000 if they have a star attached. Some with special appeal do much better (*The Sports Illustrated Swimsuit Video* sold over 200,000 units, and Jane Fonda's original *Workout* was the all-time special interest blockbuster at a million copies). This genre of special interest will usually be priced around $14.95 to $29.95.

For *quality special interest videos*—culturally relevant documentaries and performances—the market shrinks appreciably. Here, as with all home video, publicity plays a key role in how well a video or DVD will do. Well-publicized series, or videos with a "star" attached, or with special promotion or exhibition, do much better than single videos or DVDs with nothing well-known about them. For example, a performance of a well-known opera starring Placido Domingo has sold in excess of 30,000 units, while *An Evening with the Bolshoi* (containing no well-known stars) has sold about 2,500 units. In another case, a documentary on Georgia O'Keefe had sold about 400 units through normal home video channels, but when a successful exhibit of O'Keefe's work was shown at museums around the country, the video's sales increased to 40,000 units through sales at museum gift stores. The publicity surrounding the exhibit sold the video.

Without this "presold" quality so important in home video—a star, publicity, a major exhibition, or broadcast—a cultural video can expect to sell only 1,000 to 5,000 units unless its subject makes it a hit with a certain population of consumers. For titles that expect to sell below 5,000 units, selling at low prices will often not provide enough profit to keep the title in distribution. These programs will thus often be priced between $39.95 and $89.95 for the home market.

In all these cases, prices are determined by the perceived potential market for the program, by the cost of marketing the title, and by what the market will bear. For some documentaries and educational titles, however, there is yet another variable involved: the educational market.

WHY ARE SOME NON-FICTION VIDEOS PRICED OVER $100?

Public librarians are often confused at seeing certain non-fiction videos priced at $150 to $350 when they can purchase a Disney children's classic for $26.99. These higher-priced titles are videos priced for the educational—not the home video—market.

Before home video hit the video stores and library shelves, there was already a flourishing, although limited, market for media made specifically for the purpose of teaching. Before 1980, there were a small number of public libraries that, along with schools, media centers, colleges, government, business, and health organizations, purchased these educational films, filmstrips, and early videotapes. The market for these titles was extremely limited—roughly 3,000 potential institutional buyers—and a film was considered successful if it sold 300 to 500 copies. Because of this, and the fact that this business began with higher-priced 16mm film, the prices for these films and tapes were high; but because educators and media specialists placed great value in media that directly enhanced their curricula, they were willing to pay these prices.

Today, this market is in transition. The educational market has been flooded with videos and DVDs made for other markets, at low prices. This includes titles made for the consumer market, as well as series made for public television that have potential crossover to the consumer market (e.g., Ken Burns' *Lewis and Clark*, Sir David Attenborough's *The Life of Birds*, and the Peter Jennings–hosted retrospective *The Century*).

In response, the price of videos and DVDs made for the educational market has been dropping. Today, programs made primarily for the educational market may still sell at prices ranging from $50 to $500, but the average is moving down to the $99 to $200 range. Yet they are still, and may always be, priced higher than home video.

The reason is simple: their market is not big enough to warrant a very low price. For a feature film, the educational market represents a tiny part of its entire video and DVD sales. A film that sells 500,000 units will make its money from the consumer market—the few thousand units it may sell to libraries and colleges are merely icing on the cake. For consumer-oriented special interest videos, the educational market plays a more important role—perhaps accounting for 25 percent of sales or more, depending on the title—but it is still the consumer sales that drive the price point.

However, for many documentaries and educational titles there simply is no consumer interest, and their market will only be to institutions. These programs may be valuable to a very specific segment of the educational market. They may contain information that is important to educators, and they may be used for years in classrooms and be seen by hundreds of students, but they may simply not be of enough interest to consumers to warrant distribution to the home market.

For most of these educational titles, the institutional market is not currently large enough to support high numbers of sales at low prices. The current average for a non-blockbuster educational title is about 600 units. This is barely enough to promote a title, send it out for preview to the educational market, and service that market over the life of the video. So, at this time, each title will be priced according to its market potential, much like the studios price their feature films, depending on whether or not they think the numbers are there to justify initial release to sell-through.

The good news is that, gradually, the institutional market for non-fiction and independent video has increased at the departmental level at universities, at the building level in schools and organizations, and at public libraries.

The public library market is an extremely important part of this. In the early days of home video in libraries, feature films formed most core collections, but, there has been growing interest among video librarians in expanding their non-fiction collections. This is evinced by the spread of organized library consortia purchasing educational programs, as well as the good attendance at library continuing education seminars on non-fiction video evaluation and selection. Increasing awareness in the public library market for non-fiction and educational videos and DVDs can have a real impact on widening the sales universe for these programs.

The hope of many in the field is that the sales average for non-fiction videos and DVDs made for the educational market may rise to 2,000 units, allowing prices to come down to the $50 range as an average unit price.

In the meantime, interested librarians can join, or cause the creation of, local or state purchasing consortia. An increasing number of consortia organized at the state library level have made special purchasing arrangements with educational distributors. In this kind of consortia buying, the distributors offer lower prices for group purchases, enabling groups of schools or libraries to buy higher-priced titles at lower, multiple-unit rates. This method of purchase has increased the number of institutional collections of non-fiction video and DVD. This, in turn, helps to lower the price for these works.

WHAT ARE FUTURE TRENDS IN VIDEO USE?

It is important to remember that video is a market in transition and that change is gradual. In the early years of home video, most consumers were not very interested in documentaries, or even many how-to's—only feature films. While feature films still make up the bulk of the home video business, the rise in special interest and documentary activity shows that people's perception of how video can be used is evolving.

Non-fiction is currently the new frontier in home video, both for consumers and for public libraries. In early 1990, the video rental market flattened out for the first time since the arrival of home video. This meant that video rentals of feature films did not expand for the first time but stayed level or began to contract. Many in the field called this the "maturation" of the market, perceiving that the novelty of renting new feature films was wearing thin, and consumers were looking for something else. Later in that same year, Ken Burns' documentary series *The Civil War* broke all public television viewing records and set new records for non-fiction home video sales. At the same time, PBS Home Video launched its campaign to sell PBS documentaries through retail stores. Since 1990, video rentals have continued to decline, though 1999 and 2000 are seeing a serious leveling off, thanks to explosive growth in DVD rentals.

Will video ever be "used like books"? Video and books are two different forms of receiving information, and there will always be differences in the way we use them—though with the rise of e-books and other digital forms of transmission, various hybrids combining text, graphics, and full-motion video are likely to appear in the future. In addition, consumers are increasingly beginning to use video and DVD (with its ability to add numerous extras—special documentaries, source materials, etc.), especially non-fiction video and DVD, more the way they do books: collecting them, giving them as gifts, and using them for information, reference, and research.

As this happens, libraries and other institutions will continue to reflect that change in the way they select, catalog, and use media. For example, an increasing number of university libraries now put videos and DVDs on reserve for student use, along with books and periodicals, and public libraries in many areas are interfiling video and DVD with print materials. In addition, many libraries are becoming primary media sources for the teachers, non-profit organizations, and business groups in their communities. Their video and DVD collections thus reflect an expanded need for non-fiction programs as sources of information in many subject categories. With the advent of digital streaming technologies, libraries—public, school, and academic—need to be ready to explore new ways of bringing programming to their constituents.

As the market continues to evolve, and consumers and educators find new and expanded uses for non-fiction video, there will continue to be increasing public interest in alternatives to mainstream titles. Mass market features made in Hollywood that appeal to millions will certainly continue to entertain consumers on video and DVD, but the *Basic Instincts* and *Lethal Weapons* are made primarily as commercial vehicles. The vision of reality they give us, while diverting, exciting, and often amusing, is rarely sustaining.

Independent films, on the other hand, are often the works of individuals—the activist, the artist, the educator—and, as such, will often present more interesting, alternative views of the truth than those presented in more commercial films. In an era when the old "mass" ways of perceiving how the world works are fading, and new truths are arising, the vision of the individual should have renewed power. Watch for even greater consumer interest in programs made outside the Hollywood mainstream—independent feature films, documentary series and singles, non-mainstream children's films, and cultural titles. The best of these have the power to touch us, teach us, and inspire us in ways the commercial media rarely do.

NOTE

Thanks to Pamela Handman, Information Analyst for KPMG Global Financial Strategies, for literature searches that yielded many of the statistics cited in this chapter.

REFERENCES

Dretzka, Gary. 1999. "Home Video Sales in Slow Motion." *Chicago Tribune* (July 13): Business Section, 1.

Kirchedoerffer, Ed. 1999. "The Truth about Home Video: Trends for Non-fiction." *RealScreen* (July/August). http://www.realscreen.com/articles/rs26089.asp.

Kirchedoerffer, Ed. 1998. "VSDA—Video Revolution: Special-interest home video Flows into the Mainstream." *RealScreen* (June): 28. http://www.realscreen.com/articles/rs22684.asp.

Liebenson, Donald. 1995. "Niche Titles Are Where Action Is." *Los Angeles Times* (December 17): 79

Mangalindan, Mylene. 2000. "Reel.com to Shutter Operations, Citing Mounting Losses." *Wall Street Journal* (June 13): B12.

Rosenblum, Trudi M. 1999. "Audiobooks '99." *Publishers Weekly* (June 7): 42–44.

Scally, Robert. 1999. "Video/DVD: DVD, Internet Sales Peak at Same Time."*Discount Store News* 38(23) (December 13): 66.

Sporich, Brett. 2000. "States Will Have to Wait to Collect Proceeds from E-Commerce Taxes." *Video Store* (April 2): 7.

Sporich, Brett. 2000a. "Web Retailers Doomed." *Video Store* (April 16): 1.

RECOMMENDED READING

Arnold, Thomas K. 1997. "The Special Challenge of Special Interest." *Los Angeles Times* (June 17): D10.

Brown, Kimberly. 2000. "Don't Believe the Hype . . . (At least not yet): Producers Invest in e-Commerce for a Wealthier Tomorrow." *RealScreen* (April 1). http://www. realscreen.com/articles/rs28954.asp.

Brown, Kimberly. 2000a. "The Educated Buyer: Bringing Docs into the Classroom Isn't as Easy as A-B-C." *RealScreen* (May). http://www.realscreen.com/articles/ rs28954.asp.

Cella, Catherine. 1994. "Special-interest Delivery." *Billboard* 106(31) (July 30): 78 (3 pp.).

Fitzpatrick, Eileen. 1998. "Amazon.com Starts Selling VHS and DVD Titles on Internet." *Billboard* (November 28): 3.

Fitzpatrick, Eileen. 1998. "Distributors Adjust to Online Shift." *Billboard* (December 5): 105–107.

Fitzpatrick, Eileen. 1999. "Amazon Aids Indie Vid." *Billboard* (July 17): 6.

Goldstein, Seth. 1998. "Sell-Through-Dominant DVD Could Take a Big Bite Out of Video Biz's Margins." *Billboard* (December 19): 63.

Goldstein, Seth, and Fitzpatrick, Eileen. 1999. "Vid Biz in Transition." *Billboard* (July 10): 1.

Hansell, Saul. 2000. "Stock Shock Is a Signal: Tough Times for E-Tailers." *New York Times* (April 10): C1.

Jeffrey, Don. 1999. "Vid Biz: Home Video Stays on Track as the Big Get Bigger and the Small Hang On." *Billboard* (July 10): 65–67.

The National Association of Recording Merchandisers (NARM). *Annual Survey.* http:// www.narm.com/programs/research.htm. Surveys sales and rentals for various media and entertainment genres in selected markets.

Nichols, Peter M. 1999. "Catalogue Sellers Thrive On Line." *New York Times* (March 5): E38.

Nichols, Peter M. 2000. "If It's on Video, You Can Find It Someplace in Your Computer." *New York Times* (June 7): D38.

Olson, Catherine Applefeld. 1996. "Special-Interest Vids Vie for Shelf Space." *Billboard* 108(50) (December 14): 61–63

Olson, Catherine Applefeld. 2000. "The Year in Video 1999." *Billboard* (January 8): 87–92.

Rosenberg, Scott. 1995. "Will Video Stores Be Dinosaurs?" *Computer Life* (January): 69.

Shapiro, Eben. 1998. "Web Retailers Are Racing to Sell Videotapes." *Wall Street Journal* (October 2): B1.

Sweeting, Paul. 1999. "Now Downloading on a Computer Near You." *Variety* (May 24– 30): 23.

USADATA.com. 2000. "Market Research Report: The U.S. Children's Video Market." http://www.usadata.com/market_research/sml_00/sml_43.htm.

Waldrep, Mark. 1998. "Special Interest DVD-Video: From the Beginning." *EMedia Professional* (December): 66.

Chapter 17

Program Rights, or Answers to the Question, "Why Can't I Buy That Program?"

Jon Cecil

HISTORY AND OPERATION OF PUBLIC BROADCASTING

On a daily basis, PBS Video, a self-supporting department of the Public Broadcasting Service (PBS), receives inquiries about the purchase of programs that appear on public television. Too often, unfortunately, little help can be provided to the caller. The reasons are many and complex, but generally involve program use rights. What follows is an attempt to provide an overview of the complexities of video distribution, which may help to answer a variety of questions that arise in relation to program rights, availability, and cost.

Before getting into the intricacies and vagaries of program rights, however, perhaps a short review of just what PBS is and where it fits into the larger scheme of public broadcasting will help to clear up several misconceptions that continue to confound and confuse the layperson.

In the beginning, there was educational broadcasting. . . .

The first non-commercial television station, KUHT, Houston, Texas, signed on the air in 1953 and was licensed to the University of Houston. Over the next decade, 75 such stations signed on the air across the nation, nearly all licensed to colleges and school districts. Most programming was produced for local consumption and was very low-cost. *Children's Corner*, educational TV's first production for children, for example, had a weekly production budget of $150, including salaries; and this was before videotape was available. Most programs were produced live and, where budgets permitted, were recorded for posterity on a form of black-and-white 16mm film called kinescopes.

To fill their limited daily broadcast schedules, educational television stations began to share programming, "bicycling" (mailing or shipping) kinescopes, and later two-inches videotapes, from station to station. To complete a circuit would take several weeks. The need to share limited production resources moved educational television stations to band together in the mid- to late 1960s into statewide or regional "networks" that linked stations by telephone lines. These primitive linkages allowed programs to be exchanged between stations electronically. Regional program schedules could be originated from a single location, thus reducing the heavy requirement for bicycling. However, this type of network was dependent on a limited, single, one-way landline that had to be shared by many television stations.

As educational television grew and programming emphasis shifted from classroom television to general audience fare, it attracted the attention of the privately chartered Carnegie Commission on Educational Television, which in 1967 completed a landmark study that focused on both general audience and instructional programs (Carnegie Commission 1967). The Commission recommended boosts in state and local financial support, federal funding of "public TV" programming and operations, and the formation of a nationwide interconnection system to improve program distribution.

That same year Congress enacted, and President Lyndon Johnson signed, the Public Broadcasting Act (PL 90–129), adopting many of the Carnegie Commission's recommendations and establishing an ongoing federal commitment to support public broadcasting (radio and television). The act created the Corporation for Public Broadcasting (CPB), which was chartered to receive and disburse the federal revenues in support of public radio and television stations and producers. CPB was to act as a "heat shield" between stations and federal agencies, in order to protect programming from governmental influence. The legislation also called for the formation of the nationwide interconnection system recommended by the Carnegie Commission. CPB was charged with funding the interconnection system but was not permitted to operate it (see Burke 1979; United States, *Legislative History* 1971).

Subsequent consultations involving CPB and the Ford Foundation (a longtime supporter of educational television) and the stations led to the recommendation to establish the Public Broadcasting Service as a membership organization to operate the interconnection system. PBS became a reality in late 1969 and established its headquarters in Washington, DC, with a budget of $7 million and 128 member stations. The national interconnection system became operational using reduced-rate telephone lines in the fall of 1970, and during its first year it distributed such notable programs as *Washington Week in Review*, *The French Chef*, and *Civilisation*.

In 1978, PBS, with funding from CPB, moved from the single-channel terrestrial (telephone line) interconnection into the space age, establishing the nation's first satellite interconnected television system. PBS leased four C-ban transponders (10-watt channels) on a Western Union satellite (*Westar IV*) that allowed PBS to distribute four channels of programming simultaneously. The fuel load on board the satellite was scheduled to be completely exhausted in 1992, causing *Westar IV* to loose its orbit and fall into the earth's atmosphere. This forced PBS to move to its second-generation satellite service, which consists of five KU-band (100-watt) and one C-ban transponders, aboard AT&T's *Telstar 401* satellite, scheduled for launch in late 1993. Temporary arrangements were made on another satellite to cover the transition period. Advances in digital compression will ultimately permit PBS to distribute nearly 40 channels of programming simultaneously with the new system, as well as offer High Definition Television (HDTV) programming, greatly enhancing its capability to service a multitude of educational audiences.

Over the past 20 years, PBS has grown to 346 member public television stations throughout the 50 United States, Puerto Rico, the Virgin Islands, Guam, and American Samoa. The mix of license holders of public television stations has changed considerably over time. The shift has been from a predominance of educational institutions in the early years to a large proportion of community, non-profit organizations and state agencies, followed by colleges and universities and a small handful of school districts. Each member station is governed by its own board of directors. PBS' services to its member stations have grown from operating the interconnection system to program funding, acquisition, and scheduling; education services; press relations; advertising and video promotion; audience research; station development and revenue-producing activities; broadcast and technical operations; and engineering development. PBS has done the Emmy Award–winning, cutting-edge engineering work that has made possible the technologies of closed captioning for the hearing impaired, and has greatly improved reception of UHF television signals, high-fidelity stereo audio, and descriptive video services for the sight-impaired. PBS is governed by a 35-member board of directors made up of approximately 40 percent station professionals and 60 percent lay representatives, all nominated at large and all elected by a vote of the membership.

The annual operating budget has grown to over $420 million, which includes over $300 million for new program production and acquisition. Member stations account for 31 percent of the budget; 25 percent is contributed by self-supporting services like PBS Home Video, PBS Video, and National Datacast; 33 percent from corporate underwriting for program production; and 11 percent from CPB and the U.S. Department of Education (restricted to new program production and education services). It is also important to note that PBS does not produce programs. Program productions funded by PBS are produced by member stations like WNET, New York; WGBH, Boston; and a wide array of independent producers, from the highly visible and successful Children's Television Workshop, to smaller but highly regarded and well-known producers like Ken and Ric Burns, to producers who have yet to gain national recognition. PBS also provides a substantial portion of the production funds required each year by producers of programs distributed by public television stations. A more complete exploration of that area follows later in this chapter.

CPB, which once controlled and disseminated tens of millions of dollars in production funds directly to producers for full production funding, has passed that responsibility on to PBS and has assumed the responsibility for funding only the research, development, and pilot production phases of new program projects. PBS is responsible for providing the major, ongoing production funds and supplemental funding for the full production of programs or program series. Production funds from PBS may also be used to pay for the U.S. broadcast rights for works by the best foreign producers, such as the British Broadcasting Corporation, Thames Television, and Granada Television in Britain. Co-productions between American producers and Canadian, European, Asian, Australian, African, or Latin American producers may also be funded by PBS.

This quick review of PBS should make it clear that PBS is not a government agency, nor is its operation subsidized by the federal government. PBS is a membership organization that receives no direct support from the federal government. The only federal dollars that PBS receives come through CPB and are earmarked for either specific program production support or interconnection hardware and construction costs. All operations costs, including the operation of the interconnection system, are fully funded through membership dues or revenues derived from investment income and self-supporting services. Any net revenues generated by self-supporting services are used to reduce member dues.

In recent years PBS has received a number of different grants from the National Science Foundation and the U.S. Department of Education to develop and deliver a number of different professional development initiatives for teachers throughout the nation. Mathline and Scienceline were created to help teachers develop new strategies for teaching with the national curriculum standards in math and science. TeacherLine was created as an umbrella service under which professional development courses and modules in technology application, math, science, and other content areas can be offered. Using modeling techniques filmed in the classroom, in conjunction with Web-based instructional modules, learning communities, and local initiatives offered by PBS member stations, PBS has been able to maximize its technical delivery systems to extend the reach nationwide to benefit teachers and educators. This type of service would not have been possible without specially earmarked federal grants.

Perhaps an item that needs a bit more clarification is the actual contribution the federal government makes to program production. Overall, less than 10 percent of the total dollars invested in program productions distributed by PBS are provided by the federal funds available from CPB. It is true that some productions have a higher percentage of federal dollars than others, but no programs distributed by PBS are totally funded by the federal government—it is against PBS' program underwriting regulations. PBS is not the copyright owner of the programs it distributes; the producers are. And while the production funding provided by PBS may help producers to clear rights for other distribution, for example, home video, audiovisual (AV), or foreign, the producers continue to own and control those rights and are free to assign those rights to any distributor or, in order to raise additional production capital, to sell off some or all of those rights. That said, however, in recent years PBS has substantially increased its contribution to program productions and has developed a very solid video distribution business. Therefore, PBS has been more active about acquiring home and AV rights for programs in return for production funding.

Many times, however, the producer does not have the fiscal resources to be sure that all of the ancillary uses of his or her intellectual property (the television program) can be fully exploited. For most producers, there are many other people whose needs and demands must be met before the producer can benefit. What follows are the dilemmas that must be faced by producers, distributors, and ultimately, the video or program purchasers.

PROGRAM RIGHTS: PRODUCERS' DILEMMA

Virtually every television or film program involves the creative work of writers, directors, musicians, actors, and many others whose livelihood is derived from compensation received for their craft. This compensation is often based on the various uses made of these individuals' work. Like authors who receive a percentage of their total book sales from the book's publisher, the creative people behind television and film productions may also have the right to share in the dollars earned by the producer. This percentage is compensation for the creative work contributed to the production of the program.

The amount of money earned by each of the involved parties is usually determined through production contracts. In many cases, this amount is a part of a standard, predetermined fee negotiated on the individuals' behalf by the guild or craft union that represents them, such as the Writers' Guild, the Directors' Guild, the American Federation of Television and Radio Artists (AFTRA), the American Federation of Musicians (AFM), and others. In other cases, individuals negotiate separate agreements with the program producers.

In addition to the costs of the creative talents of the people directly involved in an individual production, producers must also clear—receive authorization and pay for—the various use rights for still photographs, stock film footage, music, and record cuts with the owners or copyright holders of each of those production elements. For example, a documentary program might include several hundred different still photos and pieces of film footage obtained from dozens of sources.

To further complicate the process, separate clearances and additional monies are generally required for each different type of use planned for the program— broadcast, commercial cable, educational cable, non-theatrical (educational audiovisual), closed-circuit, public performance, home video, foreign distribution, and digital reproduction.

The payment for these ancillary rights may be in the form of a single, up-front payment, a percentage of the revenues generated by the producer from a program, or a combination of the two. Additionally, the rapid advance of the Internet and the World Wide Web, coupled with broadband and fiber-optic delivery systems have further complicated the picture. The advent of video streaming across the Internet has raised major rights questions as producers, copyright holders, and distributors try to anticipate the financial risks and cost benefits implied by this newest technology.

The producer is therefore faced with what can become a formidable undertaking that involves negotiating numerous contracts; for example, in cases where a guild or union agreement does not apply, conducting extensive research into copyright ownership of various production elements, such as photographs or music. Once the copyright holder is located, the producer must then negotiate the payment for use of the property. Further, negotiating for a broad array of digital rights at a time when no one really has any working knowledge of the potential up- and downside of the new technologies causes great consternation for both producers and rights holders.

All of this work involves the time and talent of many people, and the process costs additional dollars to accomplish. It is not uncommon for a producer who wants to make a single program available for audiovisual distribution to spend between $2,000 and $25,000 to obtain all of the necessary clearances. Clearance costs for program series may exceed $250,000. If home video rights are also cleared, the costs will at minimum double.

These complicated financial realities, together with the fact that it is frequently an uphill battle just to pull together the basic funding for the production costs and broadcast rights clearances (even with the help of investors and bank loans), pose a number of hard questions for the producer. The producer must decide whether the time, energy, and costs involved in clearing ancillary rights for a program can be recovered through the revenues generated from the sale of those rights.

The entire rights clearance picture has been further complicated and muddied for producers by the newest technologies—the Internet, World Wide Web, and digitized video. Producers are now faced with additional rights clearance costs if they want to be able to explore distribution of their works through any of these new technologies. Owners of copyrighted works such as photographs, video clips, and music have found the new technologies to be a major threat in several ways. First, the Internet and the Web are, by their very nature, worldwide in scope. If a producer's work is delivered on the Web he could very easily loose control over its distribution as Web-savvy pirates across the globe can access the work and potentially reproduce it, modify it, and even sell it without legal permission or knowledge by the producer. That means individual photos, film clips, and musical works can be more easily pirated.

Digitization creates similar dilemmas for producers and copyright holders. Digital images can be reproduced with no degradation in quality and can also be easily altered from their original form through the use of a myriad of computer software programs. With the advent of digital compression, digital servers, fiber optics, video editing, computer software, CD-ROM, and interactive DVD technologies, the picture takes on a whole new view. Users no longer simply want to view whole programs; they also increasingly want random access to and use of pieces of those programs. Owners of copyrighted works are rightfully concerned about what will happen to their works if they are released in digital form, or are part of an excerpted video segment. Therefore, copyright holders and producers either refuse to, or are very reluctant to grant those digital and/ or excerpting rights to producers and/or distributors, and, quite naturally, require substantial additional money to allow those rights to be granted.

Unfortunately, many producers are either unable to afford the additional rights clearances at the time of the original rights negotiations, or they find it difficult, if not impossible, to negotiate for digital rights that they need in the current marketplace. Producers are increasingly becoming aware of the revenue potential that can be generated from the marketing of ancillary rights to their programs. Many are building the additional costs of rights clearances into their production budgets and are clearing the rights early in the production process to take advantage of those opportunities. There will, however, continue to be situations where ancillary rights are not cleared due to the lack of potential revenue to recover those costs, the lack of fiscal or staff resources to negotiate the clearance process, or the failure of the producer to plan ahead.

It is extremely important to point out that if a program is broadcast, but does not ultimately go into video or film distribution, there is no legal way for a library or school to obtain and permanently retain a copy of the program or a portion of a program, either through purchase of a prerecorded copy of the work or through off-air taping. There are thousands of programs that appear on public, commercial, and cable television that will never be made available for distribution to the audiovisual or home market, no matter what the price. The reasons will vary, but the inability to clear the rights and the financial realities of clearances and distribution will always play a major role.

The "Guidelines for Off-Air Recording," developed in connection with the 1976 copyright law, does make certain provisions for taping and short-term use of broadcast programming in educational contexts ("Guidelines for Off-Air Recording" 1981; see also Sinofsky 1984). These guidelines stipulate use and retention periods for programming recorded off-air. In order to permanently retain the material (e.g., for repeated use in the classroom, for a library collection, etc.), the user must obtain a license or similar rights from the copyright holder. If, however, the program isn't in distribution, these rights are not available, and the program must eventually be erased.

The more recently developed Fair Use Guidelines for Educational Multimedia (1996) may serve to provide guidance for the application of fair-use principles by educators, scholars, and students who develop multimedia projects using portions of copyrighted works, as part of the systematic learning activity of non-profit educational institutions. Educational multimedia projects combine students' or educators' original material (such as course notes or commentary) together with copyrighted media formats (such as motion media, music, text, graphics, illustrations, photographs, and digital software) into an integrated presentation. (See also Chapter 15 in this book for further discussion of these guidelines.)

Under the guidelines, educators may incorporate portions of lawfully acquired copyrighted works (obtained through lawful means such as purchase, gift, or license) into educational multimedia projects for curriculum-based instruction at educational institutions, and students may do so when producing their own educational multimedia projects for a specific course, subject to certain restrictions.

Because of the high cost of rights clearances, virtually all of the *Great Performances* and *American Masters* programs broadcast by public television stations are not, nor will they ever be, available for distribution. Clearance expenses for audiovisual and/or home video distribution would cost the producers several hundred thousand dollars over a single broadcast season—an amount of money that cannot be recovered through video sales.

PBS Video is committed to contacting producers at the earliest stages of their production planning to acquaint them with the needs and potentials of the audiovisual market. Perhaps with the proper amount of producer education and encouragement—and, when necessary, a little financial help from PBS Video—more of the broadcast programs libraries would wish to acquire will become available in the future.

PROGRAM POTENTIAL: DISTRIBUTORS' DILEMMA

Virtually every television program produced is of interest to someone. Many programs are produced to meet a specific educational objective or classroom need and are intended primarily for audiovisual sale to institutions and organizations. Many more programs, however, are designed to inform, educate, or entertain the population in general and are intended primarily for wider television broadcast or cablecast.

These general interest broadcast programs are very often found to have a strong, ongoing informational and educational value to institutions and agencies. Finding ways of making programs available to these markets is a task jointly shared by the producer and the distributor. The process, however, varies from program to program.

As stated earlier, the rights to a program reside with the producer, who is free to execute a distribution agreement with any distributor he or she pleases. As an alternative, the producer may decide to handle the distribution himself or herself. Programs seen on public television are handled by a wide variety of non-theatrical and home video distributors. The choice of distributor has much to do with who offered the best deal, who had the most to offer, whom the producer felt most comfortable with, or which company bought out another, thus taking over the distribution of the program.

Distributors often become aware of programs or series that are in the development, funding, or early production stages. In such cases, the distributor may approach the producer before a program has been completed to discuss the distribution potential of a program. In other cases, the producer may seek out a distributor for programs that are in production or already produced.

Producers of programs are proud of their work, and most would like to see their programs being used for more than simply open-circuit broadcast. Such ancillary uses not only reaffirm the producer's belief in his or her work but also open new avenues through which some of the production's costs can be partially recovered, or sources of funds for the development of new programming can be cultivated. And assuming that the clearances can be obtained for such ancillary uses, the producer and distributor must explore the best alternatives for marketing these rights.

Producers are interested in selecting a distributor that can best represent their programs in the various ancillary markets and assure the best financial returns. They look for a distributor they can trust to fairly represent the result of their creative energies—their programs. Distributors, on the other hand, must address several major questions about a specific program or series before they determine whether to commit to audiovisual or home distribution of programs that are broadcast on television. The answers to these questions are crucial to making the decision to distribute a specific program or series of programs.

Every program must be scrutinized, and the distributor must answer the following and other questions before committing to a contract for the distribution of a program.

- *Quality: Is it good enough?* Is the content, production quality, and technical quality of the program or series consistent with that expected by the customers? Does it meet our standards? Most distributors are selective about the programs they accept for distribution because the programs reflect on the distributor's reputation for quality. Many programs are rejected simply because the distributor doesn't feel they are of high enough quality.

- *Value: Does it meet a need?* Who might be interested in having access to a program beyond simply viewing it when it is broadcast? Why would a program be of interest to the customers that we serve? In assessing the potential for a program, the distributor must determine the value of the program to the customers it serves and what the various educational or informational uses of the program might be. Many programs are really good television but fail to work in another setting because the program format doesn't lend itself to AV use or home viewing on cassette. Sometimes the questions are easy to answer, but many times they are simply judgment calls based on experience, knowledge, and intuition. Is our judgment always right? Unfortunately, no.

- *Revenue: Will it pay for itself?* How many customers might potentially buy, license, or rent a program? Are there enough agencies and/or individuals willing and able to pay for such use? Can enough revenue be generated to recover the cost of marketing, royalties, distribution, and overhead? Distributors cannot exist unless they can pay their bills, and as is often said, "It takes money to make money." Distributors must invest in every program they distribute, and unless there is sufficient revenue to at least break even, a distributor can't exist for long.

For example, a producer might require an advance payment against future royalties or a royalty guarantee from a distributor. Normally, an advance is used by the producer to cover out-of-pocket costs for clearing the necessary rights. An advance or a guarantee is also a good-faith commitment on the part of the distributor. Such an advance or guarantee can range from $1,000 to over $50,000 for a single program to over $500,000 for a series. What happens if the program or series flops? Can the distributor take the risk to make the program or series available?

Even if there are no advances or guarantees, the distributor must invest in technical costs to create masters for duplicating, and duplicate programs for previews, rentals, and sales; marketing materials and expenses for catalogs, brochures, picture jackets for the cassettes, fliers, mailing lists, advertising, and postage; and perhaps most important, people resources—time and talent committed to one program or series cannot be committed to another.

No one distributor has the financial or human resources to represent all the possible programs or series that are broadcast on television. Therefore, we must be selective about which programs we add to our collections and cautious about taking on more than we can effectively handle. If this caution is not exercised, service to our customers will suffer, and ultimately, we will no longer be in business. However, distributors are inherent risk takers. We realize that in our business there are always programs that do not meet all of the criteria we like to judge them by. Occasionally, the content of a program is so powerful that it demands distribution even though it may be of value to a very small number of people or not have the highest production values or the potential to pay its own way. In such cases, the distributor may still decide to take the risk and offer the program, hoping that other, more successful programs will support the effort to make the program available to those relatively few people who will find it of value.

A new dilemma facing the media distributors is whether or not to invest in the DVD format for programs they distribute. The current cost for converting a standard hour of analog video into a DVD master averages about $20,000. If a distributor wants to add additional features to the DVD, the cost can easily double. The retail price for DVD programs tends to be only slightly higher than the equivalent videocassette version—$24.98 or $29.98, as compared to $19.98 for video. Hypothetically, creating an enhanced DVD set for a nine-part series like Ken Burns' *The Civil War*, for instance, could cost nearly $350,000. That is a major risk for a distributor. There certainly isn't a large enough sales potential in the AV market to make such an investment alone; a successful release in the home video market would be a necessity to make it a worthwhile business risk.

Much like the special interest video market 10 years ago, the special interest DVD market is in its infancy. It is certain that, as in video, the DVD market will be dominated by feature films, and special interest DVDs will occupy a very small niche in that market. There will be a lot of experimentation going on over the coming years, and special interest DVD may or may not be a financially sustainable business venture. Will DVD become the format of choice for video products, like CDs for audio? Or, will videostreaming, chip storage, on-demand downloading of video, or some other type of technology supplant the DVD format before it becomes fully established? These are questions that will plague video distributors as they agonize over the number of different formats they must consider in the future.

PROGRAM COSTS: PURCHASERS' DILEMMA

"Why does that program cost so much? I can go down to the video store and buy a top-rated feature film or special interest video for $20 or less. Why should I pay $50 to $150 for an educational program that was funded with federal money in the first place? I should be getting it free. After all, this is for use in my school!" This might be the reaction of an educator when he or she first sees the price of a program in the PBS Video catalog, or one from another major non-theatrical, non-home video distributor. The reaction is not unusual for those unfamiliar with the pricing structure that has developed for educational media over the years, a structure that is in large part based on the costs of program production, rights clearance, and program distribution.

Program production dollars are aggregated from limited production budgets of local public TV stations, foundations, and corporate underwriters. Funds are also garnered in some instances from a variety of federal agencies or the endowments for the arts or humanities and, occasionally, from co-production dollars from cable or foreign producers. Many times the producer must supplement these dollars with risk funds obtained through bank loans. Risk dollars are paid back with the revenues generated from sales to ancillary markets such as foreign broadcast, audiovisual, home video, and cable. Federal tax dollars rarely provide the majority of production funding for a program or series. Complete funding for a production by the federal government is almost non-existent. Unless a federal agency commissions a work, the copyright almost always remains with the producer. Even if the production is funded with tax dollars, it is virtually never distributed free, nor is it public domain.

Programs sold for AV or educational/institutional use are cleared by a producer and licensed to a distributor. The distributor, in turn, sells (i.e., licenses) the work for use in an educational setting or for educational use by an institution or organization (including patron checkout from a public library or student checkout in a school). Such a license restricts a distributor from selling directly or indirectly to home users.

The question of audiovisual pricing actually boils down to simple mathematics. The educational/institutional market for the last 25 years has consisted of approximately 20,000 to 30,000 schools, libraries, colleges, and other AV buyers who generally purchase a single copy of a program. In most cases, however, a program will not be appropriate for all potential buyers; it will typically be applicable to less than 5,000 to 10,000 buyers.

Statistics have shown that an average of only 2 to 4 percent of potential buyers purchase any given program. Therefore, a broad-appeal program (one that appeals to K–12, colleges, and libraries) can expect to sell somewhere between 400 and 800 copies over the sales life of the program (five to ten years). A more limited-appeal program may only sell 50 to 100 copies.

Producers normally receive between 25 and 30 percent of the gross dollars generated from the sale of their programs in royalties. That means that the revenues returned to the producer to cover clearance costs and any production costs must be generated through a very few sales. Thus, the price of an individual program has necessarily remained fairly high. For example: A particular program costs $250,000 to produce and $5,000 to clear for audiovisual distribution. The price of the program is $250, and 400 copies are sold over a five-year period. With a royalty of 25 percent, the producer would receive $25,000— $5,000 would be used to recover clearance costs, and only $20,000 could be applied to recover production costs or apply to another production.

By comparison, programs sold in the home market are licensed for use in the home. Home video programs may, of course, be used in educational settings; and the current sales trends in the education markets show that schools, colleges, and libraries are buying more and more home video programming, spreading their limited media acquisitions budgets as far as possible. Many educational institutions are reimbursing teachers who purchase programming with their own credit cards, and some institutions are using corporate credit cards to purchase programming, thus bypassing the cumbersome purchase order process. However, depending on the nature of the institution and the nature of the use, separate public performance rights may be required in order to comply with copyright and licensing requirements.

The home video market presently comprises about 30 million potential buyers (homes with videocassette recorders [VCRs]). Given the same ratio, a program might sell 200,000 to 400,000 copies. However, the reality is that homeowners don't buy many videos; they rent them. There are approximately 28,000 video rental stores in the United States, and most of them purchase multiple copies of a title.

A decent feature film will sell over 100,000 copies to rental stores alone. That translates to over $3.0 million for a program that retails at $59.98 and wholesales at $29.98. A producer normally receives between 10 and 15 percent of the wholesale price of a home videocassette. Based on $3.4 million in sales, the producer would receive $450,000 at the 15 percent rate.

More and more home video programs are being initially released for mass-market sales. That means the initial suggested retail price (SRP) is often less than $20. Popular children's programs such as *Teletubbies* and *Barney* have SRPs of under $15. The large retail chains like Wal-Mart and K Mart work on very small margins, further reducing the price they charge for home video programs. When a program does sell well in the retail market the number of sales can be a dramatic 300,000 or more copies. When *Toy Story 2* was released at $24.95, the initial duplication run was over 11 million copies. Sales have exceeded that initial duplication, but with a wholesale price of $13.72, Disney Home Video would have received somewhere between $15 and $30 million from the initial release.

An example of how these numbers play out is PBS' experience with *The Civil War*, the most watched public television series in history and the largest-selling audiovisual series ever by PBS Video. In just under 18 months (beginning 6 months before the series aired on PBS), schools, colleges, libraries, and other AV customers bought nearly 7,000 sets of *The Civil War*—over 60,000 video-cassettes. But compare that to the home video market, where in less than three months of retail distribution, over 40,000 sets, or 360,000 cassettes, of *The Civil War* were sold. In the same 18-month period mentioned above, it is estimated that total home video sales of *The Civil War* through a combination of direct marketing and retail exceeded 100,000 sets, or 900,000 cassettes. It is important to point out, however, that *The Civil War* was an aberration, a phenomenon that won't soon be repeated. The series does, however, provide an interesting point of reference against which to compare sales patterns for other programs.

In 1991, PBS completed two years of research and exploration into the existing home video marketplace. The results showed that the home market was really several markets, each with something to teach about the marketing of "special interest" video to home users. These three distinct marketing options were rental, retail, and direct marketing.

Rental stores make their money by moving "hot" theatrical titles in and out the door, seven days a week. The distributor only generates revenue from the sale of the video to the rental store. Subsequent revenues generated from the multiple rentals of those videos are not shared with the distributor but kept by the rental store. Therefore, most theatrical titles are initially released at somewhere between $59.95 and $89.95 to provide for a wide profit margin and maximize distributor revenue from the initial sale of the video to rental stores. Rental stores don't buy much special interest (educational/informational) programming for their rental collections. Those programs simply don't move off the shelves quickly enough.

The retail market, however, has developed into a successful outlet for special interest video, but only if those videos are priced for "sell-through." Sell-through pricing is that "magic" price that induces people to buy rather than rent. In today's video market, the sell-through price is under $20. If the program is right, and it is priced under $20, it is possible to generate enough sales to recoup a moderate investment. A handful of breakout titles can become special interest best-sellers in the retail market, but even the most successful special interest titles only have sales numbers that compare with a mediocre theatrical title. The retail market is actually a wholesale market. Distributors typically sell their videos to retailers at 40 to 50 percent below retail. A $20 video will wholesale at between $10 and $12. The margins are very tight.

Finally, there is direct selling. This marketing strategy consists of 800-number, toll-free phone ordering from television advertising, print advertising, catalog sales and, most recently, e-commerce sales over the Web. Direct selling of special interest video has good profit margins and holds much promise. The problem with direct sales is that the advertising, direct mail, and fulfillment costs are very high and can quickly destroy the profit margin on low-priced products.

After reviewing the options, PBS determined that the rental market was not viable for its type of programming. Similarly, it was perceived that PBS lacked the expertise and mechanisms to successfully compete in the retail market and could not find enough risk capital ($2 to $3 million) to get a foothold in the direct sales business. Therefore, the best option was to find a commercial video distributor who had the expertise and financial resources to establish the PBS Home Video label for PBS.

The PBS Home Video label was launched through a marketing and licensing agreement between PBS and Pacific Arts in 1991. After several years of working together to establish the PBS Home Video label in the broad home video market, PBS and Pacific Arts came to a parting of the ways. Subsequently, the PBS Home Video label has been marketed through Turner Home Video and then Warner Home Video after the merger between the two media giants. Over the nearly 10 years since entering the home video market, PBS and its various commercial partners have garnered a great deal of knowledge about the home video market for special interest videos and DVDs:

- Some programs sell much better than others. This is not surprising—the pattern of success and failure is elusive. Trying to figure out what the public will buy is like trying to read tea leaves. A seemingly sure hit will be a dud, and a high-risk program will catch the imagination and sell.

- The 800 toll-free numbers at the end of programs don't necessarily generate significant sales. A tag at the end of a program can result in orders for a few dozen copies or many thousands; it depends totally on the program and how that program grabs the interest of the viewers. Timing of the broadcast is also an important factor. If a program is popular and airs in the spring or summer, sales will be far less than if that same program were to air in the final quarter of the calendar year—Christmas sales account for a major portion of annual retail video sales. In October 1998, PBS aired the three-part *Stephen Hawking's Universe* series. In November, Ken Burns' *Lewis and Clark* documentary aired on PBS. By Christmas, PBS had sold over 30,000 copies of the

Hawkings series and 40,000 copies of *Lewis and Clark* through direct sales from catalogs, on-air tags, and e-commerce.

- E-commerce sales are a fast-growing source of video sales and should be an integral part of an overall home video sales strategy.

- Retailers will keep a title on the shelf for a very short time (30 to 90 days); if it doesn't move, back it goes to the distributor for a full credit. This is known in the industry as "selling on wheels." Shelf space is at a premium, and the only titles that get the shelf space are those that move. If a title doesn't work in the retail stores, the catalogs are sometimes the answer. People often don't react quickly enough to catch a video during its initial retail cycle. However, if they see a program in a video catalog several weeks or months after they viewed it, they frequently order it.

- The retail (read wholesale) release of programs can, and most likely will, devastate the audiovisual sales of the same program or series. The copyright law provides schools with a fair-use exemption when a program is used as a part of face-to-face classroom teaching. Thus, it is perfectly legal for a school to purchase a home video for curricular use or to put it in the school library for a student or teacher to check out and take home to view. If the home video version of a program is cheaper than the audiovisual version of the same program, it is very clear which the educator will choose.[1]

The Dilemma

Educational media materials are selected and purchased because of their value to the educational process. Textbooks are used instead of paperbacks in most cases and certainly cost substantially more. It stands to reason, therefore, that if an educational videocassette has more value as a teaching tool, it should also be included in school, college, and library video collections, even if the cost is comparatively high.

Currently, the number of educational media purchasers remains comparatively small, and the unit prices of educational video consequently continue to remain relatively high. If educational/institutional buyers are unwilling to continue to purchase these programs, but instead turn to purchasing the home video programs alone, many programs will cease to be available for purchase and others will simply not be produced. However, change is inevitable, particularly in the video marketplace.

Ten years ago, nearly all films and videocassettes were purchased by the district or regional media center in K–12 schools, by the regional or central circulating library in public libraries, and by the media center in colleges. Today, more and more videocassettes are being purchased at the school, branch library, and individual college department levels. Therefore, the number of potential audiovisual customers has grown dramatically. In fact, the trend is already having an effect on the pricing of videocassettes for audiovisual uses. PBS Video's release of *Eyes on the Prize*, at $59.95 per program, permitted hundreds of new customers to purchase the series at reduced prices. Many programs will continue to appeal to a very few purchasers, and the prices will remain relatively high. After all, it's all a numbers game. Currently, most AV programs distributed by PBS are priced at less than $59.95, and, as mentioned earlier, most of the new AV customers are purchasing the home video version of a video, rather than the higher-priced AV version.

In some ways, the reduction of prices by video distributors for broad-appeal programs was an experiment. Distributors were attempting to determine whether there are sufficient numbers of purchasers to allow the return of the same or higher royalties to producers while still being able to pay our bills. These experiments have proven to be successful; the volume of sales has increased, and the prices of nearly all programs have come down. However, it is also true that many titles are not being put into distribution because the lower prices, combined with still limited sales because of limited appeal content, make those titles a poor business risk. Some distributors have no alternative but to retain the higher prices necessitated by low-volume sales. It is also true that the reduction in video pricing by numerous distributors is in response to the realities of a marketplace that is turning to home video as a less costly alternative for video products.

In closing this overview of current video rights and distribution issues, it is important to point out that there are fundamental changes looming on the horizon. The rapid rise in demand for DVD and interactive DVD-ROM programs is forcing producers to look at a whole new rights clearance problem: excerpt or segmentation rights—the right for a portion of a video work to be lifted from the original work and inserted with other video clips, print, and data to create an entirely new product.

New digital technologies may eliminate the need for shipping hard copies of videos to educators in the not-too-distant future, as fiber-optic, digital compression of television signals, and others are brought online by both public and commercial companies and agencies. Education services and electronic or digital delivery not only will be offered through public television but also will be widely available through cable television systems and the telephone companies.

No matter where technology takes us, however, there will continue to be some basic principles that must be followed. First, copyright costs will still have to be paid for a variety of different uses that will be made of artists' creative work, that is, writing, acting, directing, music, photos, and film footage. Second, the costs of rights clearances will have to be recouped from the revenues generated from the licensing of those rights. At times the economics will simply be impossible to overcome, and rights will not be cleared for some uses of some programs. Finally, distributors and producers will have to be able to at least cover their costs, or the programs will not be marketed.

NOTE

1. It is very important to note that the home video version of a title very often does not have public performance rights attached to it (while the higher-priced educational

market version almost always does). While the use of the home video version in the classroom may be permitted under the fair-use (i.e., face-to-face teaching) provisions of the copyright law, other uses of the title—in-library programs, extracurricular school programs, and the like—may require securing separate performance rights. One of the differences between a $20 tape purchased from a retail outlet or vendor and the same tape purchased for $50 directly from an educational distributor is the inclusion of these rights.

REFERENCES

Burke, John Edward. 1979. *An Historical-Analytical Study of the Legislative and Political Origins of the Public Broadcasting Act of 1967*. New York: Arno Press.

Carnegie Commission on Educational Television. 1967. *Public Television: A Program for Action*. New York: Bantam Books.

"Guidelines for Off-Air Recording of Broadcast Programming for Educational Purposes." 1981. U.S. *Congressional Record* (October 14): E4751. See also: http://www.lib.berkeley.edu/MRC/Kastenmeier.html.

Sinofsky, Esther R. 1984. *Off-Air Videotaping in Education*. New York: Bowker.

United States. *Legislative History of the Public Broadcasting Act, 1967: PL 90–129 (S. 1160) 81 Stat. 365*. 1971. Englewood, CO: Information Handling Services.

RECOMMENDED READING

Avery, Robert K. 1979. *The Politics of Interconnection: A History of Public Television at the National Level*. Washington, DC: National Association of Educational Broadcasters.

Bullert, B. J. 1997. *Public Television: Politics and the Battle over Documentary Film*. New Brunswick, NJ: Rutgers University Press.

Jarvik, Laurence Ariel. 1997. *PBS, behind the Screen*. Rocklin, CA: Forum.

Keeffe, Mary Ann. 1982. *Public Broadcasting: History, Organization, and Funding*. Washington, DC: Library of Congress, Congressional Research Service.

Pepper, Robert M. 1979. *The Formation of the Public Broadcasting Service*. New York: Arno Press.

Stewart, David C. 1999. *The PBS Companion: A History of Public Television*. New York: TV Books.

Part VI

Resources

Chapter 18

Video Reference Tools and Selection Aids

Rebecca Albitz

INTRODUCTION

While librarians of all types face a myriad of bibliographic challenges on a daily basis, media librarians are regularly confronted by two particular pitfalls that seem to consistently mire their work. The first, which has been mentioned either directly or obliquely by other chapter authors, is locating distribution sources for titles desired for purchase, particularly non-feature titles such as educational videos, documentaries, and other works outside of the home video market. The relative ease of acquiring home video titles and the relative difficulty in identifying titles and purchase sources for the rest of the video universe is not surprising. Opportunities and venues for buying feature films and mass-marketed non-fiction videos seem to be everywhere these days—from big book jobbers, to e-commerce sellers, to retail stores and wholesale outlets (see Chapters 10 and 16 in this book on the workings of the video marketplace). Given the enormous markets involved, the videographic coverage for Hollywood features and other popular titles is better now than ever. The real difficulties lie beyond this mainstream. The small, independent nature of much of the educational and documentary video marketplace has historically worked against the development of effective, consolidated videographies for these materials. It is also the case that due to the volatility of this market, even the best-known educational or documentary titles may change distributors or go out of distribution with no notice.

The second challenge routinely faced by media librarians is locating current evaluative information about new non-feature titles. Again, while movie reviews and review indexes, both in print and online, are plentiful, evaluations and reviews of non-fiction videos continue to be limited and difficult to locate.

This chapter will provide a discussion of resources that will aid media librarians working in all types of libraries in overcoming these two daunting challenges. The first section of this chapter will focus on print and online tools designed to assist the media buyer in locating a specific title or a video on a certain topic. The second section will discuss review sources for educational video titles. The final section of this chapter will provide a bibliographic listing of those resources described throughout this chapter, as well as a number of more specialized tools.

VIDEO REFERENCE TOOLS

The single most time-consuming part of the media librarian's job is locating sources for acquiring specific non-feature videos. Even with access to complete production information, locating a distributor can be difficult. More often than not, however, a title is the only information available. Even more commonly, a patron will request a program seen on PBS or another television station, and remember the topic but not the title (and certainly not the director, producer, or other production specifics). The challenge is to know where to begin looking, whether you have complete information or only bits and pieces. A number of different reference tools, both print and electronic, are available to help the video selector locate videos primarily by title, but also by subject or genre. The following print reference resources are an excellent place to begin your search.

Print Directories

When faced with the need to confirm a specific book title, determine if it is still in print, and locate publication information, all librarians would immediately reach for *Books in Print*. Unfortunately, because of the ever-changing nature of the video market and the relatively insubstantial portion of this marketplace occupied by non-feature videos, no such single publication exists for documentary and educational video titles. Instead, a number of different directories must be consulted due, in part, to the inevitable delay between compilation and publication that occurs with print directories. When used in tandem, these references provide useful, although far from comprehensive, coverage of available non-feature video titles. While entries are organized alphabetically by title in these reference works, in all cases there is an attempt to provide some subject and production information access through cross-referencing and indexing. Two of the most comprehensive print video directories currently available are *Bowker's Complete Video Directory* and *The Video Source Book*. Both of these titles are published annually; both cover educational/documentary/special interest videos and feature films. *Bowker's* divides video titles into two distinct categories:

"Entertainment" and "Special Interest and Educational." Each entry contains production and credit information, a brief description of the contents of the program, format availability (VHS, 16mm, DVD), and ordering and pricing information. *Bowker's* has recently become available on CD-ROM (*Bowker's Complete Video Directory on Disc*), replacing Bowker's earlier CD-ROM product, *Variety's Video Directory Plus*. Updated quarterly, this electronic version also contains over 5,000 full-text reviews for those programs that have been reviewed in *Variety*, along with the same title/production/subject information provided in the print edition. As of this writing, a total of 200,000 titles, including 100,000 non-feature titles are listed in the Bowker directory.

A resource that parallels much of *Bowker's Video Directory* is *The Video Source Book* (Gale Group). Originating 21 years ago, *The Video Source Book* was the first print reference guide to available video titles, preceding *Bowker's* first appearance by 11 years. The publication currently includes information for around 160,000 videos. Organization of *The Video Source Book* is slightly different from *Bowker's*. Rather than creating separate volumes for feature/entertainment videos and educational/special interest titles, *The Video Source Book* combines all titles into one alphabetical listing. Like the Bowker directory, *The Video Source Book* provides a general subject index, utilizing broad terms such as "nursing" or "puppets." Also, feature films are grouped along with the educational titles under the same general subject categories, while *Bowker's* employs a genre-based organizational system for entertainment titles. Both the Bowker and Gale directories offer various appendix information, such as a directory of distributors and producers, awards information, and special formats indexes (e.g., closed-captioned materials, DVDs, other digital/optical formats). While there is substantial overlap in title coverage between these two directories, and while some of the data included in both tend to be out-of-date or questionable, checking both will provide the media librarian with the most comprehensive list of videos in print.

A resource that was created primarily to serve video rental stores, but may also be of use to the media librarian who regularly purchases mainstream videos, is *Videolog*. Produced in a looseleaf format, *Videolog* focuses on feature and entertainment videos produced by major studios or film production companies. This resource is organized by genre, which includes some educational and documentary titles. The most current of any of the print reference tools cited, *Videolog* is updated weekly. Because it lists studio distributors rather than standard library distributors, *Videolog* is most useful to verify purchase availability. *Videolog* is available in an electronic version, in disk format, for Windows and DOS.

Electronic Directories and Databases

Commercial Databases

The first extensive database of audiovisual information was produced by the National Information Center for Educational Media (NICEM), started at the

University of Southern California in late 1950s. Now a commercially produced product, the NICEM database is available in both CD-ROM and Web-based versions (superseding NICEM's earlier print product, *Film/Video Locator*). Web versions of the NICEM database (with slightly variant search interfaces) are currently available from SilverPlatter (AV On-line) (http://www.silverplatter. com), The Library Corporation (AV MARC), (http://www.tlcdelivers.com), EBSCOhost (NICEM AV) (http://www.epnet.com) and directly from NICEM (http://www.nicem.com). CD-ROM versions of the database are currently available from both SilverPlatter and The Library Corp. The semi-annually updated NICEM database contains plain text and MARC-formatted records for over 605,000 non-print educational items, including film, video, audio materials, and other media. These items are searchable by title, date, age level, and subject area, media type, distributor, and other fields. Subject searching is controlled by a thesaurus compiled by NICEM that incorporates both Library of Congress and Sears subject headings. Like the Bowker and Gale directories discussed above, the coverage of the NICEM database is substantial, but hardly comprehensive.

Once the hurdle of determining a video's availability and distributor has been cleared, locating contact information for the distributor can create an equally daunting challenge. Fortunately, there are several print and online resources that can be of assistance. As discussed above, both print and electronic versions of the *Bowker's Complete Video Directory*, and the print *The Video Source Book* contain useful directories of distributors, producers, and service providers. Although NICEM no longer offers direct access to its separate distributor address database, the full NICEM database allows searching by distributor and producer name (such a search pulls up all the entries for that distributor, which include address information). The Web site for the review publication *The Video Librarian* (discussed at length below) contains a searchable database of distributors whose works have been reviewed in that publication (http://videolibrarian.com /producers.html). Finally, the University of California, Berkeley Media Resources Center maintains a listing of over 1,000 video and film distributors at its Web site, http://www.lib.berkeley.edu/MRC/Distributors.html.

Bibliographic Utilities and Online Public Access Catalogs

Perhaps the single best electronic reference resource one can use to at least preliminarily identify media titles is Online Computer Library Center, Inc's. (OCLC) WorldCat. An international shared cataloging utility and union catalog containing the holdings of its member institutions, WorldCat contains over 42 million records. Of these 42 million, more than 900,000 are for titles classified as visual materials. Because WorldCat contains records from academic, public, special, and school libraries, the broadest variety of media titles are represented. A study undertaken by Joseph Palmer in 1990 (Palmer 1991) indicated that OCLC was far more current and comprehensive in its coverage of the video publication universe than either *Bowker's Video Directory* or *Video Source*

Book. Although Palmer's study is over a decade old, anecdotal evidence suggests that this situation has not changed in the intervening 10 years.

For some classes of videos, WorldCat is particularly important. It is useful for identifying videos not distributed through mainstream distribution channels, including those produced by professional, educational, and special interest groups. WorldCat also contains a large number of unique, locally produced videos from member libraries and archives—everything from regional histories, to local cable programming, to the visual documentation of scholarly research. Because OCLC records are cataloged according to Anglo-Amercan Cataloging Rules (AACR2) and use standardized subject headings, media titles can be located easily, not just by title and keyword, but also by Library of Congress or Sears subject headings. The fact that OCLC identifies libraries owning particular videos is also important, since an increasing number of libraries are willing to interlibrary-loan videos.

On the negative side, the records in WorldCat are bibliographic snapshots of the items at the time they were cataloged. Videos may no longer be in distribution, or their distributors may have changed since the time the piece was cataloged; and, because WorldCat records are primarily bibliographic records (as opposed to collection development or acquisition records), entries usually do not indicate distribution or price information (see Palmer 1993 for a discussion of this liability). Fortunately, this information can usually be obtained by using one or more of the directories or online resources discussed in the sections above.

Another union catalog that the media librarian might find useful is The Research Libraries Information Network (RLIN). An online cataloging utility and bibliographic database similar to OCLC/WorldCat, RLIN also represents the holdings of academic, public, and special member libraries, but with emphasis on large research libraries. As is the case with OCLC, holdings reflected in RLIN are cataloged using AACR2, providing thorough subject access, which is invaluable to the researcher who needs to locate media titles by topic. Despite its usefulness for media librarians, the RLIN database is not nearly as extensive as WorldCat, nor is there the variety of video genres represented.

OCLC/WorldCat and RLIN are both subscription services that some institutions may not be able to afford. An alternative online strategy that provides many of the same advantages of searching an automated national union catalog without the cost is to search the online public access catalogs (OPACs) of institutions with large existing media collections. With a modem and an Internet service provider anyone can search the catalogs of hundreds of academic and public libraries across the country. The trick to exploiting this resource fully is to know where some of the large, thoroughly cataloged collections are housed. The University of California, Berkeley (http://www.lib.berkeley.edu), Indiana University (http://www.indiana.edu/~libweb), New York University (http://www.nyu.edu/library/bobst), American University (http://www.lib.american.edu), and the Chicago Public Library (http://www.chipublib.org/cpl.html) all house substantial, diverse collections cataloged fully using AACR2 and Library of Congress subject headings. Some of these institutions, such as UC Berkeley (http://www.lib.berkeley.edu/MRC), have also produced large videographic Web sites for their holdings that allow searching topically or in other unique ways. While no single library's collection can equal OCLC or RLIN for number and variety of titles, an OPAC is certainly an inexpensive, convenient place to begin an online search when these other resources are not available.

Video Distributor Catalogs and Current Awareness Publications

The previous print and electronic resources discussed cover a broad spectrum of genres and subjects, allowing the user to see a large portion of the videos that have been or are currently in distribution. Video distributor catalogs are resources that provide a more focused and timely listing of currently available titles, sometimes concentrated on specific genres, formats, or subject areas. Printed and disseminated by video distribution or production companies as marketing tools, these catalogs can serve as extremely useful selection and current awareness tools. The challenge in using such catalogs is that they are not indexed in any one resource; the media librarian needs to be aware of the distribution companies that specialize in certain subjects or genres and request a catalog. Once on a distributor's mailing list, the flow of catalogs, for better or worse, is usually unstoppable. As one might expect in these days of e-commerce mania, many distributor catalogs, either in full or in part, have migrated to the Web.

Some major video distributor catalogs are more like substantive reference works than marketing tools. Facets Multimedia (http://www.facets.org), a Chicago-based film repertory cinema and video distribution and rental operation, produces a tome of over 600 pages, listing those video titles they either sell or rent. The catalog includes perhaps the best single collection of international cinema available on video in the United States. Facets also distributes an increasingly impressive list of non-feature works, including popular and independently produced documentaries, children's video, and educational titles. As a collection development tool, *Facets' Complete Video Catalog* is invaluable (the catalog is also available online at http://www.facets.org). The large print catalog is organized by genre, country of origin, or language in which the video was produced. Language and country of origin take precedence over genre in this organizational scheme. Some of the genre groupings are: Independent American Cinema, Animation, Documentary Cinema, and Children's Video. Entries for titles include intelligently written synopses, director, and release year. Title, director, and short film indices provide further access to this collection. The Short Film Index lists, by title, short films that are contained within a compilation tape. For example, if a copy of "A Diary for Timothy" is needed, this index says that this short documentary is on a compilation tape called *Listen to Britain*.

In addition to its main catalog Facets also regularly produces smaller, supplementary catalogs, including new titles listings, genre listings, national cinema
listings, and other specialized videographies. Facets Multimedia has also published several larger and more focused videographies in monographic form—
subsets of titles culled from their main catalog. Two of the best-known guides
are *Facets Gay and Lesbian Video Guide* (McGavin 1993) and *Facets African-
American Video Guide* (Ogle 1994). While duplicating information that is already available in Facets' main catalog, these guides are useful to the media
librarian who is concentrating purchasing efforts on specific areas of the collection.

A mass-market distributor that offers a catalog equally as impressive as Facets' (at least in physical size and number of titles included) is Movies Unlimited.
More of a mainstream, consumer-oriented operation than Facets, the Movies
Unlimited 800+ page catalog contains an astoundingly large list of videos and
DVDs, ranging from hot new movies and international cinema classics, to TV
and movie ephemera; from soft-porn to popular educational and documentary
works. Like the Facets catalog, the Movies Unlimited listing can be searched
on the Web (http://www.moviesunlimited.com). Both Facets and Movies Unlimited online catalogs have fairly crude search capabilities, and during peak use
periods their search engines slow down considerably. Both catalogs are, nonetheless, exceptionally useful collection development and acquisition tools.

Large library material jobbers, such as Baker & Taylor and Ingram, are well
established in the area of mass-market video distribution. Most of these firms
offer periodic publications that highlight new and notable offerings. Baker &
Taylor (http://www.btol.com/library.cfm), for example, publishes a newsletter
entitled *Video Alert*. This monthly publication provides new release information
for feature films, special interest video, and children's productions. Similarly,
Ingram Library Video (http://www.ingramlibrary.com) publishes a number of
Video Highlights publications that serve as a selector advisory service for video
librarians. In addition to its newsletter, Baker & Taylor also offers a number of
other online and print collection development tools and guides for video, via a
subsidiary company, Professional Media Services (http://www.promedia.com/).

Finally, for mass-market educational videos, documentaries, how-to's, and
other popular mainstream non-fiction titles, it is hard to beat the megalithic
Amazon.com or its online competitors, such as Barnes & Noble (http://www.
bn.com). By all measures Amazon's offerings are enormous. One can consequently think of the Amazon Web site as kind of electronic *Books in Print* for
popular video. Other major Internet video distributors are discussed in Chapter
10 in this book.

Besides broad-based home video distributors such as those described above,
a number of popular educational and specialized video distributors also produce
large, general catalogs. PBS Video—the bedrock of most library video collections—publishes an annual catalog as well as updates called *PBS Video News*.
For the media librarian looking for programs that are part of a series that ap-

peared on PBS (e.g., *NOVA, The American Experience*), or a single program, this is an excellent collection development tool. PBS Video also produces a weekly electronic newsletter highlighting new programming, called *PBS Preview*. Information about subscribing to this free service is available on PBS' home page at http://www.pbs.org.

The common difficulty in finding information about non-mainstream, independently produced and distributed videos—particularly videos exclusively distributed by a single firm—has been discussed earlier. In light of this difficulty, obtaining a regular supply of catalogs from key independent distributors is essential.

Knowing the content specialties and styles of particular video distributors is the key to efficiently utilizing their catalogs for collection development purposes. For example, if you are seeking an independent production in which a filmmaker addresses personal issues surrounding women and abortion, then one of the first catalogs you might consider is published by Women Make Movies (http://www.wmm.com). This distributor handles independently produced video titles made by women, and focuses on issues of importance to women in all cultures. A number of other chapters in this book provide extensive listings of independent distributors that specialize in specific topical areas (see, for example, Chapter 19 in this book on resources for building multicultural video collections, Chapter 20 on alternative media, and Chapter 5 on health science collections).

Listservs

Where can you turn when you are looking for a specific title and all of the reference resources described in the previous sections fail? The answer is VIDEOLIB, a listserv established by the ALA's Video Round Table (VRT). This discussion forum links hundreds of media librarians from all types of libraries throughout the world. The collective wisdom and experience of this group of subscribers usually results in quick, accurate answers to questions concerning video title availability, distributor information, and pricing. VIDEOLIB is also a useful vehicle for locating titles on a specific topic. For example, a recent query requesting videos about the Tennessee Valley Authority resulted in a number of useful suggestions. The sister listserv to VIDEOLIB is VIDEONEWS, an electronic bulletin board devoted to announcements from video producers and distributors about new products and services. VIDEO-NEWS is also a useful avenue through which the video collection development librarian can hear about the latest programs. Subscription and policy information for both of these listservs is available at http://www.lib.berkeley.edu/VideoLib/.

SELECTION AIDS

Locating a specific title can be a challenge, but determining the quality of a video production can be even more time-consuming for the media librarian.

Unlike the plethora of review sources available for books of all kinds, as well as for feature films, there are a limited number of current review publications for educational and special interest videos. Dishearteningly, there seem to be fewer such resources now than 10 years ago, perhaps an indication of the fragility of this portion of the video marketplace. Another means of determining the quality of programming prior to purchase is through a series of "year's best" and "notables" lists that are compiled by a variety of groups. Along with reviews these lists provide media collection development librarians with guidance as they select titles to round out their collections.

Review Sources

Indexes and Journals

The differences in availability of review sources between feature films and educational or special interest titles are dramatic. Most general interest news magazines (*Time, Newsweek*), newspapers (*U.S.A. Today*, the *New York Times*), and popular or general interest magazines (*Entertainment Weekly, New Yorker*) carry reviews for films released in theaters and which will eventually be available on video. Locating these reviews is also easy as these serials are all indexed in standard references resources like *Reader's Guide to Periodical Literature* and *ProQuest Direct* (see the appendixes to Chapter 10 in this book for a selective listing of movie review sources and indexes). Serials that review non-feature titles are scarce, primarily because the potential audience for these titles is limited. The serials that focus on these productions tend to be library trade journals, film journals, or discipline-specific academic publications. *Booklist* (http://www.ala.org/booklist/) and *Library Journal* (http://www.libraryjournal.reviewsnews.com) devote sections to video reviews. Each covers educational titles, how-to's, and some independent and unusual fiction videos. These journals are indexed by a number of print and online resources, so locating reviews for a specific title is possible. Both titles, however, have the same two drawbacks. The first is that each reviews a limited number of titles in each issue—a far lower percentage of new video titles than each journal's book coverage. The second is that the reviews tend to appear long after the video's initial release date, limiting their usefulness to the media collection development librarian who is looking for the most current information.

The best resource for special interest video reviews is *The Video Librarian* (http://www.videolibrarian.com). This bi-monthly serial focuses solely on reviewing new video titles, although feature articles and editorials are also staples of the publication. Because the number of video reviews included in each issue of *The Video Librarian* is larger than either of the other two journals mentioned above, the range and variety of titles covered are broader, and the reviews are more current.

One reference resource that gathers review information from a variety of different publications is *Media Review Digest* (MRD) (http://www.pierianpress. com). Published annually since 1973, MRD indexes both feature and non-feature films and videos reviewed in over 140 international journals, including media-related titles, subject-specialized journals, and general periodical literature. A Web-based version of MRD is also available. Both print and online versions offer a great deal of valuable information, including awards information, indications of positive or negative reviews, and short quotes from reviews. MRD offers a one-stop approach to video reviews, which can be quite useful. Unfortunately, because of standard delays in gathering, collating, and publishing this kind of reference tool, information provided in the print version of MRD tends to be dated, limiting this version's usefulness to those seeking retrospective reviews rather than current ones. The Web version of MRD purportedly resolves the timeliness issue. Updated weekly, and providing retrospective coverage back to 1989, this electronic version indexes approximately 30,000 reviews, awards, and prizes. Beginning with the information from the 1996 edition, the MRD database includes an increasing number of links to related Web resources for selected titles reviewed, including links to full-text reviews and credits from the Internet Movie Database. While the majority of these reviews are for feature films, some full-text reviews for educational titles are also available. A subscription to MRD also allows the subscribing library to link a video record in its OPAC directly to the index entry for the title in MRD through the inclusion of the 856 field in the MARC record.

Notables Lists and Core Lists

Reviews are useful collection development tools, allowing the media librarian to gain another professional's insight into the quality of a particular program. Another useful tool that can assist the buyer in locating current quality programming is "year's best" or "notables" lists. Such lists are common for books, from the National Book Awards, to the *New York Times*, to the American Library Association's *Notable Books List*. These types of lists and awards are generally selected by panels of professional experts and bear the type of authority and credibility not always present in reviews by individuals. Such lists can be quite useful as selection aids and as a way of learning about the best and brightest recent offerings. Although not as common as book lists, a number of video "best" lists of non-feature videos are currently available. Three different committees within ALA generate notable videos lists. The ALA Video Round Table (VRT) selects the best videos produced during the previous two years that are appropriate for high school and adult audiences. The VRT notables list is available on the Web at: http://www.ala.org/vrt. The Association for Library Services to Children (ALSC) publishes its list of notable children's media titles (http://www.ala.org/alsc). ALSC also annually awards the Andrew Carnegie Medal for Excellence in Children's Video (http://www.ala.org/alsc/carnegie. html) to honor outstanding video productions for children released during the previous year. Finally, the Young Adult Library Services Association (YALSA)

of ALA generates its list Selected Videos for Young Adults (http://www.ala.
org/yalsa/booklists/video). These three lists are compiled during the winter and
are available to the media librarian in the March 15 issue of *Booklist*. *Booklist*
also publishes an "Editor's Choice" issue each January that includes a section
on video and other media (the latest *Booklist* selections are available at http://
www.ala.org/booklist/).

For print materials, there exists a large and venerable body of publications
developed by librarians to define core collections for particular types of libraries
or for particular subject areas. Few such lists currently exist for video, however,
and those that do, such as *Video for Libraries: Special Interest Video for Small
and Medium-sized Public Libraries* (Mason and Scholtz 1988) and *Video Movies: A Core Collection for Libraries* (Pitman and Swanson 1990), are sadly out
of date. But, these older listings are useful when building an initial collection
or doing retrospective purchasing to fill in subject gaps. The relatively current
core video lists, most of which are compiled by non-librarians, tend to be subject
specific. Examples of these highly specialized videographies include such works
as *A Critical Guide to Management Training Media* (Ellet and Winig 1996),
and *Videos of African and African-Related Performance: An Annotated Bibliography* (Lems-Dworkin 1996). Although more of an entertaining and informative exercise among colleagues than a rigorous professional enterprise,
members of the VIDEOLIB listserv, during the spring of 2000, jointly developed
a core video list comprised of 96 series titles and over 225 individual titles for
all age groups. The list, posted at http://www.lib.berkeley.edu/MRC/corefinal.
html, will, it is hoped, continue to be updated by VIDEOLIB members.

REFERENCES

The following reference publications and review sources are those the media collection
development librarian will find most useful in ascertaining the availability and usefulness
of educational video titles.

Palmer, J. W. 1991. "Bibliographic Control of Videos: A Second Look." *Public Libraries*
(March/April): 106–111
Palmer, J. W. 1993. "Obtainability of Specialized Subject Videos Found with OCLC's
EPIC." *RQ* (Fall): 101–109.

Directories, Catalogs, and Indexes

Bowker's Complete Video Directory. Annual. New Providence, NJ: R. R. Bowker.
Ellet, William, and Winig, Laura, eds. 1996. *A Critical Guide to Management Training
Media*. Boston: Harvard Business School Publishers.
Facets' Complete Video Catalog. Annual. Chicago: Facets Multimedia. Distributed by
Academy Chicago Publishers.
Lems-Dworkin, Carol. 1996. *Videos of African and African-Related Performance: An
Annotated Bibliography*. Evanston, IL: C. Lems-Dworkin Publishers. http://
members.aol.com/lemsdworkn/.

Mason, Sally, and Scholtz, James, eds. 1988. *Video for Libraries: Special Interest Video for Small and Medium-Sized Public Libraries*. Chicago: ALA.

McGavin, Patrick Z. 1993. *Facets Gay and Lesbian Video Guide*. Chicago: Facets Multimedia. Distributed by Academy Chicago Publishers.

Media Review Digest. Annual. Ann Arbor, MI: Pierian Press (also available on the Web at http://www.pierianpress.com).

Ogle, Patrick, comp. 1994. *Facets African-American Video Guide*. Chicago: Facets Multimedia. Distributed by Academy Chicago Publishers.

Pitman, Randy, and Swanson, Elliott. 1990. *Video Movies: A Core Collection for Libraries*. Santa Barbara, CA: ABC-CLIO.

The Video Source Book. Annual. Farmington Hills, MI: Gale Group. http://www.gale.com.

Videolog. Weekly. San Diego, CA: Trade Service Publications (10996 Torreyana Road, San Diego, CA 92121–1192).

Journals and Newsletters

Library Journal. Monthly. New York: R. R. Bowker. http://www.libraryjournal.com.
PBS Video News. Washington, DC: PBS Video.
Video Alert. Monthly. Morton Grove, IL: Baker & Taylor.
The Video Librarian. Bi-monthly. Seabeck, WA: Randy Pitman. http://videolibrarian.com/.

Online Resources

Bowker's Complete Video Directory on Disc. New Providence, NJ: R. R. Bowker. Updated quarterly. (Formerly titled *Variety's Video Directory Plus*.)

RECOMMENDED RESOURCES

Directories, Catalogs, Indexes

Boyle, Virginia A. 1996. *Facets Non-Violent, Non-Sexist Children's Video Guide*. Chicago: Facets Multimedia. Distributed by Academy Chicago Publishers.

Costello, Tom, ed. 1994. *International Guide to Literature on Film*. London: K. G. Saur.

Karsten, Eileen, and Gross, Dorothy-Ellen. 1993. *From Real Life to Reel Life: A Filmography of Biographical Films*. Metuchen, NJ: Scarecrow Press.

Towers, Deirdre. 1991. *The Dance Film and Video Guide*. Princeton, NJ: Dance Horizons/Princeton Book Co.

Journals and Newsletters

The Independent. New York: Association of Independent Video and Film Makers. http://www.aivf.org/. Established in 1978, the Independent Film and Video Monthly provides valuable coverage of independent media, including both documentary and feature films. Each issue includes profiles of filmmakers, producers, and distributors, festival listings, the scoop on new technology, coverage of political trends and legislation affecting independents, and reports from film festivals and markets around the world.

Science Books and Films. Washington, DC: American Association for the Advancement of Science (1200 New York Avenue N.W., Washington, DC 20005; http://www. sbfonline.com).

Online Resources

Art on Screen Database. http://www.artfilm.org/aosdb.htm. An international compilation of bibliographic information about moving-image productions on the visual arts. Includes listings of film, video, videodisc, multimedia and CD-ROM productions. The database includes more than 25,000 records, representing productions from some 70 countries. The majority of these productions date from 1970 to the present, with selective coverage of earlier productions from 1915 through 1969. A related database includes names and addresses of more than 5,000 distributors and producers of moving-image productions.

A-V Online. Norwood, MA: SilverPlatter. Updated semiannually. http://www.silver platter.com/catalog/avol.htm.

Chapter 19

Screening Differences: Resources for Building Culturally Diverse Video Collections

Gary P. Handman

As is discussed in Chapter 9 on multicultural video collections, the terms "multiculturalism" and "diversity" are problematic on a number of levels. These and other rubrics pertaining to the heterogeneous nature of American culture have entered the contemporary lexicon as a kind of imprecise and often politically charged shorthand that can signify substantially different things, depending on the context of usage and the user. For the purposes of this resource listing, the concept of multiculturalism is employed in a broadly inclusive sense. The videographies, filmographies, and reference works provided in the list below focus largely on the provinces most traditionally associated with multiculturalism—race and ethnicity. An attempt has been made, however, to include works that consider the cinematic reflection of other cultures and communities as well, including film and video representations of gender, sexuality, and nationality. A truly inclusive list of resources dealing with multicultural film and video, one which accurately reflected the enormous diversity of American lives and American stories, could have easily been expanded to twice or three times the size of this list.

The resources discussed in this chapter fall into several broad categories. An attempt has been made to identify the more substantive print and Web-based filmographies and videographies dealing with documentary and feature works about American cultures and various cultural diasporas. Also provided is a highly selective bibliography of print and online resources focused on the representations of race, ethnicity, gender, and sexuality in mainstream Hollywood movies (for print resources, the decision has been made to include only currently in-print materials). A roster of video producers and distributors who offer particularly strong catalogs of multicultural works is provided. Last, there is a small sampling of non-profit agencies, organizations, and programs devoted to supporting, promoting, and exhibiting the works of filmmakers from diverse cultures and communities.

PRINT AND WEB RESOURCES

Like the literature of media librarianship in general, print publications specifically aimed at providing guidance for building collections of videos on culturally diverse topics have become a real rarity. While the 1980s and early 1990s saw a flurry of books and articles devoted to multicultural film and video collection and use, the years since the last edition of this book have seen few of the core lists, selection guides, or conceptual overviews one might expect in light of the continuing interest in this topic in schools, libraries, and academia. This paucity is particularly bewildering given the boom in films and videos devoted to multicultural topics and/or made by filmmakers from diverse cultural backgrounds.

The good news is that the number of valuable reference books, scholarly and popular monographs, and journal articles specifically devoted to analyzing the representation of race, ethnicity, nationality, gender, and sexuality in film and TV has continued to increase at the same time; and although still largely inchoate and unreliable (like almost everything else on the Web), the body of popular, commercial, and academic Web sites devoted to these topics is also burgeoning at an astonishing rate.

Filmographies and Other Resource Listings

American Cultures

Facets African-American Video Guide (1994); *Facets Gay and Lesbian Video Guide* (1993). Chicago: Facets Multimedia, Inc./Academy Chicago Publishers. The redoubtable film cooperative and video distributor, Facets, has produced several useful topical guides to videos in its catalog. Both annotated lists include feature and documentary works. For a more up-to-date listing of Facets offerings, libraries should write for the complete Facets catalog.

Foulke, Lori. 1998. "A Selective Guide to Latino/a Videos." *MC Journal: The Journal of Academic Media Librarianship* 6(1) (Spring). http://wings.buffalo.edu/ publications/mcjrnl/v6n1/latinos.html. An attempt to provide a representative sampling of recent and notable videos (mostly independently produced documentary works) about Latinos/as in the United States. Includes a useful background discussion of Latino/Chicano cinematic representation. Includes distributor information for the videos discussed.

Handman, Gary and Strauss, Karen. 1994. "New World, New Visions: The Immigrant

Experience on Film and Video" (Growing the Collection). *Wilson Library Bulletin*
(October): 39–45. An annotated list of feature films and documentary videos
reflecting the experiences of immigrants in the United States. Includes directory
of video distributors.

Holmlund, Chris, and Fuchs, Cynthia, eds. 1997. *Between the Sheets, in the Streets: Queer,
Lesbian, and Gay Documentary.* Minneapolis: University of Minnesota Press. An
interesting and broad-ranging compilation of essays by academics and filmmakers
dealing with the representation and reflection of queer/lesbian/gay identity in contemporary documentary works, and the connections between gay activism and
gay filmmaking. Includes a good, basic annotated filmography/videography.

Keller, Gary D. 1994. *Hispanics and United States Film: An Overview and Handbook.*
Tempe, AZ: Bilingual Review/Press. A historical overview of Hispanic participation in and representation by the Hollywood mainstream. Arranged chronologically by era, this book provides a unique view of evolving character types,
stereotypes, and genres of film featuring images of Hispanics and Hispanic culture. Includes a chapter on the post-1970s rise of Latino filmmakers and stars.
Also includes selected filmographies for individual actors, directors, and genres
discussed.

Klotman, Phyllis R., and Cutler, Janet K., eds. 1999. *Struggles for Representation: African American Documentary Film and Video.* Bloomington: Indiana University
Press. Examines over 300 non-fiction works by more than 150 African-American
film/videomakers. Includes an extremely valuable 45-page filmography of works.

Klotman, Phyllis Rauch, and Gibson, Gloria J. 1997. *Frame by Frame II: A Filmography
of the African American Image, 1978–1994.* Bloomington: Indiana University
Press. A project of the Black Film Center/Archive at Indiana University, this
filmography includes films reflecting the exceptionally broad range of African-
American contribution to both mainstream Hollywood and independently produced films—contributions ranging from screenwriting and direction, to technical
and musical, to on-screen performance. Includes production and distribution information with brief plot synopses.

McGee, Patricia B. 2000. "African-American Video Resources: A Select Guide." *MC
Journal: The Journal of Academic Media Librarianship* 7 (Fall). http://wings.
buffalo.edu/publications/mcjrnl/v7n2/mcgee.html. An annotated listing of videos
compiled in connection with the development of a projected Center for African
American Research at the Joyner Library, East Carolina University. Includes documentary works and films on video by early independent African-American filmmakers.

Richard, Alfred Charles. 1994. *Contemporary Hollywood's Negative Hispanic Image: An
Interpretive Filmography, 1956–1993.* Westport, CT: Greenwood Press. An annotated, chronological listing of over 3,100 films from the United States (and
from Latin America, the Caribbean, and Spain, selectively). See also, Richard
1992 and 1993.

Richard, Alfred Charles. 1992. *The Hispanic Image on the Silver Screen: An Interpretive
Filmography from Silents into Sound, 1898–1935.* Westport, CT: Greenwood
Press. The first in Richard's three-volume set of annotated filmographies devoted
to identifying film representations of Hispanics, Hispanic culture, and Hispanic
history. Includes listings for over 1,800 films, arranged chronologically.

Richards, Larry. 1998. *African American Films Through 1959: A Comprehensive, Illus-*

trated Filmography. Jefferson, NC: McFarland. A listing of over 1,300 titles: feature films, *soundies* (short musicals of the 1940s), trailers, shorts, and documentaries, including films that predominantly feature African-American casts or stars, or that centrally deal with African-American culture, history, and life. Alphabetical entries provide brief credits and plot synopses. Includes an appendix of actor credits.

Sampson, Henry T. 1995. *Blacks in Black and White: A Source Book on Black Films*. 2nd ed. Metuchen, NJ: Scarecrow Press. An essential reference work dealing with independently produced, all-black cast films made between 1910 and 1950. Includes an excellent overview of early black filmmaking, and chapters on notable producers and stars. Provides lengthy plot synopses and credit information for selected films, as well as a comprehensive listing with brief credits. An increasing number of these early works have become available on video from Facets and other distributors.

Viewing Race: A Videography and Resource Guide. 1999. New York: National Video Resources. http://www.ViewingRace.org/. The Viewing Race project of National Video Resources identifies a curated core collection of over 70 independently produced videos for adults and young adults dealing with a broad array of issues related to race, identity, and history. Titles in the collection were selected by a body of notable scholars, filmmakers, and media librarians. The project catalog includes excellent short essays and interviews related to media and race. The sponsors of the project have negotiated special pricing for libraries for many of the titles in the catalog.

Wood, Irene. 1999. *Culturally Diverse Videos, Audios, and CD-ROMs for Children and Young Adults*. New York: Neal-Schuman. A basic selection aid for librarians and educators compiled by the former audiovisual editor of the American Library Association's *Booklist*. Includes brief annotated listings of videos dealing with multicultural issues, African Americans, Asian Americans, and Hispanic Americans. A distributor list is provided for all items included in the book.

Worth, Fabienne. 1993. "Introduction to the Annotated Gay and Lesbian Film/Videography." *Quarterly Review of Film and Video* 15(1) (November): 89–120. An annotated filmography/videography of movies containing either overt or discrete lesbian or homosexual themes is presented. The list includes Hollywood features, experimental and independent films, documentaries, pornography, television films, and films made outside the United States. The list focuses primarily on works made in the United States since 1980.

In addition to the print resources listed above, there are currently a number of Web and CD-ROM film databases that are useful in identifying feature films by genre, theme, or national origin. Chadwyk-Healey's (Bell and Howell) costly but indispensable *American Film Institute Catalog* on CD-ROM and Web (http://afi.chadwyck.com), for example, provides access to authoritative information about U.S. films from 1893 to 1970, by key subject words such as "African American," "Hispanic American," and "Race Relations." Along with extensive credit and production information, AFI (American Film Institute) catalog entries provide very thorough plot descriptions and bibliographies of articles from which the descriptive information was taken. Chadwyck-Healey's British Film

Institute *Film Index International* (*FII*) on CD-ROM provides similarly comprehensive and authoritative information on international cinema from the beginning of the sound era to the present. The *FII* also provides links to bibliographies of journal articles and reviews for a large number of titles in the database. The popular Internet Movie Database (IMDB) (http://www.us.imdb.com), while not as authoritative or sophisticated as the above-mentioned databases, has the benefit of being free and relatively easy to use. The IMDB, which includes popular documentaries as well as features, allows keyword searching of plot synopses contributed by users of the database (although, since there's no controlled vocabulary for this searching, things can get a bit wild and woolly).

Research and Writing on Race, Gender, and Ethnicity

Writing about ethnic, racial, sexual, and gender representation in film and other mass media has become a true academic cottage industry in the past quarter century, and because film is the most postmodern of all popular culture forms, virtually every discipline under the sun seems to have jumped on the bandwagon.

The best writing in this field—represented in small part by the core listing below—can be extremely helpful to video collection developers by defining genres and styles, identifying seminal works and significant filmmakers, and providing insights into the ways in which film, culture, and politics have historically intersected. Many of these publications offer background and credit information for specific films and filmmakers that can be exceptionally useful in planning video collections, in doing video and film reference, or in teaching about the ways Hollywood has tended to reflect and shape the popular image of cultural "others." Among these publications is also an important body of writing that discusses how film and video have given an increasingly important voice to historically marginalized communities, and provided an outlet for redefining history from alternative cultural perspectives

American Cultures

Bogle, Donald. 1994. *Toms, Coons, Mulattoes, Mammies, and Bucks: An Interpretive History of Blacks in American Films*. New 3rd ed. New York: Continuum Publishing. A readable study of African-American actors and their images in motion pictures from *Uncle Tom's Cabin* and *Birth of a Nation* to the African-American superstars and new directors of the 1980s and early 1990s.

Creekmur, Corey K., and Doty, Alexander, eds. 1995. *Out in Culture: Gay, Lesbian, and Queer Essays on Popular Culture*. Durham, NC: Duke University Press. A far-flung collection of essays by academics and by popular writers, artists, and filmmakers on a wide range of subjects, ranging from Patricia White's piece on Agnes Moorehead's film career, to film critic B. Ruby Rich's essay on *Maedchen in Uniform*, to Marlon Riggs' meditation on black gay men and machismo.

Cripps, Thomas. 1993. *Slow Fade to Black: The Negro in American Film, 1900–1942*.

New York: Oxford University Press. This scholarly study, described by the author as a social history, traces the early experience of African Americans in motion pictures.

Davies, Jude, and Smith, Carol R. 2000. *Gender, Ethnicity and Sexuality in Contemporary American Film*. Chicago: Fitzroy Dearborn Publishers. Investigates the construction and representation of gender, ethnicity, and sexuality in the "new Hollywood" of the 1980s and 1990s. Includes discussions of individual feature films, including both mainstream works and independent features.

Feng, Peter. 1995. "In Search of Asian American Cinema" (Race in Contemporary American Cinema, Part 3). *Cineaste* 21 (Winter/Spring): 32–36. An attempt to define Asian American cinema and to identify unifying elements that characterize the movement. Includes a short filmography of recommended documentary works.

Fregoso, Rosa Linda. 1993. *The Bronze Screen: Chicana and Chicano Film Culture*. Minneapolis: University of Minnesota Press. Fregoso discusses the role of specific feature and documentary films in reframing identities and representations of Chicano culture in the last several decades.

Friedman, Lester D., ed. 1991. *Unspeakable Images; Ethnicity and the American Cinema*. Urbana: University of Illinois Press. This anthology of scholarly articles addresses critical theories and methodologies relating ethnic issues to the American cinema.

Gever, Martha, Parmar, Pratibha, and Greyson, John. 1993. *Queer Looks: Perspectives on Lesbian and Gay Film and Video*. New York: Routledge. An attempt to redress the "profound dearth of critical theory addressing independent productions by lesbian and gay media artists." The editors have assembled an anthology consisting of an introduction and 35 diverse "pieces" (most but not all of them essays) by critics, visual artists, or, like editors Gever, Greyson, and Parmar, " 'bitextual' figures working across media."

Guerrero, Ed. 1993. *Framing Blackness: The African American Image in Film*. Philadelphia: Temple University Press. An attempt to follow "the ceaselessly shifting black image in commercial narrative cinema, attending to its insults and injuries, its momentary illuminations and insurgencies, and its rare narratives of black empowerment." Includes interesting chapters on blaxploitation films and the new black cinema of the 1990s.

Hilger, Michael. 1995. *From Savage to Nobleman: Images of Native Americans in Film*. Lanham, MD: Scarecrow Press. Traces two recurring Native American stereotypes—"The Nobel Red Man" and "The Savage"—as reflected in the films of various decades. Includes useful filmographies for each decade/image discussed.

Hsing, Chun (Xing, Jun). 1998. *Asian America Through the Lens: History, Representations, and Identity*. Critical Perspectives on Asian Pacific Americans series, vol. 3. Walnut Creek, CA: AltaMira Press. The first, and to-date only "sustained examination of Asian American independent films," Hsing's expressed goals in this book include broadening the public exposure to new Asian American films and filmmakers, and investigating both the complex nature of Asian representations and the role of Asian American artists over the course of mainstream film history. Includes an excellent bibliography and a good selective list of films.

Keller, Gary D., ed. 1985. *Chicano Cinema: Research, Reviews and Resources*. Binghamton, NY: Bilingual Press. This book grew out of the research and scholarship for the annual Chicano Film Festival at Eastern Michigan University. It reproduces research and critical articles, an interview, and reviews on Chicano film. A directory of Chicano/Latino films and their distributors prepared by Hector Garza can be found at the back of the text.

Kilpatrick, Jacquelyn. 1999. *Celluloid Indians: Native Americans and Film*. Lincoln: University of Nebraska Press. An informative and accessible discussion of the history and nature of Native American representation in film. Kilpatrick provides useful introductory chapters on the evolution of Native American stereotypes in eighteenth- and early nineteenth-century literature and popular culture. Discusses the changing image of Native Americans in post–Vietnam War films, contemporary revisionist Hollywood Westerns, and in the recent film and documentary works of Native American filmmakers.

Klotman, Phyllis R., and Cutler, Janet K., eds. 1999. *Struggles for Representation: African American Documentary Film and Video*. Bloomington: Indiana University Press. A unique compilation of essays on the surprisingly neglected topic of African-American documentary film and video. Examines over 300 non-fiction works by more than 150 African/American film/videomakers.

List, Christine. 1996. *Chicano Images: Refiguring Ethnicity in Mainstream Film*. New York: Garland. Covers the emergence of Chicano filmmakers and Chicano film study in the context of the Chicano movement of the 1960s and 1970s. Discusses the changing representation of Chicano and Latino culture in both mainstream and independent feature films. Includes a good selective bibliography.

Moving the Image: Independent Asian Pacific American Media Arts. 1991. Edited and introduced by Russell Leong, with a Preface by Linda Mabalot. Los Angeles: UCLA Asian American Studies Center and Visual Communications, Southern California Asian American Studies Central. A collection of provocative and informative essays, interviews, and anecdotes by 50 Asian American filmmakers, media artists, and writers. Attempts to define the Asian-Pacific American media arts and describe their development from 1970 to 1990. Includes extensive resource listings and filmographies.

Noriega, Chon A. 2000. *Shot in America: Television, the State, and the Rise of Chicano Cinema*. Minneapolis: University of Minnesota Press. A detailed discussion of Chicano filmmaking and filmmakers viewed in the context of Chicano social movements, politics, and activism of the past 40 years. Noriega reveals the ways in which Chicano and other minority protests both emerged within and were regulated by the very institutions that excluded them.

Rollins, Peter, and O'Connor, John E., eds. 1998. *Hollywood's Indian: The Portrayal of the Native American in Film*. Lexington: University Press of Kentucky. Contributed essays on various aspects of the cinematic portrayal of Native Americans, from silents to Disney's *Pocahontas*. Includes interesting writings on the nature of Native American stereotypes; the films of John Ford; revisionist westerns, such as *Little Big Man* and *Dances with Wolves*. Includes several useful filmographies.

Russo, Vito. 1987. *The Celluloid Closet: Homosexuality in the Movies*. rev. ed. New York: Harper and Row. One of the earliest (first edition 1981) and perhaps the best-known popular works on the history of gay screen images in mainstream Hollywood movies. Includes a filmography and a strange but instructive necrology of gay film characters and their often untimely deaths. See also the description of the video based on this book, described below.

Smith, Valerie, ed. 1997. *Representing Blackness: Issues in Film and Video* New Brunswick, NJ: Rutgers University Press. A collection of diverse essays dealing with "black representation and questions of racial authenticity" in Hollywood films, black independent works, and popular culture in general. Includes contributions by such academic leading lights as Donald Bogle, Thomas Cripps, and Stuart Hall.

Snead, James A. 1994. *White Screens, Black Images: Hollywood From the Dark Side.* New York: Routledge. Snead's book presents an exceptionally broad range of discussions dealing with various aspects of black representation in the movies— both mainstream and black independent film. In his introduction to the book, Colin McCabe summarizes Snead's central thesis and methodology: "a refusal to read [African American] representation as merely positive or negative and a linked determination to read it in relation to the deepest of political and sexual fantasies."

Summerfield, Ellen. 1993. *Crossing Cultures Through Film.* Yarmouth, ME: Intercultural Press. Summerfield's goal in this book is to provide direction for educators in diverse curricula in the use of feature and documentary films as a means of promoting the understanding of diverse cultures in the classroom. Includes chapters on how to find and evaluate films; methods for using films in the classroom; films as a means of "unlearning" stereotypes.

Thi Thanh Nga. 1995. "The Long March from Wong to Woo: Asians in Hollywood" (Race in Contemporary American Cinema, Part 5). *Cineaste* 21(4) (Fall): 38–41. http://www.lib.berkeley.edu/MRC/LongMarch.html. Traces the stereotypical image of Asians in motion pictures, and discusses the historical difficulties faced by Asian actors and actresses in light of these representations and prejudices.

Toplin, Robert Brent, ed. 1993. *Hollywood as Mirror: Changing Views of "Outsiders" and "Enemies" in American Movies.* Westport, CT: Greenwood Press. Essays that present discussions of Hollywood films as they reflect shifting popular fears of and antipathies toward cultural outsiders and cultural and political enemies of the day. Includes a good chapter on the image of immigrants in film.

SELECTED VIDEOS ABOUT THE TREATMENT OF RACE, ETHNICITY, AND GENDER IN FILM AND TV

The Celluloid Closet. Footage from over 120 films shows the changing face of homosexuality (both male and female) in the movies from cruel stereotypes to covert love to the activist triumphs of the 1990s. Based on Vito Russo's book by the same title. 102 min. Facets and other home video distributors.

Classified X. A film by Melvin Van Peebles. Examines the treatment of black characters throughout the history of American cinema, using examples from classic films beginning with footage by Thomas Edison in 1903 to the present, tracing how Hollywood has aided and abetted the public perception of the African American. 1997 50 min. Distributor: Facets and other home video distributors.

Color Adjustment. Written and directed by Marlon Riggs. A historical view of stereotypical depictions of African Americans in television and through that depiction traces the roots of racism and race relations in America. 1991. 58 min. Distributor: California Newsreel.

Ethnic Notions. Written and directed by Marlon Riggs. Discusses the racist depiction of African Americans in American popular and material culture. 1987. 57 min. Distributor: California Newsreel.

Hollywood: An Empire of Their Own. Based on the book of the same name by film critic and historian Neal Gabler. Using archival footage, this film examines the lasting influence on the American motion picture industry of the Eastern European Jewish immigrants who founded and ran the major motion picture companies and studios. 1998. 100 min. Distributor: Facets and other home video distributors.

Image of Indians Series. A five-part series that investigates the representation of Native Americans in American popular culture, with particular focus on classical Hollywood cinema, from the silent era through the 1950s. Discusses the impact of stereotyping and negative images on Native Americans themselves. 1979. 28 minutes each installment. Distributor: VisionMaker.

Latino Hollywood. Part I: Latinos have contributed to the American film industry since its earliest days. During the silent and early talkie era, Latinos were almost always stereotyped as tempestuous lovers, bandidos, or cantina girls. This program remembers many of the early Latino actors and actresses and examines some of the stereotypical roles they portrayed. Part II: Program looks at the history and image of the Latino and Latina in Hollywoood films from the 1940s through the mid-1990s. Also reviews the roles Latino actors and actresses were given to play in popular films during this period and examines the few social-realist films of the period. It then charts the gradual shift in the 1970s and 1980s from the stereotypical Latino image to the growth of independent Latino filmmaking and the "crossover" films of the 1980s and 1990s. 1996. 18 min. Distributor: Cinema Guild.

Midnight Ramble: Oscar Micheaux and the Story of Race Movies. Recounts the story of race movies produced for Afro-Americans from the 1920s through 1950 and the role played by Oscar Micheaux, the leading Afro-American producer and director. 1994. 58 min. Distributor: Facets and other home video distributors.

The Silver Screen: Color Me Lavender. An exploration of the way Hollywood dealt with or ignored issues of homosexuality during its so-called Golden Age, when the studio system reigned supreme. 1998. 101 min. Distributor: Facets and other home video distributors.

Slaying the Dragon. A bit outdated, but still fascinating, *Slaying the Dragon* analyzes the roles and images of Asian women promulgated by the Hollywood film industry and network television over the past 50 years. Also interviews Asian-American women and their responses to the impact these stereotypes have on their relationships, their work, and themselves. 1988. 60 min. Distributor: National Asian American Telecommunications Association (NAATA).

When East Meets East. Explores the issues of ethnic and cultural identity through interviews with some of today's most prominent Asian and Chinese American filmmakers, actors, and actresses in the United States, Canada, Taiwan, and China. 199? 53 min. Distributor: Films for the Humanities & Sciences.

WEB RESOURCES

Web Sites: Institutional Catalogs, Filmographies, Videographies

Although comprehensive, up-to-date printed core listings of videos on race, gender, and ethnicity have yet to be written, it is interesting to note how many videographies, including catalogs of library holdings on these topics and listings assembled by associations, organizations, or individuals, have made their way onto the Web. The videographies listed below represent some of the more comprehensive and thoughtfully assembled Web listings of feature and documentary films broadly related to issues and themes of race, ethnicity, and gender. Taken as a whole, this collection of filmographies provides a useful starting point for surveying what's out there in the world and what other librarians and institutions have decided to collect.

American University. *Subject Mediagraphies* (http://www.library.american.edu/subject/media/index.html).
Includes substantive annotated listings for African American History Culture and Current Issues; American Indians; Gay, Lesbian, and Transgender Issues; as well as listings for world religions and various world regions. Compiled by Chris Lewis.

Asian American Film (http://www.asianamericanfilm.com/).
An interesting dot-com site devoted to building "an engaged, involved, active, and excited audience for Asian American films." Along with providing resources for filmmakers (chat and message space, employment information), the site includes a database of mostly independently produced films by Asian American filmmakers. Entries include short annotations, production and distribution information. Site includes links to online and print reviews.

Aufderheide, Patricia. *Cross-Cultural Film Guide: Films from Africa, Asia and Latin America at The American University.* (http://www.library.american.edu/subject/media/aufderheide/aufderhe.html).
A good older (1992) annotated list of feature films (and some documentaries) from Africa, Asia, and Latin America. "These are typically authorial films made as an expression of cultural identity by filmmakers who see their mandating not only as entertaining but also provoking thought." Includes an informative introduction by Aufderheide that discusses selection criteria for the list and outlines strategies for using these works in the classroom.

Carnegie Mellon University. Collections in the Arts and Humanities. Race and Ethnicity Collection. *Film/Video Materials for Programs on Hispanics.* (http://eserver.org/race/hispanic-experience.html); *Asian American Filmography.* (http://eserver.org/race/aa-filmography.html).
Short, annotated listings of documentary and feature films; site also includes interesting essays and feature articles on the broad topic of race and ethnicity.

Duke University, Lilly Library. *Jewish Film and Video Collection* (http://www.lib.duke.edu/lilly/jvid.htm). *Pacific Rim and the Asian-American Experience Film and Video* (http://www.lib.duke.edu/lilly/pacific.htm).
Annotated listings with some producer/distributor information.

Holocaust Resource Center and Archive, Queensborough Community College. *Annotated Videography on the Holocaust and Related Subjects* (http://www.holocaust-trc.org/video_res1.htm).

An excellent videography of Holocaust-related documentary and feature films, and videos dealing with related topics, such as anti-Semitism. Includes listing of vendors for materials described. Edited by Sara Roberts.

Indiana University. Department of Afro-American Studies. *Black Film Center/Archive* (http://www.indiana.edu/~bfca/index.html).

A diverse collection of over 800 historic and contemporary Hollywood and independent films; black-and-white and color, silent and sound; features, documentaries, dramatic and musical shorts, comedy shorts, newsreels, and animations in 35mm, 16mm, 8mm, and videocassette formats.

The Jewish Film Archive Online. 1999 (http://www.jewishfilm.com/; http://members.aol.com/jewfilm/index.html).

A large, annotated listing of documentary and feature films with Jewish themes and focuses. Site includes links to Jewish film festivals and film organizations. Includes distributor/producer information for films and videos listed.

Media Action Network for Asian Americans. *The MANAA Video Guide*. 1998 (http://janet.org/~manaa/video_guide.html).

The MANAA Video Guide is a well-annotated listing of feature works from Western countries with prominent Asian characters, often played by Asian American actors (both U.S.–born and immigrant). Emphasis is on those Asian characters who challenge stereotypes. Only works currently available on video are included.

National Library of Australia. 1984. *Guides to the Film Studies Collection: Towards a Black Genre: Afro-Americans on Film*. http://www.cinemedia.net/NLA/black.html.

This is a survey designed to provide a context for films in the National Library of Australia collection which portray, in varying ways, blacks and the black experience in the United States. Although dated, includes a good videographic essay that discusses the films and filmmakers cited in cultural and historical context.

Stanford University. Meyer Library Media Center. *Films on Asian American Studies* (http://www-sul.stanford.edu/depts/ssrg/adams/shortcu/films/asamfilms.html#docus); *Films on Chicano/Latino Studies* (http://www-sul.stanford.edu/depts/ssrg/adams/shortcu/films/chicfilms.html).

Annotated listings; no distributor information provided.

Teachers' Guide to the Holocaust: Videography. 1999 (http://fcit.coedu.usf.edu/holocaust/resource/films.htm).

An excellent videography of Holocaust-related films and videos compiled by Dr. William L. Schulman, Director of the Holocaust Resource Center and Archives, Queensborough Community College of The City University of New York. Site sponsored by College of Education, University of South Florida.

Television Race Initiative (PBS). 1999 (http://www.pbs.org/pov/tvraceinitiative/what.html).

The Television Race Initiative is a project focused on using selected documentary films/videos (broadcast on PBS) as the basis for fostering sustained community dialogue and problem solving around the issue of race relations. TRI has assembled an excellent, small core list of titles dealing broadly with race and ethnicity (most of these titles are available on video from distributors listed in Print and Web Resources above). Other site resources include a broadcast schedule for featured productions, and links to organizational resources, including multicultural media organizations and consortia.

University of California, Berkeley. Media Resources Center. *Ethnic Studies/Gender Studies Videographies and Area Studies Videographies* (http://www.lib.berkeley.edu/ MRC/VideographyMenu.html).

Includes extensive listings of documentary and feature films related to ethnic, gender, and sexuality studies. Also included are listings of documentary materials pertaining to area studies, and listings of holdings for various national cinemas. These Web sites include citations to reviews and articles for selected videos; links to full-text reviews; and other information about individual titles listed. Although distributor information is not included in these Web listings, some information about distribution may be obtained by searching for the titles in UC Berkeley's online catalog (PATHFINDER) (http:// sunsite2.berkeley.edu:8000/). Compiled by Gary Handman.

University of Hawaii, Manoa. Gregg M. Sinclair Library. *Wong AV Center Collections* (http://www.sinclair.hawaii.edu/HTML/wong.html).

A comprehensive collection of audiovisual materials on Hawaii and the Pacific Islands. Listing includes complete cataloging information for each entry.

Web Sites: Bibliographies

Association of College and Research Libraries (ACRL). Women's Studies Section: *Collection Development Committee Core Lists. Film* (http://www.library.wisc.edu/ libraries/WomensStudies/core/crfilm.htm).

A good basic list of English-language books and articles dealing with the representation and role of women in international cinema and television. Includes a listing of essential works of feminist film theory. Compiled by Ellen Brody, 2000.

Chicago Public Library. *African Americans in Film and Television: A Bibliography of Resources at the Harold Washington Library Center* (http://www.chipublib.org/ 001hwlc/vpaafroam.html).

This bibliography covers titles at the Harold Washington Library Center that focus on the lives, works, and presence of African Americans in the film and television industries. Works are listed alphabetically by author, editor, or compiler. Includes hypertext index to the bibliography. Compiled by William Sumner, 1996.

National Video Resources. *Viewing Race: Bibliography* (http://www.ViewingRace. org/resources/index.html).

Compiled as part of the National Video Resources Viewing Race project Web site (see Filmographies above). Includes general works about multiculturalism and race. Compiled by John Keene, 1999.

Ryerson Polytechnic University. *Gender Issues in Film* (http://www.ryerson.ca/ mgroup/filmsex.html).

A concise bibliography of books and articles concerned with gender, sexuality. Compiled by Murray Pomerance.

University of California, Berkeley. Media Resources Center. *Bibliographies Ethnic Studies/Gender Studies Media* (http://www.lib.berkeley.edu/MRC/FilmBibMenu.html).

Includes large group of Web-based bibliographies, with some annotations, relating to the representation of ethnic, racial, and gender/sexual groups in film and TV, and the history and role of these groups in the film and TV industry. Bibliographies are regularly updated. Compiled by Gary Handman, 2002.

University of Maryland Libraries. *Minorities in Broadcasting Bibliography* (http://www.lib.umd.edu/UMCP/LAB/BIBLIO/bib-minor.html).

Includes information about the Libraries' holdings on minorities in broadcasting, including books, articles, pamphlets, reports, scripts, subject files, and special collections.

University of Virginia. *Women in Cinema: A Reference Guide* (http://www.people.virginia.edu/~pm9k/libsci/womFilm.html).

An extensive compilation of bibliographies, review sources, filmographies, bibliographies, and biographical sources devoted to women in film and women in filmmaking. Compiled by Philip McEldowney, 1994.

Web Sites: Reviews, Articles, and Other Resources

Asian American Artistry (http://www.geocities.com/Hollywood/Palace/2713/film.html).

A site devoted to Asian-Pacific American culture and life, Includes an interesting selected chronology of Hollywood and international films that include both stereotypical and positive images of Asians; also includes a number of general overview articles which discuss Asian Americans and the arts. Links to Asian arts organizations and other resources. 1999.

Cho, Cindy, Hsiao, James, Hsu, Andy, and Wang, Bea. 1999(?) "Yellow Myths on the Silver Screen: The Representation of Asians in American Mainstream Cinema" (http://web.mit.edu/21h.153j/www/aacinema/intro.html).

An excellent group of student papers from MIT, done as part of an Asian American Studies class.

CinemaLuna (http://www.cinemaluna.com/).

Site dedicated to promoting alternative and independent Chicano cinema. Includes links to distributors, bibliography of books and articles about Latino/Chicano cinema, organizations, and associations.

Deeper Shade of Black (http://www.seditionists.org/black/film/).

Reviews of current and historical films featuring African-American actors, characters, themes.

Gender, Ethnicity & Class (http://www.aber.ac.uk/media/Functions/mcs.html).

A very large metasite devoted to various aspects of media and communication studies. The MCS pages devoted to gender, ethnicity, and race include full-text articles, bibliographies, and links to related sites. Topics covered include media treatment of race and gender, stereotyping, race and gender in film, media and personal and cultural identity. Compiled by Daniel Chandler, 2000.

Long Island University. B. Davis Davis Schwartz Memorial Library. *African Americans in Motion Pictures: The Past and the Present* (http://www.liunet.edu/cwis/cwp/library/african/movies.htm).

A large (although somewhat confusingly organized) site devoted to African Americans in film and African-American filmmaking. Includes a chronology, filmographies, and short essays on various aspects of African-American film history. Contains selected bibliographies of materials on films, filmmakers, and performers in the Melvin R. Sylvester and the C. W. Post Library Collection.

Midnight Ramble: The Negro in Early Hollywood (http://www.moderntimes.com/palace/black/index.html).

An exceptionally well-designed and well-written site devoted to early "race films," and filmmakers such as Oscar Micheaux. Compiled by Michael Mills, 1997.

Multicultural Audiovisual Resources (http://ublib.buffalo.edu/libraries/units/hsl/ref/av.html#lib).

A superb and extensive metasite that provides links to a wide range of resources related to multicultural film and video. Includes links to distributors, bibliographies and mediagraphies, electronic publications, organizations, libraries and archives, festivals. Also includes links to general guides and sources useful for video selection and evaluation. Compiled by Sharon Gray, State University of New York at Buffalo.

"Race and Representation in American Cinema." *Volume III: Curriculum Units by Fellows of the Yale-New Haven Teachers Institute, 1978–1997* (http://www.cis.yale.edu/ynhti/curriculum/units/1996/3/) (via Yale–New Haven Teachers Institute).

A unique and valuable collection of teaching guides and discussions dealing with various aspects of the representation of race and ethnicity and gender in film, and with the critical viewing of and thinking about film. Includes units on stereotyping, women filmmakers of color, black actors in American cinema, and discussions of particular films.

SAWnet (South Asian Women's Network) (http://www.umiacs.umd.edu/users/sawweb/sawnet/cinema.html).

An interesting site devoted to documentary and feature film and video by South Asian women filmmakers. Includes reviews, information about filmmakers, links to other sites.

PRODUCERS AND DISTRIBUTORS OF MULTICULTURAL VIDEO

Over the past decade, building collections of videos on culturally diverse topics has become a progressively easier and more satisfying task. The primary reason for these changing circumstances is simple: these past 10 years have seen a virtual big-bang explosion in the number of interesting and insightful videos about and/or originating from within the multiplicity of ethnic, racial, and sexual cultures in the United States and other parts of the world. This cinematic explosion has most notably occurred in the realm of documentary film and video— particularly documentaries by filmmakers of color, women filmmakers, and gay and lesbian filmmakers. A similarly expanding universe can, however, also been seen in the growing number of feature films available on video from the developing world, and from U.S. independent filmmakers whose stories center on themes of race, gender, and sexuality.

This is not to say that all parts of this expanding multicultural media constellation are equally scintillating. As might be expected given the intense interest in and growing market for videos on multicultural topics, this universe has also seen its share of blandly generic and slapdash non-theatrical works parading under the diversity banner. In some instances, the fairly sudden appearance of well-stocked "multicultural" sections in video distributor catalogs has simply involved decanting old wine (sometimes stale old wine) into new, trendy bottles: got a documentary on India? A feature film with an African American star? Call them "multicultural."

As is the case with collection development in other topical areas and other media, one of the first steps toward building well-rounded, effective collections that reflect a diversity of cultural and political voices and visions is learning to navigate the marketplace in which these works are sold. It is, for example, important from the outset to understand the often considerable differences between independently produced and distributed non-theatrical video works, and those productions turned out for home video or mass-market consumption. Although the distinctions between these two sectors of the marketplace aren't always absolute or clearly demarcated, there are frequently very definite differences between "indie" videos and their more commercial cousins in terms of style, point of view, artistic, and/or political agendas (and pricing!!) (For an overview and a fuller explanation of these differences, see Chapter 16 in this book.)

In attempting to become acquainted with the offerings of various video distributors, nothing can replace concentrated stretches of time spent systematically sampling the titles in their catalogs. Unfortunately, in these harried days of understaffing and mounting professional workloads, few of us have the kind of luxuriously unencumbered time to pull off such feats. One unique opportunity to preview the best and brightest new acquisitions of documentary and educational video distributors in a concentrated amount of time is to attend the annual National Media Market (NMM) (http://www.nmm.net). The Media Market is a four-day trade show during which attendees may view and/or make purchasing decisions from over 2,000 hours of programming shown in scheduled and on-demand screenings. Many of the distributors listed below are regular participants in Media Market.

While it is not possible to list the full range of sources for multicultural video here, the following list represents video distributors who offer notable selections of works by and about minority cultures in the United States, world cultures, and social and political issues and events. Many of the companies below deal primarily in independently produced works and serve as the exclusive distributor for the titles in their catalog (i.e., you won't find their offerings in the databases of Baker & Taylor or Ingram). The majority of these vendors have mounted helpful Web sites that include catalogs of their offerings, information about filmmakers, and links to related information. Despite the usefulness of these Web catalogs for obtaining information about individual titles and new offerings, perhaps the most productive way of keeping up with the universe as it continues to expand is still to ask to be placed on the mailing lists of these and similar distributors.

ArtMattan Productions, 535 Cathedral Parkway, Suite 14B, New York, NY 10025; (212) 749–6020; Fax: (212) 316–6020; E-mail: info@africanfilm.com; http://www. africanfilm.com.

Independently produced feature and documentary films focusing on the human experience of black people in Africa, the Caribbean, North and South America, and Europe. A particularly useful collection of videos relating to the African Diaspora. ArtMattan is the sponsor of the annual Contemporary African Diaspora Film Festival in New York.

Bullfrog Films, P.O. Box 149; Oley, PA 19547–0149; (610) 779–8226; Fax: (610) 370–1978; E-mail: video@bullfrogfilms.com; http://www.bullfrogfilms.com.

The Bullfrog catalog offers a notable collection of documentary videos dealing with the environment, social issues, and global politics (Bullfrog claims to be the "oldest and largest publisher of videos and films about the environment in the United States"). Also included in the Bullfrog catalog is a strong list of videos on Native American culture and history, women's studies, African studies, and global human rights issues and world development.

California Newsreel, 149 9th Street, Suite 420, San Francisco, CA 94103; (415) 621–6196; Fax: (415) 621–6522; E-mail: contact@newsreel.org; http://www.newsreel.org.

The California Newsreel catalog includes a particularly strong collection of videos related to African-American history and culture (African American Perspectives). Newsreel's *Library of African Cinema* is currently the most extensive collection of cinema works by independent African filmmakers available on video. Web site includes valuable substantive descriptions of videos and useful guides and resources related to selected titles in the catalog.

Cinema Guild, 1697 Broadway, Suite 506, New York, NY 10019; (800) 723–5522, (212) 246–5522; Fax: (212) 246–5525; E-mail: thecinemag@aol.com; http://www. cinemaguild.com.

Consistently provocative works by independent filmmakers on social, cultural, and political issues and events. Particularly strong collection of materials relating to African-American and Latino culture and history. Includes an excellent list of videos on minorities in the arts.

Documentary Educational Resources (DER), 101 Morse Street, Watertown, MA 02172; (617) 926–0491; Fax: (617) 926–9519; E-mail: docued@der.org; http://der.org/ docued.

DER is a non-profit educational organization incorporated in 1971 to produce, distribute, and promote the use of ethnographic and documentary films on world cultures. The DER catalog includes a large body of defining works of ethnographic film produced in the 1960s and 1970s as well as more recent works by a new generation of filmmakers.

Ergo Media, Inc., 668 American Legion Drive, P.O. Box 2037, Teaneck, NJ 07666–1437; (800) 695–ERGO (3746); Fax: (201) 692–0663; E-mail: ergo@jewishvideo.com; http://www.jewishvideo.com.

Videos on Judaism and Jewish culture and history, Israel, and the Jewish Diaspora. Catalog includes a small but interesting collection of feature films, including Israeli films and early Yiddish cinema.

Facets, 1517 West Fullerton Avenue, Chicago, IL 60614; (800) 331–6197, (773) 281–9075; E-mail: sales@facets.org; http://www.facets.org.

Perhaps the best one-stop shopping source of international cinema works in video format. An excellent source for Third World and independent U.S. movies. Facets also carries home video versions of many documentary titles that may be of interest to librarians building multicultural collections.

Filmakers Library, 124 East 40th Street, New York, NY 10016; (212) 808–4980; Fax: (212) 808–4983; E-mail: info@filmakers.com; http://www.filmakers.com/index.html.

A strong list of films by independent filmmakers, including many award winners. Catalog includes strong offerings in multicultural topics (including a particularly strong list of videos dealing with Jewish studies). Good coverage also of women's studies, sociological topics, and global issues.

Films for the Humanities, P.O. Box 2053, Princeton, NJ 08543–2053; (800) 257–5126, (609) 275–1400; Fax: (609) 275–3767; http://www.films.com.

Films for the Humanities' large catalog of titles in the humanities and social sciences includes a sizable number of educational and documentary videos on various multicultural groups, race and society; women's issues, international cultures, and international relations. The Films for the Humanities catalog generally stays clear of works by identifiable directors with strong points of view. FHS videos tend to be balanced, broadly focused, and generally useful, if less adventurous than works found in some of the catalogs of independent film and video distributors.

First Run/Icarus, 153 Waverly Place, 6th Floor, New York, NY 10014; (800) 876–1710, (212) 727–1711; E-mail: info@frif.com; http://www.frif.com/.

First Run offers an impressive collection of film on international culture and politics. The lists of videos on Latin America and the Middle East are particularly strong. First Run/Icarus' catalog includes the *South* series, an anthology of 27 works created by film and video makers from Latin America and the Caribbean, Asia, Africa, and the Middle East. Also included in the catalog are excellent works on women's studies, on religious cultures, and on U.S. politics.

Frameline, 346 9th Street, San Francisco, CA 94103; (415) 703–8650; Fax: (415) 861–1404; E-mail: distribution@frameline.org; http://www.frameline.org/index.html.

Frameline is the nation's only comprehensive non-profit organization dedicated to the exhibition, distribution, promotion, and funding of lesbian and gay film and video. The Frameline catalog includes a large number of excellent documentary and feature works by independent filmmakers dealing with race, gender, and sexuality. Frameline is the sponsor of the San Francisco International Lesbian and Gay Film Festival.

William Greaves Productions, 230 West 55th Street, New York, NY 10019; (212) 246–7221.

A small but interesting collection of popular video titles pertaining to African-American culture and history.

Latin American Video Archive (LAVA), 124 Washington Place, New York, NY 10014; (212) 463–0108; Fax: (212) 243–2007; E-mail: imre@igc.org; http://www.lavavideo.org.

An online searchable database and ordering service which includes thousands of Latin American titles and works by U.S. Latino filmmakers, both feature films and documentaries. The site unites the collections of hundreds of U.S. and foreign distributors and individual film/video makers into a central, online location.

Media Education Foundation (MEF), 26 Center Street, Northampton, MA 01060; (800) 897–0089; Fax: (800) 659–6882; http://www.mediaed.org/enter.html.

Founded by Professor Sut Jhally of the University of Massachusetts, MEF offers a small but significant list of videos dealing with media, gender and culture, race and representation in the media, media globalization, and media literacy. Videos feature such cultural studies heavy-hitters as Jean Kilbourne, Stuart Hall, bell hooks, and Noam Chomsky.

Multicultural Books and Videos, Inc., 28880 Southfield Road, Suite 183, Southfield, MI 48076; (800) 567–2220; E-mail: multicul@wincom.net; http://www.multiculbv.com.

A good collection of international feature films and documentaries, including titles in hard-to-find languages. Catalog includes a particularly large variety of theatrical films on video from India and the Middle East, both subtitled and not.

Multicultural Media, World Music Store, 300 Quaker Road, Chappaqua, NY 10514; (800) 283–4655; Fax: (914) 238–5944; E-mail: info@worldmusicstore.com; http:// www.worldmusicstore.com/.

A superlative selection of traditional and contemporary world music and dance compact discs, videos, books, and CD-ROMs. Multicultural Media is the co-producer of the monumental JVC/Smithsonian Folkways video collections of world music and dance. Web site allows searching of materials by geographical area.

National Asian American Telecommunications Association (NAATA), 346 Ninth Street, 2nd Floor, San Francisco, CA 94103; (415) 552–9550; E-mail: distribution@ naatanet.org; http://distribution@naatanet.org (see also Consortia).

An outstanding list of videos by and about Asian-Pacific Americans, NAATA's catalog includes both documentary and fictional works on Asian American themes. Some of the videos carried by NAATA deal with cultures (e.g., Samoans, Filipinos) that are not widely dealt with in other media resources.

National Latino Communication Center (NLCC), 3171 Los Feliz Boulevard, Suite 201, Los Angeles, CA 90039; (213) 663–8294; Fax: (213) 663–5606; E-mail: nlccemedia@ aol.com; http://latino.sscnet.ucla.edu/community/nlcc/. (See also "Associations, Cooperatives, and Consortia" and listing in Chapter 22 in this book.)

The NLCC currently has a small list of videos pertaining to Latino life and culture. The Center is in the process of establishing a National Latino Film and Video Archive project designed to accomplish two major objectives: to collect, restore, preserve, and make available for research the works of U.S. Latino film and video makers; and to serve as a moving-image source for the development of interactive educational curricular materials in a variety of disciplines, including history, the social sciences, government and politics, the arts, and ethnic studies.

National Center for Jewish Film, Lown Building 102, Brandeis University, Waltham, MA 02254–9110; (781) 899–7044; Fax: (781) 736–2070; E-mail: NCJF@logo.cc. brandeis.edu; http://www.brandeis.edu/jewishfilm/index.html.

The National Center for Jewish Film serves as both an archive and study center for Jewish films and a distribution agency for theatrical and documentary videos on Jewish history and life. The NCJF distribution catalog includes an important collection of over

30 early Yiddish film, films from Israel, and feature and documentary films on the Holocaust.

National Film Board of Canada, 22-D Hollywood Avenue, Hohokus, NJ 07423; (800) 542–2164, (212) 629–8890; Fax: (212) 629–8502. For general information, inquire at: 350 5th Avenue, Suite 4820, New York, NY 10118; http://www.nfb.ca/.

NFB's renowned catalog of documentary works includes a strong list of videos pertaining to the life, culture, and history of Native peoples of Canada and Canadian immigrant history.

Native American Public Telecommunications (NAPT), 1800 Number 33 Street, Lincoln, NE 68583; P.O. Box 83111, Lincoln, NE 68501; (402) 472–3522; Fax: (402) 472–8675; E-mail: native@unl.edu; http://nativetelecom.org/.

For NAPT video collection, see *Vision Maker*.

New Day Films, 853 Broadway, Suite 1210, New York, NY 10003; E-mail: curator @newday.com. Orders to: 22-D Hollywood Avenue, Hohokus, NJ 07423; (800) 343–5540; (201) 652–6590; Fax: (201) 652–1973; http://www.newday.com.

New Day is a cooperative of independent filmmakers that distributes films and videos about social change. New Day's catalog includes an excellent group of films on issues related to diverse American cultures, international concerns, and gender issues. The list of videos on Native Americans is especially strong.

Pacific Islander Communications, 1221 Kapiolani Boulevard, #6A-4, Honolulu, Hawaii 96814; (808) 591–0059; Fax: (808) 591–1114; E-mail: piccom@aloha.net; http:// planet-hawaii.com/pacificislander.

Videos by and about indigenous Pacific Islanders. See also: Associations, Cooperatives, and Consortia.

PBS Video, 1320 Braddock Place, Alexandria, VA 22314–1698; (800) 424–7963: Fax: (800) 344–3337; http://www.pbs.org (home video only)

As the distribution arm for many of the programs produced and aired by PBS affiliates, PBS Video offers a veritable treasure trove of important single works and series dealing with various aspects of American and international cultures.

Third World Newsreel, 335 West 38th Street, 5th Floor, New York, NY 10018; (212) 947–9277; Fax (212) 594–6417; E-mail: twn@twn.org; http://www.twn.org.

Founded in 1967, Third World Newsreel is one of the oldest alternative media arts organizations in the United States. TWN's catalog offers a strong roster of often provocative works by independently produced films by and about people of color, and the peoples of developing countries around the world.

Vision Maker, http://www.visionmaker.org/. Videos available through *Lucerne Media*, 37 Ground Pine Road, Morris Plains, NJ 07950; (800) 341–2293; Fax: 973–538–0855; E-mail: LM@lucernemedia.com; http://www.lucernemedia.com/Nat_Amer.htm.

A wide selection of programs dealing with Native American culture, history, art, and multicultural relations. The list includes many films by Native American filmmakers. Many of the titles in the Vision Maker list have been aired on public broadcasting channels.

Visual Communications, 120 Judge John Aiso Street, Los Angeles, CA 90012; (213) 680–4462; Fax (213) 687–4848; E-mail: viscom@apanet.org; http://viscom.apanet.org/.

Visual Communications offers an excellent catalog of videos by Asian American independent filmmakers dealing with issues of race, identity, gender politics, and history. Some of the titles in this catalog are also distributed by the National Asian American Telecommunications Association (see entry above). Most titles in the Visual Communications catalog are available for rental as well as purchase.

Women Make Movies (WMM), 462 Broadway, New York, NY 10013; (212) 925–0606; Fax: (212) 925–2052; E-mail: distdept@wmm.com; http://www.wmm.com/.

Currently celebrating its twenty-ninth year in business, WMM offers a superb list of provocative video documentary and performance works by and about women. The videos distributed by WMM offer unique and challenging multicultural perspectives on gender and race relations, sexual politics, and cinema studies.

ASSOCIATIONS, COOPERATIVES, AND CONSORTIA

In addition to scanning filmographies and film histories, another effective strategy involves identifying agencies, societies, broadcasting consortia, and other organizations that represent particular ethnic or gender groups. These groups often serve as an important resource base for particular filmmaking communities. Many are involved in mounting film festivals and other events devoted to the films of their particular constituencies. Some of these organizations function as distributors as part of their service to their constituents. See also Chapter 22 in this book.

American Indian Film Institute, 333 Valencia Street, Suite 322, San Francisco, CA 94103; (415) 554–0525; Fax: (415) 554–0542; E-mail: indianfilm@aifisf.com; http://www.aifisf.com/overview.html.

Asian Cinevision, 32 East Broadway, 4th Floor, New York, NY 10002; (212) 925–8685; Fax: (212) 925–8157; E-mail: acvinfo@yahoo.com, http://www.asiancinevision.org/.

Black Filmmaker Foundation (BFF), Tribeca Film Center, 375 Greenwich Street, New York, NY 10013; (212) 941–3944; Fax: (212) 941–3944.

Black Filmmakers Hall of Fame, 405 Fourteenth Street, Suite 515, Oakland, CA 94612; (510) 465–0804; Fax: (510) 839–9858; bfhfinc@aol.com; http://www.black filmmakershall.org/.

Cine Acción 346 9th Street, 2nd Floor, San Francisco, CA 94103; (415) 553–8135; Fax: (415) 863–7428; E-mail: cineaccion@aol.com; http://www.cineaccion.com.

The National Asian American Telecommunications Association, 346 Ninth Street, 2nd Floor, San Francisco, CA 94103; (415) 552–9550; E-mail: distribution@naatanet.org; distribution@naatanet.org (see also Producers and Distributors).

National Black Programming Consortium (NBPC), 761 Oak Street, Columbus, OH 43205; (614) 229–4399, ext. 228; Fax: (614) 229–4398; http://www.blackstarcon.org.

National Latino Communication Center, 3171 Los Feliz Boulevard, Suite 201, Los Angeles, CA 90039; (213) 663–8294; Fax: (213) 663–5606; E-mail: nlccemedia@aol.com; http://latino.sscnet.ucla.edu/community/nlcc/.

Native American Public Telecommunications (NAPT), 1800 North 33rd Street, Lincoln, NE 68583; P.O. Box 83111, Lincoln, NE 68501; (402) 472–3522; Fax: (402) 472–8675; E-mail: native@unl.edu; http://nativetelecom.org/.

Visual Communications, 120 Judge John Aiso Street, Los Angeles, CA 90012; (213) 680–4462; Fax: (213) 687–4848; E-mail: viscom@apanet.org; http://viscom.apanet.org/.

Local humanities councils and state art councils support regional projects that often address cultural issues, and they may also be able to provide leads to videos of interest for multicultural collections. For a listing of state humanities councils, see http://www.neh.fed.us/state/states.html (via National Endowment for the Humanities site). For a listing of state arts councils and commissions, see http://www.nasaa-arts.org/new/nasaa/gateway/gateway.html (via National Assembly of State Arts Agencies site)

FESTIVALS

Regional or ethnic film and video festivals highlight the outstanding works produced by that community, and the published programs and guides to these festivals serve as useful selection tools. Festival catalogs generally provide content description and may list sources for video and/or film rentals and purchases. Museum programs can perform a similar function. Below is a sampling of U.S. festivals devoted in part or whole to works about or by filmmakers of color or filmmakers from other defined cultural communities (see also Chapter 20 in this book). In these days of withering arts funding and high organizational overhead, festivals seem to come and go with alarming swiftness; for that reason alone, the Web is most likely the best choice for keeping up with the scene.

Festivals: A Highly Selective Sampling

African Diaspora Film Festival (Artmattan Productions); (212) 864–1760; E-mail: events@africanfilm.com; http://www.africanfilm.com/festival/.

American Indian Film Festival, 333 Valencia Street, Suite 322; San Francisco, CA 94103; (415) 554–0525; Fax: (415) 554–0542; E-mail: indianfilm@aifsif.com; http://www.aifisf.com/99fest.html.

Arab Film Festival, 416 Park Avenue, San Jose, CA 95110; (415) 564–1100; Fax: (415) 564–2203; E-mail: info@aff.org; http://www.aff.org/.

Asian American International Film Festival, Asian CineVision, 32 East Broadway, 4th Floor, New York, NY 10002; (212) 925–8685; Fax: (212) 925–8157; E-mail: ACVinNYC@aol.com; http://www.asiancinevision.org.

Chicago Asian Showcase, The Foundation for Asian American Independent Media (FAAIM), FAAIM, 3314 North Lake Shore Drive, #6D, Chicago, IL 60657; E-mail: info@faaim.org; http://www.faaim.org/showcase.htm.

Chicago Latino Film Festival, c/o Columbia College, 600 South Michigan Avenue, Chicago, IL 60605; (312) 431–1330; Fax: (312) 344–8030; E-mail: clc@galileo.colum. edu; http://www.filmfestivals.com/int/overviews/2000/chicago_latino_00.htm.

Los Angeles Asian Pacific Film and Video Festival (Visual Communications), 120 Judge John Aiso Street, Los Angeles, CA 90012; (213) 680–4462; Fax: (213) 687–4848; http://vconline.org.

Native American Film and Video Festival, Smithsonian Institution, National Museum of the American Indian, George Gustav Heye Center, Film and Video Center, 1 Bowling Green, New York, NY 10004; (212) 514–3731; Fax: (212) 514–3725; E-mail: Svensonm@ic.si.edu; http://www.si.edu/nmai_film+video.

New York International Latino Film Festival, 170 East 116th Street, New York, NY 10029; (212) 726–2358; Fax: (212) 355–6189; E-mail: info@NYLatinoFilm.com; http://www.NYLatinoFilm.com.

Red Earth American Indian Film and Video Festival, Red Earth, Inc., 2100 N.E. 52nd Street, Oklahoma City, OK 73111; (405) 427–5228; Fax: (405) 427–8079; E-mail: redearth@sprynet.com; http://www.redearth.org.

San Antonio Cinefestival, Guadalupe Cultural Arts Center, 1300 Guadalupe, San Antonio, TX 78207; (210) 271–3151; Fax: (210) 271–3480; E-mail: guadarts@aol.com; http://www.guadalupeculturalarts.org/media.html. (Film and video pertaining to the Latino community.)

San Francisco Gay and Lesbian Film Festival (Frameline), 346 Ninth Street, San Francisco, CA 94103; (415) 703–8650; Fax: (415) 861–1404; http://www.frameline.org/.

San Francisco International Asian American Film Festival (National Asian American Telecommunications Association), 346 Ninth Street, 2nd Floor, San Francisco, CA 94103; (415) 863–0814; Fax: (415) 863–7428; E-mail: festival@naatanet.org; http://www.naatanet.org/festival.

San Francisco Jewish Film Festival, Ninth Street Media Arts Center, 346 Ninth Street, San Francisco, CA 94103; (415) 621–0556; Fax: (415) 621–0568; E-mail: jewishfilm @sfjff.org; http://www.sfjff.org/.

Chapter 20

Sources for Finding Alternative Media

Nancy Goldman and Jason Sanders

Building a video collection that includes alternative media such as experimental
and independent work is challenging but worthwhile. Although works like these
can be difficult to find and evaluate due to infrequent mention in general review
compendia and other resources, including them in video collection development
is worth the effort, as they can truly enrich and broaden the scope of a video
collection. For the purposes of this discussion, *alternative media* is defined as
work that is independently made, usually by individuals and small production
companies (as opposed to large-budget, mainstream Hollywood productions, or
anonymously produced documentary and educational videos produced under
contract for other agencies).

Although some independent works express mainstream ideologies, many can
be considered "alternative," as the issues explored and the stylistic concerns
advanced often challenge and offer an alternative to the cultural, social, or political status quo. This definition includes work originally made on film and
transferred to video as well as works that originated on video. The category
includes a broad range of videos with a great diversity of styles, approaches,
and audiences: from independent narrative features and documentaries to independently produced educational works; from programs produced for public television broadcast to experimental or "art" film and video; from works presenting
a social or political perspective to works made by or about specific ethnic,
gender, or sexual groups.

The importance of including materials like this in video collections lies in the fact that they frequently offer viewpoints and address cultural issues that are not commonly acknowledged by television and mainstream media. Alternative media have also increasingly provided a voice for communities that have historically been marginalized or underrepresented in mainstream media. Making such works accessible to our schools and communities can introduce new ideas to our constituencies, broadening and enriching both their perspectives and their viewing options. Because independent artists often break away from conventions of traditional media aesthetics by experimenting with new cinematic styles and approaches, alternative media can contribute an exciting variety and vitality to a collection. Additionally, seeking out and making available regionally produced media can enrich a collection, giving it a local emphasis and demonstrating a commitment to local artists.

Alternative works are not only produced independently, they are also usually distributed and exhibited outside of the mainstream. The sale of alternative works tends to be to a narrow and fairly specialized market, a problem that is compounded by the fact that independent distributors generally don't have the resources to undertake large-scale advertising and marketing strategies. Finding and reviewing such materials consequently requires perseverance. For the majority of works produced by the independent filmmaking community, we must actively seek out reviews and evaluations in often-obscure places, rather than learn about these videos through traditional resources. This chapter will first outline methodologies for selecting and evaluating these types of works and will then list sourcebooks, Web sites, periodicals, festivals, distributors, and other resources that describe, review, and supply independent and experimental media.

METHODOLOGIES

Many alternative works are produced on shoestring budgets and often do not attract broad mention in general review sources. Although they are frequently screened in film and video festivals as well as regional exhibition programs or showcases in museums and media arts centers, they are not always picked up for national distribution. Locating and evaluating these films can be difficult. There are, however, methods for overcoming these problems; a few will be outlined here.

One first step in locating distribution for alternative media titles is checking general locators such as the National Information Center for Educational Media (NICEM) database (see http://www.nicem.com for subscription information), *The Video Source Book* (Farmington Hills, MI: Gale Group), and other resources discussed elsewhere in this book. Although these guides primarily list more conventional media, they are worth a quick look. If you are seeking a particular type of work on video, checking individual video suppliers with large collections of alternative media is a good next step. There are two major U.S. distributors of experimental films—Canyon Cinema and Filmmaker's Cooperative—and two distributors of video art—Electronic Arts Intermix and Video Data Bank. These

firms are listed in the resource section at the end of this chapter along with a
number of other distributors handling collections of experimental film on video,
experimental video art and documentary, and independent film and video. If the
work or type of work you are seeking is not listed in such resources, branching
out into resources such as non-traditional review sources, subject guides, thematic film and video festival catalogs, and showcase calendars can lead to success.

Subject guides and film histories and overviews are often useful in evaluating
and tracking down independent work. Subject filmographies and videographies
tend to address very specific areas, such as specific genres, topical areas, or
filmmakers. These reference sources generally include precise subject indices
and cite works distributed by individual artists or by small companies that may
only handle a handful of titles. They often highlight works ignored by more
general locators such as *The Video Source Book*. Although few subject filmographies exist that describe experimental media (and none have been published
recently), many film histories and theoretical texts have been written that can
be used to identify, evaluate, and locate work, and thus can be very useful for
the video collection developer. One can generally learn about subject guides and
histories by keeping abreast of the current book review literature, as well as
new publications columns in regional media arts centers' newsletters.

Subject guides to independent media, in particular for multicultural and social
issue media, proliferated in the 1980s. Unfortunately, few have been published
in recent years. However, the growth of the Web in the last few years presents
new ways to learn about and locate independent media. Individual Web sites
for both small companies and larger databases incorporating independent media
have flourished, and even though the chaotic nature of the Web can make successful searching a challenge, the Web's very existence can help provide access
to marginalized information on a plethora of subjects, including media. Whereas
in the past, published subject filmographies and videographies offered one of
the only avenues for tracking down works distributed by small companies, these
companies and works are now likely to be included in larger directories or to
be linked from webliographies. For example, the UC Berkeley Media Resources
Center Web site (http://www.lib.berkeley.edu/MRC) links numerous resources
for independent media study and video collection development, and Web sites
such as Flicker (http://www.sirius.com/~sstark) offer portals to many Web sites
relevant to experimental media study and access.

Looking beyond mainstream periodical literature for reviews can be helpful
in learning about new titles and about works newly released on video. A number
of small publications exist that focus on independent filmmaking and filmmakers. *Cineaste* and *The Independent*, as well as other journals listed below, are
excellent sources for reviews of independent film and video on many subjects,
particularly multicultural, women's, and political works. Published and Web-
based review sources and databases are also useful for locating works by subject,
title, or maker, as many of them will indicate producer and/or distributor for

works cited. Regional resources, such as local media arts centers' newsletters, often review locally produced media and will frequently identify distribution sources. National organizations such as the National Alliance of Media Arts Centers (NAMAC) and the Independent Television Service (ITVS) also publish information on independent work, and provide Web sites rich in links to distributors and media organizations.

Festival and showcase programs are another good source for locating independent media. Alternative works are often self-distributed by the media artist, and many festival and showcase programs will provide addresses. A list of guides to media arts centers and festivals with particularly strong independent media programming is provided at the end of this chapter. Most showcase calendars and media center newsletters are available by subscription, and many festivals supply complimentary copies of their programs, make them available for a low fee, or publish them on the Web. Collecting and scanning such publications can build current awareness of alternative product.

Finding out whether a work originally produced on film is available on video is another challenge. Most feature films currently available on video will be listed in *The Video Source Book* and similar print sources, as well as in large commercial Web sites specializing in mass-market video sales (amazon.com, moviesunlimited.com, etc.). More obscure titles, or ones available only through their original producers, are seldom listed in these resources. Web sites for video retailers such as Video Oyster (http://www.videooyster.com), Facets Video (http://www.facets.org), and others advertising out-of-print or more arcane titles are valuable resources in the search for the hard-to-find.

Tracking down the 16mm distributor of the film can also often be helpful. These distributors frequently know whether a work has been released on video and they often distribute works on video as well as on film. Although it is quite out-of-date, *Feature Films*, edited by James L. Limbacher (New York: R. R. Bowker, 1985), lists films alphabetically, provides 16 mm and some video distribution sources, and still serves as an excellent resource for identifying the original producer. This information can, in turn, help identify the current 16mm and video distributor of a film, since most 16mm distributors tend to handle all the product owned by specific original producers. Works like the North American Publishing Company's annual set *BiB Television Programming Source Books*, which lists films available for broadcast, can be useful in tracking rights holders and in discovering if a work at least still exists in a film format.

Searching for lesser-known films or videos involves a kind of cinematic detective work: when the printed resources fail you, you must move on to less obvious resources, including sourcebooks, distributors, and individuals. Resources created and maintained in-house, such as clippings files of film and video reviews, and distributors' address lists that note changes and mergers can help one to keep on top of the constant distribution shifts. Although systems like these require significant maintenance, they can greatly facilitate locating hard-to-find media. There are several reference services that maintain such files or databases and can aid in locating materials (sometimes for a fee), including the Pacific Film Archive Library in Berkeley, the Margaret Herrick Library at the Academy of Motion Picture Arts and Sciences in Los Angeles, and the Celeste Bartos Film Study Center at the Museum of Modern Art in New York. Numerous public, special, and university libraries and media centers may also provide film reference services; and listservs, such as AMIA-L, the listserv for the Association of Moving Image Archivists, often post queries regarding distribution sources.

The methodologies listed above are helpful in locating and evaluating alternative media. Described below are some of the specific publications and resources useful in doing so.

PUBLICATIONS AND RESOURCES

Histories and Subject Guides

Building a general understanding of the history and aesthetics of experimental and independent film and video art and becoming familiar with major filmmakers of this genre is an important first step for those involved in building representative collections. The past several decades have seen a proliferation of monographic works devoted to the cinematic avant-garde and to independent filmmakers. Additionally, exhibition catalogs describing individual and group shows can help one to learn about and locate experimental work. These are generally available through museums and showcases presenting the exhibitions. Distributors' catalogs, listed later in this chapter, can then be used to purchase the works themselves.

Following is a brief list of some representative texts covering independent and experimental media history and aesthetics, as well as several collections of interviews and analyses. Most of them include distribution sources for works discussed in the texts. See also Chapter 19 in this book for an excellent list of subject guides on materials by, for, and about diverse cultures.

Experimental and Independent Film

Ehrenstein, David. 1984. *Film: The Front Line 1984*. Denver, CO: Arden Press. Essays on 15 avant-garde and independent filmmakers from America and Europe, including credits and distribution information. Indexed by film title and name.

Levy, Emanuel. 1999. *Cinema of Outsiders: The Rise of American Independent Film*. New York: New York University Press. Defining "independent" as not just a film made outside the Hollywood studio system, but also one that showcases an edgy, challenging, and highly personal vision, Levy (film critic for *Variety*) focuses on the late 1970s and onwards, encapsulating not only David Lynch and the Coen Brothers, but also regional filmmaking, African-American, Asian American and gay and lesbian movements.

Lyons, Donald. 1994. *Independent Visions: A Critical Introduction to Recent Independent American Film*. New York: Ballantine Books.

MacDonald, Scott, ed. 1988. *A Critical Cinema: Interviews with Independent Filmmakers*. Berkeley: University of California Press.

MacDonald, Scott, ed. 1992. *A Critical Cinema 2: Interviews with Independent Filmmakers*. Berkeley: University of California Press.

MacDonald, Scott, ed. 1998. *A Critical Cinema 3: Interviews with Independent Filmmakers*. Berkeley: University of California Press. These three volumes offer collections of in-depth interviews with independent and experimental filmmakers and include bibliographies and filmographies which list distribution sources.

Merritt, Greg. 1999. *Celluloid Mavericks: A History of American Independent Film*. New York: Thunder's Mouth Press. A sweeping, generalized account of American independent work, defined as almost anything made outside of Hollywood: ethnic and "race" films, films by women, Poverty Row exploitation and horror films, documentaries, and avant-garde experimental works.

Redding, Judith, and Brownworth, Victoria. 1999. *Film Fatales: Independent Women Directors*. Seattle, WA: Seal Press. Interviews with women who make independent, documentary, and experimental films; this work is especially helpful for its focus on women-of-color directors. Includes selected filmography with distribution information.

Rees, A. L. 1999. *A History of Experimental Film and Video: From Canonical Avant-garde to Contemporary British Practice*. London: BFI Publishing. An overview of international avant-garde film and video history, from the beginning of the century to the 1990s, tracing relationships between schools and movements of film and studio arts. Includes in-depth look at British experimental work, and a lengthy bibliography.

Renan, Sheldon. 1967. *An Introduction to the American Underground Film*. New York: E. P. Dutton. This important work gives a concise history of American underground film up to the mid-1960s, includes biographical profiles on filmmakers, and has an appendix listing all films mentioned in the text and their distributors in 1966. As many avant-garde films are still distributed by the same companies today, this appendix is still useful despite its publication date.

Rosenbaum, Jonathan. 1983. *Film: The Front Line 1983*. Denver, CO: Arden Press. Critical essays on 18 international avant-garde and independent filmmakers and brief paragraphs on 22 additional filmmakers. Includes credits and indexes but not distribution information.

Russell, Catherine. 1999. *Experimental Ethnography: The Work of Film in the Age of Video*. Durham, NC and London: Duke University Press. Thorough discussion of the ethnographic and experimental documentary field, including analyses of key works made throughout the century, and discussions of film and video makers' work. Includes filmography listing distribution sources for many works cited in the text.

Sitney, P. Adams. 1979. *Visionary Film: The American Avant-garde*. 2nd ed. New York: Oxford University Press. Considered a classic work, this book presents the history of American avant-garde film within a scholarly theoretical and critical framework.

Youngblood, Gene. 1970. *Expanded Cinema*. New York: Dutton. A fascinating look at pre-digital and proto-digital avant-garde experiments with film manipulation and film abstraction, performance works, and other early incorporation of film in multimedia context.

Experimental Video Art and Documentary

Boyle, Deirdre. 1997. *Subject to Change: Guerrilla Television Revisited.* New York: Oxford University Press. Chronicles the history of three major video collectives of the 1970s and their efforts to democratize television. Includes information on archival sources for some of these early tapes.

Boyle, Deirdre. 1986. *Video Classics: A Guide to Video Art and Documentary Tapes.* Phoenix, AZ: Oryx. Designed as an acquisitions tool for media librarians, archivists, and programmers, this book lists 80 titles of experimental and documentary videos, with reviews and distribution information. Although it is out-of-date, it still serves as a useful introduction to a core collection of video art and documentary. Indexed by artists/producers and by subjects.

Hall, Doug, and Fifer, Sally Jo, eds. 1990. *Illuminating Video: An Essential Guide to Video Art.* New York: Aperture Foundation; Bay Area Video Coalition. This collection of critical essays by 42 artists, curators, critics, and scholars approaches video art from historical, aesthetic, and thematic angles. It includes a videography listing all works cited in the text and lists addresses for major video art distributors.

Hanhardt, John, ed. 1986. *Video Culture: A Critical Investigation.* Rochester, NY: Visual Studies Workshop Press. Anthology of critical writings on film, video, and television from sociological, historical, and theoretical perspectives.

Hill, Chris, Horsfield, Kate, and Troy, Maria, eds. 1996. *Rewind: Video Art and Alternative Media in the United States, 1968–1980.* Chicago: Video Data Bank. History of alternative media written to accompany the nine-tape anthology *Surveying the First Decade.* Available as photocopied manuscript, supplied at no charge with series purchase or rental. Can also be purchased separately from Video Data Bank. Includes curator's essay, program descriptions, an extensive bibliography, as well as biographies, videographies, and a guide to collections.

Renov, Michael, and Suderburg, Erika. 1996. *Resolutions: Contemporary Video Practices.* Minneapolis: University of Minnesota Press. Collection of essays by film and video artists, activists, curators, and critical theorists on wide-ranging issues concerning alternative video production, reception, aesthetics, and theory, among other topics.

Web Resources

There are also many Web sites and subscription Internet services that provide a range of information on experimental media. Some are indexed and offer sophisticated search options, and many are quite useful in locating distribution or print sources. Listed below are several that are particularly useful in learning about and locating alternative works.

Flicker (http://www.sirius.com/~sstark/).
This invaluable site offers a great variety of information on alternative media, including links to venues, resources, and film and video artists' home pages. Often the artists' pages list distribution information. Flicker also provides access to the archives of the experimental film mailing list Frameworks.

OVid (http://www.werkleitz.de/ovid).

This ambitious site offers an international searchable database for experimental film and video art, with works of over 2,000 artists currently indexed. Entries include filmographic/videographic citations, international distribution, and contact information. Currently, the catalogs of such major distributors as Light Cone and Canyon Cinema are included, with plans to add many more.

Program for Art on Film (http://www.artfilm.org).

Online access to the *Art on Film* database of over 18,000 entries of international films and videos on the visual arts. The database includes many experimental and multicultural works.

Open Directory Project (http://dmoz.org/Arts/Movies/Genres/Experimental_Film/).

The Open Directory Project relies on volunteer editors to produce "the most comprehensive directory to the web." This page provides numerous links to festivals, filmmakers, reviews, titles, venues, and other experimental film-related sites.

Independent Television Service (ITVS), 51 Federal Street, Suite 100, San Francisco, CA 94107–1447; (415) 356–8383; Fax: (415) 356–8391; E-mail: itvs@itvs.org; http://www.itvs.org.

ITVS was established by Congress to help bring independently produced programs to television. The ITVS Web site includes information on home video and education distribution sources for many of the programs it has funded.

Periodicals

Periodical literature is one of the best sources for learning about newly released films and tapes and keeping abreast of current scholarship. Many of the journals listed below regularly feature reviews and articles on independent film and video. Although reviews of experimental film and video can be difficult to find, some of the journals listed below provide a critical framework useful in evaluating experimental work. Art newsletters such as *Art News, Artforum International*, and *Art in America* also occasionally review experimental video. Unfortunately, review literature on experimental film and video is spotty. Often a more effective way to learn about new experimental work is to regularly scan calendars and programs of experimental film and video showcases and festivals.

Afterimage, Visual Studies Workshop, 31 Prince Street, Rochester, NY 14607 (http://www.vsw.org/afterimage).

Bimonthly journal of articles, interviews, and reviews on photography, independent and avant-garde film and video, and visual books.

Bright Lights Film Journal (http://www.brightlightsfilm.com).

This journal, published exclusively online since 1995, defines itself as "a popular-academic hybrid of movie analysis, history, and commentary." It frequently includes articles on experimental and independent film.

Cineaste, Cineaste Publishers, Inc., 200 Park Avenue South, New York, NY 10003.

This quarterly journal includes many reviews and articles on alternative media. Reviews include theatrical distribution sources.

Cinematograph: A Journal of Film and Media Art, Foundation for Art in Cinema, 480 Potrero Avenue, San Francisco, CA 94110.

This annual journal's focus is theoretical and critical articles on experimental film.

The Independent, Association of Independent Video and Filmmakers/Foundation for Independent Video and Film, Inc. (AIVF/FIVF), 625 Broadway, 9th Floor, New York, NY 10012 (http://www.aivf.org).

This monthly, geared to independent film and video makers, features articles on multicultural themes and productions as well as independent art and documentary films and videos.

Jump Cut, Jump Cut Associates, P.O. Box 865, Berkeley, CA 94701.

Offers a political/theoretical perspective on cinema, focusing frequently on social, independent, and feminist issues.

MAIN Newsletter, National Alliance of Media Arts Centers, 346 9th Street, San Francisco, CA 94103.

Includes news from and of interest to national media arts centers. Available on the NAMAC Web site (http://www.namac.org) to anyone; the printed version is available to NAMAC members.

Millennium Film Journal, 66 East 4th Street, New York, NY 10003.

Published approximately three times per year, this journal focuses on articles, interviews, and reviews concerning avant-garde film theory and practice.

Release Print, Film Arts Foundation, 346 Ninth Street, 2d Floor, San Francisco, CA 94103.

This newsletter from the northern California organization for independent film and video makers often includes interviews with independent media artists and spotlights independent works and events. Also lists festival and funding news.

Variety, Variety, Inc., 475 Park Avenue South, New York, NY 10016 (http://www. variety.com).

Reviews all feature films released in theaters and in film festivals and includes some television and video reviews, in addition to its thorough coverage of film industry news.

Village Voice, Village Voice Publishing Corporation, P.O. Box 1905, Marion, OH 43306.

The film section of this weekly often highlights reviews and articles on independent film and video and on New York film showcase and festival programs.

Reviews and Indexes

Some of the journals mentioned above are indexed in print and electronic periodical indexes. Unfortunately, many such journals, including regional newsletters, are not indexed anywhere; others are only indexed in specialized film and television resources. Listed below are several periodical indexes which specialize in film and video, as well as general databases of films that include reference citations and links to reviews.

American Film Institute Catalog. Alexandria, VA. 1999–. Chadwyck-Healey, Inc. (http://www.chadwyck.com).

Detailed plot summaries and extensive credits for nearly all American films made up to 1970 (work on the 1950s is not yet complete). This well-respected work boasts a high degree of scholarship, and offers keyword subject indexing and some reference citations. Also available in print from University of California Press.

Film Index International. Alexandria, VA. 1996–. Chadwyck-Healey, Inc. (http://www.chadwyck.com).

Information on over 99,000 international feature films and shorts, including key credits and brief plot synopses. Entries for films and personalities include reference citations to articles and reviews.

Film Literature Index. Albany, NY. 1973–. New York: Filmdex, Inc.

Over 200 international film journals are indexed here by subject (including film and video reviews) and author. Published quarterly, with annual cumulations. Since 1988, the index has included separate sections for film and for television/video. Indiana University is currently in negotiations to mount this index online—stay tuned!

International Index to Film/TV Periodicals. On the *FIAF International FilmArchive CD-ROM.* Brussels, Belgium. 1995–. Federation Internationale des Archives du Film (http://www.fiafnet.org).

Indexes and annotates articles from roughly 150 international film periodicals, with excellent coverage of European and eastern European titles. Covers periodical literature from 1972 to the present. Available as Internet subscription (updated monthly) or on CD-ROM (updated twice each year).

Internet Movie Database (IMDB) (http://www.imdb.com).

A smorgasbord of information on film, including synopses, links to reviews, credits, filmographies, and trivia. The quantity of information provided is extensive. However, coverage and quality is uneven, as much of it is contributed by individual fans.

Lexis-Nexis. P.O. Box 933, Dayton, OH 45401–0933 (http://www.lexis-nexis.com).

Range of subscription databases covering legal, business, government, and academic topics and publications. Among other services, offers indexing and full-text articles from thousands of national and regional publications, including general interest periodicals, newspapers and newsletters, trade journals, and other publications. Covers the past 10–20 years to the present. Very useful for locating reviews from national newspapers and trade papers.

New York Times Film Reviews. 1970–. New York: New York Times and Arno Press.

Original set presents facsimiles of all reviews published in the *New York Times* from 1913 to 1968, with title, credits, and corporate indexes. Continued by annual or biannual updates. Reviews from the last few years available on the *New York Times'* Web site (http://www.nytimes.com).

Variety Film Reviews. 1983–. New York: R. R. Bowker.

Facsimiles of all feature films reviewed in *Variety* since 1907. Compiled into one set up to 1980, with annual or biannual updates. Indexed by title only, with liberal cross-referencing for foreign-language titles. Now also available by subscription to *Variety Extra*, available on *Variety*'s Web site (http://www.variety.com).

Festivals

Film and video festivals often premiere new works, and festival catalogs can be an excellent resource for locating synopses and distribution sources for lesser-known films and tapes. Although not all festival catalogs include U.S. distribution information, most will note the original producer, who can advise about video availability. Listed below are several print and Web-based guides to festivals, which can be searched by categories including experimental film and video art. These guides are followed by a sampling of festivals offering independent and experimental film and video. Many of the festivals with ethnic and regional focuses listed in Chapter 19 in this book also feature experimental media. Collecting programs and schedules from festivals and media centers in your region can be a good resource for new and locally produced work. Although there are many foreign festivals that also screen alternative works, they are not listed here, as it is very costly and time-consuming to purchase videos from foreign sources.

Published and Web-Based Festival Guides

Film Fest Preview (http://www.variety.com/filmfest). This site posts reviews of festivals of all shapes and sizes, with good contact information.

Film Festival Server (http://www.filmfestivals.com). Lists international festivals by month, name, and country, with contact and submission information. Provides links to most festival sites as well.

Langer, Adam. 2000. *The Film Festival Guide.* Chicago: Chicago Review Press. A comprehensive reference guide that includes interviews with festival directors, contact information, a submission calendar, and over 500 festival listings.

Variety International Film Guide. Variety, 34–35 Newman Street, London W1P 3PD. This annual includes articles on new productions by country as well as listings of international film festivals, archives, bookstores, and magazines.

Festivals Featuring Alternative Media

This highly selective list includes representative festivals from around the United States presenting independent, regional, and experimental works. As almost every festival showcases some independent narrative features, they are not all included here. For additional resources, consult the guides listed above.

Ann Arbor Film Festival, P.O. Box 8232, Ann Arbor, MI 48107; (734) 995–5356; E-mail: vicki@honeyman.org; http://aafilmfest.org/festival.html.
One of the oldest and most renowned festivals of super-8 and 16mm films.

Athens International Video Festival, P.O. Box 388, Athens, OH 45701; (740) 593–1330; E-mail: bradley@ohiou.edu; http://www.athensfest.org/.

Black Maria Film Festival, c/o Department of Media Arts, Jersey City State College, 203 West Side Avenue, Jersey City, NJ 07305; (201) 200–2043; Fax: (201) 200–3490; http://ellserver1.njcu.edu/TAEBMFF.
A curated, touring program of recent avant-garde work.

Chicago Underground Film Festival, 3109 North Western Avenue, Chicago, IL 60618; (773) 327–FILM; E-mail: info@cuff.org; http://www.cuff.org/.
One of many rawer festivals catering to shorts and feature-length narrative independent works.

DoubleTake Documentary Film Festival, 317 West Pettigrew Street, Durham, NC 27705; (919) 660–3699; E-mail: ddff@duke.edu; http://www-cds.aas.duke.edu/film festival.
North Carolina's independent and experimental documentary film festival, spotlighting new American and international documentary works.

Film Arts Festival, 346 Ninth Street, Second Floor, San Francisco, CA 94103; (415) 552–FILM; E-mail: lizc@filmarts.org; http://www.filmarts.org/festival.html.
One of the premier festivals devoted to screening new independent and experimental works from the San Francisco Bay Area and beyond.

Flicker Film Festival, P.O. Box 15296, Durham, NC 27704; E-mail: flicker@ipass. net; http:// www.flickerfestival.com.
Bimonthly Chapel Hill, North Carolina festival, strong in 8mm works. Now branching out to other national locations.

Human Rights Watch International Film Festival, 485 Fifth Avenue, New York, NY 10017; (212) 972–8400; Fax: (212) 972–0905; E-mail hrwnyc@hrw.org; http://www. hrw.org/hrw/iff/festival.html.
Founded by the Human Rights Watch organization in 1990, showcasing fictional and documentary films dealing with human rights issues.

Independent Feature Film Market, 104 West 29th Street, 12th Floor, New York, NY 10001; (212) 465–8200; Fax: (212) 465–8525; E-mail: ifpny@ifp.org; http://www.ifp. org/docs.cfm/Locales/East/Film_Market.
A starting point and meeting ground between new filmmakers, producers, and distributors, now branching out to other regional markets.

LA Freewaves, 2151 Lake Shore Avenue, Los Angeles, CA 90039; (323) 664–1510; E-mail: freewaves@aol.com; http://www.freewaves.org.
LA Freewaves is a media arts network, providing services, workshops, and screening opportunities for experimental media artists. Its festival, "A Celebration of Experimental Media Arts," takes place at numerous venues in the Los Angeles area. Its Web site also serves as a resource, including links to many artists and organizations, information on classes in video production and Web design, and information on its own festival programming.

Margaret Mead Film and Video Festival, American Museum of Natural History, Department of Education, Central Park West at 79th Street, New York, NY 10024–5192; (212) 769–5305; Fax: (212) 769–5329; E-mail: meadfest@amnh.org; http://www.amnh. org/mmead/.
This annual festival of anthropological films screens and premieres many outstanding independent documentaries on world cultures, and often follows with a national touring program.

MIX—The New York Lesbian and Gay Experimental Film and Video Festival, (212) 571–4242; Fax: (212) 571–5155; E-mail: mix@echonyc.com; http://www.mixnyc.org.

New York Video Festival, Film Society of Lincoln Center, 70 Lincoln Center Plaza, New York, NY 10023; (212) 875–5600; E-mail: sbensman@filmlinc.com; http://www.filmlinc.com/nyvf/nyvf.htm.
One of the largest festivals in the United States devoted to video.

Slamdance Film Festival, 5526 Hollywood Boulevard, Los Angeles, CA 90028; (323) 466–1786; Fax: (323) 466–1784; E-mail: mail@slamdance.com; http://www.slamdance.com.
A growing alternative to the slicker Sundance Film Festival, featuring extreme and low-budget filmmaking.

Women in the Director's Chair Film and Video Festival, 941 West Lawrence Avenue, Suite 500, Chicago, IL 60640; (773) 907–0610; http://www.widc.org.

Internet Film Festivals

The Internet has greatly expanded the way researchers, librarians, and the general public view and learn about media. Although the explosion of content available over the Internet often offers quantity over quality, it still gives us ideas about technological impact on the future of the moving image. One new avenue for exhibiting alternative media is through streaming video sites. These sites seem to appear and disappear with relative frequency, and the work they exhibit is of varying artistic quality. Many of these sites primarily feature smaller, shorter versions of traditional Hollywood fare intended as calling cards to the industry, although some sites, including Atom (http://www.atomfilms.com) and Ifilm (http://www.ifilm.com), index work under headings such as "experimental." Several sites, such as ResFest (http://www.resfest.com), Digital Film Festival (http://www.dfilm.com), and the Sundance Online Film Festival (http://www.sundance.org), showcase only work that has been produced digitally. Although these sites at present function somewhat as novelties, they and others like them are worth keeping an eye on, as this method of media exhibition, and potentially distribution, is likely to increase and improve in coming years.

Independent and Experimental Showcases

In addition to festivals, archives, showcases, and regional exhibition programs screen a wide range of independent and experimental film and video. Listed below is a sampling of institutions that offer ongoing programming. Although many more exhibition programs exist that include some alternative programming, this list concentrates on those organizations offering substantive, ongoing programming of experimental works. A number of them include experimental film and video as part of their program, while others are devoted solely to screening alternative works. Calendars for some of these organizations will include program notes with print source information.

Many other regional media arts centers often present local experimental and independent works. Consult the National Alliance of Media Arts Centers

(NAMAC), 346 9th Street, San Francisco, CA 94103 (415–431–1391; http://
www.namac.org) for addresses and activities of additional regional media arts
centers. NAMAC's Web site includes a directory profiling NAMAC member
organizations, including information on their programs, collections, distribution
activities, publications, and histories, and links to their Web sites.

Anthology Film Archives, 32–34 Second Avenue, New York, NY 10003; (212) 505–
5181; Fax: (212) 477–2714; http://www.anthologyfilmarchives.org.

Artist's Television Access, 992 Valencia Street, San Francisco CA 94110; (415) 824–
3890; http://www.atasite.org.

Chicago Filmmakers, 5243 North Clark Street, Chicago IL 60640; (773) 293–1447;
Fax: (773) 293–0575; http://www.chicagofilmmakers.org.

Filmform—Los Angeles, UCLA Hammer Museum, 10899 Wilshire Boulevard, Los
Angeles, CA 90024; (310) 433–7000; http://www.filmforum.org.

The Gene Siskel Film Center, School of the Art Institute of Chicago, 289 South Columbus Drive and Jackson Boulevard, Chicago, IL 60603; (312) 443–3733; http://www.
artic.edu/saic/art/filmcntr/.

Hallwalls Contemporary Arts Center, The Tri-Main Center, 2495 Main Street, Suite
425, Buffalo, NY 14214; (716) 835–7362; Fax: (716) 835–7364; E-mail: office@
hallwalls.org; http://www.hallwalls.org/.

Image Film and Video Center of Atlanta, 75 Bennett Street NW Suite N-1, Atlanta,
GA 30309; (404) 352–4225; Fax: (404) 352–0173; http://www.imagefv.org.

The Kitchen, 512 West 19th Street, New York, NY 10011; (212) 255–5793; Fax: (212)
645–4258; http://www.thekitchen.org.

Millennium Film Workshop, 66 East 4th Street; New York, NY 10003; (212) 673–
0090.

Museum of Modern Art Film Department, 11 West 53rd Street, New York, NY 10019;
(212) 708–9400; http://www.moma.org/staticfilmvideo/current.html.

Northwest Film Center, Portland Art Museum, 1219 SW Park Avenue, Portland, OR
97205; (503) 221–1156; Fax: (503) 294–0874; E-mail: info@nwfilm.org; http://www.
nwfilm.org/.

Pacific Film Archive, 2625 Durant Avenue, Berkeley, CA 94720; (510) 642–1412;
Fax: (510) 642–4889; http://www.bampfa.berkeley.edu.

Pittsburgh Filmmakers, 477 Melwood Avenue, Pittsburgh, PA 15213; (412) 681–5449;
http://www.pghfilmmakers.org.

San Francisco Cinematheque/Foundation for Art in Cinema, P.O. Box 880338, San
Francisco, CA 94188–0338; (415) 822–2885; http://www.sfcinematheque.org.

Walker Art Center, Vineland Place, Minneapolis, MN 55403; (612) 375–7622;
information@walkerart.org; http://www.walkerart.org/.

Wexner Center for the Arts, Ohio State University, North High Street at 15th Avenue,
Columbus, OH 43210–1393; (614) 292–0330; Fax: (614) 292–3369; http://www.
wexarts.org/.

Whitney Museum of American Art, Film and Video Exhibition, 945 Madison Avenue at 75th Street, New York, NY 10021; (212) 570–3676; http://www.whitney.org/.

Distributors

Distribution sources for alternative media range from large companies handling a wide variety of titles that may include some independent work to small outlets that have a particular cultural, aesthetic, or thematic orientation. Like any business, media distribution is often adversely affected by economic climates, and consequently, changes and mergers in distribution companies occur with relative frequency. Listed below are a few of the current resources concentrating on alternative media. Be aware, however, that changes in these resources may have occurred since the publication of this volume.

Additional distributors of culturally diverse media are listed in Chapter 19 in this book. A useful listing of alternative media production and distribution groups is also posted at the Web site of activist cable access producers Paper Tiger Television: http://www.papertiger.org/roar/chap21.html.

American Friends Service Committee, Video and Film Library, 2161 Massachusetts Avenue, Cambridge, MA 02140; (617) 497–5273; Fax: (617) 354–2832; E-mail: pshannon@afsc.org; http://www.afsc.org/nero/nevlib.htm. Distributes political documentaries and activist works on video.

Arthouse Inc., (212) 334–6165; Fax: (212) 334–6273; E-mail arthouse@arthouseinc. com; http://www.arthouseinc.com/.

Strong on films by and about artists, with a good collection of experimental work.

California Newsreel, 149 9th Street, Room 420, San Francisco, CA 94103; (415) 621–6196; http://www.californianewsreel.org.

Films and videos on ethnic and political issues. Very strong emphasis on African cinema and anti-apartheid works through their collections "Black America Emerges," "Library of African Cinema," and "The Southern Africa Media Center."

Cambridge Documentary Films, Inc., P.O. Box 390385, Cambridge, MA 02139–0004; (617) 484–3993; Fax: (617) 484–0754; http://www1.shore.net/~cdf/.

Large collection of various documentary films and videos.

Canadian Filmmakers Distribution Center, 37 Hanna Avenue, Suite 220, Toronto, ONM6K 1W8 Canada; (416) 588–0725; Fax: (416) 588–7956; http://www.cfmdc.org/.

Canada's oldest artist-run center for experimental media, offering distribution services for their members. Their Web site offers a searchable catalog of works they distribute.

Canyon Cinema, 2325 Third Street, Suite 338, San Francisco, CA 94107; Phone/Fax: (415) 626–2255; http://www.canyoncinema.com.

Established in 1966 as a non-profit cooperative distribution center owned and operated by its filmmaker members, Canyon remains an important alternative distribution center for independent/experimental films. Canyon handles over 2,000 titles and distributes both film and video. Their catalogs, with filmmakers' own descriptions of their works, are a valuable resource.

Cecile Starr, 35 Strong Street, Burlington, VT 05401; (802) 863–6904.

Distributes a small but important collection of abstract and experimental films, including titles by Hans Richter, Mary Ellen Bute, Len Lye, and Alexander Alexeieff and Claire Parker.

Cinema Guild, 1697 Broadway, Suite 506, New York, NY 10019; (212) 246–5522; http://www.cinemaguild.com.

International feature and short films and videos on a wide range of social issues and multiethnic topics, as well as arts and entertainment works.

Direct Cinema, Ltd., P.O. Box 1333, Santa Monica, CA 90410; (310) 636–8200, or (800) 525–0000; http://www.directcinema.com/.

Distributes a wide selection of short independent films and videos, many of which are award-winning. Topics include anthropology, art and architecture, children's films, history and cultural studies, and the environment.

Electronic Arts Intermix, 542 West 22 Street, 3rd Floor, New York, NY 10011; (212) 337–0680; Fax: (212) 337–0679; E-mail: info@eai.org; http://www.eai.org.

One of the two largest distributors of artists' video, EAI handles a wide range of international art videos for sale or rental. Their new catalog is a significant reference resource for the field.

Facets Video, 1517 West Fullerton Avenue, Chicago, IL 60610; (800) 331–6197; Fax: (773) 929–5437; http://www.facets.org/.

One of the largest and most respected independent distributors of narrative feature films, international classics, and experimental compilations on videotape. In addition to their general catalog, Facets publishes many subject guides to works in their collection.

Filmakers Library, 124 East 40th Street, New York, NY 10016; (212) 808–4980; http://www.filmakers.com.

Films and videos on social issues, area studies, history, ecology, psychology, and more are handled by this distributor.

Filmmaker's Cooperative, 175 Lexington Avenue, New York, NY 10016; (212) 889–3820; http://www.film-makerscoop.com.

Like Canyon, Filmmaker's Cooperative is open to any filmmaker wishing to place a print on deposit for rental at a fee set by the individual artist. They distribute a wide range of experimental and personal films. Artists write their own catalog descriptions. Although they primarily handle film, FMC also distributes some experimental video.

First Run/Icarus Films, 32 Court Street, 21st Floor, Brooklyn, NY 11201; (800) 876–1710; (718) 488–8900; Fax: (718) 488–8642; http://www.frif.com.

Noted for their strong collection of works on Latin American studies, this company also handles independent works on such topics as economics, cinema studies, history, social issues, area studies, and religion.

Flower Films & Video, 10341 San Pablo Avenue, El Cerrito, CA 94530; (510) 525–0942; Fax: (510) 525–1204; http://www.lesblank.com.

Sells and rents films and videos by Les Blank, which celebrate "Real Food, Roots Music and People Full of Passion for what they do!" American ethnic and cultural topics, as well as other independent filmmakers' works.

The Iota Center, 3765 Cardiff Avenue, #305, Los Angeles, CA 90034; (310) 842–8704; http://www.iotacenter.org.

They specialize in "preserving and promoting the art of light and movement," and distribute abstract animation and video art by artists including Oskar Fischinger, Jordan Belson, Stan Brakhage, and Glenn McKay.

The Kitchen, 512 West 19th Street, New York, NY 10011; (212) 255–5793; Fax: (212) 645–4258; http://www.thekitchen.org.

In addition to their multidisciplinary programs of video, music, dance, performance, film, and literature, this New York exhibition space also distributes a wide-ranging selection of video art.

Light Cone, 12 rue des Vignoles, 75020 Paris, France; (33) 01 46 59 01 53; Fax: (33) 01 46 59 03 12; http://www.lightcone.org.

Experimental film and video, from Paris. Some of their product can also be purchased online from http://www.re-voir.com.

The Lux: Centre for Film, Video, and Digital Arts, Lux Centre, 2–4 Hoxton Square, London N1 6NU, England; (44) 020 7684 0201; http://www.lux.org.uk.www.

English distributor devoted to the avant-garde.

Museum of Modern Art Circulating Film and Video Library, 11 West 53d Street, New York, NY 10019; (212) 708–9530; http://www.moma.org.

Distributes a high-quality collection of features and shorts, with concentrations in silent film, documentary, and independent and experimental film, as well as some video art. Many works are available on both film and video for either sale or rental.

Mystic Fire Video, 19 Gregory Drive, South Burlington, VT 05407–2284; (800) 727–8433; http://www.mysticfire.com.

Distributes avant-garde film and theater on video, as well as many nature documentaries, spiritual works, and fine arts titles.

National Asian American Telecommunications Association (NAATA), 346 9th Street, 2nd Floor, San Francisco, CA 94103; (415) 863–0814; http://www.naatanet.org.

Films and videos which showcase voices, issues, and experiences from diverse Asian American and Pacific Islander communities.

New Day Films, 22-D Hollywood Avenue, Hohokus, NJ 07423; (201) 652–6590; Fax: (201) 652–1973; http://www.newday.com.

Social issue films and videotapes, with many addressing issues of gender and socialization, as well as multicultural and other independent works.

Paper Tiger TV, 339 Lafayette Street, New York, NY 10012; (212) 420–9045; Fax: (212) 420–8196; E-mail: info@papertiger; http://www.papertiger.org/.

This activist video collective produces broadcast videos that analyze and critique issues involving media, culture, and politics. They also distribute the tapes for sale or rental.

Third World Newsreel, 545 Eighth Avenue, 10th Floor, New York, NY 10018; (212) 947–9277 Fax: (212) 594–6417; E-mail: twn@twn.org; http://www.twn.org.

One of the largest and oldest distributors of alternative media in the United States.

Video Data Bank, School of the Art Institute of Chicago, 112 South Michigan Avenue, Chicago, IL 60603; (312) 345–3550; Fax: (312) 541–8073; E-mail: info@vdb.org; http://www.vdb.org.

Distributes experimental and independently produced videotapes by and about contemporary artists. Videos are available for sale or rental. Along with Electronic Arts Intermix, one of the two largest national art video distributors.

Women Make Movies, 225 Lafayette Street, Suite 212, New York, NY 10012; (212) 925–0606; http://www.wmm.com/.
Independently produced films and tapes by and about women, including many experimental works and works by black, Asian, and Latin women.

REFERENCE SERVICES

Assistance in locating distribution sources for specific film or video titles or subjects is offered by some public, special, and university library and media centers. Several that specialize in film, video, or television reference and can be helpful in locating distribution sources for independent works are listed below. Some of these services are fee-based. For additional reference services, consult national directories to libraries and media centers, as well as the *International Directory of Film and TV Documentation Collections* (1993–). The *International Directory* is available on paper and as part of the *International FilmArchive CD-ROM*, from the International Federation of Film Archives (FIAF), 1 rue Defacqz, 1000 Brussels, Belgium; http://www.fiafnet.org.

Margaret Herrick Library, Academy of Motion Picture Arts and Sciences, 333 South La Cienega Boulevard, Beverly Hills, CA 90211; (310) 247–3020. Hours: 9:00–3:00, M–Tu and Th–F. http://www.oscars.org/mhl.
Offers phone reference service at no cost for simple questions that can be answered in approximately three minutes. More in-depth reference and research requests should be directed by mail to the National Film Information Service at the same address. They will handle such requests for costs ranging from $10.00 up.

Museum of Modern Art, Department of Film, Celeste Bartos Film Study Center, 11 West 53rd Street, New York, NY 10019; (212) 708–9613. Hours: 1:00–5:00, M–F. http://www.moma.org.
Answers brief reference questions pertinent to films and films available on video. For video art questions, call the MoMA Video Study Center at (212) 708–9689.

Pacific Film Archive Library, UC Berkeley Art Museum /Pacific Film Archive (BAM/PFA), 2625 Durant Avenue, Berkeley, CA 94720–2250; (510) 642–1437. Hours: 1:00–5:00, M–Thu. http://www.bampfa.berkeley.edu.
Answers brief reference questions on any film-related topic by phone, mail, or in person. They also offer in-depth research through their consultation service, which is billed at an hourly rate. The BAM/PFA Web site includes *PFA Filmnotes*, a searchable database of PFA programs which lists distribution sources, and *CineFiles*, a growing image database of PFA's files of reviews, press kits, distributors' flyers, and other documentation.

University of Southern California (USC), Cinema-Television Library, USC, University Park, Los Angeles, CA 90089–0182; (213) 740–8906. Hours: 1:00–5:00, M–F.
Although their primary clientele is USC students and faculty, they do offer telephone reference and referral to the public as well for brief film and television-related requests.

Chapter 21

Sources of Stock and Archival Footage

Helene Whitson

WHAT IS STOCK FOOTAGE?

According to Rick DeCroix, stock footage "refers to any piece of film or video photographed by an outside source that is licensed to a producer or director for use in a separate, secondary production." Such footage is introduced by moving-image makers into a scene or setting to help illustrate their story. There are various kinds of stock footage, and in fact, any footage can be considered stock footage, depending on its use. The following are four examples of difference sources of stock footage:

1. *Footage created by a moving-image agency as a by-product of its daily activities.* Television news is a good example of this material, because it is a product of a news department's operations. Stories may be produced, and footage shot to illustrate the story, but the station may never air it. Many stations keep archives of their own material and use or reuse it in future productions, and make it available for others to use. Moving-image producers frequently gather generic footage on various topics for their own use.

2. *Generic, subject-specific footage created by moving-image makers specifically for use in other productions.* Some film production companies specialize in generating film on specific subjects, such as wildlife, urban areas, weather, people, animals, sports, or trains. Other film/video makers who do not have the time, staff, or funds to create their own footage—a shot of a car crash, for

example—may choose to incorporate such ready-made material into their productions instead.

3. *Historic factual footage, including older television news, movie newsreels, and amateur moving images (home movies/videos).* Producers frequently require actual historic footage to amplify and elaborate the story being told. A production on World War II, for example, might use archival footage of soldiers on the battlefield, interspersing it with footage created by the film/video maker, to lend an air of authenticity and immediacy to their work. Government-created footage, such as that produced by various U.S. agencies, can be quite helpful for these purposes. The portable 8mm camera and, later, home video have had the indirect effect of putting historical documentation into the hands of the general public. Amateur film and video can be a valuable source for recording specific fashions and fads, hairstyles, family life and work life, architecture, and elements of material culture.

4. *Footage from commercial productions used in other productions.* Just as television news producers may not use all the footage they have created, commercial moving-image producers rarely incorporate all their shot footage into their final work. Such unused film or video often is retained by producers or studios in their archives for use in future productions, in order to save both time and money. Examples of materials in such an archive might include footage of an interior set without actors, or perhaps a re-creation of an important event, a well-known locale, or other recognizable visual elements.

WHAT ARE STOCK FOOTAGE HOUSES?

Stock footage houses are commercial agencies that own moving-image footage or represent owners of footage. The primary purpose of such enterprises is the acquisition and sale or licensing of moving images. Such agencies may have a wide variety of materials or may specialize in certain subjects, such as wildlife or nature footage, sports, or views of cities. They may have the rights to previously produced materials, such as news collections and full-length feature films, or may create footage on commission. In order to make their collections accessible to potential clients, they organize, catalog, preserve, index in detail (often to the shot level), and reproduce whatever the customer selects. For a fee, such companies often provide prospective buyers with research assistants to find that exact scene or shot the customer needs. Stock footage agencies usually have material accessible by specific subject, and have indexed their holdings thoroughly. A stock footage house often can find the exact scenes the researcher needs, if they exist, whether they be long shots, establishing shots, or aerial overviews. Because film producers and studios often work on tight deadlines, stock footage houses are attuned to delivering customized products on fairly short order.

As mentioned previously, stock footage houses may specialize in specific types or genres of images. Depending on the nature of the collection, these companies might focus on national or international footage, on factual or entertainment footage. They may provide early syndicated newsreels, commercially prepared films and videos, industrial and educational films, or entertainment items. Stock footage houses often are not a primary source for locally produced programming, such as television news, video, or community-access programming. This type of footage may be retained by the local station, where it might be preserved or reused in other productions. Sometimes, however, this material is deposited for preservation with a local historical society, archive, library, or museum. Collections such as these are referred to as film or video archives, and their mission is quite different from that of commercial footage houses, although the materials they house may be similar.

WHAT ARE MOVING-IMAGE ARCHIVES?

Moving-image archives are agencies that collect moving-image materials (and often supporting materials as well) because of their historical importance. The primary mission of such organizations is to organize, preserve, and make that footage accessible for study, research, educational, and often commercial uses (the nature of the materials in such may define or limit particular uses). Educators and researchers may use materials from a moving-image archive for teaching, in their research, in exhibits, and in educational productions. Moving-image archives often are established to collect and preserve a very specific type of information, depending on the mission of the institution that establishes or houses the archives. In fact, such agencies, especially if they are highly specialized institutions such as museums or film centers, may have an institutional mission or scope to collect moving images. The Louis Wolfson II Media History Center, a research center supported by a consortium of the Miami-Dade Public Library, Miami-Dade Community College, and the University of Miami, was established expressly to collect moving-image materials and supporting documentation about Florida. Another example, the San Francisco Bay Area Television Archive at San Francisco State University's J. Paul Leonard Library, grew out of the concept that local television news is an additional, important nonprint source of information for scholarly research in an academic setting.

While some moving-image archives are independent entities, such as the international Museum of Photography at George Eastman House and Northeast Historic Films, most tend to have an affiliation with one or more larger institutions. Many archives have both physical and administrative ties to academic institutions, such as the UCLA Film and Television Archive, the San Francisco Bay Area Television Archive at the San Francisco State J. Paul Leonard Library, and the American Archive of the Factual Film at Iowa State University. Historical societies and public libraries also support a number of more regionally focused archival collections such as the Chicago Historical Society, the Minnesota Historical Society, and the Louis Wolfson II Media History Center. Government agencies, such as the Library of Congress, the National Archives, and the Mississippi State Department of Archives and History, tend to focus on materials of interest to national or state historians. Finally, museums such as the Museum of Modern Art in New York City will collect moving images that support their other collections. Again, no matter with which type of institution a moving-image archive may be affiliated, many of these collections were developed to be financially self-supporting. Thus, the type of highly specific, frame-by-frame access one has to images in a stock footage library is not available to those who utilize moving-image archives.

While the mission of a stock footage library is to make accessible and license or sell footage, the mission of the moving-image archive is to preserve rare moving images for future viewers. Moving-image archives describe, catalog, index, and preserve these materials according to national standards. Unfortunately, inconsistent or inadequate funding and staffing in archives and similar organizations often places serious limitation on such crucial functions as cataloging and indexing, preservation, and reference and research services. While moving-image archives may have similar footage to that held by stock footage houses, they generally cannot provide the same type of highly detailed information about these materials as their commercial counterparts (providing the in-depth, frame-by-frame analysis of materials in the collections would be the same as providing a page-by-page analysis of a book). Archives staff also may have additional, non-moving-image responsibilities, and may not always be able to address the needs of the moving-image researcher immediately. Moving-image archives that own the copyright to their materials may be more likely to provide detailed access and service because they can benefit from the funds that licensing the materials will generate.

Because of the distinct differences between these missions, it is clear that professional filmmakers often choose to utilize a stock footage collection rather than a moving-image archive, except under rare circumstances. The images owned by a stock footage library are thoroughly indexed, and they can be licensed or purchased in a timely fashion. At the present time, some moving-image archives are allowing stock footage agencies to represent their collections. Such an action is a new development in the access to moving images, and the success of such projects is unknown. An institutional decision to enter into such an agreement must be weighed carefully and considered in the context of institutional policies, rights, and control of the images.

LOCATING STOCK FOOTAGE AND STOCK FOOTAGE AGENCIES

The Library of Congress does not use "stock footage" or "archival footage" as a subject heading, so it is difficult to find monographs/books on that topic. Printed works such as *Footage: The Worldwide Moving Image Sourcebook* have assigned to them the broader headings of *Motion Picture Film Collections—*

North America—Directories; Videotape Collections—North America—Direc-
tories; Motion Pictures—Catalogs; or *Videotape—Catalogs*. While books assigned these subject headings may include information about stock footage and
stock footage companies, the subject heading does not reflect accurately the
focus of these works.

Various indices, both print and electronic, will guide researchers to information concerning stock footage, including *Film Literature Index*, the *International Index to Film Periodicals, ABI Inform, Art Abstracts*, and the
International Index to the Performing Arts. Researchers can use the heading
"stock footage" to find articles about stock footage, as well as information concerning stock footage providers.

The Internet provides a broad array of information about stock footage, including access to providers and access to research about the topic. *Google* is a
particularly good search engine. Other search engines which retrieve the largest
number of Web pages concerning stock footage include *Ixquick, Fast Search,
Northern Light, Infoseek*, and *Metacrawler*. Researchers may simply use the
search term "Stock footage."

Perhaps the most comprehensive guide to stock footage companies and their
holdings in available through the Web site Footage.net (http://www.footage.net).
This Web site is based on the print directory mentioned above, *Footage: The
Worldwide Moving Image Sourcebook*, last published in 1997. A wide variety
of stock footage companies, from WPA Films to National Geographic to CNN,
are represented on this site. A global search engine allows the user to initiate a
search from this site's home page. Links to individual company sites also are
provided. Many of these companies have set up their own search engines, allowing prospective customers to search their inventory and, in some cases, preview available footage prior to ordering. Another site, The Stock Solution (http:
//www.digitaldirectory.com/stock/html), while focusing primarily on stock
photographs, also includes links to many of the same companies found on Foot-
age.net. Other online resources include a database created by the National Archives and Records Administration, *Source and Permission Contact List* (http:
//www.nara.gov/research/ordering/source.html), which categorizes archives and
stock footage sources by very general subjects; and, the *Motion Picture Editors
Guild Newsletter* of May–June 1999, which includes a list of stock footage resources at http://www.editorsguild.com/newsletter/mayjun99/stock_footage.html.

WORKING WITH STOCK FOOTAGE HOUSES

There are a great many stock footage houses around the world, and their
services, rates, and turnaround times vary. As mentioned previously, some stock
footage houses have online subject databases researchers can access via the
Internet, search for free, and then contact the company with requests. The company will compile a screening tape (¾-inch, VHS, BetaSP, or any other format),
for a fee. The videotape of requested material has time code—a method of

numbering each video frame by hours, minutes, and seconds—burned onto the tape, so that the researcher can indicate the exact frames needed, and note the inclusive time on the tape. In addition, time code also protects the licensing institution or copyright holder from any unauthorized use of the materials. The researcher must pay for the cost of the tape itself as well as shipping costs. After the order has been placed, the stock footage company will then transfer the frames from the original medium to whichever format the researcher desires. There will be varying fees for that process, as well as fees for licensing.

Stock footage houses without online subject databases generally have research assistants who will search the collection for a fee. Even those companies that do provide access to their inventories via the Web often provide additional fee-based research services. Dubbing and licensing fees are routinely charged for selected materials as well. In most cases, stock footage houses require prepayment before they will complete the final transfer of materials from original footage to desired format copy or ship this material to the client.

COPYRIGHT/LICENSING

There are many elements to a moving image, including the location, the people, the sound, narration, musical score, or music in general (e.g., a band playing in the background). Any or all of those elements may become an issue in clearing copyright for desired footage. Those wishing to incorporate clips from other productions into their own works should be certain of the copyright status of the material, including all elements contained within the selected clip. There are two types of ownership: physical and intellectual. Physical ownership refers to having possession of the particular item. Intellectual ownership refers to the ownership of the contents.

Commercial stock footage houses generally either own the intellectual rights (copyright) to their holdings or act as agents for the copyright holders. Archives, libraries, museums, historical societies, and other moving-image archives may own the physical moving-image items in their collections, but they may or may not own the intellectual rights to those holdings. To make matters more complicated, the owner of the work may not own all of the rights to every element of a piece of footage. For example, the band in the background of a scene may be playing the "Anniversary Waltz," a work whose intellectual rights may be held by someone else. If a filmmaker is planning to use news footage that includes a reporter, she or he probably would not be able to use the footage without a release from the reporter. In these cases, the user would have to seek permission from other copyright holders.

If an institution such as a library or museum accepts a moving-image collection as a gift, then a representative from the institution should negotiate a deed of gift with the donor. This legal agreement (which should be in writing) will spell out the rights and responsibilities of both the donor and the recipient. Archives, libraries, museums, and historical societies often have an indemnification clause that assigns responsibility for rights clearance to the end user. Thus, if use of the material is challenged in terms of rights ownership or nature of use, the institution is not held liable. Institutions that allow users to duplicate moving images from their collection for any purpose should generally require the user to clear the rights to this material with the copyright owner.

Stock footage libraries charge licensing fees in order to compensate the copyright holder for use of their property. The categories and fees for licensing may differ, depending upon the requester: a student working on a class project, an individual who wants an item for personal reasons, an independent filmmaker, a producer for a public television program, or a director representing a major motion picture company. The number of times a piece of footage will be seen and the type of material into which it is being incorporated vary greatly, depending on these different classes of users. The fees charged will reflect these various uses and use contexts. Licensing usually is granted for a specific length of time; it rarely is given in perpetuity. A filmmaker or video maker may start a project with one "market" (or audience) in mind, and later want to distribute this film to other markets. Under each of these circumstances, new rights would have to be negotiated between the filmmaker and the stock footage house.

ARCHIVES CITED

For a complete list of moving image archives that are members of the International Federation of Film Archives (FIAF), search this organization's directory at http://www.cinema.ucla.edu/FIAF/english/.

The International Federation of Television Archives (FIAT) also provides a list of members and their telephone numbers, as well as some links to various member Web sites, at http://www.nb.no/fiat/fiat.html.

- UCLA Film and Television Archive (http://www.cinema.ucla.edu)
- San Francisco Bay Area Television Archive at the San Francisco State University Library (http://www.library.sfsu.edu/special/sfbata.html)
- The American Archive of the Factual Film at Iowa State University (http://www.lib.iastate.edu/spcl/aaff/aaff.html)
- Chicago Historical Society (http://www.chicagohs.org)
- Minnesota Historical Society (http://www.mnhs.org)
- Louis Wolfson II Media History Center at Miami-Dade Public Library (http://www.mdpls.org/services/departments.htm)
- Library of Congress (http://www.loc.gov)
- National Archives (http://www.nara.gov)
- Mississippi State Department of Archives and History (http://www.mdah.state.ms.us)
- The New York Museum of Modern Art (http://www.moma.org)

- Northeast Historic Films (http://www.oldfilm.org)
- George Eastman House (http://www.eastman.org)

REFERENCES

DeCroix, Rick. 1997. "A History of Stock Footage: Changing Definitions with Changing Times." In *Footage: The Worldwide Moving Image Sourcebook*. New York: Second Line Search Inc. http://www.footagesources.com/learnmore/learnmore_historyarticle.html.
Prelinger, Rick. 2000. "Beyond Copyright Consciousness." *Bad Subjects* 52 (November). http://eserver.org/bs/52/prelinger.html.

RESOURCES

Albitz, Rebecca. 2000. "Locating Moving Image Material for Multimedia Development: A Reference Strategy." *Reference Librarian* 71: 99–110.
Brown, Kimberley. 2000. "Footage.net gets eMotion(al)." *RealScreen* (February 1): 10. http://www.realscreen.com/articles/magazine/20000201/27894.html.
Christie, Brendan. 1998. "The Difference between Rights and Wrongs: Navigating Stock Footage Clearance—From the Myth of 'Fair Use' to the Peril of Libel, the Pitfalls and Policies of Leasing Footage." *RealScreen* (March 1): 37. http://www.realscreen.com/articles/magazine/19980301/21091.html.
Christie, Brendan. 2000. "Taking Stock of the Web." *RealScreen* (July 1): 41. http://www.realscreen.com/articles/magazine/20000701/29541.html.
Christie, Brendan, and Kennedy, John. 1998. "Stalking Stock." *RealScreen* (July 1): 29. http://www.realscreen.com/articles/magazine/19980701/22387.html.
Dick, Ernest J. 1998. "The Great Stock Hunt: An Archivist Passes Judgement on Footage: The Worldwide Moving Image Sourcebook." *RealScreen* (January 1): 21. http://www.realscreen.com/articles/magazine/19980101/20278.html.
Footage: The Worldwide Moving Image Sourcebook. 1997. New York: Second Line Search Inc. http://www.footagesources.com/home.html.
Keenlyside, Sarah. 2000. "The Future of Footage." *RealScreen* (February 1): 39. http://www.realscreen.com/articles/magazine/20000201/27892.html.
Morgan, Jenny, comp. 1996. *Film Researcher's Handbook: A Guide to Sources in North America, South America, Asia, Australasia and Africa*. London and New York: Routledge.
National Archives and Records Administration. *Source and Permission Contact List*. http://www.nara.gov/research/ordering/source.html. Listing of rights clearance contacts, including film archives, broadcasting sources, stock footage holders, government sources, and other moving-image resources.
News Libraries Bibliography (SLA News Division). http://www.poynter.org/research/biblio/bib_nlibs.htm.
Prelinger, Rick. 1998. "Archival Survival: The Fundamentals of Using Film Archives and Stock Footage Libraries." http://www.footage.net/info/archival_survival.html.

Rayman, Susan, and Brown, Kimberley. 2001. "Culling the Shots: Filmmakers Get En-
    trepreneurial with Their Footage." *RealScreen* (February 1): 39. http://www.
    realscreen.com/articles/magazine/20010201/Stock.html.
Slide, Anthony. 1986. *The American Film Industry: A Historical Dictionary.* Westport,
    CT: Greenwood Press.

Selected Commercial Stock Footage Houses

Below is a highly selective list of some of the larger and more well-known commercial
stock footage houses. The holdings of a number of these firms are also indexed by
Footage.net.

ABC News VideoSource (http://www.abcnewsvsource.com/welcome.html).

Along with stock footage from ABC news productions from the last 30 years, includes
newsreel footage from APTN (global news coverage), British Movietone News (1929 to
1979), and Universal Newsreels (1929 to 1967).

Archive Films (http://www.archivefilms.com).

The Archive Films library contains more than 24,000 cataloged hours of historical
stock footage and film clips, including footage from newsreels, Hollywood features, silent
films, classic documentaries, vintage industrial and educational films, TV programs, music performances, and home movies. The company also exclusively represents many other
large film libraries, including the March of Time, The Gaumont Newsreel, The Prelinger
Collection of American Life, Culture and Industry, The RKO/Pathe Library, The Rohauer
Collection, and the The Christian Science Monitor TV News Archive.

BBC Worldwide (http://www.bbcfootage.com).

The BBC collections include Broadcast Archives, News Archives, and StockVisions,
containing more than two million subject listings, captured on over 500 million feet of
film, 400,000 hours of video, and more than 500,000 sound recordings.

CNN Image Sources (http://www.cnnimagesource.com).

A large collection of stock footage gathered by CNN as part of its news production
operations. Site includes a searchable image database. Transcripts are available for some
materials.

efootage (http://www.efootage.com).

This site provides access to a large commercial, copyright-cleared stock footage collection. A representative portion of the collection is searchable from the company's Web
site. The efootage database currently offers thumbnail still frames of selected works;
streamed video samples are in the works, according to the vendor.

Video Monitoring Services of America (http://www.vidmon.com/).

A service that records broadcast news in over 100 top national markets every month
and offers this material for sale to public relations and media firms, marketing agencies,
political organizations, and others. The company's library includes over one million television commercials, the largest in the world, and will be a vital resource for you to stay
up-to-date on the latest creative efforts of your competition.

WGBH Film and Video Resource Center (http://www3.wgbh.org/wgbh/footage/).

Footage from WGBH (PBS) productions, including such programs as *NOVA, Frontline*, and *The American Experience*.

WPA Film Library (http://www.wpafilmlibrary.com).

The WPA Film Library is one of the largest sources of historical and contemporary moving images (over 40,000 hours). They are the exclusive North American distributor for the British Pathe News Library (1896–1970). Collection also includes TV programming from the 1950s and 1960s, as well as footage from the productions of MPI Media (WPA's parent company).

Chapter 22

Video and Film Associations, Organizations, and Discussion Lists

Gary P. Handman

As discussed and lamented in the introduction to this book and elsewhere, video librarianship remains a professional specialty with startlingly few practitioners. Formal training for the specialty is uneven at best, and there are few standard resources or guides upon which to rely once on the job. It is consequently natural for video librarians faced with the formidable challenge of building collections and services to turn to key professional organizations for guidance in their work. The Video Round Table and scattered ALA committees mentioned below aside, ALA has never been much interested in video (and most likely will never be). State library organizations offer little more in the way of support for the connection-hungry video librarian. Fortunately, there are greener and more productive organizational pastures existing beyond these library professional circles.

Organizations and associations devoted to various aspects of film, video, new media, and the arts in general have never been in short supply. Some of these groups are fairly well-established and long-running; others seem to pop up one month, only to go under the next. The organizations listed below (many of which have been around for awhile) provide the types of unique information and valuable connections with filmmakers, arts centers, and programs, and distributors that can be extremely useful for enterprising media librarians. Many of the groups described sponsor festivals, a particularly effective way to learn about new and important works on the market. A fair number offer workshops, seminars, conferences, and other education and information-sharing programs. In some cases, the services offered by the organization include information and resource clearinghouse functions and other forms of communication, such as online discussion lists.

For other organizations and associations focusing on film and video making by and about specific cultural communities, see Chapter 19 in this book, devoted to resources for building culturally diverse video collections.

MISCELLANEOUS

MediaWeb (http://riceinfont.rice.edu/Outreach/MediaWeb/).

MediaWeb is an educational outreach service of the Temple University Computer Center, and the Rice University Data Applications Center. MediaWeb is a loose coalition of film/TV/video webmasters that seeks to foster collaboration and coordination among media studies Web sites. The central service of this organization is a listserv devoted to the discussion of media-related Web site development. To subscribe, consult the following Web location: http://listserv.temple.edu/cgi-bin/wa?SUBED1=mediaweb&A=1.

ARTS ORGANIZATIONS—GENERAL

Americans for the Arts, 1000 Vermont Avenue NW, 12th Floor, Washington, DC 20005; (202) 371–2830; Fax: (202) 371–0424; http://www.artsusa.org/; One East 53rd Street, New York, NY 10022; (212) 223–2787; Fax: (212) 980–4857.

Americans for the Arts works with cultural organizations, arts and business leaders, and individuals to provide leadership, education, and information that will encourage national support for the arts. AFA goals include increased fiscal support of the arts; arts education for children; community development through the arts. Publications: a large catalog of monographs and reports related to arts funding and arts administration, arts education, and other topics related to art and American society.

ArtsWire, E-mail: artswire@artswire.org; http://www.artswire.org/.

A program sponsored by the New York Foundation for the Arts, Arts Wire is an online network of artists, arts workers, arts organizations, and arts funders. The ArtsWire Web site provides access to current news and information relating to the arts; informed discussion of arts-related issues; listings of grants, exhibition opportunities, and jobs in the arts. ArtsWire's WebBase database is a growing listing of arts and culture-related resources on the Web and elsewhere.

FILM ARTS ORGANIZATIONS

Organizations and associations whose central mission is to support and act as advocate for the independent film and video making community. Some of these organizations, such as the National Latino Communication Center (NLCC) and the National Asian American Telecommunications Association (NAATA), are also engaged in video distribution and in public broadcasting programming (see Chapter 19 in this book for details). Also included are organizations, such as the American Film Institute, that are concerned with film preservation and scholarship activities related to more mainstream Hollywood films.

American Film Institute (AFI), 2021 North Western Avenue, Los Angeles, CA 90027; (323) 856–7600; Fax: (323) 467–4578; E-mail: Info@afionline.org; http://www. afionline.org/.

Established in 1965 by the National Endowment for the Arts, AFI is an independent, non-profit organization dedicated to: preserving the heritage of film and television; identifying and training new talent; increasing recognition and understanding of the moving image as an art form. In 1984, the Institute established the National Center for Film and Video Preservation at AFI as a mechanism for coordinating and implementing national film and television preservation activities. Institute programs emanate from the AFI campus in Los Angeles and the AFI Theater in the John F. Kennedy Center in Washington, DC (202) 828–4000; Fax: (202) 659–1970.

American Indian Film Institute (AIFI), 333 Valencia Street, Suite 322, San Francisco, CA 94103; (415) 554–0525; Fax: (415) 554–0542; E-mail: indianfilm@aifisf.com; http: //www.aifisf.com/overview.html.

The American Indian Film Institute is a non-profit media arts center founded in 1977 to encourage Indian and non-Indian filmmakers to document Native voices, viewpoints, and stories that have been historically excluded from mainstream media; to develop Indian and non-Indian audiences for this work; and to advocate for authentic representations of Indians in the media. Sponsor of the annual AIFI Film Festival since 1975. Publications: *Indian Cinema Entertainment [ICE]* (quarterly).

Asian Cinevision (ACV), 32 East Broadway, 4th Floor, New York, NY 10002; (212) 925–8685; Fax: (212) 925–8157; E-mail: acvinfo@yahoo.com; http://www.asian cinevision.org.

ACV is a non-profit national media arts center dedicated to the development of Asian American film and video arts. Founded in 1976, Asian CineVision's year-round activities include major exhibitions in film and video, media production service, publications, and training workshops. Sponsors the Asian American International Film Festival (see http: //www.asiancinevision.org/ff2000/index.html).

The Association of Independent Video and Filmmakers (AIVF), 304 Hudson Street, New York, NY 10013; (212) 807–1400; Fax: (212) 463–8519; E-mail: info@aivf.org; http://www.aivf.org.

AIVF was established by a group of independent makers to offer support and resources to independent artists. The organization currently has 5,000 members internationally. Publications: *The Independent*. Some back issues available online to AIVF members.

Black Filmmakers Hall of Fame, 405 Fourteenth Street, Suite 515, Oakland, CA 94612; (510) 465–0804; Fax: (510) 839–9858; E-mail: bfhfinc@aol.com; http://www. blackfilmmakershall.org.

Founded in 1973, the Black Filmmakers Hall of Fame is devoted to supporting and increasing the visibility of current African-American filmmaking, and highlighting African-American filmmaking history. BFHF sponsors regular workshops, lectures, and screenings devoted to black film, and hosts an annual film festival in Oakland, California.

Cine Acción, 346 9th Street, 2nd Floor, San Francisco, CA 94103; (415) 553–8135; Fax: (415) 863–7428; E-mail: cineaccion@aol.com; http://www.cineaccion.com.

A group of Latino Bay Area film and video makers founded Cine Acción in 1980 to foster production and appreciation of Latino media arts, and to increase the participation of Latinos in the film and video industry. The organization screens film and video year-round in the Cineteca de Cine Acción, and produces the annual Festival ¡Cine Latino! Cine Acción. Distribution: distributes Cineworks, a catalog of film and video by members that contains a vast array of works addressing Latino cultural identity, politics, and imagery. Publications: monthly bulletin and quarterly newsletter.

Film Arts Foundation (FAF), 346 Ninth Street, 2nd Floor, San Francisco, CA 94103; (Cross streets are Folsom and Harrison); (415) 552–8760; Fax: (415) 552–0882; E-mail: info@filmarts.org; http://www.filmarts.org.

Established in 1979, Film Arts Foundation is one of the most venerable film arts organizations in the United States. FAF is dedicated to supporting the work of independent film and video makers in the San Francisco Bay Area and other parts of the country, through providing production facilities, a grants program, and film screenings, seminars, and workshops. The FAF Web site includes useful information about festivals and other national filmmaking activities. Publications: *Release Print Magazine* (10 issues yearly).

Media Alliance, c/o Thirteen/WNET, 450 West 33rd Street, New York, NY 10001; (212) 560–2919; Fax: (212) 560–6866; E-mail: mediaall@tmn.com; http://www.mediaalliance.org.

Media Alliance is a non-profit membership organization dedicated to advancing independent media (video, film, audio, radio, and computers) in New York State by expanding resources, support, and audiences for the media arts. Publications: bi-monthly newsletter; newsletter highlights available online at: http://www.mediaalliance.org/newsletter.html.

The National Alliance for Media Arts and Culture (NAMAC), 346 9th Street, San Francisco, CA 94103; (415) 431–1391; Fax: (415) 431–1392; E-mail: namac@namac.org; http://www.NAMAC.org.

Founded in 1980, NAMAC's member organizations include media arts centers, production facilities, university-based programs, museums, film festivals, media distributors, film archives, multimedia developers, community access TV stations, and individuals working in the field. The general goal of NAMAC is to encourage film, video, audio, and online/multimedia arts. NAMAC's regional and national members collectively provide a wide range of support services for independent media, including media education, production, exhibition, distribution, collection building, preservation, criticism, and advocacy. NAMAC sponsors an annual national conference. Publications: *Main Newsletter* (quarterly; available online via NAMAC Web site).

National Asian American Telecommunications Association (NAATA), 346 Ninth Street, 2nd Floor, San Francisco, CA 94103; Fax: (415) 863–7428; E-mail: naata@naatanet.org; http://www.naatanet.org.

Started with seed funds from the Corporation for Public Broadcasting, NAATA is one of the five Minority Consortia created to provide culturally diverse programming for public television. In addition to national public television broadcasts, NAATA's program areas have expanded to include support to media artists, international educational and cable distribution, and the annual San Francisco International Asian American Film Festival. Distribution: distributes a large catalog of award-winning videos by Asian American film and video makers and on Asian American topics. Publications: *Asian American Network*.

National Association of Regional Media Centers (NARMC), http://www.aect.org/Affiliates/narmc.html.

The National Association of Regional Media Centers is committed to promoting leadership among its membership through networking, advocacy, and support activities that will enhance the equitable access to media, technology, and information services to educational communities. The purpose of NARMC is to foster the exchange of ideas and information among educational communications specialists whose responsibilities relate to the administration of regional media centers and large district media centers.

National Latino Communication Center (NLCC), 3171 Los Feliz Boulevard, Suite 201, Los Angeles, CA 90039; (213) 663–8294; Fax: (213) 663–5606; E-mail: nlccemedia@ aol.com; http://latino.sscnet.ucla.edu/community/nlcc.

The National Latino Communications Center (NLCC) is a non-profit media arts and production center that funds, produces, and syndicates Latino programming for public television. NLCC is the largest single provider of grants to producers of Latino programming intended for public television. The archive will serve as a repository not only of Latino films and videos, but also of treatments, scripts, production stills, music scores, correspondence, and other related film/video materials. Distribution: distributes a small list of feature films and documentaries on video dealing with Chicano/Latino life and culture. Publications: quarterly newsletter that discusses issues facing Latino producers and includes updates on the center's work, such as the establishment of a National Latino Film and Video Archive.

Native American Public Telecommunications (NAPT), 1800 North 33rd Street, Lincoln, NE 68583; P.O. Box 83111, Lincoln, NE 68501; (402) 472–3522; Fax: (402) 472–8675; E-mail: native@unl.edu; http://nativetelecom.org.

The mission of Native American Public Telecommunications (NAPT) is to "inform, educate and encourage the awareness of tribal histories, cultures, languages, opportunities and aspirations through the fullest participation of American Indians and Alaska Natives in creating and employing all forms of educational and public telecommunications programs and services." Activities include producing and developing educational programs for all media, including television and public radio; various lobbying and advocacy activities. Distribution: distributes a list of videos on Native American history and culture.

Program for Art on Film (PAF), 200 Willoughby Avenue, c/o Pratt SILS, Brooklyn, NY 11205; (718) 399–4506; Fax: (718) 399–4507; E-mail: Info@Artfilm.org; http:// www.artfilm.org/PAF.htm.

Founded in 1984 as a joint venture between the J. Paul Getty Trust and the Metropolitan Museum of Art, PAF was established to foster new ways of thinking about the relationship between art and moving-image media, and to encourage critical analysis of media productions. In 1996, the Program was restructured as an independent, non-profit corporation, and relocated to Pratt Institute (Brooklyn), where it is affiliated with the Graduate School of Information and Library Science. PAF's Art On Screen database includes records for over 25,000 films, videos, videodiscs, CD-ROMs, and multimedia productions, produced from 1970 to the present, with selective coverage of earlier productions from 1915 through 1969. A related database includes names and addresses of more than 5,000 distributors and producers of moving-image productions. Publications: filmographies, reference works, and conference proceedings dealing with art, architecture, and film, and video (see http://www.artfilm.org/pubs.htm).

FILM AND VIDEO INDUSTRY ORGANIZATIONS

Association for Information Media and Equipment (AIME), P.O. Box 1173, 56 John Street, Clarksdale, MS 38614; (662) 624–9355; Fax: (662) 624–9366; E-mail: aime@ gmi.net; http://www.aime.org.

AIME assists producers of information film, video, interactive technologies, computer software, and equipment for educational and information uses by: "promoting the general welfare and improving the professional status of those engaged in information technologies; developing activities and policies to stimulate more widespread and more effective use of these technologies; analyzing the needs of organizations involved in the information industries; instituting activities to attract and interest people of talent in seeking professional careers in the information industries." Publications: *AIME News*. AIME maintains a useful Web site devoted to industry perspectives on media copyright, and on evolving issues in the area of electronic media.

ORGANIZATIONS RELATED TO FILM AND VIDEO IN LIBRARIES, ARCHIVES, AND MEDIA CENTERS

American Library Association (ALA), 50 East Huron Street; Chicago, IL 60611; (312) 944–6780, (800) 545–2433; http://www.ala.org (see: http://www.ala.org/contact_ala.html for other contact information).

ALA has served librarians for over 100 years. The ALA Conference/Convention is held in a different city each spring/summer, and the Mid-Winter Conference is held annually in Chicago. *Booklist*, the monthly journal, includes an audiovisual section with video reviews. Within the organization the following divisions and organizations are directly involved with the selection, acquisition, processing, and use of video in libraries:

Association for Library Collections & Technical Services (ALCTS) (http://www.ala.org/alcts/). Concerns include acquisition, cataloging and classification, preservation of library materials, selection, and evaluation of resources. Committees/subcommittees include: Media Resources Committee (formerly Audiovisual Committee) (http://www.ala.org/alcts/organization/div/mrc/mediaresources. html); Media Resources Committee Standards Subcommittee (http://www.ala.org/alcts/ organization/div/mrc/mrstandards.html).

Association of College and Research Libraries (ACRL) (http://www.ala.org/acrl/). Committees include: Media Discussion Group, ACRL Arts Section (including Technology in the Arts Committee; and the Film & Broadcast Discussion Group).

Association for Library Service to Children (ALSC) (http://www.ala.org/alsc/). Evaluates and recommends non-print as well as print materials for children. The Notable Films and Videos Committee selects an annual winner of the Carnegie Medal (established 1991) to recognize children's video.

Library and Information Technology Association (LITA) (http://www.lita.org/). Efforts are directed to video communications and other related aspects of media activities, as well as hardware applications in libraries.

Public Library Association (PLA) (http://www.pla.org/). Committees: PLA Audiovisual Committee.

Video Round Table (VRT) (http://www.lib.virginia.edu/dmmc/VRT/). Provides a forum and voice for video interests of ALA members working in all types of libraries. Activities include maintenance of two active listservs (VIDEOLIB and VIDEONEWS) devoted to the discussion of broad issues and specific problems related to video librarianship; sponsorship of an annual Notable Videos for Adults award. Publications: *VRT Newsletter* (tri-annual).

Young Adult Library Services Association (YALSA) (http://www.ala.org/yalsa/). Committees include: AV Producers and Distributors Liaison, Media Selection and Usage, and Selected Films and Video for Young Adults.

Association of Moving Image Archivists (AMIA), 8949 Wilshire Boulevard, Beverly Hills, CA 90211; (310) 550–1300; Fax: (310) 550–1363; E-mail: amia@amianet.org; http://www.amianet.org.

AMIA is a non-profit professional association established to foster cooperation among individuals and organizations concerned with the collection, preservation, exhibition, and use of moving-image materials. Currently, AMIA represents over 600 archivists and institutions from the United States and Canada. AMIA members are drawn from a broad cross-section of film, television, video, and interactive media: classic and contemporary Hollywood productions; newsreels and documentaries; and national, regional, and local television production, including news, public affairs, and entertainment programming. Conferences: annual conference. Publications: *AMIA Newsletter* (quarterly); *Archival Moving Image Materials: A Cataloging Manual* (draft). Sponsors AMIA-L listserv.

Consortium of College and University Media Centers (CCUMC), CCUMC Executive Office, 121 Pearson Hall—ITC, Iowa State University, Ames, IA 50011–2203; (515) 294–1811; Fax: (515) 294–8089; E-mail: donrieck@iastate.edu; http://ccumc@ccumc.org.

The mission of CCUMC is to improve the process of learning and teaching through the effective use of media/instructional technology services in higher education. Membership includes all sizes of institutions in higher education that provide media/instructional technology–related support services, as well as companies providing related products. Activities of the organization include annual conference, special satellite programs. Publications: *The Leader*, the association's newsletter, is published four times a year: three regular issues (September, January, May) and an occasional annual survey issue (June).

Dance Films Association (DFA), 48 West 21st Street, #907; New York, New York 10010; Tel./Fax: (212) 727–0764; E-mail: dfa5@juno.com; http://www.dancefilmsassn.org.

DFA acts as an information clearinghouse and meeting ground for the user, producer, and distributor of dance films and videos. DFA organizes lectures, screenings, workshops, and panel discussions in institutions around the country and participates in competitions and festivals around the world. Publications: *Dance on Camera Journal*, bimonthly newsletter; *Dance on Camera: A Guide to Dance Films and Videos* (Scarecrow Press, 1998). Conferences/Festivals: Since 1972, DFA has sponsored the annual Dance on Camera Festival, the oldest, annual competitive dance film and video festival in the world.

International Federation of Film Archives (La Federation Internationale des Archives du Film) (FIAF), 1 Rue Defacqz, B-1000; Bruxelles / Brussels, Belgique / Belgium; (32–2) 538 3065 (FIAF); (32–2) 534–6130 (P.I.P.); Fax: (32–2) 534 4774; E-mail: info@fiafnet.org; http://www.cinema.ucla.edu/fiaf/default.html.

Founded in Paris in 1938, FIAF is a collaborative association of the world's leading film archives whose purpose has always been to ensure the proper preservation and showing of motion pictures. Today, more than 100 archives in over 60 countries collect, restore, and exhibit films and cinema documentation spanning the entire history of film. Publications: *The Journal of Film Preservation, The International Filmarchive CD-ROM* (which includes *The International Index to Film Periodicals*).

National Video Resources (NVR), 73 Spring Street, Suite 606, New York, NY 10012; (212) 274–8080; E-mail: nvrinfo@nvr.org; http://www.nvr.org.

NVR is a non-profit organization established in 1990 by the Rockefeller Foundation with the goal of increasing the public's awareness of and access to independently produced media and film, including media delivered through the new digital technologies. NVR designs and implements projects that help enable individuals and organizations such as public libraries, colleges and universities, and other non-profits to acquire and use independent film and video. NVR also commissions and publishes research on issues of concern to independent media makers, distributors, educators, activists, and individuals. Publications: *NVR Reports*; publications and guides related to programming projects, including *Viewing Race*, and *From Rose to Roosevelt*.

Online Audiovisual Catalogers (OLAC) (http://ublib.buffalo.edu/libraries/units/cts/olac/).

OLAC was founded in 1980 as a forum for catalogers of audiovisual materials. OLAC provides a means for exchange of information, continuing education, and communication among AV catalogers, and with the Library of Congress and bibliographic utilities. Conferences: sponsors bi-annual conferences. Publications: *OLAC Newsletter*.

University Film and Video Association (UFVA), Robert Bassett, Chapman University, School of Film & Television, 333 North Glassell Street, Orange, CA 92866; (714) 628–7244; Fax: (714) 997–6700; E-mail: bassett@chapman.edu; http://www.ufva.org.

Founded in 1947 as the University Film Producers Council, members include college and university faculty and students, archivists, librarians, educational institutions, businesses and manufacturers, and creators of films and videos. Conferences: annual conference, featuring peer review of videos and films, media writing, presentations of papers, special screenings, production workshops, and technical exhibits. Publications: *UFVA Digest*, Annual Membership Directory; *UFVA Monographs*; *The Film/Video Production Annual*, an electronic publication of films and videotapes by UFVA members.

ADVOCACY AND MEDIA LITERACY ORGANIZATIONS

For other media literacy organizations and resources see the Center for Media Literacy's Web site (http://www.medialit.org/othersites.html#National) and Pennsylvania State University College of Education's media literacy site (http://www.ed.psu.edu/ls/multires.htm). Many of the organizations listed above in the Media Arts section could also be listed among the following media advocacy groups; many are centrally involved in lobbying for national and regional arts funding, for freedom of expression, and for the preservation of a diversity of media viewpoints.

Alliance for a Media Literate America (formerly the Partnership for Media Education [PME]), E-mail: amla@ccicrosby.com; http://www.nmec.org/.

A coalition of private and public sector organizations formed in 1997 and stimulating the growth in media literacy education through national leadership, advocacy, networking, and information exchange. Conferences: annual: The National Media Education Conference. These meetings provide an opportunity for educators to learn the principles of media education in a venue that both exemplifies and models the best practices in the field—in essence, a national forum for diverse views, visions, and voices.

The Benton Foundation, 950 18th Street NW, Washington, DC 20006; (202) 638–5770, (202) 638–5771; E-mail: benton@benton.org; http://www.benton.org/.

Founded in 1981, the Benton Foundation has undertaken a wide variety of media and public interest initiatives, including: "defining and promoting public policies that support the public interest services and capacities of new media; helping non-profit organizations use communications tools and strategies to be information providers and social advocates; creating knowledge centers in the new media that are trusted sources and guides to non-profit information and action." Publications: the Foundation offers a large number of publications and position papers related to media and public policy; many of these are available online at http://www.benton.org/Library. Also available is a free, online current awareness service that provides a bi-weekly digest of headline news items related to telecommunications and national telecommunications policy (see http://www.benton.org/Lists/home.html#comm-policy).

Center for Media Education (CME), 2120 L Street NW, Suite 200, Washington, DC 20037; (202) 331–7833; Fax: (202) 331–7841; E-mail: cme@cme.org; http://www.cme.org/.

Founded in 1991 to carry on the work of Action for Children's Television, CME is a national non-profit organization dedicated to creating a quality electronic media culture for children and youth, their families, and the community. At the national and state levels, CME is working with education, library, and child advocacy organizations to expand the access of poor and minority children to new educational technologies in school and at home. Publications: *INFOACTIVE KIDS: A Quarterly Subscription*; various special reports and resource books.

Center for Media Literacy (CML), 4727 Wilshire Boulevard, #403, Los Angeles, CA 90010; (800) 226–9494; Fax: (323) 931–4474; E-mail: cml@medialit.org; http://www.medialit.org/.

A non-profit membership organization established in 1989, CML's activities include developing and distributing, via a printed and online catalog, media literacy educational materials; conducting media literacy workshops, teacher training, seminars, and special events, as well as co-sponsoring national conferences. Publications and media: see http://www.medialit.org/Catalog/catalog.htm.

Media Education Foundation (MEF), 26 Center Street, Northampton, MA 10160; (800) 897–0089; E-mail: mediaed@mediaed.org; http://www.mediaed.org/.

MEF is a non-profit educational organization devoted to media research and production of resources to aid educators and others in fostering analytical media literacy. Distribution: MEF offers a useful and unique catalog of videos devoted to issues such as media literacy, media and society, and the politics of mass communication.

MediaRights.org, 443 Broadway, 5th Floor, New York, NY 10013; E-mail: info@mediarights.org; http://www.mediarights.org/.

Started in mid-2000, MediaRights.org is a broad-based group devoted to increasing the visibility of and access to social issue documentaries and advocacy videos. The organization's Web site is intended as a community resource and meeting place for media makers, activists, educators, and librarians. The site includes a growing, searchable database of videos from a variety of distributors and producers.

The Visual Resources Association (VRA), http://www.VRAweb.org/.

VRA is a non-profit organization established to further research and education in the field of visual resources and to promote a spirit of cooperation among the members of the profession. Membership is open to any person or institution interested in the purposes of the Association. VRA membership includes slide and photograph curators, film and video librarians, media professionals, photo archivists, slide and microform producers, rights and reproduction officials, photographers, art historians, and others concerned with visual materials. Publication: *VRA Bulletin.*

LISTSERVS AND OTHER ONLINE DISCUSSION FORUMS

The following is a very small sampling of currently active online discussion groups devoted to media studies and film and video collections and services in libraries. Unless otherwise noted, subscription to these lists is open to the general public.

For general information on online mailing lists, see Web location: http://alabanza.com/kabacoff/Inter-Links/listserv.html (Interlinks).

For a good introduction to general collection development and acquisition resources on the Internet, see Collection Development and the Internet: *A Brief Handbook for Recommending Officers in the Humanities and Social Sciences Division at the Library of Congress.* Compiled by Abby Yochelson, Cassy Ammen, John Guidas, Sheridan Harvey, Carolyn Larson, and Margo McGinnis. Web location: lcweb.loc.gov/acq/colldev/handbook.html.

VIDEO/FILM COLLECTIONS IN LIBRARIES AND ARCHIVES

ACQNET-L. A moderated listserv that aims to provide a medium for acquisitions librarians and others interested in acquisitions work to exchange information, ideas, and to find solutions to common problems. Information about ACQNET is available at http://www.library.vanderbilt.edu/law/acqs/acqnet.html. Subscription address: acqnet-l@listserv.appstate.edu. ACQ-WEB (http://www.library.vanderbilt.edu/law/acqs/acqs.html) is a sister publication of ACQNET and the gathering place for librarians and other professionals interested in acquisitions and collection development.

AMIA-L. Association for Moving Image Archivists (see listing for AMIA above). Subscription address: listserv@lsv.uky.edu.

CCUMC-L (see listing for CCUMC above). Consortium of College and University Media Centers—Discussion List). The consortium's Internet mailing list, CCUMC-L@iastate.edu, is open to all current members of CCUMC.

MC JOURNAL (Journal of Academic Media Librarianship). A peer-reviewed electronic forum for practical and scholarly information concerning academic media librarianship. Subscription address: listserv@ubvm.http://wings.buffalo.edu/publications/mcjrnl/.

VIDEOLIB (American Library Association. Video Round Table). Established to encourage the broad and lively discussion of issues relating to the selection, evaluation, acquisition, bibliographic control, preservation, and use of current and evolving video formats in libraries and related institutions. Subscription address: listproc@library.berkeley.edu. List archive at: http://www.lib.berkeley.edu/VideoLib/archive.html.

VIDEONEWS (American Library Assn. Video Round Table). An electronic clearinghouse for information about new services, products, resources, and programs of interest to video librarians and archivists, educators, and others involved in the selection, acquisition, programming, and preservation of video materials in non-profit settings. Subscription address: listproc@library.berkeley.edu.

NEW MEDIA

DIGVID-L (Digital Video Discussion). DIGVID-L is an open, unmoderated discussion list featuring digital video. Read and post discussions, advice, experiences in using, creating, and distributing digitally stored video. Practicalities of formats including, but not limited to, DVI, MPEG, and JPEG, as well as QuickTime, Video For Windows, etc. Subscription address: listserv@ucdavis.edu.

MEDIA STUDIES

CINEMA-L. Discussion of all forms of cinema, in all its aspects. Its founding is based on the understanding that most people who watch and enjoy movies do so from a variety of viewpoints, and that a general, unlimited forum is desirable. Subscription address: listserv@american.edu-bit.listserv.cinema-l.

FILM-STUDIES. General interest discussion group for film studies. Subscription address: majordomo@list.uiowa.edu.

H-FILM. Film History and the Scholarly Study of Media. Subscription address: listserv@H-Net.msu.edu.

MEDIA-L. Media In Education—serves as a network for people in the media services profession to ask questions and discuss new procedures or services. Subscription address: listserv@bingvmb.cc.binghamton.edu.

SCREEN-L. An unmoderated list for all who study, teach, theorize about, or research film and television—mostly in an academic setting, but not necessarily so. SCREEN-L ranges from the abstract (post-post-structuralist theory) to the concrete (roommate match-ups for the next SCS/UFVA conference). Pedagogical, historical, theoretical, and production issues pertaining to film and TV studies are welcomed. Subscription address: listserv@ua1vm.ua.edu.

Part VII

Fast Forward: The Future of Moving-Image Distribution and Access

Chapter 23

DVD: Not If but When

Kristine R. Brancolini

Librarians are often accused of being resistant to change. Those of us who work in the area of media collection development realize that one type of change is inevitable—changing formats for the delivery of media resources. Activity on the American Library Association Video Round Table listserv (VIDEOLIB) over the past two years indicates considerable anxiety over the adoption of the latest format, Digital Versatile Disc (DVD). While many librarians prefer to take a wait-and-see attitude with regard to this new format, others have begun serious efforts toward DVD collection building, always in addition to the dominant video format in all libraries, VHS. This chapter will assess the current status of DVD and provide a framework for planning for the adoption of this new format. The recently adopted ACRL "Guidelines for Media Resources in Academic Libraries" (1999) highlight this important role for media librarians.

[W]hile supporting these traditional formats, media librarians must assess rapidly-evolving new formats and be ready to adopt them when they stabilize. We must still evaluate new formats, but move more quickly than in the past to incorporate them into our collections. Libraries must plan for format adoption."

This statement applies to librarians in all types of libraries. Despite the potential pitfalls and the costs of adopting a new format, media librarians must incorporate this task into their responsibilities. Adopting a new format involves some risk, but it is the only way to provide access to the diversity and quality of media resources that users deserve.

Why an entire chapter devoted to DVD? Because it is the first new format for the delivery of motion video to hit the market since the advent of VHS in the 1970s, and it is likely that all libraries will eventually be adding this format to their media collections. Like laser discs and audio compact discs (CDs), DVD offers many benefits and few disadvantages. The advantages include the following:

- *Quality*. The sound and picture quality are superior to VHS and the picture quality is superior to laser discs. Like laser discs, many DVDs offer supplemental materials and features, such as alternate sound tracks, multiple versions and formats (e.g., letterbox and "pan-and-scan," dubbed and subtitled), short documentaries on "the making of the film, and commentary by the director.
- *Durability*. Unlike VHS players, in which a spinning electromagnetic device (read heads) comes into direct contact with the videotape, there is no physical contact between the DVD disc and the heads during playback. The surface of the disc is plastic-coated, to further protect it from physical damage. Unlike tape-based media, which physically deteriorate over time (even if unplayed), optical discs do not degrade simply sitting on a shelf. Nor can they be accidentally erased or damaged by a 3-M desensitizer or other magnetic devices. Like CDs, a DVD is likely to be playable long after the equipment exists to play it (for information on the permanence of CDs, see "Permanence, Care, and Handling of CDs").
- *Size*. DVDs are the same size as a CD, but packaged to be shelved with videocassettes. They can be intershelved with VHS tapes, but require less storage space.

The disadvantages are similar to those of CDs:

- *Size*. While their small size is an advantage from a storage perspective, DVDs are also prone to theft. Most libraries with open shelving find they must use security cases and take other precautions to minimize theft.
- *Surface Damage*. Despite their protective coating, DVDs are subject to surface damage, including scratches, gouges, and pits. Library collections of DVDs are especially prone to damage. Like other playback equipment, DVD players must be cleaned to prevent damage to discs and discs must be cleaned periodically. Minor damage to a disc can be remedied with polishing or buffing.
- *Durability*. Some librarians report that DVDs seem to be prone to serious damage, such as cracking and deep scratching. Rue Herbert from the University of South Florida wrote about DVDs: "Ours have already come back scratched, chipped, and needing new cases. It's too early to tell if we are actually going to have to replace DVDs more than VHS (plenty of problems there with multiple users as you all know), but it's definitely something to think about." (VIDEOLIB, June 27, 2000). However, this concern has not been expressed by many others, and in a follow-up message Rue reported less frequent damage as users became accustomed to handling the discs.

• *Packaging*. Anecdotal evidence suggests that DVD packaging is somewhat flimsy. In postings on VIDEOLIB listserv in October and November 2000, librarians reported that users often damage the center core of the DVD box while trying to remove the disc.

Another disadvantage is not inherent in the format, but related to the reluctance of libraries to invest in new formats while continuing to support the older format. Libraries are likely to be interfiling DVDs and VHS tapes for many years to come and, particularly in academic libraries, supporting the equipment for both formats. This is an unpleasant prospect for some librarians; but a realistic assessment of the situation quickly reveals that videotape is an inferior storage medium when compared to optical disc and librarians should rejoice that someday—perhaps in the not-so-distant future—we will be replacing our last videocassette.

Media librarians and industry analysts agree: DVD is the next format we will all be buying. However, unlike VHS, DVD is not just one format. It is a multipurpose optical storage medium that accommodates text, audio, video, and data. Writers in the library literature often confuse DVD-video and DVD-ROM.[1] It can be difficult to isolate information related to DVD-video specifically. It is no surprise that DVD articles published in technology journals, such as *Computers in Libraries* and *E-Media Professional*, tend to focus on DVD-ROM as a replacement for CD-ROM, rather than DVD-video as a replacement for laser disc or VHS. A search for DVD alone, without qualifying it, will produce thousands of results, many of them unrelated to DVD-video. The purpose of this chapter is to outline the issues related to adopting DVD-video for library collections, with an emphasis upon planning for the new format.

BACKGROUND ON DVD

Sometime between 1995, when librarians and other consumers first heard about development of a new digital video format, and the time it was released to the public in February 1997, DVD experienced a name-change from Digital Video Disc to Digital Versatile Disc. However, DVD is not really an acronym anymore. The Web site of the DVD Entertainment Group (http://www. dvdinformation.com/) simply uses the initials, without explanation. This name change came about in recognition of DVD's multiple uses and capabilities. The most prominent use of DVD technology is DVD-video. DVD-ROM was released in February 1998, but the proliferation of software has been a slow process. Walt Crawford pointed out in a June/July 2000 article that during a visit to his local CompUSA store he found approximately a half dozen DVD-ROM titles that were not games (Crawford 2000). The rollout of DVD-audio players (purportedly the multichannel, high-resolution successors to existing CD-audio technology) occurred in July 2000, with software releases delayed until early November 2000. Until recently, the future of DVD-audio was uncertain due to competing proprietary formats and record company concerns about copy protection. Although this chapter will focus on DVD-video, the DVD information sources include hardware and software news about all formats. (See the list at the end of the chapter.)

A DVD is a five-inch optical disc. It looks like an audio CD or a CD-ROM, but it differs in important ways. It is a high-capacity storage device that contains at least 4.7 gigabytes of data, a sevenfold increase over the current CD-ROM standard:

- DVD-5 stores 4.7 Gigabytes and has data on 1 side and 1 layer.
- DVD-9 stores 8.5 Gigabytes and has data on 1 side and 2 layers.
- DVD-10 stores 9.4 Gigabytes and has data on 2 sides and 1 layer.
- DVD-18 stores 17.0 Gigabytes and has data on 2 sides and 2 layers.

The highest-capacity discs are designed to replace CD-ROM to store large databases. DVD-video is intended to replace VHS as the primary means for distributing entertainment to the home. A DVD videodisc holds 133 minutes on each side, which means that two two-hour movies could be held on one disc, offering six discrete channels of audio. The video image encoded on a DVD disc uses MPEG-2 standard compression[2] and Dolby AC-3 (Dolby Digital) audio. Picture quality is superior to laser discs, with 500 lines of resolution to laser disc's 400; VHS contains only 250 lines of resolution. DVD offers consumers picture and sound quality superior to existing distribution formats, in a compact, durable package. DVD is primarily a format for the distribution of feature films and other home video offerings at this time, but there are indications that it will eventually replace VHS for the distribution of educational video as well.

The first DVD player was a combination DVD-laser disc player. The early adopters of DVD were expected to be laser disc owners, and that prediction has been realized. It was clear from the beginning that DVD would bring the demise of laser disc, but since laser disc players are only in approximately 2 percent of U.S. households, knocking out laser disc alone was never the goal of DVD manufacturers; they want the VHS market as well. There are two million laser disc households in the United States. There are 80–90 million VHS households. Currently, DVD offers playback only, but Panasonic demonstrated a DVD recorder in New York in September 2000 and reported plans to release the DVR-2000 DVD-R/RW deck during the first quarter of 2001 for $2,500.

DVD players were released in 12 test markets in February 1997; however, the first software was not released until March 19. By the end of the year an estimated 200,000 players (excluding combination players) were actually purchased by consumers; 1.53 million DVD discs, selling for approximately $22 each, had been sold to consumers. As of mid-October 2000 more than 10 million DVD players had been shipped to retailers. DVD-video reached this milestone faster than any other home electronics product, including the audio compact disc and VHS. Approximately 12 million DVD players were shipped to retailers in calendar year 2001, bringing the total units shipped since the format's inception to more than 48 million.

The rapid growth in sales has led to decreasing prices for DVD players. Ethan McCarty, writing for *etown.com* in July 2000, speculated that with low prices hovering around $130, some retailers might go as low as $9 by Christmas. By November, this prediction came true, with Circuit City advertising a price tag of $99 on selected models. The day after Thanksgiving, Wal-Mart offered one model for $99 (and four-head VHS VCRs for less than $70). In 2001 the average price for a player dropped to around $200. Since the format's launch in 1997, software shipments have reached 233 million units, according to the DVD Entertainment Group (http://www.dvdinformation.com/). As of mid-2001, more than 10,000 DVD titles were in print, with another 1,800 expected by the end of the year.

CURRENT STATUS OF VHS

Despite DVD's rapid market penetration, VHS continues to dominate home video. VHS holds a 93 percent market share vs. DVD's 5 percent (Ullman, 2000), with more than one VCR in 53 percent of U.S. homes (McCarty 2000a). In 1999, Americans purchased over 27 million new VCRs—a 26 percent rise from the previous year. In effect, one out of five TV households bought a new deck last year. Meanwhile, over $11.8 billion of software was sold. "IRMA [International Recording Media Association] reports estimate that, worldwide, DVD will be sold into 15 million households by the end of 2000, compared with more than 400 million households that own some 600 million still-in-use VHS VCRs," according to IRMA president Charles Van Horn (McCarty 2000a). At a panel discussion among pro-VHS tape industry experts in March 2000, participants noted two significant market trends. First, video stores are devoting increasing amounts of shelf space to DVD. For VHS to remain viable, prices must remain below DVD prices. However, the profits are higher for DVD, so retailers tend to devote more shelf space to DVD. Second, the rise of pay-per-view "Near-Video-on-Demand" (PPV/NVOD) offered by satellite and cable companies is reducing revenues from all prerecorded entertainment, including VHS. PPV/NVOD customers are major renters and buyers of movies, but once they start using NVOD, they tend to reduce their tape rentals by 60 percent and their purchases by 50 percent (Ullman 2000). The impact of digital services may not be immediate, but industry analysts anticipate that over the next two to four years, they will reduce the demand for VHS by 15 percent. In August 2000, Strategy Analytics, a market research group, concluded that "DVD will become the standard home video format within five years, largely replacing VHS cassettes" (Matzkin 2000).

DIVX (DIGITAL VIDEO EXPRESS)

In the first few years immediately following the introduction of DVD, Digital Video Express, known as DivX, was a competing digital format. The controversy surrounding this now-obsolete format was surprisingly intense. DivX lasted less than two years, from April 1998 to June 1999, and from the time it was announced until it was withdrawn from the market, an extremely vocal group of consumers, early adopters of DVD, took every public opportunity to hasten its demise. The story of DivX is important for media librarians, because it offers warning signs for early adopters of a new media format in libraries.

On September 8, 1997, Richard L. Sharp, chairman of Circuit City Stores, the nation's largest retailer of television, stereos, and other consumer electronics, announced DivX (pronounced Div-ix). DivX was conceived as the answer to film distributors' fears about DVD copying. It featured superior anti-piracy and anti-copying protection. It was also designed to eliminate VHS from the rental market. Despite the popularity of DVD, VHS continued to dominate the rental market. DivX manufacturers hoped that it would help displace VHS in the rental market by offering the quality of DVD at a cost less expensive than buying DVDs.

The consumer purchased a DivX disc for approximately $4.50 to $5.00. The disc could be watched an unlimited number of times within 48 hours. The 48 hours did not begin until the consumer played the disc for the first time. However, once the 48 hours had elapsed, the consumer was required to pay every time the disc was played again. The player needed to be attached to a phone line and the consumer's credit card was billed approximately $3.00 for each additional play. If the consumer did not want to view the disc again, he or she threw it away. If the consumer wanted to view the disc an unlimited number of times, he or she could pay to convert it to an "open" disc—approximately $12, in addition to the original purchase price.

DivX was essentially a pay-per-view system. DVD discs would play on a DivX player, but DivX discs would not play on a DVD player. DivX was released in Richmond, Virginia, as a test market in April 1998, with 65–70 titles; nationwide release did not occur until late September. Circuit City would never release figures on the number of people who had opened DivX accounts, so it is impossible to know how many machines were sold. However, early in 1999, Circuit City reported that more than 1 million discs had been sold. Industry analysts attributed some of the DivX popularity to the lack of available open DVD players at the time. All digital video players were selling briskly, including DivX; but Circuit City continued to lose money on DivX, and on June 16, 1999, it announced the immediate end of DivX.

Circuit City, parent company of Digital Video Express, supported existing DivX players until June 2001. During this time, customers who bought DivX machines and subscribed to the pay-per-view format could continue to watch

DivX discs. The company offered a $100 rebate to all those customers, which was the price difference between DivX and non-DivX players. A year later, *etown.com* reporter David Elrich reported that the DivX debacle had cost Circuit City $130 million (Elrich 2000).

Public reaction to DivX was overwhelmingly negative from the beginning. The *etown.com* Web site conducted a poll soon after the DivX announcement in September 1997. It asked one question: "Do you like the DivX concept?" It received a record 786 responses—five times higher than usual; 96.8 percent said "no" (Poll 1997). Anti-DivX Web sites appeared overnight, along with anti-DivX articles on DVD Web sites. One fascinating article was entitled "The Truth about DivX." The original title was "3 Good Things about DivX; 33 Bad Things about DivX," but the author changed the title when he discovered there were only two good things about DivX and 35 bad things. There was even an official opposition organization, the National Organization to Ban DivX. Early adopters of DVD were livid, believing that DivX posed a serious threat to the viability of DVD, or at least its rapid adoption. Retailers were worried that consumers would be confused about the competing formats, which would slow sales (Smith 1997). At first it seemed that consumers would be required to adjust. Five major film distributors, Disney, Paramount, Universal, DreamWorks SKG, and 20th Century Fox, were releasing on DivX, with no plans to release widely on DVD. Disney and Universal planned to release selectively on the open DVD format (*Partyka*, May 1998), but the others not at all. However, eventually the situation changed and all major distributors chose to release on open DVD, albeit selectively in some cases.

From a library perspective, DivX was a disaster. A DivX disc that has been "opened" can only be played on one player, the player for which it was licensed. Consequently, libraries could not lend DivX discs, even if they had paid to "open" them. For this reason, DivX was never a serious option for library collections, but it contributed to the confusion about DVD among consumers. When the ALA Video Round Table and the ACRL Media Resources Committee proposed a program at ALA 2000 about DVD, an ACRL officer responded, "Isn't that format obsolete already?" No, that's DivX.

"DivX" has become shorthand for a very bad consumer electronics idea, usually coupled with the pay-per-view or pay-per-play concept. Mentioning DivX post–June 1999 always connotes something you want to avoid. For example, in an *etown.com* article dated October 27, 1999, entitled "Uh Oh, Washington Looks at MP3," Bennett Z. Kobb alerts readers " 'SDMI [Secure Digital Music Initiative] is the new DivX' and other heart-warming tales." Even if DivX had been a legitimate option for libraries, the controversy surrounding its release should have been a signal to librarians: this format warrants a wait-and-see attitude. However, with DivX gone, it is time for libraries to move aggressively to add DVDs to their collections.

DVD IN LIBRARIES

Questions and responses concerning DVD on the VIDEOLIB listserv suggest that some libraries have begun well-planned collection development activities with regard to DVD-video, but some librarians are still wary. With the demise of DivX, DVD-video became the clear choice for a digital video format. It has no competitors. Why the reluctance to begin collecting? Misconceptions abound regarding prices for DVDs and DVD players, the availability of titles suitable for libraries, consumer demand, and more. What is the actual situation? The following questions and answers address some of the concerns expressed by librarians on VIDEOLIB and in other discussion forums, such as ALA programs.

What kind of titles are available on DVD? My library doesn't buy feature films. Is there any DVD content suitable for my library?

If your library collects feature films, there is an abundance of suitable content. However, even if your library excludes feature films, there is a growing body of performances, documentaries, and educational programs available on DVD. According to the official DVD Video Group Web site, more than 6,500 titles were available as of late 2000. To see a complete list, visit their Web site: http://www.dvdinformation.com. This list may be searched by genre, including children's/family, documentary, foreign, music, and more. One extremely useful feature is that this list can be searched specifically for wide-screen versions. Many wide-screen versions of films are available only on DVD.

Where can I find reviews of DVDs? Are they included in other video review sources? What kinds of titles are being reviewed?

DVD titles are reviewed alongside VHS titles in major review sources, such as *Video Librarian*. *Video Librarian* includes a "DVD Spotlight" section for feature films, highlighting notable new releases, with an emphasis on re-releases of older and classic films. The November–December 2000 issue of *Video Librarian* listed a number of documentaries and performances, in addition to the feature film releases and re-releases.[3] This list represents a small percentage of the total new releases, but more distributors are sure to follow. In a recent listserv posting (VIDEONEWS, November 14, 2000), Randy Pitman, editor of *Video Librarian*, described the distributors and examples of programs he is seeing on DVD:

[W]ith the costs of DVD compression dropping, more and more independent features and documentaries are coming to market, including reasonably priced titles from Acorn Media (*Bernadette Peters in Concert*), A&E Home Video (*The Brandon Teena Story*), First Run Features (*The Architecture of Doom*), Goldhil Video (*WWII in Color*), Home Vision Cinema (*Chihuly Over Venice*) Kino-on-Video (*Maniac & Narcotic*), Monterey

Home Video (*Grateful Dead: Ticket to New Year's*), MPI Home Video (*Baraka*), National Geographic (*Surviving Everest*), New Yorker Video (*Jazz on a Summer's Day*), WGBH Boston Video (*The Miracle of Life, Everest: The Death Zone*) and WinStar Home Video (*Hellhounds on My Trail*), among others.

Randy also noted that PBS is releasing many new titles on DVD, including *Jazz, The American President,* and *Stephen Hawking's Universe.*

There are also review publications focused exclusively on DVD and laser disc. Doug Pratt publishes *The DVD-LaserDisc Newletter. Doug Pratt's DVD-Video Guide* compiles Mr. Pratt's review from this publication. He includes 2,400 DVD reviews from a number of categories: feature films, music videos, documentaries, video art, historic television programs, and erotica. The most frequent online review source and guide to new releases is *DVD-Daily Magazine*, which Steven Sickles publishes twice a week. E-mail subscriptions are free; subscription information and the archives are available on the Web: http://www.dvd-daily.com. The pre-release entries link to Amazon.com, which offers pre-release discounts up to 40 percent.

Where can my library buy DVDs? Are they difficult to acquire?

DVDs conform to the same patterns of distribution as other videorecordings. Most DVDs are home video releases, which can be purchased from the same sources as VHS home video: library jobbers, including Baker & Taylor (http://www.btol.com) and Ingram (http://www.ingramlibrary.com); online retailers, including Amazon.com (http://www.amazon.com) and Barnes & Noble (http://www.bn.com); specialty retailers, such as Facets Multimedia (http://www.facets.org) and format retailers, such as Ken Crane DVDs/Laserdiscs (formerly Ken Crane's Laserdisc Superstore) (http://www.kencranes.com). As libraries with laser disc collections discovered, there may be advantages to buying a format like DVDs from a format retailer. In addition to significant discounts—30 percent off for DVDs and 20 percent for laser discs—Ken Crane stocks many more DVD titles than other sources. On the other hand, for foreign titles and independent releases, it may be necessary to go to a specialty source like Facets (http://www.facets.org). When a library needs a particular title on DVD as soon as possible, it will still be necessary to shop around for availability. For the best service and prices, educational titles must be acquired from exclusive distributors, which is the same situation that exists for these titles on VHS.

Will all DVDs play on any player or computer? What about foreign purchases? What is regional encoding?

All DVDs released in the United States will play on any player and on any computer equipped with a DVD-ROM drive sold in the United States. However, DVD presents the same problems as VHS tapes and laser discs with regard to

NTSC, PAL, and SECAM television standards. They offer the additional wrinkle of regional encoding, or "locales." Most discs and players are encoded to play back only in one global region (the reasons for this have to do with protection of international commercial markets). Each player is given a code for the region in which it is sold. The player will refuse to play discs that are not allowed in that region. This means that discs bought in one country may not play on players bought in another country. Regional codes are entirely optional for the maker of a disc. Discs without codes will play on any player in any country. Players and discs are identified by the region number superimposed on a map of the world. If a disc plays in more than one region it will have more than one number on the map. (A map with the codes is available on the Web: http://www.unik. no/~robert/hifi/dvd/world.html.)

Region 1. United States, Canada, and U.S. Territories

Region 2. Japan, Europe, South Africa, and the Middle East (including Egypt)

Region 3. Southeast Asia and East Asia (including Hong Kong)

Region 4. Australia, New Zealand, Pacific Islands, Central America, Mexico, South America, and the Caribbean

Region 5. Eastern Europe (former Soviet Union), Indian subcontinent, Africa, North Korea, and Mongolia

Region 6. China

Region 7. Reserved

Region 8. Special international venues (airplanes, cruise ships, etc.)

For more information about regional codes, see Jim Taylor's DVD FAQ on the Web: http://www.dvddemystified.com/dvdfaq.html#1.10.

Taylor also describes the relationship of regional DVD to international television standards (http://www.dvddemystified.com/dvdfaq.html#1.19). The MPEG video on DVD is stored in digital format, but it is formatted for one of two incompatible television systems: 525/60 (NTSC) or 625/50 (PAL/SECAM).[4] PAL and SECAM share the same scanning format, so discs are the same for both systems. The only difference is that SECAM players output the color signal in the format required for SECAM televisions. Some players only play NTSC discs, some players only play PAL discs, and some play both. All DVD players sold in PAL countries play both. These multi-standard players partially convert NTSC to a 60Hz PAL (4.43 NTSC) signal. In his FAQ, Taylor summarizes the situation as follows:

There are actually three types of DVD players if you count computers. Most DVD PC software and hardware can play both NTSC and PAL video and both Dolby Digital and MPEG audio. Some PCs can only display the converted video on the computer monitor, but others can output it as a video signal for a TV. (Taylor 2000: 1.19)

Libraries that plan to purchase foreign releases directly from those countries should be aware of the possible need for all-region, multi-standard players.

My library does not circulate its video collection. If we buy DVDs, we must purchase playback equipment. How much does a DVD player cost?

DVD players have become increasingly affordable for consumers and for libraries that provide on-site access for the formats they circulate. Prices range in price from $99 to thousands of dollars, but $250 is typical as of this writing. Public libraries and academic libraries view the equipment situation differently. In a public library, the majority of users borrow videorecordings to take home. Consequently, the prevalence of DVD players in the community served by the library is an important factor. However, even if adoption has been slow in a particular community to date, the drop in DVD player price to under $100 may be the impetus for a huge increase in the next year or two. Academic libraries, on the other hand, tend to provide playback in the library, so librarians must compare the cost of supporting a new format with the cost of supporting existing formats. The cost of adding DVD equipment to the library media center is not a significant factor. A DVD player is comparable in cost to a VHS player. Another consideration for academic librarians is equipment in classrooms. Unless the institution is planning to purchase DVD playback equipment for classrooms, instructors may be frustrated with the necessity of restricting student viewing to the library. Some academic library media departments also support classroom equipment, so the dilemma may be resolved easily. Beginning or significantly expanding the library's DVD collection requires discussions with campus equipment providers regarding equipment for classroom playback.

Where can I find answers to other questions regarding DVD in libraries?

At the end of this chapter you will find a bibliography of print and Web-based information sources on DVD. For questions not answered in these sources or for library-specific questions, search the archives of VIDEOLIB listserv (http://www.lib.berkeley.edu/VideoLib/archive.html), or post a query to the current subscribers. Subscription information may be found on the Web: http://www.lib.berkeley.edu/MRC/vrtlists.html. During December 2000, DVD threads on the listserv dealt with collection development policies, regional encoding and television standards, review sources, and security cases. VIDEOLIB is an essential source of information for any topic related to media librarianship, including DVD.

CONCLUSION

VHS video launched the video revolution in libraries. It has been and continues to be an incredibly popular format with consumers. Yet, librarians always knew there was something better coming. Videotape simply does not offer the sound and picture quality and the durability that we came to expect with laser discs and audio compact discs. Our wait has ended. Although DVDs do not yet provide the diversity of video programming that our users require and demand, the offerings are improving daily. Someday in the foreseeable future, mastering costs will have decreased to the point that virtually all video content will be available on DVD. In the meantime, embrace this new format for the advantages it offers our users and the conveniences it offers libraries. Then watch for the inevitable signs that VHS is on its way out.

APPENDIX

Selected Review Sources

The DVD-LaserDisc Newletter. Address: P.O. Box 420, East Rockaway, NJ 11518–0420. Web: http://www.DVDLaser.com. The current subscription price is $35.00 per year.

Pratt, Douglas. 1999. *Doug Pratt's DVD-Video Guide: More than 2000 Reviews of the Best DVD-Videos*. New York: Harbor Electronic Publishing. For selected Pratt reviews online, see: http://www.DVDLaser.com/.

Video Librarian. Address: 8705 Honeycomb Court NW, Seabeck, WA 98380, or through subscription agencies. Web: http://VIDEOLIBrarian.com/index.html. The current subscription price is $47.00 per year.

Selected DVD Web Sites

DVD Demystified. http://www.dvddemystified.com/. Jim Taylor is the author of *DVD Demystified*, now in its second edition (McGraw-Hill, 2000). This site is most notable for its excellent DVD FAQ.

DVD for Libraries. http://alexia.lis.uiuc.edu/course/fall1998/lis415/projects/buffo/lis415/DVD.html. Includes a brief history of the format, definition of terms and concepts, technical specifications of DVD and related formats, links to related resource sites, and other useful information.

DVD Info. http://www.unik.no/~robert/hifi/dvd/. Robert Aas's site in Norway is the most comprehensive DVD site in the world.

Digital Video Group. http://www.dvdinformation.com. The official site of the DVD Entertainment Group.

Etown.com: The Consumer Electronics Source. http://www.etown.com. Begun as a journalists' collective in 1995, this is one of the best sources of news about the consumer electronics industry, as well as product reviews.

NOTES

1. For a good definition of DVD-ROM and a discussion of its role as successor to CD-ROM, see Parker (1997). The industry Web site DVD-ROM.com (http://www.dvdrom.com/), by way of defining the format, offers the following comment:

While DVD-Video was the first of the DVD formats to be developed and has received most attention, DVD-ROM is potentially more important and will support a larger range of applications particularly where the CD-ROM capacity is inadequate. DVD-ROM titles include multi-disc CD-ROM games and reference titles converted to DVD, new versions of CD-ROM titles with additional, high quality MPEG-2 video and applications designed from the outset for DVD.

2. MPEG (Moving Picture Experts Group) is "the name of family of standards used for coding audio-visual information (e.g., movies, video, music) in a digital compressed format. The major advantage of MPEG compared to other video and audio coding formats is that MPEG files are much smaller for the same quality. This is because MPEG uses very sophisticated compression techniques" (from MPEG.org Web site [http://www.mpeg.org/MPEG/index.html#mpeg]).

3. This list includes: *The Battle for Citizen Kane* (VHS or DVD, WGBH Boston Video, $19.95, with public performance rights); *The Films of Charles & Ray Eames*, Volumes 1–4 (DVD, previously released on VHS, Image Entertainment, $24.95 per volume); *American Cinema* (DVD, previously released on VHS, Image Entertainment, $79.99 for 2 discs, 542 minutes); *AFI's 100 Years, 100 Movies* (DVD, previously released on VHS, Image Entertainment, $79.99, 2 discs, 460 minutes); *AFI's 100 Years, 100 Stars* (DVD, previously released on VHS, Image Entertainment, $24.99, 1 disc, 135 minutes); *The Life of Python* (VHS or DVD, A&E Home Video, $29. 95 for VHS, $39.95 for DVD, 3 videocassettes or 2 discs); *Storyville: The Naked Dance* (VHS or DVD, Shanachie Entertainment, $19.95 for VHS, $24.95 for DVD, with public performance rights); and *Genghis Blues* (VHS or DVD, New Video, $24.95 for VHS, $29.95 for DVD).

4. For a listing of television standards (NTSC, PAL and SECAM) by world region, go to http://www.fjm-media.com/worldtv.htm.

REFERENCES

ACRL. "Guidelines for Media Resources in Academic Libraries." 1999. *C&RL News* 60 (April): 304–312. Available on the World Wide Web: http://www.ala.org/acrl/guides/medresg.html.

Crawford, Walt. 2000. "The DVD Advantage: A Mixed Blessing?" *E-Content* 23(3) (June/July): 89–92. Accessed online via Academic Search Elite.

Elrich, David. 2000. "Extra: The DivX Disaster Revisited." *etown.com* (June 16). URL: http://www.etown.com/news/article.jhtml?articleID=2901.

Kobb, Bennett Z. 1999. "Uh-oh, Washington Looks at MP3." *etown.com* (October 27). URL: http://www.etown.com/news/article.jhtml?articleID=1189.

Matzkin, Jonathan K. 2000. "DVD Will Replace VHS in Five Years." *etown.com* (August 3). URL: http://www.e-town.com/news/article.jhtml?articleID=3201.

McCarty, Ethan. 2000. "$99 DVD Decks by Christmas?" *etown.com.* (July 7). URL: http://www.etown.com/news/article.jhtml?articleID=3056.

McCarty, Ethan. 2000a. "VHS Is Stayin' Alive." *etown.com* (March 7). URL: http://www.etown.com/news/article.jhtml?articleID=2220.

Parker, Dana J. 1997. "DVD-ROM: Who Needs It, Who Will Use It, and How?" *EMedia Professional* (January). URL: http://www.emedialive.com/JanEM/parker1.html.

Partyka, Jeff. 1998. "Pioneer, JVC, Twentieth Century Fox Sign up for Divx." *Emedia Professional* 11(5) (May): 12–13. Access online via Ebsco Professional Development Collection.

"Permanence, Care, and Handling of CDs." [n.d.]. *Kodak Digital Science*. Web site. URL: http://www.kodak.com:80/US/en/digital/techInfo/permanence1.shtml.

Poll: Divx Horrilibis (Final Edition). 1997. *etown.com* (September 25). URL: http://community.etown.com/cgi-bin/page_builder/display.cgi?/news/articles/polldivx intro092597mfx.html.

Pratt, Douglas. 1999. *Doug Pratt's DVD-Video Guide: More than 2000 Reviews of the Best DVD-Videos*. New York: Harbor Electronic Publishing.

Smith, Steve. 1997. "Retailers: DIVX Will Hurt DVD." *etown.com* (October 27). URL: http://www.etown.com/news/article.jhtml?articleID=334.

Taylor, Jim. 2000. DVD FAQ. *DVD Demystified*. Web site. Updated December 15. URL: http://www.dvddemystified.com/dvdfaq.html.

"The Truth about DIVX." [n.d.] *DVD Info*. URL: http://www.unik.no/~robert/hifi/dvd/divx.html.

Ullman, Lawrence. 2000. "VHS: The End Isn't Here Yet." *etown.com* (March 21). URL: http://www.etown.com/news/article.jhtml?articleID=2302.

RECOMMENDED READING

Crawford, Walt. 1999. "Up to Speed on DVD." *American Libraries* 30 (September): 71–72.

Crawford, Walt. 2000. "DVD Today and Tomorrow." Association of College and Research Libraries Program, July 8 ("Byting Into DVD"). http://home.att.net/~wcc.libmedx/dvdspch.htm.

"Digital Video Disc: The Coming Revolution in Consumer Electronics." http://www.dvd-rom.com/technology/dvd_tech.html.

Jessop, Deborah. 1998. "DVD Basics for Libraries and Information Centers." *Computers in Libraries* 18 (April): 62–67

Chapter 24

Video Collections into the Future

Rick E. Provine

Maybe not today, maybe not tomorrow, but soon, and for the rest of your
life.

—Humphrey Bogart, *Casablanca*

INTRODUCTION

Prognosticating the future and second-guessing change is risky business at best.
Entire media formats have come and gone since the last edition of this text. In
that same period, the Internet and the continuing evolution of personal computing have irrevocably changed the world in ways that were unforeseeable (or
science fiction) even a decade before. In an age of ceaselessly changing digital
technologies and hungry consumer electronics markets, only one thing is really
certain—convergence. Our computers and our televisions (and our telephones
for that matter) are rapidly moving ever closer to one another, and the lines
between entertainment, information, and human interaction continue to blur.

What implications do these current and future changes hold for media librarians? On the most basic level, the seemingly endless progression of media formats and utilities and consumer gizmos will undoubtedly continue to force
providers of media services to juggle more equipment and content formats than
ever, from VHS and DVD to online media access workstations. Although some
industry analysts predict the eventual development of a media "convergence

box" that will accommodate everything from video games, to digital video-on-demand, to Internet access, this type of utility is still a long way down the road.[1] For some types of libraries, the increasing interest in digital media production and use, whether it involves incorporating short video clips into PowerPoint presentations or shooting and editing entire digital movies, has added even more equipment to the mix, from analog and digital video cameras, to video capture and encoding hardware and software.

"Going digital" will have significant implications for our collections and services as well. While, as will be discussed below, the current telecommunications infrastructure and video compression technologies do not practically support the sending and receiving of full-length, high-resolution video programming, these bottlenecks may be relatively short term. Sooner than we think, the pendulum may swing away from ownership of physical media and toward acquiring, licensing, or mediating online access, at least for some portions of the collection. The Internet is, in a sense, a kind of enormously powerful (although spectacularly uncontrolled) publishing machine. For some libraries at least, the Net may offer possibilities for expanding the concept of collection development to include the creation and publication of unique text, image, and sound content. The speed with which we hurdle toward this over-the-wire media future is dependent on a number of complex factors, on both the production and the delivery ends of the media equation. Still, libraries need to be attuned to this possible future and to prepare now.

SHOULD I THROW AWAY MY VCR?

Turn on the TV most any night and you are bound to be assailed by glitzy Intel, Apple, Sony, and Panasonic ads hailing the birth of digital video and presaging the death of videotape and its ancillary playback hardware. It's all too cool; it's also premature hype. Just as many libraries still have 16mm films, U-MATIC videotapes, and laser discs, VHS tapes are likely to be a familiar staple for the foreseeable future, even as DVD roars into the market. The penetration of VCRs is still high enough to provide a revenue stream to the producers. Until this changes, we will continue to see VHS tapes in our collections.[2] This is especially true for the works of smaller producers and producers of documentary works, who cannot yet afford to convert their catalogs to DVD. The cost of this conversion will steadily decrease, but it will take time (for a short take on DVD from the independent filmmaking camp, see Deussing 1999).

Format changes are occurring more quickly than ever before. Witness the laser disc. Although much beloved by film scholars and a relatively small body of diehard film fans for its excellent image quality and random access capabilities, laser discs never gained a suitable foothold in the marketplace (see Jameson 1995 for an early laser enthusiast's typically elegiac ode to the format). Most libraries, wisely or not, assiduously stayed away from the format, and now, after a relatively brief life span, it's basically gone.[3] DVD promises to be more popular than laser discs (or even VHS), primarily due to the unprecedented industry support and cooperation, and a consumer market eager and willing to shell out money for new electronic toys. DVD already enjoys higher market penetration than laser disc ever did; in fact, the format is the mostly quickly selling consumer electronic medium ever. But will DVD be stable long enough to allow the smaller producers and smaller libraries to switch before a new format comes along? Maybe not. The cycle may move quickly enough to allow some to skip a generation, and enter the digital world in the next iteration of disc-based media. What is most significant about DVD for this chapter is the fact that it's a digital format. That means that producers and libraries are sitting on digital content, and that fact moves us a step closer to the convergence of the computer, television, and video.

VIDEO OVER THE WIRE: WHAT IS IT AND HOW DOES IT WORK?

Besides DVD, what types of digital collections (or quasi-collections) are available right now? As anyone who has done even perfunctory poking around online knows, the Web is crammed and littered with sight and sound bites. Although a wide variety of techniques and technologies are employed for delivering audio and video over networks, the majority of media on the Web are "streamed." Streaming is a technique for transferring video data across networks in a way that allows it to be processed and displayed as a steady and continuous stream of visual/sound information. Prior to the development of streaming technologies, the delivery of digital video across a data network such as the Internet required that the video file be treated like other types of data files: the entire file had to be uploaded by the sender and downloaded by the receiver before it could be played—an extremely time-consuming and machine memory–intensive process. Streamed video was developed to overcome some of these limitations. With streamed video, a digital video can either be broadcast live (e.g., the broadcast of a live lecture or event), or the file can be stored on a video server for later replay. To view the file or broadcast, the viewer's computer must have the appropriate player software. The viewer can see the video more or less instantly; the entire file need not be downloaded or saved on the hard drive before viewing it.[4]

Currently, most streamed video applications utilize a few standards and protocols. These include proprietary standards developed by Apple (QuickTime), Real Networks, and Microsoft (Windows Media), and internationally developed standards such as MPEG (Motion Picture Experts Group). There are a few others, but these formats dominate. These standards and protocols govern the ways in which digital video is captured, compressed, and delivered over networks. It is generally the case that video encoded for a particular protocol or standard requires a unique type of player (or "plug-in") to view.

Effective video streaming over the Web depends on a number of factors.

Perhaps primary among these is the available bandwidth between the server and the end user (client).[5] Digital video images contain enormous amounts of data (the size of a standard, uncompressed video file is about 12 megabytes per minute of video). Delivery of these files requires tremendous bandwidth compared to the text and graphics we usually see on Web pages. Video frame rates (i.e., the "smoothness" of the moving image), viewing window size, and other factors are largely determined by network bandwidth. Because of the high bandwidth requirements, most video delivered over networks is first compressed into smaller data "packages." Even compressed, however, video files are large, and the transfer of video over networks often requires that certain compromises be made when digitally encoding the image. These compromises include encoding the video image with less-than-optimum frame rates (i.e., less than the standard 30 frames per second), a necessity often resulting in a jerky image. Bandwidth limitation also generally makes it necessary to restrict picture size to a small portion of the computer monitor (less than 240 × 360 pixels). Because of bandwidth requirements and server storage limitations, most videos currently being served on the Web are short clips rather than full-length works.

Mediating between compression (on the sender's side) and decompression (on the receiving end) is a device and/or program known as a "codec"(coder/decoder or compression/decompression algorithm). Simply put, a codec squeezes the video into a smaller data package, and then unpacks it upon arrival on the viewer's desktop. Codecs use complicated algorithms to identify and sample repetition and redundancy of the moving image. For example, in many movie sequences only a small portion of the image actually moves from one frame to the next (the gunfighter draws his gun, but the cowpokes in the background and other elements of the scene remain fixed). Eliminating this redundancy offers tremendous savings in overall size and bandwidth. Different types of video require different codecs. You may have noticed that when viewing Internet content, you are occasionally prompted to download a new "codec" to play back a particular piece of video or audio. Digital media companies are continually improving, refining, and developing new codecs to more successfully deliver rich content over existing networks. For a more detailed discussion of codecs and how they operate, see Fowler 1997.

WHAT'S OUT THERE? DO WE HAVE A COLLECTION YET?

Snippets and Fragments and Clips (Oh My!)

Putting up video on the Web is not rocket science; given the daunting technical limitations discussed above, however, mounting anything other than small clips is. The abundant video and audio to be found on the Web is more often than not used in the same ways neon was employed in the 1940s and 1950s as an advertising hook: it encourages hotrodders—those speeding across the digital highway in this case—to stop and look or listen. The majority of these clips serve as enticing marketing devices for dot.com enterprises (the two-minute clip of the Victoria's Secret annual fashion preview apparently received the highest number of daily hits ever recorded for a single Web site). Not surprisingly, movie studios and other mega-media concerns were early in seizing upon the Web as a way of flacking the next big blockbuster: movie trailers, clips, and short films abound. Bored at work? Check out The Trailer Park (http://www. movie-trailers.com), or Apple's Movie Trailer site (http://www.apple.com/ trailers). Need your hip-hop fix? Rolling Stone (http://www.rollingstone.com/ videos) and other sites will provide you two minutes of MTV streamed to the desktop. News sites, such as CNN (http://www.cnn.com/videoselect) and MSNBC (http://www.msnbc.com) are beginning to offer current events sight-bites in addition to sound bites.

The small size of the video "chunks" served up by these sites is intentional: they make it easy for most people to get video content over dial-up connections. While these sight and sound snippets are intended to reach the broadest possible audience, they're also often intended to be ephemeral. For most libraries, such works do not possess either the quality or the stability to serve as video "collections." One could argue, however, that an evolving aspect of collection development and/or reference for media librarians may be ferreting out the more useful and stable of these sites and cataloging or aggregating them on library Web sites, based on the needs and wants of library users. A good example of such an endeavor is the movie page maintained by the Digital Librarian (http:// www.digital-librarian.com/movies.html).

Playing in the Broadband

While clips currently dominate the Internet media domain, with the increasing presence of broadband access we are starting to see digital video on the Internet that more closely approximates standard video, in length, if not resolution. Some sites have even started video-on-demand services, delivering feature-length content using proprietary playback software (like Windows Media). Many of these sites tend to offer older public domain works or low-end feature films, or promotional materials that never played theatrically and were consequently inexpensive to acquire (e.g., MeTV [http://www.METV.com] and Bigstar's Broadband Theater [http://www.bigstar.com]). The big studios have also begun experimenting with digital on-demand delivery, in direct competition with rental stores and pay-per-view cable. Earlier in 2001, for example, Miramax (http:// www.miramax.com/) debuted an online version of its film *Guinevere* (all 500 megabytes of it), available to the consumer as a licensed downloaded file for $3.49 ("Miramax Film Available" 2001; "Miramax Reeling Out" 2001). Other media providers are similarly jostling for position. In January 2001, for example, Arts & Entertainment (A&E) and the History Channel signed a comprehensive agreement with Intertainer (http://www.intertainer.com), a broadband service, to make selected A&E programs available on demand. In late 1999, music industry giants EMI and Microsoft cut a deal to deliver a library of over 5,000 music videos over the Internet ("EMI" 1999).

While Hollywood continues to figure out how to set its digital ducks in a row, independent and experimental movie mavericks have enthusiastically begun to jump into the pond. In a sense, the Web represents a media frontier as exciting and wide open as the landscape faced by late-nineteenth-century movie pioneers such as the Lumière brothers and Thomas Edison (Web movies bear a strong resemblance, in fact, to the Lumières' grainy little 52 second films of trains entering stations and babies being fed). "Indie" and underground filmmakers have begun exploring the Web as a medium for creating, mounting, and publicizing short works shot with digital equipment and existing far beyond the bounds of mainstream Hollywood in terms of content, length, and style. Examples of such adventurous Internet showcases include Inetfilm (http://inetfilm. com). ifilm (http://ifilm.com), and AtomFilms (http://www.atomfilms.com). In Chapter 20 in this book, other digital film sites are discussed. Michele LaMura (1997 and 1999) also provides a good, brief discussion of indie film Web sites, including a list of such sites.

The movie merchants aren't the only ones trying to get a handle on ways of turning a profit on digital video content over the Web. Streamed video has also become a staple for many university extension operations, as a way of delivering fee-based continuing education. Professional organizations and associations, such as the Institute of Electrical and Electronics Engineers (IEEE) (http://ieee. mediaplatform.com), have also begun putting fee-based video tutorials and continuing education materials on the Web. PBS' Adult Learning Service (ALS) similarly offers self-paced professional development modules for educators via streamed video, for a fee (http://www.pbs.org/als/streaming).

In addition to providing a centerpiece for these types of fee-based educational sites, streamed video and webcasting are also becoming increasingly popular ways for professional and educational associations and organizations to post proceedings and events. The educational/information technology association EDUCAUSE, for example, provides full-length presentations from its annual conference on the Web (http://www.educause.edu/conference/e98/webcast98. html). A 1999 symposium on Bioscience and Biotechnology in History sponsored by the UC Berkeley Bancroft Library, in collaboration with the Berkeley Multimedia Research, has been put up as streamed video and simultaneous text (http://www.lib.berkeley.edu/BANC/Biotech/symposium/).[6]

It is increasingly common to find academic and industrial Web sites that include video training and teaching modules, taped lectures and events, and research intended primarily for local-area use (for an interesting listing of educational webcasting and streaming archives, see the Trans-European Education Research and Networking Association [TERENA] Portal Initiative Web site: http://www.terena.nl/projects/reis/mmis/mmis-edu.html). In such environments, intranets and dedicated broadband systems using Asynchronous Transfer Mode

(ATM) or switched Ethernet networks are often used to delivery broadcast-quality digital video playback to a fairly circumscribed clientele on campus and in residence centers, or within a corporate center. The videos maintained on academic and corporate servers run the gamut, from indexed standing collections of materials available on demand, to ephemeral teaching and research resources retained for a short time only.

Content Developers as Libraries; Libraries as Content Developers

At this relatively early phase in the evolution of networked media, libraries and archives have largely stayed out of the ballgame, except, perhaps, for those instances in which the library has incorporated instructional technology or academic computing functions. While, as discussed above, academic institutions have ventured cautiously into this arena in various ways, such endeavors have almost always been project-based and developed and administered well outside of the library. Instructional/educational technology programs and academic computing operations are generally the central players in the business of taping, archiving, and delivering lectures over the network. This task is sometimes also handled by individual teaching departments. There is frequently a strong research component to video projects and collections on campus.

An interesting example of such a research-based undertaking is the Informedia Digital Video Library project at Carnegie Mellon University, which is attempting to develop ways of automatically "indexing" the content of video programs (http://www.informedia.cs.cmu.edu/dli2/). The VISION Digital Video Library System, being developed by the Electrical Engineering and Computer Science Department at the University of Kansas, is similarly attempting to develop a system for indexing a collection of unique primary resources (http://www.ittc.ukans.edu/~sgauch/DVLS.html). As academic institutions begin to experiment with the advanced networking capabilities promised by Internet2, it is altogether likely that more such video library projects will begin to come online.[7] For an example of current Internet2 digital library initiatives, see http://www.internet2.edu/html/about.html.

It is rather curious that few academic libraries have even ventured into cataloging the content of such projects, let alone spearheading or collaborating in them. The few libraries, archives, and museums that have tiptoed into the video collection arena have generally done so in conformity with the patterns discussed above; they have been forced to operate within the same technical, copyright, and user constraints as other enterprises and endeavors. Notable among these projects is the Library of Congress American Memory Project (http://memory.loc.gov). The Project includes clips—in MPEG, Real, and QuickTime formats—of early films and animation, moving-image documentation of nineteenth- and early-twentieth-century American culture and life. LC is also busy developing the National Audio-Visual Conservation Center (NAVCC), a project that "will

prototype new approaches for the storage and maintenance of digitally refor-
matted and 'born-digital' recorded sound and moving-image collections and experiment with new ways to present them to researchers." The prototype,
scheduled to come online in 2004, will deliver high-quality digital video from
its new facility in Culpeper, Virginia to Washington, DC, via dedicated line
(http://lcweb.loc.gov/rr/mopic/avprot/avprhome.html).

Although considerably less ambitious in scope than the LC or National Archives undertakings, other library-based Web video projects have been turning
up on various campuses. The UC Berkeley library has, for example, begun to
incorporate into its Media Resources Center (MRC) Web catalog video clips
from the works of San Francisco Bay Area filmmakers and distributors (http://
www.lib.berkeley.edu/MRC). The MRC site also hosts a small collection of
streamed videos of campus events as well as a growing library of streamed
audio files.

Rick Prelinger's ambitious Internet Moving Image Archive (IMIA) project
(http://www.moviearchive.org/movie/index.html) is another example of possible
things to come for moving-image archives. Although not an undertaking of a
brick-and-mortar library, the goals and intent of the Internet Moving Image
Archive are very "library-like" in nature: to make broadly accessible and without
cost a growing body of "ephemeral films," including educational, industrial,
advertising, amateur films and home movies—"genres that film historians and
archives have largely ignored, despite their profound influence on the minds of
spectators" (IMIA Web site). IMIA is a part of a larger project, the Internet
Archive (http://www.archive.org), which is attempting to amalgamate and preserve significant Web "collections" for future researchers, scholars, and the general public.[8]

Again, both fee-based and free video content such as the sites described above
and those to come provide interesting and unique challenges for collection developers (and other library staff). Many of the sites and files described—particularly the full-length works—have a number of similarities to both traditional
library materials and print-based digital resources. A library could, for example,
conceivably catalog the UCB Biotech symposium mentioned above, and add it
to its catalog and "collection." The library could similarly license access to the
IEEE symposia described above and link to the video from a Web catalog. Short
of full cataloging, there is the possibility of developing subject-based Web pages
or other library-produced resources and interfaces that point to these materials
or provide augmented access to them. As is the case in dealing with any digital
resource produced and maintained outside of the library, there are, unfortunately,
a number of fairly knotty problems in moving ahead with such projects. If the
library intends to provide in-house access to virtual video collections, the networking and computer resources obviously need to be in place. Perhaps even
more daunting is the fact that the longevity and stability of content produced
outside of the library is seldom certain.

While video components of academic library special collections and digital library initiatives will undoubtedly continue to make their way onto the Web, the role of public libraries as digital video content providers or creators is far less certain (particularly given the historically marginal role of analog video in these libraries). This is not to say that there are not roles to be played. The potential role of libraries as aggregators of links to external Web media resources has been discussed earlier. There are more "left-field" or non-traditional creative possibilities as well. In the last edition of this book (1994), Teri Schorzman offered an exceptionally interesting look at the role of libraries as collectors and producers of oral and regional history on video; and in fact, in the earliest days of library video history, the medium was embraced by a few intrepid public libraries as a way of documenting "community memory" and community events (Schiff 1984). As digital video cameras and popular digital editing software become cheaper and more common, public libraries have an unparalleled opportunity to revisit these types of projects, and to use the Web as a medium for "publishing" and publicizing them.

THE WIRES ARE GETTING BIGGER AND FASTER, AND THE FILES ARE GETTING SMALLER. WHAT NOW?

Sooner or later, the technical problems of delivering high-quality video over the wire will be worked out. Even more problematic and long-lasting than these tech hurdles, however, are the obstacles to network video delivery posed by intellectual property ownership and copyright constraints.

In terms of network delivery, owners of commercially oriented digital video content find themselves in an odd bind. In an age of rampant e-commerce and access to global audiences, the impression seems to be that *all* content is potentially golden, if only the owners could figure out the right markets, the right marketing scheme, and, perhaps most importantly, suitable protections for their real or imagined investments. Cyberpirates, hackers, and sundry information anarchists aside, John Parry Barlow's clarion call—"information wants to be free"—and nightmarish visions of Napster have struck, paralyzing fear into the hearts of most Web entrepreneurs and entrepreneurial wannabes.[9]

Studios and filmmakers spend considerable sums to create and market their works. Digital delivery of their wares to huge audiences via media such as DVD and over the Internet is enormously enticing. However, the same technologies that allow unprecedented types and scope of content delivery also hold the potential for diverting this lucrative revenue stream. Duplication in the digital age is exact and often endlessly possible, and the editing tools to change and manipulate content are also readily available. The opportunity and means to distort the message of a work or appropriate its characters or content have never been more universally at hand for the tech savvy. It is estimated, for example, that college students and hackers currently swap 400,000 bootlegged films a day "in a vast, underground file-sharing network that includes services like Freenet,

Fairshare and Filetopia and the Internet's version of CB radio, Internet Relay Chat" (Chmielewski 2001).

Competition from a rival format (DivX) and intellectual property concerns caused major delays in the release of DVD (see Chapter 23 for a discussion of DivX). Even with the rather sophisticated copy protection employed on Hollywood DVD releases, computer hackers have already found a way around it and posted it to the Internet (see Gomes 2000; Miller 2000, 2000a). Until security for the content can be assured, or until the economic model proves it can survive in spite of hacking, Hollywood will not be comfortable letting its product loose on the Net; and without Hollywood, the economic forces necessary to make sweeping, swift strides toward a digital future for feature films will not be manifested, making it more expensive for smaller content providers to get established in this arena.

For content owners and distributors with less to lose than the Hollywood industrial complex, the potential benefits of network video distribution might, even at present, outweigh the risks involved. One interesting aspect of new technologies is that they often create new markets for older materials or for materials which never made it into the mainstream. DVD, for example, has prompted the re-release of classics, hidden treasures, and oddities, often with added or supplementary features that give consumers a reason to revisit titles (Brown 2000). Similarly, a major benefit of online digital collections might be an increased audience for more esoteric and ephemeral materials. The cost of editing, duplicating, and distributing such materials on tape, disc, or other physical media is often prohibitively high, particularly given the historically specialized audiences for this material. Internet distribution might allow the distributors of these materials to dramatically cut the cost of distribution and to reach wider audiences. Peter Armitage, CEO of AfriCam, put it this way: "There are many advantages on the Internet. It allows video on demand, it is unregulated, and costs are low, as are barriers to entry. It is interactive and, above all, it allows a relationship with the viewer" ("Africam Confident" 2000).

Despite the intellectual property gridlock, some strides are being made toward developing mechanisms and business models for on-demand delivery (although these strides are often being taken well outside the province of Hollywood). In December 1999, Cinemedia Online (previously the State Film Centre of Victoria [Australia] Film & Video Library) successfully concluded the SWIFT digital media library evaluation trial (see Wright 1998). This project was designed to develop a prototype system to enable Cinemedia to deliver high-quality moving-image material (initially a core of 274 current and historical titles) to end users over broadband networks while still protecting the commercial rights of owners of the material.

The National Film Board of Canada has developed Cineroute, a pilot project to make a selection of the films in its collection available by request over the Internet. The initial audience for the 800-title collection (delivered in full-screen via the Canadian Ca*Net 2 broadband network) was students and instructors at the college level, students and professors at the university level, and those working at Canadian research centers. Phase 2 of the pilot project will include elementary schools, high schools, public libraries, and community organizations and individuals who will be given access to the collections via cable modem and satellite. "The ultimate objective of the CineRoute project is to provide a national film on demand service for all Canadian institutions and households that are connected to the Internet" (http://www.nfb.ca/E/2/5/4/index.html).

DIGITAL STORAGE: FOR THE AGES OR FOR THE MOMENT?

Does digital video mean preserved video? Digital media, as mentioned earlier, is infinitely cloneable—digitized video or audio files can be copied ad infinitum with no loss of image or sound quality. Digital copies do not deteriorate like film, photographs, or videotapes. It is not surprising, therefore, that digitization seems an attractive model for preservation. Unfortunately, digitization is far from a preservation panacea. The storage media for these digital copies *do* deteriorate over time; and storage media and technologies become obsolete fairly quickly. Effective digital preservation requires a regular conversion from aging storage media and formats to newer ones. The size of video files makes this a costly proposition on many fronts, including both the time and technology.

A series of symposia held in September 1999 at the University of South Carolina (http://www.sc.edu/filmsymposium) examined the pitfalls of digital film preservation as it relates to "orphan films" (defined by the National Film Preservation Foundation as "films that do not have commercial owners able to pay the costs necessary for preservation" (http://www.filmpreservation.com/why_orphan_films.html).[10] Many symposium attendees expressed a fear that the rush to digitize such films siphons funds away from more traditional methods of preservation, resulting in lost content. The concern was also expressed that even digitized preservation copies may not be funded to the level necessary to outlive a quality film print.

Another preservation issue is more basic. Where will today's fleeting digital streams of video go after they are seen? Commercial content providers do not think like librarians: they are seldom in the business of archiving and providing long-term access to their wares. Dealing with content that is maintained by an outside party and is out of the library's control is a problem that should be familiar to anyone who has had the frustrating experience of running into a broken or unmaintained Web link. The rapid evolution and change in digital formats and protocols is another issue; an encoding standard and player here today may well be gone next week. Unless an organization or institution archives the requisite players, plug-ins, and helper applications along with the archived content, these materials may not be playable at all in the future.

CONCLUSION

The leap from prerecorded disc and tape formats to online video access will be gradual. The hurdles discussed in this chapter, both technical and legal, are not insurmountable, but they will take time to overcome. DVD will undoubtedly conquer the large part of the feature film world and a hefty share of the mass-market special interest field as well. However, just as not all periodicals are available—and may never be available—as digital full text, neither will all videos be available in digital formats. Market economies will determine which content makes the transition and when. For some classes of materials—independent documentary works, primary source materials, educational market materials, and other non-feature titles—tape may still be around when DVD gives way to the next big digital thing.

Video on the Internet is too hot a commodity not to happen eventually. The potential markets for broadcast-quality, online, on-demand video are staggering. That fact, if nothing else, means that the technological limitations to the delivery of high-resolution moving images *will* be worked out eventually. When this evolutionary technological leap happens, the media monopolies and moguls will go into action—they're currently waiting in the wings panting at the prospects of movies to the world's desktops. Fortunately, the democratic and global nature of the Internet, maturing digital technologies, and the economies of scale made possible by Internet content distribution also bode well for the eventual availability of a broader and more diverse scope of video programming than ever before.

Where do libraries fit into this often perplexing, increasingly commodified digital future? Where we've always fit: in the role of selecting, acquiring, describing, preserving, and making accessible the best and most diverse resources for our clients, regardless of format and source. The precise nature of these central functions is, however, bound to change and to take us into strange and ambiguous new territories, as the fundamental meaning of "collections," and "collection development" continues to expand and evolve. The development of the Web and other digital resources and utilities as tools for digital video distribution and as means of creating original new works holds unprecedented challenges and opportunities for video librarians. There are new partnerships and new services to be investigated in this emerging digital media environment, new genres of artistic and documentary expression to be explored. And while we are likely to carry many of our past roles and functions with us into this digital future, there are also exciting new roles to be played: as developers of innovative types of user interfaces and finding tools; as teachers of these new resources; and as developers of unique content.

CITED AND RECOMMENDED WEB SITES

Apple QuickTime. http://www.apple.com/quicktime/.
Atomfilms. http://www.atomfilms.com/

Bigstar Broadband Theater. http://www.bigstar.com.

Carnegie Mellon Informedia Project. http://www.informedia.cs.cmu.edu/dli2/. The Informedia Digital Video Library project at Carnegie Mellon University has pioneered new approaches for automated video and audio indexing, navigation, visualization, search and retrieval, and embedded them in a system for use in education, information, and entertainment environments.

Cinemedia Online. http://www.cinemedia.net/.

CNN. http://www.cnn.com/videoselect.

CSPAN. http://www.cspan.org/.

Digital Librarian Media Page. http://www.digital-librarian.com/movies.html.
EDUCAUSE 1998 Conference. http://www.educause.edu/conference/e98/webcast98.html.

HDTV http://web-star.com/hdtv/faq.html. A FAQ that answers many basic questions about HDTV.

IFILM. http://www.ifilm.com/.

The Institute of Electrical and Electronics Engineers (IEEE). http://ieee.mediaplatform.com.

The Internet Moving Image Archive (IMIA). http://www.moviearchive.org/movie/index.html.

Intertainer. http://www.intertainer.com.

Library of Congress. American Memory Project. http://memory.loc.gov/ammem/collections/finder.html.

Library of Congress. Digital Audio-Visual Preservation Prototyping Project. http://lcweb.loc.gov/rr/mopic/avprot/.

METV.com. http://www.metv.com/.

Miramax. http://www.miramax.com.

MPEG. http://www.cselt.it/mpeg/. The home page of the Moving Picture Experts Group (MPEG), a working group of ISO/IEC in charge of the development of standards for coded representation of digital audio and video.

MSNBC. http://www.msnbc.com.

National Film Board of Canada. http://www.nfb.ca/E/2/5/4/index.html.

Orphans of the Storm Symposium. http://www.sc.edu/filmsymposium/.

PBS Adult Learning Service. http://www.pbs.org/als/streaming.

Real Networks. http://www.real.com/.

SCOLA. http://www.scola.org/. International news and TV programming delivery to educational institutions over the Internet and satellite.

SWIFT. http://www.cinemedia.net/SWIFT/project.html.

The Trailer Park. http://www.movie-trailers.com.

Trans-European Education Research and Networking Association (TERENA) Portal Initiative Web site. http://www.terena.nl/projects/reis/mmis/mmis-edu.html.

UC Berkeley Bancroft Library Bioscience and Biotechnology in History Symposium. http://www.lib.berkeley.edu/BANC/Biotech/symposium.

UC Berkeley Media Resources Center. http://www.lib.berkeley.edu/MRC.

The VISION Digital Video Library System (University of Kansas). http://www.ittc.ukans.edu/~sgauch/DVLS.html.

Windows Media. http://www.microsoft.com/windows/windowsmedia/.

NOTES

1. See Scafidi et al. (2000) for an analysis of consumer electronic media convergence trends. Not everyone has high hopes for convergence. For example, Marc Andreessen, founder of Netscape, believes that technological innovation is likely to produce greater divergence and greater specialization of devices: "Whenever anyone says 'convergence,' reach for your wallet . . . the whole concept that people will want to interact with their television set is silly. Interactive television happens when your football team loses, and you pitch a beer can at the screen" (as quoted in Anders 2001).

2. Industry predictions are that VCRs will remain a competitior to DVD for at least the next five years, particularly given the radically decreasing cost of VCR hardware, the recording capability of VCRs (as opposed to DVD currently), and the large number of prerecorded videotape titles currently available. It is predicted that DVD video player unit shipments will surpass VCR player unit shipments in 2003 (Scafidi et al. 2000)

3. For a discussion of the demise of laser discs, see Schworm 1999. One of the most disconcerting aspects of this continuous process of format evolution and supersecession is the often yawning gap that frequently develops between hardware and content development. Although laser disc technology is basically defunct, there are a great many titles that are currently only available in this format. Although it is possible that these works will eventually make their way onto DVD, this is by no means certain. The same can certainly be said of VHS titles as DVD captures an increasingly large share of the home video market.

4. "Bandwidth (the width of a band of electromagnetic frequencies) is used to mean (1) how fast data flows on a given transmission path, and (2), somewhat more technically, the width of the range of frequencies that an electronic signal occupies on a given transmission medium. Any digital or analog signal has a bandwidth. Generally speaking, bandwidth is directly proportional to the amount of data transmitted or received per unit time. In a qualitative sense, bandwidth is proportional to the complexity of the data for a given level of system performance. For example, it takes more bandwidth to download a photograph in one second than it takes to download a page of text in one second. Large sound files, computer programs, and animated videos require still more bandwidth for acceptable system performance. Virtual reality (VR) and full-length three-dimensional audio/visual presentations require the most bandwidth of all" (*whatis?com IT Encyclopedia*. http://whatis.techtarget.com).

5. For a good, basic explanation of video streaming, see: Hunter et al. (1997) and Patrick Winkler, ed., "Audio and Video Streaming," http://www.cba.bgsu.edu/amis/facstaff/smagal/commerce/skills/sub/w/wpat/.

6. The Berkeley site employs an HTML-like mark-up language known as SMIL (pronounced SMILE) (Synchronized Multimedia Integration Language), which allows the coordinated play of multiple media, such as text and images. See Robin Cover's SGML/XML Web Page (http://www.oasis-open.org/cover/smil.html) for more information and resources regarding SMIL.

7. Internet2 is a consortium of over 180 universities working in partnership with industry and government to "develop and deploy advanced network applications and technologies, accelerating the creation of tomorrow's Internet. . . . The primary goals of Internet2 are to: Create a leading edge network capability for the national research community; enable revolutionary Internet applications; and ensure the rapid transfer of new network services and applications to the broader Internet community" (http://www.internet2.edu/html/about.html).

8. "The Internet Archive is a 501(c)(3) public nonprofit that was founded to build an 'Internet library,' with the purpose of offering free access to historical digital collections for researchers, historians, and scholars. . . . The Internet Archive is working to prevent the Internet—a new medium with major historical significance—from disappearing into the past. Collaborating with institutions including the Library of Congress and the Smithsonian, we are working to permanently preserve a record of public material" [from Internet Archive Web site].

9. See Birchall (2000) for an interview with Jack Valenti, president/CEO of the Motion Pictures Association of America, regarding industry fears concerning DVD and Internet video piracy. For a discussion of DVD/CD replication and encyption, see Block (1997).

10. The types of films most at risk are newsreels, early silent films, educational shorts, avant-garde and experimental works, films no longer under copyright protection, amateur footage, and documentaries and features made outside the commercial mainstream.

REFERENCES

Ault, Susanne. 2000. "Will Digital Ever Stick?" *Broadcasting and Cable* (December 4): 50.

"AfriCam Confident Of Online Video Streaming Future." 2000. News Bytes News Network (September 6). Accessed online via EBSCOhost.

Anders, George. 2001. "Marc Andreessen: Act II : What's Still True—And What was Never True—About the Internet." http://www.fastcompany.com/online/43/andreessen.html.

Birchall, Danny. 2000. "Thieves Like Us." *Sight and Sound* 10(10) (October): 32–36.

Block, Debbie Galante. 1997. "CD DVD Piracy: The Replicator, the User, and the Technology." *EMedia Professional* 10 (December): 92 (13 pp.).

Brown, Kimberly. 2000. "Here Today, Here Tommorow: Distributors Are Dusting Off the Classics to Bring Docs to the DVD Market." *RealScreen* (October 1). http://www.realscreen.com/articles/magazine/20001001/30100.html.

Chmielewski, Dawn C. 2001. "Motion Picture Studios Release Films for Internet Download." *San Jose Mercury News* (January 28).

Duessing, Ryan. 1999. "DVD Unbound: Blowing Up the Small Screen." *The Independent* (June): 10–11.

"EMI to Deliver Extensive Music Video Library via Microsoft Windows Media." 1999. http://www.microsoft.com/presspass/press/1999/Nov99/MSEMIpr.asp.

Fowler, T. Jay. 1997. "Video Compression: A Codec Primer." *Wired Digital* (August 25). http://hotwired.lycos.com/webmonkey/97/34/index1a.html.

Gomes, Lee. 2000. "Ruling in Copyright Case Favors Film Industry." *Wall Street Journal* (August 18): B6.

Hunter, Jane, Witana, Varuni, and Antoniades, Mark. 1997. "A Review of Video Streaming over the Internet." http://archive.dstc.edu.au/RDU/staff/jane-hunter/video-streaming.html.

Jameson, Richard T. 1995. "Discs Be My Destiny." *Film Comment* 31 (July–August): 86–88.

LaMura, Michele. 1997. "Indies Online: The Future Is NOW." http://www.newenglandfilm.com/news/archives/97october/streaming.htm.

LaMura, Michele. 1999. "Stream On: The Latest in Video on the Web." http://www.newenglandfilm.com/news/archives/99february/streaming.htm.

Miller, Greg. 2000. "Another Blow against Internet DVD Piracy." *Los Angeles Times* (January 22): C1.

Miller, Greg. 2000a. "Film Industry Wins Ruling in DVD Suit." *Los Angeles Times* (January 21): C1.

"Miramax Film Available for Download." 2001. *USA Today* (January 23). http://www.usatoday.com/life/cyber/tech/review/2001-01-18-miramax.htm.

"Miramax Reeling Out Net's First Feature-Length Rental Film." 2001. *Design News* (January 23).

Scafidi, Mary Joe, Olhava, Schelley, and Schlicting, Wolfgang. 2000. "U.S. DVD Market Forecast and Analysis, 2000–2004." *IDC Bulletin* (June): 18 pp.

Schiff, Lillian. 1984. "Video and Film Programming at the Port Washington Public Library." *Film Library Quarterly* 17: 67–72.

Schworm, Peter. 1999. "The Last Days of Laserdisc?" *EMedia Professional* 12 (September): 24.

Wright, Robin. 1998. "Accessing the Moving Image: Cinemedia's SWIFT Digital Video Library: A Case Study in Developing a Digital Public Access Storage, Management and Delivery System for Audio-Visual Content." http://www.cinemedia.net/SWIFT/paper.htm.

RECOMMENDED READING

Ault, Susanne. 2000. "Will Digital Ever Stick?" *Broadcasting and Cable* (December 4): 50.

Goldsborough, R. 1999. "Video on the Internet. The Past, Present and Future." *Link-Up (USA)* (July/August): 23–24.

Klien, Leo Robert. 2000. "Media Convergence Library-style." *Library Journal* (Spring Supplement): 28–30.

May, Rebecca. 2000. "Cable Networks' Strategies for Convergence." *Electronic Media* (November 27): 42.

McCarty, Ethan. 2000. "VHS Is Stayin' Alive." *etown.com.* (March 7). URL: http://www.etown.com/news/article.jhtml?articleID=2220.

Ullman, Lawrence. 2000. "VHS: The End Isn't Here Yet." *etown.com.* (March 21) URL: http://www.etown.com/news/article.jhtml?articleID=2302.

Index

About the Editor and Contributors

REBECCA ALBITZ is the Electronic Resources and Scholarly Communications Librarian at the Pennsylvania State University. She holds a B.A. in Film from the University of Rochester, an M.A. in Film from Penn State, and an M.L.S. from the University of Pittsburgh. Ms. Albitz was Media Services Librarian at the University of Iowa and Media and Performing Arts Librarian at New York University. Most recently, she was Head Librarian at Penn State Shenango. Ms. Albitz has chaired the ALA Video Round Table, and founded the Association of College and Research Libraries' ARTS section Film and Broadcast Studies Discussion Group.

BETH BLENZ-CLUCAS has slogged through evaluation of thousands of educational videos as editor of *Video Rating Guide for Libraries* and *Recommended Videos for Schools* (ABC-CLIO), and as a contributor to *Children's Video Report* and other publications. She has since joined the dark side of the video force as a public relations consultant to producers of educational media. She is based in Portland, Oregon.

KRISTINE R. BRANCOLINI is Director of the Indiana University Digital Library Program. She was the Librarian for Media and Film Studies at Indiana University for 17 years. She is a founding member of the ALA Video Round Table, and currently serves as Chair of the Notable Videos for Adults Selection Committee. She has published widely on topics related to digital libraries and media. Recent articles include "A Bibliographic Essay on Using Film to Teach about Peace Studies and Structural Violence," in *Insights from Film into Violence and Oppression: Shattered Dreams of the Good Life* (Praeger, 1998), and "Media Reference Sources in Academic Libraries," in *Reference Librarian* (no. 65, 1999).

ROBERT X. BROWNING is Director of the C-SPAN Archives and Associate Professor of Political Science at Purdue University. In 1987, he founded the Purdue University Public Affairs Video Archives to preserve C-SPAN programming for research and education, and created an extensive database and cataloging system for the public affairs video collection. He continues to teach and research on the U.S. Congress with an emphasis on the video record.

JON CECIL, Director of PBS Video, has spent the past 30 years on the education side of public television. After building an education service for Iowa's public television network, Jon joined PBS' national headquarters in education. He has led PBS Video for the past 15 years, pioneering such innovations as home video pricing for AV programming, the PBS Videoindex product line, and the PBS Videodatabase of America's History and Culture.

KIM CHARLSON is the Assistant Director at the Braille and Talking Book Library at the Perkins School for the Blind in Watertown, Massachusetts. She is a graduate of the Library Science program at the University of Northern Texas in Denton, Texas. She is a recognized national and international authority on library and information services for people with disabilities, braille literacy, adaptive technology, and information access. Kim has chaired the American Council of the Blind Board of Publications. Her writing credits include editing the Braille Revival League's magazine *BRL Memorandum* and contributing a chapter on "Braille Library Services" in the Library of Congress book entitled *Braille: Into the Next Millennium* (2000), and she authored *Establishing a Braille Literacy Program in Your Community: A Handbook for Libraries and Other Community Organizations*. She also is a contributing author to a forthcoming guide book on audio description services for performing arts organizations.

JEFF CLARK is Director of Media Resources and Classroom Technology at James Madison University, Harrisonburg, Virginia, where he has developed media collections and services since 1986. He is also permanent Chair of the JMU Libraries Preservation Committee. Mr. Clark has reviewed books, and later media programming, for *Library Journal* since 1978, and is the current Reviews Editor for the *College and University Media Review*, published by the Consortium of College and University Media Centers (CCUMC). He presently serves as Chair of the CCUMC's Government Regulations and Public Policy Committee.

WALT CRAWFORD is an information architect at the Research Libraries Group, Inc. (RLG) in Mountain View, California. An award-winning writer and speaker, Crawford has written 14 books and more than 200 articles on libraries, technology, publishing, and personal computing. He speaks a few times a year on the future of libraries and media and on technology-related topics. His articles and columns currently appear in *American Libraries, EContent Magazine*, and *Online Magazine*, and he began *Cites & Insights: Crawford at Large*, a Web-distributed print newsletter/zine, in December 2000 (http://cical.home.att.net). His most recent book is *Being Analog: Creating Tomorrow's Libraries* (1999).

SUZANNE J. CROW is the Deputy Head Librarian of the Health Professions Library at Hunter College, City University of New York. She holds an M.S. in Information Science from the University of Michigan and an M.A. in Anthropology from George Washington University. In addition to her work at Hunter College, she is active in the Medical Library Association and serves as editor for *New York Online Access to Health* (NOAH).

OKSANA DYKYJ is the Head of Visual Media Resources at Concordia University in Montreal, Canada. For over a decade she has lectured as an adjunct at Concordia University's Cinema Department, specializing in introductory-level Film Studies courses as well as developing the university's media collections. She is an active member of the Association of Moving Image Archivists and has served as program coordinator for the AMIA annual conference; she has chaired the scholarship committee and has been on the editorial board of the publication *Moving Image*. She is a member of the Preservation Task Force of the Consortium of College and University Media Centers and Reviews Editor for *MC Journal: The Journal of Academic Media Librarianship*. Her biggest passion is watching films from the silent and early sound period.

DEBRA FRANCO is the author of *Alternative Visions: Distributing Independent Media in a Home Video World* (1990), as well as numerous articles and policy papers related to the marketing and use of independent film and video. She has produced numerous independent films, and has served as Senior Project Advisor to the Video Education for Libraries Project. She is currently developing and curating a national series of screening and discussion programs for the National Video Resources Library Project, funded by the National Endowment for the Humanities.

NANCY GOLDMAN heads the PFA Library and Film Study Center at the University of California, Berkeley Art Museum and Pacific Film Archive. Ms. Goldman is currently Head of the Cataloguing and Documentation Commission of the International Federation of Film Archives (FIAF). She designed and manages PFA's *Cinefiles* film document image database, is a contributor and editorial consultant to the *FIAF International Film Archive Database*, and has written articles and lectured on topics related to film collection development and management.

GARY P. HANDMAN has served as Head of the Media Resources Center, Moffitt Library, University of California, Berkeley since 1984. He holds an M.L.S. degree from UC Berkeley and an undergraduate degree in Anthropology from UCLA, with a minor in Film History. From 1985 to 1993, Mr. Handman regularly taught the course in media librarianship in the UC Berkeley School of Library and Information Studies. He has written, spoken, and taught widely in the field of video librarianship and educational technology. He is editor of *Video Collection Development in Multi-type Libraries: A Handbook* (Greenwood, 1994), writes a regular video review column for *American Libraries*, and is an associate editor of *Video Librarian*. Mr. Handman is a founding member of the ALA Video Round Table and was the first elected chair of the group. He is the creator and moderator of the VRT listservs (VIDEOLIB and VIDEONEWS).

THOMAS R. HARRINGTON is a Reference and Instruction Librarian at Gallaudet University, Washington, DC, with special responsibility for Gallaudet's internationally renowned special collection on deaf people and deafness, the world's largest. He previously was a media librarian for 21 years, and in 1974 was the first deaf person to earn an M.L.I.S. from the University of Maryland. He has also published articles and lectured on library services to the deaf, deaf-related research resources, and media, and has created two large online databases of deaf-related information.

CASSANDRA M. KEITH received her library degree from the University of Rhode Island in 1995. She has worked as a reference librarian at the Loomis Chaffee School and the Hotchkiss School. Before getting her library degree, Ms. Keith taught English at the secondary school level for 10 years.

CHRISTOPHER LEWIS has been a Media Reference Librarian at the American University Library in Washington, DC, since 1992. He has the been the Head of Media Services there since 1997. He received his B.A. in Film Studies from the University of Cincinnati and his M.L.S. from Indiana University in Bloomington. He has also been a documentary filmmaker and advertising copywriter.

ANITA ONDRUSEK, M.L.S., Ph.D., has been a librarian and media specialist in settings serving grade school children, health professions students, and general adult collection users. She is presently the Science/Reference Librarian at Hunter College, City University of New York.

RANDY PITMAN is the editor of *Video Librarian*, the video review guide for libraries. He is the author of *The Video Librarian's Guide to Collection Development and Management, Video Movies: A Core Collection for Libraries, The*

Librarian's Video Primer, and has written numerous articles for various library publications. An outspoken advocate for the use of video in libraries, he is also the past Chair of the ALA Video Round Table (VRT).

RICK E. PROVINE is the Technology Librarian at DePauw University. Prior to that, he served as Director of Media at the University of Virginia Libraries, where he developed the institution's first multimedia center, and eventually, the state-of-the-art Robertson Media Center and Digital Media Lab. He has published and spoken on media collections, new technologies, and multimedia. He has held several offices in the American Library Association, including Chair of the Video Round Table and Chair of ACRL's Media Resources Committee. He currently serves as Chair of the ACRL/ARTS' Film and Broadcast Studies Discussion Group.

JASON SANDERS is the Film Research Associate at the Pacific Film Archive, and also works as an editor and writer for the San Francisco International Film Festival and the San Francisco International Asian American Film Festival. His film program notes have been published in festivals from the Bay Area to Toronto to New Zealand. As an undergraduate he studied film under Richard DeCordova at Depaul University, and later received an M.A. in Cinema Studies from New York University.

JAMES C. SCHOLTZ is currently the Library Director of the Yankton (SD) Community Library. Past positions include being a library system consultant, a community college library director, a YA/AV Department Head, and a public library Associate Director. Jim is also a freelance technology consultant and has reviewed videos for *Booklist* magazine since 1985. He has been active in ALA on various committees and roundtables dealing with AV/technology issues, and is also the author of four books and numerous articles dealing with video in libraries.

DIANA VOGELSONG is Assistant University Librarian for Information Services at American University Library in Washington, DC, an institution which serves a highly diverse international student body. With an M.L.S. from the University of Maryland and an M.A. in Art History from American University, she has worked in the areas of intellectual property, media, and the arts, including more than 10 years as a media librarian. She served on numerous film juries and has been active in the Consortium of College and University Media Centers. She has published in the subject areas of fine arts and media management and is author of *Landscape Architecture Sourcebook: A Guide to Resources on the History and Practice of Landscape Architecture in the United States* (1997).

MICHAEL VOLLMAR-GRONE is the Audiovisual Librarian of the Amos Memorial Public Library, Sidney, Ohio. For the past decade he has developed and defined the Audiovisual Department, which includes the movies, music, and audiobook collections. Prior to joining the library, Vollmar-Grone was employed as an award-winning photojournalist and corporate photographer.

MARY WATKINS is the Outreach Manager for WGBH's Media Access Group. Ms. Watkins is responsible for directing communications activities for WGBH's Access Services unit (The Caption Center and Descriptive Video Service®) and the research, development, and public policy efforts of the CPB/WGBH National Center for Accessible Media. In addition to developing print and online materials and conducting workshops and presentations about access technologies for diverse audiences—deaf, hard-of-hearing, blind and visually impaired consumers, the television and film industries, educators, and corporations and technology companies in the United States and abroad—Ms. Watkins oversees the division's press relations and consumer affairs activities. She has a B.A. in Philosophy from Boston College.

HELENE WHITSON, Special Collections Librarian/Archivist, and Curator, San Francisco Bay Area Television Archive, San Francisco State University Library, has been at San Francisco State since 1966 in various librarian assignments. She is the author/creator of a number of books and videotapes including *Strike!* (1979); *The California State University and Colleges Trustees Almanac* (1981); *KQED Film Archives Preservation Project* (Videotape, 1987); *Unearthing the Past: Access to Local Television News* (Videotape, 1989); and *The San Francisco Bay Area Television Archive at San Francisco State University* (Videotape, 1996.) She was a member of the California Cooperative Preservation Program task force, which drafted California's resource materials preservation plan. She is a 1999 recipient of the Governor's Citation for Life Achievement, San Francisco/Northern California Chapter, National Academy of Television Arts and Sciences, and the California Heritage Preservation Commission's 2000 Archivist Award of Excellence.